FUTURES GUIDE 2022

The Top Prospects For Every MLB Team and more

Edited by Cliff Corcoran

Trevor Andresen, Steve Givarz, Nathan Graham, Kevin Johnson, Keanan Lamb, Tyler Oringer, Jeffrey Paternostro, Jarrett Seidler, Ben Spanier, John Trupin, Brandon Williams

Bret Sayre, Consultant Editor
Robert Au, Harry Pavlidis and Amy Pircher, Statistics Editors

Library of Congress Cataloging-in-Publication Data:
paperback
ISBN-10: 1950716945
ISBN-13: 978-1950716944

Project Credits
Cover Design: Ginny Searle
Interior Design and Production: Amy Pircher, Robert Au
Layout: Amy Pircher, Robert Au

Cover Photos
Front Cover: George Valera. © Jeff Lange, Akron Beacon Journal

Baseball icon courtesy of Uberux, from https://www.shareicon.net/author/uberux

Manufactured in the United States of America
10 9 8 7 6 5 4 3 2 1

Table of Contents

Top 101 Prospects

by Jeffrey Paternostro, Jarrett Seidler and John Trupin

1. Bobby Witt Jr., SS/3B, Kansas City Royals

Witt was already one of the 10 best prospects in the game when he started tormenting Cactus League pitchers last spring. He looked so good that the Royals nearly took him north as a 20-year-old with no professional game experience other than 37 post-draft tilts in the complex. Instead, they gave him a merely aggressive assignment to Double-A—bypassing both A-ball levels—and he absolutely mashed for the entire first half before carbon copying his performance in Triple-A in the second half. Overall, Witt hit .290/.361/.575 while only taking two plate appearances all season against pitchers younger than him. That slugging percentage is more than 70 points higher than Adley Rutschman posted at the same levels . . . and Witt is 28 months younger. Witt is a fine defender at shortstop, but a mix of his readiness and an impending infield playing-time logjam might slide him over to third; he could win Gold Gloves there. With absolutely no disrespect to the next two players on this list, Witt is now the best prospect in the minors.

2. Adley Rutschman, C, Baltimore Orioles

Rutschman was the incumbent. He was second on last year's list behind Wander Franco. He was first on our Midseason Top 50. He is a switch-hitter who hit for average, got on base and hit for power in the upper minors in 2021 while showing off one of if not the best defensive skill sets among minor-league catchers. When comparing the elite prospects in baseball, it often comes down to minor quibbles. We're not completely convinced Rutschman will have an obviously plus offensive tool set, as he doesn't always make ideal contact, especially from the left side. He was a little bit old for his levels, as the Orioles could have easily had him up in the majors around the same time as Wander Franco; like Franco, Rutschman was probably ready in 2020. Finally, catching prospects tend to see more offensive regression once the realities of the day-to-day grind of being a major-league backstop set in. Those are ultimately minor quibbles though, and Rutschman is likely to be one of the three or four best catchers in baseball as soon as he gets the call.

3. Julio Rodríguez, OF, Seattle Mariners

From Everett, Washington, to Little Rock, Arkansas, with an impressive layover as the star of the Dominican Republic's bronze-medal-winning Olympic team in Tokyo, Rodríguez terrorized opposing pitchers in 2021. With the physical and mental makeup that presidents of baseball and business operations, alike, dream of, Rodríguez ran an OPS over 1.000 despite facing pitchers who were his elders in every single game of his season. Rodríguez's towering frame is lean and muscular, and he managed to add speed, both on the stopwatch and in the box score, stealing 21 bases in 26 attempts with his stateside affiliates. The potential for 40-home-run power remains self-evident from both his frame and the eye-popping exit velocities his quick wrists generate. Though there's always the risk he wobbles in the process of refining his swing for elevation, his barrel control should entrench him in the middle of a contending lineup sooner rather than later.

4. Spencer Torkelson, 3B/1B, Detroit Tigers

Torkelson was the first-overall pick in 2020—not a surprise. He was announced as a third baseman—that was a bit of a surprise. The nicest thing you can say about his defense at the hot corner is that he battles it to a draw, at times. He also hits like a premier first baseman, so it's really not going to matter where he stands on the field. Torkelson did exactly what you would want your top college bat to do in his first taste of the minors; he laid waste to them. He's a patient hitter and picks the right pitches to hit hard. The only thing keeping him from making the top troika on this list a Fab Four is that there was a little more swing-and-miss in the upper levels than expected. So, he might only hit .280 with 30-plus homers. Ah well.

5. Grayson Rodriguez, RHP, Baltimore Orioles

Rodriguez is everything you could ask for in a pitching prospect. Start with his amateur background: a well-built, projectable, 6-foot-5 Texas prep arm drafted in the first half of the first round in 2018. Since debuting as a pro, he has continually leveled up in every look we've had. His fastball now sits consistently in the upper 90s with late life. His slider now projects as plus-plus. His changeup projects as a plus offering and tunnels very well off his slider. He has great feel for spin, enough so that his curveball would be the best off-speed pitch for half of the pitchers on this list. He flashes a good cutter he doesn't really need. He throws strikes and paints corners. Last year, we wrote in this space that if Rodriguez ever threw 100 innings in a season there was a pretty good chance he'd be one of the best pitching prospects in baseball by the end of it. He threw 103 innings in 2021, but we were wrong: he's not one of the best, he's *the* best.

6. Riley Greene, OF, Detroit Tigers

In 2020, Greene torched spring training, the alternate site, and the fall instructional league to such a degree that one could mentally fill in his player card as if he had a great season at the full-season A-ball levels. The Tigers sure acted like he did, sending him to ~~the Eastern League~~ Double-A Northeast as a 20-year-old. He tore it up there and then shredded Triple-A even more for a 40-game denouement. He has a majestic, balanced, left-handed swing and hits the ball hard to all fields, projecting for plus-or-better hit and power. He's capable of making spectacular highlight-reel catches in the outfield, although he might end up being more suited to a corner than center if he continues to grow. Torkelson vs. Greene has been a common debate since Torkelson was drafted two years ago. We give the ever-so-slight edge to Tork right now, but it's extremely close; they're both tracking to be major forces in Detroit's rebuild.

7. Jordan Walker, 3B, St. Louis Cardinals

Well more than half of all qualified major-league hitters socked more than 20 home runs last year. It has become a power hitter's game. But there are power hitters, and then there is Jordan Walker. At 19 years old and with a fair amount of physical projection left in his 6-foot-5 frame, Walker already hits the ball about as hard as your favorite major-league slugger. Power is the carrying tool here, but it's far from the only notable one. Walker has an advanced approach for his age and experience level, and while he swings hard enough that batting titles are likely not in his future, his selectivity and quality of contact in the zone portend a potential plus hit tool. He runs well and plays an average third base, at present, but the physical gains he is likely to experience should send him to an outfield corner or even first base. As with Torkelson, the bat will play anywhere.

8. Shane Baz, RHP, Tampa Bay Rays

Baz is certainly a less-perfect pitching prospect than Rodriguez. He barely throws his changeup, relying very heavily on his fastball and his two breaking pitches. He has a past history of significant command and control issues; he'd never had a walk rate below four per nine innings prior to 2021. His arm path is on the shorter side, so his delivery looks less visually pleasing. But here's the most important part, the reason Baz is a Top-10 prospect: Baz throws the easiest 80-grade fastball you'll ever see. It effortlessly comes out of his hand in the upper 90s with high spin and an optimized approach angle. With that profile, he's going to befuddle a hell of a lot of hitters with high fastballs, and the elite-stuff profile doesn't stop there. His slider grades out with plus-plus potential, too, and obliterated right-handed hitters after his call-up. Against lefties, he relied more on his soft stuff: a loopier curveball and the occasional change, both with success. Baz's command improved greatly last year, enough that the "bullpen risk" dial was turned way down, and he was impressive enough that he started Game 2 of the Division Series for the Rays. If he keeps throwing strikes, he could be a front-line starter as soon as this year.

9. Marco Luciano, SS, San Francisco Giants

Electrifying batting practices turned into eye-opening game power for the 19-year-old Luciano last year. Some of the best bat speed anywhere and a swing geared for elevation make Luciano a particularly promising bet to reach his offensive ceiling. He stands slightly open and crouched at the plate, engaging his stout lower half to great effect with a short stroke that can help him adjust when fooled. The Giants did not handle the teenage slugger with kid gloves, and there were periods when he did, indeed, get fooled. Luciano got reps at Low-A, High-A, the Futures Game and the Arizona Fall League. Considering his tools and performance despite relatively minimal game experience, we're bullish on Luciano's ability to adjust and prosper. Luciano's foot speed and glovework suggest the hot corner lies in his future, but his arm is strong, and the bat has the potential to play anywhere on the diamond.

10. Francisco Álvarez, C, New York Mets

Álvarez hits the ball as hard as any prospect in the minors and knows what pitches to swing at. He slugged .538 as a teenager at High-A after his Ted Williams–like slash line at Low-A forced a promotion before Memorial Day. With no real red flags on his health or defense, Álvarez is likely to stay at catcher. Does anything else *really* matter? Yes, he's short and stout. His swing setup is a little funky and open. He doesn't run well and has no obvious fallback position if he has to move out from behind the dish. Who cares? He's a catcher who hits nukes all over the field! That's one of the most valuable profiles in baseball.

11. CJ Abrams, SS, San Diego Padres

Abrams was well on his way to a spot in the top 10—and perhaps one in the San Diego lineup, as well—when he fractured his left tibia and sprained the medial collateral ligament in that knee during an infield collision last July. For a prospect that derives a lot of his value from speed and up-the-middle defense, this is concerning. Let's look at the bright side, though. Abrams jumped to Double-A as a 20-year-old with only 34 pro games under his belt. He hit a smidge under .300, showed off elite-level speed and a smooth glove at shortstop. He's not likely to be one of the 60-odd percent of qualified hitters smacking 20 bombs, but anything he hits to the outfield is a threat to be a double, and anything in the gap is a threat to be a triple, and those extra bases add up, too. Hopefully he'll be back on the field this year showing no lingering effects from his injury or lost time, because he's a potential impact player for San Diego in the near-term.

12. Oneil Cruz, SS, Pittsburgh Pirates

Cruz is a unique prospect: a 6-foot-7 shortstop flashing 80-grade raw power and enough agility and instincts to play the position. For years, everyone assumed something in that profile had to give—most likely either the power wouldn't translate to games, or his body would fill out and move him to a corner spot. He needed to keep the swing-and-miss manageable while not sacrificing hard contact to reach his offensive potential—a tall task given his very long levers—and he's three inches taller than any regular shortstop in MLB history. Then Cruz made it up last September . . . still a perfectly adequate defensive shortstop, with manageable swing-and-miss, now showing top-of-the-line hard-hit data in games (his second big-league hit registered the hardest exit velo for a Pirate in 2021). We're still not sure he's going to remain at shortstop for very long, and we're not sure he's going to make enough contact because we're deep in uncharted water, but some of the data points we can chart show him navigating towards "superstar."

13. Brett Baty, 3B/OF, New York Mets

Baty has a tremendous swing, makes great swing decisions, and can flash 80 raw power on the right day. A 6-hit/7-game-power projection is firmly within reach, and his production at High-A and Double-A last year was certainly strong. One caveat from the data that bears out in live looks: he hits the ball on the ground a *lot* right now. This may be a partially fixable approach issue more than a swing issue; for better and worse, he likes taking what the pitcher gives him instead of trying to uppercut everything to Mars. His swing *does* have some natural loft to it, and, when he swings up, he can lift balls to places almost no one else can, especially the opposite-field power alley. But if you've got top-end raw, you really don't want to hit wormburners half the time. Defensively, he has solid building blocks at third base—plus arm with the actions and agility for the hot corner—but his inconsistency there and the major-league team's potential needs have led the Mets to start playing him in the outfield, as well. Early reviews of his performance on the grass suggest that he should be fine in a corner outfield slot in due time.

14. Anthony Volpe, SS, New York Yankees

Last year, in a season evenly split between Low-A and High-A, Volpe put up one of the most dominant performances relative to league and age context in the minors, mashing at a .294/.423/.604 clip, good for a combined 144 DRC+. It was his first full-season experience, and he turned 20 just a week before the minor-league season started. It was a surprising slugging output, particularly given that he'd been a hit-over-power prospect coming out of the draft. But Volpe got a lot stronger and optimized his swing mechanics during the pandemic year while working with former Baseball Prospectus prospect writer and professional scout Jason Lefkowitz; Volpe was one of the few prospects who may have demonstrably benefited from the break. His overall defensive abilities are above-average, though his foot speed and range may slide him to second or third eventually. Given that he maintained his feel for contact with vastly improved power, Volpe now projects as a difference-maker no matter where he ends up.

15. Noelvi Marte, SS, Seattle Mariners

One of the youngest players in full-season affiliated baseball last year, Marte held his own against older and more experienced competition. As top-tier international signees from the same class on the same big-league arrival schedule within organizations whose affiliates play in the same leagues at all but one level, Marte and Marco Luciano have frequently been contrasted against one another and likely will continue to be. Luciano's offensive ceiling is higher and more explosive, while Marte's agility and glovework give him slightly more of a fighting chance to stick up the middle. Marte's swing is keyed off a leg-kick load that tends to produce backspin, though most of his power is to the pull side. His arm strength fits on the left side of the infield, like Luciano's, and Marte runs better, but the truth is both players are brimming with star-level potential.

16. Jeremy Peña, SS, Houston Astros

Peña seemed poised for a 2021 breakout coming off strong reports from the Dominican Republic Professional Baseball League (LIDOM) the prior winter. A left-wrist injury at the alternate site in April put the kibosh on that until August, but he more than made up for the lost time upon his return, scorching the ball for a month in Triple-A and putting himself in contention for a spot on the Astros' playoff roster. He didn't end up contributing to the American League pennant and will have to settle for being the heir apparent for Carlos Correa in Houston. Peña doesn't have Correa's upside with the bat, although the fact that his power gains continued even after a wrist injury is promising. He is close to Correa's equal on defense, a silky shortstop with a plus arm and plus foot speed who should compete for Gold Gloves. We'd like to see a slightly longer track record of this kind of offensive performance, but any confirmation or refutation is now likely to come in the majors.

17. Marcelo Mayer, SS, Boston Red Sox

Although health and Boston's willingness to let him play right away meant we've seen Mayer handle the disparate array of talent levels that make up the Florida Complex League, nothing he did there altered the expectations we had for him when he was drafted fourth-overall last July. The projection here is primarily built on, well, projection. Mayer is smooth in the field, and his arm is plenty strong, so even with middling foot speed he shouldn't struggle to stick at shortstop. The lanky, 6-foot-3 teenager has the frame to add muscle, which could help him build out his simple, sweet swoosh of a swing to produce laser line drives and towering big flies to pair with his already-patient approach. If the power comes, it would complete a superstar's tool kit. If it doesn't, well, J.P. Crawford panned out alright.

18. Henry Davis, C, Pittsburgh Pirates

Sure, Davis was the number-one overall pick last year in part because he signed for a well-below-slot $6.5 million (less than what any of next three picks signed for) which, in turn, allowed the Pirates to select three top prep prospects—lefty Anthony Solometo, outfielder Lonnie White Jr. and righty Bubba Chandler—with their next three picks and sign them to big-money deals. Still, Davis was a viable 1.1 selection on talent alone given his profile as an advanced, power-hitting catcher coming out of Louisville. He lifts the ball easily with plus bat speed, leading to hard, elevated contact, though his oddball setup and uppercut swing path leaves some unanswered hit-tool questions against higher-level pitching. Behind the dish, he has a very strong arm but is still rounding out the framing and receiving elements. If he doesn't get all the way there and has to move to another position down the road, he's fast and agile enough to fallback on third base or the outfield. If he's a catcher all the way up, his power output will make him an All-Star.

19. Cade Cavalli, RHP, Washington Nationals

Due to injuries and inconsistent command when he was on the mound, Cavalli never put together the kind of dominant college campaign that would have landed him among the top arms in the 2020 draft. So how do you go from the 22nd-overall pick to 19th best prospect in baseball? Well, the stuff was never in question with Cavalli, and he finally had that full, healthy season to show off his potential top-of-the-rotation wares in 2021. He made it all the way to Triple-A, striking out 12 per nine inings, flashing triple-digit heat and two potential plus breaking balls. His 123 innings last year were more than he threw across three seasons for the Sooners, and while he still has a little more injury risk and a shorter history of strike-throwing than the arms ranked ahead of him, Cavalli has very much the same upside.

20. Jack Leiter, RHP, Texas Rangers

Prepare to be reminded early and often for the next decade or two that Jack is the son of Al, the retired effectively wild lefty with a killer cutter. The younger Leiter was a high school classmate of Volpe's at Delbarton Prep in Morristown, New Jersey, and was a comparable or even better prospect at the time, but Leiter was considered unsignable and matriculated at Vanderbilt. By the 2021 season, he was the top collegiate pitching prospect in the country, although he wasn't the Friday-night starter for Vandy due to the presence of 2019 College World Series hero Kumar Rocker. Leiter regularly gets his fastball into the mid-90s and shapes it with a high, flat approach angle that hitters perceive as rise; he can also throw a nifty sinker to mix it up. His curveball has graded as a future out-pitch since high school, and his slider caught up to it in college. As you'd expect, given that his father is both a former MLB All-Star and a current MLB Network pitching analyst, his mechanics are sound and repeatable. As far as pitching prospects with no professional innings go, Leiter is about as high-probability as it gets.

21. George Kirby, RHP, Seattle Mariners

If you gauge it by his own track record, Kirby's trademark command cratered in 2021, but relative to almost every other pitcher in minor-league baseball, he continued on one of the higher-floor trajectories a starting pitcher can travel. In 2021, the 2019 first-rounder issued his first walk in a competitive game since May 4, 2019, when he was pitching for Elon University. He'd ultimately yield a handful more free passes but made short work of High-A and looked impressive in his first few tastes of Double-A. Kirby's motion is simple and repeatable, the only flare in it is a slight coil in his leg lift that helps him reach back for impressive velocity. After working in the low 90s in college, Kirby now sits 95–98 with his fastball and has clipped triple-digits repeatedly. His changeup is his most impressive secondary, and he rounds out his repertoire with a solid slider and a slower, more vertically breaking curveball. The limiting factor on Kirby, at the moment, is the lack of a wipeout off-speed pitch, but if he maintains something close to his present velocity and command, his blend of security and potential will continue to be one that few pitching prospects can rival.

22. Gabriel Moreno, C, Toronto Blue Jays

Moreno is ranked third among catchers on this year's 101, although, if we were more certain of a full-time future behind the plate, he'd be above Henry Davis. Moreno's 2021 season was truncated at both ends—first by a groin injury and then by a thumb fracture—but he hit .360 when he was on the field. That will get your attention. A reincarnated Rogers

Hornsby with modern swing analytics and training might not hit .360 in the majors, but Moreno has the kind of blink-and-you-miss-it bat speed and advanced ability to barrel pitches that suggest .300 is very much in play. His defensive development is not quite as far along. The injuries cost him some much needed reps, and the Blue Jays were already planning to try him out at other spots when he hit the injured list in June. Moreno is a little undersized for an everyday catcher, and his receiving remains rough, but 70 hit and 55 power is a nice fit at any spot, and he should be able to don the tools of ignorance a few days a week, at least.

23. Tyler Soderstrom, C/1B, Oakland Athletics

Like Moreno, Soderstrom's ranking is hurt by a lack of confidence that he'll catch in the majors. He was a first-round pick on the strength of his future hit and power tools more than his glove, and while he has the arm to control the running game, 15 passed balls in 38 games behind the plate last year—he missed time with a back injury—is an indication of how far the rest of the defensive profile has to go. There's going to be a temptation to move him to a corner soon, because the bat is ready for tougher challenges than A-ball, and he has already been exposed to first base. Soderstrom has 30-home-run pop and an already-selective approach for a teenager in full-season ball. He could easily be the best offensive catcher in baseball, if he can stick there as even a passably below-average defender, but he's more likely to be a very good slugger at another position.

24. Max Meyer, RHP, Miami Marlins

The single best off-speed pitch of any player on this list—any player in the entire minors, in fact—is Meyer's slider. If it's not an 80-grade projection, it's close. The pitch sits in the high 80s and nips the low 90s with sharp downward tilt and hard break. He can use it to get chases out of the zone or called strikes in the zone. We expect to name it one of the best breaking pitches in the majors in a future version of this book. His fastball has plus-plus velocity but is not a true plus-plus pitch, at present, due to its shape and natural sinking action. Meyer barely threw his changeup in college because he didn't need to, but he's been focusing on developing it as a pro. He's in the right system for that, and the pitch showed signs of advancing into at least a credible third offering in 2021. While he still carries some of the relief risk stereotypical of a short, slider-heavy righty, he went straight to Double-A and cruised for most of the season as a starter. He could be the next great one out of Miami's underrated pitching development factory.

25. Zac Veen, OF, Colorado Rockies

The Cody Bellinger/Kyle Tucker lookalikes will not all pan out, but when you see Veen get into a baseball, it's easy to see why folks buy in. Veen's body is 84 percent legs and arms, long levers that he wields in a back-thumping uppercut swing that can get exposed by elevated velocity but punishes nigh anything else. He's a long strider, and despite speed that will likely take a step back as he adds muscle to his lean frame, he may remain a reasonable threat on the bases. Veen's patience at the plate and obvious power will help him get on base, but his ability to consistently put the bat on the ball will be the question mark that bobs above his head all the way through the minors, particularly after he racked up 126 punchouts in 479 plate appearances at Low-A. A Veen that navigates that challenge skillfully could prompt fans to bring their gloves when they ascend to The Rooftop in right field at Coors Field.

26. Robert Hassell III, OF, San Diego Padres

A decade after Bryce Harper graced the cover of Sports Illustrated, the powers that be of baseball prospectdom convened at the summit of Mt. Scout. "What," they wondered, "if we gave that same swing to a new prospect, but this time, instead of a muscle-bound former catcher, it belonged to a lithe outfielder whose power was a question mark?" And so it was that we were provided with Hassell, whose barrel control helps set him apart from many teenage hitters. His ability to get the best part of the bat to the ball all over the plate with plus bat speed helps him project to be an above-average hitter who could eventually feature 20- to 25-home-run power. As a 20-year-old, Hassell will still be quite young for High-A this year, and he'll hope to improve upon last year's numbers there while shoring up his defensive acumen to solidify himself as a tri-positional outfielder.

27. Brennen Davis, OF, Chicago Cubs

Neither Davis' stat line—an .860 OPS across 99 games and three levels—nor his raw tool grades scream top-30 prospect. But he doesn't have a real weakness in his game, either. We will first note that he played almost all of those 99 games in the upper minors as a 21-year-old. Then we will add that Davis is a plus runner who should be a fine defender in center field. We'll further strengthen our case by mentioning that his above-average bat speed and barrel control mean he's already hitting for more game power than his batting practices or still-projectable frame would suggest. Perhaps Davis doesn't have a standout carrying tool at present, but he has a chance to roll a bunch of 6s on his scout sheet. That is the kind of center fielder that makes All-Star games.

28. Nolan Gorman, 2B/3B, St. Louis Cardinals

Gorman has been passed as a prospect by Jordan Walker, the other power-hitting third baseman in Cardinal red—or occasionally powder blue—and isn't even a primary third baseman anymore. Likely in deference to Nolan Arenado and the six years left on his contract, Gorman started taking grounders at second base this past spring. Gorman moves well enough there that, with advanced positioning data, he should be average, and his plus arm will be a weapon on double-play turns. More importantly, the keystone is an available spot to get his bat in the lineup, and, despite the added responsibility of learning a new position on the fly, Gorman continued to show a potential average-hit/plus-plus-power combo at the plate in the upper minors. Pretty soon, Arenado won't be the only Nolan shining on the dirt in St. Louis.

29. Nick Gonzales, 2B, Pittsburgh Pirates

For a short guy, Gonzales takes some mighty hacks. He has slugged better than .550 at nearly every level he has played at: all three years of college, 2019 on the Cape and 2021 in High-A. The one exception is that he slugged "only" .549 in the Arizona Fall League last year. Gonzales' hands are tremendously quick to the ball, he's strong and he swings up. His approach is advanced, and he has hit for average at all levels so far, although the ferocity of his swing does lead to a moderate amount of swing-and-miss. Second base is an excellent fit for his solid actions and footwork but so-so arm strength. The Pirates were conservative in his first pro season, leaving him in A-ball, but he could move quickly now.

30. Luis Matos, OF, San Francisco Giants

Matos was one of the breakout prospect bats of 2021. He had very few pro reps after being one of the Giants top international-free-agent signings in 2018, but his full-season debut flashed all five tools in abundance. Matos has a smaller, squarish frame, but his plus bat speed, quick wrists and torquey swing should generate plus game power down the line. Matos will need to refine his approach against better competition, but he already shows the kind of advanced bat-to-ball ability that will give him plenty of runway to make those kinds of adjustments. His defensive tools range from average to slightly above, but the 19-year-old has a good shot to stick in center, where his potential plus offensive tools would make him a first-division regular.

31. Josh Jung, 3B, Texas Rangers

Jung isn't the, er, youngest prospect in this group—in fact, Adley Rutschman is the only position player in the top 50 who is older, and by all of six days. (Both will turn 24 right around when this book will reach most of you. Happy birthday, guys!) We haven't held Jung's veritably wizened status against him, however. The 2019 draftee has mashed every step of his pro career and splashed some paint on one gray area in his game: whether or not he had big-league power. Jung used the 2020 layoff to refine his swing for a bit more loft, and while he did swing and miss a touch more often in 2021, he was comfortably within the realm of lesser concern for his first season in the high minors. He's no Adrían Beltré at the hot corner, but, at both Frisco and Round Rock, Jung looked like the future of the third-base position in Arlington. In a suddenly invigorated infield, that future could arrive as soon as Opening Day 2022.

32. Hunter Greene, RHP, Cincinnati Reds

Greene regularly sits above 100 miles per hour with his fastball. If he keeps that up in the majors, he'll be the first starting pitcher of the verified-pitch-data era to do so. That's enough propane that concerns about the shape of his fastball aren't going to matter a whole lot. Greene's tremendous arm speed also leads to a high aptitude for the slide piece; his slider should get to at least plus and isn't far from there already. Given that he was a first-round prospect as a shortstop, as well, he's very fluid and moves well on the mound. His changeup needs further development—get ready to read that a lot in the rest of this list—and he missed a lot of time around Tommy John surgery several years ago, but Greene is closing in on the majors, and, you know, he throws it up to 104 mph with a plus slider.

33. George Valera, OF, Cleveland Guardians

It's difficult to identify a major-league hitter that has a swing quite like Valera's. It's funky and violent, with a seemingly purposeful kind of awkwardness to it. Perhaps it's best described it as resembling a drawing of Bryce Harper's swing made from memory . . . with your non-dominant hand . . . while blindfolded. That swing allows Valera to hit absolute laser beams to all fields despite being listed at a probably generous 5-foot-11 and 185 pounds. It would be easier to project Valera as a perennial 30-home-run hitter in the majors if his swing looked like that of the *actual* Bryce Harper—who, to be fair, was already an All-Star at this age—but sometimes unusual swings lead to unusual results. For all the hitchy, twitchy weirdness that precedes Valera squaring up a fastball, he does square them up, and he knows which ones to square up. Knowing is in fact half the battle here. The rest should be covered by his prodigious bat speed.

34. Corbin Carroll, OF, Arizona Diamondbacks

It was . . . one week in the month of May
When Carroll was destroying balls like Juan Uribe
Five tools, that's what we expect
And soon we'd rate him as a top prospect
Sweet swing from the left-hand side
He hits, but he can also run, just look at his slide
Eventually, he had surgery
Separated shoulder means his future's murky . . .

35. MJ Melendez, C, Kansas City Royals

The 2019 Wilmington Blue Rocks may have been the last Carolina League champions, but that season was an unmitigated disaster for some of Kansas City's best hitting prospects. The team put up a .618 OPS. Nick Pratto hit .191 with no power and struck out 34.7 percent of the time. Kyle Isbel hit an empty .216. And Melendez, the number-67 prospect on the 2019 Top 101, hit .163 and struck out in 39.4 percent of his plate appearances. We don't really know what happened there. Frawley Stadium is one of the worst places in affiliated baseball to hit, but even that doesn't explain it all. (Wilmington changed affiliations to Washington in 2021, and a way-less-talented Blue Rocks squad of Nats "prospects" put up a .692 OPS last year.) What we do know is that Melendez came out in 2021 and ran it back to 2018—and then some—shrugging off his ghastly 2019. The lefty hit 41 dingers between Double-A and Triple-A along with by far the best contact rates of his career, pushing himself forward towards the City of Fountains. One slight problem he's about to run into: Salvador Perez just set the single-season record for home runs hit by a primary catcher, and Perez is a better defender by reputation.

36. Miguel Vargas, 3B, Los Angeles Dodgers

An old scouting cliché is that the doubles a player hits when he's 19 or 20 will naturally turn into home runs as he physically matures. That conventional wisdom predated the widespread industry realization that organizations can use player development to increase prospects' game power irrespective of a projectable teenaged bat filling out. The Dodgers are one of the best developmental organizations for hitters. Miguel Vargas is significantly bigger and stronger than he was two years ago. Those powers combined to lift Vargas from seven home runs in 2019 to 23 home runs last year. Consequently, his 38 doubles in 2019 shrunk to 27 in 2021. This is all an oversimplification, but nevertheless a very good result for Vargas' prospect status. Oh, and he kept hitting .300 and getting on base, as well. Vargas is significantly bigger than most third basemen now, but he has seen more supplemental time at second base than first, which is also a very Dodgers thing.

37. Alek Thomas, OF, Arizona Diamondbacks

Consistent, young and big league-ready, Thomas hails from the five-average-or-better-tools school of prospects. Though often treated as safe, there is risk in a player reliant on doing everything decently, and we've seen even more impressive bats than Thomas struggle out of the gate or put together uneven performances early in their careers (see: Kelenic, Jarred; or Benintendi, Andrew). To muddle things further, while Thomas has enough speed to stretch doubles into triples, he has never shown a knack for base stealing. Still, the 5-foot-11 outfielder has a lot to fall back on. He moves fluidly in the outfield and will be able to handle center field if called upon. That gives a bit more leeway to his production at the plate, where he converts his athletic frame into a max-effort lefty swing that has met the high minors with great success. Thomas has a floaty leg lift that he uses to time pitches but could be exposed against big-league breaking balls. He'll be just 22 in 2022, however; there will be time to adjust.

38. Liover Peguero, SS, Pittsburgh Pirates

Peguero was acquired from Arizona in the first Starling Marte trade, a deal the Diamondbacks would very much like to have back right now. Peguero was assigned to High-A to be Nick Gonzales' double-play partner in one of the better keystone-prospect pairings in recent memory. Evaluators came away split as to who was the better prospect; after a season of watching them side by side, we ever so slightly lean towards Gonzales and his greater present skills. Peguero has excellent feel for the bat and plus bat speed, projecting to above-average outcomes for both his hit and power tools. He's a fluid defender at shortstop, and he's now on the cusp of being a 70 runner, too. He's still rounding out his game, but he was better than average with the stick at the age of 20 in High-A, and he is filled with offensive and defensive upside.

39. Keibert Ruiz, C, Washington Nationals

At long last, 2021 freed Ruiz from the yoke and crushing pressure of needing to outperform Will Smith to win a role on the perennially World Series–contending Dodgers. Sent to the nation's capital, Ruiz can finally focus on the simpler things in this game, like replacing the superstar(s) he was traded for by quickly becoming an All-Star catcher, thus helping convince Juan Soto to stay with the Nationals. You know, normal rebuilding-club things. Beyond his change of scenery, things went quite well for Ruiz in 2021. He put his disappointing 2019 season well behind him with a stellar performance at the plate between Triple-A and the bigs, and his 24 home runs across the two levels doubled his prior career high. Considering that slugging came with no expense to his typical contact-geared approach, Nationals fans may be treated to a rare profile behind the dish in coming years: single-digit walk and strikeout rates/easy double-digit home-run rates. Trea bien.

40. Nick Yorke, 2B, Boston Red Sox

Yorke was considered a reach when Boston selected him in the first round of the 2020 draft. Ideally, you want your first-round prep bat to have oodles of tools projection and/or a fair bit of defensive value. Yorke was a hit-tool-driven, mostly filled-out, high school second baseman. The consensus was his hit tool was an easy plus, but there have been many prep bats given similar accolades who never really hit to that level, even in the minors. Well, Yorke promptly went out and hit .323 in Low-A. He then hit .333 in High-A. He showed a little more pop than expected, to boot. It gets harder now. Double-A is often a stern test of the performance-over-tools profile, but Yorke's performance has passed every test so far, and we reckon, if you re-ran the 2020 draft today, he'd go a bit higher than 17th.

41. Mick Abel, RHP, Philadelphia Phillies

Abel was on the verge of a huge breakout in the first half of 2021, regularly sitting mid-90s and touching 99 with impressive spin and vertical break on his hellacious fastball. He was ramping up towards fuller outings and reached a season high of 79 pitches on July 21st, when the Phillies backed off over a mix of workload concerns, COVID and minor shoulder fatigue. Abel did not pitch again until fall instructs, where he was throwing just as hard as he threw during the regular season. Abel spent much of his game action throwing a lot of fastballs and trying to improve his command, but he also threw a plus-flashing slider. Whether he can get either his curveball or changeup to become a viable pitch is an open question, as is his workload, but, all in all, it was a successful debut for one of the highest-upside arms in the minors.

42. Nick Lodolo, LHP, Cincinnati Reds

A sinker/slurve command guy? In this economy?!? As modern pitch design has developed, we've come to realizations about certain things we always sort of knew. A main one is that four-seam fastballs with high life—like Abel's—are, as a general rule, going to strike out a heck of a lot more batters than lower-velocity, lower-spin sinkers down in the zone—like Lodolo's. That doesn't mean Lodolo doesn't have an effective fastball, it just means he's probably never going to dominate with it, unless he discovers Dustin May-quality, seam-shifted wake. Lodolo's best off-speed pitch is a slurvy, sweeping breaking ball which he manipulates quite a lot in speed and movement; it's right on the borderline of being a distinct slider or curveball, if you care about pitch nomenclature. His changeup adds another usable offering. He has superlative command of everything and should be in the majors soon, so long as the shoulder fatigue that ended his season doesn't turn into a long-term issue.

43. Daniel Espino, RHP, Cleveland Guardians

Velocity only earns the scrutiny of others. Once that scrutiny is focused upon a player, it's incumbent upon them to make something of it. Espino was one of a few prospects to earn pre-draft notoriety due to heavy publicity from his baseball-focused prep school. His stuff was genuinely explosive, but his size and motion were polarizing, with some confident his health was a ticking time bomb due in part to his lengthy arm action. Two years later, Espino has made nearly every positive move that could be reasonably expected of him. His fastball sits in the mid-to-upper 90s, and his slider trails only Max Meyer's for bat-missing electricity. Espino's arm action has been shortened dramatically, helping him lower and center his vertical approach angle, as well, adding deceptiveness to both pitches. You'd like to see a third pitch round out the repertoire, but you'd also like it if ice cream cleaned your gums and whitened your teeth. He'll be 21 next year and should reach Triple-A. There's already plenty going right.

44. Triston Casas, 1B, Boston Red Sox

Major-league first basemen, as a class, hit .257/.338/.454 last year. It doesn't pop as a line, but it was more than 50 points of OPS better than all shortstops and 10 percent better than league-average. The offensive bar is high at the cold corner. As in Lake Wobegon, all the first basemen are above average. The best first baseman—a cohort Casas certainly has a shot at joining—are 30- to 40-percent better than league average. Broadly speaking, to get there you need three things:

1. 30-home-run power: This won't be an issue for Casas, who creates lift and plus-plus raw power with a long stride and minimal hand load.
2. Above-average plate discipline: Casas already has a strong command of the strike zone and a two-strike, contact-heavy approach that will keep him in counts when he falls behind.
3. A plus hit tool: Ah, the open question. Casas has good barrel control and can sting the ball from any part of the zone, but likes to hunt fastballs and can get out on his front foot against off-speed pitches. The breakers and changeups only get better from here on out, and if Casas ends up merely average as a first baseman, which is above-average overall, that may be why.

45. Kahlil Watson, SS, Miami Marlins

Watson was almost universally considered one of the top half-dozen or so prospects in the 2021 draft class—he was number five in our rankings—yet fell to Miami at the sixteenth pick amidst rumors about his bonus demands. The Marlins ultimately offered him every last dollar they had left in their pool plus overage after signing all their other picks: $4,540,790. Watson signed right at the deadline and then dominated in a Florida Complex League cameo. He possesses innate barrel control from the left side of the plate and smashes the ball hard and up from his compact frame. Whether or not his approach will hold up against more advanced pitching is the largest question he'll face offensively as he moves up the chain. His future position is a bit up in the air, too, although we expect he'll be able to stay somewhere on the dirt. Watson has a chance to be a star, if he can swing at the right pitches.

46. Colton Cowser, OF, Baltimore Orioles

It was not at all a surprise that Cowser went to a model-heavy team like Baltimore in the draft: his draft-year performance at Sam Houston State (.374/.490/.680) was exemplary. After he signed, he took a quick pit stop in the complex and made his way to Low-A, where he hit .347 while walking more than he struck out. Cowser has exceptional plate discipline, pitch recognition and contact ability, as you could probably guess from the stat lines. His power projection is more muted; until he shows over-the-fence power with wood bats, it's hard to project him as anything more than an average hitter for power. He played mostly center in his pro debut, but he has more of a corner-masher profile long-term, so some extra pop would be nice.

47. Brayan Rocchio, SS, Cleveland Guardians

With the recent acquisitions of Gabriel Arias, Amed Rosario and Andrés Giménez, it seems as if the Guardians may be trying to replace Francisco Lindor with some sort of shortstop Voltron. Rocchio is the homegrown entry, fresh off a breakout season with the bat in which he added potential above-average power to his plus hit and glove. He has a chance to have the best bat of the group, but may be only the third-best defender. Perhaps he will slide over to second base—Cleveland has plenty of infield holes to fill beyond the large, Lindor-shaped one at short—where he'd be among the better defenders in baseball, and his merely above-average arm would be a weapon rather than occasionally stretched.

48. Jordan Lawlar, SS, Arizona Diamondbacks

Lawlar was our top draft prospect in July, but he suffered a torn shoulder labrum in the Arizona Complex League only two games into his pro career. The subsequent surgery ended his season and cost him reps that were a tad more important given he was an older prep; Lawler turned 19 less than a week after the draft. While he's expected to be ready early this year, significant shoulder rehabs can be nearly as tricky for hitters as pitchers, and we're in a bit of a wait-and-see mode until he takes the field again. His pre-draft reports showed a mix of advanced hitting and game power, albeit with only above-average-type projection and some swing-and-miss concerns. He's likely to stay at shortstop and provide good-but-not great offense, health willing.

49. Jackson Jobe, RHP, Detroit Tigers

The third-overall pick in 2021, Jobe received a whopping $6.9 million bonus to leapfrog Ole Miss and start his pro career. The logic is understandable, even for a prep arm: MLB is increasingly a league ruled by potent breaking balls, and a projectable teenage arm who already boasts a wipeout slider has cleared one of the most challenging hurdles to big-league success. What awaits now is his professional debut and the always-fraught journey of a teenager who throws low-to-mid-90s and spins his breaker more than 3,000 revolutions per minute. Jobe's polish, velocity, solid changeup as a third pitch and low-effort delivery earned him this lofty ranking in spite of his age and distance from the majors. Like the Tigers, we see the outline of a top-of-the-rotation starter.

50. Justin Foscue, 2B, Texas Rangers

Though he shares much in his profile with fellow Texas prospect Josh Jung, Foscue's polished offensive profile has a slightly less impressive defensive one affixed to it. He generates excellent power with an aggressive stride that drives him forward in the box as he swings to thunderous impact, albeit with unsurprising swing-and-miss risk. His subpar foot speed, range and arm will keep him at second base, or perhaps corner outfield, and his size (he's listed at six-feet tall) makes him unlikely to shift to first base. Texas has loved targeting pure hitters who may lack a position, à la Nick Solak and Willie Calhoun, and it would be no surprise to see them give Foscue a chance to figure things out. With Marcus Semien and Corey Seager in the fold, however, Foscue may soon be swinging as an audition for other organizations.

51. Ronny Mauricio, SS, New York Mets

Mauricio is one of the highest-upside players on this list. He has most of the tools for stardom: feel for the barrel from both sides of the plate, big bat speed, raw power he can get to in games, and good defensive instincts and body control. He just doesn't make good swing decisions, so much so that his OBP started with a two last season. This appears to be both a spin-recognition and plate-aggressiveness issue, especially from the left side of the plate. That's a problem, because switch-hitters predominantly bat lefty, and that's also Mauricio's better power side. Whether Mauricio can get to even a mediocre level of discipline and pitch recognition will make or break his profile, because everything else is there. All he needs to do is one of the hardest things in baseball: manage the strike zone better.

52. Austin Martin, SS/OF, Minnesota Twins

Martin was a strong candidate to go first overall in the 2020 draft and ended up receiving the second-highest signing bonus. He was an advanced college bat at a premium defensive spot. To an extent, the Jays were betting on certainty over ceiling. Martin was never likely to be a middle-of-the-order thumper, but you'd have expected his slugging percentage to start with a four last year, not a three. Perhaps that's part of the reason Toronto was willing to deal such a recent top pick at the deadline, sending Martin to the Twins for righty José Berríos. Martin has an unorthodox setup that cuts off his ability to consistently lift the ball, or even hit it as hard as you'd expect given his good wrists and bat speed. His approach is still sterling—he had a .414 OBP last year—and he split time between shortstop and center field, the two most valuable non-catcher spots in the field. The thing is, he's not an ideal shortstop or center fielder, which might just mean he's a really good second baseman or left fielder, or that he plays a bit of everywhere. We still think he's a very good prospect, but there's a little more uncertainty heading into this year than last.

53. Joey Bart, C, San Francisco Giants

Once again, we ask you to Meet Joey Bart. "What do we do now?" is a fair question for the Giants with regards to the 25-year-old backstop, who watched a rested Buster Posey go out on top for the shockingly dominant NL West champs before retiring at the end of 2021. Bart hasn't exactly seized the mantle, struggling over the past two seasons with a strength-over-speed swing that can generate moonshots but too often creates power for wind turbines. As a receiver, Bart is talented, and the slugging, whiffing, venerable gamecaller profile may be enough to satiate San Francisco. But his track record of hitting would make that at least a slight disappointment—we still hold out hope for more at the plate.

54. Eury Perez, RHP, Miami Marlins

Perez is the highest-ranked prospect on this list that most prospect observers hadn't heard of coming into 2021. He was a low-six-figure international-free-agent signing from 2019 who had yet to pitch in official games. The Marlins sent him straight to full-season ball just a few weeks after his 18th birthday. Given his age and lack of experience, his workload was very closely monitored; he made most of his starts on six days of rest and only saw one hitter a third time in a game all season. But when unleashed, he was often electric, throwing an impressive mid-90s bowling ball of a sinker from his 6-foot-8 frame. He paired the downhill sinker with a slurvy breaker and a firm change which both flashed, as well. He even made five late-season starts in High-A and shined there, too. Perez is physically mature for a teenager and has relief risk in his mechanics and command, but he has a chance for a big rotation outcome, as well.

55. Diego Cartaya, C, Los Angeles Dodgers

A hamstring injury limited Cartaya to a mere 137 Low-A plate appearances in 2021, but it was an impressive cameo. He has always received high marks for his power potential, and his future plus pop is present given how he scorched the ball for Rancho Cucamonga. Yes, that is one of the most hitter-friendly places around, but Cartaya is so strong that his simple, short swing will rocket balls out of parks at lower, more humid elevations, as well. The hit tool might lag behind a bit, as Cartaya has to adjust to spin—which may come once he gets more than 137 plate appearances—but he has the same offensive upside as the top catchers on this list. So why is he down here? Well, he's a 19-year-old catcher with a whole 137 plate appearances above the complex, for one, but the bigger concern is that he has a rather large frame for a backstop, and his defense is a little stiff. This is something that should get smoothed out with full, healthy seasons behind the plate, but the hope for the glove is that it ends up scraping average. If it gets there, you will gladly pencil Cartaya into the middle of your lineup.

56. Kyle Muller, LHP, Atlanta Braves

Nearly-graduated prospects like Muller can be useful mile markers for how we judge prospects against established big-leaguers. Muller was a competent starter in both Triple-A and the majors last year. Seeing him have success at the highest level already is reassuring, given that he's almost fully formed but not quite entirely polished. The massive lefty could stand to locate better, but we've been saying that for years, and he has continued to make it work well enough. At 92–95 from the left side, with tremendous downward plane on both his slider and curveball, Muller will always be an uncomfortable at-bat, and he should offer hitters plenty of those while in the reigning champions' rotation in 2022.

57. Gabriel Arias, SS, Cleveland Guardians

An often-underexplored facet of the *Warhammer 40,000* franchise lore is its dedication to pockets of realism, even in a world defined by absurdist, over-the-top sci-fi sprawl. One such kernel of truth is that, in the fictional city of Mecha-Cleveland, the farm system of the local baseball club has a seemingly inexhaustible reserve of promising shortstop prospects. Arias is not a *psyker* from the post-apocalyptic fantasy future, but he is the most advanced of those still prospect eligible from Cleveland's bumper crop of middle infielders. Acquired from the Padres in the 2020 deadline deal for Mike Clevinger, Arias delivers decent thump for his size, with a precocious knack for driving the ball to right-center field. He spent all of 2021 in Triple-A, an impressive feat for someone who topped out in High-A in 2019 and won't turn 22 until late February. Between Brayan Rocchio, Arias and Andrés Giménez, the Guardians could have three under-23 true shortstops making bids for playing time by mid-2022.

58. Michael Harris II, OF, Atlanta Braves

Harris is yet another Atlanta-area prep that the Braves have scouted, drafted and developed into a Top-101 prospect. This has been going on for decades now. Georgia is a baseball hotbed, after all, but Harris' trend lines are Disco-Stu-approved after a strong 2021 campaign in which Harris raked in High-A. He's a plus runner who should end up a good center fielder. He shows the kind of bat-to-ball skills that could lead to the occasional .300 season in the majors. His game power shows up more as doubles right now, but his batting practices suggest more pop to come. The total package is a potential five-tool center fielder and plus regular.

59. Luis Campusano, C, San Diego Padres

Yanked out of the oven a bit early for the second straight year only to cool his heels in San Diego for a month, Campusano is still one of the most promising offensive backstops in the league. He's not quite the mound of offensive singularity that we've seen emerge elsewhere from ostensible backstops such as Alejandro Kirk, but Campusano is a sturdy youth with a sweeping swing that aims to pull with power. That uppercut gave him a bit more time strolling back to the dugout after strike three last year than in years past, but not so much to be concerned. The task of managing a big-league staff is a tall order for a now-23-year-old, but Campusano's glovework is passable, at least. As he gains acuity against high-level pitching from both sides of the plate, it is easy to envision Campusano becoming a quality backstop with a .260 average and 20–25 home runs year in and year out.

60. Jordan Groshans, SS/3B, Toronto Blue Jays

Groshans looks the part of a slugging third baseman, but that's a little deceptive. He's still pretty okay at shortstop, despite his size and fringy range. Conversely, his plus raw power has played more average in games, as his contact profile is more solid than spectacular and he likes to use the big part of the ballpark. He's hitterish, which is a descriptor we often use when we don't think a prospect is a particularly great hitter but seems to get it done. Groshans can get it done at the plate, and he can get it done at shortstop or third base. He's highly likely to be at least an average regular, but he's honestly a little bit boring as top prospects go. We generally avoid player comps so, instead, how about this: Groshans is that trendy indy band from your 20s that has settled into making a string of well-crafted pop albums that get 6.8s from *Pitchfork*.

61. Oswald Peraza, SS, New York Yankees

The launch angle revolution has even come for your slash-and-dash, glove-first shortstops. Peraza always had bat speed that generated loud contact, but his swing plane and approach kept his ISO under .100 as a pro. Sometime during lockdown, he figured out how to swing up, and he started belting home runs as soon as the minor-league season resumed in 2021. He has sacrificed some barrel control for the more-than-occasional bomb, but that hasn't stopped him from squaring balls in the upper minors. The shortstop glove and foot speed remain plus, so Peraza is a good bet to have a long career, even if his batting average dips into the .250 range once he starts facing the best off-speed stuff. There's also more upside now, as he's shown the potential to be a 20–20, up-the-middle and middle-of-the-lineup bat.

62. Orelvis Martinez, SS/3B, Toronto Blue Jays

The highest-paid international-amateur signee of the 2018 class, Martinez stands out for his bat speed, mature approach and impressive physicality at just 19. He lacks the famous bloodlines of Toronto's current infield stars, but he has the swing to match. Much like Groshans, Martinez is defined by his bat and has already begun seeing consistent time at third base. That should be of little concern. As he gains experience, the combination of his strength, bat speed and ability to loft pitches anywhere in the zone could make him one of the most impressive finished offensive products on this list.

63. Bobby Miller, RHP, Los Angeles Dodgers

The Dodgers haven't picked higher than 15th overall since 2006, but their investments in scouting and player development have turned up gem after gem. Their 2020 first-rounder, Miller is a massive righty who went to Louisville but seems to have learned his craft at Hole In A Boat University: "Where Everything Sinks." His mid- to upper-90s heat was enough to overpower hitters in the low minors thanks to passable control, but his medley of offspeeds is what will likely make Miller so exciting as he progresses. His slider and changeup occupy the same mid- to upper-80s velocity band with hard, late break, and Miller's comfort using each pitch keeps platoon bats honest. He'll modulate his slider at times to generate cut, which can further trouble lefties. Miller was one of the more impressive arms in the minors last year, and, as things spiraled with their pitching staff in the postseason, there was reason to think the Dodgers might pull him from the AFL up to their playoff roster. Instead, Miller may make his major-league debut this year, but the progress of his command will be the speed governor of his ascension.

64. Reid Detmers, LHP, Los Angeles Angels

It was a tale of two halves for Detmers. In the first half of the season, he added a new slider and picked up several ticks on his fastball, hitting the mid-90s with some regularity and sitting a touch lower, as opposed to on either side of 90. That gave him the ability to whiff Double-A batters with something other than his majestic curve, and, with his new weapons, he quickly raced his way to the Angels around midseason. But his fastball got pasted by major-league hitters, even with the additional velo, and, after four dreadful starts, Detmers tested positive for COVID-19. He came back for the very last game of the season and got rocked again, failing to make it out of the second inning. On balance, this was still a positive season for the former Louisville star, and we expect him to settle in as a mid-rotation starter, but the downside risk with his profile is more "swingman" than "short reliever."

65. Matthew Liberatore, LHP, St. Louis Cardinals

How far can a pitcher go with two solid secondaries but a fastball that doesn't miss bats? Liberatore looks the part, standing 6-foot-5 and bearing down on hitters from the left side with a picturesque curveball and a fading changeup that pairs well with his sinking, low-90s fastball. Liberatore commands his secondaries well, and, at 21 years old, held his own in Triple-A, skipping there straight from Low-A. Critiquing Liberatore so heavily can feel nitpicky given his youth, but we've seen similar beautiful curveballs fade in effectiveness at higher levels, and Liberatore is already not an above-average bat-misser. Late in the season, he began to show a firmer version of the breaking ball. That could help raise his promising, but presently capped, trajectory.

66. Brady House, SS, Washington Nationals

A Boras client ending up with the Nats, you say? House slid in last year's draft to number 11, where Washington picked him up for an above-slot $5 million bonus. He hit very well in the Florida Complex League after signing, showing off big power upside and continuing to make improvements in making contact. He's a shortstop for now, but he's 6-foot-4 with a full frame, so the most likely scenario is that he outgrows the position and ends up fitting best at third base or an outfield corner. He has had swing-and-miss issues resulting from stiffness and rigidity in his swing, so the hit tool bears watching as he advances. House will take some time to develop, but he could be a corner bat to watch in the latter half of the decade.

67. Owen Caissie, OF, Chicago Cubs

Canada's most notable exports:

1. Pro Wrestling Legend Bret "Hitman" Hart
2. The "Love and Sausages" sketch from *Kids in the Hall*
3. Owen Caissie?

That's heady company for a teenaged outfield prospect, even one with the precocious pop Caissie has shown so far. Hailing from Burlington (dramatic pause), Ontario, Canada, he was San Diego's second-round pick in 2020. The Padres then sent him to the Cubs for Yu Darvish before Caissie even made his pro debut. Debuting in the complex this past summer, Caissie spit out exit velocities that probably required a technician call or two to confirm TrackMan was calibrated properly. He hasn't even started to fill out his 6-foot-4 frame yet. Once he does, he will look the part of a classic first-division right fielder. That's not the best there is, the best there was, or the best there ever will be, but like we said, it's a lofty company.

68. Andy Pages, OF, Los Angeles Dodgers

In a fantasy world, more hitters would be able to thrive with the convoluted swing Pages utilizes. In the fantasy-baseball world, Pages may be one of the most prized youngsters in the minors. In the real world, he's simply one of the most powerful hitters in MiLB, blasting 31 home runs last year. The muscle-bound Cuban is a quintessential right fielder, with a missile for an arm and enough speed to handle a corner, though not likely center. Every swing from Pages appears intent on driving the ball, and he is frequently successful thanks to quick hands that help scoop pitches no matter where they cross the plate. However, we know that last bit because Pages made little distinction about where pitches came in as he chose to swing and has already struggled with elevated strikeout rates. The respect afforded to him in High-A helped him push his walk rate over 14 percent, but better pitching will force him to be more selective. With a stance that begins standing fully upright, his leg-lift- and bat-waggle-laden swing are fascinating to watch, but may need paring down to allow him to reach his power at higher levels.

69. Edward Cabrera, RHP, Miami Marlins

Future Stars Edward Cabrera was an unstoppable force in MLB The Show 21, akin to Tecmo Super Bowl Bo Jackson, to the point that teammate and gamer Jazz Chisholm did an in-game interview on the virtual-Cabrera phenomenon when he was called up to the real Show. For some reason, Sony's San Diego Studio gave Cabrera's card a 100-mph sinker with a completely unhittable attack angle and movement—let's call it virtual seam-shifted wake—which even the best e-baseball players in the world couldn't touch. The real Cabrera doesn't throw a sinker at all, and his four-seam fastball is actually pretty hittable, although it does touch triple-digits every now and again. His bread-and-butter pitch is a plus, hard-diving changeup—notch another one for the Miami changeup farm—and he also works with power breaking balls that show promise. He has had a difficult time staying healthy and walked an awful lot of batters in both Triple-A and the majors last year, so there's significant bullpen risk. But, hey, who knows, maybe he'll suddenly pick up the greatest sinker of all time from his video-game self.

70. Elly De La Cruz, SS/3B, Cincinnati Reds

De La Cruz was not a seven-figure, or even six-figure, international free agent. He's already playing more third base than shortstop. And he strikes out about as often as Milhouse Van Houten with Lisa Simpson (we assume that's still a trope, we haven't watched regularly since before De La Cruz was born). De La Cruz also features some of the loudest tools outside of your local Lowe's (no, no, that's Globe Life Field, you took the wrong exit). De La Cruz has plus, bordering on plus-plus, raw power and the speed to match it. The approach *is* raw, but he also jumped from his stateside complex debut to full-season ball in a cool 55 plate appearances and wasn't overwhelmed by the ex-Florida-State League. All of these are positive markers for further growth and refinement, and the upside here is . . . well, early-seasons *Simpsons*.

71. Cristian Pache, OF, Atlanta Braves

Congratulations to the current holder of the Alex Reyes Award for managing to thread the needle of retaining prospect eligibility *and* at least a glimmer of Top-101 sheen two or more years past when they might've been expected to graduate. Since debuting in 2020, Pache has appeared in 14 postseason games and just 24 regular-season tilts. While being the next Terrance Gore is an admirable and appealing goal for well over 99 percent of aspiring baseball players, Pache has cause to aspire higher. Even as Atlanta's outfield depth was stretched like filo dough in 2021, Pache struggled to hit well enough to justify an extended run. We don't close the book on development for 23-year-olds, particularly those with Pache's baseline of perennial Gold Glove defense and benchmark-setting range in the outfield, but we do wonder if we'll ever make it to the final chapter.

72. Nick Pratto, 1B, Kansas City Royals

Delaware is home to the president, a whole bunch of post office boxes for credit-card companies, and one possibly cursed High-A baseball park. As we noted with teammate MJ Melendez, Pratto was not the only notable Royals prospect to deal with whatever bad vibes were emanating from Frawley Stadium in 2019, but hitting .190 as a first-base prospect is, to quote the Phillies current skipper, "not what you want." Last season, on the other hand, is what you want, what you really, really want. Pratto quadrupled his home run total from his High-A campaign and did it at higher levels; his 36 taters trailed only Melendez among Royals farmhands. Pratto is about the most traditional, three-true-outcomes, corner slugger on this list. Just keep him away from whoever cursed him by touching his face on the steps of the Wilmington stadium while whispering "stop hitting."

73. Nate Pearson, RHP, Toronto Blue Jays

One of the tallest drinks of water around drank deeply from the highest-hung bird feeder on the Blue Jays' farm in 2021, growing strong and poising himself to take flight. Yet an emu painted blue is still bound by gravity, and an adductor strain on the cusp of the season opener sent the fireballing bluebird plummeting to the injured list and towards another disappointing season. Shifted to the bullpen in reaction to Toronto's solid rotation yet deeply disappointing relief corps, Pearson struggled to stabilize. Letting him rub elbows with Tyler Chatwood may have been a mistake, as Pearson managed to miss bats with regularity yet lost the strike zone entirely at times and continued to look like a two-pitch wonder. Pearson's tool kit is still too enticing, and a full season of health could quickly wipe away many of these worries, but he needs to stabilize or risk a crash landing.

74. Sixto Sánchez, RHP, Miami Marlins

Sánchez missed the entire 2021 season. Expected to anchor the Miami rotation and graduate from prospect eligibility in April, he instead got off to a late-spring start between visa and COVID-19-testing issues. He then started having shoulder problems when ramping up. After months of trying to get his season underway, he had surgery to repair a small tear in his posterior capsule in July, which is one of the most concerning arm-related diagnoses a pitcher can have. He was the number-four prospect in baseball just one year ago given the overwhelming quality of his demonstrated major-league stuff—in 2020 he was throwing a high-90s four-seamer and sinker along with a plus-plus changeup and plus slider—but we have no idea if he's going to be the same pitcher the next time he takes the mound.

75. Shea Langeliers, C, Atlanta Braves

Langeliers' star hasn't shone quite as brightly since he was mentioned in the same breath as Adley Rutschman as a potential first-overall draft pick back in 2019. Langeliers' progress has been steady, though, and he remains a potential plus power bat with advanced catch-and-throw skills behind the plate. There's some stiffness to his swing that allows him to lift baseballs when he gets the fat part of the barrel on them, but leaves him swinging-and-missing more often than you'd like for a potential middle-of-the-order bat. Behind the plate, Langeliers shows off a real howitzer that keeps the running game in check, although he didn't grade out particularly well by Baseball Prospectus' minor-league framing metric. He sets a big target and has soft-enough hands that you could see him improve to become an average to slightly-above-average defender on balance, which, combined with his plus game power, should make him a fine everyday backstop.

76. Dax Fulton, LHP, Miami Marlins

Fulton got $2.4 million from the Marlins in 2020 while rehabbing from Tommy John surgery from the previous fall. Over the course of 2021, it became clear why Miami coveted the 6-foot-7 Oklahoma prep so much. His command was shaky early in the season as he continued to work his way back into form, but, by midseason, he was throwing enough good strikes. He sits in the low 90s with both a four-seam fastball and a sinker and gets strong downhill plane. His out-pitch is a big, biting curveball he can throw for strikes and get batters to chase. His changeup projects as above-average, as well, and his pitch mix tunnels together and forces hitters to guess. Fulton needs to continue sharpening his command and stretch out further, but the mid-rotation upside is clear.

77. Matt McLain, SS, Cincinnati Reds

Matthew Michael McLain ment mo mhe Muniversity mof Mouthern Malifornia, mhere me mashed many mi-*cough**cough* Pardon, something lodged in the throat. Whew. McLain has the sort of low-variance skills that could produce significant outcome variance year over year. He is asked to play shortstop full-time for a club without other strong infield defenders? Things could get dicey. Manfred rejuices the baseballs to personally spite Max Scherzer? McLain's plus hit tool and line-drive swing suddenly make him a 15- to 20-home-run threat. More likely, however, McLain's best role will be as a multi-positional infielder that starts five to six days a week, extending a lineup and keeping the rest of the club fresh. If he cannot generate enough power, or the hit tool slips, however, it's a quick path to the Romine Zone.

78. Jordan Balazovic, RHP, Minnesota Twins

A plus fastball with life || and a curve that can miss bats
The rest needs refinement || we'd prefer you not scout stats
The bullpen may call him || despite the renewed ardor
But our young righty's fate || may still be a third starter

79. Reginald Preciado, SS/3B, Chicago Cubs

When the Cubs acquired Preciado from the Padres in the the Yu Darvish trade, they hoped he would make good on his sky-high ceiling as a 6-foot-4, switch-hitting shortstop. One of the few players born in 2003 on this list, Preciado skipped the Dominican Summer League and headed straight to the Arizona Complex League, turning heads with his athleticism and ability to drive the ball with power already. A good offseason in the weight room and a spring and summer in affiliated ball could push the Panamanian way up this list next year.

80. D.L. Hall, LHP, Baltimore Orioles

We're not so mature that we can pretend we've never made a quip about an Orioles pitching prospect being named D.L., but Hall finding himself on the IL for most of the 2021 season with a "stress reaction" in his pitching elbow was truly unfortunate. He showed dominant stuff in his brief Double-A season and enough control and command for us not to have to squint too hard to see a starter. He regularly pumps upper 90s from the left side, resulting in very uncomfortable swings from batters, especially when he bores it in on righties. Hall's curve is potential plus, and both the slider and change are more than mere arsenal filler. He's just never really thrown enough strikes for us to be confident he's a starter, and now he has had a vague, season-ending elbow issue. With a full, healthy season, Hall would easily be in the top half of this list, but he's also far from the only pitching prospect in this half we could say that about.

81. Jarren Duran, OF, Boston Red Sox

While we had concerns that Duran's stomp-and-lift swing overhaul would lead to more swing-and-miss at the highest level, we did not expect well over a third of his plate appearances to end with a K. The endgame of all prospect writing is projecting major-league performance, but 112 poor plate appearances in the majors can be an adjustment period or a bellwether. Duran has gone from being a hit-tool-driven college second baseman to a slugging outfielder more suited to a corner spot despite plus-plus run times. One way to project major-league performance is that most hitters will hit for a lower average in the majors than they did in the minors. Duran hit .258 in Triple-A. With that came plenty of power, more than enough to support a corner-outfield profile. Getting to enough of that pop when you hit .240 though, that can be tricky. We think those 112 PAs were mostly an adjustment period, but there are reasons to be concerned that he won't fully max out his power/speed profile.

82. Andrew Painter, RHP, Philadelphia Phillies

Get ready for a lot of puns about painting the corners. Painter was touching 100 mph in instructs last fall after going to the Phillies with the number-13 pick. He's another skyscraper hurler, 6-foot-8 to be exact, and, while he'd been more mid-90s than high 90s in the past, he has the physical projectability to throw in the higher velocity band regularly. He also throws a curveball, slider and changeup that have above-average potential, and he can manipulate his offspeeds to disrupt hitter timing. It's a long way from post-draft backfield work to the majors, but Painter's on the same path as organization-mate Mick Abel, just a year behind him.

83. Jairo Pomares, OF, San Francisco Giants

Few teams had a concentration of breakouts to rival the Low-A San Jose Giants' last year. Between a starting rotation that included three pitchers in the top 10 for strikeouts in MiLB, and a lineup that for much of the year featured Marco Luciano, Luis Matos, Patrick Bailey and Pomares, it was a near-constant vacillation between gasoline, fireworks, and smoke. For his part, Pomares brought as much aggression to the plate as anyone in the minors, with a lefty stroke designed to swat the ball out of the infield and, ideally, deep into the night sky. The Cuban slugger has the bat speed to make it work despite an atypical frame for raw power. This is a profile that lives or dies with the bat, however, as he's already a corner-outfield glove and has not shown much acumen for adding danger on the bases. Pomares has proven he can put a hurting on pitches, but the next step will be learning to take free passes when offered, now that teams respect his power.

84. Gavin Williams, RHP, Cleveland Guardians

Williams went from undrafted in 2020, after three years of inconsistency and injuries mostly in East Carolina University's bullpen, to a clear-cut first-rounder with a dominant campaign as ECU's Friday-night starter. He throws a robust fastball that sat in the upper 90s at times last spring and has hit triple digits in the past. Both his curveball and his slider project as above-average offerings. He's a hulking presence on the mound and threw strikes for the entire collegiate season. The Guardians are one of the best player-development groups specifically at maximizing pitching, so he's in the right place to keep figuring everything out. It's only his pre-2021 priors that prevent Williams from ranking among the better pitching prospects in baseball, and if he keeps firing like this in the pros, he will be one of them.

85. Spencer Strider, RHP, Atlanta Braves

Strider made it to the majors a little more than a year after being drafted, under the guise that he might help Atlanta's pursuit of a World Series. He didn't end up throwing in the playoffs, but he's a World Series champion nonetheless, a stunning rise for a fourth-rounder who didn't pitch a lot at Clemson and often didn't throw strikes when he did. Strider is nominally a starting-pitching prospect, but he leans heavily on two great pitches: his high-90s fastball with great characteristics high in the strike zone, and a plus slurvy breaking ball. Given the mostly theoretical nature of his changeup, his past durability and command issues, and that Atlanta was willing to put him on the 40-man as a reliever so quickly, he's the single most likely pitcher on this list to end up in the bullpen. It's not a lock—more and more teams are willing to start guys who basically throw only two pitches, and amorphous roles do exist—but it's the best bet.

86. Sam Bachman, RHP, Los Angeles Angels

We're still in a holding pattern on Bachman, who, much like Strider, has the stocky, short frame and tough-as-nails top two pitches to be a high-leverage arm in the bigs as early as 2022. His conservative usage in the wake of last year's draft didn't show us much we didn't know, but a club with the ability to be patient could comfortably continue working Bachman as a starter to see if the third pitch comes along. His running fastball sits 94–98, the sharp, late-breaking slider is 85–89, and his situational changeup clocks similarly. The changeup flashes plus but is not nearly as refined as the first two offerings, which would be headlined further if a club that was desperate to contend and always needed pitching wanted to get him to the majors as soon as possible. Hey, which team drafted him again? Oh.

87. Emerson Hancock, RHP, Seattle Mariners

As recently as 10 or even five years ago, Hancock would have been a top-three draft pick. He has the look and the pedigree, with an athletic 6-foot-4 frame, and starred when healthy for the Georgia Bulldogs in the SEC. His stuff ticks the boxes, with mid-90s heat and a couple of impressive secondaries that flash plus in his slider and changeup. But Hancock was instead selected sixth, the third pitcher and second righty taken last year, trailing Marlins draftee Max Meyer then as he does now on this list. Health is one major concern, as Hancock struggled with arm fatigue off and on throughout the season, limiting his innings load. When he was pitching, he was often working specific gameplans and attempting to overhaul the fastball traits (read: unexceptional sinker) that saw his skill set deprioritized.

88. Gunnar Henderson, SS/3B, Baltimore Orioles

Will the real Gunnar Henderson please stand up? After looking overmatched at the alternate site in 2020—fair enough for a 19-year-old who hadn't played above the complex—he went to instructs and, against more age-appropriate competition, looked the part of a future power-hitting infielder. Assigned to Low-A to start 2021, the now-20-year-old blew the doors off the level, then scuffled a bit after a promotion. Henderson is playing almost as much third base as shortstop already, and the hot corner is his likely major-league home. We think the plus raw power will play nicely there, we'd just like to see it all come together for an entire season first.

89. Roansy Contreras, RHP, Pittsburgh Pirates

As velocity continues to tick up across baseball, some teams are starting to embrace the idea that it's easier to add fastball velocity to a pitcher with command of a deep arsenal than to teach their flamethrowers to throw better strikes. Michael Baumann of *The Ringer* delved into this idea with Reid Detmers, but it applies to Contreras, as well. A solid-enough pitching prospect when he was wearing Yankee pinstripes, he mostly sat low 90s but filled up the zone with all three pitches (fastball, curve and a promising sinking change). Now a Pirates prospect—he was dealt last offseason for Jameson Taillon—he sits mid-90s, touches higher, and the velocity bump has tightened up his curve into a true power breaker. While fastball velocity isn't everything, when you have most everything else, it can be a big boon. Conversely, Contreras is a shorter righty who needs to refine that third pitch and dealt with a minor forearm strain last year, so there is some relief risk in the profile.

90. Randy Vasquez, RHP, New York Yankees

As if the Yankees needed another hard-throwing, pop-up pitching prospect. Vasquez is an undersized right-hander and was an overaged international free agent who showed up in full-season ball this year pumping two different versions of a plus fastball and then dropping a big power breaker on a parade of unsuspecting hitters across three levels. It's a very simple gameplan. The righties get a steady diet of mid-90s two-seamers under the hands. Assuming they don't shatter their bats while grounding out to shortstop, once ahead he drops the big 10–5 breaker on 'em. Lefties get a four-seamer with a tick more velocity and riding life, then the same hook, but to their back foot. Vasquez's delivery is unorthodox, with more than a bit of tornadic effort. The changeup is below-average, albeit with some projection. So, there are more than a few reliever markers here. Vasquez would be a very good reliever, but we also think he has a shot to be quite a good starter.

91. Cole Winn, RHP, Texas Rangers

The rare Rangers pitching prospect who was neither put under the knife nor acquired during the 2021 season, Winn has a repertoire that elicits a relieved nod more than Bugs-Bunny-meets-Lola eyes, but he should be starting games in the The Shed for Texas as a 22-year-old next year, and he is impressively short on flaws. His four pitches, led by a fading changeup, typically fill a compass rose of movement profiles, though they can at times blend into varying speeds of pure drop. The quality of the change should give Winn an edge against platoon bats, leaving him to hopefully further refine his breaking balls. Consistency with either could lock Winn into the middle of the rotation for the next decade.

92. Kyle Harrison, LHP, San Francisco Giants

It can be difficult for mid-round prep arms to stand out quickly, as many are selected on promise and projectability—rainy day projects for the player-development staff. Ranking fifth among qualified stateside minor-league starters in strikeout rate when you're 19 years old is one way to break the mold. Harrison's slider has dramatic sweep and sink, and his slightly herky-jerky motion adds a bit of deception to help his low-90s fastball play up. He will throw both his slider and changeup to righties and lefties alike, and while he lives around the zone, he rarely sets up shop in its heart. The positive is evident in his 35.7-percent strikeout rate, with ground-ball tendencies to boot. What's unknown is whether he can hew to the corners consistently without walking so many hitters that he constantly places himself under siege.

93. Bryson Stott, SS, Philadelphia Phillies

Stott hit well at three levels in 2021 and capped it off with a strong performance in the Arizona Fall League. He's a well-rounded player who has no clear plus tool but no below-average tools, either. He's likely to hit for moderate average and power while taking a healthy but not overwhelming share of walks. His arm and hands allow him to play shortstop credibly despite average range, and he has experience at both second and third, as well. It is not an exciting skill set, but he's likely an average to above-average regular in the middle infield, and that's a very valuable profile.

94. Garrett Mitchell, OF, Milwaukee Brewers

After having his skill set picked apart ad nauseum ahead of the 2020 draft, Mitchell both thrived and struggled in 2021, much as he did in college. An advanced older bat, he shone in High-A on the back of his excellent athleticism and patient approach, but was stymied in his first month and change at Double-A. The big question is what exactly Milwaukee sees as a necessary next step for the speedy former UCLA Bruin; can he be enough of an impact player with his current approach, or does he need to overhaul his swing to turn his solid exit velocities into over-the-fence power at the risk of losing entirely what has helped him succeed thus far? His ceiling and track record earns him the respect of this ranking, but any extended struggles akin to his shoddy finale with Biloxi would be deeply worrisome.

95. Vidal Bruján, IF/OF, Tampa Bay Rays

There's unlikely to be much interest in a 2022 reboot of Bruce Campbell's turn-of-the-century syndicated period dramedy *Jack of All Trades*, but Bruján would be the ideal candidate to step into the role of secret agent Jack Stiles. He can do a little bit of everything. He played six different positions in 2021, and he is at least competent at each of them. He's a plus-plus runner, although he wasn't a particularly proficient base stealer last year. He's a switch-hitter and can hit a bit from both sides. He has added some game power, enough that 10–15 home runs isn't out of the question. The problem with being a jack of all trades—other than being a genre-bending, low budget, 22-minute show with no clear audience—is that you are often a master of none. Bruján doesn't really have that one obvious skill that would make him more than a useful regular. He should last far longer in the majors than Campbell's two-season star vehicle, though.

96. Joe Ryan, RHP, Minnesota Twins

Ryan found out he was traded from Tampa Bay to Minnesota for Nelson Cruz while eating breakfast in Tokyo's Olympic Village. He then went out and shoved as one of the best pitchers in the tournament, winning the semifinal game to help propel Team USA to a silver medal. Ryan continued to deal when he got back to North America with a pair of one-run starts in Triple-A, leading to a successful September call-up. All Ryan has done as a professional is get outs of all kinds—especially strikeouts—and avoid walks. He does not have overwhelming velocity or spin on his fastball, and only his curveball rates much above average amongst his current crop of offspeeds, but he throws a ton of good strikes and gets enough whiffs to get by while gobbling up innings. He's a high-probability mid-rotation starter.

97. Geraldo Perdomo, SS, Arizona Diamondbacks

Exhibit A in player development not being linear: On July 8, Perdomo was transferred to the Developmental List. If you aren't a baseball-operations employee, you might not know what that is. It removes the player from counting against the roster maximum for the minors, while allowing him to work on . . . well, development at the team complex. You rarely see this happen to top prospects, but, at the time, Perdomo was running a .509 OPS in Double-A; that from a player who was considered an especially polished shortstop prospect who could fall out of bed and hit .280 just about anywhere while showing an advanced glove. Whatever Perdomo worked on at Salt River Field took, as he looked very much like the Top

101 prospect of years past upon his return to Double-A in August. He played well enough to earn a September cup of coffee back in Arizona with the big club, and has started to show signs of growing into more game power, which would lift the profile from solid regular to occasional All-Star.

98. Sal Frelick, OF, Milwaukee Brewers

Milwaukee doubled down on outfielders with Garrett Mitchell's present offensive profile when they selected Frelick in the first round this year. They were rewarded with a near-identical season, statistically, albeit condensed, as Frelick throttled Low-A Carolina and had more tempered results in High-A Wisconsin. Unlike Mitchell, Frelick's frame and swing do not suggest untapped potential; what you see is what you get. Fortunately, though you might have to squint a bit more to see it, what you do get with Frelick is someone who should reach first base quite often and can get himself into scoring position from there. The Lilliputian lefty's swing is demonstrably geared towards making contact, with a tiny stride that helps with timing but hardly generates torque, and little semblance of a power hack. Given 600 plate appearances, a few of the pitchers on this list might hit more balls over the fence than Frelick, but as long as he's roaming center field, spraying singles, and stretching gappers into triples, he has a path to success.

99. Ezequiel Duran, IF, Texas Rangers

The trade return for Joey Gallo was never going to bring back a prospect that could match him in the power department, but Duran has plenty of thunder in his swing. He led the Penn League in homers in 2019, but his power was more of the plus variety. It looks plus-plus now, with 30-home-run seasons possible if he tones down some of his free-swinging tendencies. Duran played mostly second base as a Yankees prospect, usually in deference to better gloves to his right, but saw more time at shortstop and some at third base after the trade. His average foot speed isn't ideal for the six, but his soft hands, smooth actions, and plus arm should make him above-average at the other infield spots.

100. Aaron Ashby, LHP, Milwaukee Brewers

I recommend getting your sinker up on to 96, yeah
I recommend whiffin' batters with your plus slider's zoom, yeah
Throw it down (what a jagged little pill)
It feels so good (spinning with plummet)
Wait until the curve settles
You pitch, you learn
You win, you learn
You miss, you learn
You lose, you learn
You bend, you learn
You deal, you learn

101. James Triantos, 2B/SS, Chicago Cubs

It's rare for a second-rounder with only 25 games in the Arizona Complex League to be a Top 101 prospect the year after he was drafted, but we simply cannot deny Triantos' ability to hit. The suburban-Virginia prep infielder signed for a well-overslot $2.1 million after reclassifying from the 2022 draft class. Reports from the desert backfields immediately flagged him with a potential plus or plus-plus hit tool, and those kept coming in all summer and fall. He has high-end bat-to-ball abilities for his age, and his quick bat puts some thump into the ball when he makes contact, which is a combination you're not going to see out of many 18-year-olds making their pro debut. He's already sliding down the defensive spectrum—he played more innings at second than short as a pro—and his clunky-looking swing is not going to win any aesthetic awards. But on hitting talent alone, Triantos has a shot for big offensive outcomes.

Arizona Diamondbacks

The State of the System:

Good depth remains, but injuries plagued the Diamondbacks' system, and some of the advanced college arms from recent drafts scuffled, as well.

The Top Ten:

1 **Corbin Carroll OF** OFP: 60 ETA: 2024

Born: 08/21/00 Age: 21 Bats: L Throws: L Height: 5'10" Weight: 165 lb. Origin: Round 1, 2019 Draft (#16 overall)

YEAR	TEAM	LVL	AGE	PA	R	2B	3B	HR	RBI	BB	K	SB	CS	AVG/OBP/SLG	DRC+	BABIP	BRR	FRAA	WARP
2019	DIA	ROK	18	137	23	6	3	2	14	24	29	16	1	.288/.409/.450		.366			
2019	HIL	SS	18	49	13	3	4	0	6	5	12	2	0	.326/.408/.581		.452			
2021	HIL	A+	20	29	9	1	2	2	5	6	7	3	1	.435/.552/.913	113	.571	-0.4	CF(7) 0.7	0.2
2022 non-DC	*ARI*	*MLB*	*21*	*251*	*22*	*10*	*2*	*4*	*23*	*22*	*75*	*11*	*2*	*.210/.288/.336*	*73*	*.295*	*1.1*	*CF 1, LF 0*	*0.3*

Comparables: Josh Hart, Austin Meadows, Jason Martin

The Report: Carroll only played a week of games before suffering a season-ending shoulder injury. Nonetheless, that was enough to mostly confirm his reported break out behind closed doors at the 2020 alternate site. The only tool that didn't show as better than average was his throwing arm, which is fringy but accurate and perfectly acceptable in center field (at least prior to the injury). The rest of the defensive tools pop. Carroll has plus-plus speed and a potential plus glove up the middle. At the plate, strong hands and wrists generate loud contact despite a smaller frame, and Carroll roped line drives to all parts of the field and showed over-the-fence power to the opposite field. It was an incredibly impressive week, and we expect he would have established himself as one of the top position-player prospects in baseball with a full season laser show. Obviously that didn't happen, and the nature of his injury is concerning for his long-term projection. But assuming Carroll looks more or less the same come spring training, his breakout was probably only deferred for a year.

OFP: 60 / First-division center fielder

Variance: High. He's coming off a significant shoulder injury. That's it. That's the tweet.

Darius Austin's Fantasy Take: We don't have any specific information to suggest that Carroll should be moved out of the upper echelon of fantasy prospects. He could be rather pedestrian in the first few weeks of his return and still quickly be a top-10 dynasty prospect purely because so many of the names ahead of him could graduate by midseason. His speed gives him fantasy upside beyond even the promise of his bat. I doubt it's likely, but if you can find someone who is so freaked out about the shoulder injury that they'll trade him for anything less than that kind of value, jump on it. While it might backfire horribly, this kind of upside isn't easy to come by.

2 Alek Thomas OF   OFP: 60   ETA: 2022

Born: 04/28/00 Age: 22 Bats: L Throws: L Height: 5'11" Weight: 175 lb. Origin: Round 2, 2018 Draft (#63 overall)

YEAR	TEAM	LVL	AGE	PA	R	2B	3B	HR	RBI	BB	K	SB	CS	AVG/OBP/SLG	DRC+	BABIP	BRR	FRAA	WARP
2019	KC	A	19	402	63	21	7	8	48	43	72	11	6	.312/.393/.479	132	.372	0.3	CF(76) -10.6, LF(7) 0.0, RF(7) 0.9	1.7
2019	VIS	A+	19	104	13	2	0	2	7	9	33	4	5	.255/.327/.340	78	.373	0.0	CF(23) 2.4	0.3
2021	AMA	AA	21	329	54	18	8	10	41	37	65	8	5	.283/.374/.507	119	.335	-0.6	CF(45) -1.2, RF(18) 0.5, LF(10) -0.3	1.6
2021	RNO	AAA	21	166	32	11	4	8	18	15	34	5	4	.369/.434/.658	119	.439	0.4	CF(31) 4.1, LF(1) -0.0, RF(1) -0.1	1.4
2022 non-DC	*ARI*	*MLB*	*22*	*251*	*25*	*11*	*2*	*5*	*26*	*20*	*59*	*5*	*3*	*.255/.323/.404*	*97*	*.322*	*0.6*	*CF 1, RF 0*	*1.1*

Comparables: Austin Meadows, David Dahl, Byron Buxton

The Report: Now *here* was a season-long breakout for a Diamondbacks outfield prospect, although it was slightly more complicated than the gaudy stat line. Thomas has long been a favorite of the BP Prospect team due to his whippy bat speed and subsequent loud, line-drive contact. He has an unorthodox swing, with a bit of a Hokey Pokey leg kick and short load that can create intermittent sync issues. When everything is on time, Thomas sprays bullets line to line, and he started to tap into more of his raw power in 2021. He keeps the bat in the zone for a good long while and can stay back against off-speed pitches, but made more weak ground-ball contact in games than his slash line suggests. Thomas is fast enough to beat out some of those slow rollers, and his plus speed also covers for inefficient routes in center. His arm is average but accurate, and he would likely be an above-average defender in either corner. Thomas certainly benefited from favorable home parks, but, when he's locked in, it's not hard to see a plus-hit/plus-power center fielder at the highest level. There's just more hit-tool variance than you'd expect for someone who posted a .300 batting average in the upper minors.

OFP: 60 / First-division center fielder

Variance: Medium. Thomas is likely to be at least an average major leaguer given the varied ways he can impact a game, but, for a plus runner with good closing speed, he's not a lock to stick in center, and for a polished bat-to-ball prospect, there's more hit-tool collapse risk than you'd prefer.

Darius Austin's Fantasy Take: It's very difficult to draw much distinction between Thomas and Carroll as far as overall value goes. Admittedly, there's more power and a little less speed here, but Arizona is likely to have two top-10 dynasty prospects this year, and it's plausible they'll both be top-five by the end of the season. We're all too familiar with tooled-up prospects seeing their hit tool collapse at the highest level, but if Thomas is only a four-category juggernaut who frustrates in batting average sometimes, you'll have no trouble living with it.

3 Jordan Lawlar SS   OFP: 60   ETA: 2025

Born: 07/17/02 Age: 19 Bats: R Throws: R Height: 6'2" Weight: 190 lb. Origin: Round 1, 2021 Draft (#6 overall)

The Report: In a 2021 draft class loaded with high-end prep shortstop talent, Lawlar ended up number one on our draft board. He does not have the most upside of his cohort, but there are no weaknesses in his game. He's likely to not only stick at shortstop, but be at least above-average there. He's a plus-plus runner, which makes him both rangy on the infield and a threat on the basepaths. Offensively, his contact ability is going to carry the day. Lawlar needs to clean up some of his swing decisions, but that should come with professional reps, and the fundamentals of his stroke are good. He should get to average-ish power, although he doesn't have a ton of physical projection left. Lawlar would have been number one on the Diamondbacks' list if he didn't suffer a tear in his left shoulder shortly after starting his pro career. It's his non-throwing arm, and he should be ready for spring training, but, like with Carroll, this will require some monitoring.

OFP: 60 / First-division shortstop

Variance: High. He has limited pro reps, not a ton of tools projection, and there's the shoulder injury.

Darius Austin's Fantasy Take: It's weird to think of a prep draftee with a pesky shoulder issue as safe. While we shouldn't lose sight of either of those factors when we get our next looks at Lawlar, he is one of the most secure prospects out there for our purposes, albeit one who lacks the explosive upside of Thomas and Carroll. Whether he's a fantasy star or not is likely to depend on his ability to combine plus averages with 30-plus swipes in the majors (or whatever will be difference-making by the time he arrives, which might be closer to 20 than 30).

4 Geraldo Perdomo SS OFP: 55 ETA: Debuted in 2021

Born: 10/22/99 Age: 22 Bats: S Throws: R Height: 6'2" Weight: 203 lb. Origin: International Free Agent, 2016

YEAR	TEAM	LVL	AGE	PA	R	2B	3B	HR	RBI	BB	K	SB	CS	AVG/OBP/SLG	DRC+	BABIP	BRR	FRAA	WARP
2019	SRR	WIN	19	97	17	3	1	1	5	13	21	2	3	.316/.417/.418		.407			
2019	KC	A	19	385	48	16	3	2	36	56	56	20	8	.268/.394/.357	124	.318	-1.7	SS(80) 1.8, 2B(11) -0.1	2.3
2019	VIS	A+	19	114	15	5	0	1	11	14	11	6	5	.301/.407/.387	131	.325	-0.3	SS(26) -1.2	0.5
2021	AMA	AA	21	344	51	8	5	6	32	47	81	8	5	.231/.351/.357	104	.299	0.3	SS(82) 1.6	1.4
2021	ARI	MLB	21	37	5	3	1	0	1	6	6	0	0	.258/.378/.419	103	.320	-0.2	SS(10) 0.1	0.1
2022 DC	*ARI*	*MLB*	*22*	*92*	*9*	*3*	*0*	*1*	*7*	*10*	*18*	*2*	*2*	*.223/.323/.325*	*77*	*.282*	*0.3*	*SS 0*	*0.1*

Comparables: Jonathan Villar, Richard Ureña, Luis Sardinas

The Report: Perdomo started the year in the majors, found himself off any minor-league roster and on the developmental list over the summer, then played well enough down the stretch to end the season back with the Diamondbacks. It was a roller-coaster season for a prospect that, coming into 2021, had more of a surety profile given his advanced bat-to-ball approach and shortstop glove. The top-line stats in Double-A don't look great, but he finished the season strong, and, even during his early struggles, his defense never went into a slump. Perdomo has a somewhat-limited ceiling, but his above-average hit tool and on-base skills, coupled with an above-average shortstop glove, make him a good bet to be at least an average regular with perhaps a bit more in the tank if he grows into some of the pop he flashed in August and September. His 2021 campaign bumps the variance, but he's coming off a lost 2020 season, and his early-season struggles last year are most likely a blip in the rearview mirror now.

OFP: 55 / Above-average shortstop

Variance: Medium. Perdomo doesn't have sustained upper-minors success, and it's a performance-over-tools profile.

Darius Austin's Fantasy Take: The best thing we can say about Perdomo, right now, is that he already arrived. Even that comes with a caveat: since Nick Ahmed is under contract for two more years, I'm not sure how much playing time there really is for Perdomo in the short term. Perdomo is only 22 and might find some more power, but his current profile is one of a deep-league middle infielder who needs every single plate appearance to squeeze out some value—kind of like most of Nick Ahmed's career, actually.

5 Drey Jameson RHP OFP: 55 ETA: 2022

Born: 08/17/97 Age: 24 Bats: R Throws: R Height: 6'0" Weight: 165 lb. Origin: Round 1, 2019 Draft (#34 overall)

YEAR	TEAM	LVL	AGE	W	L	SV	G	GS	IP	H	HR	BB/9	K/9	K	GB%	BABIP	WHIP	ERA	DRA-	WARP
2019	HIL	SS	21	0	0	0	8	8	11^{2}	14	1	6.9	9.3	12	41.7%	.371	1.97	6.17		
2021	HIL	A+	23	2	4	0	13	12	64^{1}	60	9	2.5	10.8	77	52.6%	.319	1.21	3.92	95	0.7
2021	AMA	AA	23	3	2	0	8	8	46^{1}	38	6	3.5	13.2	68	38.5%	.327	1.21	4.08	79	0.8
2022 non-DC	*ARI*	*MLB*	*24*	*2*	*2*	*0*	*57*	*0*	*50*	*46*	*7*	*3.8*	*8.8*	*48*	*39.1%*	*.289*	*1.35*	*4.29*	*103*	*0.1*

Comparables: Michael King, Keegan Thompson, Scot Shields

The Report: Jameson's story fluctuated and warped throughout the year, but it built, constructively, into one well worth monitoring. The undersized righty out of Ball State made no drastic alterations to his repertoire, but a series of smaller adjustments have left us with a player boasting three above-average pitches and results in the mid-minors to match. Jameson's fastball seemed the most obvious beneficiary of his mechanical refinements. Though he worked 94–98 all year, major worries in the past stemmed from the violence of his motion and the pitch's sink and run. Early in 2021, his motion appeared toned down, but the fastball still could get hittable, as was noted in a midseason "Ten Pack" while Jameson churned through High-A. As the season progressed, Jameson appeared to incrementally raise his release point, helping to cull much of the sink and create a pitch that made enemies at the top of the zone.

That only augmented the effectiveness of the righty's hard slider, which he'll throw for whiffs to hitters on either side of the plate. The repertoire is still control over command, but Jameson is comfortable throwing the slider in all counts, locating a more cutting version in the zone, at times, before burying the hard-dropping variant. The changeup is average, good enough to trouble lefties with a healthy velocity gap. His athleticism no doubt aided him in making adjustments as the season went on, and, insomuch as it means anything, he was chosen by the league for the Gold Glove among all MiLB pitchers. He's still undersized, so the bullpen and durability vultures will circle all the way up until he proves he can handle himself in a big-league rotation, but that process could begin as soon as late 2022.

OFP: 55 / No. 3–4 starter

Variance: Medium. It's not hard to see Jameson pitching like a number-two if health and durability are no object. It's also plausible he ends up a high-caliber arm who only works about five innings a night, or less cheerily, as a high-end bullpen burner. Until the pitching leaderboards are filled with Sonny Grays and José Berríoses, however, pitchers of Jameson's stature will face doubts until they're doing it.

Darius Austin's Fantasy Take: Inevitable concerns about reliever risk aside, Jameson has a lot of what we're looking for: obvious strikeout potential, three potential MLB-quality weapons and relative proximity. He's working his way into top-101-dynasty-prospect contention. Take a shot that there's even more to come, and hope we don't end up pouring another one out for a once-promising starter doomed to the bullpen.

6 Ryne Nelson RHP OFP: 55 ETA: 2022

Born: 02/01/98 Age: 24 Bats: R Throws: R Height: 6'3" Weight: 184 lb. Origin: Round 2, 2019 Draft (#56 overall)

YEAR	TEAM	LVL	AGE	W	L	SV	G	GS	IP	H	HR	BB/9	K/9	K	GB%	BABIP	WHIP	ERA	DRA-	WARP
2019	HIL	SS	21	0	1	0	10	7	18^{2}	15	1	4.8	12.5	26	45.0%	.359	1.34	2.89		
2021	HIL	A+	23	4	1	0	8	8	39^{1}	21	3	3.2	13.5	59	29.5%	.240	0.89	2.52	85	0.6
2021	AMA	AA	23	3	3	0	14	14	77	66	13	3.0	12.2	104	38.0%	.312	1.19	3.51	89	0.9
2022 non-DC	*ARI*	*MLB*	*24*	*2*	*3*	*0*	*57*	*0*	*50*	*47*	*8*	*4.1*	*9.7*	*53*	*40.0%*	*.295*	*1.40*	*4.69*	*111*	*-0.1*

Comparables: Joe Kelly, Jordan Montgomery, Wil Crowe

The Report: Every bit the prototypical projectable arm visually that Jameson is not, Nelson also managed to take significant strides in 2022. Whereas his motion used to resemble a PowerPoint presentation of a pitcher's delivery, with an almost robotic stage-by-stage progression through to the plate, he has simplified and smoothed things to great effect. Pitching primarily out of the stretch now, Nelson can more easily whip his lengthy limbs through his over-the-top motion, delivering pitches to the catcher's target with excellent extension. That improved control helped Nelson work deeper into games and avoid punishment on the occasional gopher ball, which his high-spin heater is liable to elicit on occasion. The fastball is Nelson's primary weapon, sitting 93–96 and missing bats anywhere from the belt up.

His lean 6-foot-4 frame could still add weight, but the governor on Nelson's ascension is not concern about his durability or velocity. The larger question is whether any of his secondaries can climb past average, or if his brilliant heater will be enough to anchor him in the rotation. His 12–6 curveball has the right shape to pair, but its upper-70s velocity makes for a less knee-buckling bite. His slider works in the low 80s and is passable but not eye-catching. Nelson worked his mid-80s changeup with greater frequency in 2021, but not necessarily to greater effect. He'll work out the kinks in Triple-A before likely getting a big-league showcase in the back half of 2022.

OFP: 55 / No. 3–4 starter

Variance: Medium. The improvement in command is an immense stabilizer; it gets Nelson in this conversation. But MLB is more and more a game dominated by breaking balls, while the minors remain solvable for those with simply excellent fastballs. If Nelson's offspeed takes a step forward, he's in great shape for a rotation role. If not, well, we'll find out just how good that fastball really is, likely in one-to-two-inning bursts instead of five to seven.

Darius Austin's Fantasy Take: It's tempting to think that Nelson has a fairly similar fantasy outlook to Jameson, not least because the two exhibited similar levels of dominance while playing on the same teams. Nelson has more reliever risk, however, and may prove to be more of a WHIP liability when facing more advanced hitters. Given his history and the relatively recent development of his other secondaries, he's certainly worth monitoring in all leagues in case he moves more firmly into starting contention. He remains a watchlist guy unless your league has more than 200 prospects rostered.

7 Blake Walston LHP OFP: 55 ETA: 2024

Born: 06/28/01 Age: 21 Bats: L Throws: L Height: 6'5" Weight: 175 lb. Origin: Round 1, 2019 Draft (#26 overall)

YEAR	TEAM	LVL	AGE	W	L	SV	G	GS	IP	H	HR	BB/9	K/9	K	GB%	BABIP	WHIP	ERA	DRA-	WARP
2019	DIA	ROK	18	0	0	0	3	2	5	2	0	0.0	19.8	11	83.3%	.333	0.40	1.80		
2019	HIL	SS	18	0	0	0	3	3	6	6	0	3.0	9.0	6	41.2%	.353	1.33	3.00		
2021	VIS	A	20	2	2	0	8	8	43^{1}	34	4	3.5	12.5	60	43.7%	.303	1.18	3.32	86	0.6
2021	HIL	A+	20	2	3	0	11	11	52^{1}	52	12	2.8	9.8	57	36.8%	.288	1.30	4.13	120	-0.2
2022 non-DC	*ARI*	*MLB*	*21*	*2*	*3*	*0*	*57*	*0*	*50*	*53*	*8*	*4.3*	*7.7*	*42*	*39.4%*	*.305*	*1.55*	*5.79*	*132*	*-0.7*

Comparables: Jeanmar Gómez, Matt Wisler, Sterling Hitchcock

The Report: Coming into the 2019 draft, Walston was a projection bet with a plus-flashing breaking ball, and while his 2021 season was successful enough on the mound, we are still waiting for the stuff to jump. He has filled out some, but his 6-foot-5 frame is still lithe and limby. Walston can ramp the fastball up to 96 from a loose, athletic delivery, but generally sits in the low 90s. And the heater plays a bit below the Stalker readings, as hitters pick it up well from his lower slot. To keep opposing lineups off the number one, he employs two breaking balls—a loopy, 11–5 curve with good shape but not a ton of late snap and a firmer, sliderish option that misses more bats. Walston also works in a reasonably advanced changeup for a recent prep pick, although the pitch works more off arm speed and velocity separation than movement. His profile remains mostly in a holding pattern for now. A few more ticks on the fastball might help cover for his command, which lags behind the raw strike throwing, and tighten up the curveball. Walston looks like he will add strength and velocity in the coming years, but until it happens, it hasn't happened.

OFP: 55 / No. 3–4 starter

Variance: High. Walston has an advanced arsenal that he can throw for strikes, and it's easier to teach velocity than the rest of the profile, but it's a hittable fastball, at present.

Darius Austin's Fantasy Take: There's a lot of projection and development required to get Walston from where he is now to viable fantasy starter. The fastball seems like it's going to get demolished by right-handed hitters, and that's a tough obstacle to overcome. If he can sit in the mid-90s from the left side, command the heater well and bring along those secondaries, there's an every-league fantasy starter here. Why does it feel like I just made a lot of unreasonable demands?

8 Slade Cecconi RHP OFP: 50 ETA: 2023

Born: 06/24/99 Age: 23 Bats: R Throws: R Height: 6'4" Weight: 219 lb. Origin: Round 1, 2020 Draft (#33 overall)

YEAR	TEAM	LVL	AGE	W	L	SV	G	GS	IP	H	HR	BB/9	K/9	K	GB%	BABIP	WHIP	ERA	DRA-	WARP
2021	HIL	A+	22	4	2	0	12	12	59	53	5	3.1	9.6	63	43.8%	.310	1.24	4.12	101	0.4
2022 non-DC	*ARI*	*MLB*	*23*	*2*	*3*	*0*	*57*	*0*	*50*	*53*	*7*	*4.2*	*7.0*	*38*	*36.0%*	*.299*	*1.52*	*5.36*	*123*	*-0.4*

Comparables: Rocky Coppinger, Liam Hendriks, Shawn Boskie

The Report: An injury to his non-throwing hand delayed the start to Cecconi's season, and elbow soreness ended it early in August, though he did return to throw 15 innings in the Arizona Fall League and looked healthy. For better or worse, Cecconi did little to alter any priors on his profile in 2021. The former Hurricane looked, quacked and released pitches that resembled ~~an ibis~~ duck that should be a mid-rotation starter. And then hitters swing, and they don't miss nearly as often as they should. The well-built, 6-foot-4 righty reliably finds the zone with his 94–96-mph four-seamer and a tight slider with depth in the zone, and his get-me-over curveball can be located, as well, but it's fair to worry about his repertoire beyond the first two offerings, as neither his curve nor changeup appear more than fringy.

OFP: 50 / No. 4 starter or high-leverage relief

Variance: High. The 2021 season was technically Cecconi's pro debut, beyond work at the alternate site in 2020, so it's a bit unfair to be genuinely impatient with him. Cecconi has perhaps a better chance to never reach the majors than any any of the other arms listed here, but the same profile that saw him recruited to Miami got him drafted 33rd overall, and it will keep him in the pros long enough that he can hopefully figure out how to stop being quite so hittable.

Darius Austin's Fantasy Take: For a player who already had potential—say it with me now—reliever flags, missing a good chunk of time in his pro debut wasn't ideal. Cecconi still has the upside that we thought was worth chasing last year, and he certainly looks the part. At some point, he actually has to pitch those consistent starting innings to back that up, but it's a little too early to be mentally banishing him to the bullpen.

9 Bryce Jarvis RHP   OFP: 50   ETA: Late 2022/Early 2023

Born: 12/26/97 Age: 24 Bats: L Throws: R Height: 6'2" Weight: 195 lb. Origin: Round 1, 2020 Draft (#18 overall)

YEAR	TEAM	LVL	AGE	W	L	SV	G	GS	IP	H	HR	BB/9	K/9	K	GB%	BABIP	WHIP	ERA	DRA-	WARP
2021	HIL	A+	23	1	2	0	7	7	37^{1}	30	4	3.1	10.1	42	31.6%	.283	1.15	3.62	95	0.4
2021	AMA	AA	23	1	2	0	8	8	35	32	8	4.4	10.3	40	43.6%	.286	1.40	5.66	106	0.1
2022 non-DC	*ARI*	*MLB*	*24*	*2*	*3*	*0*	*57*	*0*	*50*	*51*	*8*	*4.5*	*7.9*	*43*	*44.6%*	*.299*	*1.54*	*5.47*	*126*	*-0.5*

Comparables: Williams Pérez, Aaron Slegers, Mitch Talbot

The Report: Jarvis maintained his fastball jump from his junior year at Duke into the pros, regularly hitting 95 with high spin from a high slot and maintaining his velocity deep into starts. He hasn't held his college command quite as well and can get hit early in counts when his fastball catches too much of the plate. When Jarvis does get ahead, both his slider and change tunnel well off the heater and can get swings-and-misses down and out of the zone. The slider is ahead of the change, at present, showing hard, 11–5 tilt. His delivery is high octane and uptempo, adding to the questions around his ultimate command projection. If Jarvis can improve his efficiency with his fastball early in counts, he has mid-rotation stuff, on balance, but, given the command issues in 2021, reliever risk remains.

OFP: 50 / No. 4 starter or set-up

Variance: Medium. Jarvis has a strong three-pitch mix and missed plenty of bats in Double-A. The topline results weren't as good as you'd expect given the stuff, and the arsenal may play better in short bursts or bulk-innings work.

Darius Austin's Fantasy Take: Sure, the extra walks carry a higher-than-normal reliever risk, but Jarvis's ability to maintain his velocity deep into starts provides a little more optimism about future fantasy prospects. There are lots of flashier names than Jarvis, but, between his stuff and proximity, I'd prefer to roll the dice on this type of profile in 15-team dynasty leagues. The strikeouts are there. If even a little control comes, Jarvis could be an easy SP3 for your fantasy rotation. Jarvis might be the best dynasty pitching prospect in the system.

10 Seth Beer 1B   OFP: 50   ETA: Debuted in 2021

Born: 09/18/96 Age: 25 Bats: L Throws: R Height: 6'3" Weight: 213 lb. Origin: Round 1, 2018 Draft (#28 overall)

YEAR	TEAM	LVL	AGE	PA	R	2B	3B	HR	RBI	BB	K	SB	CS	AVG/OBP/SLG	DRC+	BABIP	BRR	FRAA	WARP
2019	SRR	WIN	22	80	9	5	1	1	12	5	14	1	0	.315/.375/.452		.379			
2019	FAY	A+	22	152	24	8	0	9	34	14	30	0	3	.328/.414/.602	157	.359	-1.6	1B(16) -0.1, LF(15) -0.6	1.2
2019	CC	AA	22	280	40	9	0	16	52	24	58	0	0	.299/.407/.543	141	.333	-2.6	1B(46) 0.4, LF(8) -0.1	2.0
2019	JXN	AA	22	101	8	7	0	1	17	8	25	0	1	.205/.297/.318	85	.270	-0.3	1B(14) -0.6, LF(10) -0.6	0.0
2021	RNO	AAA	24	435	73	33	0	16	59	39	76	0	0	.287/.398/.511	117	.321	-3.0	1B(91) 0.4	1.7
2021	ARI	MLB	24	10	4	1	0	1	3	1	3	0	0	.444/.500/.889	80	.600	0.0		0.0
2022 DC	*ARI*	*MLB*	*25*	*305*	*34*	*15*	*0*	*9*	*36*	*22*	*64*	*0*	*0*	*.245/.337/.413*	*100*	*.292*	*-0.5*	*1B 0, LF 1*	*0.7*

Comparables: David Cooper, Ryan O'Hearn, Mark Trumbo

The Report: It's now been more than a half decade since Beer's freshman season at Clemson. That year, he posted a frankly ludicrous 1.235 OPS with twice as many walks as strikeouts in the ACC. That got him shortlisted for the Golden Spikes and established him as the favorite to go first overall in 2018. His prospect stock has gone through a controlled skid since then, but he's never really been bad at the plate, either in college or the pros. It's easy to nitpick the profile, as draftniks and amateur scouts did his sophomore and junior years. Beer has kind of a length-and-strength swing and fringe bat speed, although he marries it with a sterling approach and better barrel control than you'd expect. Arizona isn't even trying to have him stand in the outfield anymore, and he's more likely to be a DH in the majors than a first baseman. He hits the ball hard, but it's not elite power. Both of his offensive tools are likely to end up plus, but, with little to no defensive value, that's merely useful.

OFP: 50 / Second-division designated hitter or first baseman.

Variance: Low. The biggest impact on Beer's immediate major-league future is whether or not the universal DH is in the new Collective Bargaining Agreemet. The tools variance isn't high here, but there also aren't really roster spots for a role-45 DH, so he has to hit the projection to avoid the dreaded Quad-A label.

Darius Austin's Fantasy Take: "National League player relying on the reintroduction of a DH" is not so much precarious as halfway off the cliff already, hoping for the CBA to extend a helping hand. I have little doubt that Beer will be a good hitter, but he may well not be a great one. We should know before the season starts whether he gets that DH opportunity, but I don't think Arizona will let him stand at first instead of Christian Walker often enough to make a difference. It's not that far from there to . . . well, Renato Núñez.

The Prospects You Meet Outside the Top Ten:

#11

Deyvison De Los Santos 3B Born: 06/21/03 Age: 19 Bats: R Throws: R Height: 6'1" Weight: 185 lb. Origin: International Free Agent, 2019

YEAR	TEAM	LVL	AGE	PA	R	2B	3B	HR	RBI	BB	K	SB	CS	AVG/OBP/SLG	DRC+	BABIP	BRR	FRAA	WARP
2021	DIA	ROK	18	95	19	4	2	5	17	13	24	1	1	.329/.421/.610		.415			
2021	VIS	A	18	160	26	12	0	3	20	13	43	2	0	.276/.340/.421	95	.374	1.0	3B(35) 5.8, 1B(1) -0.0	1.0
2022 non-DC	*ARI*	*MLB*	*19*	*251*	*18*	*11*	*1*	*2*	*20*	*14*	*85*	*0*	*1*	*.205/.257/.297*	*49*	*.310*	*-0.2*	*3B 4, 1B 0*	*-0.6*

Signed out of the Dominican Republic for $200,000 in 2019, De Los Santos smashed his way onto the radar this year by hitting baseballs very hard and very far. It's a true power hitter's swing: he coils himself like a spring and explodes with plus bat speed and serious lift. It's a violent-enough stroke to lend itself to whiffs in the zone—and De Los Santos struggled with offspeed out of the zone in a late-season promotion to Visalia—but he has impact power potential with the bat. Even if he gets fooled a bit, if he gets the barrel on the ball, it will go far. There's some semblance of an approach, too, so once he gets more reps and sees more age-appropriate competition, there's the potential for at least an average hit tool, as well. De Los Santos is a better runner than you'd think given the frame and rangy at third base, but his hands and arm can be a bit inconsistent; he may end up sliding over to first long-term.

#12

Stuart Fairchild OF Born: 03/17/96 Age: 26 Bats: R Throws: R Height: 6'0" Weight: 205 lb. Origin: Round 2, 2017 Draft (#38 overall)

YEAR	TEAM	LVL	AGE	PA	R	2B	3B	HR	RBI	BB	K	SB	CS	AVG/OBP/SLG	DRC+	BABIP	BRR	FRAA	WARP
2019	DBT	A+	23	281	32	17	2	8	37	25	60	3	5	.258/.335/.440	122	.306	-0.8	CF(39) -3.3, LF(15) 2.9	1.5
2019	CHA	AA	23	179	25	12	1	4	17	19	23	3	2	.275/.380/.444	128	.302	-1.2	CF(29) -0.4, RF(10) 1.4, LF(4) 0.3	1.3
2021	RNO	AAA	25	182	27	7	4	9	28	22	39	7	1	.295/.385/.564	113	.336	1.2	RF(26) -0.9, LF(10) -0.4, CF(3) -0.3	0.8
2021	ARI	MLB	25	17	3	1	0	0	2	1	3	0	0	.133/.235/.200	101	.167	-0.2	CF(5) -0.3, LF(2) -0.1, RF(1) 0.0	0.0
2022 non-DC	*ARI*	*MLB*	*26*	*251*	*24*	*11*	*1*	*6*	*26*	*20*	*61*	*4*	*3*	*.228/.304/.375*	*85*	*.286*	*0.3*	*CF 0, RF 0*	*0.5*

Comparables: Chris Heisey, Mitch Haniger, Drew Stubbs

Fairchild missed some time with a hamstring injury in 2021, but otherwise continued his trajectory towards becoming a useful fourth outfielder/fringe starter. He's unlikely to maintain a .562 slugging percentage outside of the PCL, but he does have fringe-average pop along with some on-base ability and platoon leverage to back a solid center-field glove.

Prospects on the Rise

Jorge Barrosa CF Born: 02/17/01 Age: 21 Bats: S Throws: L Height: 5'9" Weight: 165 lb. Origin: International Free Agent, 2017

YEAR	TEAM	LVL	AGE	PA	R	2B	3B	HR	RBI	BB	K	SB	CS	AVG/OBP/SLG	DRC+	BABIP	BRR	FRAA	WARP
2019	HIL	SS	18	252	25	12	2	1	26	21	32	8	4	.251/.335/.336		.289			
2021	VIS	A	20	163	30	8	0	3	16	7	31	9	4	.333/.389/.449	111	.404	1.4	CF(20) 2.0, LF(14) 1.5, RF(2) 0.1	1.3
2021	HIL	A+	20	272	41	18	3	4	21	22	48	20	7	.256/.332/.405	110	.304	-0.2	CF(60) 6.5	1.9
2022 non-DC	*ARI*	*MLB*	*21*	*251*	*20*	*11*	*1*	*2*	*21*	*13*	*52*	*12*	*5*	*.238/.289/.336*	*69*	*.296*	*1.2*	*CF 3, RF 1*	*0.4*

Barrosa is listed at 5-foot-9 and 165 pounds, but that doesn't stop him from really letting it rip at the plate. It's controlled aggression and above-average bat speed, but he can get a bit swing-happy at times, and the lack of real game power means upper-level arms will challenge him; he will have to refine his approach. Barossa is a high-end plus runner but an inefficient base stealer. The speed certainly plays in center field though, and he is a potential impact defender given his closing speed and willingness to leave it all out in the field. The glove should get him a shot in the majors, but how the bat develops will determine if he's a fifth outfielder, fringe starter, or something in between.

Ryan Bliss SS Born: 12/13/99 Age: 22 Bats: R Throws: R Height: 5'9" Weight: 165 lb. Origin: Round 2, 2021 Draft (#42 overall)

YEAR	TEAM	LVL	AGE	PA	R	2B	3B	HR	RBI	BB	K	SB	CS	AVG/OBP/SLG	DRC+	BABIP	BRR	FRAA	WARP
2021	VIS	A	21	175	22	9	1	6	23	13	40	11	4	.259/.322/.443	108	.310	-1.5	SS(37) -0.8	0.5
2022 non-DC	*ARI*	*MLB*	*22*	*251*	*21*	*10*	*1*	*4*	*23*	*14*	*80*	*10*	*5*	*.219/.271/.335*	*62*	*.312*	*1.1*	*SS -2*	*-0.4*

Comparables: Nico Hoerner, Kyle Seager, Brent Morel

The Diamondbacks' second-round pick last July, Bliss is an undersized, wiry college infielder who generates surprising pull-side power from his frame. He struggled a bit with better velocity in his pro debut but tracked and adjusted to offspeed well. His below-average arm will eventually limit him to second base, but he should end up above average at the keystone due to plus hands and actions. If he can continue to show average game pop up the ladder, Bliss could end up a fringe starter or useful bench infielder.

Jeferson Espinal OF Born: 06/07/02 Age: 20 Bats: L Throws: L Height: 6'0" Weight: 180 lb. Origin: International Free Agent, 2018

YEAR	TEAM	LVL	AGE	PA	R	2B	3B	HR	RBI	BB	K	SB	CS	AVG/OBP/SLG	DRC+	BABIP	BRR	FRAA	WARP
2019	DSL DB1	ROK	17	206	36	9	2	2	14	15	45	22	9	.358/.412/.460		.464			
2019	DIA	ROK	17	43	6	1	0	0	7	8	11	4	1	.286/.419/.314		.417			
2021	DIA	ROK	19	83	17	6	1	1	10	10	21	9	1	.352/.446/.507		.490			
2021	VIS	A	19	170	22	8	0	1	13	16	63	7	2	.216/.288/.288	66	.356	1.2	RF(16) 3.0, CF(13) 0.5, LF(9) -2.4	0.1
2022 non-DC	*ARI*	*MLB*	*20*	*251*	*16*	*10*	*0*	*2*	*17*	*16*	*103*	*9*	*4*	*.178/.235/.256*	*30*	*.307*	*1.0*	*CF 1, LF 0*	*-1.3*

Espinal was too advanced for the complex this time around but overmatched by the velocity and spin of full-season ball. If only there were a level in between the two that would have been an age- and experience-appropriate step up for him. Anyhoo, Espinal is a bit physically immature but has a good tools foundation of speed and center-field defense. The next step is filling out his frame and adjusting to full-season stuff on the second go-round.

Prospects on the Farm

Luis Frías RHP Born: 05/23/98 Age: 24 Bats: R Throws: R Height: 6'3" Weight: 245 lb. Origin: International Free Agent, 2015

YEAR	TEAM	LVL	AGE	W	L	SV	G	GS	IP	H	HR	BB/9	K/9	K	GB%	BABIP	WHIP	ERA	DRA-	WARP
2019	HIL	SS	21	3	3	0	10	10	49^2	36	0	3.1	13.0	72	42.5%	.340	1.07	1.99		
2019	KC	A	21	3	1	0	6	6	26^2	22	1	4.0	9.8	29	36.6%	.300	1.28	4.39	92	0.3
2021	HIL	A+	23	2	0	0	2	2	11	5	0	3.3	12.3	15	42.9%	.238	0.82	0.82	89	0.1
2021	AMA	AA	23	5	6	0	16	16	78^2	69	16	2.9	10.4	91	44.1%	.269	1.19	5.26	86	1.1
2021	RNO	AAA	23	2	1	0	5	5	21^2	21	1	6.6	8.3	20	50.8%	.323	1.71	5.82	92	0.2
2021	ARI	MLB	23	0	0	0	3	0	3^1	2	0	13.5	8.1	3	37.5%	.250	2.10	2.70	173	-0.1
2022 DC	*ARI*	*MLB*	*24*	*4*	*3*	*0*	*40*	*3*	*45.3*	*45*	*6*	*5.0*	*8.8*	*44*	*47.2%*	*.310*	*1.57*	*5.43*	*121*	*-0.3*

Comparables: Bryan Mitchell, Brad Peacock, Trent Thornton

Frias didn't really put it together as a starter in the upper minors, but the Diamondbacks gave him a late-season cup of coffee out of their major-league pen. The fastball ticked up a bit—he's more mid-90s as a starter—which helped cover for fringy command and fairly nondescript shape. His power breaker can miss bats, and his change can flash a little split/sink action at times, although he uses it sparingly, even when starting. It hasn't quite clicked for Frias, but he could still be a valuable pen piece for the Diamondbacks in 2022, if he smooths out his command issues just a bit.

Conor Grammes RHP Born: 07/13/97 Age: 24 Bats: R Throws: R Height: 6'1" Weight: 200 lb. Origin: Round 5, 2019 Draft (#152 overall)

YEAR	TEAM	LVL	AGE	W	L	SV	G	GS	IP	H	HR	BB/9	K/9	K	GB%	BABIP	WHIP	ERA	DRA-	WARP
2019	HIL	SS	21	0	1	0	9	6	15^1	11	0	4.7	11.7	20	48.6%	.314	1.24	4.11		
2021	HIL	A+	23	0	2	0	8	7	25^1	35	5	4.3	11.4	32	43.4%	.429	1.86	7.46	90	0.3
2022 non-DC	*ARI*	*MLB*	*24*	*2*	*3*	*0*	*57*	*0*	*50*	*53*	*8*	*4.7*	*7.8*	*43*	*42.0%*	*.308*	*1.59*	*5.87*	*133*	*-0.7*

Arizona's strategy of jamming its system with pitcher after pitcher featuring modernized repertoires and less-than-Rolex-quality consistency all but ensures some breakouts (see: Jameson, Drey), some disappointments (see: Jarvis, Bryce), and some injury-shortened flashes. Grammes came out of Xavier University a raw fireballer with a horseradish-sharp slider and still is mostly that. The two planes he works on with the sharp, vertical break of his high-spin slider and the solid carry of his upper-90s fastball make him a nightmare to square up for righties and lefties, alike. July 2021 Tommy John surgery will keep him out for most of this year, but the silver lining is it should hasten his inevitable transition to a more sensible high-leverage bullpen role, assuming the signature stuff returns.

Tommy Henry LHP Born: 07/29/97 Age: 24 Bats: L Throws: L Height: 6'3" Weight: 205 lb. Origin: Round 2, 2019 Draft (#74 overall)

YEAR	TEAM	LVL	AGE	W	L	SV	G	GS	IP	H	HR	BB/9	K/9	K	GB%	BABIP	WHIP	ERA	DRA-	WARP
2021	AMA	AA	23	4	6	0	23	23	115²	116	24	4.1	10.5	135	38.7%	.335	1.46	5.21	84	1.8
2022 non-DC	*ARI*	*MLB*	*24*	*2*	*3*	*0*	*57*	*0*	*50*	*51*	*9*	*5.0*	*8.6*	*47*	*35.6%*	*.303*	*1.59*	*5.66*	*128*	*-0.5*

Comparables: Scott Diamond, Luke French, Thomas Pannone

Henry popped a little more velocity at the alternate site in 2020, but, in a return to regular game action in 2021, the fastball settled back into the low 90s. The change remains an above-average pitch with good sink and fade, while his two breaking-ball looks remain fringy but with potential. The slider is ahead right now, as it's a viable left-on-left option when he keeps it down in the zone. Henry's junior year at Michigan was the only season he really filled up the zone, and his control wavered again in Double-A last year. His arm action is a little stiff and a little slingy, and his fastball location can get a little scattershot. The heater is a bit too hittable at 90–92, so he is going to need to find those extra ticks again or a bit finer command to get back to that average-major-league-starter projection.

Top Talents 25 and Under (as of 4/1/2022):

1. Corbin Carroll, OF
2. Alex Thomas, OF
3. Jordan Lawler, SS
4. Daulton Varsho, OF/C
5. Geraldo Perdomo, SS
6. Drey Jameson, RHP
7. Ryne Nelson, RHP
8. Blake Walston, LHP
9. Slade Cecconi, RHP
10. Bryce Jarvis, RHP

Little and less went right for the Diamondbacks in 2021, and their division may have three potential juggernauts in it, but other than that, Mrs. Lincoln, how did you enjoy the play? Fortunately for Arizona, their system features more upside than those of much of the league, and much of its top talent should reach Phoenix in 2022. Additionally, the Diamondbacks have the luxury of a few players still under contract for some time, like center fielder/second baseman Ketel Marte and righty Zac Gallen, that they can either choose to build around or deal away for significant prospect recompense.

Players like Thomas, Perdomo, Beer and at least a few of the pitchers will join Varsho in the majors consistently this coming season, and Arizona has to hope Varsho can be an example for them. The enigmatic speedster has a profile matched by precious few in the league, capably handling all three outfield positions and mixing in behind the dish as needed. His overall offensive profile is sufficient to start, with a 94 DRC+ in 315 plate appearances in 2021, but he's best suited playing five days a week or so as a fourth outfielder and second-and-a-half catcher. Let him give Carson Kelly a rest once a week when a righty is on the mound and spend the rest of his time helping Arizona extend its bench with his versatility. They just need to focus on extending their starting lineup first.

Atlanta Braves

The State of the System:

The defending world champs have graduated most of the impact players from their farm, but they do still have a reserve of potential near-term big-league contributors.

The Top Ten:

1 **Kyle Muller LHP** OFP: 60 ETA: Debuted in 2021
Born: 10/07/97 Age: 24 Bats: R Throws: L Height: 6'7" Weight: 250 lb. Origin: Round 2, 2016 Draft (#44 overall)

YEAR	TEAM	LVL	AGE	W	L	SV	G	GS	IP	H	HR	BB/9	K/9	K	GB%	BABIP	WHIP	ERA	DRA-	WARP
2019	MIS	AA	21	7	6	0	22	22	111^2	81	5	5.5	9.7	120	39.2%	.286	1.33	3.14	108	0.2
2021	GWN	AAA	23	5	4	0	17	17	79^2	66	9	4.7	10.5	93	41.6%	.286	1.36	3.39	78	2.0
2021	ATL	MLB	23	2	4	0	9	8	36^2	26	2	4.9	9.1	37	37.5%	.261	1.25	4.17	106	0.2
2022 DC	*ATL*	*MLB*	*24*	*4*	*3*	*0*	*33*	*4*	*46.7*	*42*	*6*	*5.2*	*9.6*	*49*	*40.9%*	*.293*	*1.49*	*5.09*	*116*	*0.0*

Comparables: Robbie Erlin, Eduardo Rodriguez, Jake Thompson

The Report: Muller pitched a whole bunch in the majors this year for the eventual World Series champions; he was just three or four starts from graduating. He was basically as advertised: big stuff, questionable command and control. His fastball was more above average in velocity than the huge velocity he'd flashed previously, sitting around 93–94 most nights, but it's also a very high-spin pitch. He used a hard downward-tilting slider as his primary secondary offering, and it was very effective. So was his previously plus-flashing curveball in more limited usage; it ran a 48.1 percent whiff rate, so he might want to try showing that off more, especially against lefties (when he barely threw it). Muller's changeup has shown above-average potential in the past, but he barely threw it in 2021.

He throws a lot more strikes than he used to. It's still not quite enough to be a reliable frontline starting pitcher yet. But maybe there's another big gain coming here. We've been believers in Muller's profile for years now and nothing that happened in 2021 raised any additional red flags.

OFP: 60 / No. 2–3 starter

Variance: Medium. He's no more than a grade of consistent command from hitting his OFP outright (maybe only half a grade), but we could write that about two pitching prospects on every list if we're being honest.

Mark Barry's Fantasy Take: Last year at this time, we were hearing rumblings of a magical uptick to Muller's command at the alternate site. Those improvements didn't really translate to his performance in 2021, as he still walked more than 12 percent of opposing hitters between Triple-A and a major-league debut. Between those extreme bouts of charitability and his failure to average five innings per appearance, I have serious doubts about Muller's ability to stick in a rotation.

2 Michael Harris II OF OFP: 60 ETA: 2024

Born: 03/07/01 Age: 21 Bats: L Throws: L Height: 6'0" Weight: 195 lb. Origin: Round 3, 2019 Draft (#98 overall)

YEAR	TEAM	LVL	AGE	PA	R	2B	3B	HR	RBI	BB	K	SB	CS	AVG/OBP/SLG	DRC+	BABIP	BRR	FRAA	WARP
2019	BRA	ROK	18	119	15	6	3	2	16	9	20	5	2	.349/.403/.514		.414			
2019	ROM	A	18	93	11	2	1	0	11	9	22	3	0	.183/.269/.232	84	.246	-0.5	RF(18) 5.3, CF(4) 0.8	0.7
2021	ROM	A+	20	420	55	26	3	7	64	35	76	27	4	.294/.362/.436	116	.349	1.9	CF(76) 5.5, RF(9) -0.3, LF(7) 6.2	3.5
2022 non-DC	*ATL*	*MLB*	*21*	*251*	*21*	*11*	*1*	*2*	*21*	*17*	*55*	*8*	*2*	*.240/.299/.338*	*73*	*.305*	*0.6*	*CF 2, RF 0*	*0.4*

Comparables: Christian Yelich, Albert Almora Jr., Austin Meadows

The Report: Another entry in Atlanta's now decades-long pipeline of local prep picks, Harris was a two-way star in high school about a half hour down I-75. He has focused solely on hitting as a pro, and it started to pay dividends in his first full professional season. Harris emerged from the lost pandemic season with a sweet lefty swing and an advanced approach for his experience level. The raw power is well ahead of the game power at this point, but he hits the ball hard and can already drive the gaps. As he gains more upper-body strength and game experience, some of those copious doubles should turn into home runs. Harris is a high-end plus runner who should stick in center field and has 20–20 potential at an up-the-middle spot. Even if his game power ends up fringier, the approach, plus hit tool and speed would all play well at the top of a lineup.

OFP: 60 / First-division outfielder

Variance: High. Harris only has low-minors experience, and his game power is gap power at present.

Mark Barry's Fantasy Take: In 2021, minor-league stolen bases were less impressive than ever. Still, Harris snagged a buncha bags and did so pretty efficiently. His approach is improving, and, despite not hitting for a ton of power (or even above-average power), he's well on his way to being a five-category contributor. He's a pretty clear top-35 dynasty prospect, for me.

3 Cristian Pache OF OFP: 55 ETA: Debuted in 2020

Born: 11/19/98 Age: 23 Bats: R Throws: R Height: 6'2" Weight: 215 lb. Origin: International Free Agent, 2015

YEAR	TEAM	LVL	AGE	PA	R	2B	3B	HR	RBI	BB	K	SB	CS	AVG/OBP/SLG	DRC+	BABIP	BRR	FRAA	WARP
2019	MIS	AA	20	433	50	28	8	11	53	34	104	8	11	.278/.340/.474	119	.351	-2.0	CF(58) 1.1, RF(23) 3.0, LF(22) 0.1	2.8
2019	GWN	AAA	20	105	13	8	1	1	8	9	18	0	0	.274/.337/.411	96	.329	-1.4	CF(23) -3.2, RF(3) 3.5	0.2
2020	ATL	MLB	21	4	0	0	0	0	0	0	2	0	0	.250/.250/.250	96	.500		LF(2) 0.2	0.0
2021	GWN	AAA	22	353	50	15	0	11	44	30	97	9	7	.265/.330/.414	89	.347	0.6	CF(79) -3.9, RF(4) 0.1	0.5
2021	ATL	MLB	22	68	6	3	0	1	4	2	25	0	0	.111/.152/.206	65	.162	1.2	CF(22) -1.8	-0.1
2022 DC	*ATL*	*MLB*	*23*	*335*	*35*	*15*	*2*	*6*	*34*	*21*	*99*	*6*	*4*	*.224/.277/.353*	*67*	*.306*	*0.6*	*CF -1*	*-0.2*

Comparables: Manuel Margot, Anthony Gose, Melky Cabrera

The Report: Pache is the best defensive outfielder in the minors and one of the best at any level. As long as we write about his defense, and his defense only, this will be an absolutely glowing report. Our internal system notes on Pache from others include "generational defender" and "an 8 in center and not debatable." He's fast, he has a quick and accurate first step, he takes exceptional routes to balls, and his arm is plus-plus. He will be a joy to watch in the field in the same ways Kevin Kiermaier long has been. Because of that, if Pache can hit .250 with some power, he'll be an absolute superstar. Well, about that...

We have been more optimistic that Pache's offensive game was improving at times in the past than we are right now, which is reflected in this report and in his Top 101 ranking. He swings at too many pitches he can't hit, and he can't hit velocity up in the zone or offspeed low, so that's a problem. The swing-and-miss limits his game power substantially. He was comically overmatched in the majors and, at times, in Triple-A, too. Yet, we have slight reason for optimism in his strong finish at Triple-A and the knowledge that he doesn't need to hit *that* much.

OFP: 55 / Many Gold Gloves, many below-average offensive seasons

Variance: High. Pache was a Top-25 prospect each of the last two years, and his latent offensive potential isn't totally gone, but we're not at all confident he's going to get there.

Mark Barry's Fantasy Take: Pache's first real opportunity in the big leagues went about as well as Marissa Cooper's debut to society in the first season of the television series *The O.C.* (read: bad, it went bad). For those who prefer their glass half full, his demotion to Triple-A resulted in the exact production you'd hope for from the 22-year-old: decent average, decent power and decent speed. I'm not expecting superstardom by any stretch, but now might be a good time to get in on the basement floor for Pache, with decent production on the horizon.

4 Shea Langeliers C OFP: 55 ETA: Late 2022/Early 2023

Born: 11/18/97 Age: 24 Bats: R Throws: R Height: 6'0" Weight: 205 lb. Origin: Round 1, 2019 Draft (#9 overall)

YEAR	TEAM	LVL	AGE	PA	R	2B	3B	HR	RBI	BB	K	SB	CS	AVG/OBP/SLG	DRC+	BABIP	BRR	FRAA	WARP
2019	ROM	A	21	239	27	13	0	2	34	17	55	0	0	.255/.310/.343	89	.325	-1.0	C(42) 2.6	0.6
2021	MIS	AA	23	370	56	13	0	22	52	36	97	1	0	.258/.338/.498	136	.299	0.3	C(79) -12.9	1.6
2022 non-DC	*ATL*	*MLB*	*24*	*251*	*25*	*10*	*0*	*7*	*28*	*19*	*75*	*0*	*0*	*.224/.290/.376*	*77*	*.299*	*-0.4*	*C -3*	*0.1*

Comparables: José Briceño, Elias Díaz, Will Smith

The Report: It was a scant three years ago, before the 2019 college season, that Langeliers was considered right alongside Adley Rutschman as a potential first-overall pick. Langeliers had a strong junior season for Baylor, while Rutschman had one of the best college seasons of all time, won the Golden Spikes and heard his name called first from the dais. Langeliers still ended up a top-10 pick on the strength of his advanced defensive profile and plus power potential. He started 2021 in Double-A and mostly played to that projection, with one notable exception.

Let's start with the bat. Langeliers uses a small leg kick for timing and then looks to lift. It's not a particularly long swing, and, although there is some stiffness and leverage, he never gets overly pull-happy. The bat speed is merely average, and he will flail over your better breaking stuff, but the power plays line to line. The hit tool has always projected on the fringy side of average, and he might only hit in the.230–.240 range, but given the potential for 20-plus bombs, Langeliers should eek out an averagish offensive line on balance. You'll take that from your everyday catcher.

But now, the exception. Coming out of college, Langeliers had a sterling defensive reputation, an advanced glove with a plus arm. The arm strength has shown up. He pops an accurate 1.9 and threw out more than 40 percent of base stealers last year. But if you are reading a prospect blurb on this website, you likely know that the framing is the thing, and Langeliers graded out well below average in that regard statistically. We don't know precisely how much we should care about that at this exact point in time, but you can see some of those issues behind the plate. While his body stays quiet, and he sets a big target, his receiving can be alternatively stabby or tentative. This is an improvable skill, but the bar for acceptable framing is a lot higher in the majors than Double-A, and the glove was supposed to be the set-it-and-forget-it part of the profile.

OFP: 55 / Cromulent starting catcher

Variance: Medium. The hit tool questions aren't new, the defensive questions are.

Mark Barry's Fantasy Take: In the land of one-catcher leagues, the dude that strikes out more than a quarter of the time at Double and Triple-A is, well, whatever the opposite of king would be. The peasant? The jester? Langeliers flashed some pop this year, but there wasn't much else to get excited about. You'll probably be able to find a reasonable facsimile of that skill set on the waiver wire.

5 Spencer Strider RHP OFP: 55 ETA: Debuted in 2021

Born: 10/28/98 Age: 23 Bats: R Throws: R Height: 6'0" Weight: 195 lb. Origin: Round 4, 2020 Draft (#126 overall)

YEAR	TEAM	LVL	AGE	W	L	SV	G	GS	IP	H	HR	BB/9	K/9	K	GB%	BABIP	WHIP	ERA	DRA-	WARP
2021	AUG	A	22	0	0	0	4	4	15^1	6	0	2.9	18.8	32	25.0%	.300	0.72	0.59	53	0.5
2021	ROM	A+	22	0	0	0	3	3	14^2	9	1	3.7	14.7	24	43.3%	.276	1.02	2.45	82	0.3
2021	MIS	AA	22	3	7	0	14	14	63	48	6	4.1	13.4	94	30.7%	.321	1.22	4.71	80	1.3
2021	ATL	MLB	22	1	0	0	2	0	2^1	2	1	3.9	0.0	0	25.0%	.143	1.29	3.86	145	0.0
2022 DC	*ATL*	*MLB*	*23*	*7*	*3*	*0*	*55*	*3*	*58*	*49*	*9*	*4.7*	*11.5*	*74*	*42.3%*	*.295*	*1.38*	*4.43*	*104*	*0.2*

Comparables: Tyler Thornburg, Joe Ryan, Armando Galarraga

The Report: Strider raced to the majors just more than a year out from the draft with the thought that his dominant two-pitch mix might help Atlanta's playoff push out of the bullpen. He got into two games, which was enough to confirm that he has a high-90s fastball with elite characteristics and not a whole lot else. Down in the minors earlier in the season, Strider made stops at all four full-season levels, quickly emerging as a top pitching prospect on the way back from college Tommy John surgery. In addition to the high, hard-to-hit heaters coming in from tough angles, he mixes in a sharp, downward-tilting, slurvy breaking ball, which is an easy plus pitch. His changeup is theoretical at this point in his pro career. While we've seen more two-pitch starters recently, Atlanta probably did tell us what they actually think of his future by putting him on the 40-man so soon as a relief pitcher.

OFP: 55 / Long-term closer

Variance: Medium. Maybe the world has changed enough that he can start? We're not betting on it or anything, but variance can be positive too.

Mark Barry's Fantasy Take: It feels like Strider might be on the fast track to high-leverage bullpen work. That's useful, but it's also less exciting for fantasy purposes.

6 Ryan Cusick RHP OFP: 55 ETA: 2023

Born: 11/12/99 Age: 22 Bats: R Throws: R Height: 6'6" Weight: 235 lb. Origin: Round 1, 2021 Draft (#24 overall)

YEAR	TEAM	LVL	AGE	W	L	SV	G	GS	IP	H	HR	BB/9	K/9	K	GB%	BABIP	WHIP	ERA	DRA-	WARP
2021	AUG	A	21	0	1	0	6	6	16^{1}	15	1	2.2	18.7	34	57.1%	.519	1.16	2.76	57	0.5
2022 non-DC	*ATL*	*MLB*	*22*	*2*	*2*	*0*	*57*	*0*	*50*	*44*	*7*	*4.1*	*10.5*	*58*	*40.9%*	*.300*	*1.36*	*4.22*	*102*	*0.1*

Comparables: Taylor Widener, Steven Jennings, John Carver

The Report: Cusick already cuts an imposing figure on the mound, his sturdy 6-foot-6 frame unleashing upper-90s heat with downhill plane from a high-three-quarters slot. He pairs the fastball with a short power curve that also gets under bats. Cusick was drafted in the back half of the first round rather than the top half, because he didn't really have the third pitch or command profile that suggested a sure-shot starter, and the delivery is uptempo with moderate effort, on top of that. Cusick threw plenty of strikes and racked up plenty of strikeouts in his brief pro debut, though. If the headline offerings continue to dominate, the lack of a third pitch might be less noticeable.

OFP: 55 / No. 3–4 starter or second-division closer

Variance: Medium. Velocity isn't everything, but high 90s is high 90s, and a plus curve is a plus curve. Cusick should move quickly, as long as he throws enough good strikes. There's profile risk, but the line between starter and reliever is getting blurrier every year.

Mark Barry's Fantasy Take: As Pythagoras taught us, $a^2 + b^2 = c^2$. As Billywagneras taught us, high velo + power breaking ball = reliever. Sorry, I don't make the rules. It's science.

7 Jared Shuster LHP OFP: 55 ETA: 2023

Born: 08/03/98 Age: 23 Bats: L Throws: L Height: 6'3" Weight: 210 lb. Origin: Round 1, 2020 Draft (#25 overall)

YEAR	TEAM	LVL	AGE	W	L	SV	G	GS	IP	H	HR	BB/9	K/9	K	GB%	BABIP	WHIP	ERA	DRA-	WARP
2021	ROM	A+	22	2	0	0	15	14	58^{1}	47	10	2.3	11.3	73	34.7%	.272	1.06	3.70	95	0.6
2021	MIS	AA	22	0	0	0	3	3	14^{2}	19	5	3.1	10.4	17	36.2%	.341	1.64	7.36	90	0.2
2022 non-DC	*ATL*	*MLB*	*23*	*2*	*3*	*0*	*57*	*0*	*50*	*52*	*8*	*3.5*	*8.2*	*45*	*33.2%*	*.302*	*1.43*	*5.11*	*122*	*-0.4*

Comparables: Danny Duffy, Jeanmar Gómez, Zach Jackson

The Report: During our time at the Cape, we were able to catch many looks at the Braves' 2020 first-round pick. The Wake Forest lefty sat 88–91 on his running fastball, with a ridiculous changeup that flashed elite and a below-average slider. After our time at the Cape, we were informed that the lefty was sitting at 93–95 and touching 97 with an improved slider in his COVID-shortened college season, pre-draft.

Now, Shuster's fastball seems to have slotted in between the spike at Wake Forest and his Cape season. He sits 90–92 and has touched 94. The changeup is still a plus pitch, flashing higher. His slider has shown improvement. The fastball has developed more run than his college days, and where Shuster's slider was a sweeping, hanging pitch, almost mimicking a slurve, now there is tighter break and less 10–4 action.

The arm action is as deceptive as ever and further accentuates his fall-off-the-table changeup. While he has a bit of a stubby, short-armed release, it plays well given that his biggest strength is the change. How much you like the profile depends heavily on if you think the slider will continue to refine itself into a functional third offering. A potential top-of-the-scale changeup and a fastball that flashes above average paired with consistent command is a great base from which to start, but the third offering is likely to be the difference between starter and reliever.

OFP: 55 / No. 3–4 starter

Variance: High. Shuster has good command and one of the best left-handed changeups in Minor League Baseball but needs to develop his slider to become an above-average major-league starter.

Mark Barry's Fantasy Take: So, the slider development is the only thing standing in the way of a long, fruitful and lucrative career as a big-league hurler? Oh, no pressure. Shuster's changeup is enough to get him in the door, but it remains to be seen if he can actually turn over a lineup. That difference ultimately might not be as important IRL, but for fantasy, it's the difference between the watchlist and a set-and-forget starter.

8 Drew Waters OF   OFP: 55   ETA: 2022

Born: 12/30/98 Age: 23 Bats: S Throws: R Height: 6'2" Weight: 185 lb. Origin: Round 2, 2017 Draft (#41 overall)

YEAR	TEAM	LVL	AGE	PA	R	2B	3B	HR	RBI	BB	K	SB	CS	AVG/OBP/SLG	DRC+	BABIP	BRR	FRAA	WARP
2019	MIS	AA	20	454	63	35	9	5	41	28	121	13	6	.319/.366/.481	108	.436	-2.1	LF(55) 8.1, CF(38) 6.7, RF(18) -1.0	3.3
2019	GWN	AAA	20	119	17	5	0	2	11	11	43	3	0	.271/.336/.374	66	.429	0.7	RF(16) 2.4, LF(7) 0.4, CF(3) 0.7	0.3
2021	GWN	AAA	22	459	70	22	1	11	37	47	142	28	9	.240/.329/.381	85	.341	2.1	LF(44) 4.3, CF(38) 6.2, RF(25) 2.8	2.2
2022 DC	*ATL*	*MLB*	*23*	*337*	*38*	*17*	*2*	*5*	*32*	*27*	*106*	*9*	*3*	*.224/.295/.354*	*75*	*.324*	*0.7*	*LF 3, RF 2*	*0.6*

Comparables: Colby Rasmus, Byron Buxton, Alex Verdugo

The Report: Waters made the last three Top-101 lists based on the premise that his natural bat-to-ball ability and beautiful swing would carry the day over his hyper-aggressive approach. That did not even carry the day through Triple-A, where his entire offensive profile collapsed in a sea of strikeouts and weak contact. His wrists remain quick, but his swing has too much length to work if he's going to swing at everything. He beat the ball into the ground over and over and over again, and not all that hard, so the above-average power projection simply isn't getting into games, at present. It was a bad season, though not all is lost; he is an extremely obvious swing-change and approach-revamp candidate. Defensively, he's a capable center fielder who has more often played in the corners in the high-minors in deference to Pache.

OFP: 55 / Starting outfielder, though probably not center if it's in the same outfield as Pache

Variance: High. Hitters do have to actually hit.

Mark Barry's Fantasy Take: November 2020 was a simpler time. Wait, nevermind. It absolutely was not. Anyway, last year Waters was earmarked for fantasy-stud status, as he displayed four near-elite tools with a budding ability to hit. The bud didn't bloom in 2021, and now there are serious questions about his eventual offensive role. On the bright side for dynasty managers, his hit tool is now baked into his value, so those with a strong stomach will have an easier time bringing Waters into the fold.

9 Tucker Davidson LHP   OFP: 50   ETA: Debuted in 2020

Born: 03/25/96 Age: 26 Bats: L Throws: L Height: 6'2" Weight: 215 lb. Origin: Round 19, 2016 Draft (#559 overall)

YEAR	TEAM	LVL	AGE	W	L	SV	G	GS	IP	H	HR	BB/9	K/9	K	GB%	BABIP	WHIP	ERA	DRA-	WARP
2019	MIS	AA	23	7	6	0	21	21	110^2	88	5	3.7	9.9	122	48.6%	.311	1.20	2.03	83	1.7
2019	GWN	AAA	23	1	1	0	4	4	19	20	0	4.3	5.7	12	49.2%	.345	1.53	2.84	114	0.1
2020	ATL	MLB	24	0	1	0	1	1	1^2	3	1	21.6	10.8	2	28.6%	.333	4.20	10.80	126	0.0
2021	GWN	AAA	25	2	2	0	4	4	23	11	2	2.0	11.0	28	54.9%	.184	0.70	1.17	85	0.5
2021	ATL	MLB	25	0	0	0	4	4	20	15	3	3.6	8.1	18	42.1%	.226	1.15	3.60	100	0.2
2022 DC	*ATL*	*MLB*	*26*	*2*	*2*	*0*	*9*	*9*	*41.7*	*40*	*5*	*4.3*	*9.1*	*42*	*47.4%*	*.308*	*1.46*	*4.72*	*110*	*0.1*

Comparables: Travis Wood, Gavin Floyd, Jakob Junis

The Report: Davidson should have had more of a chance to establish himself at the back end of Atlanta's rotation in 2021, but forearm soreness cost him four months of the season. One assumes it's not a serious issue going forward, as the team was willing to bring him back to start against Houston in the World Series. Even if his name is not written in ink on the 2022 staff, Davidson should see plenty of major-league time, as he can still help the club in a number of ways. His fastball runs up into the mid-90s, and he shows two different breaking ball looks that can get swings and misses. The slider is the better of the two breakers at present, showing sharp tilt in the mid-80s, while the curve has more depth but can be a bit humpy. Davidson is on the older side, dealt with an arm issue and may not have a plus offering, but he's a major league–ready utility arm who can fill in the back of your rotation competently.

OFP: 50 / No. 4 starter or good swingman or bulk guy, all of which adds up to 120 innings or so

Variance: Low. Yeah, there's the forearm soreness, that's not great, but Davidson looked more or less like himself in the World Series—granted a version of himself that hadn't really pitched in four months—and should continue to be himself in whatever role Atlanta needs in 2022.

Mark Barry's Fantasy Take: Hey, utility arms can be valuable in fantasy leagues, too. I'm not expecting volume from Davidson, but he can definitely be used as a matchup-specific streamer for your fantasy squad with the upside for a little more.

10 Vaughn Grissom IF

OFP: 50 ETA: 2024

Born: 01/05/01 Age: 21 Bats: R Throws: R Height: 6'3" Weight: 180 lb. Origin: Round 11, 2019 Draft (#337 overall)

YEAR	TEAM	LVL	AGE	PA	R	2B	3B	HR	RBI	BB	K	SB	CS	AVG/OBP/SLG	DRC+	BABIP	BRR	FRAA	WARP
2019	BRA	ROK	18	184	22	7	1	3	23	16	27	3	0	.288/.361/.400		.323			
2021	AUG	A	20	328	52	15	4	5	33	34	49	13	3	.311/.402/.446	127	.360	1.6	SS(35) -3.2, 3B(23) 1.8, 2B(10) 3.0	2.3
2021	ROM	A+	20	52	12	2	0	2	10	11	5	3	0	.378/.519/.595	139	.375	0.9	SS(8) -0.8, 2B(2) 0.1	0.4
2022 non-DC	*ATL*	*MLB*	*21*	*251*	*23*	*10*	*1*	*3*	*23*	*20*	*47*	*4*	*1*	*.246/.318/.358*	*87*	*.296*	*0.2*	*SS -1, 3B 1*	*0.5*

Comparables: Yairo Muñoz, Johan Camargo, Yamaico Navarro

The Report: Disciplined, athletic, projectable. That's what we like to hear. There is real potential here for Grissom to succeed at the higher levels. 6-foot-3 and 185 pounds with tons of upside, Grissom shows a really quick bat with some lift and gap power and a ton of positive projection. He has displayed incredibly impressive discipline and will regularly swing at pitches middle in and in his hitting zone. With an approach that helps him cover most of the plate, a quick bat path (albeit still fairly flat) and loud tools, the young shortstop has turned himself into a very exciting player to watch. I think we are testing a higher OFP here if Grissom adjusts that plane when moving the bat through the zone. Grissom is still thin but has gained noticeable muscle from 2019 to 2021. There are concerns about whether he can last at shortstop, but maybe center could work?

OFP: 50 / Average infielder

Variance: High. Grissom is still pretty thin, and his arm strength is still not sufficient to project him as a shortstop, but he has the tools and strike-zone recognition to be an everyday big-league infielder.

Mark Barry's Fantasy Take: Outside of Harris, Grissom might be the most interesting fantasy name on this list. He is slowly but surely getting to some power and has even displayed a knack for swiping a base or two. But for me, the real reason for optimism is his approach at the plate and extreme knack for contact. With continued physical development, Grissom might soon find himself featuring as a top-101 dynasty prospect, if he's not there already.

The Prospects You Meet Outside the Top Ten

#11

Bryce Elder RHP Born: 05/19/99 Age: 23 Bats: R Throws: R Height: 6'2" Weight: 220 lb. Origin: Round 5, 2020 Draft (#156 overall)

YEAR	TEAM	LVL	AGE	W	L	SV	G	GS	IP	H	HR	BB/9	K/9	K	GB%	BABIP	WHIP	ERA	DRA-	WARP
2021	ROM	A+	22	2	1	0	9	9	45	38	2	4.0	11.0	55	58.6%	.316	1.29	2.60	79	0.9
2021	MIS	AA	22	7	1	0	9	9	56	39	7	2.7	9.6	60	58.7%	.244	1.00	3.21	86	1.0
2021	GWN	AAA	22	2	3	0	7	7	36^{2}	18	1	4.9	9.8	40	53.5%	.200	1.04	2.21	81	0.9
2022 non-DC	*ATL*	*MLB*	*23*	*2*	*2*	*0*	*57*	*0*	*50*	*47*	*5*	*4.6*	*8.8*	*48*	*26.4%*	*.300*	*1.45*	*4.31*	*104*	*0.1*

Comparables: Chad Kuhl, Scott Baker, Robert Gsellman

Elder mixes his pitches really well and has a true plan of attack for most batters he faces. He does seem to shy away from the elite hitters he faced (Wander Franco) and might struggle against true big-league talent right away, due to his lack of an above-average fastball (it can run a bit straight), but his slider and curveball might make him a very dark horse contender for a spot on the Braves Opening Day roster in 2022. Our own Nathan Graham had the best adjective to describe Elder: "polished." Nothing really pops out overall—his slider at least flashes plus—but he is consistent, developed and probably ready for the next step. —Tyler Oringer

#12

Braden Shewmake SS Born: 11/19/97 Age: 24 Bats: L Throws: R Height: 6'4" Weight: 190 lb. Origin: Round 1, 2019 Draft (#21 overall)

YEAR	TEAM	LVL	AGE	PA	R	2B	3B	HR	RBI	BB	K	SB	CS	AVG/OBP/SLG	DRC+	BABIP	BRR	FRAA	WARP
2019	ROM	A	21	226	37	18	2	3	39	21	29	11	3	.318/.389/.473	128	.359	2.8	SS(39) -0.2	1.7
2019	MIS	AA	21	52	7	0	0	0	1	4	11	2	0	.217/.288/.217	90	.278	-0.1	SS(14) 2.0	0.3
2021	MIS	AA	23	344	40	14	3	12	40	17	75	4	2	.228/.271/.401	100	.262	-0.4	SS(79) 5.3	1.5
2022 non-DC	*ATL*	*MLB*	*24*	*251*	*22*	*11*	*1*	*5*	*24*	*13*	*57*	*3*	*2*	*.233/.282/.359*	*72*	*.288*	*0.2*	*SS 2*	*0.3*

Comparables: Niko Goodrum, Brad Miller, Asdrúbal Cabrera

Despite his lack of success in early 2021, Shewmake has the tools to start at the highest level (probably as a long-legged second baseman). He has a level swing and a pretty quick bat. There's room for the former first-round pick to fill out, and since he has shown some occasional power, it could be an exciting profile for an up-the-middle player. He makes loud contact at times, and while he appears to be more of a gap hitter, we believe his average raw power will show up when he takes that next step. He has an all-fields approach, and, while his habit of chasing pitches hurt him this year, we expect he will adjust. Shewmake should stick at shortstop for now, but he must repeat this season for us to believe he has the instincts to play everyday at the highest level at the premium infield spot.

#13

Jesse Franklin V OF Born: 12/01/98 Age: 23 Bats: L Throws: L Height: 6'1" Weight: 215 lb. Origin: Round 3, 2020 Draft (#97 overall)

YEAR	TEAM	LVL	AGE	PA	R	2B	3B	HR	RBI	BB	K	SB	CS	AVG/OBP/SLG	DRC+	BABIP	BRR	FRAA	WARP
2021	PEJ	WIN	22	66	10	1	0	1	5	12	23	0	0	.098/.303/.176		.148			
2021	ROM	A+	22	406	55	24	2	24	61	34	115	19	4	.244/.320/.522	126	.284	-0.2	RF(40) -2.2, CF(32) -4.0, LF(18) -0.9	1.9
2022 non-DC	*ATL*	*MLB*	*23*	*251*	*25*	*11*	*1*	*8*	*28*	*16*	*82*	*8*	*3*	*.217/.278/.384*	*75*	*.298*	*0.7*	*RF 0, CF -1*	*0.1*

Franklin is a premium athlete with above-average raw power, future game power and speed. With a very relaxed stride towards the mound and a powerful bat with home-run power and loft, he should continue his home run–hitting ways from this year. The issue here is his swing is max effort, despite a controlled bottom half, leading to over-exerted swings and misses. Franklin is pretty dang filled out, and we think what you saw in High-A last year is what the profile will be until he cracks the 26-man roster in two years or so.

The hit tool is a concern, but the game power will carry Franklin through the minors and could force Atlanta to consider him for a starter role in left field in a couple of years. While he has only had one season in pro ball, we feel confident tagging him as one of those 45-hit/60-power guys that can give you a serviceable season, but not much more, year after year.

Prospects on the Rise

Joey Estes RHP Born: 10/08/01 Age: 20 Bats: R Throws: R Height: 6'2" Weight: 190 lb. Origin: Round 16, 2019 Draft (#487 overall)

YEAR	TEAM	LVL	AGE	W	L	SV	G	GS	IP	H	HR	BB/9	K/9	K	GB%	BABIP	WHIP	ERA	DRA-	WARP
2019	BRA	ROK	17	0	1	0	5	5	10	10	0	6.3	7.2	8	22.6%	.323	1.70	8.10		
2021	AUG	A	19	3	6	0	20	20	99	66	7	2.6	11.5	127	34.2%	.259	0.96	2.91	100	0.9
2022 non-DC	*ATL*	*MLB*	*20*	*2*	*3*	*0*	*57*	*0*	*50*	*50*	*8*	*4.0*	*8.1*	*45*	*39.1%*	*.294*	*1.44*	*5.04*	*119*	*-0.3*

Comparables: Edgar Gonzalez, Luis Patiño, Jeff D'Amico

Command is what sticks out when evaluating Estes. He has shown the ability to locate all three of his pitches. He has an aggressive delivery to the plate, and he extends well and hides the ball better than most in the lower minors. Estes mixes the pitches in his arsenal well, and, when the slider is working, it is very difficult for batters to get on base against him. With his running fastball and 10–4-type slider, which has good shape to it, we expect him to succeed consistently against minor-league hitters. Estes was initially projected to be a swingman-type reliever, but he has flashed the command (and sometimes stuff) to succeed as a back-end starter.

The big issue here is that Estes only has three pitches, with a 93-mph running fastball as the anchor. While the secondaries are good, he needs to take a step forward with his velocity and changeup to be a starter. His lanky frame does project to add some velocity as he progresses.

Spencer Schwellenbach RHP Born: 05/31/00 Age: 22 Bats: R Throws: R Height: 6'1" Weight: 200 lb. Origin: Round 2, 2021 Draft (#59 overall)

Schwellenbach's Tommy John surgery will delay the start of his pro career until 2023 or so, but, as an amateur, it was quite clear his fastball is a plus pitch with some arm-side run and riveting life. There is little doubt in our minds that Schwellenbach could succeed as a two-pitch, late-inning reliever with that dart of a heater. The arm action on his fastball and slider are quite similar. Given that the slider has sharp, tight break and a 12–14-mph dropoff from the fastball, the potential is there for it to be a truly effective pitch. His mechanics are repeatable and crisp, but his lack of a third pitch will likely be what the Braves focus on as he rises their ranks (and the fact that he might be a true two-way player). Given the profile, we definitely think reliever long-term here, but there is so much that remains to be seen about Schwellenbach as he recovers from surgery and progresses through the minors.

Factors on the Farm

Trey Riley RHP Born: 04/21/98 Age: 24 Bats: L Throws: R Height: 6'3" Weight: 205 lb. Origin: Round 5, 2018 Draft (#142 overall)

YEAR	TEAM	LVL	AGE	W	L	SV	G	GS	IP	H	HR	BB/9	K/9	K	GB%	BABIP	WHIP	ERA	DRA-	WARP
2019	ROM	A	21	2	7	0	17	12	58^{2}	71	4	7.1	6.3	41	42.5%	.360	1.99	7.67	182	-2.0
2021	ROM	A+	23	5	1	0	26	0	38^{1}	26	5	2.6	7.5	32	61.2%	.214	0.97	3.29	93	0.4
2022 non-DC	*ATL*	*MLB*	*24*	*2*	*3*	*0*	*57*	*0*	*50*	*56*	*6*	*5.6*	*6.0*	*33*	*42.3%*	*.309*	*1.75*	*6.14*	*138*	*-0.8*

Pitching only from the stretch, Riley has an aggressive delivery with an almost-over-the-top slot. He was used as a reliever last year and certainly seems best fit in that role. His fastball sits 92–95 without much movement, and he'll also deploy a slider with late break and a slow curve. The slider almost looks like a cutter, at times. When evaluating Riley, the biggest change from 2019 and 2020 to this year is his repetition of his delivery. His mechanics in 2020 were a bit wonky and, at times, he was overthrowing and almost falling off the mound. We saw a massive improvement in 2021, with his release appearing more controlled, repeatable and far less aggressive. He attacks hitters with all of his pitches and could be a name to keep an eye on if the command and curveball start to round into shape.

Freddy Tarnok RHP Born: 11/24/98 Age: 23 Bats: R Throws: R Height: 6'3" Weight: 185 lb. Origin: Round 3, 2017 Draft (#80 overall)

YEAR	TEAM	LVL	AGE	W	L	SV	G	GS	IP	H	HR	BB/9	K/9	K	GB%	BABIP	WHIP	ERA	DRA-	WARP
2019	BRA	ROK	20	0	1	0	3	3	8	3	1	1.1	10.1	9	50.0%	.118	0.50	3.38		
2019	FLO	A+	20	3	7	0	19	19	98	105	6	3.3	7.5	82	36.5%	.330	1.44	4.87	106	0.9
2021	ROM	A+	22	3	2	0	7	5	28^{1}	21	6	4.1	15.2	48	34.5%	.306	1.20	4.76	74	0.6
2021	MIS	AA	22	3	2	0	9	9	45	35	2	3.0	12.2	61	33.3%	.324	1.11	2.60	81	0.9
2022 DC	*ATL*	*MLB*	*23*	*3*	*2*	*0*	*25*	*3*	*32.3*	*28*	*4*	*4.4*	*9.6*	*34*	*50.5%*	*.282*	*1.37*	*4.33*	*105*	*0.1*

Comparables: Michael Fulmer, Michael Bowden, Nathan Eovaldi

Tarnok continued to miss copious amounts of bats in High-A and Double-A, but the medium-term profile still fits best in the pen. He can pump mid- to upper-90s heat in short bursts, but a high-effort delivery means the fastball command isn't particularly fine. That would be less of an issue if Tarnok's curve and change were more consistent, but while the breaker flashes above average, it can lack for late, bat-missing dive, and the changeup is on the firm side. Tarnok could be a 2022 pen factor, if Atlanta elects to slide him into relief, but, given his relative lack of mound experience, it might be worth seeing what one more year stretched out will bring.

Top Talents 25 and Under (as of 4/1/2022):

1. Ronald Acuña Jr., OF
2. Ozzie Albies, 2B
3. Austin Riley, 3B
4. Ian Anderson, RHP
5. Mike Soroka, RHP
6. Huascar Ynoa, RHP
7. Kyle Muller, LHP
8. Michael Harris II, OF
9. Cristian Pache, OF
10. Shea Langeliers, C

It's downright absurd to think the reigning World Series champions are also one of the clubs best suited to improving internally purely based on the age curve of their core. And yet, and yet . . . Assuming full recovery from his ACL injury, or even a slight reduction in foot speed, Acuña should still threaten perpetual 30–30 seasons, or at least 40–20 seasons for a decade to come. Acuña was improving most aspects of his game in his age-23 season, with a career-low strikeout rate, career-high barrel rate and, at least through 82 games, a career-best 137 DRC+. He had simplified his already streamlined swing, reducing the floatiness of his leg lift and getting his quicksilver hands engaged all the more judiciously. Few players impact the game the way a healthy Acuña can, and hopefully we'll see 150-plus games of that once more in 2022.

The steadiness of Albies is a gift that keeps on giving for Atlanta, as Acuña's partner in crime continued to deliver first-division numbers day in and day out. His third season of more than 680 plate appearances ahead of his 25th birthday was his most powerful at the plate, with Albies incorporating a good deal more loft. It was a nice bump for his counting stats, as Albies racked up a 30–20 season without adding much to his strikeout rate, but, in many ways, he simply found a slightly different route to the same solid production. Slap that onto his usual top-notch glovework and baserunning, and it's a recipe Atlanta will continue to enjoy supping on for another six seasons at least.

Though there was reason to believe a 2021 breakout was possible for Riley, the hulking Tennessean should have considered how his stellar campaign after an uninspired first couple of years and roughly 500 plate appearances in MLB would be wielded to defend dozens of slow-starting, bat-first prospects for years to come. Deeply inconsiderate. Overlooking that culpability, Riley made the adjustments to be expected of a quality young hitter adjusting to big-league pitching. He swung less overall, but especially out of the zone, and upped the quality of his contact when he did swing while also improving his contact rate. Going forward, he may dip slightly from his 123 DRC+, as he's coming off a .368 BABIP, but the pieces are there for an above-average bat, though his defensive home may ultimately lie in a Jay Bruce-ian 1B/strong-armed-corner-OF nexus.

Ian Anderson waxed enough hitters with his waning changeup to make the tides off the coast of Savannah ebb and flow. The postseason goliath had a solid regular season, as well, and will be merely 24 years old in 2022. Fellow 24-year-old Mike Soroka will hopefully join him in the rotation. Despite Soroka's ill fortune, a torn Achilles is not the same specter of doom for a pitcher as it might be a shooting guard, particularly one that young. Almost a year and a half away from the mound will likely slow Soroka's return to his 2019 eminence as Atlanta's precocious then-ace, but it should be a delay more than a total deterrent. Atlanta should also have Ynoa back at full bore in 2022, with the tanky righty pumping his two-pitch combo at top speeds to seemingly reasonable effect in a rotation role. Ynoa could be one of the great losers from the likely universal designated hitter, as his comparatively competent swings at the dish do add some panache to what is ultimately a high-leverage bullpen profile.

If you're the type to snarkily respond to such a consortium of talent with a time-tested witticism such as "is that it?" then let me assure you, George Carlin reincarnate, no it is not. Kyle Wright may, at long last, exceed the cutoff for this list, but Touki Toussaint and William Contreras do not. Perhaps Toussaint will never reach the ceiling he occasionally flirted with, but a 103 DRA– in 2021 is in line with his 99 DRA– for the career thus far, suggesting an average, if inefficient, starting pitcher. That's the sort of arm a club like Atlanta may continue to need, particularly given the careful manner in which they'll likely handle Soroka and others on return from injury.

Baltimore Orioles

The State of the System:

The best 1-2 prospect punch in the minors highlights a top-tier system that is especially deep in position players.

The Top Ten:

1 Adley Rutschman C

OFP: 70 ETA: 2022, right after whatever the new service time claw-back date is

Born: 02/06/98 Age: 24 Bats: S Throws: R Height: 6'2" Weight: 220 lb. Origin: Round 1, 2019 Draft (#1 overall)

YEAR	TEAM	LVL	AGE	PA	R	2B	3B	HR	RBI	BB	K	SB	CS	AVG/OBP/SLG	DRC+	BABIP	BRR	FRAA	WARP
2019	ORI	ROK	21	16	3	0	0	1	3	2	2	1	0	.143/.250/.357		.091			
2019	ABD	SS	21	92	11	7	1	1	15	12	16	0	0	.325/.413/.481		.387			
2019	DEL	A	21	47	5	1	0	2	8	6	9	0	0	.154/.261/.333	104	.138	0.1	C(6) 0.1	0.2
2021	BOW	AA	23	358	61	16	0	18	55	55	57	1	2	.271/.392/.508	141	.279	0.3	C(53) 13.8, 1B(20) 0.1	4.4
2021	NOR	AAA	23	185	25	9	2	5	20	24	33	2	2	.312/.405/.490	123	.364	-0.6	C(29) 4.8, 1B(8) -1.3	1.4
2022 DC	*BAL*	*MLB*	*24*	*371*	*47*	*15*	*1*	*10*	*44*	*40*	*67*	*1*	*1*	*.243/.333/.399*	*97*	*.277*	*-0.4*	*C 7*	*2.3*

Comparables: Will Smith, Yan Gomes, Sean Murphy

The Report: Despite being the consensus choice for the first-overall pick in 2019 and a top-five prospect in baseball as soon as he signed, Rutschman had very little professional track record coming into 2021. His pro debut was delayed by a bout of mono, and his performance—in a small sample size—was fairly pedestrian. In 2020, he wasn't assigned to the alternate site until major-league games had started—perhaps to make sure he didn't look too good and win a job—and, although the reports were strong out of Bowie, and we had little doubt he was one of the best prospects in baseball, we would've liked to have had a validating campaign at some point.

Well, 2021 mostly sufficed. Rutschman posted a .899 OPS in the upper minors while walking almost as often as he struck out. He hit for average. He hit for power. He should have been in Triple-A by July and the majors by August. He is one of the best prospects in baseball.

All that said, it was not the most dominant offensive campaign you've ever seen. The switch-hitting Rutschman was tinkering with his left-handed swing, and he went through spates of suboptimal contact or even outright swing-and-miss against fairly pedestrian stuff. He has plus raw power, but, despite the minor-league home-run totals, we expect it to play more towards average in games. There's some risk he's merely an average, or slightly above, hitter in the majors.

Even in that outcome though, Rutschman is a potential All-Star. He is probably the best defensive catcher in the minors. He is certainly the best defender that is also a significant prospect. He's an elite framer, and his arm is average but accurate. As best as we can decipher the soft skills, he seems great there, as well. If he figures out the left-handed swing and posts anything close to that .899 OPS in the majors, he's the best catcher in baseball. He's likely to be in the top five catchers in the majors for a long time, regardless.

OFP: 70 / All-Star catcher

Variance: Medium. There's really no reason Rutschman couldn't have been up in the majors around midseason 2021, but we do think there is some offensive-regression risk in the majors, as well as the chance that an automatic ball/strike system nerfs some of his long-term top-line defensive value.

Darius Austin's Fantasy Take: Rutschman's defensive talent looks set to make him so valuable to the Orioles overall that there's a risk his prospect reputation outpaces his fantasy worth. While he's clearly capable of being the number-one catcher in fantasy, his sometimes-uneven performance against inferior pitching to that which he'll see in the majors leads me to suspect that Rutschman won't provide the truly elite-level performance in the short term that many are expecting. To be clear, it's still quite likely that Rutschman is a comfortable top-10 catcher as soon as he's up, I just think people aren't going to be that impressed if he does what Eric Haase did in 2021. Rutschman remains the most reliable catching prospect in the game, with a considerable amount of offensive upside, and he's more than talented enough to prove me wrong this year, too.

Eyewitness Report: Adley Rutschman

Evaluator: Jeffrey Paternostro

Report Date: 06/08/2021

Dates Seen: 6/1, 6/3-6/5

Risk Factor: Medium

Physical/Health: Has more or less maintained his physique since 2019 look. Tall, solidly built. Big target behind the plate, but with good twitch and flexibility.

Tool	Future Grade	Report
Hit	50	Setup is a mirror image from right and left. Right side has more lift; left side, more rotational and stays in the zone a while. Advanced approach, but was out of sync against marginal stuff. Looked good hunting fastballs early, but could get indecisive deeper in counts. Can foul off tough stuff, but quality of contact from the left side wasn't great. Pulled groundballs and not as loud as you'd like. Hits the ball hard enough that you'd expect him to sort this out.
Power	50	Not a power hitter's swing per se, but strong and the ball jumps from the right side. Plus raw but would expect game power to play to average.
Baserunning/ Speed	30	4.38-4.51. Aggressive baserunner, and he plays above his raw speed on the bases. Not fast, but not a station-to-station guy either.
Glove	80	Elite receiver. Quiet and soft hands. Steals strikes down and off the corners. Moves well laterally. Pitchers not afraid to throw their best stuff in the dirt.
Arm	50	Gets out of the crouch well, smooth transfer and gets the ball out quickly. Only average arm strength, but puts the ball right to the base in 2.0 seconds more often than not.

Conclusion: The allure of Rutschman has always been the possibility of a plus, two-way catcher. There's probably only three or so in the majors right now, and there's rarely more than that at any time. The glove more than holds up its end of the bargain, and even if he hits .200, he will be employed in the majors for a good long while. He should hit a fair bit more than that, but didn't show obvious plus offensive tools in this look. .260 and 15-20 home runs with this glove is still an All-Star though, at least under the game's current reliance on the human element for ball/strike calls.

2 Grayson Rodriguez RHP OFP: 70 ETA: 2022, maybe the same day as Rutschman

Born: 11/16/99 Age: 22 Bats: L Throws: R Height: 6'5" Weight: 220 lb. Origin: Round 1, 2018 Draft (#11 overall)

YEAR	TEAM	LVL	AGE	W	L	SV	G	GS	IP	H	HR	BB/9	K/9	K	GB%	BABIP	WHIP	ERA	DRA-	WARP
2019	DEL	A	19	10	4	0	20	20	94	57	4	3.4	12.4	129	44.2%	.262	0.99	2.68	76	2.0
2021	ABD	A+	21	3	0	0	5	5	23^{1}	11	2	1.9	15.4	40	42.5%	.237	0.69	1.54	69	0.6
2021	BOW	AA	21	6	1	0	18	18	79^{2}	47	8	2.5	13.7	121	37.8%	.252	0.87	2.60	83	1.4
2022 DC	*BAL*	*MLB*	*22*	*4*	*3*	*0*	*12*	*12*	*64.7*	*52*	*9*	*3.6*	*11.2*	*80*	*37.7%*	*.283*	*1.21*	*3.51*	*87*	*1.0*

Comparables: Carlos Villanueva, Danny Salazar, Chris Archer

The Report: Rodriguez is simply a superlative pitching prospect in nearly every way we evaluate pitching prospects in the 2020s. He sits in the mid-to-upper 90s with late life; his fastball, which he commands well, is at least a plus-plus offering. His slider also projects as plus-plus; he throws it with incredible confidence as both a chase and freeze pitch. His changeup projects as above average and might play higher given how well it tunnels with his slider, and he has feel for a curveball and cutter, both of which are distinct from his slider.

Rodriguez throws pretty easy gas from a large frame. We know of no significant health concerns. He struck out 40.5 percent of the batters he faced last year and barely walked anyone. He has dominated everywhere he's pitched as a pro, and his velocity has been gradually ticking up year-over-year, even month-over-month—one of our favorite traits to see when evaluating pitchers. He has close to no red flags at all; if you really want to stretch: at times in the past, his breaking balls have bled together, and he has a little bit of mechanical effort. He has clear ace upside, with only Shane Baz coming close in that department amongst current pitching prospects, and low downside variance for a top pitching prospect.

OFP: 70 / Top-of-the-rotation starter

Variance: Low. He's likely to be very good.

Darius Austin's Fantasy Take: While Rutschman would have to dramatically disappoint not to be a starting-caliber catcher in almost any league, I have more confidence in Rodriguez being a truly great fantasy option when he arrives in 2022. There isn't anything more you could ask for here. The only real knock is that he's going to have to pitch in a typically stacked AL East and make most of his starts in hitters' parks. It still wouldn't surprise me if he's a fantasy ace this year, and, despite the TINSTAAPP of it all, it's hard to think of many pitchers you're likely to want more a half decade down the line.

3 Colton Cowser OF OFP: 55 ETA: 2023

Born: 03/20/00 Age: 22 Bats: L Throws: R Height: 6'3" Weight: 195 lb. Origin: Round 1, 2021 Draft (#5 overall)

YEAR	TEAM	LVL	AGE	PA	R	2B	3B	HR	RBI	BB	K	SB	CS	AVG/OBP/SLG	DRC+	BABIP	BRR	FRAA	WARP
2021	ORIO	ROK	21	25	8	3	0	1	8	3	4	3	2	.500/.560/.773		.588			
2021	DEL	A	21	124	22	5	0	1	26	22	19	4	2	.347/.476/.429	124	.418	-1.1	CF(16) -2.8, RF(4) 3.0	0.7
2022 non-DC	*BAL*	*MLB*	*22*	*251*	*22*	*10*	*0*	*2*	*20*	*25*	*46*	*3*	*2*	*.228/.315/.317*	*78*	*.278*	*0.1*	*CF -2, RF 1*	*0.1*

Comparables: Andrew Stevenson, Adam Haseley, Mallex Smith

The Report: Cowser makes exceptionally good swing decisions and puts the bat on the ball a heck of a lot when he swings. That combination of attributes, alone, is fairly rare—especially for a player with only 32 games of pro experience. It led Cowser to put up Bonds-esque numbers at Sam Houston State (.374/.490/.680 in his draft year) and dominate full-season ball after the draft.

The flip side is that, in our current estimation, Cowser's college power was mostly a metal-bat/environmental mirage; he projects as more of an average hitter for pop as a pro. Given that he's likely to end up in a corner and not center, that puts an awful lot of pressure on his vaunted plate discipline and contact to hold up all the way through—or for more power with wood bats to emerge than we currently expect.

OFP: 55 / On-base machine in a corner

Variance: Low. Cowser has a pretty well-developed skill set for a recent draftee.

Darius Austin's Fantasy Take: You know how we're not all thrilled with Christian Yelich now that he has gone from MVP candidate to a guy who still gets on base a ton but doesn't hit for much power? I'm not saying Cowser will struggle to reach double-digit homers, and the Orioles would obviously be delighted if Cowser can walk close to that much and combine it with a little more batting average. If we're looking at a 15–20-homer guy, nobody's going wild in fantasy. He might be able to run enough to increase the excitement level a tick, as long as he truly is an on-base machine.

4 D.L. Hall LHP OFP: 55 ETA: Late 2022/Early 2023

Born: 09/19/98 Age: 23 Bats: L Throws: L Height: 6'2" Weight: 195 lb. Origin: Round 1, 2017 Draft (#21 overall)

YEAR	TEAM	LVL	AGE	W	L	SV	G	GS	IP	H	HR	BB/9	K/9	K	GB%	BABIP	WHIP	ERA	DRA-	WARP
2019	FRE	A+	20	4	5	1	19	17	80^2	53	3	6.0	12.9	116	34.1%	.301	1.33	3.46	79	1.6
2021	BOW	AA	22	2	0	0	7	7	31^2	16	4	4.5	15.9	56	59.3%	.240	1.01	3.13	80	0.6
2022 DC	*BAL*	*MLB*	*23*	*0*	*0*	*0*	*3*	*3*	*14.3*	*11*	*2*	*6.0*	*12.3*	*19*	*33.3%*	*.290*	*1.45*	*4.41*	*100*	*0.1*

Comparables: Josh Hader, Jason Schmidt, Franklin Morales

The Report: Hall was starting to build a case as a long-term starter when he was felled, in June, by elbow tendinitis that eventually ended his season. He doesn't have a great track record on the strike-throwing front, but he was starting to show average command of the fastball and better than that on his breaking balls. His fastball sat upper 90s, although he would dial it back at times to get a bit finer with his location. Either way, batters don't see the heater well, and it bores in on righties. Hall gets grounders down in the zone, swing-and-miss up and the fastball could be a true plus-plus offering if he can throw good strikes with it in the top end of his velocity range.

Hall's curveball is his best secondary, although the shape can be inconsistent, and it isn't always a true plus bat-misser. The slider has come along nicely, and while it's his third pitch, it is potentially average and is particularly useful left-on-left as another way to get weak ground-ball contact. Hall's changeup has good velocity separation, but doesn't really do all that much and can look like a typical rough, Double-A change. He doesn't really need it against righties when the curve is working, but getting it to a consistent 40 or 45 would be helpful for the days when the hook isn't as snappy. Hall's arm action can be a bit rigid, but he generates plus arm speed with good extension and creates a tough angle for hitters. There are certainly reliever markers in the mechanics, and the elbow injury muddles his future more, but the stuff is good enough to start.

OFP: 55 / Number-three-quality stuff, perhaps with number-five volume of innings, or maybe he's just a late-inning reliever.

Variance: High. Hall needs a consolidation season in which he throws 100-plus innings as a starter showing at least average command/control. He has always carried relief risk and now has an elbow injury on top of that.

Darius Austin's Fantasy Take: Hall isn't a bad guy to go after if you're not harboring any intentions of competing in the immediate future, especially if you're trading with someone who is. The fantasy upside is as obvious as the risk that Hall gets sidelined by another injury—or merely his inconsistent control—and ends up in the bullpen. I can't help but feel like we've seen this story a hundred times before, and it hardly ever ends with a starter who makes 30 turns in the rotation. He'd be a great reliever, though.

5 Gunnar Henderson SS OFP: 55 ETA: 2023

Born: 06/29/01 Age: 21 Bats: L Throws: R Height: 6'2" Weight: 210 lb. Origin: Round 2, 2019 Draft (#42 overall)

YEAR	TEAM	LVL	AGE	PA	R	2B	3B	HR	RBI	BB	K	SB	CS	AVG/OBP/SLG	DRC+	BABIP	BRR	FRAA	WARP
2019	ORI	ROK	18	121	21	5	2	1	11	11	28	2	2	.259/.331/.370		.338			
2021	DEL	A	20	157	30	11	1	8	39	14	46	5	1	.312/.369/.574	108	.404	0.8	SS(20) 3.2, 3B(11) 0.2	1.0
2021	ABD	A+	20	289	34	16	3	9	35	40	87	11	1	.230/.343/.432	98	.313	-1.9	SS(40) 4.2, 3B(23) -0.7	0.9
2022 non-DC	*BAL*	*MLB*	*21*	*251*	*22*	*11*	*1*	*5*	*25*	*20*	*81*	*3*	*2*	*.207/.278/.346*	*65*	*.294*	*0.2*	*SS 1, 3B 0*	*-0.1*

Comparables: Jazz Chisholm Jr., Didi Gregorius, Gavin Cecchini

The Report: Henderson had an up-and-down 2020, looking overmatched against the Orioles' suite of polished, upper-minors arms at the Bowie alternate site before looking more like the seven-figure prep shortstop Baltimore drafted against more age-appropriate competition in instructs. Last year flipped the script. Henderson got off to a scorching start in Low-A before scuffling a bit during subsequent promotions. His barrel control got tested against better arms, and while he should grow into the role of a power-hitting third baseman in time, he can fall in love with taking big cuts, leading to length and some stiffness as he swings over breaking balls. When Henderson can drop the barrel, he looks like a future 20-plus-home-run hitter. He is solidly built, with room to add strength. He played mostly shortstop in 2021, and while he's fine on the routine stuff, he's a little mechanical with his actions and can look awkward throwing on the move or on the turn. He's an above-average runner, but should slow down in his twenties and is a better fit for the hot corner.

OFP: 55 / Power-hitting third baseman

Variance: High. Henderson needs to clean up his swing decisions a little bit, and it will never be a rock-solid plus hit tool given the length and lift. A longer stint in Double-A will clarify things further.

Darius Austin's Fantasy Take: Henderson is likely to be a starting fantasy player of some sort while also feeling like one of those guys who you're going to want to draft coming off a year when his average tanked and shy away from when he just hit .270. Maybe the decision-making and the swing gets a little smoother with time, and the annual slash lines look more like 2014–16 Kyle Seager than 2017–18 Kyle Seager. I also don't expect him to run as much as his minor-league numbers suggest. A test in Double-A against better pitching with no unusual stolen-base rules—we presume—should be revealing.

6 Jordan Westburg SS/3B OFP: 55 ETA: Late 2022/Early 2023

Born: 02/18/99 Age: 23 Bats: R Throws: R Height: 6'3" Weight: 203 lb. Origin: Round 1, 2020 Draft (#30 overall)

YEAR	TEAM	LVL	AGE	PA	R	2B	3B	HR	RBI	BB	K	SB	CS	AVG/OBP/SLG	DRC+	BABIP	BRR	FRAA	WARP
2021	DEL	A	22	91	18	5	1	3	24	12	24	5	1	.366/.484/.592	114	.500	0.8	3B(11) -1.3, SS(8) -0.8	0.3
2021	ABD	A+	22	285	41	16	2	8	41	35	71	9	4	.286/.389/.469	114	.372	0.5	SS(40) 4.4, 3B(20) -2.1	1.6
2021	BOW	AA	22	130	15	6	2	4	14	14	32	3	0	.232/.323/.429	96	.282	0.3	SS(21) 1.7, 3B(5) 0.0	0.5
2022 non-DC	*BAL*	*MLB*	*23*	*251*	*23*	*11*	*1*	*4*	*24*	*21*	*68*	*3*	*2*	*.227/.308/.356*	*80*	*.304*	*0.2*	*SS 1, 3B 0*	*0.4*

Comparables: Chris Taylor, Dansby Swanson, Brad Miller

The Report: A college performer in the SEC without any standout tools, Westburg has kept on hitting in the pros. Approach isn't one of the five tools, of course, but if you wanted to find a plus grade in his profile, that's where you'd start. It's not all that hard in A-ball to keep the bat on your shoulder and draw walks, but Westburg never expands and is comfortable taking close pitches. When he does get something in the zone, he's short to the ball while keeping the barrel in the zone well. He stings line drives but doesn't really get consistent lift or try to pull the ball, and, consequently, his game power tends towards doubles in the gaps. The frame, approach and bat control suggest there could be more power growth here, but, for now, that tool projection remains average. The hit tool can be found on the sunnier side of 5, but Westburg runs a lot of deep counts, and pitchers can get in his kitchen with better velocity, so even that is more solid average than plus. He should get on base plenty and is sure-handed at third base with a quick release and a strong, accurate arm.

OFP: 55 / Well-rounded third baseman

Variance: Medium. Westburg had a fairly conservative 2021 track for a polished college bat, albeit one who had a truncated junior season. Given that he doesn't have a clear carrying tool, the performance will need to continue up the ladder.

Darius Austin's Fantasy Take: I'm getting a little déjà vu from the Cowser profile. Westburg feels about as safe as Cowser, given his approach, while lacking some of the potential variance and, thus, upside. He looks like a boring, reliable corner infielder who gets a boost in OBP formats.

7 Coby Mayo 3B OFP: 55 ETA: 2024/2025

Born: 12/10/01 Age: 20 Bats: R Throws: R Height: 6'5" Weight: 215 lb. Origin: Round 4, 2020 Draft (#103 overall)

YEAR	TEAM	LVL	AGE	PA	R	2B	3B	HR	RBI	BB	K	SB	CS	AVG/OBP/SLG	DRC+	BABIP	BRR	FRAA	WARP
2021	ORIB	ROK	19	84	17	6	0	3	13	11	13	6	0	.324/.429/.535		.364			
2021	DEL	A	19	125	27	8	1	5	26	16	26	5	0	.311/.416/.547	118	.373	1.3	3B(27) -3.3	0.4
2022 non-DC	*BAL*	*MLB*	*20*	*251*	*22*	*10*	*1*	*4*	*23*	*19*	*68*	*4*	*1*	*.218/.287/.336*	*69*	*.292*	*0.3*	*3B -1, SS 0*	*-0.3*

Comparables: Mat Gamel, Joey Gallo, Ke'Bryan Hayes

The Report: After signing Heston Kjerstad for significantly under slot in the 2020 draft, the Orioles spread the extra pool money across several picks. A power-hitting prep third baseman taken in the fourth round, Mayo got the biggest over-slot bonus. He dealt with a knee injury in spring training last year that delayed the start to his pro career, but, once he got on the field, he showed the kind of easy-plus raw power that gets you a seven-figure bonus as a prep bat. Mayo is more physically mature than your average 20-year-old baseball player, with a strong upper body and quick hands that get the bat through the zone with good lift. He loads a little late and swings very hard, which can affect his bat control, but he has a two-strike approach to help mitigate some of the swing-and-miss and is so strong he can dump a pitch into the outfield even when he doesn't square it. Defensively, Mayo looks the part of a solid third baseman. He has a quick first step, soft hands and an accurate plus arm. There's certainly some hit-tool risk up the ladder, as the swing is a little unorthodox, and he'll need to show he can handle better offspeed and sequencing, but that's true of just about every prep bat in A-ball, and most aren't as advanced as Mayo.

OFP: 55 / Power-hitting third baseman

Variance: High. Mayo has limited pro reps and is unlikely to add a ton more physicality. He doesn't need to get bigger, but he will need to keep hitting up the ladder given the corner profile.

Darius Austin's Fantasy Take: If you're looking for a spoonful of upside, you might have more luck here. Mayo is not as safe as Westburg, given the extra whiffs. He does have the raw pop to suggest he might be the best single-category contributor of anyone on the Orioles' list. Being able to retain that two-strike approach all the way up through the majors will go a long way towards ensuring he gets the playing time to maximize his homer potential. Those dingers might not come with much average or speed, but, sandwiched between healthy run and RBI totals, they'll make for a satisfying combination.

8 Heston Kjerstad OF

Born: 02/12/99 Age: 23 Bats: L Throws: R Height: 6'3" Weight: 205 lb. Origin: Round 1, 2020 Draft (#2 overall)

The Report: Kjerstad had an episode of myocarditis—in plain English, heart inflammation—before instructs in fall 2020. He was unable to ramp up in spring and summer 2021, but did get back on the field in 2021 instructs and faced some live pitching. The latest update we had, as of publication, was that Kjerstad has reportedly made a full recovery and is expected to be ready for spring training, and there's an encouraging precedent in former Orioles prospect Eduardo Rodríguez, who missed the 2020 season with similar heart problems and was back to his old form in 2021.

Before he was sidelined, Kjerstad was a top prospect due to his combination of barrel control and huge power. The hope was that he would improve his pitch selection as a pro and become an elite masher in an outfield corner. Right now, we just hope he's well moving forward.

Darius Austin's Fantasy Take: Sometimes the fantasy take is that it's best to stop thinking about fantasy and recognize that there are more important things. We all hope that, next year, we can use this space to merely consider whether Kjerstad will make good on his promise out of the draft.

9 Kyle Bradish RHP OFP: 50 ETA: 2022

Born: 09/12/96 Age: 25 Bats: R Throws: R Height: 6'4" Weight: 220 lb. Origin: Round 4, 2018 Draft (#121 overall)

YEAR	TEAM	LVL	AGE	W	L	SV	G	GS	IP	H	HR	BB/9	K/9	K	GB%	BABIP	WHIP	ERA	DRA-	WARP
2019	IE	A+	22	6	7	0	24	18	101	90	9	4.7	10.7	120	43.9%	.314	1.42	4.28	97	0.5
2021	BOW	AA	24	1	0	0	3	3	13^{2}	7	0	3.3	17.1	26	47.6%	.333	0.88	0.00	84	0.2
2021	NOR	AAA	24	5	5	0	21	19	86^{2}	85	10	4.1	10.9	105	43.2%	.336	1.43	4.26	93	1.5
2022 DC	*BAL*	*MLB*	*25*	*0*	*0*	*0*	*3*	*3*	*14*	*13*	*2*	*4.5*	*9.1*	*14*	*31.9%*	*.295*	*1.45*	*4.66*	*107*	*0.1*

Comparables: Wes Parsons, Taylor Jungmann, Brock Stewart

The Report: After we got strong reports on Bradish from the 2020 alternate site, he came out and torched Double-A in May, earning a quick promotion to Norfolk. His Triple-A performance was more uneven. Bradish has a potentially dominant fastball/slider combo, but command-and-control issues persist. The heater is mid-90s from a high slot with good extension. He can create downhill plane with it or ride it up in the zone as a put-away pitch. However, his arm stroke and release point on the fastball can be inconsistent, leading him into hitters' counts a bit more than you'd like. His slider is mid-80s with plus razorblade action. At its best, it disappears under hitters' bats, but it can get slurvy and show as a more 12–5, glove-side chase pitch that better lineups will lay off. Bradish also has a slower, spinny, 12–6 curve for a different breaking ball look, but that can be a bit humpy or back up. There's a firm change, as well. His delivery has some effort, the fastball velocity and command play better in short bursts, and he may fit better as a multi- or late-inning reliever, as the fastball and slider could both be high-end plus in the late innings.

OFP: 50 / No. 4 starter/good bulk guy/average set-up guy

Variance: Medium. There's some command and role risk, but Bradish has the present stuff to miss bats in the majors.

Â Darius Austin's Fantasy Take: I like Bradish as a guy who has the components to suddenly wildly outperform his current fantasy stock. He's not someone you should be rostering unless your league is deep into 400-plus-prospect territory, since the chances are he'll never develop the consistency to make it all come together as a good fantasy starter. If he can refine that fastball/slider combo and develop one of those existing secondaries, though, I think he's a regular fantasy starter with big strikeout upside.

10 Terrin Vavra 2B/CF OFP: 50 ETA: Late 2022/Early 2023

Born: 05/12/97 Age: 25 Bats: L Throws: R Height: 6'1" Weight: 200 lb. Origin: Round 3, 2018 Draft (#96 overall)

YEAR	TEAM	LVL	AGE	PA	R	2B	3B	HR	RBI	BB	K	SB	CS	AVG/OBP/SLG	DRC+	BABIP	BRR	FRAA	WARP
2019	ASH	A	22	453	79	32	1	10	52	62	62	18	9	.318/.409/.489	144	.350	-0.4	SS(53) -1.5, 2B(41) 4.5	4.0
2021	BOW	AA	24	184	28	10	1	5	20	29	42	6	1	.248/.388/.430	115	.314	-1.0	2B(27) -1.7, CF(9) -1.0, SS(2) 0.3	0.6
2022 DC	*BAL*	*MLB*	*25*	*100*	*11*	*4*	*0*	*1*	*10*	*10*	*21*	*2*	*1*	*.224/.316/.348*	*80*	*.279*	*0.1*	*SS 0, 2B 0*	*0.2*

Comparables: Ryan Flaherty, Wilmer Difo, Vimael Machín

The Report: The Orioles don't just draft college bats with strong plate discipline and solid bat-to-ball skills, they trade for them, as well. Vavra, part of the return for Mychal Givens in August 2020, isn't quite as loud at the plate as Cowser or Westburg, and he can occasionally get caught in between against offspeed with two strikes, but, otherwise, he shows a knack for consistent line-drive contact. Vavra clearly knows the zone, although his approach can border on passive at times, and he should get on base at a good clip. He'll flash enough pull-side lift that 15 home runs or so isn't out of the question, but the ball doesn't exactly jump off his bat, and he has a lean frame that's unlikely to add much more strength in his mid-twenties.

Vavra is fluid and rangy at the keystone, but his arm limits him to the right side of the infield. Baltimore has given him some reps in center field, and while he's not a burner, he has enough foot speed to have some outfield flex. There's isn't anything in the profile that will wow you, and he wasn't quite as good at the plate after coming back from a midseason back issue, but Vavra is likely to be a near-term major-league contributor on the strength of his broad set of average tools.

OFP: 50 / Second-division second baseman/good super-utility

Variance: Medium. You'd like to have seen a little more upper-minors performance given the age and lack of tools projection, but some of that could be attributed to the back and hip injuries he dealt with. On the other hand, Vavra also dealt with back and hip injuries and can't afford to give much twitch and athleticism back.

Darius Austin's Fantasy Take: Is that *more* déjà vu? Given that his bat is less loud than Cowser and Westburg's, Vavra is not creating much buzz that I can tell. Then again, we are at number 10, and it's a credit to the Orioles that, once more, we've got a player who looks likely to be a solid major-league contributor. It's not exciting for our purposes, but many of us need a deeper-league middle infielder. The hope is that Vavra can squeeze some 15–15-type seasons out of this skill set while doing so in a lineup that should be fairly formidable in the coming years.

The Prospects You Meet Outside the Top Ten

#11

Connor Norby 2B Born: 06/08/00 Age: 22 Bats: R Throws: R Height: 5'10" Weight: 187 lb. Origin: Round 2, 2021 Draft (#41 overall)

YEAR	TEAM	LVL	AGE	PA	R	2B	3B	HR	RBI	BB	K	SB	CS	AVG/OBP/SLG	DRC+	BABIP	BRR	FRAA	WARP
2021	DEL	A	21	126	17	4	1	3	17	21	28	5	3	.283/.413/.434	113	.352	0.3	2B(26) -0.1	0.6
2022 non-DC	*BAL*	*MLB*	*22*	*251*	*21*	*10*	*1*	*3*	*21*	*24*	*77*	*5*	*3*	*.208/.293/.310*	*66*	*.302*	*0.4*	*2B 0*	*-0.2*

Comparables: Ty Washington, Ryan Dorow, Wilver Perez

It's an oversimplification to say that Norby is Vavra only on a longer timeline to major-league performance, but there are some similarities. Like Vavra, he's second-base-only on the dirt and is less likely to be able to roam the grass. He has a similarly advanced approach, and he also likes to work the big part of the park. Norby stays back well on offspeed and has enough bat speed to trigger late. He does have a bit of sneaky pop due to his strong wrists, but is very inconsistent at lifting the ball. Weirdly, there's a little more surety in Norby's bat despite his being further away, but he is further away and doesn't really have significantly more upside than Vavra.

Prospects on the Rise

Mishael Deson LF Born: 07/07/02 Age: 19 Bats: R Throws: R Height: 6'3" Weight: 155 lb. Origin: International Free Agent, 2018

YEAR	TEAM	LVL	AGE	PA	R	2B	3B	HR	RBI	BB	K	SB	CS	AVG/OBP/SLG	DRC+	BABIP	BRR	FRAA	WARP
2019	DSL ROC	ROK	16	112	16	5	1	1	8	12	17	11	4	.268/.345/.371		.313			
2019	DSL COL	ROK	16	174	22	9	1	0	12	17	31	12	7	.242/.316/.314		.296			
2021	ORIB	ROK	18	114	19	2	2	3	16	9	23	11	2	.369/.416/.515		.449			
2021	DEL	A	18	25	0	0	0	0	2	0	5	1	0	.174/.160/.174	103	.200	-0.2	RF(4) -0.1	0.1
2022 non-DC	*BAL*	*MLB*	*19*	*251*	*18*	*10*	*1*	*2*	*19*	*13*	*55*	*13*	*5*	*.214/.262/.299*	*53*	*.271*	*1.4*	*LF 0, RF 0*	*-0.5*

The player to be named later in the Givens trade, Deson is now a name prospect. His stateside debut in the complex went smashingly and earned him a late-season cup of coffee in Low-A Delmarva as an 18-year-old. He looked overmatched against full-season arms but showed enough hand-eye to make contact in A-ball despite a raw, aggressive approach. It wasn't good contact, mind you, but it's something to build on. Deson has a stomp-and-lift swing with plus bat speed, potential plus pop and projection left in his 6-foot-3 frame. It's a right-field profile all the way, but the tools are loud enough to flag him as a potential breakout bat next year.

Kyle Stowers OF Born: 01/02/98 Age: 24 Bats: L Throws: L Height: 6'3" Weight: 200 lb. Origin: Round 2, 2019 Draft (#71 overall)

YEAR	TEAM	LVL	AGE	PA	R	2B	3B	HR	RBI	BB	K	SB	CS	AVG/OBP/SLG	DRC+	BABIP	BRR	FRAA	WARP
2019	ABD	SS	21	228	19	13	1	6	23	20	53	5	1	.216/.289/.377		.259			
2021	ABD	A+	23	161	25	6	1	7	32	27	55	3	3	.275/.404/.496	101	.414	-0.2	RF(18) -0.6, LF(10) 0.3, CF(5) -0.1	0.5
2021	BOW	AA	23	276	38	15	0	17	42	34	84	4	1	.283/.377/.561	110	.362	-0.8	RF(48) -2.5, LF(9) 0.1	0.9
2021	NOR	AAA	23	93	10	2	0	3	11	12	32	1	0	.272/.366/.407	82	.413	0.1	RF(19) -0.2, LF(2) -0.2	0.1
2022 DC	*BAL*	*MLB*	*24*	*65*	*7*	*2*	*0*	*2*	*7*	*6*	*23*	*0*	*0*	*.217/.303/.377*	*79*	*.325*	*0.0*	*RF 0*	*0.0*

Comparables: Jake Goebbert, John Mayberry Jr., Steven Moya

A Stanford hitter with almost 30 home runs, you say? What heresy is this? Stowers finally tapped into his raw power in the minors last year with some added length and loft in his stroke. He traded off a fair bit of swing-and-miss, as he has a steep swing plane now and only average bat speed. If you want to look at the bright side, his K rate held pretty steady at around 30 percent with each minor-league promotion. If he can manage that for one more promotion—watch out, that last step is slippery—Stowers looks the part of a three-true-outcome, second-division right fielder.

Factors on the Farm

Mike Baumann RHP Born: 09/10/95 Age: 26 Bats: R Throws: R Height: 6'4" Weight: 235 lb. Origin: Round 3, 2017 Draft (#98 overall)

YEAR	TEAM	LVL	AGE	W	L	SV	G	GS	IP	H	HR	BB/9	K/9	K	GB%	BABIP	WHIP	ERA	DRA-	WARP
2019	FRE	A+	23	1	4	0	11	11	54	40	2	4.0	12.8	77	43.1%	.317	1.19	3.83	77	1.1
2019	BOW	AA	23	6	2	1	13	11	70	45	2	2.7	8.4	65	41.4%	.242	0.94	2.31	93	0.8
2021	BOW	AA	25	3	2	0	10	10	38^{2}	29	6	4.2	9.1	39	44.2%	.237	1.22	4.89	96	0.4
2021	NOR	AAA	25	1	1	0	6	6	27	18	0	4.3	8.7	26	37.7%	.261	1.15	2.00	97	0.4
2021	BAL	MLB	25	1	1	0	4	0	10	13	2	5.4	4.5	5	36.8%	.306	1.90	9.90	133	-0.1
2022 DC	*BAL*	*MLB*	*26*	*7*	*6*	*0*	*65*	*6*	*77.7*	*77*	*11*	*4.8*	*8.0*	*68*	*40.9%*	*.296*	*1.53*	*5.18*	*117*	*-0.3*

Comparables: Austin Voth, Travis Harper, Justin Haley

Now going by Mike and ruining all our jokes about *Ringer* writer (and BP alum) Michael Baumann, Baumann The Pitcher made the majors in 2021 and threw 10 relief innings in which he mostly looked like a 95-and-a-slider guy. In the minors, hs changeup had improved from "definitely going to be a reliever" levels of fringiness to "there's a shot he can start" levels of fringiness, and whether or not he's able to hold that and throw some more strikes will probably carry the day on whether he can start in the majors or not. Lord knows Baltimore is going to be the land of opportunity for starting chances while they manipulate everyone's service time. But Baumann also might just be a 95-and-a-slider middle reliever.

Joseph Ortiz IF Born: 07/14/98 Age: 23 Bats: R Throws: R Height: 5'11" Weight: 175 lb. Origin: Round 4, 2019 Draft (#108 overall)

YEAR	TEAM	LVL	AGE	PA	R	2B	3B	HR	RBI	BB	K	SB	CS	AVG/OBP/SLG	DRC+	BABIP	BRR	FRAA	WARP
2019	ABD	SS	20	228	23	2	0	1	17	30	37	2	1	.241/.345/.267		.293			
2021	ABD	A+	22	89	14	7	2	0	8	10	18	3	0	.289/.382/.434	104	.373	0.2	SS(14) -0.3, 2B(5) 0.6, 3B(2) 0.3	0.4
2021	BOW	AA	22	67	11	2	0	4	9	6	14	1	0	.233/.313/.467	113	.238	0.8	SS(6) -0.1, 2B(5) 0.3, 3B(2) 0.4	0.4
2022 non-DC	*BAL*	*MLB*	*23*	*251*	*22*	*10*	*1*	*4*	*23*	*18*	*58*	*1*	*1*	*.224/.291/.338*	*74*	*.284*	*-0.1*	*SS 1, 2B 0*	*0.2*

Johnny Rizer OF Born: 11/07/96 Age: 25 Bats: L Throws: L Height: 6'0" Weight: 192 lb. Origin: Round 7, 2019 Draft (#198 overall)

YEAR	TEAM	LVL	AGE	PA	R	2B	3B	HR	RBI	BB	K	SB	CS	AVG/OBP/SLG	DRC+	BABIP	BRR	FRAA	WARP
2019	ABD	SS	22	107	16	9	2	3	19	6	18	1	1	.305/.374/.537		.347			
2019	DEL	A	22	153	18	6	2	1	22	9	27	2	1	.310/.359/.401	100	.377	-0.4	RF(33) 3.7, LF(2) -0.2	0.8
2021	ABD	A+	24	67	9	6	0	3	8	5	17	2	1	.288/.373/.542	108	.359	-0.4	RF(7) 0.9, CF(3) -0.5	0.3
2021	BOW	AA	24	337	48	9	3	11	45	21	87	11	4	.247/.300/.401	86	.307	1.8	CF(43) 1.0, LF(23) 3.6, RF(10) 0.0	1.2
2022 non-DC	*BAL*	*MLB*	*25*	*251*	*21*	*9*	*1*	*4*	*23*	*13*	*69*	*3*	*2*	*.226/.277/.338*	*63*	*.303*	*0.2*	*CF 1, RF 1*	*-0.1*

The Orioles have significant upper-minors position-player depth. Joey Ortiz had the best shot at something approaching a second-division-regular role given his positional flex, passable shortstop defense and plus raw pop, but he went under the knife for labrum surgery on his left shoulder last summer. That muddles the projection until we see him back on the field this spring.

Conversely, Rizer is the most likely to have a five-year career as a useful bench player. He's a perfectly adequate center fielder with good feel for contact against righties and sneaky pop. He's very uncomfortable against southpaws, and you'd prefer he was more of a true burner, both for defense and baserunning reasons, but he can handle all three outfield spots and hit righties well enough to carve out a nice little major-league career.

Kevin Smith LHP Born: 05/13/97 Age: 25 Bats: R Throws: L Height: 6'5" Weight: 200 lb. Origin: Round 7, 2018 Draft (#200 overall)

YEAR	TEAM	LVL	AGE	W	L	SV	G	GS	IP	H	HR	BB/9	K/9	K	GB%	BABIP	WHIP	ERA	DRA-	WARP
2019	STL	A+	22	5	5	0	17	17	85^{2}	83	5	2.5	10.7	102	44.1%	.359	1.25	3.05	80	1.9
2019	BNG	AA	22	3	2	0	6	6	31^{1}	25	1	4.3	8.0	28	39.3%	.289	1.28	3.45	92	0.4
2021	BOW	AA	24	0	1	1	6	5	26	18	1	3.5	12.8	37	50.0%	.315	1.08	1.04	85	0.4
2021	NOR	AAA	24	3	6	0	16	15	56^{1}	56	14	7.8	10.9	68	35.8%	.307	1.86	6.23	103	0.7
2022 DC	*BAL*	*MLB*	*25*	*2*	*2*	*0*	*17*	*3*	*27.3*	*26*	*4*	*5.7*	*10.5*	*32*	*38.4%*	*.309*	*1.59*	*5.43*	*119*	*-0.1*

Comparables: Harrison Musgrave, Dillon Peters, Asher Wojciechowski

Smith came into 2021 showing fringy stuff by the eyeball test—fastball topping out in the low 90s, average slider—but faring well in analytical models. It should be no surprise, then, that he was traded from a then-very eye-scouting-heavy team in the Mets to a very analytical team in the Orioles. He shoved in Double-A at the start of the season, but he'd already pitched well at the level in 2019, and he lost the strike zone after being promoted to Triple-A. Things completely unraveled at the end of the season; he walked six in each of his last two starts. The Orioles added him to the 40-man over the winter, anyway. If he's throwing strikes, he projects as a back-end starter with obvious LOOGY fallback.

Personal Cheeseball

Jean Pinto RHP Born: 01/09/01 Age: 21 Bats: R Throws: R Height: 5'11" Weight: 175 lb. Origin: International Free Agent, 2019

YEAR	TEAM	LVL	AGE	W	L	SV	G	GS	IP	H	HR	BB/9	K/9	K	GB%	BABIP	WHIP	ERA	DRA-	WARP
2019	DSL ANG	ROK	18	0	1	0	3	3	12	12	0	2.3	14.3	19	57.1%	.429	1.25	2.25		
2021	ORIB	ROK	20	1	1	0	5	4	20	11	2	1.8	12.6	28	47.6%	.220	0.75	1.80		
2021	DEL	A	20	1	1	0	9	7	46²	29	1	2.5	10.8	56	52.7%	.257	0.90	2.51	81	0.9
2022 non-DC	*BAL*	*MLB*	*21*	*2*	*3*	*0*	*57*	*0*	*50*	*49*	*6*	*4.2*	*8.0*	*44*	*41.0%*	*.300*	*1.46*	*4.77*	*113*	*-0.2*

If it was still 2005, we could get Pinto onto this list proper, but, as one scout said to us while discussing him, "We know too much now." He's a short, stocky, 20-year-old changeup specialist in the low minors. This is a profile near and dear to our hearts, and he racked up the kind of strikeout numbers you'd expect for a prospect with a potential above-average cambio in A-ball. He manipulates his breaking ball and commands that well, too. There's even a little more fastball than you'd think. It sits in the low 90s, but there is not much else going for the pitch. We expect the fastball to be too hittable further up the chain. We also expect we'll be keeping a close eye on him as he meanders through the system.

Top Talents 25 and Under (as of 4/1/2022):

1. Adley Rutschman, C
2. Grayson Rodriguez, RHP
3. Colton Cowser, OF
4. Ryan Mountcastle, 1B/OF
5. DL Hall, LHP
6. Gunnar Henderson, SS/3B
7. Jordan Westburg, 3B
8. Coby Mayo, 3B
9. Heston Kjerstad, OF
10. Kyle Bradish, RHP

The Orioles' system is unsurprisingly strong given the team's draft picks after being 95 games below .500 over the past four years. What is distressing is the molassas-like pace at which the big-league club appears to be improving. Center fielder Cedric Mullins appears to be a sorely needed glimmer of light at the end of the tunnel, but, like most of Baltimore's current roster, he has already entered his typical athletic prime, and it's unclear that there's another star who can join him on the current roster. Ryan Mountcastle had an impressive rookie campaign at the plate, clubbing 33 home runs and looking like a capable big-league bat. The lumbering slugger is far from graceful when he's stuck in a corner outfield spot, but as a second-division first baseman who can high-five Trey Mancini as they take turns between right field and the cold corner, he's reasonably tasked. Despite the thump he brings, he's a righty swinger who rarely walks, creating a field of landmines he must traverse to maintain his profile.

Boston Red Sox

The State of the System:

A trio of potentially plus regulars don't entirely make up for the overall lack of depth in this system, but it's easier to find or develop depth than potentially plus regulars.

The Top Ten:

1 Marcelo Mayer SS OFP: 70 ETA: 2024/2025

Born: 12/12/02 Age: 19 Bats: L Throws: R Height: 6'3" Weight: 188 lb. Origin: Round 1, 2021 Draft (#4 overall)

YEAR	TEAM	LVL	AGE	PA	R	2B	3B	HR	RBI	BB	K	SB	CS	AVG/OBP/SLG	DRC+	BABIP	BRR	FRAA	WARP
2021	RSX	ROK	18	107	25	4	1	3	17	15	27	7	1	.275/.377/.440		.361			

Comparables: Luis Guillorme, Adrian Valerio, Nelson Molina

The Report: Mayer was one of the top overall talents in last year's draft class and had a strong case to go first overall based on his upside. The Red Sox were the beneficiary of his "falling" to them at the fourth pick, and they now have one of the top shortstop prospects in baseball. He has a sweet, left-handed swing that forms the basis for a potential plus-hit/plus-power offensive profile. Mayer is mostly hitting line drives, at present, but should grow into more pop in his twenties and get to most of it in games due to his advanced approach and bat-to-ball skills. Defensively, he's almost as aesthetically pleasing. He shows off good hands and smooth actions but is perhaps not as twitchy as you'd like for a long-term shortstop projection. His arm will play fine at third base, if he has to slide over, and, given the rest of his defensive skills, Mayer would be a plus glove at the hot corner.

OFP: 70 / All-Star infielder

Variance: High. Mayer had quite a solid post-draft pro debut, but he has only played complex ball, and the plus-power projection remains mostly projection at present.

Mark Barry's Fantasy Take: There are dudes from the 2021 draft that have a higher fantasy ceiling (thanks to threatening on the bases), but Mayer likely has the highest floor, thanks to a sweet swing and an already advanced bat. He's a top-40 dynasty prospect right now, and, if a few line drives turn into dingers, he'll be much higher than that.

2 Nick Yorke 2B OFP: 60 ETA: Late 2023/Early 2024

Born: 04/02/02 Age: 20 Bats: R Throws: R Height: 6'0" Weight: 200 lb. Origin: Round 1, 2020 Draft (#17 overall)

YEAR	TEAM	LVL	AGE	PA	R	2B	3B	HR	RBI	BB	K	SB	CS	AVG/OBP/SLG	DRC+	BABIP	BRR	FRAA	WARP
2021	SAL	A	19	346	59	14	4	10	47	41	47	11	8	.323/.413/.500	144	.353	-4.9	2B(66) 7.0	3.0
2021	GVL	A+	19	96	17	6	1	4	15	11	22	2	1	.333/.406/.571	116	.407	0.3	2B(19) -1.0	0.4
2022 non-DC	*BOS*	*MLB*	*20*	*251*	*24*	*10*	*1*	*5*	*25*	*19*	*51*	*4*	*3*	*.251/.316/.378*	*90*	*.304*	*0.3*	*2B 2*	*0.8*

Comparables: Delino DeShields, Jonathan Schoop, Xavier Edwards

The Report: In the space of a little over a year, Yorke went from surprise first-round pick to top prospect on the strength of his potentially plus-plus hit tool. As an amateur, he didn't offer much defensive value, and it was an open question how much power he'd develop. While scouts generally thought he'd hit, he would have to hit a lot, and we've all seen plenty of supposed future-.300 hitters come out of high school and not even hit .300 in the minors. Well, Yorke hit .320 with good underlying contact rates, and he added some physicality to his whippy swing and plus bat speed. The end result was that his power came even more quickly than expected, and while he's unlikely to be a consistent 20-plus-home-run guy, average pop with plenty of doubles is certainly in play. Yorke is an aggressive hitter, but he recognizes spin well, and there wasn't much in A-ball he couldn't barrel. He stays back on offspeed, has really good wrists and bat control and will take a walk when offered. He is okay at second, certainly passable, but his hit tool remains the carrying tool here. So far, so good.

OFP: 60 / First-division second baseman

Variance: High. Double-A will be an important test of Yorke's bat and approach. There's little reason to believe he won't keep hitting, but if he is more of a .270 hitter in the end, there isn't much else to carry his profile beyond average regular.

Mark Barry's Fantasy Take: Get the sensation of biting into a Yorke Dynasty Prospect Stock! In reality, Yorke's fantasy profile isn't all that different from Mayer's. Neither is going to run, and both are relying on advanced hit tools that presently produce a bunch of line drives and doubles. I have more faith in Yorke's ability to consistently hit for average, so, for me, he's a better fantasy prospect than Mayer right now, especially since we're not terribly interested in defense, in which Yorke only nominally participates.

3 Triston Casas 1B OFP: 60 ETA: Late 2022/Early 2023

Born: 01/15/00 Age: 22 Bats: L Throws: R Height: 6'4" Weight: 252 lb. Origin: Round 1, 2018 Draft (#26 overall)

YEAR	TEAM	LVL	AGE	PA	R	2B	3B	HR	RBI	BB	K	SB	CS	AVG/OBP/SLG	DRC+	BABIP	BRR	FRAA	WARP
2019	GVL	A	19	493	64	25	5	19	78	58	116	3	2	.254/.349/.472	134	.300	-0.6	1B(94) -4.7, 3B(8) -1.1	2.5
2019	SAL	A+	19	7	2	1	0	1	3	0	2	0	0	.429/.429/1.000	94	.500	0.1	1B(2) -0.1	0.0
2021	SCO	WIN	21	97	19	6	0	1	11	17	18	0	1	.372/.495/.487		.475			
2021	POR	AA	21	329	57	12	2	13	52	49	63	6	3	.284/.395/.484	128	.323	-0.8	1B(73) -6.2	1.4
2021	WOR	AAA	21	42	6	3	1	1	7	8	8	1	0	.242/.381/.485	107	.280	-0.4	1B(7) 0.0	0.1
2022 DC	*BOS*	*MLB*	*22*	*334*	*43*	*15*	*2*	*9*	*40*	*36*	*78*	*1*	*1*	*.238/.328/.401*	*98*	*.295*	*-0.1*	*1B -1*	*0.4*

Comparables: Ronald Guzmán, Josh Naylor, Rowdy Tellez

The Report: It's hard out there for a true first-base prospect, but Casas ticks most of the boxes to be a middle-of-the-order run producer. He has a power hitter's swing with lift and plus-plus raw power to match. He should get to most of that power, as he demonstrates a good approach, and, while it's a strength swing—and he's very strong—there's plus bat speed and not a ton of length. Casas is able to generate most of his hand/hip separation with a long stride out of a narrow stance. His power plays to all fields. With two strikes, he widens his base and focuses on contact, which has helped keep his strikeout rates low for a power bat, but the quality of his two-strike contact isn't always great. His ultimate hit tool looks more solid-average than plus, which, coupled with 30 home runs, is a very nice regular at first base. It's tough to be a star there without a few more decibels from the offensive tools, though. Defensively, Casas will add some supplemental value to the profile, as he's an above-average defender with a sneaky-good arm.

OFP: 60 / First-division first baseman, occasional All-Star

Variance: Medium. For all the batting practices shows he's capable of, Casas hasn't consistently gotten his over-the-fence power into games yet. He's only 21 and was facing much more experience competition, so there isn't cause for concern, per se. But as a first-base prospect, he's eventually going to have to thump it a bit more.

Mark Barry's Fantasy Take: There aren't a ton of guys in the minors that could perennially flirt with 35 homers—a total fewer than 20 big-league sluggers reached in 2021. Casas is as big as a house (or houses, if you speak Spanish) and has that kind of pop. There are adjustments he'll have to make to get to all of it into games, sure, but, even now, he's the best dynasty prospect in this system.

Eyewitness Report: Triston Casas

Evaluator: Trevor Andresen
Report Date: 11/17/2021
Dates Seen: 11/8 - 11/13 (Arizona Fall League)
Risk Factor: Medium
Physical/Health: XL 6'4 250 lb. frame. Well proportioned w/ strength throughout. Surprising athleticism given size

Tool	Future Grade	Report
Hit	55	Hits from a crouched stance. Simple swing w/ minimal wasted mvmt. Quick, strong hands w/ above-avg bat control. Mature approach w/ a strong command of the strike zone. Puts together consistent, high quality at-bats. Shortens up & competes w/ 2K's. Likely performs above true hit tool due to discipline/walk rates
Power	60	Easy plus power that plays to all fields. 30+ HR bat at maturity
Baserunning/ Speed	30	Bottom of the scale runner w/ no value on the basepaths
Glove	55	Big target at 1B & displays above-avg body control around the bag. Will save runs & help prevent errors on errant throws across the diamond
Arm	50	Avg strength. Can make all the necessary throws (double plays, relays, etc.)

Conclusion: Casas fits the mold of a middle-of-the-order run producer, and should step into an everyday role by 2023

4 Jarren Duran OF

OFP: 55 ETA: Debuted in 2021

Born: 09/05/96 Age: 25 Bats: L Throws: R Height: 6'2" Weight: 212 lb. Origin: Round 7, 2018 Draft (#220 overall)

YEAR	TEAM	LVL	AGE	PA	R	2B	3B	HR	RBI	BB	K	SB	CS	AVG/OBP/SLG	DRC+	BABIP	BRR	FRAA	WARP
2019	PEJ	WIN	22	101	15	5	2	1	9	10	20	7	2	.267/.337/.400		.329			
2019	SAL	A+	22	226	49	13	3	4	19	23	44	18	5	.387/.456/.543	140	.480	3.9	CF(50) 0.9	2.3
2019	POR	AA	22	352	41	11	5	1	19	23	84	28	8	.250/.309/.325	83	.335	6.2	CF(80) -3.6	0.9
2020	CAG	WIN	23	70	14	2	0	0	10	12	14	6	0	.236/.386/.273		.310			
2021	WOR	AAA	24	283	46	11	2	16	36	30	66	16	3	.258/.357/.516	117	.288	1.8	CF(49) -3.3, RF(7) -1.0, LF(2) 0.4	1.3
2021	BOS	MLB	24	112	17	3	2	2	10	4	40	2	1	.215/.241/.336	58	.318	0.5	CF(28) -2.9, LF(1) -0.0	-0.4
2022 DC	*BOS*	*MLB*	*25*	*474*	*57*	*20*	*4*	*10*	*49*	*31*	*141*	*22*	*8*	*.235/.298/.373*	*76*	*.327*	*2.3*	*LF 4, CF 0*	*0.7*

Comparables: Brett Gardner, Tyler Naquin, Lorenzo Cain

The Report: It should be pretty simple. Despite being drafted as a second baseman, Duran should be a power/speed center fielder. He's a plus-plus runner who started generating plus pop by throwing his whole body into a stomp-and-lift swing. It's not all that different an approach from Casas's, although the much-smaller-framed Duran requires much more physical exertion and sacrifices a lot more barrel control in the process. But after spending the 2020 season at the alternate site overhauling his swing mechanics for power, Duran came out and crushed dingers in Triple-A, eventually earning a midseason callup to Fenway.

Here's where it gets complicated. Facing major-league stuff and sequencing, he struck out . . . a lot. His new approach was always going to tilt towards the three true outcomes, but you figured he'd hit .240 and sock enough dingers to make it work. He didn't. There's also the issue of his defense. While Duran has plenty of foot speed for center, his reads and routes remain below average. Again, he was a college second baseman that didn't become a full-time outfielder until 2019, but you'd like to have seen more improvement by this point. Duran still could be a power/speed center fielder, but it's not been quite that simple.

OFP: 55 / Above-average outfielder

Variance: Medium. For a prospect that hit in Triple-A and already has some major-league time, there remain hit-tool and positional questions, but if he does click enough at the plate, and Duran does develop into an average defender, he still has plus-regular upside.

Mark Barry's Fantasy Take: The speed is nice, and, as we've learned over the last handful of years, it's rare. Still, it's hard to steal bases if you strike out all the time. #Expertanalysis. I'd feel better about Duran settling into a role if he defense was better, as it would afford him more opportunities to figure it out on the job. Until his approach improves, I'm not all that interested in Duran.

5 Brayan Bello RHP OFP: 55 ETA: Late 2022/Early 2023

Born: 05/17/99 Age: 23 Bats: R Throws: R Height: 6'1" Weight: 170 lb. Origin: International Free Agent, 2017

YEAR	TEAM	LVL	AGE	W	L	SV	G	GS	IP	H	HR	BB/9	K/9	K	GB%	BABIP	WHIP	ERA	DRA-	WARP
2019	GVL	A	20	5	10	0	25	25	117^{2}	135	9	2.9	9.1	119	46.7%	.362	1.47	5.43	106	0.6
2021	GVL	A+	22	5	0	0	6	6	31^{2}	25	3	2.0	12.8	45	52.9%	.328	1.01	2.27	69	0.8
2021	POR	AA	22	2	3	0	15	15	63^{2}	66	5	3.4	12.3	87	44.8%	.381	1.41	4.66	83	1.1
2022 DC	*BOS*	*MLB*	*23*	*0*	*0*	*0*	*14*	*0*	*12.7*	*12*	*1*	*3.7*	*9.0*	*12*	*36.7%*	*.317*	*1.40*	*4.58*	*106*	*0.0*

Comparables: Yordano Ventura, Tommy Hanson, Alex Cobb

The Report: Bello's power stuff will have him in the major-league picture for the Red Sox sooner rather than later. His fastball sits comfortably mid-90s, routinely touching higher, and its boring action from his three-quarters slot can make for a distinctly uncomfortable at-bat for lefties. It gets worse for southpaws, as Bello's best secondary is a turbo sinker that can get into the 90s, as well, and shows power sink and fade. His best changeups are plus-plus, but his feel is inconsistent enough, at present, to tamp down the projection to merely a 60-grade bat-misser. A mid-80s slider with 10–4 tilt rounds out his arsenal, but it does not have ideal depth to consistently get underneath barrels.

Bello's 2021 breakout was driven in part by an uptick in command, but he has a very up-tempo delivery with noticeable late arm effort that can cause him to yank his fastball or not quite finish turning over the change. Double-A hitters were able to wait him out and find their pitch too often, but, with some refinement, Bello should be missing bats in the majors in short order.

OFP: 55 / Garrett Whitlockian multi-inning arm

Variance: Medium. Bello just needs a bit more consistency with his delivery and command to really unlock a meaningful major-league role. It's not impossible for him to stick as a starter, as his breaking ball has average projection, but, given his slighter frame and continued command issues, his best fit is letting it rip for four to nine outs.

Mark Barry's Fantasy Take: For dynasty prospects, a mid-rotation starter projection isn't the greatest compliment. Obviously, we all want those stud aces that could eventually anchor a rotation, but there's always a need for the guys just a tier below. Or Bello, I guess. There's a deep pitch mix here, and, despite somewhat struggling for the first time against Double-A hitters, Bello isn't all that far off from being MLB ready. He's currently a dart throw for leagues that roster 200 prospects, but he's close-ish and has the solid foundation of, well, a mid-rotation starter.

6 Jeter Downs SS OFP: 50 ETA: 2022

Born: 07/27/98 Age: 23 Bats: R Throws: R Height: 5'11" Weight: 195 lb. Origin: Round 1, 2017 Draft (#32 overall)

YEAR	TEAM	LVL	AGE	PA	R	2B	3B	HR	RBI	BB	K	SB	CS	AVG/OBP/SLG	DRC+	BABIP	BRR	FRAA	WARP
2019	RC	A+	20	479	78	33	4	19	75	54	97	23	8	.269/.354/.507	126	.304	2.2	SS(91) -6.0, 2B(10) -1.1	2.1
2019	TUL	AA	20	56	14	2	0	5	11	6	10	1	0	.333/.429/.688	114	.333	0.8	SS(11) -0.9, 2B(1) -0.0	0.3
2021	SCO	WIN	22	72	9	0	0	5	14	14	18	4	2	.228/.389/.491		.235			
2021	WOR	AAA	22	405	39	9	0	14	39	38	131	18	3	.190/.272/.333	73	.249	2.7	SS(79) -9.3, 2B(21) -1.1	-0.7
2022 non-DC	*BOS*	*MLB*	*23*	*251*	*24*	*9*	*0*	*7*	*26*	*20*	*76*	*7*	*3*	*.201/.276/.348*	*67*	*.268*	*0.6*	*SS -2, 2B 0*	*-0.3*

Comparables: Jonathan Villar, Javier Báez, Jorge Polanco

The Report: Downs was overmatched in Triple-A, there's no real way to sugarcoat it. His approach was a little bit too aggressive, his swing a little bit long, and his bat a little bit slow. The reports from the Arizona Fall League were better (as was his performance). He has improved in the field, and while he's still a better fit at second base than shortstop, he might be able to handle short for a while longer. He has continued to hit for some power—even amongst his 2021 offensive struggles—and could still fill out more in his upper body and add some strength. Downs does look like a power-over-hit bat at this point, and it's not sure shot above-average power, so that would tend to make us a little concerned about the hit tool. Granted, hitting .190 for almost 100 games would do that, anyway.

OFP: 50 / Average infielder

Variance: High. The 2022 season is a significant tipping point for Downs. He will get another shot at Triple-A as a 23-year-old, and a lot more will become clearer.

Mark Barry's Fantasy Take: It makes perfect sense, when you think about it. It's a long con. A dude named Jeter goes to the Red Sox and flashes all of his namesake's prowess on defense and none of it on offense. Admittedly, that's a little harsh, I'm sorry. Proximity keeps Downs in the dynasty consciousness, but his production relegates him to AL-only, for now.

7 Bryan Mata RHP OFP: 55 ETA: 2023

Born: 05/03/99 Age: 23 Bats: R Throws: R Height: 6'3" Weight: 238 lb. Origin: International Free Agent, 2016

YEAR	TEAM	LVL	AGE	W	L	SV	G	GS	IP	H	HR	BB/9	K/9	K	GB%	BABIP	WHIP	ERA	DRA-	WARP
2019	SAL	A+	20	3	1	0	10	10	51^{1}	38	1	3.2	9.1	52	64.0%	.270	1.09	1.75	95	0.6
2019	POR	AA	20	4	6	0	11	11	53^{2}	54	6	4.0	9.9	59	50.3%	.350	1.45	5.03	97	0.5

Comparables: Carlos Martínez, Beau Burrows, Franklin Pérez

The Report: Keanan Lamb noted last year in Mata's blurb that, "big physical gains can sometimes be troublesome for a pitcher's arm." Now, we don't consider ourselves orthopedic oracles or anything—although you will never go broke betting on pitchers to get hurt—but, sure enough, Mata went down with triceps soreness that led to Tommy John surgery. It's a shame, as he could have been a 2021 option for the big club if things had continued apace. He routinely touched the upper 90s with his fastball and flashed an above-average cutter, as well as a useable curve and changeup. There was reliever risk before the surgery due to Mata's at-times-well-below-average command, and that will only be amplified now, but we'll see where he is this Summer.

OFP: 55 No. 3–4 starter or late-inning reliever

Variance: Extreme. Mata is in the midst of Tommy John rehab and had a high variance profile before that.

Mark Barry's Fantasy Take: Last year, I narrowed down the dynasty options for Mata to speculative closer or right-handed Martín Pérez. That was before Tommy John surgery in April 2021. Needless to say, I'm not super enthused about Mata's dynasty prospects.

8 Gilberto Jimenez OF OFP: 50 ETA: 2024

Born: 07/08/00 Age: 21 Bats: S Throws: R Height: 5'11" Weight: 212 lb. Origin: International Free Agent, 2017

YEAR	TEAM	LVL	AGE	PA	R	2B	3B	HR	RBI	BB	K	SB	CS	AVG/OBP/SLG	DRC+	BABIP	BRR	FRAA	WARP
2019	LOW	SS	18	254	35	11	3	3	19	13	38	14	6	.359/.393/.470		.413			
2021	SAL	A	20	408	64	16	6	3	56	19	86	13	8	.306/.346/.405	102	.381	-1.0	CF(46) -3.8, RF(30) 3.6, LF(14) 0.8	1.5
2022 non-DC	*BOS*	*MLB*	*21*	*251*	*19*	*9*	*1*	*2*	*20*	*10*	*61*	*6*	*5*	*.242/.282/.327*	*65*	*.318*	*0.8*	*CF -2, RF 1*	*-0.2*

Comparables: Victor Robles, Manuel Margot, Ender Inciarte

The Report: Before the lost 2020 season, Jimenez was an undersized, slashy contact merchant. He showed up in A-ball in 2021 having added 25 pounds or so of good weight while maintaining his plus-plus foot speed. He's now an averagely built, slashy contact merchant. Jimenez uses a wide base and stooping stance to help shorten the distance from barrel to ball, and then he loops, lines or beats the ball into the ground and starts running. His left-handed swing, especially, is almost an auto jailbreak, so he will load up on infield hits, probably bunt his way on a bit and lead some teams in triples. He will not hit for much home-run power, and he's aggressive enough at the plate that he doesn't see many deep counts, let alone walks. Jimenez is a solid-enough center fielder, although his defense plays below his raw speed. If he can play an above-average center in the majors, he doesn't have to hit .300 to be a regular, but it would probably help.

OFP: 50 / Second-division starter or good fourth outfielder

Variance: High. Jimenez is only going to see better velocity, stuff and defense as he progresses through the minors. His feel for contact is real, but there are very fine margins for this offensive profile.

Mark Barry's Fantasy Take: I, too, put on 25(ish) pounds during the 2020 quarantine. Unlike Jimenez, though, I unfortunately did not maintain my foot speed, which, if were being honest, wasn't all that great to begin with. Where was I? Right. If you want to toss Jimenez on the watchlist, I wouldn't begrudge you, but too many things need to break just right for him to be an above-average fantasy guy for me to take the plunge.

9 Connor Seabold RHP OFP: 50 ETA: Debuted in 2021

Born: 01/24/96 Age: 26 Bats: R Throws: R Height: 6'2" Weight: 190 lb. Origin: Round 3, 2017 Draft (#83 overall)

YEAR	TEAM	LVL	AGE	W	L	SV	G	GS	IP	H	HR	BB/9	K/9	K	GB%	BABIP	WHIP	ERA	DRA-	WARP
2019	PHE	ROK	23	0	1	0	1	1	2^1	6	0	0.0	7.7	2	54.5%	.545	2.57	11.57		
2019	PHW	ROK	23	0	0	0	2	2	5	1	0	0.0	18.0	10	83.3%	.167	0.20	0.00		
2019	CLR	A+	23	1	0	0	2	1	9	4	1	1.0	10.0	10	50.0%	.158	0.56	1.00	99	0.1
2019	REA	AA	23	3	1	0	7	7	40	35	2	2.3	8.1	36	45.5%	.303	1.13	2.25	102	0.3
2021	WOR	AAA	25	4	3	0	11	11	54	43	6	3.2	8.7	52	30.9%	.261	1.15	3.50	109	0.5
2021	BOS	MLB	25	0	0	0	1	1	3	3	1	6.0	0.0	0	40.0%	.222	1.67	6.00	137	0.0
2022 DC	*BOS*	*MLB*	*26*	*3*	*3*	*0*	*20*	*6*	*42*	*43*	*6*	*3.5*	*7.6*	*35*	*32.7%*	*.304*	*1.43*	*4.99*	*116*	*0.0*

Comparables: Anthony Ranaudo, Ryan Vogelsong, Ben Lively

The Report: Seabold dealt with an elbow issue that cost him the first couple months of the 2021 minor-league season, and his stuff wasn't quite consistently sharp once he was back on the mound. He could still sit in the average range with his fastball but would often dip more into the low 90s. At times, his slider looked like it was morphing into an out-pitch, showing good, sharp depth. Other times, it could be a bit slurvy. His changeup was too firm, or he couldn't start it in the zone enough. Broadly speaking, Seabold still has a collection of average pitches, throws strikes and is major-league-ready. But overall, his profile feels a bit riskier this time around. Arm injuries will do that, we suppose.

OFP: 50 / No. 4 starter

Variance: Medium. Seabold doesn't have a clear and consistent out-pitch and dealt with an elbow issue.

Mark Barry's Fantasy Take: Seabold? More like Land-shy. Amirite? Whatever. Nevermind. You don't need to worry about Seabold for fantasy.

10 Blaze Jordan CI OFP: 50 ETA: 2024/2025

Born: 12/19/02 Age: 19 Bats: R Throws: R Height: 6'2" Weight: 220 lb. Origin: Round 3, 2020 Draft (#89 overall)

YEAR	TEAM	LVL	AGE	PA	R	2B	3B	HR	RBI	BB	K	SB	CS	AVG/OBP/SLG	DRC+	BABIP	BRR	FRAA	WARP
2021	RSX	ROK	18	76	12	7	1	4	19	6	13	1	0	.362/.408/.667		.396			
2021	SAL	A	18	38	7	1	0	2	7	2	8	0	0	.250/.289/.444	113	.269	0.3	3B(5) -1.3, 1B(2) 0.2	0.1
2022 non-DC	*BOS*	*MLB*	*19*	*251*	*20*	*10*	*1*	*3*	*22*	*14*	*83*	*0*	*1*	*.217/.268/.320*	*58*	*.321*	*-0.2*	*3B -1, 1B 0*	*-0.9*

Comparables: Luis García, Vladimir Guerrero Jr., Darling Florentino

The Report: Jordan is among the more famous third-round prep picks you will find, on account of the elite raw power he had flashed for years on the showcase circuit. He also reclassified to make himself eligible a year early, meaning he was 17 years old when drafted. So, Jordan is young with top-of-the-scale raw power. That's good. He also gets it from a physically maxed, length-and-strength swing and is already playing an awful lot of first base. That's less good. All in all, it was a perfectly fine pro debut for the now 18-year-old, although he struggled with offspeed and better velocity after a late-season promotion to Low-A. Jordan's perfectly fine at first base, with above-average mobility and pretty good hands, already. He's stretched a bit at third, as his general athleticism is a little short for the hot corner. Ultimately, his power is the carrying tool and will have to carry his profile, so 2021 can be considered a qualified success, in that regard.

OFP: 50 / Average first baseman

Variance: High. Jordan has a power-hitter's swing, but his bat speed only scrapes average, so his approach and swing decisions will have to improve as he moves up the ladder to keep the dingers coming.

Mark Barry's Fantasy Take: If this were purely a fantasy list, Jordan would probably slide in at number four, behind your pick of Mayer or Yorke. His power is real, but it's not particularly close to helping you in the big leagues. That's okay, but the combination of Jordan's name value and power potential means that he's overvalued in dynasty circles right now. If he's on my roster, I'm floating him in trade talks.

The Prospects You Meet Outside the Top Ten:

Prospects on the Rise

Alex Binelas 3B Born: 05/26/00 Age: 22 Bats: L Throws: R Height: 6'3" Weight: 225 lb. Origin: Round 3, 2021 Draft (#86 overall)

YEAR	TEAM	LVL	AGE	PA	R	2B	3B	HR	RBI	BB	K	SB	CS	AVG/OBP/SLG	DRC+	BABIP	BRR	FRAA	WARP
2021	BRWG	ROK	21	27	4	0	0	0	2	5	6	1	1	.286/.444/.286		.400			
2021	CAR	A	21	132	29	11	0	9	27	12	33	0	0	.314/.379/.636	126	.364	0.7	3B(20) -4.9, 1B(5) -0.4	0.3
2022 non-DC	*MIL*	*MLB*	*22*	*251*	*25*	*11*	*1*	*7*	*28*	*16*	*82*	*0*	*0*	*.233/.290/.390*	*81*	*.327*	*-0.3*	*3B -4, 1B 0*	*-0.4*

We are not the first to report that Binelas hits the ball incredibly hard. It's kind of his whole thing, really. He just doesn't hit it as often as you'd like. He was a potential first-round pick coming into last spring, but slid down to the third round after hitting just .250 for Louisville. A bit of a hitch opens him up to barrel control and swing-and-miss issues, but he does do a lot of damage on contact. Binelas is a burly dude with fringe athletic tools, so he might end up at first base—where he played more often in college, anyway. As with Blaze Jordan, it's all going to come down to how often he's registering those 100-plus-mph exit velocities.

Wilkelman Gonzalez RHP Born: 03/25/02 Age: 20 Bats: R Throws: R Height: 6'0" Weight: 167 lb. Origin: International Free Agent, 2018

YEAR	TEAM	LVL	AGE	W	L	SV	G	GS	IP	H	HR	BB/9	K/9	K	GB%	BABIP	WHIP	ERA	DRA-	WARP
2019	DSL RS1	ROK	17	0	3	0	14	14	46^1	34	3	4.7	8.5	44	39.2%	.267	1.25	3.30		
2021	RSX	ROK	19	4	2	0	8	7	35	29	1	2.1	11.8	46	40.5%	.337	1.06	3.60		
2021	SAL	A	19	0	0	0	4	4	17^2	13	1	4.1	10.2	20	34.8%	.279	1.19	1.53	106	0.1
2022 non-DC	*BOS*	*MLB*	*20*	*2*	*3*	*0*	*57*	*0*	*50*	*55*	*8*	*5.4*	*7.3*	*40*	*44.6%*	*.308*	*1.70*	*6.49*	*141*	*-0.9*

Comparables: Kyle Drabek, Chris Flexen, Jordan Lyles

A low-six-figure interntional-free-agent signing in 2018, the 6-foot Gonzalez is undersized for a starting-pitching prospect, but showed plus arm speed and a full arsenal during his successful stateside debut. He requires effort in his mechanics to ramp it up to 95, but his fastball has some riding life to it from his three-quarters slot. Gonzalez's primary secondary is a sweepy, big-breaking slide piece, but he mixes in a promising changeup and a curve with a bit more depth that's also more of a work in progress. It's hard to see a starter here long-term, despite the deep repertoire, but Gonzalez has plenty of time to iron out his mechanics and command.

Brandon Walter LHP Born: 09/08/96 Age: 25 Bats: L Throws: L Height: 6'2" Weight: 200 lb. Origin: Round 26, 2019 Draft (#797 overall)

YEAR	TEAM	LVL	AGE	W	L	SV	G	GS	IP	H	HR	BB/9	K/9	K	GB%	BABIP	WHIP	ERA	DRA-	WARP
2019	RSX	ROK	22	4	1	0	13	0	33^1	26	2	2.2	10.5	39	48.3%	.286	1.02	2.70		
2021	SAL	A	24	1	1	2	13	2	31	21	0	1.7	13.4	46	67.1%	.288	0.87	1.45	67	0.8
2021	GVL	A+	24	4	3	0	12	12	58^1	46	6	2.2	13.3	86	58.3%	.317	1.03	3.70	73	1.4
2022 non-DC	*BOS*	*MLB*	*25*	*2*	*2*	*0*	*57*	*0*	*50*	*46*	*5*	*3.0*	*9.7*	*53*	*40.4%*	*.310*	*1.27*	*3.61*	*90*	*0.5*

Comparables: Josh Edgin, Charlie Furbush, Jacob deGrom

Walter was a 26th-round draft pick as a fourth-year junior in 2019. He was a 24-year-old pitching at two A-ball levels in 2021. Generally, those aren't great markers for prospectdom. His better markers are a fastball that can touch 95 and a potentially above-average changeup. Walter has a little short slider, as well, and it all comes from a funky lefty delivery that makes his stuff hard to pick up. Deception can often explain prodigious strikeout rates in the low minors, but Walter's total package has back-of-the-rotation potential.

Factors on the Farm

Victor Santos RHP

Born: 07/12/00 Age: 21 Bats: R Throws: R Height: 6'1" Weight: 191 lb. Origin: International Free Agent, 2016

YEAR	TEAM	LVL	AGE	W	L	SV	G	GS	IP	H	HR	BB/9	K/9	K	GB%	BABIP	WHIP	ERA	DRA-	WARP
2019	LWD	A	18	5	10	0	27	13	105^1	106	11	1.5	7.6	89	38.8%	.315	1.18	4.02	101	0.8
2021	JS	A+	20	2	1	1	9	1	20^1	17	2	2.2	11.1	25	54.7%	.294	1.08	1.33	82	0.4
2021	POR	AA	20	4	2	0	10	8	45^1	43	5	1.2	8.9	45	47.1%	.290	1.08	2.58	100	0.4
2021	REA	AA	20	1	1	0	4	4	20^2	17	2	1.7	6.5	15	37.1%	.254	1.02	3.05	104	0.1
2022 non-DC	*BOS*	*MLB*	*21*	*2*	*3*	*0*	*57*	*0*	*50*	*53*	*7*	*2.4*	*6.4*	*35*	*51.8%*	*.296*	*1.33*	*4.61*	*112*	*-0.1*

The player to be named later for C.J. Chatham, Santos has long been a Prospect Team favorite. He has added a few ticks on his fastball since his time with the Phillies, and while that only gets him into the average range, his command and deception make it play a bit past its station. He will bore it in to lefties, sink it a bit to righties and generally keep it off the good part of the lumber. His changeup and slider are both around average, with the change flashing better than that, at times. He has very little margin for error and no clear out-pitch, but Santos has a shot to be a back-end starter soon, although, granted, Fenway isn't the most inviting abode for this kind of profile.

Josh Winckowski RHP

Born: 06/28/98 Age: 24 Bats: R Throws: R Height: 6'4" Weight: 202 lb. Origin: Round 15, 2016 Draft (#462 overall)

YEAR	TEAM	LVL	AGE	W	L	SV	G	GS	IP	H	HR	BB/9	K/9	K	GB%	BABIP	WHIP	ERA	DRA-	WARP
2019	LAN	A	21	6	3	0	13	13	73^2	62	3	3.2	8.7	71	54.5%	.299	1.19	2.32	99	0.6
2019	DUN	A+	21	4	5	1	11	10	53^2	48	5	2.9	6.2	37	49.1%	.261	1.21	3.19	107	0.4
2021	POR	AA	23	8	3	0	21	20	100	100	10	2.7	7.9	88	50.3%	.300	1.30	4.14	100	0.8
2021	WOR	AAA	23	1	1	0	2	2	12	5	1	2.3	9.8	13	50.0%	.148	0.67	2.25	94	0.2
2022 DC	*BOS*	*MLB*	*24*	*0*	*0*	*0*	*14*	*0*	*12.7*	*13*	*1*	*3.6*	*6.7*	*9*	*58.9%*	*.309*	*1.47*	*4.89*	*113*	*0.0*

Comparables: Corey Oswalt, Taylor Clarke, Luis Cessa

We have more player-to-be-named-later action, this time from the Andrew Benintendi deal. Winckowski tossed more than 120 innings last year between Double-A, Triple-A and fall ball and has a frame built to log innings. However, he may fit better as a reliever, as his changeup has never really come around to even average. He does have a potentially above-average slider that can show razor-blade depth, and that he will also manipulate into a slower, slurvier offering. Winckowski works primarily off a low- to mid-90s fastball with some ride. You'd like to see him make it as a back-end starter, as we don't know how much his stuff misses bats, even in short bursts, but he should be ready to log major-league innings in some role in 2022.

Connor Wong C

Born: 05/19/96 Age: 26 Bats: R Throws: R Height: 6'1" Weight: 181 lb. Origin: Round 3, 2017 Draft (#100 overall)

YEAR	TEAM	LVL	AGE	PA	R	2B	3B	HR	RBI	BB	K	SB	CS	AVG/OBP/SLG	DRC+	BABIP	BRR	FRAA	WARP
2019	RC	A+	23	302	39	15	6	15	51	21	93	9	2	.245/.306/.507	104	.310	1.4	C(59) -5.4, 2B(10) 1.1, 3B(2) -0.0	0.8
2019	TUL	AA	23	163	17	9	1	9	31	11	50	2	1	.349/.393/.604	91	.467	0.2	C(24) -1.6, 3B(10) -0.7, 2B(4) -0.2	0.1
2021	WOR	AAA	25	208	22	13	0	8	26	9	58	7	1	.256/.288/.442	87	.323	0.7	C(44) 0.0, 2B(1) -0.4	0.5
2021	BOS	MLB	25	14	3	1	1	0	1	1	7	0	0	.308/.357/.538	71	.667	0.6	C(5) -0.1	0.1
2022 DC	*BOS*	*MLB*	*26*	*60*	*7*	*3*	*0*	*2*	*8*	*3*	*19*	*0*	*0*	*.242/.295/.414*	*82*	*.337*	*0.0*	*C 0*	*0.1*

Comparables: Grayson Greiner, Nick Hundley, Michael Perez

The third piece in the Mookie Betts trade, Wong has started filling out his punch card to get into the Fraternal Order of Backup Catchers. He's a solid catch-and-throw backstop with enough game pop that you won't mind seeing him on the lineup card a couple times a week. Wong swings hard and swings often, with enough stiffness that strikeouts will be an issue, so you'll likely mostly catch his starts over Sunday brunch.

Top Talents 25 and Under (as of 4/1/2022):

1. Rafael Devers, 3B
2. Alex Verdugo, OF
3. Marcelo Mayer, SS
4. Tanner Houck, RHP
5. Nick Yorke, 2B
6. Triston Casas, 1B
7. Jarren Duran, OF
8. Jeter Downs, IF
9. Brayan Bello, RHP
10. Bryan Mata, RHP

The two-season playoff drought in Boston, following their World Series title in 2018, ended in 2021, as the Red Sox overcame the Yankees in the Wild Card Game and swept the Rays aside in the Division Series before falling to Houston in the American League Championship Series. At the root of that resurgence was a return to form for Devers, whose 2020 was troubling but seems distantly removed now. The 24-year-old star cracked 38 home runs and ran a career-high walk rate of 9.3 percent while lowering his career strikeout rate and matching his lifetime batting average, which is to say everything either continued to go well or improved. Now 25, he is entering his penultimate year under team control, so prepare for plenty of extension discussion akin to that which surrounded Mookie Betts, but, for at least one more season, Boston should be able to enjoy a star left side of the infield few clubs can match.

In contrast to Devers' bounce-back season, while Verdugo was not a bad player in 2021, he did not quite take another step forward at the plate, and slippage in his defensive play and baserunning efficiency hurt his otherwise solid profile. Still, not much is worth fretting over with Verdugo's profile between the lines, as he has shown the ability to make contact consistently and for acceptable power while handling a rotating defensive role. He's not likely a star but is a positive part of a contender.

More emergent was Houck, who exceeded most expectations with a nice 69-inning stint in the majors, holding his velocity and the bite of his slider better than expected and putting hitters in binds. His 78 DRA– and 30.5-percent strikeout rate lined up well with his results, which is to say that the needle points far more firmly towards mid-rotation starter than bullpen arm compared to this stage last year, much less before that.

Chicago Cubs

The State of the System:

The Cubs have completely remade their system through trades. While it came at significant cost to the major-league roster, this is now one of the top systems in baseball, although it leans heavily towards high-upside bats a ways off from helping that major-league squad.

The Top Ten:

1 Brennen Davis OF OFP: 60 ETA: Late 2022/Early 2023

Born: 11/02/99 Age: 22 Bats: R Throws: R Height: 6'4" Weight: 210 lb. Origin: Round 2, 2018 Draft (#62 overall)

YEAR	TEAM	LVL	AGE	PA	R	2B	3B	HR	RBI	BB	K	SB	CS	AVG/OBP/SLG	DRC+	BABIP	BRR	FRAA	WARP
2019	SB	A	19	204	33	9	3	8	30	18	38	4	1	.305/.381/.525	132	.346	0.2	LF(23) -1.2, CF(23) -2.0, RF(2) 0.7	1.1
2021	SB	A+	21	32	6	2	0	2	5	3	6	2	0	.321/.406/.607	113	.350	0.0	CF(5) -0.3	0.1
2021	TNS	AA	21	316	50	20	0	13	36	36	97	6	4	.252/.367/.474	105	.344	-1.0	CF(33) 1.0, RF(29) -1.6, LF(8) 1.4	1.1
2021	IOW	AAA	21	68	10	3	0	4	12	11	15	0	0	.268/.397/.536	113	.297	-0.9	RF(9) -2.0, CF(4) -0.2, LF(2) 0.3	0.1
2022 DC	*CHC*	*MLB*	*22*	*31*	*4*	*1*	*0*	*1*	*4*	*2*	*9*	*0*	*0*	*.232/.319/.418*	*94*	*.314*	*0.0*	*CF 0*	*0.1*

Comparables: Teoscar Hernández, Dalton Pompey, Lewis Brinson

The Report: Physically lean and extremely raw when drafted 62nd overall in 2018, Davis was seen as a slow-burn-type prospect who would have a long road ahead of him before becoming a big-league player. He has since exceeded expectations, becoming physically stronger and showing an ability to turn his raw tools into offensive production. He added good weight without losing any of his top-flight athleticism, meaning he'll be able to stick in center for the early portion of his career. When the time comes for a move to a corner, his arm is strong enough to be adequate in either right or left. At the plate, Davis has made adjustments, shortening up his swing and showing a willingness to use the entire field. The 2021 season proved he can get to the plus raw pop in games, and it will improve as he continues to gain muscle. Given that he has less than 600 professional at-bats, we'll need to see him tested more against advanced pitching, but the high upside makes him a likely core piece in the Cubs' next window of contention.

OFP: 60 / First-division outfielder who makes the occasional All-Star Game.

Variance: Medium. There's a chance for hit-tool regression when facing big-league arms, but the solid tools across the board should carry him to an everyday role.

Mark Barry's Fantasy Take: It's a little disappointing that Davis's speed hasn't translated to success in base thievery, but that's really the only knock against him, from a fantasy angle. There's a whiff of Justin Upton–esque production for Davis's ceiling, and while that might not seem eye-poppingly exciting for a top-10 dynasty prospect, that's still really, really good.

2 Owen Caissie OF OFP: 55 ETA: 2025

Born: 07/08/02 Age: 19 Bats: L Throws: R Height: 6'4" Weight: 190 lb. Origin: Round 2, 2020 Draft (#45 overall)

YEAR	TEAM	LVL	AGE	PA	R	2B	3B	HR	RBI	BB	K	SB	CS	AVG/OBP/SLG	DRC+	BABIP	BRR	FRAA	WARP
2021	CUB	ROK	18	136	20	7	1	6	20	26	39	1	2	.349/.478/.596		.500			
2021	MB	A	18	90	15	4	0	1	9	16	28	0	0	.233/.367/.329	92	.356	-0.4	LF(14) 0.7	0.2
2022 non-DC	*CHC*	*MLB*	*19*	*251*	*18*	*10*	*1*	*2*	*18*	*23*	*86*	*0*	*0*	*.182/.263/.269*	*46*	*.283*	*-0.3*	*RF 0, LF 0*	*-1.1*

Comparables: Juan Soto, Agustin Ruiz, Eric Jenkins

The Report: A Canadian prep outfielder with a sweet, power-hitting swing from the left side, Caissie hits the ball so hard that you could put Clayton Kershaw in a Bugatti Chiron with the highest-performance tires Hankook offers, and he's not tracking it down. Caissie has enough bat speed to handle plus velocity, but there is enough length and lift that swing-and-miss will be a long-term issue. We got a brief preview of that, as he struggled with stuff moving down and out of the zone after a promotion to full-season ball in 2021. However, given the contact profile, if he cleans up his swing decisions with more reps—and he does have a semblance of an approach, at least at present—he should run batting averages close enough to .250–.260 to make the power play in games. It's impact power potential, but it will need to get there, as he is already playing mostly left field and can be a bit awkward out there.

OFP: 55 / Middle-of-the-lineup masher

Variance: High. Caissie may not offer much value past a power bat. Given his age, experience level and horizon to the majors, a lot can go wrong before he's mashing dingers in the bigs.

Mark Barry's Fantasy Take: When it comes to nursery rhymes, Caissie's favorite involves blind mice. He really enjoys Christmas stories about wisemen. "The Magic Number" by De La Soul is in the running for his future walkup song. He's a fan of threes, is what I'm saying. Or at least, that's something his professional production would lead one to believe. Caissie still has a year and a half before he can legally order a Three Weavers on a road trip to Los Angeles, so there's time for him to iron out the swing-and-miss. Otherwise, he's likely to hit a bunch of homers, work a bunch of walks and tally a bunch of strikeouts. You know, the truest of outcomes.

3 Reginald Preciado IF OFP: 55 ETA: 2025

Born: 05/16/03 Age: 19 Bats: S Throws: R Height: 6'4" Weight: 185 lb. Origin: International Free Agent, 2019

YEAR	TEAM	LVL	AGE	PA	R	2B	3B	HR	RBI	BB	K	SB	CS	AVG/OBP/SLG	DRC+	BABIP	BRR	FRAA	WARP
2021	CUB	ROK	18	154	28	10	3	3	25	11	35	7	1	.333/.383/.511		.423			

Comparables: Pedro Guerrero, Seth Moranda, Jose Luis Javier

The Report: While Caissie had the louder contact and hit his way out of the complex, the buzzier piece from the Yu Darvish deal had a more-than-respectable summer in the desert, himself. As weird as this is to say about an 18-year-old with an indeterminate defensive home, Preciado has a higher floor than Caissie given his broader set of tools. Preciado didn't send the Trackman machine haywire like a seismograph perched on the San Andreas—that's how we visualize TM working in our heads—but he had a very solid contact profile given the projection left in his teenaged frame. The swing works well from both sides of the plate, and there's plenty of bat speed and barrel feel to let him tap into whatever raw power comes in his twenties. There may not be elite offensive upside, but Preciado has a good chance to end up with plus hit and power tools while sticking on the left side of the infield—although that is unlikely to be at shortstop, and it's not impossible that he grows off the dirt entirely.

OFP: 55 / Above-average infielder, probably

Variance: High. Okay, I said he had a higher floor. He also has a long way to go to the majors, as the ETA above indicates, so it's not a high floor, per se.

Mark Barry's Fantasy Take: Preciado has been one of the buzziest names in dynasty circles despite playing just 34 games, all against lower-level competition. It's easy to understand why: He does a little bit of everything from both sides of the plate at a premium position. Still, he's just 18 years old and hasn't yet appeared beyond the complex. The window for acquiring Preciado at a reasonable cost has long closed, so if you believe in the ceiling, you're going to have to pay up for it. There's some Corey Seager–y vibes emanating from his write-ups, and the talent is there, but I'm a little skittish going all in.

4 James Triantos SS OFP: 55 ETA: 2025

Born: 01/29/03 Age: 19 Bats: R Throws: R Height: 6'1" Weight: 195 lb. Origin: Round 2, 2021 Draft (#56 overall)

YEAR	TEAM	LVL	AGE	PA	R	2B	3B	HR	RBI	BB	K	SB	CS	AVG/OBP/SLG	DRC+	BABIP	BRR	FRAA	WARP
2021	CUB	ROK	18	109	27	7	1	6	19	7	18	3	3	.327/.376/.594		.351			

Comparables: Angel Rodriguez, Yoelfi Suriel, Beicker Mendoza

The Report: We got turned on to Triantos fairly early in the amateur season, as he was a bit of an analytics darling combining premium bat-to-ball with high exit velocities. The Cubs grabbed him in the second round and went almost a million dollar-over slot to keep him from matriculating at North Carolina. He's not the most physical or most projectable high-school bat—we wouldn't be shocked if his listed height and weight are a bit generous—but he wrings everything out of his swing without sacrificing contact. Triantos has split time up the middle as a pro, but his long-term home is probably third base. He's a bit of a rough defender, at present, but his arm should play well at the hot corner while the rest of the defensive profile catches up.

OFP: 55 / Above-average infielder

Variance: High. The bat looks legit, but legit in the complex is a different thing than legit further up the ladder. He's unlikely to add a ton of value through infield defense, so the bat is going to have to be legit.

Mark Barry's Fantasy Take: Sure, it would be nice if Triantos drew a few more walks, but asking for more free passes from a dude that hit .327 and nearly slugged .600 is a little like going to pick up a million-dollar prize and then asking for parking validation. Triantos's true fantasy value likely won't reveal itself until he faces better pitching, but, unlike Preciado, there's still room to get in on Triantos before it gets too costly. He's a back-end first/early second rounder in most first-year player drafts.

5 Kevin Alcantara CF OFP: 55 ETA: 2025/2026

Born: 07/12/02 Age: 19 Bats: R Throws: R Height: 6'6" Weight: 188 lb. Origin: International Free Agent, 2018

YEAR	TEAM	LVL	AGE	PA	R	2B	3B	HR	RBI	BB	K	SB	CS	AVG/OBP/SLG	DRC+	BABIP	BRR	FRAA	WARP
2019	DSL NYY	ROK	16	46	7	3	1	0	6	5	9	2	0	.237/.348/.368		.300			
2019	YAE	ROK	16	128	19	5	2	1	13	3	27	3	3	.260/.289/.358		.326			
2021	CUB	ROK	18	107	27	3	5	4	21	13	28	3	0	.337/.415/.609		.443			
2021	YNK	ROK	18	31	5	1	0	1	3	4	8	2	0	.370/.452/.519		.500			

Comparables: Mikey Edie, Yovanny Cuevas, Jose Paez

The Report: Perhaps the highest-upside bat in a system suddenly flush with them, Alcantara has even more projection than production, at present, and he absolutely crushed the complex league. A lean 6-foot-6 with a commensurately long swing, that length leads to loud contact when he squares his pitch up, but he doesn't consistently lift the ball yet. He's a plus runner with a plus arm but is more likely to end up in right field than center field as he physically matures. Alcantara has consistently been one of the youngest players on his teams—the Yankees brought him stateside as soon as he turned 17 in 2019, and, even back in the complex last season, he had only 16 plate appearances against a pitcher younger than him. Between consistently facing older and more-experienced competition and the long levers in his stroke, he has, at times, struggled with swing-and-miss. If Alcantara can refine that a bit as he gets more game reps, he is a potential plus regular in the outfield.

OFP: 55 / Above-average outfielder

Variance: Extreme. This cuts in both directions. Alcantara is a physical outlier given his frame and present athletic tools, that puts true-superstar outcomes on the table if he sticks up the middle, it also might eventually leave him a corner outfielder with strikeout issues.

Mark Barry's Fantasy Take: Look, striking out over a quarter of the time in complex ball is extremely Not What You Want. That said, there's so much to like with the rest of Alcantara's production, I'm still snapping him up and keeping my fingers crossed for some development in the contact department. He's not particularly close, but Alcantara's plate discipline would be impressive for, like, Joey Votto, let alone a teenager. He's a top-101 name for me.

6 Pete Crow-Armstrong CF OFP: 55 ETA: 2024

Born: 03/25/02 Age: 20 Bats: L Throws: L Height: 6'0" Weight: 184 lb. Origin: Round 1, 2020 Draft (#19 overall)

YEAR	TEAM	LVL	AGE	PA	R	2B	3B	HR	RBI	BB	K	SB	CS	AVG/OBP/SLG	DRC+	BABIP	BRR	FRAA	WARP
2021	SLU	A	19	32	6	2	0	0	4	7	6	2	3	.417/.563/.500	119	.556	0.1	CF(5) 1.6	0.3
2022 non-DC	*CHC*	*MLB*	*20*	*251*	*19*	*10*	*1*	*2*	*19*	*21*	*74*	*6*	*5*	*.199/.275/.290*	*57*	*.285*	*0.7*	*CF 4*	*0.0*

The Report: As far as "recent first-round pick who had a good first week and then suffered a significant shoulder injury" goes, Crow-Armstrong's 2021 wasn't quite as good as Corbin Carroll's, but it wasn't far off. He scorched the ball for St. Lucie, suggesting the louder contact behind closed doors in 2020 that we heard about might be real. He then tore the labrum in his non-throwing shoulder and was dealt at the deadline for Javier Báez. As with Carroll, we don't really have enough information to assume a breakout would have continued going forward, so we are functionally holding his projection more or less steady. Crow-Armstrong has plus speed and a center-field glove with some offensive upside if he does start to hit for a little more game power. Even more pop probably tops out around fringe-average, but that would be enough to make him a plus regular given the rest of the profile. We'll have to wait until play resumes to see if that's truly on offer, or if what we saw last year was just a good week of at-bats down in Florida.

OFP: 55 / Table-setting, good-glove center fielder

Variance: High. He's coming off a significant shoulder injury. That's it. That's the tweet.

Mark Barry's Fantasy Take: It's hard to imagine a better pro debut than PCA's first six games in 2021. Unfortunately, we couldn't see him build on that success thanks to a torn labrum, which also kept us from *really* understanding what kind of player he might be moving forward. There are hit-tool questions, and his future power will still determine his ultimate fantasy upside, but his glove will give him opportunities. I'm taking advantage of the injury to try and add PCA at a discount, hoping for a 2021 replication—with a little more volume.

7 Jordan Wicks LHP OFP: 55 ETA: 2023

Born: 09/01/99 Age: 22 Bats: L Throws: L Height: 6'3" Weight: 220 lb. Origin: Round 1, 2021 Draft (#21 overall)

YEAR	TEAM	LVL	AGE	W	L	SV	G	GS	IP	H	HR	BB/9	K/9	K	GB%	BABIP	WHIP	ERA	DRA-	WARP
2021	SB	A+	21	0	0	0	4	4	7	7	0	3.9	6.4	5	37.5%	.304	1.43	5.14	117	0.0
2022 non-DC	*CHC*	*MLB*	*22*	*2*	*3*	*0*	*57*	*0*	*50*	*58*	*8*	*5.5*	*6.5*	*36*	*38.8%*	*.314*	*1.78*	*7.18*	*149*	*-1.1*

Comparables: Jayson Aquino, Mike Rayl, Zack Dodson

The Report: Nabbing Wicks with the 21st selection last July, the Cubs got the consensus top lefty in the draft, a potent college arm who should move quickly through the organization. He set single-season and career strikeout records at Kansas State using his double-plus change. It's a spin-killing offering, thrown in any count, generating plenty of weak swings as it falls off the table. He replicates the arm speed well, which allows his average fastball to play above its velocity. He has added a curve since being drafted to accompany an already-established slider as his primary breaking pitches. Wicks is a quick worker on the mound and utilizes an easy, repeatable delivery, giving hope for future plus command. That ability to control the zone and his four pitch repertoire should allow him to become a mid-rotation constant in the near future.

OFP: 55 / No. 3–4 starter

Variance: Medium. We're fairly confident that Wicks' ability to throw strikes and command the secondaries will make him a future big-league starter, but there is a chance the stuff improves and he exceeds our expectations in 2022.

Mark Barry's Fantasy Take: As it stands, Wicks seems like a streaming option whose fantasy contributions can be easily found on the waiver wire. That doesn't mean you should ignore him, however. Toss Wicks on the watchlist for now and monitor his velocity and control against (likely) Double-A bats.

8 Brailyn Márquez LHP OFP: 55 ETA: Debuted in 2020

Born: 01/30/99 Age: 23 Bats: L Throws: L Height: 6'4" Weight: 185 lb. Origin: International Free Agent, 2015

YEAR	TEAM	LVL	AGE	W	L	SV	G	GS	IP	H	HR	BB/9	K/9	K	GB%	BABIP	WHIP	ERA	DRA-	WARP
2019	SB	A	20	5	4	0	17	17	77^1	64	4	5.0	11.9	102	50.8%	.337	1.38	3.61	82	1.3
2019	MB	A+	20	4	1	0	5	5	26^1	21	1	2.4	8.9	26	44.4%	.282	1.06	1.71	91	0.4
2020	CHC	MLB	21	0	0	0	1	0	0^2	2	0	40.5	13.5	1	33.3%	.667	7.50	67.50		
2022 DC	*CHC*	*MLB*	*23*	*5*	*3*	*0*	*47*	*3*	*51.7*	*50*	*8*	*5.7*	*9.1*	*52*	*37.9%*	*.305*	*1.61*	*5.48*	*118*	*-0.2*

Comparables: Luiz Gohara, Brad Hand, Chris Tillman

The Report: Márquez was a Top-101 name coming into the 2021 season on the strength of a power arsenal featuring a fastball that touched triple digits and a swing-and-miss slider. Given that he debuted at the end of the 2020 season, you would have guessed that he'd have graduated from prospect lists last year. However, he's a pitcher. A shoulder strain cost Marquez all of 2021, and his outlook for 2022 is still a bit murky. Even as a top prospect, he had significant relief risk given his mechanics and inconsistency with his command and third pitch. The shoulder issue makes it more likely he'll be relief-only when he returns. Beyond that, given that it's a significant shoulder issue, we'll need to see his stuff come all the way back before we're sure he's a late-inning reliever.

OFP: 55 / Mid-rotation starter, but more likely an eighth-inning guy

Variance: Extreme. He's a pitcher coming off a significant shoulder injury. That's it. That's the tweet.

Mark Barry's Fantasy Take: For a dude that posted a 67.50 ERA in 2020, I suppose missing the entire 2021 campaign counts as an improvement. It's awfully hard to bet on the come with shoulder injuries, though, so Marquez's high ceiling a year ago has significantly lowered. I'm out until he shows a little (read: *any*) health.

9 Alexander Canario OF   OFP: 50   ETA: 2024

Born: 05/07/00   Age: 22   Bats: R   Throws: R   Height: 6'1"   Weight: 165 lb.   Origin: International Free Agent, 2016

YEAR	TEAM	LVL	AGE	PA	R	2B	3B	HR	RBI	BB	K	SB	CS	AVG/OBP/SLG	DRC+	BABIP	BRR	FRAA	WARP
2019	GIO	ROK	19	46	13	3	1	7	14	2	9	1	0	.395/.435/1.000		.370			
2019	SK	SS	19	219	38	17	1	9	40	18	71	3	1	.301/.365/.539		.419			
2021	SJ	A	21	274	43	14	3	9	29	33	79	15	3	.235/.325/.433	98	.307	1.0	LF(22) 1.9, RF(20) 0.3, CF(14) -1.3	1.0
2021	SB	A+	21	182	19	6	1	9	28	10	46	6	5	.224/.264/.429	106	.248	-1.7	CF(26) 2.1, RF(18) 0.7	0.8
2022 non-DC	*CHC*	*MLB*	*22*	*251*	*21*	*9*	*1*	*5*	*24*	*16*	*78*	*6*	*4*	*.207/.262/.335*	*60*	*.286*	*0.8*	*CF -1, RF 1*	*-0.3*

Comparables: Dalton Pompey, Ender Inciarte, Gregory Polanco

The Report: Among the trio of high-upside, low-minors Giants bats (Canario, Luis Matos and Luis Toribio), Canario's performance split the difference between the breakout of Matos and the scuffling of Toribio. He did not appear to see any long-term effects from his own shoulder surgery in 2020, still hitting for big time power when he got wood on the ball. That didn't happen as often as you'd like, though. Acquired in the Kris Bryant trade, Canario has big bat speed and generates easy-plus raw power line to line from a rather average-looking frame, but he likes to swing and will struggle with better fastballs in the zone and expand out of it too often. He has some semblance of an approach, at times, and he will continue to do damage on contact, but his hit tool is fringy, at best, and there's a chance he gets found out even further in the upper minors. Canario is a perfectly fine right fielder given his average foot speed and plus arm, but he's going to have to hit like a right fielder up the chain. The raw power fits the bill, but it remains to be seen if he can get it into games against better pitching.

OFP: 50 / Average right fielder

Variance: High. There's big-time hit-tool risk here. Canario could hit more than 30 homers in the majors, but he could also hit below .200 in Double-A.

Mark Barry's Fantasy Take: Since graduating from Rookie Ball, Canario has done two things with aplomb: 1) wow scouts with his bat speed and 2) strike out. The latter will make it tough for the former to yield results against good pitching.

10 Caleb Kilian RHP   OFP: 50   ETA: Late 2022

Born: 06/02/97   Age: 25   Bats: R   Throws: R   Height: 6'4"   Weight: 180 lb.   Origin: Round 8, 2019 Draft (#236 overall)

YEAR	TEAM	LVL	AGE	W	L	SV	G	GS	IP	H	HR	BB/9	K/9	K	GB%	BABIP	WHIP	ERA	DRA-	WARP
2019	GIO	ROK	22	0	0	0	6	5	12	6	0	1.5	8.3	11	57.1%	.214	0.67	0.00		
2021	EUG	A+	24	3	0	0	4	4	21^{2}	9	0	0.4	13.3	32	57.1%	.214	0.46	1.25	81	0.4
2021	RIC	AA	24	3	2	0	11	11	63	51	2	1.1	9.1	64	49.4%	.292	0.94	2.43	96	0.6
2021	TNS	AA	24	1	2	0	4	4	15^{2}	15	3	2.3	9.2	16	38.6%	.293	1.21	4.02	95	0.2
2022 non-DC	*CHC*	*MLB*	*25*	*2*	*2*	*0*	*57*	*0*	*50*	*49*	*6*	*2.3*	*7.7*	*42*	*44.8%*	*.297*	*1.25*	*3.94*	*97*	*0.3*

Comparables: Gonzalez Germen, Shane Greene, Craig Stammen

The Report: Kilian posted a near 10:1 strikeout-to-walk ratio in the minors last year. While his stuff isn't quite that dominant, it ticked up as the year went on, and improving secondaries give him a shot at being a rotation piece for the Cubs in the near term. His fastball works mostly in an average velocity range, although he showed a bit more in short bursts in the Arizona Fall League. His delivery is easy and repeatable, and the fastball shows a bit of plane given his height. After coming over with Canario in the Bryant trade, Kilian made more use of his potentially average mid-80s slider with tight, cutter action, and his curve—which was slurvy and inconsistent early in the season—showed added depth. He has some feel for the change, as well. While nothing here stands out, he has a well-rounded mix and throws enough quality strikes—that he profiles as a relatively safe back-end starter.

OFP: 50 / No. 4 starter

Variance: Medium. Kilian was a little old for his levels and may lack a true put-away pitch at the top level. However, he has made enough improvement with his secondaries that he should have some utility at the back of a rotation, even if the stuff is more hittable when facing major leaguers.

Mark Barry's Fantasy Take: Killian is probably my favorite arm in the Cubs' organization for fantasy purposes, mostly because we have a pretty good idea of his ultimate role. The righty averaged a shade under 5 ⅔ innings per start in 2021, which pretty much qualifies him as an ironman workhorse in this era. I think he'll be an innings-eater type in the big leagues with the potential for more if/when his secondaries improve.

The Prospects You Meet Outside the Top Ten:

#11

Ryan Jensen RHP Born: 11/23/97 Age: 24 Bats: R Throws: R Height: 6'0" Weight: 190 lb. Origin: Round 1, 2019 Draft (#27 overall)

YEAR	TEAM	LVL	AGE	W	L	SV	G	GS	IP	H	HR	BB/9	K/9	K	GB%	BABIP	WHIP	ERA	DRA-	WARP
2019	EUG	SS	21	0	0	0	6	6	12	7	0	10.5	14.3	19	68.2%	.318	1.75	2.25		
2021	SB	A+	23	2	7	0	16	16	62	42	8	3.5	10.9	75	53.3%	.239	1.06	4.50	78	1.4
2021	TNS	AA	23	1	0	0	4	4	18	14	2	3.5	7.5	15	60.4%	.261	1.17	3.00	99	0.2
2022 non-DC	*CHC*	*MLB*	*24*	*2*	*3*	*0*	*57*	*0*	*50*	*50*	*6*	*4.5*	*7.9*	*44*	*56.9%*	*.302*	*1.50*	*4.87*	*113*	*-0.2*

Comparables: Brandon Bielak, Alex Colomé, Yennsy Díaz

Take away a rough four-game stretch in June, and Jensen's overall numbers were solid, with opposing hitters batting .194 over two levels in his first full professional season. Jensen pounds the zone with a sinking, mid-90s fastball that gets good movement with both two and four seams. The change and curve lag behind his sharp slider, which has the potential to be a future plus offering. There's still plenty of reliever risk in his profile considering his size and inconsistent command, but the stuff will play up if he pares down his repertoire out of the bullpen.

#12

DJ Herz LHP Born: 01/04/01 Age: 21 Bats: R Throws: L Height: 6'2" Weight: 175 lb. Origin: Round 8, 2019 Draft (#252 overall)

YEAR	TEAM	LVL	AGE	W	L	SV	G	GS	IP	H	HR	BB/9	K/9	K	GB%	BABIP	WHIP	ERA	DRA-	WARP
2019	CUB2	ROK	18	0	1	0	6	6	10^1	10	0	7.0	7.0	8	41.2%	.294	1.74	2.61		
2021	MB	A	20	3	4	0	17	17	65^2	32	6	5.2	14.4	105	30.9%	.252	1.07	3.43	81	1.3
2021	SB	A+	20	1	0	0	3	3	16	10	1	3.4	14.6	26	51.6%	.300	1.00	2.81	76	0.4
2022 non-DC	*CHC*	*MLB*	*21*	*2*	*3*	*0*	*57*	*0*	*50*	*42*	*8*	*5.9*	*11.1*	*61*	*43.9%*	*.284*	*1.49*	*5.08*	*113*	*-0.2*

Comparables: Jaret Wright, Brad Hand, Franklin Morales

An eighth-round selection in 2019, Hertz emerged from the lost season of 2020 to become the breakout pitcher in the organization. His strikeout numbers were gaudy, as he punched out 131 in just 81 ⅔ innings combined between High- and Low-A. On the surface, his stuff is not overpowering. He throws a fastball that sits in the low 90s and two good, but not great, secondaries, but the whole package plays up due to his delivery. Herz generates plenty of late, awkward swings with his deceptive, low-three-quarters arm slot and extreme crossfire delivery. There's a bit of projection left in the frame, and if the secondaries continue to develop, Herz could become a future mid-rotation starter on the North Side.

Eyewitness Report: DJ Herz

Evaluator: Nathan Graham

Report Date: 09/29/2021

Dates Seen: 9/4/21

Risk Factor: High

Delivery: Large frame, thin and athletic build, plenty of projection remaining; Semi-wind up with a crossfire delivery that features moderate effort and a lower three-quarters arm slot, works from the far 1B side of the rubber

Pitch Type	Future Grade	Sitting Velocity	Peak Velocity	Report
Fastball	60	90-92	93	Average velocity, will tick up with physical maturity. Delivery angle, arm slot, and deception make it hard for hitters to pick up helping the pitch play up.
Changeup	60	82-85	86	Inconsistent currently, but has swing and miss potential when he gets it right, has depth and he replicates the arm action well. Good velocity separation.
Curveball	50	80-85	85	Solid offering with 1-7 movement, will use it to steal a strike or can bury it away from left handed hitters.

Conclusion: An overslot eighth rounder in 2019, Herz is young, projectable lefty who has been dominate in his first full professional season. The advanced secondaries and deception help the fastball play up. The three-pitch mix and remaining physical projection give him a profile of a future back of the rotation starter.

#13

Miguel Amaya C/DH Born: 03/09/99 Age: 23 Bats: R Throws: R Height: 6'2" Weight: 230 lb. Origin: International Free Agent, 2015

YEAR	TEAM	LVL	AGE	PA	R	2B	3B	HR	RBI	BB	K	SB	CS	AVG/OBP/SLG	DRC+	BABIP	BRR	FRAA	WARP
2019	MB	A+	20	410	50	24	0	11	57	54	69	2	0	.235/.351/.402	132	.259	-3.4	C(91) 6.2	3.0
2021	TNS	AA	22	106	11	4	0	1	13	21	22	2	0	.215/.406/.304	127	.281	1.0	C(12) 0.6, 1B(2) -0.4	0.8
2022 non-DC	*CHC*	*MLB*	*23*	*251*	*26*	*10*	*0*	*6*	*26*	*29*	*62*	*0*	*0*	*.215/.325/.363*	*90*	*.271*	*-0.3*	*C 0, 1B 0*	*0.8*

Comparables: Francisco Mejía, Christian Vázquez, Wilson Ramos

Once one of the top prospects in the organization and the heir apparent to Willson Contreras, Amaya's star has faded due to injuries and the inability to make consistent hard contact. Despite his struggles, he had some early-season successes that gave hope that he could return to his 2018 form. He spent time in early April at the alternate site getting reps behind the plate and working with many of the pitchers who would see time in Chicago. Offensively, during his brief stint at Double-A he displayed an improved eye, compiling a career-high walk rate. The 2022 season is likely a wash, with Amaya undergoing Tommy John surgery on his throwing arm last November, but he's still young and could contribute at the big-league level in 2023.

Prospects on the Rise

Drew Gray LHP Born: 05/10/03 Age: 19 Bats: L Throws: L Height: 6'3" Weight: 190 lb. Origin: Round 3, 2021 Draft (#93 overall)

The Cubs' 2021 third-round pick out of IMG Academy is a lanky lefty with a big, spinning fastball he can run up to 95 mph and a mid-70s hammer curve. His delivery has a lot of long levers, and he has had both mechanical and strike-throwing issues. He doesn't really have much of a changeup to speak of, but the fastball and breaker are exactly what you want in a modern pitching prospect. If Gray unlocks some more consistency in a professional developmental program, he could quickly become one of the better pitching prospects in this system.

Cristian Hernandez SS Born: 12/13/03 Age: 18 Bats: R Throws: R Height: 6'2" Weight: 175 lb. Origin: International Free Agent, 2021

YEAR	TEAM	LVL	AGE	PA	R	2B	3B	HR	RBI	BB	K	SB	CS	AVG/OBP/SLG	DRC+	BABIP	BRR	FRAA	WARP
2021	DSL CUBB	ROK	17	191	38	5	1	5	22	30	39	21	3	.285/.398/.424		.345			

Comparables: Pedro Guerrero, Yefry Rivas, Anthony Chavez

Look, you could certainly make a case for Hernandez to have a spot in the top 10, or at least a number next to his name. In a shallower system, we'd probably have to slot him there, but the variance on Dominican Summer League prospects—even high bonus ones—is beyond extreme. The building blocks are there for a future Top-101 prospect: sure-shot shortstop, plus arm, plus run, knack for contact. He's also the same age as the 2022 prep draft class. Let's see him stateside first.

Kevin Made SS Born: 09/10/02 Age: 19 Bats: R Throws: R Height: 5'10" Weight: 160 lb. Origin: International Free Agent, 2019

YEAR	TEAM	LVL	AGE	PA	R	2B	3B	HR	RBI	BB	K	SB	CS	AVG/OBP/SLG	DRC+	BABIP	BRR	FRAA	WARP
2021	MB	A	18	243	19	13	3	1	20	6	57	2	0	.272/.296/.366	88	.356	-2.6	SS(41) -1.7, 3B(13) 1.2	0.1
2022 non-DC	*CHC*	*MLB*	*19*	*251*	*18*	*11*	*1*	*1*	*19*	*9*	*68*	*0*	*1*	*.234/.267/.318*	*57*	*.320*	*-0.1*	*SS 1, 3B 0*	*-0.5*

Comparables: Ronny Mauricio, Adrian Marin, Ruddy Giron

Perhaps a couple of years ago, Made would have spent the first few months of his first pro season in Mesa before a summer spent with short-season Eugene. To get regular game time in 2021, he had to go to full-season ball, and he struggled to stay above water. Cover up that slash line with your hand, and we'll tell you there was some stuff to like. Made has above-average bat speed and a power hitter's stroke. He doesn't really have the physicality yet to consistently drive the ball, but you can see the outline of future power growth. Defensively, he has a shot to stick at short, with solid hands and actions and enough arm for the left side. The main issue Made encountered in 2021 was his swing decisions were: swing. That's it, just swing. Given that, it's impressive that he hit .270 against significantly older and more-experienced pitching, but the hit-tool risk is significant, and you are betting on future physical gains that may or may not come—and might force him off shortstop when they do.

Factors on the Farm

Ben Leeper RHP Born: 06/15/97 Age: 25 Bats: R Throws: R Height: 6'0" Weight: 195 lb. Origin: Undrafted Free Agent, 2020

YEAR	TEAM	LVL	AGE	W	L	SV	G	GS	IP	H	HR	BB/9	K/9	K	GB%	BABIP	WHIP	ERA	DRA-	WARP
2021	TNS	AA	24	1	2	1	10	0	14^{1}	9	0	2.5	13.8	22	28.1%	.281	0.91	1.26	84	0.3
2021	IOW	AAA	24	3	1	2	17	0	20^{2}	6	2	3.9	13.5	31	41.7%	.118	0.73	1.31	74	0.6
2022 DC	*CHC*	*MLB*	*25*	*1*	*1*	*0*	*22*	*0*	*19.3*	*16*	*3*	*4.3*	*11.6*	*25*	*33.8%*	*.302*	*1.34*	*4.36*	*97*	*0.1*

A 2020 undrafted free agent, Leeper was a pleasant surprise for the Cubs in 2021. After an unremarkable tenure in Stillwater as Oklahoma State's closer, he was dominant in his pro debut, showing improved command and holding opposing hitters to a .125 average over 35 innings. He'll sprinkle in the occasional curve, but his bread and butter is a heavy, mid-90s fastball that pairs well with his plus slider. He's likely to begin 2022 at Triple-A Iowa but should be first in line to provide depth if the Cubs' patchwork bullpen struggles early.

Zachary Leigh RHP Born: 11/14/97 Age: 24 Bats: R Throws: R Height: 6'0" Weight: 170 lb. Origin: Round 16, 2021 Draft (#484 overall)

YEAR	TEAM	LVL	AGE	W	L	SV	G	GS	IP	H	HR	BB/9	K/9	K	GB%	BABIP	WHIP	ERA	DRA-	WARP
2021	SB	A+	23	0	0	0	3	0	5	3	0	5.4	14.4	8	27.3%	.273	1.20	1.80	93	0.1
2022 non-DC	*CHC*	*MLB*	*24*	*2*	*3*	*0*	*57*	*0*	*50*	*50*	*8*	*5.2*	*9.0*	*50*	*37.1%*	*.308*	*1.60*	*5.83*	*130*	*-0.6*

A 16th-round college senior who lacked eye-popping numbers in the Sun Belt Conference, Leigh did not generate a lot of post-draft ink. That's likely to change after his brief, impressive pro debut, in which he struck out 17 in just eight innings. A starter at Texas State, Leigh saw his stuff play up after he transitioned to a bullpen role at High-A South Bend, with his fastball velocity jumping into the high 90s. That heat plus his power curve and developing change will make Leigh a quick mover in the organization.

Because You Were Going to Ask

Ed Howard SS Born: 01/28/02 Age: 20 Bats: R Throws: R Height: 6'2" Weight: 185 lb. Origin: Round 1, 2020 Draft (#16 overall)

YEAR	TEAM	LVL	AGE	PA	R	2B	3B	HR	RBI	BB	K	SB	CS	AVG/OBP/SLG	DRC+	BABIP	BRR	FRAA	WARP
2021	MB	A	19	326	33	9	3	4	31	18	98	7	2	.225/.277/.315	75	.318	0.2	SS(58) -0.1, 2B(21) -4.4	-0.4
2022 non-DC	*CHC*	*MLB*	*20*	*251*	*17*	*9*	*1*	*2*	*19*	*12*	*83*	*3*	*1*	*.202/.246/.286*	*40*	*.300*	*0.2*	*SS 0, 2B -1*	*-1.2*

Comparables: Luis Sardinas, Jonathan Araúz, Cole Tucker

There is no way to parse a .591 OPS that is going to make Howard's season look all right, and his performance at the plate was often that level of overmatched. He too often threw his whole upper body at pitches, sacrificing bat control and timing. Like Made, he could have used a short-season assignment, but, generally speaking, a full-season assignment for a high prep pick isn't outrageously aggressive. Howard was one of our favorite prospects in the 2020 draft, and that player doesn't completely disappear after a bad season. He's still a solid middle-infield glove and is young enough to run it back in 2022, but, in a rapidly improving, deep Cubs system, he has ground to make up.

Top Talents 25 and Under (as of 4/1/2022):

1. Nick Madrigal, 2B
2. Nico Hoerner, SS/2B
3. Brennen Davis, OF
4. Owen Caissie, OF
5. Reginald Preciado, IF
6. James Triantos, 2B
7. Kevin Alcantara, OF
8. Pete Crow-Armstrong, OF
9. Jordan Wicks, LHP
10. Brailyn Márquez, LHP

Chicago's hard reset came amidst the ascendance of the Brewers and rejuvenation of the Cardinals; however, the Bears in Blue could quickly return to NL Central contention with more financial infusions beyond rotation additions Marcus Stroman and Wade Miley, as well as the continued progression of their young double-play duo. Those are two sizable "ifs," but their middle infield features a pair of former Top-50 prospects with profiles featuring the same theme at different extremes.

One of the more polarizing (and, thus, heavily publicized) prospects in the last several years, Madrigal has roughly half a season of games under his belt but looks exactly as advertised: a no-pop, no-whiff, no-walk second baseman with an excellent glove and a trophy case he purchased on layaway that he should soon start filling with batting titles. He's a threat to finish each season with a higher OBP than SLG, though he should leg out enough doubles and triples to avoid that, and his 114 DRC+ thus far is an encouraging sign that what you see, as it has been since his time starring at Oregon State, is what you get. A torn hamstring cut short his 2021 campaign, marking back-to-back campaigns ended by injury (in 2020, he separated his non-throwing shoulder), and durability will continue to be a concern for a keystoner who might've had to look up to make eye contact with Pee Wee Reese.

Across the bag from Madrigal is Hoerner, who the Cubs are currently slated to roll out every day at shortstop. There are teams doing worse than that, but Hoerner is best-served as a second baseman who can spell another shortstop, as he did when the club still employed Javy Báez. Chicago moved him around the field when he was healthy, getting him reps at every spot in the other than first and catcher, not exactly offering a ringing endorsement of his competence at short. "When healthy" carries a lot of weight as well here, as Hoerner took three different trips to the 10-day injured list in 2021 with hamstring and oblique issues. Hoerner's only year as a pro in which he didn't miss roughly half the season due to injury of some sort was 2020, and there was only half a season to play that year. His bat-to-ball skills are excellent, and, like Madrigal, he should scatter the ball well enough to stick in the lineup. If they can stay on the field, the "Spray-to-Play" brothers should both be average big leaguers, useful players who genuinely improve their clubs. Whereas Madrigal's physicality will likely make him a highly polished finished product, Hoerner's role as pretender to shortstop likely depends on him tapping into another tier of power at the plate, or else he could see himself shifted into a utility role as Chicago looks elsewhere for an upgrade.

Chicago White Sox

The State of the System:

At least the White Sox have the young core of a major-league playoff team in place already.

The Top Ten:

1 Colson Montgomery SS OFP: 55 ETA: 2025

Born: 02/27/02 Age: 20 Bats: L Throws: R Height: 6'4" Weight: 205 lb. Origin: Round 1, 2021 Draft (#22 overall)

YEAR	TEAM	LVL	AGE	PA	R	2B	3B	HR	RBI	BB	K	SB	CS	AVG/OBP/SLG	DRC+	BABIP	BRR	FRAA	WARP
2021	WSX	ROK	19	111	16	7	0	0	7	13	22	0	1	.287/.396/.362		.375			

Comparables: Jordan McCants, Trace Loehr, Engelb Vielma

The Report: A high-school basketball star, as well, Montgomery's tall, projectable frame is more that of a shooting guard than a long-term shortstop, but he should add enough physicality to his offensive profile that a slide over to third base won't impact his long-term major-league future. He projects for above-average game power and already shows plenty of bat speed, although his approach is a bit raw, and his swing mechanics can get a little inside-out, limiting his ability to tap into even his present game pop. Defensively, he has the kind of fluid movements and body control you'd associate with a kid that drew the interest of Division I basketball teams, and he has enough arm for either left-side infield spot. Montgomery has a collection of potentially solid-average tools, but there is also some upside in his bat past the present 55-hit/55-power projection given that he was a cold-weather, multi-sport athlete as a high schooler.

OFP: 55 / Above-average third baseman

Variance: High. Montgomery is well-rounded for a prep pick. He was also a little old for his class and hasn't played outside of the complex yet.

Darius Austin's Fantasy Take: This kind of profile can cut two ways, since focusing on baseball and facing stiffer competition could either make Montgomery look like a total bargain or a guy who only succeeded because he was a supreme athlete facing others who couldn't devote all their time to baseball. As he's not going to cost you an early first-year-player-draft pick, I lean on betting on the athleticism and the upside. He's not far outside the top-100, as things stand, and will move up rapidly if he takes well to pro ball.

2 Yoelkis Céspedes CF OFP: 55 ETA: 2023

Born: 09/24/97 Age: 24 Bats: R Throws: R Height: 5'9" Weight: 205 lb. Origin: International Free Agent, 2021

YEAR	TEAM	LVL	AGE	PA	R	2B	3B	HR	RBI	BB	K	SB	CS	AVG/OBP/SLG	DRC+	BABIP	BRR	FRAA	WARP
2021	GDD	WIN	23	78	8	3	0	0	1	2	22	2	0	.181/.244/.222		.260			
2021	WS	A+	23	199	34	17	0	7	20	13	56	10	2	.278/.355/.494	89	.372	0.5	CF(21) -1.5, RF(3) -0.4	0.2
2021	BIR	AA	23	100	14	3	2	1	7	3	27	8	4	.298/.340/.404	81	.409	-0.2	CF(26) 3.9	0.5
2022 non-DC	*CHW*	*MLB*	*24*	*251*	*21*	*11*	*1*	*3*	*22*	*12*	*83*	*10*	*5*	*.223/.277/.335*	*64*	*.329*	*1.0*	*CF 4, RF 0*	*0.3*

Comparables: Henry Ramos, Elier Hernandez, Angel Morales

The Report: Despite possessing a stocky frame not unlike his older brother's, Céspedes runs well and is currently a plus defender in center. Combine that with his tools at the plate, and the White Sox might have something here. However, there are things that need to be ironed out if he is going to make this "something" a reality. His raw power is real and spectacular when it shows up in games. His swing is beautifully explosive and leads to a loud and satisfying conclusion when he turns on a mistake. It's the non-mistakes that are concerning; Céspedes (understandably) seems to enjoy tapping into that power, and his swing seems geared to handle a certain type of pitch in a certain location. When he intends to drive the ball the other way, he is able to, but, at times, he will look stiff against both decent breaking stuff down and away and hard stuff up in the zone. He did seem to get better as last summer went on, so perhaps some of his early struggles were due to rust.

OFP: 55 / His power-and-speed combo creates above-average outfield production

Variance: High. We need to see his hit tool play against top pitching.

Darius Austin's Fantasy Take: Céspedes essentially didn't play in any pro games for a couple of years, and it showed. That's kind of what we're hanging our hat on here as far as our fantasy hopes go: that his first year back was chiefly a product of the aforementioned rust. His age is somewhat deceptive, given the loss of development time, but that doesn't make the need for his hit tool to come around less pressing. His raw pop will certainly play, and he can run, so his other tools are there for fantasy, if you can afford to wait around a bit longer and see if there's another hit-tool-fuelled gear here.

Eyewitness Report: Yoelkis Céspedes

Evaluator: Ben Spanier

Report Date: 08/31/2021

Dates Seen: several while at High-A

Risk Factor: Medium

Physical/Health: Short, stocky frame, strength visible throughout but especially in upper body. Possesses more athleticism than might be expected given that description.

Tool	Future Grade	Report
Hit	45	Open stance, closes in conjunction with moderate leg kick. Fairly quiet but uses steep, aggressive, power-oriented swing that is designed to hit mistakes and pitches middle-in. Can get very pull-oriented and is vulnerable against decent breaking stuff down and away, doesn't always get to good velocity up.
Power	60	Isn't yet getting to it with regularity in-game, but it's a beautiful power-hitter's cut and when he zones a pitch he cans send it a long way. Will also hit his share of doubles into the gap. Above-average bat speed, good hip rotation, and plenty of upper body strength.
Baserunning/ Speed	60	Plus runner who is aggressive, will take the extra base, stretch extra base hits, and grab a few steals.
Glove	60	Very smooth. Gets good jumps and runs clean routes, hardly ever has to rush to make up for mistakes.
Arm	55	Strong arm and throws get good carry, but don't really pop.

Conclusion: I see Céspedes as someone who, even with hit tool concerns, can be an average regular with a profile built on power, defense, and speed. Has more value as a center fielder but should be able to handle all three spots.

3 Jake Burger 3B OFP: 55 ETA: Debuted in 2021

Born: 04/10/96 Age: 26 Bats: R Throws: R Height: 6'2" Weight: 230 lb. Origin: Round 1, 2017 Draft (#11 overall)

YEAR	TEAM	LVL	AGE	PA	R	2B	3B	HR	RBI	BB	K	SB	CS	AVG/OBP/SLG	DRC+	BABIP	BRR	FRAA	WARP
2021	CLT	AAA	25	340	46	16	2	18	54	24	91	0	0	.274/.332/.513	102	.330	-2.4	3B(65) 0.0, 2B(5) -0.3	0.9
2021	CHW	MLB	25	42	5	3	1	1	3	4	15	0	0	.263/.333/.474	74	.409	-0.2	3B(8) -0.6	-0.1
2022 DC	*CHW*	*MLB*	*26*	*122*	*14*	*5*	*0*	*4*	*15*	*8*	*36*	*0*	*0*	*.231/.291/.400*	*83*	*.302*	*-0.1*	*3B 0, 2B 0*	*0.1*

Comparables: Todd Frazier, Danny Valencia, Brent Morel

The Report: It's somewhat incredible that Burger made it back at all from a pair of Achilles tears that kept him out of organized baseball games for three seasons. To come back and immediately play to his previous, power-hitting prospect projection despite three gap years is frankly flabbergasting. Burger has slimmed down from his college days but still has plenty of oomph behind his swing. There's a bit of noise as he loads, but he has enough bat speed and bat control that it doesn't significantly impact his contact profile, although he can be vulnerable to better spin moving away from him. He still battles at third base well enough to play there—and the White Sox have talked about making him their 2022 second baseman—which is good, since there might not be quite enough impact in the bat to be a regular as a right/right first baseman. Regardless, we won't be fading to black and rolling to credits after his first major-league home run. This comeback tale has a few more story beats left in its run time.

OFP: 55 / Above-average third baseman

Variance: Low. There's a chance that swing-and-miss will eat up some of his offensive value in the majors—and his underlying swing stats in his Southside cup of coffee weren't great—but, given the time off, some adjustment period is to be expected.

Darius Austin's Fantasy Take: That both infield corners are closed off as routes to playing time complicates matters for Burger. If he can play first, second and third, stand in an outfield corner in an emergency and mash righties whenever he plays, he should work his way into being a handy, multi-positional, three-category player in most leagues. I wouldn't count on him as an everyday option, and, if the White Sox sign a more established second baseman, things get a little trickier.

4 Norge Vera RHP OFP: 50 ETA: 2024

Born: 06/01/00 Age: 22 Bats: R Throws: R Height: 6'4" Weight: 185 lb. Origin: International Free Agent, 2021

YEAR	TEAM	LVL	AGE	W	L	SV	G	GS	IP	H	HR	BB/9	K/9	K	GB%	BABIP	WHIP	ERA	DRA-	WARP
2021	DSL WSX	ROK	21	1	0	0	8	7	19	9	0	2.4	16.1	34	73.3%	.300	0.74	0.00		

The Report: The White Sox' other major Cuban international-free-agent signing from 2021, Vera's development got more of a slow roll as he spent the summer in the Dominican complex. He's a pitcher, less advanced then Céspedes, generally, and didn't even play all that much in Serie Nacional, so none of this is a surprise. Nor is it a bombshell that he was pumping upper 90s at times in the Dominican Summer League. His secondaries are more of a work in progress, but arm strength is arm strength, and Vera's upside makes him the best pitching prospect in a system admittedly shallow on arms.

OFP: 50 / No. 4 starter or late-inning reliever

Variance: Extreme. Vera has only a handful of complex starts, and his secondaries need development. He could also be a prospect for whom it clicks once he gets his mound legs back under him in pro ball.

Darius Austin's Fantasy Take: It turns out you can teach velocity, but Vera already has it, so that's one thing you don't need to worry about. Stick him on the watchlist and monitor the reports for anything that suggests he might have developed those secondaries enough for a regular starting role.

5 Jose Rodriguez SS OFP: 50 ETA: 2024

Born: 05/13/01 Age: 21 Bats: R Throws: R Height: 5'11" Weight: 175 lb. Origin: International Free Agent, 2018

YEAR	TEAM	LVL	AGE	PA	R	2B	3B	HR	RBI	BB	K	SB	CS	AVG/OBP/SLG	DRC+	BABIP	BRR	FRAA	WARP
2019	WSX	ROK	18	200	28	7	3	9	31	9	45	7	1	.293/.328/.505		.343			
2021	GDD	WIN	20	66	5	1	1	1	13	4	10	2	0	.226/.273/.323		.255			
2021	KAN	A	20	361	58	22	4	9	32	21	57	20	5	.283/.328/.452	111	.317	1.8	SS(71) -8.9, 2B(3) 0.1	0.9
2021	WS	A+	20	126	19	4	1	5	19	5	13	10	5	.361/.381/.538	138	.369	-1.7	SS(29) -4.0	0.4
2022 non-DC	*CHW*	*MLB*	*21*	*251*	*22*	*11*	*1*	*4*	*24*	*10*	*49*	*9*	*4*	*.263/.297/.380*	*83*	*.315*	*0.9*	*SS -1, 2B 0*	*0.4*

Comparables: Jorge Polanco, Ryan Mountcastle, Richard Ureña

The Report: Rodriguez is the rare White Sox prospect who was an unqualified success in 2021, performing very well at Low-A Kannapolis in his first full-season assignment and somehow improving on it after a promotion to High-A. He's a fun player to watch, as he plays with energy and evinces more personality than your average minor leaguer. His production to this point is predicated almost entirely on great bat speed and excellent hand-eye coordination; he swings often, and he swings hard. He is visibly strong, but his frame is on the smaller side, so it's hard to see a power-based profile developing here, and it will be interesting to see if he can keep up the same rate of contact as he begins to face higher-level pitching. He does add value with his speed, and, though he isn't a good shortstop at present, he has the tools to improve there. He would likely handle second or third a bit better and could profile as a utility infielder of sorts if necessary. Wherever it goes from here, Rodriguez will be an interesting name to follow.

OFP: 50 / Average infielder or utility type who can hit a bit and run a little

Variance: High. Rodriguez's defense isn't great, and it's hard to guarantee offensive production, at present.

Darius Austin's Fantasy Take: As a smaller middle infielder with great bat speed and control, Rodriguez is probably going to be a regular feature on lists of underrated fantasy prospects, but he doesn't quite have the discipline the projection models are going to love, as he swings at everything. Still, if his approach keeps playing through the two highest levels of the minors, the questions about contact will diminish, and he could at least be a solid, versatile, speed-and-average-driven middle infielder. He's a top-200 prospect who needs to defy those power projections to move up much more.

6 Wes Kath 3B OFP: 50 ETA: 2025

Born: 08/03/02 Age: 19 Bats: L Throws: R Height: 6'3" Weight: 200 lb. Origin: Round 2, 2021 Draft (#57 overall)

YEAR	TEAM	LVL	AGE	PA	R	2B	3B	HR	RBI	BB	K	SB	CS	AVG/OBP/SLG	DRC+	BABIP	BRR	FRAA	WARP
2021	WSX	ROK	18	115	15	0	2	3	15	8	42	1	0	.212/.287/.337		.322			

Comparables: Gavin Conticello, Nick Moore, Nolan Jones

The Report: Chicago doubled up on prep bats last summer, taking the Scottsdale, Arizona, shortstop in the second round. Kath only had to drive a half hour down the road to get to his first pro game, so no doubt White Sox scouts got plenty of looks at the big-framed high-school shortstop with big power. Kath was announced as a third baseman—where he played on the showcase circuit—and that's his short, medium and hopefully long-term home. He has just enough arm for the hot corner, and is athletic enough, for now, to handle it with aplomb. His swing is long and lofted but features plenty of bat speed and generates plenty of raw power.

OFP: 50 / Average, power-hitting third baseman

Variance: High. Kath has only played 28 pro games in the Arizona Complex League, and one of them was in right field. It's not impossible that he fills out enough to be forced off the dirt. So, there is some positional risk in addition to the general hit-tool risk you'd find for any second-round prep bat.

Darius Austin's Fantasy Take: Kath's statistical outlook isn't all that different from Burger's. He's just four or five years away, and Burger has already arrived. Keep an eye on Kath to see whether he can hack it defensively and if the power holds up after he moves up the levels, but don't worry about rostering him unless you're way past 300-prospects deep.

7 Matthew Thompson RHP OFP: 50 ETA: 2025

Born: 08/11/00 Age: 21 Bats: R Throws: R Height: 6'3" Weight: 195 lb. Origin: Round 2, 2019 Draft (#45 overall)

YEAR	TEAM	LVL	AGE	W	L	SV	G	GS	IP	H	HR	BB/9	K/9	K	GB%	BABIP	WHIP	ERA	DRA-	WARP
2019	WSX	ROK	18	0	0	0	2	2	2	2	0	0.0	9.0	2	33.3%	.333	1.00	0.00		
2021	KAN	A	20	2	8	0	19	19	71^2	83	7	4.8	9.7	77	42.9%	.384	1.69	5.90	96	0.8
2022 non-DC	*CHW*	*MLB*	*21*	*2*	*3*	*0*	*57*	*0*	*50*	*57*	*8*	*5.9*	*7.1*	*39*	*40.8%*	*.314*	*1.80*	*6.82*	*143*	*-1.0*

Comparables: Anthony Swarzak, Nick Bierbrodt, Matt Manning

The Report: Thompson was statistically awful for Kannapolis in 2021, *and* dealt with injury issues. So, why is he ranked in the top 10? Well, it's a pretty shallow White Sox system this year, but it's not just that. Thompson is still very talented and showed big-league flashes at times throughout the 2021 season. He's 93–96 with his fastball, but excellent extension lets it play up and explode through the zone. His upper-70s to low-80s curve varies in shape, appearing beautiful at 12–6 or sharp at 10–4. Both versions feature depth and late bite, creating a legitimate future plus swing-and-miss pitch. His changeup is well behind, and it's control over command, at present, but this is still a potential major-league profile.

OFP: 50 / Solid back-end starter or decent reliever

Variance: High. Thompson needs to demonstrate consistency and improved command and hasn't performed yet. There is some positive variance potential here, too.

Darius Austin's Fantasy Take: Anyone in the market for all the risk indicators plus a fairly limited ceiling and a long lead time? No, didn't think so.

8 Jonathan Stiever RHP OFP: 50 ETA: Debuted in 2020

Born: 05/12/97 Age: 25 Bats: R Throws: R Height: 6'2" Weight: 210 lb. Origin: Round 5, 2018 Draft (#138 overall)

YEAR	TEAM	LVL	AGE	W	L	SV	G	GS	IP	H	HR	BB/9	K/9	K	GB%	BABIP	WHIP	ERA	DRA-	WARP
2019	KAN	A	22	4	6	0	14	14	74	88	10	1.7	9.4	77	43.8%	.363	1.38	4.74	99	0.6
2019	WS	A+	22	6	4	0	12	12	71	56	7	1.6	9.8	77	40.4%	.278	0.97	2.15	73	1.6
2020	CHW	MLB	23	0	1	0	2	2	6^1	7	4	5.7	4.3	3	40.9%	.167	1.74	9.95	142	-0.1
2021	CLT	AAA	24	5	5	0	17	17	74	80	13	3.4	10.7	88	32.9%	.330	1.46	5.84	96	1.2
2021	CHW	MLB	24	0	0	0	1	0	0	4	0			0	0.0%	1.000				
2022 DC	*CHW*	*MLB*	*25*	*2*	*2*	*0*	*8*	*8*	*36.3*	*37*	*6*	*3.3*	*8.2*	*33*	*55.8%*	*.297*	*1.39*	*5.01*	*116*	*0.0*

Comparables: Dylan Covey, Cy Sneed, Alfredo Figaro

The Report: Stiever didn't record an out in his one major-league appearance of 2021, leading to the always-unfortunate career ERA of infinity. His Triple-A results weren't much better, and there's no single explanation for his struggles and stagnation. He can still pop above-average velocity above the barrel, but he's touching mid-90s now rather than sitting there like he did in A-ball. His breaker is a little softer, his control and command significantly worse, and his changeup hasn't really progressed. Stiever, like most prospects, has had his last two seasons of development disrupted. He went from a fringe 101 candidate—who pitched well across two A-ball levels—in 2019, to the majors in 2020 (by way of the alternate site), and then to Triple-A in 2021. We often write that development is not linear, but that path probably didn't help. Stiever's 2021 season ended in August due to a lat injury that required surgery. Hopefully that's a reset button that lets him tap back into the stuff that made him a mid-rotation pitching prospect just two years ago.

OFP: 50 / No. 4 starter

Variance: Medium. The stuff still flashes, but that stops being something to hang your hat on in Triple-A. Baseball is a very "what have you done for me lately" industry, and Stiever has struggled for a bit now.

Darius Austin's Fantasy Take: I liked Stiever in recent years as a proximity candidate who had strikeout stuff, but this has gone about as badly as it could have outside of his just being hurt the entire time . . . oh, and he got hurt, as well. If he can turn the clock back to the performance and stuff that he had in 2019, then I'm still interested. It's hard to find a reason why we'd believe in that happening now, though.

9 Jared Kelley RHP OFP: 50 ETA: 2025

Born: 10/03/01 Age: 20 Bats: R Throws: R Height: 6'3" Weight: 230 lb. Origin: Round 2, 2020 Draft (#47 overall)

YEAR	TEAM	LVL	AGE	W	L	SV	G	GS	IP	H	HR	BB/9	K/9	K	GB%	BABIP	WHIP	ERA	DRA-	WARP
2021	KAN	A	19	0	5	0	10	10	21	21	1	9.4	10.7	25	49.2%	.328	2.05	6.86	108	0.1
2022 non-DC	*CHW*	*MLB*	*20*	*2*	*3*	*0*	*57*	*0*	*50*	*55*	*8*	*8.2*	*8.0*	*44*	*42.5%*	*.317*	*2.02*	*7.59*	*150*	*-1.1*

Comparables: J.B. Wendelken, Edgar García, Oscar Villarreal

The Report: Chicago's 2020 second-round pick had a rough go of it last season. He was injured for much of the year, and, when he pitched, he got knocked around in short outings. His talent hasn't simply evaporated, of course. Kelley's mid-to-upper 90s fastball has plenty of life and heft and really shouldn't be easy to square up, though a jump in command is necessary for it to be as effective as it should be. His mid-80s slider looks very good, at times, but, given the brevity of his outings, it was generally difficult for us to get a good feel for his secondary stuff. Kelly will look to turn the page in 2022.

OFP: 50 / Back-end starter or reliever

Variance: Very High. He has stuff, he just needs to stay healthy and perform.

Darius Austin's Fantasy Take: Look, guys, I don't know what to tell you. This is not a great system for pitching prospects. Kelley sounds like a reliever based on the above, but he didn't get a chance to do much other than pitch in brief outings. Either way, it's not exciting.

10 Micker Adolfo RF/DH OFP: 50 ETA: 2022

Born: 09/11/96 Age: 25 Bats: R Throws: R Height: 6'4" Weight: 225 lb. Origin: International Free Agent, 2013

YEAR	TEAM	LVL	AGE	PA	R	2B	3B	HR	RBI	BB	K	SB	CS	AVG/OBP/SLG	DRC+	BABIP	BRR	FRAA	WARP
2019	GDD	WIN	22	61	5	0	0	4	6	5	27	0	0	.167/.262/.389		.217			
2019	WSX	ROK	22	58	8	5	0	2	3	7	21	0	0	.260/.362/.480		.407			
2019	BIR	AA	22	95	5	7	0	0	9	14	36	0	3	.205/.337/.295	67	.372	-3.3		-0.5
2021	BIR	AA	24	242	33	15	0	15	46	19	85	1	0	.249/.318/.525	113	.328	0.4	RF(39) -2.0	0.9
2021	CLT	AAA	24	163	23	9	1	10	23	12	53	3	0	.240/.301/.513	91	.299	-0.1	RF(30) 0.0, LF(10) 1.2	0.4
2022 DC	*CHW*	*MLB*	*25*	*131*	*16*	*6*	*0*	*4*	*15*	*9*	*49*	*0*	*0*	*.222/.290/.407*	*82*	*.334*	*-0.1*	*LF 1, RF 0*	*0.1*

Comparables: Steven Moya, Teoscar Hernández, Abraham Almonte

The Report: This is one of those cases in which the stat line does a good job of describing the player. Adolfo's front foot is interesting in that it almost turns toward the inside of his body pre-swing but plants towards the first-base line straight following a leg kick that generates some big torque and genuine plus-plus raw power. Adolfo appears to lean a bit on his back leg pre-pitch and transfers his weight to his front foot as he explodes through the baseball on his swing.

This is also one of those cases in which the hit tool might actually be two full grades lower than the power tool (40 vs. 60). Adolfo has a long, free-swinging stroke that generates plenty of whiffs, but he is absolutely one of the strongest players in all of minor-league baseball. When he connects, his 70 raw power is likely to keep @MLBHRVideos busy. He's a well-below-average runner, which really limits his ability to play the field, but Adolfo isn't going to be in any lineups for his defense.

OFP: 50 / Slugging designated hitter and occasional corner outfielder

Variance: Low. This is who Micker Adolfo is, but while his variance is low, he doesn't have much of a floor if he isn't hitting 30-plus bombs.

Darius Austin's Fantasy Take: Adolfo is out of options, so if we're going to see the monster, highlight home runs in a White Sox uniform, we ought to be seeing them soon. They are also his only source of value, and it's hard not to feel like the "good" outcome here is Wily Mo Pena. Honestly, Adolfo's going to have trouble striking out as infrequently as Wily Mo, since he has managed to run a strikeout rate north of 30 percent—often considerably so—at almost every stop in the minors. Adolfo could hit 35 dingers and still get the Chris Carter treatment: designated for assignment at the end of the year.

The Prospects You Meet Outside the Top Ten:

Prospects on the Rise

Sean Burke RHP Born: 12/18/99 Age: 22 Bats: R Throws: R Height: 6'6" Weight: 230 lb. Origin: Round 3, 2021 Draft (#94 overall)

YEAR	TEAM	LVL	AGE	W	L	SV	G	GS	IP	H	HR	BB/9	K/9	K	GB%	BABIP	WHIP	ERA	DRA-	WARP
2021	KAN	A	21	0	1	0	5	5	14	9	0	6.4	12.9	20	43.3%	.321	1.36	3.21	92	0.2
2022 non-DC	*CHW*	*MLB*	*22*	*2*	*3*	*0*	*57*	*0*	*50*	*49*	*7*	*6.3*	*9.2*	*51*	*35.1%*	*.305*	*1.68*	*5.90*	*129*	*-0.6*

Comparables: Zach Lewis, Dallas Beeler, Abdiel Saldana

Burke is a massive, 6-foot-6 righty who likes to pound mid-90s riding fastballs above hitter's hands. His heater can be a bat-misser on its own, but Burke struggled with the free pass for much of his college career, and that bled over into his pro debut, as well. He works a spike curve with good depth and a shorter slider into his repertoire, as well, but both are inconsistent, and he often struggles to get ahead in the count to deploy them. His delivery is fairly simple, but that makes his control issues a bit more worrisome and a move to the bullpen more likely.

Andrew Dalquist RHP Born: 11/13/00 Age: 21 Bats: R Throws: R Height: 6'1" Weight: 175 lb. Origin: Round 3, 2019 Draft (#81 overall)

YEAR	TEAM	LVL	AGE	W	L	SV	G	GS	IP	H	HR	BB/9	K/9	K	GB%	BABIP	WHIP	ERA	DRA-	WARP
2019	WSX	ROK	18	0	0	0	3	3	3	2	0	6.0	6.0	2	33.3%	.222	1.33	0.00		
2021	KAN	A	20	3	9	0	23	23	83	87	1	6.1	8.6	79	42.8%	.345	1.72	4.99	117	0.0
2022 non-DC	*CHW*	*MLB*	*21*	*2*	*3*	*0*	*57*	*0*	*50*	*58*	*8*	*7.1*	*7.0*	*38*	*43.8%*	*.321*	*1.96*	*7.44*	*152*	*-1.2*

Comparables: Jamey Wright, Elieser Hernandez, Chase De Jong

The 2019 third-rounder Dalquist had an uneven Low-A campaign in 2021, striking out just under a batter an inning and recording an ERA just under five. Diminutive as starting-pitching prospects go, Dalquist is athletic at 6-ish feet and 175 pounds, but it is hard to project significant velocity gains here. He currently sits low- to mid-90s, though his fastball is lively. He has two interesting breaking pitches, an 11–5 curve in the mid-70s and a somewhat subtle, low–80s slider. Both pitches break sharply, at times, but not consistently, and his changeup seems fairly undeveloped. We've seen all four get knocked around, and command improvements will be necessary in order to stop this from happening.

Bryan Ramos DH Born: 03/12/02 Age: 20 Bats: R Throws: R Height: 6'2" Weight: 190 lb. Origin: International Free Agent, 2018

YEAR	TEAM	LVL	AGE	PA	R	2B	3B	HR	RBI	BB	K	SB	CS	AVG/OBP/SLG	DRC+	BABIP	BRR	FRAA	WARP
2019	WSX	ROK	17	218	36	10	2	4	26	19	44	3	4	.277/.353/.415		.331			
2021	KAN	A	19	504	64	23	6	13	57	51	110	13	4	.244/.345/.415	103	.295	1.4	3B(34) 1.1, 2B(25) -0.2	1.8
2022 non-DC	*CHW*	*MLB*	*20*	*251*	*21*	*10*	*1*	*4*	*23*	*17*	*70*	*3*	*2*	*.213/.280/.334*	*65*	*.288*	*0.3*	*3B 0, 2B 0*	*-0.4*

Comparables: Dilson Herrera, Brandon Drury, Jeimer Candelario

Ramos didn't light up the leaderboards this year, but he held his own as a 19-year-old in full-season ball. Signed out of Cuba in 2018, he has emerged as an under-the-radar factor in this system thanks to his innate hitting ability and power potential. Listed at 6-foot-2 and 190 pounds, Ramos has a large fraame and appears to carry a bit more weight than that official number. He's a good athlete for his size, so there is no real issue there, but it is slightly curious to us that he split his time in the field almost evenly between second and third. We think he can handle third, though he might have to migrate across the diamond as he grows into his body. His power is immediately evident and plays to all fields, and his bat just might develop enough for the pop to play. His swing isn't stiff, and a good approach allows him to get on base at a decent clip and select pitches he can drive. Ramos is someone to keep an eye on.

Factors on the Farm

Romy Gonzalez IF Born: 09/06/96 Age: 25 Bats: R Throws: R Height: 6'1" Weight: 215 lb. Origin: Round 18, 2018 Draft (#528 overall)

YEAR	TEAM	LVL	AGE	PA	R	2B	3B	HR	RBI	BB	K	SB	CS	AVG/OBP/SLG	DRC+	BABIP	BRR	FRAA	WARP
2019	KAN	A	22	405	35	22	4	4	45	38	108	11	3	.244/.329/.364	94	.337	2.1	LF(68) 8.9, 1B(14) -0.8, 2B(7) -0.4	1.9
2021	BIR	AA	24	344	52	11	0	20	47	38	97	21	6	.267/.355/.502	122	.328	-0.4	SS(61) -0.8, 2B(10) 0.9	1.9
2021	CLT	AAA	24	60	9	6	0	4	14	5	15	3	0	.370/.417/.704	102	.444	1.4	SS(10) -1.8, 2B(3) -0.3, 3B(2) -0.5	0.1
2021	CHW	MLB	24	33	4	3	0	0	2	1	11	0	0	.250/.273/.344	70	.381	0.4	3B(4) -0.3, RF(3) -0.2, 2B(1) -0.1	0.0
2022 DC	*CHW*	*MLB*	*25*	*129*	*14*	*5*	*0*	*3*	*14*	*9*	*40*	*3*	*1*	*.231/.296/.386*	*83*	*.316*	*0.2*	*2B 0, SS 0*	*0.1*

Comparables: Danny Valencia, Ryon Healy, Wilmer Difo

Gonzalez hit his way to the majors in 2021, but his swing can be inconsistent. At times, he flashes above-average power potential. At others, his bat looks slower and is just an average stroke with loose mechanics. An intriguing combination of speed and power, Gonzalez has a chance to be a .260-average, 20–20 guy at his very peak. However, the 25-year-old likely tracks as a fringe-hit-with-power bat that can swipe a base and play a few infield spots. One of those will be shortstop, although he appears to be one of those guys who can *play* shortstop but isn't a *shortstop*. Although it's easy to poke holes in his game, his entire profile makes for a useful bench piece or fringe starter.

Yolbert Sanchez MI Born: 03/03/97 Age: 25 Bats: R Throws: R Height: 5'11" Weight: 176 lb. Origin: International Free Agent, 2019

YEAR	TEAM	LVL	AGE	PA	R	2B	3B	HR	RBI	BB	K	SB	CS	AVG/OBP/SLG	DRC+	BABIP	BRR	FRAA	WARP
2019	DSL WSX	ROK	22	127	19	8	1	2	12	15	12	3	3	.297/.386/.441		.320			
2021	WS	A+	24	239	28	7	0	5	29	18	33	2	1	.286/.340/.387	110	.318	0.3	2B(34) -3.6, SS(24) -2.0	0.5
2021	BIR	AA	24	155	15	6	0	4	13	5	16	3	0	.343/.369/.469	122	.366	0.7	2B(19) 0.7, SS(16) 2.3, 3B(3) -0.0	1.2
2022 non-DC	*CHW*	*MLB*	*25*	*251*	*22*	*9*	*0*	*3*	*23*	*13*	*37*	*2*	*1*	*.269/.311/.363*	*84*	*.307*	*-0.1*	*2B -1, SS 0*	*0.3*

Comparables: Brian Dozier, Matt Tolbert, Jordan Pacheco

A former top international prospect—he signed for $2.5 million in 2019—Sanchez played at High-A and Double-A in 2021, slashing .286/.340/.387 at the former and .343/.369/.469 at the latter. He's not an overly explosive player, but he can handle both middle-infield spots and probably third, as well. With good barrel control and a bit of pop, he could be a utility option in the near future.

Emilio Vargas RHP Born: 08/12/96 Age: 25 Bats: R Throws: R Height: 6'3" Weight: 220 lb. Origin: International Free Agent, 2013

YEAR	TEAM	LVL	AGE	W	L	SV	G	GS	IP	H	HR	BB/9	K/9	K	GB%	BABIP	WHIP	ERA	DRA-	WARP
2019	DIA	ROK	22	0	2	0	3	3	10[1]	9	1	1.7	10.5	12	32.0%	.333	1.06	4.35		
2019	JXN	AA	22	5	3	0	17	17	85[2]	74	10	2.4	7.4	70	43.1%	.261	1.13	3.78	102	0.5
2021	BIR	AA	24	7	4	0	21	15	83[2]	69	9	3.0	10.6	99	39.5%	.296	1.16	2.90	94	1.1
2022 non-DC	*CHW*	*MLB*	*25*	*2*	*2*	*0*	*57*	*0*	*50*	*48*	*8*	*3.7*	*8.4*	*46*	*34.7%*	*.289*	*1.37*	*4.65*	*109*	*0.0*

Comparables: Conner Greene, Zach Davies, Brian Bass

Vargas is the type of prospect who has more than enough stuff to get minor-league hitters out, but may struggle some in the majors. The well-rounded right-hander's best offering is a sweeping slider, which flashes above-average potential, as it has a big, horizontal movement that plays up against righties but not ideal depth given his three-quarters slot. His fastball sits low 90s with some wiggle, and he has an average changeup, as well. Vargas is consistent in his delivery, and while, overall, the profile is a little below major-league average, he's ready to be a little below major-league average in the majors.

Top Talents 25 and Under (as of 4/1/2022):

1. Luis Robert, OF
2. Eloy Jiménez, OF
3. Michael Kopech, RHP
4. Andrew Vaughn, 1B/OF
5. Garrett Crochet, LHP
6. Colson Montgomery, SS
7. Yoelkis Céspedes, OF
8. Gavin Sheets, 1B/OF
9. Jake Burger, IF
10. Norge Vera, RHP

The time is now for the ChiSox, whose consolidation of early- to mid-20s talent is the envy of much of the league. They comfortably claimed control of the American League Central in 2021 en route to a division title. Credit is due, in great part, to their thunderous outfielders and lightning-hurling young arms. Despite a torn hip flexor in early May that cost him roughly three months of 2021, Robert actually returned better than before, with improvements to nearly every facet of his offensive game. He ran a 121 DRC+ and appeared for all the world a possible superstar given his brilliant defensive capabilities at full health. "La Pantera" can hopefully retain the offensive strides, namely his improved contact profile and pitch selection, while seeing rejuvenation in his speed reflected in his defensive and baserunning numbers from day one in 2022.

In left field, the Southsiders have another much-heralded yet often-injured potential standout. Jiménez missed nearly four months with a torn left pectoral and took several days of recovery with lesser groin and knee injuries, to boot. That heat map of full-body undermining is a relatively straightforward first step to understanding the disappointing numbers the young slugger put up in 2021, but it does not guarantee better results going forward. Jiménez is a massive athlete with a history of, frankly, injuries borne of clumsiness. While that is a relatable and endearing trait, it could be worrisome going forward if he continues to struggle to stay on the field and mash the ball to his obvious capability. Still, few players can hit like a healthy Jiménez, both for power and a respectable average, if aggressive in his swinging zeal.

Chicago's young fireballers, Kopech and Crochet, each had stellar seasons out of the the pen and will be rewarded with the opportunity to continue attempting to develop as starters, or at least see consideration as such. The righty Kopech and lefty Crochet have each demonstrated dominant stuff from the pen, though the latter did see his triple-digit averages dip to sitting at a still-solid 96–98. Chicago's bullpen was and is a masterpiece on paper, and they can afford to give both players a bit of time to stretch out, particularly given that the division they play in is unlikely to feature any other serious competitors, once again. The White Sox' rotation, conversely, could seriously use the upside both players offer.

Considering Vaughn's big-league welcome featured him playing primarily in left field, and 856 ⅔ of his 956 ⅓ defensive innings somewhere other than first base, the only non-pitching position he'd played through his entire professional and collegiate career . . . things could have gone worse? If you subscribe to the notion that asking a player to learn new roles defensively is detrimental to their production on the other side of the ball, Vaughn's thinly stretched debut—which saw him move from left field to right field to third base and even second—was hardly a surprise. That said, for one of the most polished college bats in the minors, the lack of thump in Vaughn's first major-league foray was underwhelming. To his credit, he did avoid swinging and missing too much and was merely a league-average bat moonlighting as a utility player, something that hopefully will get easier in Year Two. His less-heralded compatriot in peculiar defensive profile had a slightly stronger year at the dish, though the hulking Sheets is even more likely to need DH time on a roster that already features Jiménez, José Abreu, and Vaughn. While Sheets has hit enough to merit starting somewhere or, at least, a role on the strong side of a platoon, his fit on Chicago's roster at present is something they'll need to sort out.

Cincinnati Reds

The State of the System:

While the Reds' system could use the influx of talent from, say, trading Luis Castillo and Sonny Gray, it might not be in a spot to provide the core of the next Reds playoff team even after dealing major-league pieces.

The Top Ten:

1 Hunter Greene RHP OFP: 60 ETA: 2022

Born: 08/06/99 Age: 22 Bats: R Throws: R Height: 6'5" Weight: 230 lb. Origin: Round 1, 2017 Draft (#2 overall)

YEAR	TEAM	LVL	AGE	W	L	SV	G	GS	IP	H	HR	BB/9	K/9	K	GB%	BABIP	WHIP	ERA	DRA-	WARP
2021	CHA	AA	21	5	0	0	7	7	41	27	2	3.1	13.2	60	41.2%	.301	1.00	1.98	92	0.6
2021	LOU	AAA	21	5	8	0	14	14	65^1	59	11	3.4	10.9	79	45.2%	.306	1.29	4.13	84	1.4
2022 DC	*CIN*	*MLB*	*22*	*4*	*4*	*0*	*16*	*16*	*68*	*63*	*10*	*3.9*	*9.7*	*73*	*40.0%*	*.302*	*1.37*	*4.54*	*102*	*0.5*

Comparables: Zach Davies, Wily Peralta, Jake Odorizzi

The Report: Greene is one of the hardest-throwing pitchers in the history of affiliated baseball. He spent much of 2021 regularly hitting the low 100s and sometimes touching the mid-100s in the high minors, phrases that don't even look right on paper. His slider also projects as a plus pitch and already flashes that on good nights. Given his arm speed, that shouldn't be a surprise, and he's well-rounded enough as a baseball player (he'd have been drafted in the first round as a shortstop, even if he never set foot on a mound) that he has fluid and repeatable motions on the mound. Suffice it to say, he's starting with a heck of a skills base.

Greene does have a few downsides that he will have to overcome to be a star. His fastball has hittable shape to it. (It may not matter given the velocity.) His changeup is still in development. (It may not matter if the fastball and slider play like they could in the majors.) And he missed a *lot* of time surrounding a 2018 elbow injury which led to Tommy John surgery. So sure, there are relief markers, but also, holy shit, it's 104 with a plus breaking pitch!

OFP: 60 / No. 2–3 starter or first-division closer

Variance: High. With just a few more adjustments, he's an ace. Or he could end up as a reliever. We'll see soon.

Mark Barry's Fantasy Take: So back to that upside. Routinely hitting triple digits on the gun is a pretty good way to raise your ceiling. I've been skeptical about Greene's ability to start, but he managed to prove me wrong this year, averaging a little more than five innings per start. If his change develops, he could be a no-doubt ace. If it doesn't, he won't get the volume, but he'll be good in short spurts.

2 Nick Lodolo LHP OFP: 55 ETA: 2022, health permitting

Born: 02/05/98 Age: 24 Bats: L Throws: L Height: 6'6" Weight: 205 lb. Origin: Round 1, 2019 Draft (#7 overall)

YEAR	TEAM	LVL	AGE	W	L	SV	G	GS	IP	H	HR	BB/9	K/9	K	GB%	BABIP	WHIP	ERA	DRA-	WARP
2019	BIL	ROA	21	0	1	0	6	6	11^1	12	1	0.0	16.7	21	32.0%	.458	1.06	2.38		
2019	DAY	A	21	0	0	0	2	2	7	6	0	0.0	11.6	9	50.0%	.333	0.86	2.57	86	0.1
2021	CHA	AA	23	2	1	0	10	10	44	31	1	1.8	13.9	68	53.3%	.337	0.91	1.84	77	1.0
2021	LOU	AAA	23	0	1	0	3	3	6^2	7	2	2.7	13.5	10	56.2%	.357	1.35	5.40	87	0.1
2022 non-DC	*CIN*	*MLB*	*24*	*3*	*2*	*0*	*57*	*0*	*50*	*42*	*6*	*2.9*	*9.9*	*54*	*48.7%*	*.289*	*1.17*	*3.24*	*79*	*0.7*

Comparables: Tim Crabtree, Travis Miller, Joba Chamberlain

The Report: Do you prefer the command lefty who might not have a true swing-and-miss pitch, or the righty throwing pure smoke with a TJ and relief risk? It was a somewhat close call for us, but Lodolo's own injury issues—he was shut down at the end of August with shoulder fatigue that was later called a strain—slots him in second. When he was on the mound in

2021, he very much looked the part of an advanced college lefty. Lodolo has a narrow frame, which is about 70 percent legs, and throws across his body, creating a little extra deception for his fastball, which often seems to get on hitters faster than its low-90s radar readings. He can also pop a four-seamer by you on occasion at 95. The slider isn't a true plus pitch, but he can manipulate its shape across a low-80s velocity band. At the higher end, it shows some short cut/tilt that he can backdoor to righties or front-hip to lefties. At the lower end, it's a longer, slurvier breaker with more depth. It's not a pitch that will rack up strikeouts, but it will miss enough bats and catch guys lunging for weak grounders. The changeup has improved, and although it's firm—at times only a few miles per hour slower than the fastball—Lodolo sells it well, and it has a little late sink. He moves his stuff around the zone well and dominated the upper minors. The only questions now are short-term health and long-term durability, not minor questions for a pitching prospect, mind you.

OFP: 55 / No. 3–4 starter

Variance: Medium. The only real question here is arm health. If he's healthy, Lodolo is likely to be a rotation piece for the Reds at some point in 2022. If not, well, he is a pitcher, after all.

Mark Barry's Fantasy Take: I don't know, man. Lodolo's walks were up, like, 2,000 percent or something this season. Maybe that's because he didn't walk a single hitter in 2019, and his control in 2021 was merely really good as opposed to otherworldly. In all seriousness, Lodolo is one of my favorite minor-league arms. He might not have the same upside as Greene, but I think his floor is high. He's a top-10 dynasty arm for me, no question.

3 Elly De La Cruz SS   OFP: 60   ETA: 2025

Born: 01/11/02 Age: 20 Bats: S Throws: R Height: 6'2" Weight: 150 lb. Origin: International Free Agent, 2018

YEAR	TEAM	LVL	AGE	PA	R	2B	3B	HR	RBI	BB	K	SB	CS	AVG/OBP/SLG	DRC+	BABIP	BRR	FRAA	WARP
2019	DSL REDS	ROK	17	186	24	11	1	1	26	14	45	3	6	.285/.351/.382		.380			
2021	RED	ROK	19	55	13	6	2	3	13	4	15	2	0	.400/.455/.780		.531			
2021	DBT	A	19	210	22	12	7	5	29	10	65	8	5	.269/.305/.477	89	.372	-0.7	3B(28) 7.0, SS(20) 2.7	1.2
2022 non-DC	*CIN*	*MLB*	*20*	*251*	*19*	*11*	*3*	*3*	*22*	*11*	*86*	*4*	*5*	*.218/.258/.338*	*58*	*.327*	*1.0*	*3B 3, SS 2*	*0.0*

Comparables: Mat Gamel, Juan Silverio, Ozzie Albies

The Report: By the time De La Cruz made his stateside debut in the Arizona Complex League at the end of June, we'd already been hearing for months about his spring backfield exploits; he was one of the top whispered names amongst desert-faring scouts. The switch-hitter disposed of that level in less than three weeks, then posted elite exit velocities at the Low-A level for the rest of the season. He has a whippy swing from both sides of the plate and is already flashing plus game power with the chance for plus-plus. He's big and fast at present, and the Reds already started playing him at third base quite often after his full-season promotion.

The downside here is that De La Cruz's pitch recognition and plate approach are fairly brutal, which manifested in his Low-A statline, if not quite in the topline numbers. De La Cruz struck out more than 30 percent of the time and barely reached a five-percent walk rate. That's not going to be sustainable as he moves up. He seemed to struggle on both breaking-ball recognition and swing decisions. We've seen many hitters over the years with a great-looking swing but poor approach crush the ball against lower-level competition and then get eaten alive at the upper levels. That's a concern here, too.

OFP: 60 / First-division infielder

Variance: Extreme. De La Cruz is the position player on our Top 101 Prospects list least likely to ever make the majors, and also one of the most likely to be a star.

Mark Barry's Fantasy Take: I totally understand the merit of speculating on guys like De La Cruz. He offers insane power and great speed on the dirt, sure. But he struck out a lot, and I'm not sure his approach is good enough to offset all of the whiffs. He's definitely a boom-or-bust type, but I'm a little more risk averse when it comes to this profile.

4 Matt McLain IF   OFP: 55   ETA: 2023

Born: 08/06/99 Age: 22 Bats: R Throws: R Height: 5'11" Weight: 180 lb. Origin: Round 1, 2021 Draft (#17 overall)

YEAR	TEAM	LVL	AGE	PA	R	2B	3B	HR	RBI	BB	K	SB	CS	AVG/OBP/SLG	DRC+	BABIP	BRR	FRAA	WARP
2021	DAY	A+	21	119	15	6	0	3	19	17	24	10	2	.273/.387/.424	111	.329	0.4	SS(27) 1.3	0.7
2022 non-DC	*CIN*	*MLB*	*22*	*251*	*21*	*10*	*0*	*3*	*21*	*22*	*61*	*11*	*4*	*.213/.291/.314*	*66*	*.276*	*0.9*	*SS 2*	*0.2*

Comparables: Dixon Machado, Jean Segura, Tim Anderson

The Report: "Polished college bat" can be a bit of a sneaky pejorative. The draft is for dreamers and upside, and McLain doesn't really have a projectable plus tool in his shed. He did, however, hit the ground running in his pro career, showing no ill effects from a thumb injury that cost him some of his junior season at UCLA. McLain's advanced approach and compact swing make him a tough out at the plate, and, if any tool gets to plus, it might be hit. He's physically mature and unlikely to develop anything more than fringe-average power but should make up for the below-average slugging with plenty of on-base. Defensively, McLain's a "good enough" shortstop, for now, but his future is likely moving around the dirt as needed—he has the arm for the left side and the hands for up the middle—to get his table-setting bat in the lineup.

OFP: 55 / Better-than-the-sum-of-his-parts infield regular

Variance: Medium. The double-edged sword of an "advanced" bat is you can't really wish-cast on development. McLain will have to prove he can hit at every level, and if the bat starts to slide, there isn't much else to carry the profile. At present, though, the profile looks like it could move fast.

Mark Barry's Fantasy Take: Only 10 guys hit 20 homers and stole 20 bases in 2021. McLain might not have that kind of power, at present, but that's the kind of outcome you should be hoping for. Even if he doesn't get to that peak with the pop, he's close enough to the big leagues that his bat and wheels make him a top-75 prospect.

5 Jay Allen II CF

OFP: 55 ETA: 2025

Born: 11/22/02 Age: 19 Bats: R Throws: R Height: 6'3" Weight: 190 lb. Origin: Round 1, 2021 Draft (#30 overall)

YEAR	TEAM	LVL	AGE	PA	R	2B	3B	HR	RBI	BB	K	SB	CS	AVG/OBP/SLG	DRC+	BABIP	BRR	FRAA	WARP
2021	RED	ROK	18	75	20	3	1	3	11	8	12	14	1	.328/.440/.557		.362			

Comparables: Marlin Almonte, Frank Tolentino, Eudy Pina

The Report: A multi-sport athlete in high school who was also a Division I quarterback prospect, Allen is more advanced as a baseball player than that description often suggests. He makes loud contact with an ideal swing plane and already shows off plus-plus bat speed, but the most impressive thing here might be how advanced his approach is, and he whiffs much less than you'd think. You can dream on 30-home-run pop given the projectablity and swing plane—although the exit velocities are just "fine" for his age—and I expect you will see more power year over year as he fills out his lower half and gets a better base at the plate. Allen is only an average runner, but an aggressive one who could add 20 steals along with his power projection. He might slow down a bit more as he matures, so he's not a lock to stick in center. As an amateur, his hit tool was inconsistent, but you can chalk some of that up to his split attention as a high school athlete. Given his approach and a full spring as a full-time baseball player, I'd expect everything to click perhaps even as soon as this year. The profile isn't without risk, of course, but Allen might have the most upside of any bat in the Reds' system, and that includes a low-minors, loud-tools, Top 101 prospect in De La Cruz. We may soon look back at this year's OFP and ranking as a needless hedge. Ah well.

OFP: 55 / Above-average outfielder

Variance: High, and a fair bit of that is positive variance. Allen was a three-star football recruit who has only focused on baseball for the last year or so. If he had been a more traditional prep prospect, perhaps he goes in the top half of the first round and is on the 101. Of course, even then he would carry the usual hit-tool risks of a top prep bat.

Mark Barry's Fantasy Take: My oh my, that 30–20 suggestion above is quite a tease. McLain is going to be the first Cincinnati Red taken in this year's FYPDs, but you could do much worse by waiting and snagging more ceiling with Allen later in drafts. Outside of the top couple of names, I'd argue you should be targeting upside, so there's a case to be made for Allen as the top dynasty option in this system.

6 Austin Hendrick RF

OFP: 50 ETA: Late 2024

Born: 06/15/01 Age: 21 Bats: L Throws: L Height: 6'0" Weight: 195 lb. Origin: Round 1, 2020 Draft (#12 overall)

YEAR	TEAM	LVL	AGE	PA	R	2B	3B	HR	RBI	BB	K	SB	CS	AVG/OBP/SLG	DRC+	BABIP	BRR	FRAA	WARP
2021	DBT	A	20	266	30	16	0	7	29	51	100	4	2	.211/.380/.388	93	.363	0.3	RF(56) 3.0, CF(5) -0.3	0.9
2022 non-DC	*CIN*	*MLB*	*21*	*251*	*21*	*11*	*0*	*3*	*20*	*28*	*105*	*1*	*1*	*.172/.275/.285*	*53*	*.306*	*-0.2*	*RF 2, CF 0*	*-0.7*

Comparables: Rymer Liriano, Sócrates Brito, Josh Reddick

The Report: You expect some fits and starts in the development track of a cold-weather prep outfielder, even one a little old for his class, as Hendrick was. There really isn't a neat-and-tidy equivalent on the position-player side to an "arm-strength prospect," but Hendrick might be close. He's a "bat-speed prospect." Given his combination of plus-plus whip and plenty of loft, you'd expected him to slug north of .400, at least, especially playing his home games in one of the friendlier hitter's parks in the former Florida State League. Hendrick hit for more power as the season wore on—he dealt with a groin strain midseason—but there are real questions about his approach and how he will handle spin. The bat is going to have to carry the day, as he's a right fielder now and for the foreseeable future, and he can't get by merely hunting fastballs forever. There's still a tremendous amount of upside in his bat if something clicks, but the track record of hitting prospects that posted low-.200s batting averages with near-40 percent K-rates in A-ball is not encouraging.

OFP: 50 / Starting outfielder

Variance: High. You could even go extreme here, although I don't love doing that with hitters in full-season leagues without real injury concerns. But given the hit-tool variance here, Hendrick is more likely to be a 3 or a 6 than anything in between.

Mark Barry's Fantasy Take: You could argue that a pair of injured-list stints hampered Hendrick's inaugural season as a pro. You could also argue that his own performance was the main culprit, as the former-first rounder struck out, like, all the time. J.P. Breen's analysis from last season still holds: when cold-weather bats pop, they tend to pop quickly. Hendrick did work a ton of walks in his debut, so he has some idea at the plate. Still, I like him *a lot* less right now than I did at this time last year, and I think he's droppable in leagues with fewer than 200 prospects.

7 Tyler Callihan 2B   OFP: 50   ETA: 2024/2025

Born: 06/22/00   Age: 22   Bats: L   Throws: R   Height: 6'1"   Weight: 205 lb.   Origin: Round 3, 2019 Draft (#85 overall)

YEAR	TEAM	LVL	AGE	PA	R	2B	3B	HR	RBI	BB	K	SB	CS	AVG/OBP/SLG	DRC+	BABIP	BRR	FRAA	WARP
2019	GRN	ROA	19	217	27	10	5	5	26	9	46	9	3	.250/.286/.422		.297			
2019	BIL	ROA	19	21	3	0	1	1	7	1	4	2	0	.400/.429/.650		.467			
2021	DBT	A	21	99	14	6	0	2	10	8	13	5	1	.299/.351/.437	113	.324	-0.1	2B(23) 2.9	0.7
2022 non-DC	*CIN*	*MLB*	*22*	*251*	*21*	*10*	*1*	*3*	*22*	*16*	*56*	*10*	*3*	*.240/.294/.337*	*70*	*.305*	*0.8*	*2B 2*	*0.3*

Comparables: Kyle Seager, Jimmy Paredes, Everth Cabrera

The Report: The Reds had a fun group of prospect bats at Daytona this year, but all dealt with injuries that limited their time on the field. Callihan's might have been the most unfortunate, as it looked like he was in the process of taking a real step forward before an elbow injury—eventually necessitating Tommy John surgery—ended his season in June. TJ recovery for a position player is a little less complicated than for a pitcher, and Callihan was already playing second base exclusively before the injury, so arm strength isn't a foremost concern. The lost time does mean we will have to wait a bit longer to see if his hit tool has taken a real step forward, but there's plus potential here. The profile is a little bit limited by the lack of anything above an average power projection—although he hits the ball hard, it's not a swing geared to lift—but Callihan could end up an everyday player if the bat continues to play to what we saw in his 2021 cameo.

OFP: 50 / Average second baseman

Variance: High. The injury isn't a long-term concern beyond the lost reps, but given that he's a somewhat stout second baseman without above-average power, there will be continued pressure to keep hitting.

Mark Barry's Fantasy Take: Callihan is probably a little too far away to get excited about in most dynasty formats. If he comes back from surgery and mashes (perhaps with a little more lift), then go out and add him. But for now, he's a watchlist guy, if that.

8 Christian Roa RHP   OFP: 50   ETA: Late 2023

Born: 04/02/99   Age: 23   Bats: R   Throws: R   Height: 6'4"   Weight: 220 lb.   Origin: Round 2, 2020 Draft (#48 overall)

YEAR	TEAM	LVL	AGE	W	L	SV	G	GS	IP	H	HR	BB/9	K/9	K	GB%	BABIP	WHIP	ERA	DRA-	WARP
2021	RED	ROK	22	1	0	0	2	1	6^{1}	1	0	2.8	12.8	9	46.2%	.077	0.47	0.00		
2021	DBT	A	22	1	1	0	5	5	17^{2}	18	2	4.6	10.7	21	47.9%	.348	1.53	3.57	97	0.2
2021	DAY	A+	22	2	2	0	8	7	34^{2}	32	4	3.9	9.6	37	37.2%	.311	1.36	4.15	103	0.3
2022 non-DC	*CIN*	*MLB*	*23*	*2*	*3*	*0*	*57*	*0*	*50*	*54*	*8*	*5.1*	*7.7*	*42*	*37.9%*	*.311*	*1.67*	*6.16*	*136*	*-0.8*

Comparables: Nick Martínez, Daniel Mengden, Erik Johnson

The Report: Concerns regarding Roa's control dating back to college have held up as he walked nearly four per nine last year. Despite this, his stuff proved effective. The raw pitches are all likely average or better, and it's a deep repertoire including a four-seam fastball he runs up to 96, a mid-80s 10–4 slider, an upper-80s cutter with late movement and a split-changeup. The fastball has inconsistent shape and command and isn't a bat-misser despite the above-average velocity. There are consistency issues with command of the secondaries, as well, but the breaking pitches have tight break, good movement and have caused some very ugly swings. Roa has an ideal pitcher's build at 6-foot-4 and 220 pounds and could find his way into the Reds' rotation in a few years, pending substantial improvement to his command.

OFP: 50 / No. 4 starter

Variance: Medium. The stuff is good enough to get through Double-A, but the command might undo him (or move him to the pen) after that.

Mark Barry's Fantasy Take: The caveat is almost always the same: if the command comes, maybe there's starter potential. If not, well, you know. I'm not sure Roa is a buzzy-enough name to require a speculative add before finding out whether or not he can start.

9 Rece Hinds 3B OFP: 50 ETA: Late 2024 or 2025

Born: 09/05/00 Age: 21 Bats: R Throws: R Height: 6'4" Weight: 215 lb. Origin: Round 2, 2019 Draft (#49 overall)

YEAR	TEAM	LVL	AGE	PA	R	2B	3B	HR	RBI	BB	K	SB	CS	AVG/OBP/SLG	DRC+	BABIP	BRR	FRAA	WARP
2019	GRN	ROA	18	10	1	0	0	0	1	2	3	0	0	.000/.200/.000					
2021	RED	ROK	20	41	6	3	2	2	5	4	13	1	1	.294/.390/.676		.400			
2021	DBT	A	20	185	33	10	2	10	27	13	52	6	2	.251/.319/.515	105	.302	0.6	3B(33) -0.7	0.6
2022 non-DC	*CIN*	*MLB*	*21*	*251*	*23*	*10*	*1*	*6*	*26*	*14*	*84*	*5*	*2*	*.218/.272/.362*	*69*	*.312*	*0.4*	*3B 1*	*-0.2*

Comparables: Starling Marte, Jorge Soler, Brandon Drury

The Report: The last of the Daytona trio who missed a chunk of time, along with Hendrick and Callihan, Hinds' injury was a meniscus tear, although he was back on the field in Florida for the last month of the season. He certainly hits for more power than Callihan and has a stroke geared for it: leveraged and uppercutty. Swing-and-miss is always going to be a concern with that swing plane, although Hinds' strikeout rates were more below-average than bad (albeit in A-ball). A three-true-outcomes third baseman is unusual but useful, but Hinds is more likely to end up in an outfield corner or perhaps even first base, meaning the whiffs need to stay in check, and the power needs to keep playing.

OFP: 50 / Average corner masher

Variance: High. The familiar melange of hit-tool and positional risk.

Mark Barry's Fantasy Take: It has been 2.5 true outcomes for Hinds so far, but he hasn't stayed healthy enough to hone his approach and (hopefully) scale back on the strikeouts. You can keep an eye on him if you must, but I don't know that the profile is terribly exciting at present.

10 Lyon Richardson RHP OFP: 50 ETA: Late 2024 or 2025

Born: 01/18/00 Age: 22 Bats: S Throws: R Height: 6'2" Weight: 192 lb. Origin: Round 2, 2018 Draft (#47 overall)

YEAR	TEAM	LVL	AGE	W	L	SV	G	GS	IP	H	HR	BB/9	K/9	K	GB%	BABIP	WHIP	ERA	DRA-	WARP
2019	DAY	A	19	3	9	0	26	26	112^{2}	126	10	2.6	8.5	106	39.9%	.341	1.41	4.15	106	0.5
2021	DAY	A+	21	2	5	0	19	18	76	74	9	4.5	10.8	91	51.4%	.325	1.47	5.09	100	0.8
2022 non-DC	*CIN*	*MLB*	*22*	*2*	*3*	*0*	*57*	*0*	*50*	*52*	*7*	*4.7*	*7.7*	*42*	*43.6%*	*.305*	*1.58*	*5.50*	*124*	*-0.5*

Comparables: Anthony Banda, Yordano Ventura, Albert Abreu

The Report: Richardson's stat line is a bit drab, as he was a little too wild and a little too hittable given that he has a fastball he can run up to 96 and an advanced changeup. He works primarily off an average two-seamer with arm-side run but needs to develop a breaking ball (he might have a better arm slot for a slider than the inconsistent curve he throws at present). The mechanics are uptempo and a bit relievery, but despite his struggles in 2021, Richardson still has a chance to be an average starter given more developmental time—he only really started focusing on pitching in his draft year—and a better breaking ball.

OFP: 50 / No. 4 starter or set-up arm

Variance: High. Richardson needs a third pitch and better command, but, given the present strength of the changeup, he also has the potential to jump past this if he gets them.

Mark Barry's Fantasy Take: Wild and hittable sounds like a recipe for, let's say, a lack of managerial faith. Maybe he could be more with time and the development of that fabled third pitch, but you won't need to pay attention until that happens.

The Prospects You Meet Outside the Top Ten:

#11

Graham Ashcraft RHP Born: 02/11/98 Age: 24 Bats: L Throws: R Height: 6'2" Weight: 240 lb. Origin: Round 6, 2019 Draft (#174 overall)

YEAR	TEAM	LVL	AGE	W	L	SV	G	GS	IP	H	HR	BB/9	K/9	K	GB%	BABIP	WHIP	ERA	DRA-	WARP
2019	GRN	ROA	21	2	4	0	13	13	53^{2}	51	2	3.5	10.1	60	55.9%	.329	1.34	4.53		
2021	DAY	A+	23	4	1	0	8	8	38^{2}	28	0	3.0	12.8	55	54.5%	.322	1.06	2.33	63	1.2
2021	CHA	AA	23	7	3	0	14	14	72^{1}	58	4	3.0	9.2	74	59.6%	.287	1.13	3.36	87	1.2
2022 non-DC	*CIN*	*MLB*	*24*	*2*	*2*	*0*	*57*	*0*	*50*	*49*	*5*	*3.9*	*8.4*	*46*	*42.8%*	*.309*	*1.43*	*4.37*	*103*	*0.1*

Comparables: David Phelps, Rogelio Armenteros, Anthony Reyes

Pitching out of the stretch, Ashcraft comes quickly and aggressively towards the plate. He's a fastball-reliant righty who teters on the edge of starter or reliever, where he falls hinging on the development of his changeup as a third pitch. The fastball is a scorcher, upper 90s with life, and it hits the glove with relative ease. The problem is that is his only pitch that fits the latter description. Ashcraft throws a heavy diet of heaters (clearly his best pitch), which helped push his walk rate way down from 2019. You can't really blame him, the fastball is an advanced pitch and appears effortless for the stocky righty, but the slider is potentially above-average, and the changeup could get to a 45. The Reds were using him as a starter in Chattanooga in 2021, but this appears to be a two-pitch-reliever profile through and through, especially given his bullpenish mechanics. That fastball might make him a really good reliever though.

Prospects on the Rise

Bryce Bonnin RHP Born: 10/11/98 Age: 23 Bats: R Throws: R Height: 6'2" Weight: 190 lb. Origin: Round 3, 2020 Draft (#84 overall)

YEAR	TEAM	LVL	AGE	W	L	SV	G	GS	IP	H	HR	BB/9	K/9	K	GB%	BABIP	WHIP	ERA	DRA-	WARP
2021	DBT	A	22	4	0	0	7	7	32	18	0	2.3	12.4	44	43.3%	.269	0.81	1.41	84	0.6
2021	DAY	A+	22	0	2	0	3	3	11	7	4	6.5	16.4	20	50.0%	.188	1.36	7.36	74	0.3
2022 non-DC	*CIN*	*MLB*	*23*	*2*	*3*	*0*	*57*	*0*	*50*	*48*	*7*	*4.8*	*10.6*	*58*	*44.6%*	*.316*	*1.50*	*5.48*	*122*	*-0.4*

Comparables: Tyler Thornburg, Trevor Bell, Kris Wilson

From the windup, it's a Cueto-esque delivery as Bonnin turns his torso almost fully past the third base bag towards shortstop. His arm slot is high three-quarters, and he doesn't repeat it as well as you might hope, but that is something that can be ironed out as Bonnin rises through the ranks. His arsenal features a plus fastball that sits mid-90s and touches 98 with life and some cutting action. His mid-80s slider has sharp, tight break which plays really well against righties thanks to his almost crossfire delivery. He also features an average-ish changeup, which could be scrapped if he moves into a reliever role. The 23-year-old had an incredible 2021 season between Low- and High-A, but it seems that his mechanics need some tweaking before the Reds are ready to push him to that next step. They might continue trying to make him a starter, but to the eye, he appears far more comfortable out of the stretch and much more intimidating in short bursts, despite what his dazzling numbers might say. Bonnin could be a really fun multi-inning stopper.

Ivan Johnson MI Born: 10/11/98 Age: 23 Bats: S Throws: R Height: 6'0" Weight: 190 lb. Origin: Round 4, 2019 Draft (#114 overall)

YEAR	TEAM	LVL	AGE	PA	R	2B	3B	HR	RBI	BB	K	SB	CS	AVG/OBP/SLG	DRC+	BABIP	BRR	FRAA	WARP
2019	GRN	ROA	20	210	27	10	1	6	22	18	46	11	4	.255/.327/.415		.309			
2021	SUR	WIN	22	70	12	4	0	6	11	8	30	1	1	.250/.343/.617		.360			
2021	DBT	A	22	216	27	14	2	6	23	27	61	8	5	.263/.366/.457	106	.361	-0.8	SS(50) 5.8	1.3
2021	DAY	A+	22	114	17	5	0	4	18	14	39	3	2	.265/.368/.439	90	.400	0.0	2B(14) 0.6, SS(9) 0.3	0.3
2022 non-DC	*CIN*	*MLB*	*23*	*251*	*22*	*11*	*1*	*4*	*23*	*21*	*89*	*6*	*4*	*.208/.284/.328*	*64*	*.320*	*0.6*	*SS 2, 2B 0*	*0.0*

Comparables: Emmanuel Burriss, Micah Johnson, Brandon Lowe

The report here is fairly simple: Johnson has a balanced swing with quick wrists and a disciplined approach. The 2019 Reds' fourth-round selection, he tends to pull his head off of the ball, which suggests the swing could use some fine tuning. Perhaps the biggest negative here is that good breaking pitches will give him fits from time to time, though he takes them as often as he chases. Johnson has posted minimal splits as a switch-hitter, but his swing is more max effort as a righty. Defensively, Johnson projects as an average second baseman who could fill in it at short if needed. Nothing really pops out on the basepaths, but he certainly possesses good base-running instincts and turns corners well. This seems like a true, rock-solid 45 and the type of player who could play 130 games as a starter on a non-playoff team.

Jose Torres SS Born: 09/28/99 Age: 22 Bats: R Throws: R Height: 6'0" Weight: 171 lb. Origin: Round 3, 2021 Draft (#89 overall)

YEAR	TEAM	LVL	AGE	PA	R	2B	3B	HR	RBI	BB	K	SB	CS	AVG/OBP/SLG	DRC+	BABIP	BRR	FRAA	WARP
2021	DBT	A	21	107	15	4	3	4	17	8	17	6	2	.337/.383/.568	119	.364	-1.1	SS(18) 0.8	0.5
2022 non-DC	*CIN*	*MLB*	*22*	*251*	*22*	*10*	*2*	*4*	*24*	*15*	*59*	*8*	*3*	*.244/.295/.362*	*76*	*.311*	*0.8*	*SS -1*	*0.1*

Most third-round college shortstops aren't long-term shortstops, but Torres has smooth enough actions to stick there while also being able to slide over to second or third, as needed. Torres hit better as a pro than he did at NC State, and while he has very advanced barrel control, his swing can get long, and there's not a ton of bat speed, he just beats pitchers to their spots. I don't know if that keeps working up the ladder, and the contact profile is fairly pedestrian, but given his (albeit limited) pro success and ability to stick up the middle, he's worth a follow in a shallow system.

Factors on the Farm

Lorenzo Cedrola OF Born: 01/12/98 Age: 24 Bats: R Throws: R Height: 5'8" Weight: 152 lb. Origin: International Free Agent, 2015

YEAR	TEAM	LVL	AGE	PA	R	2B	3B	HR	RBI	BB	K	SB	CS	AVG/OBP/SLG	DRC+	BABIP	BRR	FRAA	WARP
2019	DBT	A+	21	381	41	10	7	1	28	17	43	18	10	.277/.330/.356	111	.310	-0.8	CF(42) -4.8, LF(32) 4.1, RF(24) -1.6	1.3
2020	LAG	WIN	22	76	13	3	0	0	8	4	13	4	0	.314/.355/.357		.379			
2021	LAG	WIN	23	130	15	7	1	0	7	8	13	5	2	.250/.300/.325		.278			
2021	CHA	AA	23	437	68	16	7	9	61	17	50	8	8	.320/.356/.461	126	.345	3.7	CF(51) 4.3, RF(50) 6.6, LF(7) -0.2	4.0
2021	LOU	AAA	23	39	5	3	0	1	1	2	2	2	0	.257/.333/.429	111	.250	0.4	CF(9) 1.9	0.4
2022 non-DC	*CIN*	*MLB*	*24*	*251*	*21*	*9*	*2*	*2*	*22*	*10*	*37*	*7*	*5*	*.265/.308/.364*	*84*	*.305*	*0.8*	*CF 1, RF 1*	*0.8*

Three descriptors come to mind on first glance at Cedrola: small, skinny and fast. However, there might be more to the puzzle than what you see with a quick look. The former Top-10 Red Sox prospect possesses a barely closed stance with a noticeable leg kick and a quick, contact-oriented bat. The hands move very quickly as his load moves from his backside to get to point of contact. Cedrola's swing entails a lot of effort, and the ball rarely goes very far, but when the he barrels a pitch, he has surprising gap power and potential home-run power. Defensively, Cedrola can stick as a major-league center fielder. He is a high-end plus runner, and while his first step could use a bit of work, he has the makings to be an average defensive center fielder or slightly above-average corner outfielder in the bigs. Did we just become the biggest Lorenzo Cedrola fans in the world?

Dauri Moreta RHP Born: 04/15/96 Age: 26 Bats: R Throws: R Height: 6'2" Weight: 185 lb. Origin: International Free Agent, 2015

YEAR	TEAM	LVL	AGE	W	L	SV	G	GS	IP	H	HR	BB/9	K/9	K	GB%	BABIP	WHIP	ERA	DRA-	WARP
2019	DBT	A+	23	1	0	2	35	0	57^{1}	46	6	1.4	10.0	64	33.1%	.288	0.96	2.35	79	1.3
2021	CHA	AA	25	4	0	0	18	0	26^{2}	17	3	1.7	12.5	37	39.7%	.255	0.82	1.35	86	0.5
2021	LOU	AAA	25	2	0	8	24	0	26^{1}	14	2	1.4	7.2	21	36.5%	.169	0.68	0.68	93	0.5
2021	CIN	MLB	25	0	0	0	4	0	3^{2}	2	1	2.5	9.8	4	22.2%	.125	0.82	2.45	106	0.0
2022 DC	*CIN*	*MLB*	*26*	*2*	*3*	*0*	*59*	*0*	*51.7*	*51*	*9*	*2.8*	*7.7*	*44*	*56.1%*	*.289*	*1.29*	*4.52*	*105*	*0.1*

"Ninety-five and a slider" can also be a bit of a backhanded description for a prospect. Nowadays, those are the table stakes for a right-handed relief pitcher, but there are also a fair amount of good relievers that fit that description. Moreta might well be one of them. An overaged international free agent who struggled with his control throughout most of his minor-league career, Moreta now fills the zone with a lively fastball that sits mid-90s and a mid-80s slider that drops off the deck with 11–6 action. He locates the fastball arm-side and up, and the slider glove-side and down. It's a pretty simple and very modern formula, but one that will miss major-league bats. He doesn't have the longest track record of this kind of command, but if Moreta maintains it, the stuff will play in the late innings.

Reiver Sanmartin LHP Born: 04/15/96 Age: 26 Bats: L Throws: L Height: 6'2" Weight: 160 lb. Origin: International Free Agent, 2015

YEAR	TEAM	LVL	AGE	W	L	SV	G	GS	IP	H	HR	BB/9	K/9	K	GB%	BABIP	WHIP	ERA	DRA-	WARP
2019	DBT	A+	23	2	5	0	13	13	64^1	68	5	2.0	8.4	60	56.3%	.325	1.27	3.78	110	0.4
2019	CHA	AA	23	2	7	0	12	12	58	61	6	2.6	8.4	54	42.6%	.313	1.34	4.34	96	0.5
2021	EST	WIN	25	0	2	0	7	7	31	16	0	3.2	5.5	19	55.2%	.186	0.87	1.45		
2021	CHA	AA	25	2	0	0	4	3	18	8	0	2.5	11.5	23	62.2%	.216	0.72	0.50	90	0.3
2021	LOU	AAA	25	8	2	0	21	14	82^1	80	6	2.5	9.7	89	54.1%	.335	1.25	3.94	93	1.4
2021	CIN	MLB	25	2	0	0	2	2	11^2	12	0	1.5	8.5	11	47.1%	.353	1.20	1.54	80	0.2
2022 DC	*CIN*	*MLB*	*26*	*11*	*9*	*0*	*71*	*19*	*132.7*	*136*	*15*	*2.7*	*8.4*	*123*	*38.3%*	*.317*	*1.33*	*4.15*	*97*	*1.2*

Comparables: Framber Valdez, Rafael Montero, Taylor Clarke

Sanmartin already got his first crack at the highest level, and, boy, was he effective. It's a low southpaw slot, with ground-ball inducing stuff (especially when that changeup is working). His release point is consistent and difficult to pick up as his arm angle keeps the ball hidden well. His fastball is his third pitch and sits around 90, but Sanmartin possesses above-average command and two above-average secondaries in his changeup and slider, with the latter playing way up to lefties. We would not be surprised in the slightest if Sanmartin succeeds against major-league lefties for years to come.

Top Talents 25 and Under (as of 4/1/2022):

1. Jonathan India, 2B
2. Hunter Greene, RHP
3. Nick Lodolo, LHP
4. Tyler Stephenson, C
5. Elly De La Cruz, SS/3B
6. Matt McLain, SS
7. Jose Barrero, SS
8. Jay Allen II, OF
9. Tony Santillan, RHP
10. Austin Hendrick, OF

After a playoff appearance in the expanded format of 2020, Cincinnati started slow and faded late in 2021, finishing third behind Milwaukee and St. Louis but with a second straight winning record. The organization has put out confusing, occasionally mixed messages at times, but, coming into this winter, they've been operating like a club with serious budgetary restrictions perhaps looking at a retool in lieu of a heavy rebuild. They're fortunate to have a few impressive pieces at the top of the tally. In a world in which the Reds were imbued with a more competitive ownership spirit, this might be a club building on the emergence of its Rookie of the Year, instead of seeking to deal off core pieces.

India's excellent debut campaign began on Opening Day and grew stronger as the season progressed. It was easy to envision him becoming an above-average regular on the dirt over time, but his immediate arrival as one was the result of solid returns on a total position shift—from his traditional third base to playing second exclusively in Year One in the majors—as well as the emergence of long-hinted but oft-fleeting power. The power threshold for the keystone is typically lower, and while India didn't hit half as many big flies Marcus Semien did, it's more than fair to call India's initial showing a rousing success. Given the uncertainty across the bag from him at shortstop, as well as Eugenio Suárez's possible decline, it's possible India could earn more time back at the hot corner, but, wherever he plays, Cincinnati has the makings of a set-him-and-forget-him building block in Jonathan India.

The first full run of big-league time for Stephenson wasn't quite as blistering, but it was plenty encouraging, enough so that the Reds dealt away longtime backstop Tucker Barnhart to seemingly cede the job to the big Georgian. More than four years have passed since injuries last took more than a handful of days away from the former 11th-overall pick, and he's already hitting well enough to make his way into the lineup most days of the week, be it behind the dish, spelling Joey Votto at first, or perhaps in the NL's anticipated designated-hitter role. Despite his size, Stephenson offers a more balanced offensive approach than many current backstops with their all-or-nothing power. Putting the ball in play is a solid recipe for success for a hitter who plays half his games at Great American Ballpark, whether Stephenson ever adapts to utilize more of his raw power or not.

Despite handling Double-A Chattanooga and Triple-A Louisville with relative ease, Barrero's festival of free-swinging faced stiffer competition in the bigs. The Cuban who formerly went by the name of Jose Garcia is still a possible solution to Cincy's shortstop conundrum, but the club is already working him in at several spots around the diamond, even though he typically has handled shortstop well. Barrero has a solid frame, but his struggles with contact at the dish were always going to be a question mark. Whether he can adapt or not will determine if he is a utility piece long-term or an everyday shortstop with attainable game pop.

The bullpen may remain home for Santillan, who worked an 85 DRA– in his first 43 ⅓ innings in the majors, pumping mid-90s fastballs and double servings of sliders to great effect. Santillan may get an extended audition in the rotation to try to shape his command into something more manageable. However, depending on how much of the current rotation Cincinnati deals away, it's likely he has shown enough out of the pen to handle increased-leverage roles if the Redlegs decide not to mess with a good thing.

Cleveland Guardians

The State of the System:

Cleveland can only play one shortstop per game, which might pose an issue for a system this deep in middle infielders. It's deep generally, too.

The Top Ten:

1 George Valera OF OFP: 60 ETA: 2023

Born: 11/13/00 Age: 21 Bats: L Throws: L Height: 5'11" Weight: 185 lb. Origin: International Free Agent, 2017

YEAR	TEAM	LVL	AGE	PA	R	2B	3B	HR	RBI	BB	K	SB	CS	AVG/OBP/SLG	DRC+	BABIP	BRR	FRAA	WARP
2019	MV	SS	18	188	22	7	1	8	29	29	52	6	2	.236/.356/.446		.296			
2019	LC	A	18	26	1	0	1	0	3	2	9	0	2	.087/.192/.174	76	.143	-1.1	RF(3) 1.2, LF(2) 1.6	0.2
2021	LC	A+	20	263	45	2	4	16	43	55	58	10	5	.256/.430/.548	157	.276	0.4	RF(38) 3.1, CF(12) -0.8, LF(9) -0.5	2.8
2021	AKR	AA	20	100	6	3	0	3	22	11	30	1	0	.267/.340/.407	93	.357	-0.4	RF(10) 3.5, LF(8) 0.6, CF(4) -0.4	0.6
2022 non-DC	*CLE*	*MLB*	*21*	*251*	*25*	*8*	*1*	*6*	*25*	*29*	*71*	*4*	*3*	*.211/.315/.354*	*83*	*.283*	*0.5*	*RF 1, CF 0*	*0.5*

Comparables: Victor Robles, Manuel Margot, Eloy Jiménez

The Report: Who doesn't love to gush about a pretty left-handed swing? Grizzled scout or newly minted fan, you can watch a Ken Griffey Jr. highlight package and get it, right? It's like a classic Fred Astaire and Ginger Rogers number, iconic and accessible.

In his first prospect-list entry at Baseball Prospectus, we gushed about Valera's pretty left-handed swing, but we're weirdos, and this is not a sweeping, MGM-musical set piece. It is, instead, a one-off scribble on Merce Cunningham's notepad, deemed unsuitable for even his stage.

Writing about Valera often leads us to flights of weird metaphor, in part because he never really got a sustained chance to show what he could do on the field before 2021. All we had was that swing. His 2018 was truncated by a hamate injury. In 2019, he only played in short-season. The 2020 season was lost to a pandemic.

Okay, the swing—yeah it's weird. Valera starts narrow and very open, with some rhythmic twitchiness. He uses a little leg kick to close it, and sometimes it hangs there for a little bit; it's an irregular tempo but always down on time. Then the bat explodes through the zone. There's minimal load and loud contact. Sometimes he will take what looks like an emergency hack and hit a laser beam over the left fielder's head. Valera shows good plate discipline and doesn't expand, but, given how hard he swings, there will always be some swing-and-miss. Everything here is a little three true outcome–ish, but we doubt you will think of him that way. He's an above-average runner, at present, but will likely slow down enough that center field won't be an ideal defensive home. He should be a fine left fielder. You won't think about his defense too much, either. You will just watch the swing.

OFP: 60 / First-division outfielder and modern-dance muse

Variance: Medium. This is the boring part where we tell you that there's hit-tool and positional risk in the profile.

Mark Barry's Fantasy Take: After a couple of seasons in which Valera's fantasy prospects were mostly just hypothetical, he finally started flashing the skills that had our boss dancing around the office professing his love. The average hasn't gotten all the way there, as he suffered from the strikeouts at Double-A, but he worked walks more than 18 percent of the time and hit for plenty of power. He's a top-25 dynasty prospect and a monster in the making. And if your league rewards extra swag, may I present to you some bat flips?

Eyewitness Report: George Valera

Evaluator: Nathan Graham
Report Date: 09/22/2021
Dates Seen: Multiple July 2021
Risk Factor: High
Physical/Health: Large frame with an athletic build, plenty of room for additional good weight to be added.

Tool	Future Grade	Report
Hit	50	Open stance, minimal load with a mild leg kick for timing. Confident hitter, plus bat speed, with natural loft in the swing which can cause some swing and miss in the zone. Recognizes spin well, rarely expands the zone to chase, has the ability to make loud contact to all fields.
Power	60	Easy plus raw power generated by bat speed and strength, natural loft to the swing with the ability to take it out to all fields, crushes mistakes.
Baserunning/ Speed	50	Current above-average raw foot speed, will play average with maturity, aggressive base runner.
Glove	50	Can handle center field well enough for now but lacks the range to stick there long term, will end up at a corner with physical maturity; currently raw, doesn't get a good first step and will take poor routes, athleticism will allow the glove to play average with additional experience.
Arm	50	Throws show good carry, strong enough to play average in RF and above average elsewhere in the outfield.

Conclusion: The pandemic and a broken hamate bone limited Valera to less than 200 professional at-bats prior to 2021 but he's now healthy and showing off the loud tools that make him the top young hitter in the organization. The power is plus but he's more than just a slugger. His command of the strike zone and ability to consistently square up pitches will make him a future impact bat.

2 Daniel Espino RHP OFP: 60 ETA: Late 2023/Early 2024

Born: 01/05/01 Age: 21 Bats: R Throws: R Height: 6'2" Weight: 205 lb. Origin: Round 1, 2019 Draft (#24 overall)

YEAR	TEAM	LVL	AGE	W	L	SV	G	GS	IP	H	HR	BB/9	K/9	K	GB%	BABIP	WHIP	ERA	DRA-	WARP
2019	INDR	ROK	18	0	1	0	6	6	13^2	7	1	3.3	10.5	16	48.4%	.207	0.88	1.98		
2019	MV	SS	18	0	2	0	3	3	10	9	1	4.5	16.2	18	31.8%	.381	1.40	6.30		
2021	LYN	A	20	1	2	0	10	10	42^2	34	2	4.9	13.5	64	48.4%	.352	1.34	3.38	68	1.2
2021	LC	A+	20	2	6	0	10	10	49	30	7	2.9	16.2	88	31.1%	.280	0.94	4.04	58	1.6
2022 non-DC	*CLE*	*MLB*	*21*	*2*	*2*	*0*	*57*	*0*	*50*	*43*	*7*	*4.9*	*11.1*	*61*	*37.3%*	*.294*	*1.41*	*4.42*	*105*	*0.0*

Comparables: Sandy Alcantara, Zach McAllister, Jeurys Familia

The Report: It doesn't always work out, but oftentimes we use the last couple of spots on the 101 to flag a prospect we think is poised for a breakout. Well, it worked out with Espino, who we ranked 100th last year and has since raised his stock to be among the top pitching prospects in the game. He came out in 2021 pumping mid- to upper-90s heat along with a bat-missing power slider, and his new, shorter arm action and repeatable, athletic delivery will give him every chance to start. We can still quibble about the command—he was a little more hittable in A-ball than you'd expect given the big-time stuff—or the lack of an obvious third pitch, although both the curve and change will flash. Espino has time to figure that out, and, even if he doesn't, it's a lot easier to be a two-pitch starter nowadays. He also has plenty of stuff for the late innings if he does end up in relief.

OFP: 60 / No. 3 starter or late-inning reliever

Variance: Medium. Espino answered every question you might have had of him in 2021, but given that he's a prep arm that hasn't pitched in the high minors yet, there's always more to be asked.

Mark Barry's Fantasy Take: Last year, I called Espino my favorite non-marquee pitching prospect. You're not getting the righty for non-marquee prices anymore. He's a top-10 fantasy pitching prospect, and there's serious ace-level upside if circumstances break right and his body doesn't.

3 Brayan Rocchio SS OFP: 60 ETA: Late 2022/Early 2023

Born: 01/13/01 Age: 21 Bats: S Throws: R Height: 5'10" Weight: 170 lb. Origin: International Free Agent, 2017

YEAR	TEAM	LVL	AGE	PA	R	2B	3B	HR	RBI	BB	K	SB	CS	AVG/OBP/SLG	DRC+	BABIP	BRR	FRAA	WARP
2019	MV	SS	18	295	33	12	3	5	27	20	40	14	8	.250/.310/.373		.276			
2021	LAG	WIN	20	76	11	6	1	2	6	5	5	2	2	.391/.440/.594		.403			
2021	LC	A+	20	288	45	13	1	9	33	20	65	14	6	.265/.337/.428	108	.319	1.0	SS(36) -1.4, 2B(16) 2.2, 3B(12) 0.3	1.3
2021	AKR	AA	20	203	34	13	4	6	30	13	41	7	4	.293/.360/.505	112	.350	-1.1	SS(43) 1.5, 2B(2) 0.2	1.0
2022 non-DC	*CLE*	*MLB*	*21*	*251*	*22*	*11*	*1*	*4*	*23*	*14*	*59*	*9*	*5*	*.236/.292/.355*	*74*	*.299*	*1.0*	*SS 0, 2B 0*	*0.3*

Comparables: Amed Rosario, Addison Russell, Enrique Hernández

The Report: Because of pandemic-related travel restrictions, Rocchio didn't even get alternate-site or instructs reps in 2020, having to make do with virtual training sessions, instead. He then came out in 2021 and started hitting for power that wasn't in the profile the last time we saw him on the field. Some of this is sustainable; Rocchio is up there looking to lift now, and he stays balanced as he lets it rip through the zone with his plus bat speed. It's an aggressive, power-over-hit approach, and there's a balance to be struck there if he's going to have major-league success—he can tend to swing over better breaking stuff, even in Double-A. It's pretty easy power when he lets his hands go, though, and, even if his frame limits the projection to more solid-average pop, he has a good chance to get to all of it. If he gets to all of it while maintaining his plus hit tool from both sides of the plate, he could make a few All-Star Games. That's a big if at this point, though.

Rocchio is a plus shortstop, showing smooth hands and actions with enough arm for the left side. The "problem" is he might be the third-best defender at the position in the organization right now, behind Andrés Giménez and Gabriel Arias. Of course, Rocchio might be plus-plus at second base, so that problem can solve itself pretty easily, if need be.

OFP: 60 / First-division shortstop

Variance: Medium. We don't know if Rocchio can maintain this kind of power without generating more swing-and-miss, at which point he might no longer make enough contact to maintain this kind of power. But he should hit enough or pop enough bombs that he's at least an average regular at one of the middle-infield spots.

Mark Barry's Fantasy Take: I don't entirely know what to make of Rocchio's 2021 emergence. He more than doubled his career home-run output, smacking 15 dingers while snagging 21 bags across two levels. That said, he's still on the smaller side, and I wouldn't really expect the power to show up against advanced-level pitching. He also wasn't very efficient on the bases, getting tossed out almost a third of the time. I understand how a switch-hitting middle infielder that can hit for a little power and flash a little speed can be useful, but I don't think there's a lot of upside.

4 Gabriel Arias SS OFP: 60 ETA: 2022, as needed

Born: 02/27/00 Age: 22 Bats: R Throws: R Height: 6'1" Weight: 217 lb. Origin: International Free Agent, 2016

YEAR	TEAM	LVL	AGE	PA	R	2B	3B	HR	RBI	BB	K	SB	CS	AVG/OBP/SLG	DRC+	BABIP	BRR	FRAA	WARP
2019	LE	A+	19	511	62	21	4	17	75	25	128	8	4	.302/.339/.470	114	.378	1.6	SS(104) -11.6, 3B(10) 1.3, 2B(2) -0.5	1.1
2021	COL	AAA	21	483	64	29	3	13	55	39	110	5	1	.284/.348/.454	101	.351	-1.1	SS(82) 0.3, 3B(19) -1.9, 2B(9) -0.3	1.3
2022 DC	*CLE*	*MLB*	*22*	*30*	*3*	*1*	*0*	*0*	*3*	*1*	*8*	*0*	*0*	*.251/.306/.390*	*84*	*.339*	*0.0*	*SS 0*	*0.0*

Comparables: Wilmer Flores, Willy Adames, Isaac Paredes

The Report: We had strong reports on Arias in 2019, and he continued to play to the scout sheet in the upper minors. The jump straight to Triple-A in 2021 was aggressive, even given his 2020 alternate-site time, but the bat held up just fine. Arias likes to swing, but it's a balanced, power-hitter's stroke that should flip some of those doubles into homers as he moves through his twenties. His approach has improved, as well, and while the offensive projection remains in the .260, 20-home-run range, we are more confident he will get there after his 2021 season. The glove remains the carrying tool here. Arias is sure-handed and rangy—he's a plus runner, although not a particularly active base thief—with plus-plus actions and arm. Cleveland is about to have a bit of a logjam at shortstop, and while Arias could slide over to third without much issue, you want this glove at the 6 every day.

OFP: 60 / First-division shortstop

Variance: Low. I suppose there's still some chance the hit tool slides some against major-league pitching—you never can be sure that prospects will hit those high-test, right-on-right sliders until they do—but the glove and pop should carry Arias to become at least an average shortstop.

Mark Barry's Fantasy Take: I wish Arias had a slightly better approach at the plate. He doesn't strike out a ton, but he does strike out. He walks sometimes, but he's not as patient as you'd like. I worry that he doesn't do anything exceptionally well, offensively, so the fantasy ceiling is lower for Arias than some of the other middle-infielders on this list. The rest of his skills are solid, though, and he should spend plenty of seasons as a safe MI option, if nothing else.

5 Gavin Williams RHP OFP: 55 ETA: 2023

Born: 07/26/99 Age: 22 Bats: L Throws: R Height: 6'6" Weight: 238 lb. Origin: Round 1, 2021 Draft (#23 overall)

The Report: Williams saw his draft stock explode as a fourth-year player last year after he went undrafted in 2020 (he previously went unsigned after Tampa Bay took him in the 30th round in 2017). After he spent three years battling injuries and inconsistency, mostly out of the bullpen, he excelled as East Carolina University's Friday-night starter, pushing his way all the way into the first round.

Williams has a premium fastball. He sat 95–97 in the AAC tournament in May and has touched triple-digits in the past. He also has two distinct, above-average breaking balls, a slider in the mid-80s and a curveball in the high 70s. He threw strikes and was unhittable for large portions of the season. His mechanics look sound, and he's a huge guy.

OFP: 55 / Mid-rotation starter or high-leverage reliever

Variance: High. Williams' track record consists of one outstanding college campaign and a long, pre-2021 injury history. On the flip side, Cleveland is quite good at pitching development.

Mark Barry's Fantasy Take: If you were playing *Family Feud*, and they surveyed 100 people on the top five intriguing traits of a Guardians pitching prospect, rest assured "premium fastball," "throws strikes" and "sound mechanics" would all appear on the list. Still, "injuries," "inconsistency," and "reliever" would all get the dreaded red X, and you'd probably get excommunicated by your family members, so I guess it's not all sunshine and puppy dogs for the righty. I'm intrigued enough by the skill set to have Williams hovering around the top-101 dynasty prospects, but I'm still skeptical enough to not quite go all in.

6 Tyler Freeman IF OFP: 55 ETA: Late 2022

Born: 05/21/99 Age: 23 Bats: R Throws: R Height: 6'0" Weight: 190 lb. Origin: Round 2, 2017 Draft (#71 overall)

YEAR	TEAM	LVL	AGE	PA	R	2B	3B	HR	RBI	BB	K	SB	CS	AVG/OBP/SLG	DRC+	BABIP	BRR	FRAA	WARP
2019	LC	A	20	272	51	16	3	3	24	18	28	11	4	.292/.382/.424	137	.320	2.6	SS(57) 1.7, 2B(3) -0.3	2.5
2019	LYN	A+	20	275	38	16	2	0	20	8	25	8	1	.319/.354/.397	119	.350	0.8	SS(57) 0.3	1.4
2021	AKR	AA	22	180	26	14	2	2	19	8	21	4	2	.323/.372/.470	122	.357	-0.8	SS(26) 0.5, 2B(7) -0.2, 3B(7) 0.9	1.1
2022 DC	*CLE*	*MLB*	*23*	*65*	*7*	*3*	*0*	*0*	*6*	*3*	*8*	*1*	*1*	*.264/.318/.361*	*87*	*.298*	*0.1*	*SS 0, 2B 0*	*0.1*

Comparables: Yairo Muñoz, Yamaico Navarro, Eugenio Suárez

The Report: One of the more consistently internally contentious prospects at BP over the last several years, Freeman has very clear pluses and minuses. To steal our own old format . . .

The Good: Freeman has fantastic bat-to-ball skills, even though his swing is not visually pleasing. He rarely strikes out and bloops the ball all over the field onto green grass. He has hit for consistently high averages at all levels. He is likely to stay somewhere on the dirt up the spectrum from first base.

The Bad: Freeman has no discernible power projection to speak of. He almost never walks, because he puts the ball in play before the pitcher gets to four balls. Thus, nearly all of his contribution is driven by his batting average on balls in play. He just missed most of the 2021 season after re-tearing his left shoulder labrum, and recurring shoulder injuries are a major concern for a prospect whose entire profile is driven by his hit tool. He might be a second baseman instead of a shortstop.

OFP: 55 / Hit-tool-driven starting middle infielder

Variance: Medium. Hit tools are tricky, and players without fallback carrying tools can fail more than you'd think.

Mark Barry's Fantasy Take: How strong is your stomach? Freeman was working on a .470 slugging percentage through 41 games last year before losing the rest of his season to a shoulder injury. Sure, that slugging came with only two homers, but the bat-to-ball skills plus *any* pop would feel very DJ LeMahieu-y, so, pretty useful for fantasy. Now, that's obviously best case scenario, and the injury concerns me, but if you can handle rolling the dice on Freeman (I can), now might be the time to inquire.

7 Nolan Jones 3B/RF OFP: 55 ETA: 2022

Born: 05/07/98 Age: 24 Bats: L Throws: R Height: 6'4" Weight: 195 lb. Origin: Round 2, 2016 Draft (#55 overall)

YEAR	TEAM	LVL	AGE	PA	R	2B	3B	HR	RBI	BB	K	SB	CS	AVG/OBP/SLG	DRC+	BABIP	BRR	FRAA	WARP
2019	MSS	WIN	21	68	8	2	0	4	8	8	31	1	0	.200/.294/.433		.320			
2019	LYN	A+	21	324	48	12	1	7	41	65	85	5	3	.286/.435/.425	134	.399	-1.4	3B(72) -3.3	1.7
2019	AKR	AA	21	211	33	10	2	8	22	31	63	2	0	.253/.370/.466	112	.346	1.1	3B(44) 1.1	1.1
2021	COL	AAA	23	407	60	25	1	13	48	59	122	10	2	.238/.356/.431	99	.327	3.8	3B(67) 2.4, RF(25) 1.0, 1B(1) -0.1	1.8
2022 DC	*CLE*	*MLB*	*24*	*306*	*41*	*14*	*1*	*8*	*34*	*35*	*100*	*0*	*1*	*.220/.319/.376*	*88*	*.319*	*-0.3*	*RF 0, 3B 0*	*0.2*

Comparables: Jeimer Candelario, Brandon Drury, Marwin Gonzalez

The Report: Jones seems like one of the top prospects most hurt by losing the 2020 season. He has long paired good walk rates with high swing-and-miss that limits his plus-plus raw power in games, but, after his 2019 season, we had some signs that things were converging positively. There was a clear backslide during the lost year, and, instead of those rates continuing to tick in a positive direction, his batting average tanked. The raw power still isn't getting above average in games, and the Guardians started playing him in right field as his third-base defense continued to be unreliable. Jones still possesses a patient approach and can hit it a mile when he connects. If he can ever figure out the rest, the building blocks for stardom remain.

OFP: 55 / Starting corner outfielder, three-true-outcomes division

Variance: Medium. He's likely to be a useful walks-and-power contributor, even if he never fully figures it out.

Mark Barry's Fantasy Take: Jones is the kind of prospect that I love to target while rebuilding. His recent struggles have driven him down most lists, but he still has power, he still has a great eye at the plate, and he's spending time at a few different spots defensively, which could lead to a clearer path for playing time. Jones should reach Cleveland this year, and while he won't win any batting titles, you know what you're getting. (Hint: it's one of three outcomes.)

8 Jose Tena SS OFP: 50 ETA: Late 2023/Early 2024

Born: 03/20/01 Age: 21 Bats: L Throws: R Height: 5'10" Weight: 160 lb. Origin: International Free Agent, 2017

YEAR	TEAM	LVL	AGE	PA	R	2B	3B	HR	RBI	BB	K	SB	CS	AVG/OBP/SLG	DRC+	BABIP	BRR	FRAA	WARP
2019	INDB	ROK	18	199	30	7	6	1	18	6	44	6	2	.325/.352/.440		.418			
2021	SCO	WIN	20	75	16	6	1	0	9	10	10	2	1	.387/.467/.516		.444			
2021	LC	A+	20	447	58	25	2	16	58	27	117	10	5	.281/.331/.467	102	.355	1.6	SS(81) -7.3, 3B(13) 0.3, 2B(11) 1.0	1.0
2022 non-DC	*CLE*	*MLB*	*21*	*251*	*21*	*11*	*1*	*4*	*23*	*13*	*75*	*4*	*3*	*.231/.277/.346*	*64*	*.320*	*0.3*	*SS -2, 3B 0*	*-0.4*

Comparables: Jorge Polanco, Richard Ureña, Luis Sardinas

The Report: Cleveland should soon be spoiled for choice in the middle infield, and while Rocchio had the louder breakout, his double-play partner at High-A Lake County wasn't far behind. Tena has a handsy swing but quick wrists and enough bat control to usually make it work. Although he doesn't consistently lift the ball, his above-average bat speed generates fringe-average pop from an undersized frame, although I suspect there may need to be an adjustment period for his free-swinging ways this year in Double-A.

Tena moved around the infield prior to Rocchio's promotion to Akron, then was the everyday shortstop thereafter. He might fit best at second base in the majors, even if he wasn't behind three or four better shortstop gloves in the organization. To be more confident in an everyday-second-base projection, we'll need to see Tena's swing work further up the ladder, but there's a .270, 15-home-run outcome here with pretty good defense at the keystone.

OFP: 50 / Average middle infielder

Variance: High. There's long-term hit-tool risk given Tena's approach—or lack thereof—and he's likely a better fit for second than short, which means he is going to have to hit a little bit.

Mark Barry's Fantasy Take: With a big 2021 and a scorching-hot performance in the Arizona Fall League, Tena has firmly put himself onto the fantasy radar. I think he's a watchlist candidate, for now, and am keeping an especially close watch on his approach as he faces Double-A pitching this season. If he's even a little bit more selective, scoop Tena up ASAP.

9 Jhonkensy Noel 3B OFP: 50 ETA: Late 2023/Early 2024

Born: 07/15/01 Age: 20 Bats: R Throws: R Height: 6'1" Weight: 180 lb. Origin: International Free Agent, 2017

YEAR	TEAM	LVL	AGE	PA	R	2B	3B	HR	RBI	BB	K	SB	CS	AVG/OBP/SLG	DRC+	BABIP	BRR	FRAA	WARP
2019	INDB	ROK	17	209	32	12	0	6	42	18	39	5	1	.287/.349/.455		.317			
2021	LYN	A	19	162	36	10	1	11	40	7	27	2	1	.393/.426/.693	148	.421	0.3	1B(18) 0.8, 3B(13) 1.5	1.6
2021	LC	A+	19	111	13	3	0	8	25	9	31	3	1	.280/.351/.550	124	.328	-1.0	3B(17) 0.5	0.6
2022 non-DC	*CLE*	*MLB*	*20*	*251*	*27*	*10*	*1*	*9*	*31*	*12*	*70*	*2*	*2*	*.259/.303/.431*	*92*	*.331*	*0.1*	*1B 0, 3B 0*	*0.4*

Comparables: Vladimir Guerrero Jr., Ronald Acuña Jr., Anthony Rizzo

The Report: Noel started absolutely crushing the ball last May as a teenager in full-season ball and never looked back, only interrupted for a month by an ankle injury. He pushed his way from relative obscurity all the way to a 40-man-roster assignment.

The calling card here is power. Noel's impressive raw pop quickly converted to game power in 2021. He hit 19 home runs in 64 full-season games, and he has an easy plus-power projection now. He wasn't in obscene offensive environments, and he also hit .340 for the season, so it's not like he's a power-only player; he could use improvements to his breaking-ball recognition, and he's a bit open, so the hit tool projects as more average, overall. Defensively, well, he's just not a third baseman at all. He should be fine at first base, in time. His bat and, more specifically, pop are enough for the position, thankfully.

OFP: 50 / Power-hitting regular first baseman

Variance: Medium. Noel made great strides, but the bar for right/right first basemen is very high.

Mark Barry's Fantasy Take: While the bar is high for a prospect to reach the big leagues as a right/right first baseman only, once you're there, the bar isn't super high to sneak into the top-10 at the position. Noel posted the numbers last season, but the big test will come at Double-A this year. You're going to have to make the move to acquire him now, though, as few prospects announced their presence from relative obscurity better than Noel.

10 Steven Kwan OF OFP: 50 ETA: 2022, as needed

Born: 09/05/97 Age: 24 Bats: L Throws: L Height: 5'9" Weight: 170 lb. Origin: Round 5, 2018 Draft (#163 overall)

YEAR	TEAM	LVL	AGE	PA	R	2B	3B	HR	RBI	BB	K	SB	CS	AVG/OBP/SLG	DRC+	BABIP	BRR	FRAA	WARP
2019	LYN	A+	21	542	68	26	7	3	39	53	51	11	7	.280/.353/.382	118	.305	-2.2	CF(91) 3.7, LF(16) 0.4	3.1
2021	AKR	AA	23	221	42	12	3	7	31	22	23	4	2	.337/.411/.539	135	.354	1.8	CF(24) -1.8, LF(12) 1.7, RF(11) 0.5	1.9
2021	COL	AAA	23	120	23	3	1	5	13	14	8	2	0	.311/.398/.505	137	.300	1.6	CF(21) 2.6, LF(3) -1.2	1.2
2022 DC	*CLE*	*MLB*	*24*	*236*	*30*	*10*	*2*	*3*	*28*	*19*	*21*	*2*	*2*	*.266/.333/.389*	*97*	*.282*	*0.1*	*LF 2, CF 0*	*1.0*

Comparables: Ezequiel Carrera, Starling Marte, Cedric Mullins

The Report: Kwan would be your favorite prospect in 2005, and, honestly, he's still a pretty good prospect today. The gaudy strikeout-to-walk rate grabs your attention, and he is certainly that kind of pesky hitter: short to the ball, good hand-eye, willing and able to waste your two-strike stuff out of the zone. Despite the power bump last year, you shouldn't expect that to be a long-term part of his profile—he doesn't hit the ball all that hard—but Kwan should be able to slap enough doubles to keep pitchers honest. Daric Barton the Outfielder is more exciting than . . . well, regular Daric Barton, but Kwan's best fit is left field—although he is fast enough to handle center—so he may be more of a fourth-outfielder type than a starter. Still, we can't help but feel he will do enough to be an average regular, even if the shape of the performance is unusual.

OFP: 50 / OBP-driven starter

Variance: Medium. Kwan doesn't have much left to prove in the minors, even after missing a chunk of 2021 with a hamstring strain. However, this profile can have sneaky risk, as it's incredibly reliant on pitchers not throwing enough strikes. There's a reason its popularity got left behind with trucker hats and skinny jeans.

Mark Barry's Fantasy Take: Oh man, Daric Barton. I remember reading *Moneyball* (a couple years late) and rushing out to try to acquire Barton's OBP in *MLB: The Show*. Unfortunately, my personal playing style (read: swinging at pretty much everything) didn't let Barton spread his wings to fly, or, uh, walk to first base. Anyway, unless Kwan's 2021 power turns into 25 big-league homers, I'm not sure how useful he'll be outside of an empty OBP—which obviously only works in certain formats.

The Prospects You Meet Outside the Top Ten:

#11

Logan Allen LHP Born: 09/05/98 Age: 23 Bats: R Throws: L Height: 6'0" Weight: 190 lb. Origin: Round 2, 2020 Draft (#56 overall)

YEAR	TEAM	LVL	AGE	W	L	SV	G	GS	IP	H	HR	BB/9	K/9	K	GB%	BABIP	WHIP	ERA	DRA-	WARP
2021	LC	A+	22	5	0	0	9	9	51^{1}	37	3	2.3	11.7	67	44.1%	.296	0.97	1.58	80	1.1
2021	AKR	AA	22	4	0	0	12	10	60	40	9	2.0	11.4	76	28.8%	.238	0.88	2.85	96	0.6
2022 non-DC	*CLE*	*MLB*	*23*	*2*	*2*	*0*	*57*	*0*	*50*	*47*	*8*	*3.3*	*9.2*	*51*	*43.1%*	*.293*	*1.31*	*4.24*	*104*	*0.1*

Comparables: Brian Matusz, Derek Holland, Matt Moore

He'll be known as Logan T. Allen for a while, to differentiate him from Logan S. Allen—that's the one that pitched for the major-league team last year—and you don't get much more to separate them beyond that middle initial. Both are lefties. Both work off a fastball/slider/change mix. Logan T. Allen is shorter and slimmer, but generates low-90s heat with plenty of deception and potential above-average command. The change is his best secondary, and he can parachute it inside to righties with good sink. The slider is a tough angle for lefties, given his three-quarters slot and tendency to throw across his body a little, but neither secondary is consistently sharp enough to be a true plus pitch. That's going to put pressure on the fastball command to keep playing up the ladder, but the building blocks are here for an average major-league starter.

#12

Petey Halpin OF Born: 05/26/02 Age: 20 Bats: L Throws: R Height: 6'0" Weight: 185 lb. Origin: Round 3, 2020 Draft (#95 overall)

YEAR	TEAM	LVL	AGE	PA	R	2B	3B	HR	RBI	BB	K	SB	CS	AVG/OBP/SLG	DRC+	BABIP	BRR	FRAA	WARP
2021	LYN	A	19	246	34	14	6	1	18	21	50	11	9	.294/.363/.425	101	.376	0.4	CF(29) 2.2, LF(17) 4.0	1.5
2022 non-DC	*CLE*	*MLB*	*20*	*251*	*19*	*11*	*2*	*1*	*20*	*15*	*58*	*6*	*6*	*.230/.284/.326*	*67*	*.300*	*1.0*	*CF 2, LF 2*	*0.3*

Halpin had some buzz after Cleveland took him in the third round of the 2020 draft, but he had to wait until last summer to make his pro debut. He handled a somewhat aggressive Low-A assignment with aplomb, spraying line drives all over Low-A East fields. Despite a wide-open stance that has him facing the pitcher—and a big step in to close—Halpin's timing is usually in sync, and he shows some advanced bat-to-ball. There's above-average bat speed, as well, although it's not a swing geared to lift despite some raw-power projection. Halpin is a plus runner with a shot to stick in center, and I'd expect him to move up this list once he has a little bit more of a pro track record. His upside isn't far off that of those in the middle of the Guardians' top 10.

#13

Tommy Mace RHP Born: 11/11/98 Age: 23 Bats: R Throws: R Height: 6'6" Weight: 230 lb. Origin: Round 2, 2021 Draft (#69 overall)

Mace was probably the best undrafted college prospect in 2020; he had signability concerns and went back to the University of Florida. His 2021 with the Gators was a mixed bag, but he still went off the board after the second round with a Comp-B selection. He's an imposing presence on the mound, with a tall, large frame and throws a heavy, mid-90s fastball that currently outpaces his slider and changeup. Mace has relief risk, but he has a big, live arm, and the Guardians are one of the best teams at developing arms into effective major-league pitchers.

Prospects on the Rise

Xzavion Curry RHP Born: 07/27/98 Age: 23 Bats: R Throws: R Height: 5'11" Weight: 190 lb. Origin: Round 7, 2019 Draft (#220 overall)

YEAR	TEAM	LVL	AGE	W	L	SV	G	GS	IP	H	HR	BB/9	K/9	K	GB%	BABIP	WHIP	ERA	DRA-	WARP
2021	LYN	A	22	3	0	0	5	5	25^1	12	1	1.4	13.5	38	27.5%	.220	0.63	1.07	72	0.6
2021	LC	A+	22	5	1	0	13	13	67^2	53	10	1.6	10.6	80	30.9%	.261	0.96	2.66	91	1.0
2022 non-DC	*CLE*	*MLB*	*23*	*2*	*3*	*0*	*57*	*0*	*50*	*50*	*9*	*2.6*	*8.0*	*44*	*34.2%*	*.290*	*1.29*	*4.48*	*112*	*-0.1*

Comparables: Kyle Kendrick, Jason Vargas, Fernando Romero

A seventh-round pick out of Georgia Tech in 2019, Curry dominated the minors last year, although the stuff isn't quite as loud as the stat line. He is a shorter righty with a high slot which helps his fastball get a little plane and late life. The pitch sits in an average velocity range, but should play up more in short bursts. He pairs the heater with a high-70s curve that is inconsistent but flashes the kind of 12–6, bat-missing shape you'd want. The change is flat, the profile is control over command, and he's listed at 5-foot-11, so he sounds like a reliever long-term, but Curry's strong 2021 campaign likely keeps him in the rotation a bit longer, in an organization that is known for developing atypical starters.

Alexfri Planez OF Born: 08/17/01 Age: 20 Bats: R Throws: R Height: 6'2" Weight: 180 lb. Origin: International Free Agent, 2017

YEAR	TEAM	LVL	AGE	PA	R	2B	3B	HR	RBI	BB	K	SB	CS	AVG/OBP/SLG	DRC+	BABIP	BRR	FRAA	WARP
2019	INDR	ROK	17	25	3	2	0	1	3	1	7	0	0	.333/.360/.542		.438			
2021	LYN	A	19	413	61	19	5	16	53	13	121	11	3	.264/.294/.462	89	.339	0.7	CF(44) -1.8, LF(27) 2.4, RF(26) -2.4	0.8
2022 non-DC	*CLE*	*MLB*	*20*	*251*	*21*	*10*	*1*	*5*	*25*	*8*	*86*	*3*	*3*	*.220/.252/.349*	*58*	*.319*	*0.5*	*CF 0, RF -1*	*-0.5*

One of the top international free agents in the 2017 class, Planez had a bumpy transition to full-season ball as a 19-year-old last year. He offers plus bat speed and premium raw pop, but his swing gets on the longer side, and he has issues picking which pitches he should try to launch into low-earth orbit. His strike-zone discipline is so rough it's hard to feel confident that he'll hit even in Double-A, but the power is tantalizing, and the swing itself isn't the problem here, despite a rather unique setup with his front heel pointing towards the pitcher. Perhaps another go-round with Low-A Lynchburg wouldn't hurt.

Factors on the Farm

Tanner Burns RHP Born: 12/28/98 Age: 23 Bats: R Throws: R Height: 6'0" Weight: 180 lb. Origin: Round 1, 2020 Draft (#36 overall)

YEAR	TEAM	LVL	AGE	W	L	SV	G	GS	IP	H	HR	BB/9	K/9	K	GB%	BABIP	WHIP	ERA	DRA-	WARP
2021	LC	A+	22	2	5	0	18	18	75^2	64	10	3.4	10.8	91	39.7%	.300	1.23	3.57	88	1.3
2022 non-DC	*CLE*	*MLB*	*23*	*2*	*3*	*0*	*57*	*0*	*50*	*51*	*8*	*4.4*	*8.2*	*45*	*37.2%*	*.302*	*1.52*	*5.27*	*122*	*-0.4*

Comparables: Jeff Hoffman, Jim Parque, Justin Wayne

Burns is perhaps a little far away for this designation—he spent all of 2021 in High-A—but he's likely to move pretty quickly given his advanced three-pitch mix. You might have preferred a polished college arm to be a little more dominant in the High-A Central than Burns was in 2021, but command has been a long-standing issue. The fastball, slurvy breaker and change are all average-ish, and the fastball is especially sneaky at 94 due to Burns' extension. At this point, it would be excessive to repeat ourselves about how Cleveland has a history of getting pitch jumps with this back-end starter profile, so we'll just say, he's likely to be a back-end starter in a year or two, and leave it at that, for now.

Richie Palacios 2B Born: 05/16/97 Age: 25 Bats: L Throws: R Height: 5'10" Weight: 180 lb. Origin: Round 3, 2018 Draft (#103 overall)

YEAR	TEAM	LVL	AGE	PA	R	2B	3B	HR	RBI	BB	K	SB	CS	AVG/OBP/SLG	DRC+	BABIP	BRR	FRAA	WARP
2021	SCO	WIN	24	93	17	8	1	3	11	13	15	4	1	.269/.387/.513		.300			
2021	AKR	AA	24	283	53	24	3	6	36	33	42	10	3	.299/.389/.496	128	.338	2.3	2B(42) 6.1, CF(10) -0.5, LF(6) -0.0	2.6
2021	COL	AAA	24	145	19	9	1	1	12	25	28	10	0	.292/.434/.416	107	.376	0.8	2B(26) 1.2, CF(6) -0.8	0.7
2022 DC	*CLE*	*MLB*	*25*	*65*	*8*	*3*	*0*	*0*	*6*	*6*	*12*	*0*	*1*	*.242/.325/.362*	*87*	*.299*	*0.1*	*LF 1*	*0.2*

Comparables: Jordany Valdespin, Zach McKinstry, David Bote

A torn right shoulder labrum cost Palacios all of 2019, so the 2018 third-rounder had very few professional reps under his belt entering the 2021 season. He made up for lost time, getting all the way to Triple-A and then adding some extra at-bats to his ledger in Arizona, as well. He broadly has the same kind of pesky profile as Steven Kwan, and a similar narrow stance and big leg kick. Palacios, though, is looking to obliterate pitches, and he did smack 33 doubles despite lacking a power-hitter's frame. But his swing tends to have timing issues, resulting in out-of-balance, max-effort hacks. Palacios's contact ability has kept his K rates low, and he's perfectly happy working a walk, but we're a little less confident in him keeping that up in the majors than Kwan. Palacios does have more positional flex than Kwan, as he's a perfectly fine second baseman in addition to getting some outfield time, although his arm limits him to second, and he really shouldn't see right field much for the same reason. We don't know if Palacios will hit enough to break into the Guardians' crowded middle infield, but his defensive flexibility should procure him a bench role for a while.

Because You Were Going to Ask

Ethan Hankins RHP Born: 05/23/00 Age: 22 Bats: R Throws: R Height: 6'6" Weight: 200 lb. Origin: Round 1, 2018 Draft (#35 overall)

YEAR	TEAM	LVL	AGE	W	L	SV	G	GS	IP	H	HR	BB/9	K/9	K	GB%	BABIP	WHIP	ERA	DRA-	WARP
2019	MV	SS	19	0	0	0	9	8	38²	23	1	4.2	10.0	43	55.1%	.253	1.06	1.40		
2019	LC	A	19	0	3	0	5	5	21¹	20	3	5.1	11.8	28	47.2%	.340	1.50	4.64	104	0.1

Comparables: Adys Portillo, Daison Acosta, Trevor Clifton

Hankins suffered an elbow injury ramping up in extended spring training last year. That led to Tommy John surgery, which cost him all of 2021 and is likely to impact his 2022 as well. He needed reps more than anything, and he's losing a lot of them. Given the already-present relief and command risk, we've dropped him off the list for now, but the power, three-pitch mix might still be present upon his return this summer or fall.

Bo Naylor C Born: 02/21/00 Age: 22 Bats: L Throws: R Height: 6'0" Weight: 195 lb. Origin: Round 1, 2018 Draft (#29 overall)

YEAR	TEAM	LVL	AGE	PA	R	2B	3B	HR	RBI	BB	K	SB	CS	AVG/OBP/SLG	DRC+	BABIP	BRR	FRAA	WARP
2019	LC	A	19	453	60	18	10	11	65	43	104	7	5	.243/.313/.421	103	.296	-0.1	C(85) 16.4	3.3
2021	AKR	AA	21	356	41	13	1	10	44	37	112	10	0	.188/.280/.332	82	.255	-0.5	C(73) 6.7	1.1
2022 non-DC	*CLE*	*MLB*	*22*	*251*	*20*	*9*	*1*	*4*	*22*	*19*	*79*	*2*	*2*	*.192/.260/.312*	*51*	*.272*	*0.3*	*C 3*	*-0.1*

Comparables: Ben Rortvedt, Christian Vázquez, Chance Sisco

If you've been reading these reports for the last few years, you probably know Naylor as a bat-first catching prospect whose glove was going to have to catch up to his bat. Then he hit .188 and struck out more than 30 percent of the time in Double-A last year. Now he's a bat-first catching prospect with significant questions about the bat, or, to put another way, not a top-10 prospect in an absolutely loaded system.

Top Talents 25 and Under (as of 4/1/2022):

1. George Valera, OF
2. Daniel Espino, RHP
3. Brayan Rocchio, SS
4. Gabriel Arias, SS
5. Andrés Giménez, SS/2B
6. Triston McKenzie, RHP
7. Gavin Williams, RHP
8. Tyler Freeman, SS
9. Emmanuel Clase, RHP
10. Nolan Jones, 3B/OF

Cleveland spent a healthy portion of 2021 attempting to undo the Mets' efforts to extract more power from Giménez by encouraging an uppercut swing he never seemed comfortable with. That did not work out well at the big-league level, but Giménez looked more comfortable at Triple-A as the season went on. He'll be just 23 this season, and while projection is not part of the equation, he does enough things well up the middle and on the basepaths to be a capable regular with a merely below-average bat.

There was hope that we'd see a resurgence in velocity from McKenzie last year, and all things are possible under the sun, including adding any degree of bulk onto his lithe 6-foot-5 frame, but it has not arrived yet. That meant a respectable-but-unremarkable age-23 campaign, as he struggled to keep the bases clear even while pumping fastballs more often than almost any other starter in baseball. He has two distinct breaking balls that have been bat-missers, which makes him a reasonable bet to develop into at least a number-four-starter type, and we've said that before about Cleveland arms.

In terms of pure relievers, it's hard to recall many as young with as few flaws as Clase. He's the type of player whose tool kit would have prompted cries of witchcraft in the nineteenth century or earlier and might've given Jimmie Foxx a heart attack. Clase's repertoire is a two-pitch mix, a cutter and a slider, with the former accounting for roughly 70 percent of his offerings and an unfathomably high ground-ball rate. Oh, and it averages 100 mph. The slider is an excellent offering in its own right, a sharp-breaking 91–92-mph devastator, and it is his best bat-misser. The cutter, however, is a barrel-dodging anomaly, the reason for his staggering 68.3 percent ground-ball rate. The only knock on Clase is that he has already been pigeon-holed as a one-inning reliever at the age of 23.

The best of Cleveland's remaining 25-and-under graduates are in the bullpen. Sam Hentges and Nick Sandlin will likely cycle between Triple-A Columbus and Cleveland as optionable arms. Cleveland is a club in a tricky spot due to its stinginess, but on a club where Anthony Gose is the only player on the 40-man roster over 30, and most of the "established names" are barely ineligible (e.g., Amed Rosario, Franmil Reyes, Shane Bieber, Aaron Civale, and Zach Plesac), there is more youth than most clubs, even among the veterans.

Colorado Rockies

The State of the System:

There's some improvement here due to an interesting 2021 draft class and a couple of low-minors breakouts, but Colorado has a ways to go on the scouting, draft, and development fronts.

The Top Ten:

1 Zac Veen OF OFP: 60 ETA: 2024

Born: 12/12/01 Age: 20 Bats: L Throws: R Height: 6'4" Weight: 190 lb. Origin: Round 1, 2020 Draft (#9 overall)

YEAR	TEAM	LVL	AGE	PA	R	2B	3B	HR	RBI	BB	K	SB	CS	AVG/OBP/SLG	DRC+	BABIP	BRR	FRAA	WARP
2021	FRE	A	19	479	83	27	4	15	75	64	126	36	17	.301/.399/.501	117	.396	-1.7	RF(69) -0.2, LF(26) 2.2	2.6
2022 non-DC	*COL*	*MLB*	*20*	*251*	*22*	*11*	*1*	*4*	*23*	*21*	*79*	*11*	*7*	*.214/.288/.332*	*67*	*.309*	*1.2*	*RF 2, LF 1*	*0.1*

Comparables: Travis Snider, Josh Bell, Juan Soto

The Report: Veen got off to a slow start in his professional debut, but there were process-related signals (pitch recognition and swing decisions, to name two) that hinted at breakout on the horizon. It took Veen a month to find his groove, but he ultimately became one of the best hitters in the Low-A West, finishing with a 301/.399/.501 line and 15 home runs over 479 plate appearances. Long and lean with room to add good weight, Veen projects for plus-plus raw power at maturity. There is some length to his swing that will result in some swing-and-miss, but he has a sound approach and realistically projects as a 30-HR bat. He lacks the pure speed to handle center field, but runs surprisingly well underway and has enough arm strength to profile in right field.

OFP: 60 / First-division outfielder

Variance: Medium. Veen has a high offensive bar to clear as a corner bat, but his advanced approach and plus impact should help him produce enough to profile as a middle-of-the-order masher.

Mark Barry's Fantasy Take:

Zac Veen, Zac Veen, Zac Veen, Zac Veeeeeeen
I'm begging of you please cut down the fan
Zac Veen, Zac Veen, Zac Veen, Zac Veeeeeeen
With less whiffs you'll be the roto man

Plus-plus pop and good approach
Your Low-A stats were past reproach
Your 36 steals seem a bit obscene
When you swing, you turn it loose
So the final form might be Jay Bruce
But that's not a bad Coors outcome for Zac Veen

Eyewitness Report: Zac Veen

Evaluator: Trevor Andresen
Report Date: 08/08/2021
Dates Seen: 7/27/21-8/1/21
Risk Factor: Medium
Physical/Health: XL 6'4 200 lb. frame. Lean build w/ long limbs & room to add more good weight.

Tool	Future Grade	Report
Hit	45	Upright, slightly open stance w/a leg kick load. Advanced approach overall; w/ a good feel for the strike zone, pitch recognition ability & swinging w/ intent in positive counts. There is some length to the swing (thanks to his long levers & how hard he swings) that results in swing/miss & will lead to high strikeout rates, but he should have the aptitude to make some adjustments when behind in the count. It might wind up as more of a .240-.250 bat, but should come w/ high walk rates.
Power	60	Easy plus raw power at present & will likely grow into plus-plus at physical maturity. Natural loft in the stroke & swings to do damage. Impact to all fields. 25-30 HR type power bat.
Baserunning/ Speed	45	Roughly average runner at present & will likely lose a half step as he continues to fill out. Stolen base count is misleading, but he does have solid instincts on the bases.
Glove	50	Speed limits him to an outfield corner. Instincts are just OK. A bit of a stiff athlete w/ average range. Won't be an asset, but should be able to profile as an average glove in RF.
Arm	55	Above-average strength. RF fit.

Conclusion: There's impact upside here accompanied w/ a good bit of hit tool variance, but Veen realistically projects as a an above-average middle of the order run producer.

2 Benny Montgomery CF OFP: 55 ETA: 2025

Born: 09/09/02 Age: 19 Bats: R Throws: R Height: 6'4" Weight: 200 lb. Origin: Round 1, 2021 Draft (#8 overall)

YEAR	TEAM	LVL	AGE	PA	R	2B	3B	HR	RBI	BB	K	SB	CS	AVG/OBP/SLG	DRC+	BABIP	BRR	FRAA	WARP
2021	RCK	ROK	18	52	7	0	1	0	6	5	9	5	1	.340/.404/.383		.421			

Comparables: Marlin Almonte, Frank Tolentino, Eudy Pina

The Report: It's rare to be able to glean much from a scouting standpoint from a spectacle like a home-run derby given the sterilized and specific environment. In the case of Montgomery, his performance at the Perfect Game All-American Classic in Oklahoma City was about as eye-opening as such an event can be. Even with a hitchy swing that begins with an odd hand-cock and glides through the zone with an unusually flat bat path, Montgomery was able to routinely barrel and lift the ball. Evaluators came away thinking he was immensely athletic and projectable, that he was coachable, and that he was one of the prospects with the most potential heading into the 2021 draft. Montgomery's frame is presently lean, but he is adding strength each day, and there is a chance for a five-tool profile at maturation.

OFP: 55 / Above-average outfielder

Variance: Extreme. Montgomery is raw yet toolsy. There will be some growing pains as his swing mechanics are re-worked and he adjusts to a professional schedule. Reports from the Arizona Complex League after the draft were not kind; we'll grant some latitude to begin with.

Mark Barry's Fantasy Take: B-B-B-Benny! Just kidding. Montgomery's combination of age and athleticism offers a ton of upside. Pair those traits with his numbers from the complex, and it's easy to dream on a five-category stud. Still, his swing hitch and troubling Complex-League reports give me some pause. He's a back-end top-101 guy for me, but his volatility and lead time would probably have me gauging the trade market.

3 Ezequiel Tovar SS OFP: 55 ETA: 2024

Born: 08/01/01 Age: 20 Bats: R Throws: R Height: 6'0" Weight: 162 lb. Origin: International Free Agent, 2017

YEAR	TEAM	LVL	AGE	PA	R	2B	3B	HR	RBI	BB	K	SB	CS	AVG/OBP/SLG	DRC+	BABIP	BRR	FRAA	WARP
2019	GJ	ROA	17	86	12	2	2	0	3	10	17	4	1	.264/.357/.347		.339			
2019	BOI	SS	17	243	22	4	2	2	13	16	52	13	0	.249/.304/.313		.315			
2021	SRR	WIN	19	96	10	2	0	3	10	5	20	2	0	.161/.219/.287		.167			
2021	FRE	A	19	326	60	21	3	11	54	14	38	21	4	.309/.346/.510	132	.320	2.5	SS(64) 8.1	3.3
2021	SPO	A+	19	143	19	9	0	4	18	3	19	3	2	.239/.266/.396	115	.252	-1.0	SS(32) -1.8	0.4
2022 non-DC	*COL*	*MLB*	*20*	*251*	*21*	*11*	*1*	*4*	*24*	*9*	*42*	*10*	*3*	*.249/.282/.369*	*74*	*.285*	*0.9*	*SS 1, 2B 0*	*0.3*

Comparables: Rougned Odor, Gleyber Torres, Starlin Castro

The Report: The Rockies signed Tovar for $800,000 as part of their 2017 July 2nd class, and while he performed fairly well throughout the first two years of his career, he truly broke out in 2021, hitting .287/.322/.475 over 469 plate appearances between both A-ball levels. Plus bat control drives his offensive profile, but his increased physicality combined with easy bat speed gives him a chance to hit 15–20 home runs if he can rein in the free-swinging nature of his approach slightly. Tovar is a plus runner, and the athleticism plays in the infield, with fluid actions, soft hands and a plus arm that enable him to fit comfortably at shortstop.

OFP: 55 / Above-average middle infielder

Variance: Medium. Tovar's feel for contact and defense at a premium position give him a relatively high floor, and there's all-star potential if he can continue to tap into his newfound raw power.

Mark Barry's Fantasy Take: Well that was fun.

From here, it gets a little more bleak on the fantasy side. If not bleak, at least a lot more speculative. Tovar flashed some pop for the first time in his career during a 72-game stint at Low-A, which means we could be looking at a 15–20 dude in the power and speed categories. That's not bad, but it's also not terribly exciting as an apex.

4 Drew Romo C OFP: 55 ETA: 2024/2025

Born: 08/29/01 Age: 20 Bats: S Throws: R Height: 6'1" Weight: 205 lb. Origin: Round 1, 2020 Draft (#35 overall)

YEAR	TEAM	LVL	AGE	PA	R	2B	3B	HR	RBI	BB	K	SB	CS	AVG/OBP/SLG	DRC+	BABIP	BRR	FRAA	WARP
2021	FRE	A	19	339	48	17	2	6	47	19	50	23	6	.314/.345/.439	121	.348	1.2	C(69) 12.8	3.2
2022 non-DC	*COL*	*MLB*	*20*	*251*	*20*	*10*	*1*	*2*	*21*	*11*	*48*	*10*	*4*	*.246/.284/.334*	*69*	*.298*	*0.9*	*C 2*	*0.5*

Comparables: John Ryan Murphy, Salvador Perez, Francisco Mejía

The Report: A Comp A pick in the shortened 2020 draft, Romo has gotten off to the kind of start that makes you wonder if we've all made too much of a fuss over the poor track record of prep catchers. The concern with that cohort is how much defensive work/projection they need, but Romo already shows the potential for a plus glove. He has excellent body control behind the plate, which helps with both blocking and receiving and gets him out of the crouch quickly enough to let his above-average arm strength play to the full tool grade.

At the plate, he's more divisive, although the offensive upside here is higher than Tovar's. Romo's short stroke with good barrel control looks the same from either side of the plate, but his pitch recognition and swing decisions limit the hit and power upsides to fringy at present. If he can get to more of his above-average raw pop as he adds reps up the organizational ladder, he could shoot up both the Rockies' and national lists. Romo has a clearer path to be a Top-50 prospect in a year's time than Tovar, but the uncertainty around Romo's bat leaves him slightly behind his Fresno teammate at present.

OFP: 55 / Above-average starting catcher, but more glove than hit

Variance: High. Our Cal League contingent was split on Romo. The instructs reports leaned towards the high side, but 19-year-old catchers remain one of the worst cohorts to bet on. The advanced glove does mitigate some of that here.

Mark Barry's Fantasy Take: While this might seem like a Golden Age for dynasty catching prospects, that really just means that the pool is even more flooded now than before, putting an even higher premium on the top end. It's unlikely that Romo hits that fantasy peak, so he's probably a waiver-wire guy in the big leagues.

5 Jaden Hill RHP OFP: 55 ETA: 2025

Born: 12/22/99 Age: 22 Bats: R Throws: R Height: 6'4" Weight: 234 lb. Origin: Round 2, 2021 Draft (#44 overall)

The Report: On talent alone, Hill was mentioned amongst the very best draft prospects heading into last spring at LSU. What needed to be demonstrated in his junior year—after an injury-riddled freshman campaign and short 2020 season coming out of the bullpen—was that he could handle a Friday-night starter's workload for the duration of the campaign. Hill's talent was never the question. Hill throws an electric fastball that hit the upper 90s and two potentially plus (or better) secondaries in his slider and changeup, which were inconsistent despite their flashes. After getting out of the gates quickly, his velocity began to dip. Hill tried to pitch through it, but eventually underwent Tommy John surgery. He went from what could have been a top-10 pick to the top of the second round, where the Rockies bought the upside hoping he can recover and develop as a starter.

OFP: 55 / No. 3–4 starter or late-inning reliever

Variance: Extreme. The typical hesitancy that is built in for any pitcher who has had a major elbow surgery is exacerbated by the fact Hill has yet to demonstrate a full season's workload. It's not impossible rhat he ends up as a front-of-the-rotation starter, but it's equally likely that his massive arm talent cannot sustain the rigors of normal baseball activity.

Mark Barry's Fantasy Take: Hill's profile and history of production point to an excellent, high-leverage bullpen arm, even in fantasy circles. Still, he's not terribly close and is currently recovering from TJS, so it's hard to justify clogging a roster spot with Hill's skills.

6 Adael Amador SS OFP: 55 ETA: 2025/2026

Born: 04/11/03 Age: 19 Bats: S Throws: R Height: 6'0" Weight: 160 lb. Origin: International Free Agent, 2019

YEAR	TEAM	LVL	AGE	PA	R	2B	3B	HR	RBI	BB	K	SB	CS	AVG/OBP/SLG	DRC+	BABIP	BRR	FRAA	WARP
2021	RCK	ROK	18	200	41	10	1	4	24	27	29	10	7	.299/.394/.445		.331			

Comparables: Pedro Guerrero, Seth Moranda, Jose Luis Javier

The Report: A switch-hitting shortstop who signed for $1.5 million in the 2019 international-free-agent class, Amador came stateside and raked in the complex. He has an unorthodox swing, garnering a "not how I would draw it up" from one evaluator, but despite a big leg kick and an indirect, often top-hand dominated bat path, he makes consistent good contact. It's not super loud at present, and Amador will need physical development to get to an above-average-hit and average-power projection, but those are in play. Defensively, Amador isn't a sure-shot shortstop, although he shows decent hands and range at present. He'd be an ideal "On the Rise" type in a deeper system, but in the Rockies' system . . . well, he's here.

OFP: 55 / Above-average infielder

Variance: Extreme. Amador is a complex-league prospect with a bit of a weird swing and an unclear defensive home. He could end up a Top-101 name in short order. He could also peter out by Double-A.

Mark Barry's Fantasy Take: I wouldn't discourage you if you wanted to toss Amador onto your watchlist in deeper formats, but he doesn't offer a ton of ceiling, and he's still super far away, so I'm not all that interested.

7 Ryan Rolison LHP OFP: 50 ETA: 2022

Born: 07/11/97 Age: 24 Bats: R Throws: L Height: 6'2" Weight: 213 lb. Origin: Round 1, 2018 Draft (#22 overall)

YEAR	TEAM	LVL	AGE	W	L	SV	G	GS	IP	H	HR	BB/9	K/9	K	GB%	BABIP	WHIP	ERA	DRA-	WARP
2019	ASH	A	21	2	1	0	3	3	14^2	8	0	1.2	8.6	14	37.8%	.216	0.68	0.61	98	0.1
2019	LAN	A+	21	6	7	0	22	22	116^1	129	22	2.9	9.1	118	43.6%	.327	1.44	4.87	103	0.1
2021	RCK	ROK	23	0	0	0	2	2	6^1	10	0	2.8	12.8	9	27.8%	.556	1.89	7.11		
2021	HFD	AA	23	2	1	0	3	3	14^2	11	1	1.2	12.3	20	52.9%	.303	0.89	3.07	88	0.2
2021	ABQ	AAA	23	2	2	0	10	10	45^2	51	7	3.2	8.9	45	41.3%	.336	1.47	5.91	103	0.1
2022 DC	*COL*	*MLB*	*24*	*3*	*3*	*0*	*12*	*12*	*54.3*	*58*	*9*	*3.3*	*7.4*	*44*	*37.5%*	*.304*	*1.44*	*5.24*	*119*	*-0.1*

Comparables: Wade LeBlanc, Dallas Braden, Luis Cessa

The Report: After missing all of 2020, Rolison had hard luck in 2021. He missed significant time after having his appendix removed and then got hit on the left hand during batting practice as he was ramping back up. All told, he threw only 71 innings last season and mostly confirmed our priors. Rolison is not the most exciting lefty pitching prospect you will see. He's a polished college-lefty type with an advanced breaking ball that sits around 80 miles per hour and isn't a true bat-misser. The pitch was sharper early in the season, a 55 offering that he moved around the zone effectively and could drop in for a strike or get Double-A hitters to chase. The fastball sits in the low 90s with some tail at the lower end of the velocity band, but it can be a bit too hittable at times. He also has also a mid-80s changeup that is used sparingly and hasn't really shown a ton of major-league utility. I suspect he has the ability to leverage the breaker enough for back-end starterdom, but fair warning: this is a brutal profile to roll out in Coors Field.

OFP: 50 / No. 4 starter

Variance: Medium. The fastball might be too hittable. There's not an obvious high-end relief fallback, but there's also not a ton of performance risk in the profile, for good or ill.

Mark Barry's Fantasy Take: Brutal profile for Coors, you say? Where do I sign up? I don't think Rolison's stuff is good enough to overcome his home digs and recent deficiencies with giving up the long ball.

8 Elehuris Montero CI   OFP: 50   ETA: Mid 2022

Born: 08/17/98 Age: 23 Bats: R Throws: R Height: 6'3" Weight: 235 lb. Origin: International Free Agent, 2014

YEAR	TEAM	LVL	AGE	PA	R	2B	3B	HR	RBI	BB	K	SB	CS	AVG/OBP/SLG	DRC+	BABIP	BRR	FRAA	WARP
2019	GDD	WIN	20	60	5	3	1	0	3	9	17	1	0	.200/.333/.300		.303			
2019	SPR	AA	20	238	23	8	0	7	18	14	74	0	1	.188/.235/.317	78	.245	0.1	3B(52) -6.2	-0.8
2021	EST	WIN	22	158	12	4	1	2	15	16	35	1	0	.221/.297/.307		.276			
2021	HFD	AA	22	379	46	11	1	22	69	43	90	0	0	.279/.361/.523	124	.309	0.2	3B(42) -0.4, 1B(40) -3.0	1.9
2021	ABQ	AAA	22	121	23	9	1	6	17	10	20	0	0	.278/.355/.546	114	.293	-1.2	3B(19) 0.2, 1B(9) -0.9	0.4
2022 DC	*COL*	*MLB*	*23*	*30*	*3*	*1*	*0*	*1*	*3*	*2*	*6*	*0*	*0*	*.242/.310/.412*	*89*	*.290*	*0.0*	*SS 0*	*0.1*

Comparables: Cheslor Cuthbert, Miguel Andújar, Miguel Sanó

The Report: After a rather pedestrian start to his 2021 campaign, Montero heated up during the summer months, getting all of his plus raw power into games. His home parks in Hartford and Albuquerque are about as friendly as it gets, but he was just as effective on the road. Montero's swing is a coiled, leveraged, mighty hack geared for power over hit and launch over barrel control. He can get long or pull off righty spin and pops up his fair share while trying to lift the ball, but he could sneak out above-average game power despite a below-average hit-tool projection.

Montero looked to be in better shape this year and played a passable third base, but is a better fit at first, although his footwork wasn't great there either. A lot of things have to go right for Montero to be a regular, but his ability to play both infield corners and mash lefties should allow him to carve out a bench role if the swing-and-miss doesn't get significantly worse in the majors. Despite his gaudy 2021 stat line, Montero doesn't have huge upside given the hit-tool and defensive limitations, but the pop might be enough for him to continue to air it out every day at a corner in the friendly confines of Coors.

OFP: 50 / Second-division corner masher

Variance: Medium. It's not low, as there is still some risk that he just won't make enough contact, or enough good contact, to get his power into games, even in the thin air of Denver. However, Montero has all but conquered the upper minors.

Mark Barry's Fantasy Take: Thanks to proximity and power, Montero might be the third-best fantasy prospect on this list. Even though there are very valid hit-tool concerns, he struck out less than 17 percent of the time this season in Triple-A, so there's some hope he could make enough contact to flash that pop. It wouldn't surprise me to see Montero become a sneaky Quad-A type that could be really useful as early as this season in deep dynasties or onlies.

9 Michael Toglia 1B   OFP: 50   ETA: Late 2022/Early 2023

Born: 08/16/98 Age: 23 Bats: S Throws: L Height: 6'5" Weight: 226 lb. Origin: Round 1, 2019 Draft (#23 overall)

YEAR	TEAM	LVL	AGE	PA	R	2B	3B	HR	RBI	BB	K	SB	CS	AVG/OBP/SLG	DRC+	BABIP	BRR	FRAA	WARP
2019	BOI	SS	20	176	25	7	0	9	26	28	45	1	1	.248/.369/.483		.290			
2021	SRR	WIN	22	105	10	2	1	3	12	12	26	1	0	.264/.343/.407		.328			
2021	SPO	A+	22	330	50	10	2	17	66	42	91	7	3	.234/.333/.465	108	.275	2.0	1B(67) 11.8	2.5
2021	HFD	AA	22	169	16	10	1	5	18	23	51	3	0	.217/.331/.406	93	.295	-2.3	1B(41) 4.3	0.5
2022 non-DC	*COL*	*MLB*	*23*	*251*	*24*	*9*	*1*	*6*	*25*	*23*	*81*	*1*	*1*	*.203/.285/.346*	*70*	*.285*	*-0.1*	*1B 3*	*-0.2*

Comparables: Ike Davis, Matt Adams, Brandon Belt

The Report: Toglia picked up in 2021 where he left off after the draft in 2019, hitting baseballs incredibly hard but swinging and missing often enough to generate several kilowatts of green energy for the Spokane Valley. A late-summer promotion to Double-A produced more of the same. You can't tease out the power from the whiffs here, as Toglia has a lot of inefficient hand movement from both sides of the plate that is responsible for both the prodigious home-run totals and the near–30 percent K-rate. And because of the length and stiffness of his swing, his contact profile can be suboptimal, even when he is getting the bat to the ball. While he is patient and draws his walks, the track record of this profile for a player already hitting just .230 at these levels is not great. Toglia played some outfield in college, but has only worn a first-base glove in the minors. He's a solid defender there, but the only thing that will move the needle at the cold corner is 30-plus-home-run, .330-plus on-base seasons (adjust for altitude as you see fit). The risk of the hit tool just not getting there is high.

OFP: 50 / Average first baseman

Variance: High. There is truly elite power potential here, especially when you factor in his home park. It's hard to have a bad 40-home-run season, and Toglia offers potentially decent glovework and on-base, as well. It's also hard to have a truly good .200 batting average season, and that's certainly in play here, too.

Mark Barry's Fantasy Take: Look, I'm hip and attuned to the trendy stats and everything, but a .228 batting average across 499 plate appearances in Double- and Triple-A doesn't inspire a ton of confidence that Toglia will be able to make enough contact against big-league pitching. The short lead time is nice and probably keeps Toglia in the top-250 or so, but I worry that he could be a batting-average black hole.

10 Joe Rock LHP

OFP: 50 ETA: 2024

Born: 07/29/00 Age: 21 Bats: L Throws: L Height: 6'6" Weight: 200 lb. Origin: Round 2, 2021 Draft (#68 overall)

YEAR	TEAM	LVL	AGE	W	L	SV	G	GS	IP	H	HR	BB/9	K/9	K	GB%	BABIP	WHIP	ERA	DRA-	WARP
2021	RCK	ROK	20	1	0	0	4	2	8	5	0	1.1	12.4	11	70.6%	.294	0.75	1.13		

The Report: Ah, nominative determinism at work. Joe Rock was the Rockies second-round pick and added a little velocity after signing. The 6-foot-6 slinger still looks like he should throw harder than he does, but he was bumping 95 in the complex and pairs it with a potential plus slider. The delivery is repeatable enough for a tall, lanky southpaw, but the low arm-slot will always leave reliever risk lurking in the profile. And yes, he's *likely* to be a reliever, but he's got a chance to start given the present strike-throwing ability and the potential to add more fastball velocity if he fills out his frame a bit more.

OFP: 50 / Look, he's probably a reliever

Variance: Medium. The fastball/slider combo and low arm-slot should give Rock a solid bullpen fallback, but he also has a whole eight pro innings under his belt and might not hold above-average velocity in longer stints.

Mark Barry's Fantasy Take: If you're looking for a drive-time deejay that plays the greatest hits from the '70s and '80s, then do I have the guy for you! Unfortunately, I don't think Rock's profile points to a stud reliever, so his fantasy viability will depend on whether he can shoulder a starter's workload without losing effectiveness.

The Prospects You Meet Outside the Top Ten

#11

Ryan Vilade OF Born: 02/18/99 Age: 23 Bats: R Throws: R Height: 6'2" Weight: 226 lb. Origin: Round 2, 2017 Draft (#48 overall)

YEAR	TEAM	LVL	AGE	PA	R	2B	3B	HR	RBI	BB	K	SB	CS	AVG/OBP/SLG	DRC+	BABIP	BRR	FRAA	WARP
2019	LAN	A+	20	587	92	27	10	12	71	56	95	24	7	.303/.367/.466	119	.342	2.4	SS(83) -4.0, 3B(46) -4.6	2.2
2021	SRR	WIN	22	90	12	2	1	0	12	10	16	3	0	.253/.344/.304		.317			
2021	ABQ	AAA	22	518	82	28	5	7	44	38	92	12	5	.284/.339/.410	91	.336	5.6	LF(60) -5.3, RF(41) -1.2, CF(18) -1.9	0.8
2021	COL	MLB	22	7	0	0	0	0	0	1	1	0	0	.000/.143/.000	106		-0.1	LF(2) 0.1	0.0
2022 DC	*COL*	*MLB*	*23*	*80*	*7*	*3*	*0*	*0*	*7*	*5*	*16*	*1*	*1*	*.242/.304/.344*	*74*	*.301*	*0.1*	*RF 0, LF 0*	*0.0*

Comparables: L.J. Hoes, José Peraza, Jorge Polanco

Superficially, Vilade kept chugging along in 2021, but there's a lot to be worried about under the hood. He continued to make a decent amount of contact and continued to hit for average, which he has done basically everywhere (albeit just a good average, not superlative.) Yet, the hoped-for power surge didn't emerge at all, with single-digit homer production over a full season. Worse yet, that lack of power was happening in Albuquerque—among the best places in affiliated baseball to hit—in a Triple-A league filled with a number of the other best places in affiliated baseball to hit. There's plus raw pop here, and Vilade didn't look terribly out of place at Futures Game batting practice, but he has to get to it in games, and that's not happening yet. Given that he's already seen some run in The Show and should be competing for a 2022 major-league spot, the big power spike needs to happen soon.

Defensively, well, just a few years ago he was a shortstop we hoped might stick at third base. In the present, he's primarily a corner outfielder whose only time on the dirt this year was at first base. This puts a lot of pressure on his bat if he's going to be a first-division regular, thus, without big offensive gains, that outcome is getting further away.

Prospects on the Rise

Warming Bernabel 3B Born: 06/06/02 Age: 20 Bats: R Throws: R Height: 6'0" Weight: 180 lb. Origin: International Free Agent, 2018

YEAR	TEAM	LVL	AGE	PA	R	2B	3B	HR	RBI	BB	K	SB	CS	AVG/OBP/SLG	DRC+	BABIP	BRR	FRAA	WARP
2019	DSL ROC	ROK	17	79	11	6	1	0	14	3	9	0	1	.300/.342/.414		.328			
2019	DSL COL	ROK	17	162	26	7	1	4	17	13	20	3	6	.225/.309/.373		.233			
2021	RCK	ROK	19	86	18	5	0	6	31	5	12	5	1	.432/.453/.743		.426			
2021	FRE	A	19	94	9	6	0	1	7	7	14	4	1	.205/.287/.313	111	.232	-0.9	3B(17) 0.6	0.4
2022 non-DC	*COL*	*MLB*	*20*	*251*	*18*	*10*	*1*	*2*	*19*	*14*	*49*	*4*	*4*	*.210/.264/.294*	*54*	*.257*	*0.4*	*3B 1*	*-0.7*

Comparables: Gio Urshela, Dilson Herrera, Alex Liddi

We flagged Bernabel on last year's list as one to watch due to his bat speed and barrel control, and those played to the report in 2021, as well. He tore up the complex, earning a late-season promotion to Fresno as a 19-year-old. The offensive profile is hit-over-power at present, and his body and arm strength might force him down the defensive spectrum, but Bernabel's bat could carry him to the majors regardless.

Brayan Castillo RHP Born: 09/11/00 Age: 21 Bats: R Throws: R Height: 6'0" Weight: 145 lb. Origin: International Free Agent, 2017

YEAR	TEAM	LVL	AGE	W	L	SV	G	GS	IP	H	HR	BB/9	K/9	K	GB%	BABIP	WHIP	ERA	DRA-	WARP
2019	DSL COL	ROK	18	2	7	0	11	11	52^{1}	46	1	4.0	8.3	48	44.9%	.310	1.32	3.61		
2021	RCK	ROK	20	3	1	0	8	5	24^{2}	27	0	5.8	10.2	28	39.7%	.380	1.74	5.11		

Castillo, who turned 21 at the end of the season, is on the older side for a complex-league arm. He's on the smaller side for a pitching prospect (it's never optimal to have the listed height and weight of a Baseball Prospectus writer). Unlike most BP writers, Castillo throws 96 with feel for a full suite of three secondaries. Given his size and age, you might hope Castillo picks the best secondary and works out as a two-pitch bullpen arm, but there might be a bit more here, even if time isn't on his side.

Brenton Doyle OF Born: 05/14/98 Age: 24 Bats: R Throws: R Height: 6'3" Weight: 200 lb. Origin: Round 4, 2019 Draft (#129 overall)

YEAR	TEAM	LVL	AGE	PA	R	2B	3B	HR	RBI	BB	K	SB	CS	AVG/OBP/SLG	DRC+	BABIP	BRR	FRAA	WARP
2019	GJ	ROA	21	215	42	11	3	8	33	31	47	17	3	.383/.477/.611		.484			
2021	SPO	A+	23	424	70	16	2	16	47	30	134	21	6	.279/.336/.454	96	.388	-0.5	RF(44) 0.1, CF(39) 2.7	1.4
2022 non-DC	*COL*	*MLB*	*24*	*251*	*22*	*9*	*1*	*5*	*24*	*14*	*87*	*7*	*3*	*.222/.273/.344*	*64*	*.328*	*0.7*	*CF 1, RF 1*	*-0.1*

Comparables: Kevin Pillar, Chas McCormick, Scott Van Slyke

A 2019, Day 2, small-college pick, Doyle came out firing in rookie ball and then, like most minor leaguers, had to cool his jets in 2020. His 2021 season was more fits and starts. "Defense never slumps" is an old canard, but Doyle's plus speed and arm lets him man any spot on the grass, and his advanced tracking and routes give him a potential above-average center-field projection. At the plate, it was a year of swing tweaks for Doyle, and he went through fallow stretches at the plate. Even when he was hitting, the swing-and-miss was at concerning levels for a 23-year-old college bat in High-A. There's a chance for an average hit tool with the right swing tweak, which would give him enough offensive value given the average pop to be a starter in center, but we are a ways away from that future at present.

Factors on the Farm

Chris McMahon RHP Born: 02/04/99 Age: 23 Bats: R Throws: R Height: 6'2" Weight: 217 lb. Origin: Round 2, 2020 Draft (#46 overall)

YEAR	TEAM	LVL	AGE	W	L	SV	G	GS	IP	H	HR	BB/9	K/9	K	GB%	BABIP	WHIP	ERA	DRA-	WARP
2021	SPO	A+	22	10	3	0	22	20	114^{1}	119	13	2.5	9.4	119	39.4%	.335	1.32	4.17	115	-0.1
2022 non-DC	*COL*	*MLB*	*23*	*2*	*3*	*0*	*57*	*0*	*50*	*54*	*7*	*3.5*	*7.0*	*38*	*37.1%*	*.303*	*1.47*	*5.26*	*123*	*-0.4*

Comparables: Doug Waechter, Jeanmar Gómez, Jason Jacome

Perhaps it's a bit of a stretch to call McMahon a Factor on the Farm when he spent all of 2021 in Spokane, but he is the kind of polished college arm that could move quickly now that he has a full, normalish season under his belt. However, if we were more confident in the stuff playing at higher levels (and the majors), he'd be a top 10 prospect in a still-very-shallow Rockies system. McMahon's fastball was down a couple of ticks as a pro, more low 90s than the mid-90s he showed in college. There's sink on the fastball, a good changeup with sink and a slider that flashes average depth but is inconsistent. McMahon keeps the ball down and commands everything well enough. There's back-end-starter potential in relatively short order here, but the Rockies have struggled to develop this kind of arm recently, and we don't know that you can simply blame the home park.

Sam Weatherly LHP Born: 05/28/99 Age: 23 Bats: L Throws: L Height: 6'4" Weight: 205 lb. Origin: Round 3, 2020 Draft (#81 overall)

YEAR	TEAM	LVL	AGE	W	L	SV	G	GS	IP	H	HR	BB/9	K/9	K	GB%	BABIP	WHIP	ERA	DRA-	WARP
2021	FRE	A	22	4	6	0	15	15	69	59	7	4.2	12.5	96	34.2%	.344	1.32	4.83	104	0.2
2022 non-DC	*COL*	*MLB*	*23*	*2*	*3*	*0*	*57*	*0*	*50*	*48*	*8*	*5.3*	*8.7*	*48*	*39.4%*	*.289*	*1.56*	*5.70*	*128*	*-0.5*

Comparables: Jo-Jo Reyes, Josh Rogers, Nick Margevicius

Weatherly flashed starter traits during the pandemic-shortened 2020 season, but wasn't able to prove that he could maintain it over a full spring as a junior at Clemson. The Rockies selected him in the third round anyway, betting on his size, athleticism and raw stuff from the left side. Weatherly's first professional season went as expected, flashing two plus offerings (a mid-90s fastball and a sweeping slider) along with below-average command that seemed to worsen over the course of an outing. There's still room to dream that the command can improve enough for him to profile as a number 3 or 4 starter, but the most realistic outcome is that of a late-inning reliever.

Colton Welker CI Born: 10/09/97 Age: 24 Bats: R Throws: R Height: 6'1" Weight: 235 lb. Origin: Round 4, 2016 Draft (#110 overall)

YEAR	TEAM	LVL	AGE	PA	R	2B	3B	HR	RBI	BB	K	SB	CS	AVG/OBP/SLG	DRC+	BABIP	BRR	FRAA	WARP
2019	SRR	WIN	21	97	10	2	0	0	7	12	13	3	0	.229/.340/.253		.271			
2019	HFD	AA	21	394	37	23	1	10	53	32	68	2	1	.252/.313/.408	112	.281	-2.4	3B(63) -2.3, 1B(27) 1.9	1.3
2021	SPO	A+	23	35	5	1	0	3	7	2	10	0	0	.194/.257/.516	101	.158		3B(5) -0.8	0.0
2021	ABQ	AAA	23	98	13	5	1	3	18	12	20	0	0	.286/.378/.476	101	.339	0.8	3B(14) -0.8, 1B(6) 0.8	0.4
2021	COL	MLB	23	40	7	1	0	0	2	3	11	0	0	.189/.250/.216	84	.269	-0.4	3B(5) -0.5, 1B(2) 0.1	0.0
2022 DC	*COL*	*MLB*	*24*	*258*	*26*	*11*	*0*	*5*	*28*	*20*	*52*	*1*	*1*	*.235/.302/.366*	*77*	*.281*	*-0.3*	*3B -1, 1B 1*	*-0.1*

Comparables: Neil Walker, Renato Núñez, Miguel Andújar

Welker missed most of the 2021 season while serving an 80-game suspension for testing positive for a performance-enhancing drug, but he hit well enough in Triple-A after his return to earn a late-season promotion to Colorado. Welker swings incredibly hard and tries to lift and pull a bit too much. He can hit absolute lasers when he gets something in the zone, but he is vulnerable to swinging over soft stuff down and struggles to adjust to offspeed generally. Welker has spent time at both corners, but his arm and range aren't ideal for third. If he can rein in some of the violence in his swing, he could serve as a useful corner bench bat against lefties, but that's a very precarious roster spot in modern baseball.

Top Talents 25 and Under (as of 4/1/2022):

1. Zac Veen, OF
2. Brendan Rodgers, IF
3. Benny Montgomery, OF
4. Ezequiel Tovar, SS
5. Drew Romo, C
6. Jaden Hill, RHP
7. Adael Amador, SS
8. Ryan Rolison, LHP
9. Elehuris Montero, IF
10. Michael Toglia, 1B

Rockies fans reading this book know the frustrating truth about the big-league club: the overall trajectory of the franchise is far worse than their 2021 record suggested. The names on the list above point to the root of the issue: much of what kept the Rockies from being a 90-loss team last year was competent play by aging or departing veterans. At the winter's outset, Rodgers and righty Peter Lambert were the lone members of the 40-man roster no longer prospect eligible yet still under the age of 26.

Gracing the top of these lists for years, Rodgers put together a respectable season, at last, posting average offensive numbers on a high-contact, high-grounder, low-walk profile that was enough for encouragement and concern. However, the next stolen base attempt Rodgers makes in the majors will be his first, a reminder that, despite decent glovework, his destiny will be determined at the dish. The force of Rodgers's contact promises that an above-average bat will bloom, and Trevor Story's departure clears a path to full-time shortstop reps, but at the cost of Trevor Story.

Lambert's return to big-league action in 2021 wasn't impressive statistically, but it was encouraging after Tommy John surgery erased his 2020 and nearly all of last year, as well. His velocity was back, sitting 93–94 in his shortened outings, and he'll compete for a rotation spot in Colorado this year. Back in 2019, Lambert struggled immensely to miss bats, posting a 121 DRA– and a ghastly 13.6 percent strikeout rate, but his changeup is indeed a plus pitch. Lambert used it much more frequently in his late-season cameo, a glimmer of hope that the Rockies are adapting.

There is plenty of promise in this prospect list, but Colorado's current depth chart is a consortium of 27- to 30-year-olds that the club spent years waiting to see realize their potential. Not enough broke through from that wave. Perhaps this coming batch will find greater provenance, but with mostly the same decision makers at the helm, skepticism feels warranted.

Detroit Tigers

The State of the System:

Do you want to know the terrifying truth about the Tigers' system after years of rebuilding, or do you want to see Torkelson and Greene sock some dingers?

The Top Ten:

1 Spencer Torkelson 3B/1B OFP: 70 ETA: 2022

Born: 08/26/99 Age: 22 Bats: R Throws: R Height: 6'1" Weight: 220 lb. Origin: Round 1, 2020 Draft (#1 overall)

YEAR	TEAM	LVL	AGE	PA	R	2B	3B	HR	RBI	BB	K	SB	CS	AVG/OBP/SLG	DRC+	BABIP	BRR	FRAA	WARP
2021	WM	A+	21	141	21	11	1	5	28	24	28	3	2	.312/.440/.569	128	.363	0.4	3B(16) -0.1, 1B(15) 0.0	0.9
2021	ERI	AA	21	212	33	10	0	14	36	30	50	1	1	.263/.373/.560	139	.278	-0.5	3B(27) -1.5, 1B(23) 0.0	1.4
2021	TOL	AAA	21	177	35	8	1	11	27	23	36	1	0	.238/.350/.531	120	.233	-0.1	1B(37) -1.0	0.7
2022 DC	*DET*	*MLB*	*22*	*496*	*59*	*20*	*2*	*17*	*58*	*53*	*119*	*2*	*1*	*.232/.323/.411*	*103*	*.276*	*-0.4*	*1B 1*	*1.3*

Comparables: Miguel Andújar, Brandon Drury, Jeimer Candelario

The Report: Diehard Tiger fans might have gotten a little nervous about their top prospect after reading tepid reports out of the 2020 alternate site and seeing his cold start to 2021, but those fears vanished when Torkelson's bat came alive as the weather warmed last year. By the end of the season, he had slugged 30 home runs across three levels, cementing himself as one of the top prospects in baseball. Defensively, he played an adequate third base, but Detroit has signaled that the hot-corner experiment is likely over, and a permanent move to first is imminent. He'll be fine there, maybe even a little bit better than that, but it really doesn't matter. The easy power is double-plus, generated by physical strength and a quick bat. It's not just batting-practice pop, it plays in-game to all fields with his patient approach and ability to control the zone. Torkelson is the best power-hitting prospect in the game and should be a middle-of-the-order masher in Detroit very soon.

OFP: 70 / Perennial All-Star, impact bat

Variance: Medium. The power is for real, but there is the chance that the contact rate falters against big-league pitching.

Mark Barry's Fantasy Take: Remember when we were collectively nervous about Torkelson's slow start? We're idiots. Collectively. Anyway, I'm not sure there's anything more I can tell you about Tork. He might be the best hitter in the minors, he is a ready-made 30-plus-homer bat, and he'll probably hit for average, too.

Eyewitness Report: Spencer Torkelson

Evaluator: Nathan Graham
Report Date: 07/14/2021
Dates Seen: 5/5/21
Risk Factor: Medium
Physical/Health: Extra-large frame, athletic with a thick lower half, physically mature.

Tool	Future Grade	Report
Hit	60	Balanced, slightly open stance; quiet, easy swing; Excellent feel for the barrel, hits the ball hard to all fields; Patient hitter who commands the zone well, recognizes spin and has the ability to make adjustments at the plate.
Power	70	Easy, double-plus raw power generated by bat speed and physical strength. Has some natural loft in his swing path, ball jumps off of the bat; Gets to it easy in-game to all fields and does not need to sell out for power.
Baserunning/ Speed	40	Current average raw speed, will play below average as he matures; Solid baserunner with good instincts.
Glove	50	Better glove than what he's given credit for, will be able to handle either corner infield position playing average defense at third and above-average at first; Shows good instincts in the field with a quick first step, lacks lateral quickness but charges well and shows soft hands when fielding.
Arm	50	Arm is strong and accurate enough to play as average from the left side of the diamond.

Conclusion: Wherever Torkelson lands defensively it doesn't matter, the bat is going to play at a high level. His combination of contact and near elite power will make him a constant middle of the order run producer in a major league lineup.

2 Riley Greene OF OFP: 70 ETA: 2022

Born: 09/28/00 Age: 21 Bats: L Throws: L Height: 6'3" Weight: 200 lb. Origin: Round 1, 2019 Draft (#5 overall)

YEAR	TEAM	LVL	AGE	PA	R	2B	3B	HR	RBI	BB	K	SB	CS	AVG/OBP/SLG	DRC+	BABIP	BRR	FRAA	WARP
2019	TIW	ROK	18	43	9	3	0	2	8	5	12	0	0	.351/.442/.595		.478			
2019	CON	SS	18	100	12	3	1	1	7	11	25	1	0	.295/.380/.386		.403			
2019	WM	A	18	108	13	2	2	2	13	6	26	4	0	.219/.278/.344	87	.268	1.1	CF(20) 1.4, RF(4) -0.1	0.4
2021	ERI	AA	20	373	59	16	5	16	54	41	102	12	1	.298/.381/.525	112	.386	1.8	CF(73) 5.6, RF(6) -0.5, LF(5) -1.0	2.4
2021	TOL	AAA	20	185	36	9	3	8	30	22	51	4	0	.308/.400/.553	105	.406	1.5	RF(15) -0.0, LF(13) -1.7, CF(13) -0.8	0.6
2022 DC	*DET*	*MLB*	*21*	*130*	*14*	*4*	*2*	*3*	*13*	*10*	*38*	*1*	*1*	*.234/.307/.395*	*87*	*.320*	*0.3*	*LF -1*	*0.1*

Comparables: Andrew McCutchen, Ronald Acuña Jr., Jay Bruce

The Report: Greene more than confirmed strong alternate-site and instructs reports from 2020 by hitting .300 with power in the upper minors. He has reshaped his body since his post-draft summer, adding 20-or-so pounds of good weight without losing any of his twitch or straight-line speed. We suspect there's more physical development to come, which might bleed enough of his presently solid-average speed to slide him from center field to left field—but he's a fearless defender with enough closing speed to handle the more premium defensive spot, for now.

If and when he does slide to a corner, the bat will play there. Greene doesn't have the prettiest left-handed swing you'll ever see. His hands still drift and load late, and the swing is muscled up, but he knows which pitches he can uncoil against and has turned his plus raw power into plus game power; he could end up regularly socking 30-plus bombs further down the line. It's not an impact hit tool, as we expect swing-and-miss against premium velocity will be an occasional issue in the majors, but, given his approach and ability to cover the high strike and drive the ball the other way, it should be a 55 or so. That should be more than enough to keep Greene's bat in the middle of the Tigers' lineup.

OFP: 70 / All-Star outfielder

Variance: Medium. There's some hit-tool risk, and, if he slides to left field, he might be more of a good everyday guy than a star.

Mark Barry's Fantasy Take: If you wanted to call Greene the best dynasty prospect in this system, I wouldn't argue with you too much. The strikeouts could keep him from matching Torkelson in the batting-average category, but Greene offers enough on the bases to make up for it. At a certain point, we're picking nits on these premium prospects, so make no mistake, both Greene and Torkelson are top-five prospects for dynasty.

3 Jackson Jobe RHP OFP: 60 ETA: 2025

Born: 07/30/02 Age: 19 Bats: R Throws: R Height: 6'2" Weight: 190 lb. Origin: Round 1, 2021 Draft (#3 overall)

The Report: In the span of a year, Jobe went from notable shortstop prospect to the best prep arm in the draft. You were certainly drafting him with the idea that his inexperience on the mound could lead to greater projection down the road than your typical, highly-ranked high-school pitcher, but Jobe already has the kind of stuff that gets you taken in the top five, regardless. He shows a mid-90s fastball and an advanced, high-spin slider that could get to plus-plus—and, if you told us it ends up elite, we would not be shocked. Jobe's not the most projectable of arms, but with the present arsenal, it's not like he needs to add much. Well, a changeup down the line, but that applies to almost every highly-ranked high-school pitcher.

OFP: 60 / Mid-rotation starter

Variance: High. Jobe has yet to throw a pro pitch, has limited mound experience even considering that, and he will likely need to expand his arsenal to stay a starter. He also might be one of the top pitching prospects in baseball at this time next year.

Mark Barry's Fantasy Take: There's a pretty large gulf between the top-two dudes in this system and everyone else. There's also a pretty large gulf between Jobe's ceiling and floor. The skills are tantalizing enough to keep him in the mix for the back-end of the top 101, even though all of the caveats related to inexperienced pitchers still apply. The fastball/slider combo is enough to warrant a pick in the top 10–12 of most first-year player drafts, or a spot on the watchlist with a finger hovered over the add button.

4 Dillon Dingler C OFP: 55 ETA: 2023

Born: 09/17/98 Age: 23 Bats: R Throws: R Height: 6'3" Weight: 210 lb. Origin: Round 2, 2020 Draft (#38 overall)

YEAR	TEAM	LVL	AGE	PA	R	2B	3B	HR	RBI	BB	K	SB	CS	AVG/OBP/SLG	DRC+	BABIP	BRR	FRAA	WARP
2021	WM	A+	22	141	25	6	1	8	24	13	36	0	0	.287/.376/.549	127	.342	2.1	C(24) 4.8	1.5
2021	ERI	AA	22	208	24	3	3	4	20	9	62	1	0	.202/.264/.314	82	.272	-0.3	C(40) 5.5	0.8
2022 non-DC	*DET*	*MLB*	*23*	*251*	*21*	*9*	*1*	*5*	*23*	*14*	*74*	*0*	*0*	*.211/.271/.332*	*62*	*.289*	*-0.1*	*C 1*	*0.1*

Comparables: Danny Jansen, Devin Mesoraco, Francisco Cervelli

The Report: We received multiple positive reports on Dingler last year out of the alternate site, raving about his makeup and all-around game, so it came as no surprise when he got off to a hot start at High-A West Michigan last year. Slashing .287/.376/.549 and playing strong defense behind the plate, he looked like a future stalwart of the Detroit lineup. His first taste of adversity at the professional level occurred after an aggressive late-season promotion to Double-A, where he struggled to make consistent contact and was sidelined with a fractured finger.

Despite the setbacks, there are still plenty of positives in Dingler's profile. The bat is not nearly as bad as his stat line in Erie. In our early-season live looks, he showed a solid approach and the ability to hit the ball hard to all fields. There is always going to be some swing-and-miss, which will limit his plus raw power, but he should be able to eventually get to 20–25 home runs annually. Defensively, he is currently where you would expect a young, inexperienced catcher to be. There's plenty of work to be done in terms of framing and game-calling, but Dingler is a premium athlete with an excellent throwing arm. With experience, he should become an above-average backstop.

OFP: 55 / First-division catcher

Variance: Medium. We need to see the bat perform against advanced pitching before he can be crowned the future everyday catcher in the Motor City, but his defensive ability provides a high floor.

Mark Barry's Fantasy Take: I'm admittedly softening a little on my aversion to fantasy backstops, as this does seem to be the golden age of dynasty prospects behind the dish. Dingler isn't really an elite option offensively, though, when compared to some of his peers at the position. I don't think you need to waste a roster spot with him until he makes it to Detroit and starts producing–especially in one—catcher leagues.

5 Ty Madden RHP OFP: 55 ETA: 2023-ish

Born: 02/21/00 Age: 22 Bats: R Throws: R Height: 6'3" Weight: 215 lb. Origin: Round 1, 2021 Draft (#32 overall)

The Report: The workhorse of a University of Texas team that made it all the way to Omaha, Madden attacks hitters with a mid-90s fastball and then puts them away with a mid-80s slider. It's a very simple approach, but his fastball velocity and command can waver, and the pitch can play down a bit because of that. The slider is more plus-flashing than true plus, but should get there. A 6–6 pitch profile is fine but not special nowadays, and Madden will need a third pitch—he throws an occasional curve and very occasional changeup, as well—and/or better command to stick in a rotation. He certainly looks the part of a mid- or back-of-the-rotation innings eater—and he has proven generally durable—but, even as we expand the definition of who can start in the majors, Madden currently doesn't look like an ideal fit.

OFP: 55 / No. 3–4 starter or late-inning reliever

Variance: Medium. The advanced, two-pitch mix should lead to the same kind of dominance in the low—and perhaps even upper—minors that Madden showed in the Big 12, but he will need to add to his arsenal to get all the way up the ladder as a starter.

Mark Barry's Fantasy Take: You don't really need to wait around to find out whether a guy can turn into a back-end starter or a reliever. If Madden pops, BOOM! (RIP to the legend), scoop him up. Otherwise, the profile is fantasy nondescript.

6 Ryan Kreidler SS OFP: 50 ETA: 2022

Born: 11/12/97 Age: 24 Bats: R Throws: R Height: 6'4" Weight: 208 lb. Origin: Round 4, 2019 Draft (#112 overall)

YEAR	TEAM	LVL	AGE	PA	R	2B	3B	HR	RBI	BB	K	SB	CS	AVG/OBP/SLG	DRC+	BABIP	BRR	FRAA	WARP
2019	CON	SS	21	257	28	13	4	2	20	20	61	9	4	.232/.307/.351		.304			
2021	ERI	AA	23	388	67	15	0	15	36	32	119	10	4	.256/.325/.429	96	.341	3.2	SS(88) -4.1	0.9
2021	TOL	AAA	23	162	28	8	0	7	22	24	39	5	2	.304/.407/.519	108	.374	2.4	SS(35) -1.4, 3B(7) -0.6	0.7
2022 non-DC	*DET*	*MLB*	*24*	*251*	*24*	*10*	*0*	*6*	*25*	*20*	*80*	*4*	*2*	*.222/.293/.353*	*73*	*.313*	*0.2*	*SS -1, 3B 0*	*0.0*

Comparables: Danny Espinosa, Jed Lowrie, Tommy Edman

The Report: After a prolonged slump to start 2021, Kreidler was almost as good at the plate as Torkelson and Greene and was promoted alongside them to Triple-A, where he kept on mashing. Despite the slugging numbers last season, Kreidler really isn't looking to launch it over the fence. He's very short to the ball, and while he generates more carry than you'd expect, his contact profile isn't particularly noteworthy. There's probably a way to unlock more game power at the highest level—he's at least as big and strong as Greene—but his current swing means the game power likely plays in the average range, at best. The swing itself can be a bit stiff with fringe barrel control, limiting the hit tool to average, as well, although Kreidler has a solid-enough approach.

The average offensive tools would be fine if Kreidler was a little bit better at the six. He can handle shortstop a couple times a week, but lacks the first-step read and quickness to be a clear everyday option. His throwing can be a little scattershot, as well. Kreidler has average arm strength, but he likes a sidearm slot, which can lead to throws tailing and suboptimal carry. His hands and actions are both fine, and he should be able to handle all three infield spots with second base being his best fit.

OFP: 50 / Average second baseman or good fifth infielder

Variance: Low. Kreidler is major league ready, but the defensive and offensive tools may end up a little short for a clear everyday role.

Mark Barry's Fantasy Take: The best-case scenario for Kreidler is that he can be next in line for the Chris Taylor Award for multi-positional, Swiss Army–knife excellence, previously named for Ben Zobrist and also held by Chris Davis the outfielder, nay, first baseman (shout out to the positional series, coming soon to a Baseball Prospectus near you). Flexibility is valuable, so if you want to use a churn spot on a guy like Kreidler due to his production and proximity, that's completely reasonable.

7 Joey Wentz LHP OFP: 50 ETA: Late 2022/Early 2023

Born: 10/06/97 Age: 24 Bats: L Throws: L Height: 6'5" Weight: 220 lb. Origin: Round 1, 2016 Draft (#40 overall)

YEAR	TEAM	LVL	AGE	W	L	SV	G	GS	IP	H	HR	BB/9	K/9	K	GB%	BABIP	WHIP	ERA	DRA-	WARP
2019	ERI	AA	21	2	0	0	5	5	25^{2}	20	3	1.4	13.0	37	19.3%	.315	0.94	2.10	74	0.5
2019	MIS	AA	21	5	8	0	20	20	103	90	13	3.9	8.7	100	32.6%	.283	1.31	4.72	139	-1.5
2021	LAK	A	23	0	3	0	5	5	18^{2}	23	5	3.9	11.6	24	34.6%	.383	1.66	6.75	110	0.1
2021	ERI	AA	23	0	4	0	13	13	53^{1}	41	7	5.6	9.8	58	33.3%	.256	1.39	3.71	109	0.2
2022 DC	*DET*	*MLB*	*24*	*2*	*2*	*0*	*8*	*8*	*34.7*	*35*	*5*	*5.4*	*8.8*	*34*	*50.7%*	*.299*	*1.61*	*5.76*	*132*	*-0.3*

Comparables: Pedro Payano, Scott Elarton, Adalberto Mejía

The Report: It has been a few years now since Wentz was a Top-101 name. His command backslid while he was still with Atlanta, and then he had Tommy John surgery shortly after the trade to Detroit for Shane Green at the 2019 deadline. Wentz got back on the mound in May of last year, 14 months post-surgery, and you can view 2021 as mostly a rehab year. His fastball still sits mostly low 90s, still utilizing a short arm stroke and nearly over-the-top slot. Wentz's fastball has good vertical action, but his command was fringy last year, although that is not uncommon post-TJ. The changeup is his best secondary, at present, showing hard split/sink action in the low 80s, but it is inconsistent enough for us to eschew a plus projection, for now. The curve, which was the party piece when Wentz was an amateur prospect, still looks the part, with a pretty 1–7 shape, but it sits in the mid-to-upper 70s and lacks bat-missing snap. Wentz throws a slider more nowadays, but that also can tend to roll in there and doesn't have the kind of depth that will miss bats, either. He has been a long-time Prospect Team favorite, and it's tricky to evaluate him this soon after elbow surgery, but he looks like a polished lefty with a collection of four pitches, each a half-grade off average either way, and not quite enough command to make it all play up.

OFP: 50 / No. 4 starter

Variance: Medium. Maybe there's still a bit more to come for the 23-year-old as he gets further away from Tommy John surgery, but the early returns are more or less in line with the pre-injury looks that suggested a back-of-the-rotation starter.

Mark Barry's Fantasy Take: If you're in the middle of your contention window, Wentz is more interesting than Madden for fantasy purposes. The lefty is closer to the big leagues and already has a starter's arsenal. His ceiling is considerably lower than Madden's, but he could eat innings as soon as 2022, and there's room for rate improvements the farther he gets from TJS.

8 Colt Keith 3B/2B OFP: 50 ETA: 2024

Born: 08/14/01 Age: 20 Bats: L Throws: R Height: 6'3" Weight: 211 lb. Origin: Round 5, 2020 Draft (#132 overall)

YEAR	TEAM	LVL	AGE	PA	R	2B	3B	HR	RBI	BB	K	SB	CS	AVG/OBP/SLG	DRC+	BABIP	BRR	FRAA	WARP
2021	LAK	A	19	181	32	6	3	1	21	30	39	4	1	.320/.436/.422	117	.422	1.4	3B(27) 3.3, 2B(14) -1.3	1.2
2021	WM	A+	19	76	7	1	1	1	6	8	27	0	0	.162/.250/.250	80	.250	0.9	3B(15) 1.1, 2B(2) -0.4	0.2
2022 non-DC	*DET*	*MLB*	*20*	*251*	*20*	*9*	*1*	*2*	*19*	*23*	*70*	*1*	*1*	*.211/.290/.301*	*62*	*.297*	*0.0*	*3B 1, 2B -1*	*-0.4*

Comparables: Blake DeWitt, Mat Gamel, Joey Gallo

The Report: The 19-year-old Keith made fairly quick work of the complex and Low-A levels in 2021 before looking a little overmatched while finishing the year in the former Midwest League. Keith utilizes a fairly big leg kick and swings hard, generating potentially average power from his strong wrists and forearms. He didn't show much game power last season, but he was often just trying to stay afloat and make contact against older and more experienced pitching. He also needs to add some upper-body strength, but that should come in his twenties, and he certainly has a frame that could add some good weight.

Keith is a perfectly fine third baseman with an easy-plus arm and has seen some time at second, as well. He is an average runner, at present, and should be rangy enough for the keystone. There isn't necessarily going to be a standout tool here, but Keith has an advanced bat for a recent prep draftee and should grow into a well-rounded two-way infielder.

OFP: 50 / Average third baseman

Variance: High. A day-two prep bat having that kind of success in full-season ball is encouraging, but Keith will need to tap into more power and continue to hit up the ladder.

Mark Barry's Fantasy Take: You might be surprised to hear that Colt Keith is indeed a third baseman in the Tigers' organization and not the quarterbacks coach for a high school in south Texas. Where was I? Right. Keith was impressive in his debut as a teen, but fantasy managers don't really need to pay attention until Keith shows some (read: any) power.

9 Roberto Campos OF OFP: 50 ETA: 2025/2026

Born: 06/14/03 Age: 19 Bats: R Throws: R Height: 6'3" Weight: 200 lb. Origin: International Free Agent, 2019

YEAR	TEAM	LVL	AGE	PA	R	2B	3B	HR	RBI	BB	K	SB	CS	AVG/OBP/SLG	DRC+	BABIP	BRR	FRAA	WARP
2021	TIGW	ROK	18	155	20	5	0	8	19	17	41	3	0	.228/.316/.441		.261			

Comparables: Jose Pena, Jesus Marriaga, Jean Montero

The Report: Campos looks like a major leaguer already, which is good and bad. He has the physique of an NFL linebacker with raw power that not many in the organization can match. His swing produces loud contact; even when he doesn't fully square up a ball, it "stays hit." His swing is often stiff, and he is often looking to do damage in the air, which leads to a higher-than-comfortable amount of swing-and-miss and weak contact. A 26.5-percent K rate in complex ball isn't ideal and leads to concerns about the quality of adjustments he can make in the future.

Defensively, he is a good athlete and does not look out of place playing center field, but lacks the ideal range and foot speed to cover the space. His profile fits better in right, where his plus arm will profile well.

OFP: 50 / Average right fielder

Variance: Extreme. Campos is extremely aggressive at a young age, which can torpedo the overall approach. He's unlikely to be a center fielder, which will put more pressure on his bat to lead the way.

Mark Barry's Fantasy Take: Boom or Bust (actually, I hate the "bust" term, let's just say boom or not-boom) would be an appropriate category for Campos. Dude has big power and a decent knack for working walks at the dish. Still, he struck out a shade under 30 percent of the time in Rookie ball, which is not ideal. He could be a three-true-outcome guy, which is useful, but Campos isn't a guy you need to rush out to add without seeing some sort of improvement.

10 Wilmer Flores RHP OFP: 50 ETA: 2024/2025

Born: 02/20/01 Age: 21 Bats: R Throws: R Height: 6'4" Weight: 225 lb. Origin: International Free Agent, 2020

YEAR	TEAM	LVL	AGE	W	L	SV	G	GS	IP	H	HR	BB/9	K/9	K	GB%	BABIP	WHIP	ERA	DRA-	WARP
2021	TIGW	ROK	20	2	1	0	3	2	13	15	0	1.4	12.5	18	58.8%	.441	1.31	4.85		
2021	LAK	A	20	4	3	0	11	11	53	47	1	3.7	12.2	72	52.4%	.368	1.30	3.40	99	0.6
2022 non-DC	*DET*	*MLB*	*21*	*2*	*3*	*0*	*57*	*0*	*50*	*51*	*6*	*5.1*	*8.4*	*46*	*39.9%*	*.310*	*1.60*	*5.74*	*127*	*-0.5*

The Report:A decade junior to his brother, the Mets cult hero and current Giants platoon bat, the youngest of the Wilmers Flores—their father and another brother share the first name—is a power righty that spent most of 2021 in A-ball. He works primarily off a high-spin heater that runs up to 96, or so, and pairs it with a 12–6 curve with above-average potential. He's already larger than his big-league brother, and his mechanics suggest the bullpen might be his long-term home. But there's enough potential in the cutter and change that round out his arsenal to keep Flores stretched out a bit longer.

OFP: 50 / No. 4 starter or set-up arm

Variance: High. Flores is relatively inexperienced in pro ball and has reliever markers throughout his profile.

Mark Barry's Fantasy Take: It might be fun to pick up Wilmer Flores and then trade him for Wilmer Flores. Or to team the brothers together and collect all of the Wilmers Flores, as if they're infinity stones. Then maybe snag the brothers Rougned Odor and mortgage the farm for a trio of Wanders Franco. Then you can call your team the Family Tree or the Bloodline or whatever. If you're not in that specific scenario, I think you can pass on this version of Wilmer Flores.

The Prospects You Meet Outside the Top Ten

Prospects on the Rise

Tanner Kohlhepp RHP Born: 05/27/99 Age: 23 Bats: L Throws: R Height: 6'3" Weight: 215 lb. Origin: Round 5, 2021 Draft (#135 overall)

A fifth-round selection out of Notre Dame, Kohlhepp spent a majority of his time at South Bend in a multi-inning relief role but should get the opportunity to start in the professional ranks. The fastball is average, but he finds success by leaning heavily on his advanced secondaries. A low arm slot helps the slider sweep out of the zone, or he can speed it up and give it the action of a cutter. Mix in an average changeup, and Kohlhepp has the stuff to keep hitters off balance.

Tyler Mattison RHP Born: 09/05/99 Age: 22 Bats: R Throws: R Height: 6'4" Weight: 235 lb. Origin: Round 4, 2021 Draft (#104 overall)

The Tigers nabbed Mattison as an under-slot signee after he dominated the Northeast Conference as the ace for Bryant University. He is a solidly built righty with a big arm who is likely to be a quick mover in the organization as a bullpen arm. You can anticipate that his fringy curve and cutter will be trimmed from his repertoire, yielding to his heavy, mid-90s fastball and above-average change. It's the type of stuff that will play up in short bursts, giving Mattison the profile of a future reliever.

Izaac Pacheco SS Born: 11/18/02 Age: 19 Bats: L Throws: R Height: 6'4" Weight: 225 lb. Origin: Round 2, 2021 Draft (#39 overall)

YEAR	TEAM	LVL	AGE	PA	R	2B	3B	HR	RBI	BB	K	SB	CS	AVG/OBP/SLG	DRC+	BABIP	BRR	FRAA	WARP
2021	TIGW	ROK	18	125	16	4	2	1	7	18	43	1	0	.226/.339/.330		.371			

Comparables: Luis Guillorme, Adrian Valerio, Nelson Molina

The club's second-rounder last July, Pacheco had some of the best raw power in the class, but concerns about his overall profile (and signing ask) pushed him to the second round. His batting practice is a pleasure to watch, as he can take the ball out to all parts of the field with relative ease at the plate. His initial introduction to pro ball was marked by a lack of adjustments and a fair amount of swing-and-miss. While he sees the ball fine, he struggled to make contact, as he would get too big and fly open. Quite large at more than 6-foot-4 and 220 pounds, he lacks the first-step quickness and range to play the six but has plenty of arm to profile at third base, where his lack of range will be less of an issue.

Factors on the Farm

Alex Faedo RHP Born: 11/12/95 Age: 26 Bats: R Throws: R Height: 6'5" Weight: 225 lb. Origin: Round 1, 2017 Draft (#18 overall)

YEAR	TEAM	LVL	AGE	W	L	SV	G	GS	IP	H	HR	BB/9	K/9	K	GB%	BABIP	WHIP	ERA	DRA-	WARP
2019	ERI	AA	23	6	7	0	22	22	115^1	104	17	2.0	10.5	134	32.5%	.299	1.12	3.90	90	1.5

Comparables: Jerad Eickhoff, Nick Pivetta, Kyle Brnovich

The second of three consecutive first-round arms taken by the Tigers during this rebuild, Faedo turned 26 this offseason and has yet to see a major-league mound. Most of that was out of his hands, as, following a serviceable 2019 season in Double-A, he tested positive for COVID-19 and then dealt with a forearm strain shortly after getting to the alternate site. That necessitated offseason Tommy John surgery that cost him all of 2021. Last we saw Faedo, he looked like a potential back-end starter, mostly on the strength of a plus slider, but we'll obviously know more when he's back on a mound in 2022.

Garrett Hill RHP Born: 01/16/96 Age: 26 Bats: R Throws: R Height: 6'0" Weight: 185 lb. Origin: Round 26, 2018 Draft (#765 overall)

YEAR	TEAM	LVL	AGE	W	L	SV	G	GS	IP	H	HR	BB/9	K/9	K	GB%	BABIP	WHIP	ERA	DRA-	WARP
2019	WM	A	23	2	1	0	7	7	38^1	19	0	3.1	9.9	42	43.5%	.207	0.83	1.41	110	0.1
2019	LAK	A+	23	6	6	0	16	16	85^2	53	3	3.6	9.1	87	37.3%	.243	1.02	2.63	97	1.1
2021	WM	A+	25	3	0	0	13	13	56	47	2	2.9	11.4	71	42.8%	.319	1.16	2.57	79	1.2
2021	ERI	AA	25	3	1	0	4	4	19^2	15	1	4.6	12.8	28	53.3%	.326	1.27	3.20	89	0.3
2022 non-DC	*DET*	*MLB*	*26*	*2*	*2*	*0*	*57*	*0*	*50*	*47*	*6*	*4.3*	*8.6*	*47*	*33.8%*	*.295*	*1.44*	*4.63*	*109*	*-0.1*

A 26th-round redshirt junior out of San Diego State, Hill is a shorter, physically maxed righty that sits in the low 90s. That's a series of descriptors that do not usually portend prospect status, even after a fine season between High-A, Double-A and the Arizona Fall League. But Hill has some arm-side run and sink on the fastball that keeps it off the fat part of the lumber and allows him to get some groundballs early in counts. It also allows him to set up his above-average changeup, which will flash Wiffle-ball-like sink and fade. He's willing to throw the change to both lefties and righties, in part because his right-on-right breaking ball options aren't ideal—a short, slurvy slider and a mid-70s curve with a little bit of depth. Hill throws strikes with everything, though, and has enough command to project as a potential back-end starter or swingman as soon as 2022.

Reese Olson RHP Born: 07/31/99 Age: 22 Bats: R Throws: R Height: 6'1" Weight: 160 lb. Origin: Round 13, 2018 Draft (#395 overall)

YEAR	TEAM	LVL	AGE	W	L	SV	G	GS	IP	H	HR	BB/9	K/9	K	GB%	BABIP	WHIP	ERA	DRA-	WARP
2019	WIS	A	19	4	7	0	27	14	94^2	104	8	4.5	8.0	84	47.2%	.343	1.60	4.66	123	-0.4
2021	WM	A+	21	1	0	0	2	2	11	6	0	1.6	11.5	14	44.0%	.240	0.73	0.00	87	0.2
2021	WIS	A+	21	5	4	0	14	14	69	58	5	4.6	10.3	79	43.4%	.312	1.35	4.30	88	1.2
2021	ERI	AA	21	2	1	0	5	5	24^2	18	1	5.1	7.7	21	49.3%	.250	1.30	4.74	110	0.1
2022 non-DC	*DET*	*MLB*	*22*	*2*	*3*	*0*	*57*	*0*	*50*	*52*	*7*	*5.6*	*7.7*	*43*	*39.2%*	*.308*	*1.68*	*5.90*	*130*	*-0.6*

Comparables: Shawn Chacon, Tony Saunders, Kyle Drabek

Top Talents 25 and Under (as of 4/1/2022):

1. Spencer Torkelson, 1B/3B
2. Riley Greene, OF
3. Casey Mize, RHP
4. Jackson Jobe, RHP
5. Tarik Skubal, LHP
6. Dillon Dingler, C
7. Matt Manning, RHP
8. Akil Baddoo, OF
9. Ty Madden, RHP
10. Ryan Kreidler, SS

While the Tigers have wallowed for half a decade in a mire, arguably obfuscated from its true depths by the fact that their division has been MLB's weakest since their rebuild began, 2021 was an undeniable stride in the right direction. This winter, the club has made further improvements and investments that put the Tigers in position to hunt the playoffs once more—at least if things go well with their many young cogs. As they've seen in the stalled progression of former high-profile prospects like Isaac Paredes and Daz Cameron, however, that's no guarantee.

While Tork and Greene should arrive soon to spark the still-woeful offense, the rotation is where Detroit should be seeing some stability. Mize was the closest to that in 2021, making 30 starts, albeit at an understandably cautious innings pace given both his history and the wonkiness of 2020. His 3.71 ERA belies a more uneven 5.03 DRA (108 DRA–), but there were tweaks and improvements that Mize appeared to make over the season, including refinements to his slider. Even for a pitcher who can get grounders at will when his splitter is working, however, Mize must find a way to miss bats more often.

The inverted image of Mize, in many ways, was Skubal, a sturdy southpaw whose high-spin four-seam fastball is a prototypical bat-misser at the top of the zone. Unfortunately, it is also a prototypical barrel-finder literally anywhere else in the zone. Among pitchers with at least 140 innings pitched last year, only Jordan Lyles and Patrick Corbin yielded more home runs than Skubal's 35, and he barely trailed the two despite facing more than 115 fewer batters than each. Skubal was, in essence, a three-true-outcomes pitcher, but, aesthetics be damned, two-thirds of the TTO trichotomy favor hitters. The upshot for the lefty is he has several pitches with bat-missing traits, but improved control needs to be the focus to avoid giving up so many Skuby Snacks.

Then there's Manning, whose challenging 2021 highlighted long-standing concerns about his arsenal. The 6-foot-6 righty turned 24 in January, so he has plenty of time to refine aspects of his skill set, but little of what he showed in his first 18 big-league games resembled a workable starter's repertoire. He sat 93–94 with his four-seamer as the primary offering, but the pitch spins less than the changeups of many pitchers, undermining its effectiveness at the top of the zone. None of his secondaries seemed to pick up the slack, either, as he ran a staggeringly poor 14.8 percent strikeout rate with a sub-10-percent swinging-strike rate on all five of his pitches. He missed spots repeatedly, setting up shop with all his offerings in a glitzy plaza right on the heart of the plate, and big-league hitters bought big. He's far from the first minors-shredding pitcher to hit a roadblock that can be overcome with experience and refinement, but there's a great deal currently separating him from being an effective MLB starter.

Houston Astros

The State of the System:

The lack of high draft picks continues to catch up with Houston, and 2021 brought a spate of significant injuries, as well.

The Top Ten:

1 **Jeremy Peña SS** OFP: 70 ETA: 2022
Born: 09/22/97 Age: 24 Bats: R Throws: R Height: 6'0" Weight: 202 lb. Origin: Round 3, 2018 Draft (#102 overall)

YEAR	TEAM	LVL	AGE	PA	R	2B	3B	HR	RBI	BB	K	SB	CS	AVG/OBP/SLG	DRC+	BABIP	BRR	FRAA	WARP
2019	PEJ	WIN	21	101	11	5	1	1	10	6	35	2	1	.183/.248/.290		.281			
2019	QC	A	21	289	44	8	4	5	41	35	57	17	6	.293/.389/.421	121	.357	3.3	SS(60) -1.7, 2B(2) -0.3	1.8
2019	FAY	A+	21	185	28	13	3	2	13	12	33	3	4	.317/.378/.467	108	.383	1.6	SS(29) -0.7, 2B(11) 0.2, 3B(1) -0.0	0.7
2020	EST	WIN	22	129	18	2	2	3	9	7	23	7	0	.306/.349/.430		.358			
2021	EST	WIN	23	134	18	6	1	2	15	11	32	7	2	.291/.364/.410		.381			
2021	AST	ROK	23	27	3	1	1	0	2	2	6	1	0	.348/.444/.478		.471			
2021	SUG	AAA	23	133	22	4	2	10	19	6	35	5	1	.287/.346/.598	106	.325	1.1	SS(25) 2.2, 3B(2) 0.0	0.8
2022 DC	*HOU*	*MLB*	*24*	*470*	*67*	*17*	*3*	*13*	*60*	*31*	*135*	*9*	*5*	*.236/.301/.386*	*85*	*.312*	*0.9*	*SS -1*	*0.9*

Comparables: Erik González, Zach Walters, Pat Valaika

The Report: Peña might not be the reason Carlos Correa is gone, but it is easier to sell Correa's departure when there's a replacement this good on the horizon. We've been high on Peña as a plus-plus defensive infielder with strong bat-to-ball skills and approach since 2019. He wasn't invited to the alternate site until late in 2020 due to Houston's veteran-heavy approach, but we received strong reports on him in instructs and out of winter ball that suggested a breakout might be coming.

Then Peña suffered a poorly-timed wrist injury that cost him most of 2021. But a funny thing happened after he came back: he started driving the ball for real over-the-fence power, not just gap power anymore. We honestly didn't see that coming, and we're still not sure it's sustainable, but the idea that Peña might add that tool to his kit . . . it's tantalizing, to say the least. With everything else accounted for, if he's even a consistent 20-homer bat, he's a star, and we think that's at least a 50/50 proposition now.

OFP: 70 / Makes All-Star Games but probably isn't *quite* as good as Correa

Variance: Medium. Peña has only hit for power very recently, and he did just miss most of last season with an injury. On the other hand, there's a decent shot he's up by May Day, and his defense and feel for the barrel provide a high floor.

Mark Barry's Fantasy Take: You guys aren't gonna believe this, but sometimes prospect development isn't linear. I know, I know, I'll give y'all a moment to digest that one. Old adages aside, we didn't think much of Peña over the last handful of lists, at least for fantasy purposes. Great glove and some speed? Fine, but perhaps not must-have in terms of rosterability. Well, Peña found some pop. And now that Carlos Correa is out the door, Peña should have a chance to fill in at the six sooner rather than later. I'm still not sure if there's elite fantasy talent here, but perhaps something in the Didi Gregorius realm (with more speed, maybe less power) is a back-end top-10 shortstop outcome.

2 Korey Lee C   OFP: 55   ETA: Late 2022

Born: 07/25/98   Age: 23   Bats: R   Throws: R   Height: 6'2"   Weight: 210 lb.   Origin: Round 1, 2019 Draft (#32 overall)

YEAR	TEAM	LVL	AGE	PA	R	2B	3B	HR	RBI	BB	K	SB	CS	AVG/OBP/SLG	DRC+	BABIP	BRR	FRAA	WARP
2019	TRI	SS	20	259	31	6	4	3	28	28	49	8	5	.268/.359/.371		.328			
2021	GDD	WIN	22	71	8	2	0	1	6	9	19	1	0	.258/.352/.339		.357			
2021	ASH	A+	22	121	24	5	0	3	14	12	24	1	0	.330/.397/.459	112	.402	-0.6	C(20) -0.5, 3B(2) 0.3	0.5
2021	CC	AA	22	203	25	9	1	8	27	17	35	3	1	.254/.320/.443	116	.275	1.3	C(38) -1.6, 3B(4) -0.1, 1B(3) 0.2	1.1
2021	SUG	AAA	22	38	2	4	0	0	4	2	9	0	0	.229/.263/.343	83	.296	0.1	C(4) -0.5, 1B(2) -0.6	-0.1
2022 DC	*HOU*	*MLB*	*23*	*31*	*4*	*1*	*0*	*0*	*3*	*2*	*6*	*0*	*0*	*.239/.294/.349*	*75*	*.291*	*0.0*	*C -1*	*0.0*

Comparables: Francisco Cervelli, Yasmani Grandal, Devin Mesoraco

The Report: Lee is a solid, two-way catching prospect, and those can be a little boring to write about. His best tool is his throwing arm. Throwing has slid down the list of important catching skills over the last decade, but Lee's might be a true plus-plus cannon played up by a quick transfer that lets him consistently pop an accurate 1.8. Unsurprisingly then, Lee threw out more than 40 percent of would-be base thieves last season. The rest of his defensive skill set is fine, if not as loud. He receives better north-south than east-west and can be a little stiff trying to shift to block balls, especially out of the one-knee-down stance. But on the whole, the defensive package is at least solid-average.

At the plate, a longer swing and some bat wrap can leave him vulnerable on the outer half of the plate, but Lee has enough bat speed to turn 95 around and generally makes hard, line-drive contact. He runs pretty well for a catcher, too. The hit and power tools project to average, which, combined with the glove, makes him a perfectly cromulent starting catching prospect.

OFP: 55 / First-division catcher

Variance: Medium. There's the usual risk of offensive regression with the trials and tribulations that come with everyday work behind the plate, but Lee merely needs some consolidation time in Triple-A before he is ready for the bigs. The defensive profile should keep him employed for a while, even if the offensive tools only ended up in the 40–45 range.

Mark Barry's Fantasy Take: While having a plus-plus, laser, rocket arm is great for a backstop, for fantasy purposes that only means that Lee has a great chance to log playing time behind the dish in Houston. Aside from that, Lee is better IRL than in fantasy, as I don't know if he will hit enough to rack up meaningful counting stats.

Eyewitness Report: Korey Lee

Evaluator: Trevor Andresen

Report Date: 11/16/2021

Dates Seen: 11/8 - 11/13 (Arizona Fall League)

Risk Factor: Medium

Physical/Health: LG 6'2 210 lb. frame. Physical build. Looks the part

Tool	Future Grade	Report
Hit	40	Hits from a wide base w/ a 60/40 weight distribution on his back side. Simple swing w/ quick wrists, plus bat speed & avg bat control. Peppers line drives all over the yard in BP. Displays strong feel for the strike zone, but the pitch recognition/swing decisions are below-avg, resulting in sw/miss both in & out of the zone against spin/offspeed. Will get himself out early in counts. Refinement necessary in order to get to a .240-.250 bat
Power	50	Bat speed/frame help him generate plus raw power. Hit tool limits playability some, but still projects as a 20 HR bat
Baserunning/ Speed	40	Athleticism plays above pure speed
Glove	55	Impressive mobility behind the dish. Works from a knee, but displays strong blocking skills & ability to move laterally. Avg hands/receiving ability
Arm	60	Plus-plus raw strength, but plays down due to arm action, transfer & accuracy

Conclusion: Lee projects as a defense/power oriented regular behind the plate and should be ready to step into an everyday role by 2023

3 Pedro Leon SS OFP: 55 ETA: Late 2022/Early 2023

Born: 05/28/98 Age: 24 Bats: R Throws: R Height: 5'10" Weight: 170 lb. Origin: International Free Agent, 2021

YEAR	TEAM	LVL	AGE	PA	R	2B	3B	HR	RBI	BB	K	SB	CS	AVG/OBP/SLG	DRC+	BABIP	BRR	FRAA	WARP
2021	GDD	WIN	23	84	9	3	0	1	9	13	20	4	1	.257/.381/.343		.347			
2021	CC	AA	23	217	29	7	1	9	33	25	67	13	8	.249/.359/.443	101	.339	0.3	SS(41) -3.9, CF(9) 0.1	0.3
2021	SUG	AAA	23	75	11	2	0	0	2	14	23	4	2	.131/.293/.164	77	.211	0.2	SS(7) -0.5, 3B(6) -1.2, CF(4) 0.4	-0.1
2022 non-DC	*HOU*	*MLB*	*24*	*251*	*22*	*9*	*1*	*4*	*22*	*24*	*79*	*10*	*5*	*.192/.284/.309*	*63*	*.276*	*1.0*	*SS -3, CF 1*	*-0.4*

Comparables: José Rondón, Matt Tuiasosopo, Deven Marrero

The Report: The Astros used almost their entire bonus pool to ink Leon last winter. The 22-year-old Cuban wasn't your typical international free agent in terms of age or horizon to the bigs and spent most of 2021 in the upper minors. The acclimation back to the day-in, day-out grind after three years off was rough at times, and Leon is still adjusting to seeing better off-speed pitches. He has a patient approach and tracks spin acceptably. The biggest reason for his struggles at the plate was chasing out of the zone. When he's hunting fastballs early, Leon is direct to the ball with plus bat speed and the ability to gap plenty of doubles, even if the over-the-fence power might end up fringy. He has mostly played shortstop with some center field reps mixed in. He has the range and arm for short, but he can get a little loose with his hands. Leon might be a better fit for center—certainly a better fit for the Astros—where his plus speed and arm would be weapons. Given the time off from games, Leon has upside well past his age and 2021 performance, but there's risk in the profile, as well, until we see a bit more consistency at the plate.

OFP: 55 / Above-average regular somewhere up the middle

Variance: High. The time off muddles a lot, and there are underlying hit-tool questions.

Mark Barry's Fantasy Take: I don't really know what to do with Leon. The profile is mostly good: there's some power, some speed and high walk rates, all things that translate nicely to fantasy. But he strikes out a lot and hasn't been particularly efficient on the bases. The whiffs make me anticipate a lower batting average, and his caught-stealing tally could lead to a red light pretty quickly. He's still a top-75ish guy thanks to his proximity, pedigree and ceiling, but I sure wish he chased *a little bit* less often.

4 Forrest Whitley RHP

Born: 09/15/97 Age: 24 Bats: R Throws: R Height: 6'7" Weight: 238 lb. Origin: Round 1, 2016 Draft (#17 overall)

YEAR	TEAM	LVL	AGE	W	L	SV	G	GS	IP	H	HR	BB/9	K/9	K	GB%	BABIP	WHIP	ERA	DRA-	WARP
2019	PEJ	WIN	21	3	2	0	6	6	25	22	3	3.2	11.5	32	43.5%	.322	1.24	2.88		
2019	AST	ROK	21	0	2	0	2	2	4^1	2	0	18.7	20.8	10	50.0%	.333	2.54	8.31		
2019	FAY	A+	21	1	0	0	2	2	8^1	4	0	1.1	11.9	11	44.4%	.222	0.60	2.16	81	0.2
2019	CC	AA	21	2	2	0	6	6	22^2	18	2	7.5	14.3	36	46.7%	.372	1.63	5.56	74	0.4
2019	RR	AAA	21	0	3	0	8	5	24^1	35	9	5.5	10.7	29	30.7%	.400	2.05	12.21	111	0.0

Comparables: Arodys Vizcaíno, Amalio Diaz, Phillippe Aumont

The Report: Unless you're counting the Arizona Fall League more than you should, 2021 was the fourth-straight lost or mostly lost season for the one-time best pitching prospect in baseball. Whitley had Tommy John surgery in the spring after being off the mound for most of 2020 with ill-defined arm soreness. He started throwing in September and should be back sometime during the 2022 campaign.

When healthy and right, Whitley showed four plus-or-better pitches: a heater up to the mid-90s, a nasty diving change and two distinct breaking balls. He just hasn't been that pitcher since his suspension/injury-truncated 2018 season, and we have very little to go off as to whether or not he can regain that form. We're rooting for it, because he was a heck of a prospect not *that* long ago.

OFP: A giant dartboard

Variance: Sometimes you miss the board and shatter a window.

Mark Barry's Fantasy Take: I'm not really sure how you hang on to Whitley with any confidence. If he's on the waiver wire, you have roster space, and you're feeling lucky, well then shoot your shot. Unfortunately, dude just seems snake-bitten.

5 Hunter Brown RHP OFP: 50 ETA: 2022

Born: 08/29/98 Age: 23 Bats: R Throws: R Height: 6'2" Weight: 212 lb. Origin: Round 5, 2019 Draft (#166 overall)

YEAR	TEAM	LVL	AGE	W	L	SV	G	GS	IP	H	HR	BB/9	K/9	K	GB%	BABIP	WHIP	ERA	DRA-	WARP
2019	TRI	SS	20	2	2	0	12	6	23^2	13	0	6.8	12.5	33	52.9%	.255	1.31	4.56		
2021	CC	AA	22	1	4	1	13	11	49^1	45	6	5.3	13.9	76	45.5%	.379	1.50	4.20	96	0.4
2021	SUG	AAA	22	5	1	0	11	8	51	47	6	3.7	9.7	55	52.5%	.311	1.33	3.88	84	0.7
2022 non-DC	*HOU*	*MLB*	*23*	*2*	*2*	*0*	*57*	*0*	*50*	*46*	*6*	*4.9*	*9.4*	*52*	*41.4%*	*.302*	*1.48*	*4.55*	*106*	*0.0*

Comparables: Paul Maholm, Nick Tropeano, Casey Coleman

The Report: Welcome to the "high-slot, high-spin fastball paired with a breaking ball down" portion of the Astros' list. Settle in, we will be here a while. The Astros have had plenty of success targeting certain types and pushing certain buttons in pitching development. However, it is going to make these blurbs sound a bit repetitive. Brown's fastball sits in the average velo band as a starter, but he can grab an extra tick in short bursts, and the pitch has some good ride to it. The "breaking ball down" part of the equation is a potential plus curve around 80 mph with tight, 12-to-6 depth, but it can roll in a little lazily at the lower end of the velocity range, and that inconsistency may make it more of a 55 offering. Brown has a cutter and change, as well, with the cutter the more useful of the two looks against lefties at present, as it shows a little tilt and he can backdoor it, while the change tends to be flat. That's the outline of the 30-start/150-inning arm the Astros have leaned on heavily in recent years, but Brown's command is well below average and may only improve to the point at which he's a solid one-inning reliever.

OFP: 50 / No. 4 starter or set-up man

Variance: Medium. Brown allowed a few too many walks and homers in the upper minors last year, but Brown *was* in the upper minors.

Mark Barry's Fantasy Take: Valuing Astros hurlers presents quite the conundrum. Tossing three or four solid innings can be helpful for real teams, but it doesn't provide the volume you're counting on for your fantasy squad. Like, Lance McCullers Jr. was great in '21, but still averaged less than 5 ⅔ frames per outing. Maybe one of these guys distinguishes himself as a legit mid-rotation option in Houston (Brown is the best bet), but I don't think that chance is a great use of a roster spot.

6 Alex Santos II RHP OFP: 50 ETA: 2025

Born: 02/10/02 Age: 20 Bats: R Throws: R Height: 6'4" Weight: 194 lb. Origin: Round 2, 2020 Draft (#72 overall)

YEAR	TEAM	LVL	AGE	W	L	SV	G	GS	IP	H	HR	BB/9	K/9	K	GB%	BABIP	WHIP	ERA	DRA-	WARP
2021	FAY	A	19	2	2	1	12	7	41^2	31	2	6.5	10.4	48	26.9%	.284	1.46	3.46	114	0.0
2022 non-DC	*HOU*	*MLB*	*20*	*2*	*3*	*0*	*57*	*0*	*50*	*56*	*10*	*7.7*	*8.3*	*46*	*42.8%*	*.320*	*1.99*	*7.91*	*160*	*-1.4*

Comparables: Tyler Skaggs, Chad Gaudin, Daryl Thompson

The Report: Houston's first pick in last year's draft came in the third round. Getting Santos there was about the best they could have hoped for; the NYC prep arm had some first-round buzz at points. His fastball hasn't jumped quite yet and still sits in the low 90s, but he throws it with a spin rate that would be well above average for a major leaguer and with near-elite extension. This allows Santos to miss A-ball bats even at 92 mph or so. The main secondary pitch is a short, low-80s slider with enough tilt to get swing-and-miss when it's down in the zone, but Santos can struggle to stay on top of it and get it below the hitter's waist; it often just helicopters or rides high. The change is a bit rough at present, but for a prep arm with limited pro experience, he sells it okay and is willing to throw it against righties.

There were some concerns about Santos's frame around the draft, and while Santos is close to physically maxed, he looked more sturdy than bulky this year. His arm action can be a bit labored and stiff, dragging behind the rest of his delivery, which may account for some of his control issues in 2021. That can be smoothed out with more reps, but Santos is going to be a slow burn and will need a bit more velocity or a secondary jump to fit in a major-league rotation long-term.

OFP: 50 / No. 4 starter

Variance: High. Santos has thrown all of 40 professional innings, and, while the building blocks for a mid-rotation pitching prospect are there, he's a ways away at present.

Mark Barry's Fantasy Take: See: Brown, Hunter (above)

7 Tyler Whitaker OF

OFP: 50 ETA: 2025

Born: 08/02/02 Age: 19 Bats: R Throws: R Height: 6'4" Weight: 190 lb. Origin: Round 3, 2021 Draft (#87 overall)

YEAR	TEAM	LVL	AGE	PA	R	2B	3B	HR	RBI	BB	K	SB	CS	AVG/OBP/SLG	DRC+	BABIP	BRR	FRAA	WARP
2021	AST	ROK	18	114	16	2	1	3	6	9	40	8	1	.202/.263/.327		.290			

Comparables: Marlin Almonte, Frank Tolentino, Eudy Pina

The Report: In the final year of the draft penalties handed down by the league, the Astros again followed the familiar pattern of using their first pick on a high-ceiling prospect in an attempt to catch lightning in a bottle. Whitaker has big-time tools, especially when it comes to the power department. His swing creates natural lift and backspins the ball with ease, although it does tend to get all-or-nothing, which calls into question whether he will hit enough to tap into the game juice regularly. Solely a position player now, he did pitch often as a high schooler, and his strong arm profiles well in any of the outfield spots, where his wheels can also provide very good coverage. His tools and physical projection far exceed his third-round draft slot, but his future is dependent on how much contact he makes.

OFP: 50 / Power corner bat

Variance: High. There are so many parts of his game to really like, but the one major question mark—the hit tool—is enough to drag his stock down.

Mark Barry's Fantasy Take: Bishop Gorman High School, you say? It would certainly be nice to finally get a useful big-league outfielder from the Las Vegas high school circuit. Anyway, grabbing Whitaker for your fantasy team would follow the same thought process utilized here by the Astros: you're rolling the dice (get it? cuz Vegas?) on tools. There is big power in the stick, but so far, there's not much else. There are worse projects to gamble on (fine, I'll stop), but Whitaker is a project, nonetheless.

8 Yainer Diaz C/DH

OFP: 50 ETA: 2024

Born: 09/21/98 Age: 23 Bats: R Throws: R Height: 6'0" Weight: 195 lb. Origin: International Free Agent, 2016

YEAR	TEAM	LVL	AGE	PA	R	2B	3B	HR	RBI	BB	K	SB	CS	AVG/OBP/SLG	DRC+	BABIP	BRR	FRAA	WARP
2019	INDR	ROK	20	88	15	6	0	5	22	4	8	0	0	.451/.477/.707		.457			
2019	MV	SS	20	140	13	6	2	2	18	4	22	0	0	.274/.293/.393		.313			
2021	FAY	A	22	49	3	2	0	1	7	0	4	1	0	.229/.224/.333	115	.227	0.0	C(5) 1.3, 1B(2) 0.2	0.4
2021	LYN	A	22	258	30	19	1	5	50	15	42	1	1	.314/.357/.464	115	.361	-1.3	C(36) 1.4, 1B(2) -0.2	1.2
2021	ASH	A+	22	105	28	4	0	11	33	8	17	2	0	.396/.438/.781	156	.391	-0.4	C(12) -1.2, 1B(8) -0.1	0.9
2022 non-DC	*HOU*	*MLB*	*23*	*251*	*23*	*11*	*0*	*5*	*26*	*12*	*54*	*0*	*1*	*.261/.301/.390*	*85*	*.318*	*-0.3*	*C -1, 1B 0*	*0.5*

Comparables: Francisco Cervelli, Kennys Vargas, Josmil Pinto

The Report: From overaged international free agent to second piece in the Myles Straw trade to top-10 prospect in the Astros system. Yes, this isn't a good or even average system, but Diaz was one of the more pleasant organizational surprises for Houston in 2021. A glance at the stat line suggests a bat-first backstop, but it's a bit more nuanced than that. Diaz can drive the ball hard to all fields and flashes enough lift to portend perhaps 20-home-run pop. He is also very aggressive early in counts and can be vulnerable to spin from right-handers in all counts, but that's not too worrying at this point in his development track. Despite a bit of noise, a double toe tap and a mighty rip, he moves the bat around the zone well enough, but the lift is inconsistent, as is his quality of contact despite good bat-to-ball numbers. That might cause his hit tool to play more fringy in the end, and that might limit how much of his plus raw power gets into games.

Diaz's offensive tools are ahead of his glove, but there's stuff to like defensively, as well. He's a bit of a trundler on the bases, but has some short-burst athleticism and is twitchy behind the plate. His receiving is better east-west than north-south, where he can get a bit snatchy, but, overall, the glove projects as average. His arm strength is above-average, but a somewhat slow trigger means he tends to pop only 2.0. Diaz has a fair bit of runway left on his development path, but he has the potential to be a 60-start-a-year backstop, with starter upside past that if the bat continues to play in the upper levels.

OFP: 50 / Second-division starter

Variance: High. The swing is going to have to show out in Double-A before we buy the bat as good enough to start—even in more of a timeshare—and the defense needs refinement, as well.

Mark Barry's Fantasy Take: There's stuff to like about Diaz, but the profile sounds very much like a guy with a backup/spot-starter upside. Sometimes things break right and you get a top-10 fantasy catcher season from a guy like Diaz, but, more often than not, guys like Diaz are readily available on the waiver wire.

9 Jose Siri OF

OFP: 45 ETA: Debuted in 2021

Born: 07/22/95 Age: 26 Bats: R Throws: R Height: 6'2" Weight: 175 lb. Origin: International Free Agent, 2012

YEAR	TEAM	LVL	AGE	PA	R	2B	3B	HR	RBI	BB	K	SB	CS	AVG/OBP/SLG	DRC+	BABIP	BRR	FRAA	WARP
2019	GIG	WIN	23	125	18	4	1	6	24	10	34	4	0	.196/.264/.411		.216			
2019	CHA	AA	23	405	46	15	1	11	50	33	126	21	6	.251/.313/.388	80	.349	-0.5	CF(98) 22.6, RF(1) -0.0	3.1
2019	LOU	AAA	23	112	10	4	1	0	3	9	39	5	2	.186/.252/.245	61	.302	1.1	CF(26) 2.1, RF(4) -0.1	0.2
2020	GIG	WIN	24	122	21	7	0	3	14	12	34	7	3	.282/.352/.427		.384			
2021	GIG	WIN	25	77	11	2	0	2	3	7	19	6	0	.217/.289/.333		.271			
2021	SUG	AAA	25	397	70	29	4	16	72	26	122	24	3	.318/.369/.552	96	.436	2.6	CF(42) -3.5, RF(30) -0.2, LF(12) 1.0	1.1
2021	HOU	MLB	25	49	10	0	1	4	9	1	17	3	1	.304/.347/.609	88	.400	0.5	RF(9) -1.1, CF(5) -0.3, LF(4) -0.3	0.0
2022 DC	*HOU*	*MLB*	*26*	*228*	*32*	*9*	*1*	*7*	*31*	*13*	*70*	*10*	*3*	*.229/.280/.398*	*78*	*.304*	*1.1*	*CF 1, RF 0*	*0.3*

Comparables: Teoscar Hernández, Aaron Altherr, Eury Pérez

The Report: It's pretty rare to find a 26-year-old former minor-league free agent on one of these lists, especially one that was DFA'd by two different organizations in 2020. Siri has always had loud, major-league quality tools, but the on-field performance hasn't matched the scout sheet since 2017. A strong winter ball campaign got him signed by the Astros, and he went out and mashed in Triple-A in 2021 on his way to Houston's playoff roster. Yes, it was far from his first crack at the upper minors, and his K-rate is still higher than you'd like—Siri swings hard and still has issues with long levers and pitch recognition—but he does a lot of damage on contact. He's a plus-plus runner whose foot speed can cover for less-than-ideal routes at times, and he has a 70-grade arm to match. There's some Quad-A potential here, but, in a system this shallow, a ready-now power bat with at least platoon utility who can play all three outfield spots is hard to argue against. And hey, this might just be a late-blooming tools profile.

OFP: 45 / Good fourth outfielder, fringe/platoon starter

Variance: Medium. Siri may not hit enough once he's seeing major-league stuff everyday, but he also doesn't need to hit a ton to have value. And if he hits a little, he's a starter, though perhaps not a starter for the Astros.

Mark Barry's Fantasy Take: Alexa, show me a streaky outfielder that will both win you plenty of weeks and make you want to tear your hair out. Siri is the kind of bat I like to bet on in leagues in which I'm either rebuilding or retooling. Scooping up older, potentially Quad-A outfielders that find themselves in line for playing time is a good way to accumulate stats without giving up the farm for established stars. Even if Siri's fantasy peak is merely an OF3, that's still pretty solid considering the cost.

10 Colin Barber OF

OFP: 50 ETA: 2024

Born: 12/04/00 Age: 21 Bats: L Throws: L Height: 6'0" Weight: 194 lb. Origin: Round 4, 2019 Draft (#136 overall)

YEAR	TEAM	LVL	AGE	PA	R	2B	3B	HR	RBI	BB	K	SB	CS	AVG/OBP/SLG	DRC+	BABIP	BRR	FRAA	WARP
2019	AST	ROK	18	119	19	5	1	2	6	19	29	2	1	.263/.387/.394		.353			
2021	ASH	A+	20	53	10	1	0	3	7	9	22	1	1	.214/.365/.452	76	.353	0.7	RF(7) 0.5, LF(5) -0.5, CF(3) -0.8	0.0
2022 non-DC	*HOU*	*MLB*	*21*	*251*	*19*	*9*	*0*	*4*	*20*	*22*	*103*	*2*	*1*	*.168/.252/.277*	*42*	*.286*	*0.0*	*CF -1, LF 0*	*-1.2*

Comparables: Rymer Liriano, Jordan Schafer, Billy McKinney

The Report: If you like prospects with big power upside, Barber is your guy in a system that doesn't have a lot of high position-player ceilings. He has a smooth, quick swing that generates big game power already. He has had a bit of a weird trip in pro ball so far—he played in independent ball with Houston's approval in 2020 to get reps and was good enough there to get invited to the alternate site—and there are significant unanswered hit-tool questions. But he hits the ball loud and far, and that's a strong basis for future development.

As seems to be an unfortunate theme in this list, Barber missed most of 2021 after shoulder surgery. He had received an aggressive assignment to High-A, and the organization seems quite high on him. He's a potential 2022 breakout, if healthy.

OFP: 50 / Power-and-speed starting outfielder

Variance: High, in all directions. Barber has barely played in affiliated ball, and we're unsure he'll hit for average, but there's a lot of talent here.

Mark Barry's Fantasy Take: If this were purely a fantasy list, I'd have Barber number three behind Peña and Leon. There are significant risks (most notably the swing-and-miss and the shoulder surgery), but there's a legitimate four-category contributor lurking, and I'd much rather speculate on a guy like Barber than one of the pitchers or catchers on this list.

The Prospects You Meet Outside the Top Ten

Prospects on the Rise

Jordan Brewer OF Born: 08/01/97 Age: 24 Bats: R Throws: R Height: 6'1" Weight: 195 lb. Origin: Round 3, 2019 Draft (#106 overall)

YEAR	TEAM	LVL	AGE	PA	R	2B	3B	HR	RBI	BB	K	SB	CS	AVG/OBP/SLG	DRC+	BABIP	BRR	FRAA	WARP
2019	TRI	SS	21	56	5	0	0	1	3	2	6	2	0	.130/.161/.185		.128			
2021	FAY	A	23	297	49	12	2	6	41	34	80	21	2	.275/.375/.410	105	.375	0.6	CF(35) 3.3, LF(10) 0.3, RF(10) 0.0	1.6
2022 non-DC	*HOU*	*MLB*	*24*	*251*	*20*	*10*	*1*	*3*	*20*	*19*	*75*	*9*	*2*	*.211/.282/.308*	*60*	*.300*	*0.7*	*CF 1, RF 0*	*-0.2*

An integral part of the 2019 Michigan team that made it to the College World Series finals, Brewer is the kind of prospect that makes a couple of plays every game that make you think, "yeah, that's what a big leaguer looks like." However, his swing produces far more groundballs then you'd like to see. If there is a player development machine that can make the most of someone willing to make changes to their game, it's the Astros, who have as good a chance as any to help Brewer max out his potential with a retooled swing. His 2021 season looks good on paper, but we will be waiting to see that kind of success at a more age-appropriate level in 2022.

Julio Robaina LHP Born: 03/23/01 Age: 21 Bats: L Throws: L Height: 5'11" Weight: 170 lb. Origin: International Free Agent, 2017

YEAR	TEAM	LVL	AGE	W	L	SV	G	GS	IP	H	HR	BB/9	K/9	K	GB%	BABIP	WHIP	ERA	DRA-	WARP
2019	AST	ROK	18	3	1	0	10	1	29	21	0	3.7	12.7	41	47.7%	.323	1.14	2.48		
2019	TRI	SS	18	0	1	1	3	0	7	8	0	6.4	12.9	10	55.6%	.444	1.86	5.14		
2019	QC	A	18	0	1	1	2	0	5^{2}	2	0	12.7	9.5	6	58.3%	.167	1.76	0.00	121	0.0
2021	FAY	A	20	4	1	0	11	4	44^{2}	39	1	3.6	9.3	46	46.9%	.299	1.28	3.63	95	0.5
2021	ASH	A+	20	3	2	0	6	5	32^{1}	32	3	1.9	11.7	42	53.9%	.337	1.21	3.90	96	0.3
2022 non-DC	*HOU*	*MLB*	*21*	*2*	*3*	*0*	*57*	*0*	*50*	*55*	*6*	*4.8*	*7.7*	*42*	*42.1%*	*.323*	*1.65*	*5.85*	*129*	*-0.6*

Comparables: Matt Wisler, Eduardo Rodriguez, Tyler Chatwood

Robaina broadly fits the Astros' type: he has short arm action, a higher slot and a fastball with some ride. His fastball, however, sits around 90, and the command is a bit fringy. The profile is buoyed by an above-average secondary pitch: the expected 12–6 curve, a short breaker he can move up and down in the zone to spot or bury, or add some tilt to get lefties to chase it down and away. Robaina also offers a firm changeup that flashes average scroogie action and a short slider with more sweep than depth for a different breaking-ball look. Robaina throws strikes and spams the curve enough to handle A-ball lineups, but he is a short, stocky lefty without much more to ring out of his frame or delivery. If the curve develops into a plus weapon that he can throw 40 percent of the time in the majors, he could be quite effective in a long-relief or bulk-innings role.

Misael Tamarez RHP Born: 01/16/00 Age: 22 Bats: R Throws: R Height: 6'1" Weight: 206 lb. Origin: International Free Agent, 2019

YEAR	TEAM	LVL	AGE	W	L	SV	G	GS	IP	H	HR	BB/9	K/9	K	GB%	BABIP	WHIP	ERA	DRA-	WARP
2019	DSL AST	ROK	19	2	2	0	7	4	23^{1}	20	0	5.0	10.0	26	52.4%	.323	1.41	2.70		
2019	AST	ROK	19	1	2	0	7	0	15^{1}	14	1	6.5	10.6	18	40.5%	.317	1.63	2.35		
2021	FAY	A	21	4	2	1	12	6	43	28	3	5.9	13.4	64	38.0%	.281	1.30	3.98	70	1.1
2021	ASH	A+	21	2	1	0	7	7	33^{2}	30	4	2.7	10.4	39	34.1%	.310	1.19	3.48	99	0.3
2022 non-DC	*HOU*	*MLB*	*22*	*2*	*3*	*0*	*57*	*0*	*50*	*50*	*8*	*5.5*	*9.1*	*50*	*47.4%*	*.306*	*1.62*	*5.79*	*130*	*-0.6*

Comparables: Dylan Cease, Elieser Hernandez, Daniel Mengden

Like Robaina, Tamarez had a solid, if unspectacular, 2021 campaign between Fayetteville and Asheville. The shape of his performance was very different, though, and so is his stuff. Tamarez has big arm strength, sustainin mid-90s heat deep into his outings (well, as deep as Astros pitching prospects are allowed to go). It's easy cheese that gets swing-and-miss up in the zone and mostly overpowered A-ball hitters. The secondaries need work, however. There's a slider which is slurvy without true depth to it, and while he can spot it gloveside, it's not a bat-misser. The change is firm, although he maintains his arm speed well enough to give it some projection. Tamarez is a set-up-level relief arm with a ways to go to get there, but he merits some monitoring in a system this shallow in the low minors.

Factors on the Farm

Ross Adolph OF Born: 12/17/96 Age: 25 Bats: L Throws: R Height: 6'1" Weight: 190 lb. Origin: Round 12, 2018 Draft (#350 overall)

YEAR	TEAM	LVL	AGE	PA	R	2B	3B	HR	RBI	BB	K	SB	CS	AVG/OBP/SLG	DRC+	BABIP	BRR	FRAA	WARP
2019	QC	A	22	288	45	15	5	6	24	37	99	9	8	.223/.354/.403	92	.351	2.3	CF(51) -3.8, LF(9) 2.0, RF(8) 0.9	0.7
2019	FAY	A+	22	172	24	5	1	1	16	24	43	2	1	.236/.360/.306	92	.330	1.2	CF(21) -0.1, LF(15) -0.7, RF(6) -0.5	0.4
2021	CC	AA	24	248	33	9	3	10	37	24	77	3	3	.245/.339/.454	97	.331	0.3	LF(21) -0.2, CF(20) 1.6, RF(20) -1.6	0.7
2022 non-DC	*HOU*	*MLB*	*25*	*251*	*22*	*10*	*1*	*4*	*23*	*21*	*86*	*4*	*3*	*.202/.286/.329*	*65*	*.304*	*0.4*	*CF 1, LF 0*	*-0.1*

It would be trickier to sneak Adolph—long one of my personal cheeseballs—onto a prospect list in a deeper system. He continues to have swing-and-miss issues against off-speed pitches, and his comfort in working deeper counts can open him up to those two-strike breakers. But he's an average runner with good enough acceleration and instincts to play center field. If he can hit .240, he offers medium pop—although he needs to lift the ball more—and enough on-base ability to be a useful fourth outfielder.

Shawn Dubin RHP Born: 09/06/95 Age: 26 Bats: R Throws: R Height: 6'1" Weight: 171 lb. Origin: Round 13, 2018 Draft (#402 overall)

YEAR	TEAM	LVL	AGE	W	L	SV	G	GS	IP	H	HR	BB/9	K/9	K	GB%	BABIP	WHIP	ERA	DRA-	WARP
2019	QC	A	23	1	0	2	3	1	12	7	0	3.0	14.3	19	69.6%	.304	0.92	0.75	104	0.1
2019	FAY	A+	23	6	5	1	22	18	98^{2}	71	3	3.8	12.0	132	49.4%	.294	1.15	3.92	67	2.6
2021	SUG	AAA	25	4	3	1	16	8	49^{2}	35	4	3.4	12.5	69	41.9%	.307	1.09	3.44	74	1.0
2022 DC	*HOU*	*MLB*	*26*	*0*	*0*	*0*	*11*	*0*	*9.7*	*7*	*1*	*4.2*	*10.8*	*11*	*45.2%*	*.285*	*1.28*	*3.61*	*86*	*0.1*

Comparables: Rob Zastryzny, Dustin McGowan, Mike MacDougal

Dubin missed a couple of months with a forearm issue but was dominant in short bursts for Sugarland. He's a big guy with big effort in his delivery, but he features upper-90s heat and a snappy plus slider with good depth. He's already 26, and, given the relief markers here, I don't know if it's worth trying to stretch him out as a starter again. He's ready to be a multi-inning reliever for the big club, arm health permitting.

Peter Solomon RHP Born: 08/16/96 Age: 25 Bats: R Throws: R Height: 6'4" Weight: 211 lb. Origin: Round 4, 2017 Draft (#121 overall)

YEAR	TEAM	LVL	AGE	W	L	SV	G	GS	IP	H	HR	BB/9	K/9	K	GB%	BABIP	WHIP	ERA	DRA-	WARP
2019	FAY	A+	22	0	0	0	2	2	7^{2}	7	1	4.7	16.4	14	33.3%	.429	1.43	2.35	83	0.1
2021	SUG	AAA	24	8	1	1	21	18	97^{2}	89	16	3.9	10.3	112	35.9%	.289	1.34	4.70	95	0.7
2021	HOU	MLB	24	1	0	0	6	0	14	10	0	5.1	6.4	10	51.4%	.270	1.29	1.29	115	0.0
2022 DC	*HOU*	*MLB*	*25*	*0*	*0*	*0*	*11*	*0*	*9.7*	*9*	*1*	*4.3*	*8.7*	*9*	*40.0%*	*.297*	*1.46*	*4.88*	*114*	*0.0*

Comparables: Alex Colomé, Alfredo Figaro, Austin Voth

Solomon came back from Tommy John surgery down a few ticks from his previous mid-90s heat. His curveball still misses bats, though, with power 12–5 break. He also has a slider/cutter-type offering and a potentially average change. You'd prefer a little more fastball or a little more command/control (ideally both), but, perhaps after a year of building back strength, he will come out in 2022 with more of his pre-injury form. He should be a useful depth starter or middle-innings reliever, even if that rebound doesn't come to pass.

Top Talents 25 and Under (as of 4/1/2022):

1. Kyle Tucker, OF
2. Yordan Alvarez, DH/OF
3. Luis Garcia, RHP
4. Jeremy Peña, SS
5. Cristian Javier, RHP
6. Korey Lee, C
7. Pedro Leon, SS/OF
8. Jake Meyers, OF
9. Forrest Whitley, RHP
10. Bryan Abreu, RHP

Some fans would relish seeing the Astros spiral out of contention for a while, particularly given the minimal consequences for their cheating scandal, but the immense talent of the names above gives Houston a bulwark against decline. While the players in the farm proper leave something to be desired, the heart of the major-league order boasts two of the most impressive young bats in MLB. Tucker finally emerged from his three-year chrysalis to post a 130 DRC+ in 140 games in 2021. Alvarez put up another strong season, as well, capped by a massive playoff run. The two sluggers flanked Meyers and Chas McCormick in the outfield in the back half of 2021, following Houston's trade of Myles Straw, but the Astros should be looking to upgrade in center, particularly with Meyers set to miss Opening Day following surgery on his left shoulder labrum.

Houston's rotation is a consortium of solid upside arms under the age of 30, including Garcia, who salsaed his way to a 90 DRA– and a rightful spot as a Rookie of the Year finalist. Garcia's emergence was crucial given the absences of Justin Verlander and Framber Valdez, as well as disappointing campaigns from Zack Greinke and Jake Odorizzi. Houston also got quality innings from Javier in a swing role, effective in nine starts early in the year before shifting to multi-inning relief. Fleeting control limited Javier, even as he ground out good results, but his likeliest scenario for 2022 seems to be to begin in the pen and spot-start as needed. He may be joined in the bullpen by Abreu, though Abreu's sense of where the ball is headed is even more limited than Javier's. The immense quality of Abreu's stuff still gives him the repertoire of a high-leverage arm, but as an impending 25-year-old who is out of options, he may need the innings only a non-contender can offer.

Kansas City Royals

The State of the System:

The Royals have one of the deeper systems in baseball, after picking up another strong draft class. It also didn't hurt that their best hitting prospects were not playing in Wilmington last year.

The Top Ten:

1 Bobby Witt Jr. SS OFP: 70 ETA: 2022

Born: 06/14/00 Age: 22 Bats: R Throws: R Height: 6'1" Weight: 200 lb. Origin: Round 1, 2019 Draft (#2 overall)

YEAR	TEAM	LVL	AGE	PA	R	2B	3B	HR	RBI	BB	K	SB	CS	AVG/OBP/SLG	DRC+	BABIP	BRR	FRAA	WARP
2019	ROY	ROK	19	180	30	2	5	1	27	13	35	9	1	.262/.317/.354		.323			
2021	NWA	AA	21	279	44	11	4	16	51	25	67	14	8	.295/.369/.570	120	.339	1.1	SS(50) -1.7, 3B(8) -1.1	1.4
2021	OMA	AAA	21	285	55	24	0	17	46	26	64	15	3	.285/.352/.581	114	.314	-0.1	SS(52) -4.8, 3B(10) -1.4	0.8
2022 DC	*KC*	*MLB*	*22*	*471*	*62*	*23*	*3*	*16*	*64*	*33*	*123*	*17*	*5*	*.246/.306/.428*	*97*	*.305*	*1.5*	*3B -8, SS 0*	*0.6*

Comparables: Freddy Galvis, Asdrúbal Cabrera, Willi Castro

The Report: Well, that was an impressive full-season debut. Sourced data about improvements in Witt's contact ability and two-strike approach made us pretty confident that his hit tool had improved behind 2020's closed doors. After torching the Cactus League in the spring, Witt nearly became the first prep player in recent memory to jump straight from a complex league to the majors. The Royals opted for a still-aggressive Double-A assignment instead, and he just never stopped hitting there or in Triple-A. He will enter spring training as a favorite for a major-league job, subject to whatever service-time shenanigans come out of the next CBA (though it's worth noting that, in the past, the Royals have prioritized player development over service time more than most teams).

Witt looks the part of an elite prospect. His right-handed swing is classically pretty: slightly open stance, even weight balance, mild leg kick, quiet hands until he explodes with phenomenal bat speed in a short, violent movement to the ball. He keeps the bat in the zone while coming forth with big loft. He hits the ball quite hard and rarely on the ground—that's the batted-ball profile you want in the 2020s—so his game power projects as plus-plus. About the only knock here is swing-and-miss against breaking stuff. You can beat him that way, but given the continued improvements in his hit ability since 2019, the quality of contact he makes, and his impressive performance, we think he might get to a 6 hit tool anyway.

Defensively, Witt is a potential plus at shortstop in both glove and arm. The Royals have exposed him to third base—where we'd expect him to be plus or better—and talked about playing him some at second base, as well. Nicky Lopez unexpectedly emerged as one of the best defensive shortstops in the majors last year, and Adalberto Mondesi and Whit Merrifield are around, too, so Witt's long-term position is going to be up in the air for a bit due to organizational needs.

Why does Bobby Witt Jr. top our 101 prospects list? Well, we just projected him as a 55- or 6-hit, 7-power player with great defensive chops on the dirt (and, just to top it all off, he stole 29 bases last season; he can run, too). So, that's part of the argument. The rest of the argument is that he is 28 months younger than Adley Rutschman and slightly outperformed him in 2021 at the same levels.

OFP: 70 / Frequent All-Star

Variance: Low. We suppose there are some latent contact questions, and his defensive home is more uncertain than you'd expect. But, seriously now, Witt jumped from the complex league to the high-minors at 20 years old and crushed the ball at both Double-A and Triple-A. We can't nitpick much at all.

Darius Austin's Fantasy Take: There's not much more you can ask for in a fantasy prospect, either. *Maybe* the difficulty with breaking stuff caps his batting average in the early running, but Witt is a legitimate five-category threat who also has a fairly immediate path to playing time. His ADP is going to get wild in redraft leagues; Witt's potential is so high, it might be worth it anyway.

2 MJ Melendez C OFP: 60 ETA: 2022

Born: 11/29/98 Age: 23 Bats: L Throws: R Height: 6'1" Weight: 190 lb. Origin: Round 2, 2017 Draft (#52 overall)

YEAR	TEAM	LVL	AGE	PA	R	2B	3B	HR	RBI	BB	K	SB	CS	AVG/OBP/SLG	DRC+	BABIP	BRR	FRAA	WARP
2019	WIL	A+	20	419	34	23	2	9	54	44	165	7	5	.163/.260/.311	58	.259	-0.7	C(71) 5.7	-0.2
2021	NWA	AA	22	347	58	18	0	28	65	43	76	2	4	.285/.372/.628	143	.286	-0.7	C(52) -3.5	2.6
2021	OMA	AAA	22	184	37	4	3	13	38	32	39	1	2	.293/.413/.620	128	.310	-1.4	C(29) -2.3, 3B(9) 0.5	0.9
2022 DC	*KC*	*MLB*	*23*	*30*	*4*	*1*	*0*	*1*	*4*	*3*	*8*	*0*	*0*	*.235/.319/.441*	*104*	*.290*	*0.0*	*C -1*	*0.1*

Comparables: Gary Sánchez, Wilson Ramos, Rowdy Tellez

The Report: Melendez struggled mightily in 2019, coming off a Top-101 ranking. Wilmington is a bad place to hit, and he wasn't the only highly-regarded Royals prospect to fail there, but a .163 batting average is a .163 batting average. Reports were better from the alternate site in 2020, but we needed to see the good side of the hit tool variance show up. Well, take a gander up top at the stats box. Melendez has a true power-hitter's swing, with a big leg kick and some length but also plus bat speed with whip and loft. There's a lot going on in that swing, and he can get off balance, but it's hard contact when he thumps one. He was the minor-league leader in home runs this year, and there's certainly 30-home-run potential in the bat.

Melendez was considered an advanced defender for a prep catcher when he was drafted, but the tools behind the plate haven't advanced as quickly as the skills at it. Live reports and our catching metrics both have him as a below-average receiver, and the Royals started to get him some third-base time in Omaha. Some of that might be because the defending major-league home-run leader is entrenched behind the plate in Kansas City, and some of it might be wanting to get Melendez's bat in the lineup as soon as possible. He's a good enough runner and athlete that third base, or perhaps left field, is a viable option. He certainly has the power for either.

OFP: 60 / First-division catcher, but maybe not for Kansas City

Variance: Medium. Moving off catcher to take most of his at-bats in a corner will put pressure on the bat to play to the power projection. There's still some risk of hit-tool regression against major-league arms. A .240 average and 20 home runs is more than viable for a backstop, but less so for a third baseman. Of course, Melendez did post a 1.000 OPS in the high minors as a 22-year-old.

Darius Austin's Fantasy Take: Melendez's potential positional move is a testament to what the Royals think of his bat. It's not particularly what we want in fantasy, although, in the short term, it offers the possibility of a catcher-eligible season in which he's getting considerably more at-bats than the average backstop. The power could be difference-making at any position. It would all be a lot more exciting—and a mediocre average more palatable—if he were catcher-eligible, but Salvador Perez isn't going anywhere. You'd be brave to do it after a 41-homer season . . . but it might not be the worst time to sell high?

3 Nick Pratto 1B/OF OFP: 55 ETA: 2022

Born: 10/06/98 Age: 23 Bats: L Throws: L Height: 6'1" Weight: 215 lb. Origin: Round 1, 2017 Draft (#14 overall)

YEAR	TEAM	LVL	AGE	PA	R	2B	3B	HR	RBI	BB	K	SB	CS	AVG/OBP/SLG	DRC+	BABIP	BRR	FRAA	WARP
2019	WIL	A+	20	472	48	21	1	9	46	49	164	17	7	.191/.278/.310	66	.286	0.3	1B(123) 4.6	-0.1
2021	NWA	AA	22	275	44	13	4	15	43	46	80	7	5	.271/.404/.570	121	.349	-1.8	1B(61) -0.8	1.2
2021	OMA	AAA	22	270	54	15	3	21	55	37	77	5	0	.259/.367/.634	119	.282	1.0	1B(52) -1.0, RF(3) -0.1	1.2
2022 non-DC	*KC*	*MLB*	*23*	*251*	*28*	*12*	*1*	*9*	*31*	*26*	*85*	*5*	*3*	*.221/.311/.416*	*92*	*.314*	*0.5*	*1B 0, RF 0*	*0.3*

Comparables: Rowdy Tellez, Logan Morrison, Matt Olson

The Report: Another top Royals prospect who was on the interstate for the 2019 Blue Rocks, Pratto had a strong bounce back of his own in 2021. MJ Melendez just snapped him off for the organizational home run lead, but Pratto generates 30-plus-home-run pop of his own out of a now-stocky frame. He is looking to lift and do damage, and while he has less-than-ideal bat speed for a true power hitter, he moves the barrel around the zone well. Pratto is also strong enough that even suboptimal contact can produce extra-base hits. Overall, the profile tilts towards three true outcomes, but Pratto should have a roughly average hit tool. He's selective at the plate and knows what he can and should try to drive. There will still be whiffs, in part due to the bat speed and swing plane, but he is comfortable working deep into counts. Pratto is a perfectly fine defensive first baseman, but, ultimately, this is a bat-only profile. When the bat offers .260, 30 homers and plenty of walks, though, that's fine.

OFP: 55 / Mashing first baseman

Variance: Medium. The power is here, but there are still questions about the ultimate hit tool, and your first baseman, ultimately, has to hit.

Darius Austin's Fantasy Take: If Pratto doesn't hit for average, you might be hearing "more valuable in OBP leagues" an awful lot over the next few years. The upside is clearly middle-of-the-order slugger who will rack up the homers and RBI while also giving you a little average boost. While first-base-only with hit-tool questions is one of the more precarious profiles, the walks should at least afford Pratto the opportunity to keep hitting dingers, even if you aren't thrilled with the batting average.

4 Asa Lacy LHP OFP: 55 ETA: 2023

Born: 06/02/99 Age: 23 Bats: L Throws: L Height: 6'4" Weight: 215 lb. Origin: Round 1, 2020 Draft (#4 overall)

YEAR	TEAM	LVL	AGE	W	L	SV	G	GS	IP	H	HR	BB/9	K/9	K	GB%	BABIP	WHIP	ERA	DRA-	WARP
2021	QC	A+	22	2	5	0	14	14	52	41	5	7.1	13.7	79	33.0%	.346	1.58	5.19	81	1.1
2022 non-DC	*KC*	*MLB*	*23*	*2*	*3*	*0*	*57*	*0*	*50*	*48*	*9*	*7.7*	*11.5*	*64*	*34.1%*	*.321*	*1.82*	*6.86*	*139*	*-0.8*

Comparables: A.J. Murray, Joaquin Benoit, Jeff Brigham

The Report: The good news for Lacy is that he has all the tools to become a future frontline starter. Physical and strong, the former fourth-overall selection has a repertoire that features four potential plus offerings. A high-90s fastball, a pair of sharp breaking pitches and an improved change helped him strike out nearly 14 per nine during his time in High-A. On the negative side, he lacks polish and is still more of a thrower than a pitcher. That was also on display at Quad Cities; the control wavered at times and led to a walk rate that went north of seven per nine in his 14 starts. A shoulder issue shut him down in July, but his return to action in instructs and the Arizona Fall League offered some promise. He was reportedly in better physical shape upon his return, and there were no visible negative effects from the injury, with his fastball even touching triple digits. Lacy's elite stuff doesn't require him to have pinpoint control, but the command needs to be tightened up if he is going to become the Royals' ace of the future.

OFP: 55 / No. 3 starter

Variance: High. Lacy's shoulder issue and inflated walk rate give plenty to be concerned about, but, if he's healthy and can throw strikes more consistently, he's a potential ace.

Darius Austin's Fantasy Take: There's probably still a buy-low window open on Lacy, especially if league-mates aren't paying too much attention to instructs or the AFL. If you've got the time to wait, then there are few higher-upside plays to make on the pitching side. Just be aware that there's plenty of risk that Lacy will be an electric but inconsistent WHIP destroyer, or that he doesn't make it at all.

5 Frank Mozzicato LHP OFP: 55 ETA: 2025/2026

Born: 06/19/03 Age: 19 Bats: L Throws: L Height: 6'3" Weight: 175 lb. Origin: Round 1, 2021 Draft (#7 overall)

The Report: A true pop-up prospect—it was weeks into the high school season before we started getting texts asking if we'd seen the lefty yet—Mozzicato pitched his way into the first round off a strong senior year that, at one point, featured four consecutive no-hitters. The relative merits of Connecticut high school baseball aside, Mozzicato is a very modern left-handed prep prospect. He is young for his draft class, having turned 18 just a few weeks before the Royals selected him seventh overall. He's a projectable 6-foot-3 with broad shoulders and a narrow waist. There's certainly room to wring more velocity out of both the frame and the delivery, and his fastball mostly sat 88–91, although he could touch higher, especially earlier in the spring season. We'd expect him to bump at least into the low 90s as he matures, and the pitch already has some riding life and advanced command for a high school arm.

The reason he got $3.5 million, though, is the curveball. It has high spin and good shape, and he can already manipulate the pitch to spot or bury. His best curves were mid-70s to the backfoot of righties, and he snaps those off more consistently than you'd expect from a raw, cold-weather arm. If you told us the pitch will eventually get to plus-plus, we'd believe you, but we'll be conservative and give it a firm plus projection, for now. Mozzicato threw exactly one changeup in our looks. The arm speed was fine, but the pitch is obviously going to need a lot of development.

The Royals are viewed, probably correctly, as a more traditional scouting organization, and Mozzicato doesn't check the same boxes as, say, Chase Petty. In some ways, due to his age and pitch type characteristics, he is more model-friendly. Whether using scouts or stats, though, you'll land in the same place: a potential mid-rotation lefty with a very long runway to get there.

OFP: 55 / No. 3–4 starter

Variance: High. Mozzicato hasn't thrown a pitch in organized ball yet, and while he already has a good hook, he will need more physical growth (and more fastball) and a viable third pitch to get to the mid-rotation projection.

Darius Austin's Fantasy Take: It's going to be a looooong wait for potential mid-rotation upside. Mozzicato wouldn't be the first cold-weather, young-for-his-class prospect to make spectacular development in pro ball. Investing in that is another matter. Let's see him add some velocity, a third pitch and actually face pro hitters before diving in.

6 Nick Loftin IF OFP: 55 ETA: Late 2022/Early 2023

Born: 09/25/98 Age: 23 Bats: R Throws: R Height: 6'1" Weight: 180 lb. Origin: Round 1, 2020 Draft (#32 overall)

YEAR	TEAM	LVL	AGE	PA	R	2B	3B	HR	RBI	BB	K	SB	CS	AVG/OBP/SLG	DRC+	BABIP	BRR	FRAA	WARP
2021	QC	A+	22	410	67	22	5	10	57	42	60	11	2	.289/.373/.463	122	.323	1.6	SS(47) -3.9, 2B(21) 1.0, 3B(11) -0.2	2.1
2022 non-DC	*KC*	*MLB*	*23*	*251*	*22*	*11*	*1*	*3*	*23*	*19*	*42*	*3*	*1*	*.243/.309/.355*	*81*	*.284*	*0.1*	*SS -3, 2B 0*	*0.0*

Comparables: Chris Taylor, Matt Duffy, Josh Rutledge

The Report: Loftin is not the guy to look to if you are compiling a list of the loudest tools in the organization. All aspects of his game are solid, but none stand out. Offensively, despite having just one professional season under his belt, Loftin has the look of a seasoned veteran. He's a difficult out who controls the zone well and rarely swings and misses. There's also some sneaky pop in his bat which should continue to improve as he gains more reps. Fluid in the field with soft hands and good instincts, he's able to adequately handle the rigors of shortstop. It's more likely, however, that the Royals take advantage of his versatility and use him in a Chris Taylor–type role, plugging him in any he's needed on defense.

OFP: 55 / First-division regular at a few different spots

Variance: Medium. There's some risk that his power will stall against more advanced pitching, but the advanced bat and defensive versatility gives him a reasonable chance to be at least an everyday player.

Darius Austin's Fantasy Take: A Chris Taylor mention might oversell Loftin's fantasy prospects just a touch. Nevertheless, the possibility of multi-position eligibility plus full-time playing time is appealing. Even if Loftin's major-league power-speed numbers don't look dissimilar to his High-A numbers, he'd be a useful supplementary piece who is extra valuable in deep leagues. Getting that homer total to 20 would make the line look more like . . . well, Chris Taylor's.

Eyewitness Report: Nick Loftin

Evaluator: Nathan Graham

Report Date: 09/29/2021

Dates Seen: Multiple August 2021

Risk Factor: Low

Physical/Health: Large frame, thin and athletic build, room for some additional growth but will always be on the lean side.

Tool	Future Grade	Report
Hit	60	Balanced, quiet swing geared for hard line drives. Hands start high with a slight toe tap for timing, above average bat speed, shows a knack for hard contact to all fields. Excellent plate discipline, recognizes spin well and rarely expands the zone.
Power	45	Lacks the frame and physical strength to generate power but the swing produces hard contact and some sneaky pop; Mostly gap to gap doubles, but will attack in hitters counts and pull it out of the park. Future fringe average power for a middle infielder.
Baserunning/ Speed	50	Average raw speed but is an aggressive, smart baserunner; Will not rack up huge stolen base numbers but chooses his spots well and is capable at swiping the occasional bag.
Glove	50	Solid hands and good instincts help to make up for average range; He's not flashy but will be able to handle short at the big league level.
Arm	50	Accurate throwing arm, shows good carry across the diamond, quick transfers helps him get rid of it in a hurry, has enough strength to handle any position in the infield; will play average at short, above average elsewhere.

Conclusion: Drafted 32nd overall in 2020, Loftin lacks loud tools but makes up for it with his solid overall game. His contact ability and defensive versatility give him a high floor of a utility role player. However, it's not difficult to envision a scenario where the hit tool develops enough to become a top of the order impact bat.

7 Kyle Isbel OF   OFP: 55   ETA: Debuted in 2021

Born: 03/03/97 Age: 25 Bats: L Throws: R Height: 5'11" Weight: 190 lb. Origin: Round 3, 2018 Draft (#94 overall)

YEAR	TEAM	LVL	AGE	PA	R	2B	3B	HR	RBI	BB	K	SB	CS	AVG/OBP/SLG	DRC+	BABIP	BRR	FRAA	WARP
2019	SUR	WIN	22	91	8	4	1	1	16	14	20	6	1	.315/.429/.438		.407			
2019	ROY	ROK	22	27	9	2	0	2	7	2	5	3	1	.360/.407/.680		.389			
2019	WIL	A+	22	214	26	7	3	5	23	15	44	8	3	.216/.282/.361	92	.253	1.6	CF(32) -2.6, RF(12) 0.4	0.4
2021	OMA	AAA	24	451	62	18	3	15	55	45	91	22	5	.269/.357/.444	108	.314	-1.1	CF(55) -5.5, RF(26) 5.0, LF(19) -1.9	1.6
2021	KC	MLB	24	83	16	5	2	1	7	7	23	2	0	.276/.337/.434	83	.385	1.1	RF(14) -0.1, CF(9) -0.4, LF(4) 0.1	0.2
2022 DC	*KC*	*MLB*	*25*	*318*	*34*	*13*	*2*	*6*	*35*	*24*	*73*	*11*	*3*	*.235/.306/.369*	*81*	*.295*	*1.0*	*RF 2, CF 0*	*0.5*

Comparables: Kevin Kiermaier, Alex Presley, Andrew Stevenson

The Report: Isbel rounds out our troika of top Royals prospects that scuffled in Wilmington in 2019, joining Melendez and Pratto. We got stronger alternate-site reports in 2020, and Isbel promptly hit his way onto the Royals' Opening Day roster this past spring. He scuffled a bit in April, staying afloat but not hitting for any power, then got his feet under him in Omaha before closing the 2021 campaign with a scorching September back in the bigs. There's nothing particularly noteworthy about Isbel's profile. He has a pretty left-handed swing with good barrel control, but his contact rates are only average-ish, and he doesn't consistently tap into his pull-side pop due to a very all-fields—at times even slashy—approach. Isbel will add additional value on the margins with his on-base and subsequent base-stealing ability, but, on balance, his 2021 major-league line might be fairly indicative of his skill set going forward. But when you combine average (or a tick above) production at the plate with the ability to handle all three outfield spots (he's likely plus in a corner given how well he runs), you get a useful every day player. If Isbel does figure out how to yank a few more fastballs down the right-field line, he might be a good every day player.

OFP: 55 / Solid-average regular in the outfield

Variance: Low. Isbel is barely eligible for this list and should be a starting outfielder on the 2022 Royals. How much pop he can consistently get into games will determine whether he is average or a bit more, but he has arguably the least variant profile on these lists.

Darius Austin's Fantasy Take: Isbel needs the volume of an everyday starter. It's never a great idea to totally buy into minor-league stolen base success (not least because of the rule changes), and his approach clearly isn't set up to give us the power we want before we even consider his home park. If he can get to 15 steals, he'll be a just-fine starting outfielder, but unless he learns to cash in on some pull-side dingers, just fine is the ceiling.

8 Vinnie Pasquantino 1B   OFP: 55   ETA: 2022

Born: 10/10/97 Age: 24 Bats: L Throws: L Height: 6'4" Weight: 245 lb. Origin: Round 11, 2019 Draft (#319 overall)

YEAR	TEAM	LVL	AGE	PA	R	2B	3B	HR	RBI	BB	K	SB	CS	AVG/OBP/SLG	DRC+	BABIP	BRR	FRAA	WARP
2019	BUR	ROA	21	248	43	17	2	14	53	27	40	0	0	.294/.371/.592		.293			
2021	QC	A+	23	276	44	20	3	13	42	33	38	4	0	.291/.384/.565	144	.298	-1.5	1B(52) 5.0	2.5
2021	NWA	AA	23	237	35	17	0	11	42	31	26	2	0	.310/.405/.560	140	.307	0.1	1B(54) -2.8	1.5
2022 non-DC	*KC*	*MLB*	*24*	*251*	*27*	*13*	*1*	*7*	*29*	*23*	*38*	*0*	*1*	*.259/.334/.426*	*104*	*.284*	*-0.3*	*1B 1*	*0.7*

Comparables: Kila Ka'aihue, Corey Dickerson, Ben Paulsen

The Report: We expected more than the normal amount of out-of-nowhere breakouts in 2021, because all of the 2020 breakouts that happened behind closed doors didn't go public until 2021. Pasquantino falls into that group; he crushed the ball in the Appy League back in 2019, but crushing the ball in the Appy League as a college first baseman who signed for a post-10th-round slot bonus doesn't get you noticed at a national level.

Pasquantino is a prototypical Baseball Prospectus darling as that term might have been applied two decades ago; he is a hulking, power-hitting lefty bat who swings hard and up and takes his fair share of walks. Pasquantino is limited to first base without any pretension that he can fool around in the outfield. Where he separates from the type is that he makes an unusual amount of contact; he only struck out 12.5 percent of the time last season. That number improved from High-A to Double-A, and he walked more than he struck out at the higher level. For a large power bat, that's an unusual amount of contact, and pairing this level of bat-to-ball ability with plus power gets you into some fun offensive outcomes. He did struggle some against lefties this season, and he has an open stance and length to his swing, so he might end up as an awfully good, positionally limited platoon bat. That's why he's not higher here.

OFP: 55 / Absolutely mashes righties and sits against Max Fried or Chris Sale

Variance: Medium. This is a tough profile with no real fallbacks if he doesn't hit, and he's stuck behind Pratto on the organizational depth chart. If he continues to hit like this, well, that's why there's a DH.

Darius Austin's Fantasy Take: If Pratto's profile is somewhat precarious, this is as precipitous as it gets. I adore this kind of ludicrous strikeout-to-walk performance, however. The platoon concern isn't a totally disqualifying factor, either, since it's a short-side issue: just ask Joc Pederson. Pasquantino might be a matchup option until a clearer path to playing time appears, but I think, when he does play, you'll want to start him. I can see him being a DFS darling in the not-too-distant future.

9 Jackson Kowar RHP OFP: 50 ETA: Debuted in 2021

Born: 10/04/96 Age: 25 Bats: R Throws: R Height: 6'5" Weight: 200 lb. Origin: Round 1, 2018 Draft (#33 overall)

YEAR	TEAM	LVL	AGE	W	L	SV	G	GS	IP	H	HR	BB/9	K/9	K	GB%	BABIP	WHIP	ERA	DRA-	WARP
2019	WIL	A+	22	5	3	0	13	13	74	68	4	2.7	8.0	66	44.9%	.305	1.22	3.53	101	0.6
2019	NWA	AA	22	2	7	0	13	13	74^{1}	73	8	2.5	9.4	78	45.5%	.323	1.26	3.51	84	0.8
2021	OMA	AAA	24	9	4	0	17	16	80^{2}	66	7	3.8	12.8	115	43.8%	.331	1.24	3.46	76	2.1
2021	KC	MLB	24	0	6	0	9	8	30^{1}	43	7	5.9	8.6	29	35.0%	.375	2.08	11.27	156	-0.6
2022 DC	*KC*	*MLB*	*25*	*5*	*4*	*0*	*26*	*12*	*71*	*67*	*9*	*4.3*	*9.2*	*72*	*41.3%*	*.299*	*1.42*	*4.73*	*111*	*0.1*

Comparables: Josh Rogers, A.J. Cole, Joe Kelly

The Report: Well, that could have gone better. Since his college days, the main impediments to Kowar being an obvious major-league starting-pitching prospect have been his command issues and lack of even an average breaking ball. There was far less concern that the fastball/change combo wouldn't be effective up the ladder. Well, about that . . .

Kowar's fastball sits 95 plus, but the pitch doesn't have much spin or movement, and his major-league heat map was a dark red blob in the middle of the plate. Hitters looked very comfortable against his heater. It was 95 coming in, but 95 going back out, too. The changeup, at its best, was a mid-80s power sinker with good, late dive that batters would swing over, but Kowar hung it in the zone enough that they'd eventually see one to drive. He threw those two pitches more than 85 percent of the time in the majors, so that's a problem. He now primarily uses a low- to mid-80s slider as his glove-side option. It has a little tilt, but he twists it off too much and can struggle to start it in the zone.

Kowar's fastball/change combination was good enough to handle Triple-A hitters in 2021, in between his two rough stints with the big club. He still wasn't as dominant as you'd like, and while we'd expect the change to be better in the long term, the questions about fastball command and shape are now the concerning ones.

OFP: 50 / No. 4 starter

Variance: Medium. I'd expect Kowar to get a fair bit of major-league time in 2022. I don't know how much more he can "refine" in Triple-A, but he really could use even an average breaking-ball option to help keep righties off the fastball. Perhaps this works better in short bursts when he can dial it up to 97 plus in the pen.

Darius Austin's Fantasy Take: I'm out on Kowar until we see significant improvements. It's always alarming when a fastball is treated like this by opposing hitters. If Kowar had a great breaking ball, we might be able to suggest a shift in pitch mix to mitigate some of the problem. As long as he's relying on an extremely hittable heater paired with a changeup that he isn't commanding well, blow-up outings are going to be a constant risk.

10 Ben Hernandez RHP OFP: 50 ETA: 2024

Born: 07/01/01 Age: 21 Bats: R Throws: R Height: 6'2" Weight: 205 lb. Origin: Round 2, 2020 Draft (#41 overall)

YEAR	TEAM	LVL	AGE	W	L	SV	G	GS	IP	H	HR	BB/9	K/9	K	GB%	BABIP	WHIP	ERA	DRA-	WARP
2021	COL	A	19	1	2	0	9	9	31^{1}	32	2	4.9	8.9	31	48.3%	.353	1.56	4.31	95	0.4
2022 non-DC	*KC*	*MLB*	*20*	*2*	*3*	*0*	*57*	*0*	*50*	*55*	*7*	*5.9*	*6.8*	*37*	*41.2%*	*.309*	*1.77*	*6.51*	*139*	*-0.8*

The Report: The good news on Hernandez is that he has a calm, easy delivery that portends future command gains and a strong, sturdy frame that indicates a theoretical ability to handle a starter's workload. His best pitch is also quite good: a mid- to upper-80s change that projects to at least future plus. The pitch doesn't have the subtle fade generally associated with changeups. Instead it drops sharply out of the hitting zone after initially presenting as a fastball. The fastball itself is a decent pitch, topping out around 95 and flashing run and sink. The third offering is a slurvy, 80-ish-mph breaking ball that he doesn't really control. Hernandez lost more than half of 2021 to injury and didn't dominate when he was pitching, but he doesn't turn 21 until July, and there is still a lot to like here.

OFP: 50 / Back-end starter

Variance: High. A prep arm with questions remaining, he hasn't yet demonstrated the ability to hold his stuff deep into outings and has a third pitch that is presently suspect.

Darius Austin's Fantasy Take: Hernandez is a free agent in my 30-team dynasty league with more than 600 prospects owned. In other words, wait until he's a back-end starter in the majors before picking him up for a friendly streaming opportunity.

The Prospects You Meet Outside the Top Ten

#11

Ben Kudrna RHP Born: 01/30/03 Age: 19 Bats: R Throws: R Height: 6'3" Weight: 175 lb. Origin: Round 2, 2021 Draft (#43 overall)

Thanks to the selection of Mozzicato, whom the Royals knew they could sign to an under-slot bonus after taking him seventh overall last June, the Royals were able to target Kudrna with their next pick. A bit of a late bloomer after a sluggish summer prior to his senior season, Kudrna had an impressive fall that had his stock rising to the tune of a signing bonus commensurate with a pick 20 spots higher than his 43rd-overall draft slot. His direct and downhill motion and very projectable frame has evaluators believing Kudrna is just beginning to scratch the surface of his potential. His fastball sits comfortably in the low to mid-90s with running life, and he could add a couple extra ticks of velo soon. His downward-breaking slider and changeup are inconsistent, but are likely to round into form as his body maxes out.

#12

Carter Jensen C/DH Born: 07/03/03 Age: 19 Bats: L Throws: R Height: 6'1" Weight: 210 lb. Origin: Round 3, 2021 Draft (#78 overall)

YEAR	TEAM	LVL	AGE	PA	R	2B	3B	HR	RBI	BB	K	SB	CS	AVG/OBP/SLG	DRC+	BABIP	BRR	FRAA	WARP
2021	ROYG	ROK	17	65	8	1	1	1	7	10	19	4	0	.273/.385/.382		.400			

In 2021's unusually deep prep-catcher class, Jensen might have had the most offensive upside, which raises the question whether he'll remain a catcher in the long run. While not overly athletic, he's just fine behind the plate and has the arm to stick there. The real highlight to his profile is a sweet left-handed swing that seems grooved to handle all types of pitches and handedness without succumbing to a platoon split. His power is increasing with added strength, meaning he'll either outpace his defensive development as a catcher and need to move to a corner-outfield spot or first base, or, if everything comes along in a linear fashion, he'll be a rare offensive-minded backstop.

Prospects on the Rise

Shane Panzini RHP Born: 10/30/01 Age: 20 Bats: R Throws: R Height: 6'3" Weight: 220 lb. Origin: Round 4, 2021 Draft (#108 overall)

The last of the Royals' 2021 bounty of prepsters—they opted for volume in a deep class rather than target high-end value—Panzini has the fastball characteristics you love to see in a developing youngster. Metrics say he can generate high spin, inducing late movement on the pitch that can baffle hitters, even when they think they've timed it up. The problem is the command. He's more of a thrower than you'd like, and his back-side mechanics tend to lag behind, leading towards some of those control issues. His secondaries are behind, as well, and Panzini needs to focus on the delivery first before working on the rest of his arsenal.

Will Klein RHP Born: 11/28/99 Age: 22 Bats: R Throws: R Height: 6'5" Weight: 230 lb. Origin: Round 5, 2020 Draft (#135 overall)

YEAR	TEAM	LVL	AGE	W	L	SV	G	GS	IP	H	HR	BB/9	K/9	K	GB%	BABIP	WHIP	ERA	DRA-	WARP
2021	QC	A+	21	7	1	4	36	0	70^{1}	43	4	5.6	15.5	121	50.8%	.312	1.24	3.20	80	1.5
2022 non-DC	*KC*	*MLB*	*22*	*2*	*3*	*0*	*57*	*0*	*50*	*42*	*6*	*6.5*	*11.7*	*64*	*33.8%*	*.303*	*1.56*	*5.17*	*112*	*-0.1*

Selected in the fifth round of the 2020 draft, Klein was a dominant force at Quad Cities last year while working primarily as a multi-inning reliever. Despite logging just 70 innings, his 121 strikeouts were the third most in the High-A Central. His extra-large frame and fastball that occasionally touches triple digits might appear to make him a lock to remain working in short bullpen bursts, but the Royals reportedly intend to stretch him out as a starter next season. If his newly developed changeup can become serviceable, it will give him another weapon to pair with his high-octane heater and give him a shot at sticking as a rotation piece.

Peyton Wilson 2B Born: 11/01/99 Age: 22 Bats: S Throws: R Height: 5'9" Weight: 180 lb. Origin: Round 2, 2021 Draft (#66 overall)

YEAR	TEAM	LVL	AGE	PA	R	2B	3B	HR	RBI	BB	K	SB	CS	AVG/OBP/SLG	DRC+	BABIP	BRR	FRAA	WARP
2021	ROYG	ROK	21	41	7	3	1	1	7	5	10	2	2	.219/.366/.469		.273			
2021	COL	A	21	46	6	3	1	0	1	4	10	5	0	.231/.326/.359	106	.300	0.4	2B(11) 0.3	0.2
2022 non-DC	*KC*	*MLB*	*22*	*251*	*19*	*10*	*1*	*2*	*20*	*16*	*68*	*13*	*3*	*.208/.271/.301*	*58*	*.284*	*1.2*	*2B 0*	*-0.4*

A veritable Swiss Army knife while at Alabama, the undersized Wilson has a compact frame that could be used in a similar, multi-position fashion in the pro ranks, but he exclusively played second base after being drafted last year. While he is more comfortable from the left side, his switch-hitting ability provides a ton of bench flexibility, though he has an aggressive approach and will attack early in the count with regularity. There isn't a ton of upside to get excited about, but the pieces are there to eventually contribute at the big-league level.

Factors on the Farm

Jonathan Bowlan RHP Born: 12/01/96 Age: 25 Bats: R Throws: R Height: 6'6" Weight: 240 lb. Origin: Round 2, 2018 Draft (#58 overall)

YEAR	TEAM	LVL	AGE	W	L	SV	G	GS	IP	H	HR	BB/9	K/9	K	GB%	BABIP	WHIP	ERA	DRA-	WARP
2019	LEX	A	22	6	2	1	13	11	69^2	55	4	1.3	9.6	74	47.3%	.283	0.93	3.36	92	0.9
2019	WIL	A+	22	5	3	0	13	12	76^1	66	5	1.5	9.0	76	40.5%	.307	1.03	2.95	79	1.5
2021	NWA	AA	24	2	0	0	4	4	17	13	0	1.6	13.2	25	50.0%	.342	0.94	1.59	83	0.3
2022 non-DC	*KC*	*MLB*	*25*	*2*	*2*	*0*	*57*	*0*	*50*	*45*	*6*	*2.5*	*8.7*	*48*	*38.2%*	*.288*	*1.20*	*3.71*	*91*	*0.4*

Comparables: Adam Russell, Carlos Fisher, Mark Leiter Jr.

It might take a bit longer for Bowlan to be a factor after early-season Tommy John surgery, but he should be back on a mound towards the end of the 2022 season. Before his injury, he looked like a quick mover, and system riser, on the strength of his zippy mid-90s fastball. Bowlan pounds the edges of the zone with the number one and pairs it with a firm slider that has enough cutting action to keep it off barrels. He has an equally firm change—that's less of a positive descriptor in this case—and a fair bit of reliever risk, especially after elbow surgery. Nevertheless, Bowlan is worth keeping an eye on in rehab and could be a factor for the big-league club by 2023.

Alec Marsh RHP Born: 05/14/98 Age: 24 Bats: R Throws: R Height: 6'2" Weight: 220 lb. Origin: Round 2, 2019 Draft (#70 overall)

YEAR	TEAM	LVL	AGE	W	L	SV	G	GS	IP	H	HR	BB/9	K/9	K	GB%	BABIP	WHIP	ERA	DRA-	WARP
2019	IDF	ROA	21	0	1	0	13	13	33^1	30	5	1.1	10.3	38	44.4%	.294	1.02	4.05		
2021	NWA	AA	23	1	3	0	6	6	25^1	20	4	4.6	14.9	42	44.0%	.348	1.30	4.97	69	0.6
2022 non-DC	*KC*	*MLB*	*24*	*2*	*2*	*0*	*57*	*0*	*50*	*43*	*7*	*5.1*	*11.5*	*63*	*31.8%*	*.303*	*1.44*	*4.69*	*107*	*0.0*

Comparables: Ethan Martin, José Cisnero, Ross Stripling

Injuries have limited Marsh to just 58 ⅔ professional innings since the Royals drafted him 70th overall in 2019. He was performing well at Northwest Arkansas before arm soreness shut him down and limited his AFL return to just one outing. If he can ever return to health, his impressive four-pitch arsenal will make him a solid option for the Royals' rotation.

Michael Massey 2B Born: 03/22/98 Age: 24 Bats: L Throws: R Height: 6'0" Weight: 190 lb. Origin: Round 4, 2019 Draft (#109 overall)

YEAR	TEAM	LVL	AGE	PA	R	2B	3B	HR	RBI	BB	K	SB	CS	AVG/OBP/SLG	DRC+	BABIP	BRR	FRAA	WARP
2019	BUR	ROA	21	192	32	7	0	5	25	13	28	4	0	.272/.339/.399		.298			
2021	QC	A+	23	439	76	27	2	21	87	33	68	12	2	.289/.351/.531	132	.297	1.0	2B(81) -4.0	2.6
2022 non-DC	*KC*	*MLB*	*24*	*251*	*24*	*11*	*1*	*6*	*27*	*15*	*48*	*3*	*1*	*.246/.299/.391*	*85*	*.286*	*0.1*	*2B -1*	*0.3*

Finally healthy after back issues caused him to fall to the fourth round in 2019, Massey flourished with the bat in his first full professional season. He has shown the ability to make contact with his smooth left-handed swing ever since his days with the Illini, but 2021 was the first year in which his power began to play. Massey's 21 home runs placed him fourth in the High-A Central in just 99 games. Defensively, he's limited to second base, but he should be a solid defender there. That puts a lot of pressure on the glove, but the bat is strong enough that, if he can stay healthy, Massey will contribute on the big-league level.

Because You Were Going to Ask

Erick Peña CF Born: 02/20/03 Age: 19 Bats: L Throws: R Height: 6'3" Weight: 205 lb. Origin: International Free Agent, 2019

YEAR	TEAM	LVL	AGE	PA	R	2B	3B	HR	RBI	BB	K	SB	CS	AVG/OBP/SLG	DRC+	BABIP	BRR	FRAA	WARP
2021	ROYB	ROK	18	156	14	10	1	3	15	15	57	4	4	.161/.256/.314		.244			

Comparables: Raysheron Michel, Dalton Pompey, Devon Torrence

This is a really deep system, one of the deepest in the game, so Peña's exclusion from the Top 10 (or 12) isn't a sign that we're totally out on him. All of the tools that got him onto the back of the 101 last year are still present, and he'd have easily made the Top 10 in weaker systems, like those of the Mets or Rockies. Still, the buzz that started after Peña signed in 2019, and continued throughout 2020, got softer in 2021. He struggled to make contact during the spring, then hit .161 and struck out more than a third of the time in the complex. We've debated even publishing complex-league stats in the past, because they are only one short slice of a longer year in development, and Peña is 18 and faced tougher competition this year than in traditional complex ball. But .161 is .161, and that coincides with greater hit-tool questions that we started hearing as early as last March. Let's see if he can start making good and better contact to correspond to his great visual swing evaluations.

Top Talents 25 and Under (as of 4/1/2022):

1. Bobby Witt Jr., SS/3B
2. MJ Melendez, C
3. Brady Singer, RHP
4. Nick Pratto, 1B
5. Asa Lacy, LHP
6. Daniel Lynch, LHP
7. Frank Mozzicato, LHP
8. Nick Loftin, SS
9. Kyle Isbel, OF
10. Jackson Kowar, RHP

The Royals have designed the first wave of their rebuild to revolve around a young rotation, but things have looked a bit wobbly thus far. Singer has had the best go of it, looking like a league-average starter through his first two seasons with a 92 DRA– in 192 ⅔ inning. He has been functionally a coin-flip pitcher thus far, throwing sinkers or sliders almost 95 percent of the time in 2021. Though he has been the same effective bulldog stretching back to his days at the University of Florida, his changeup's stagnation is a continued impediment to what could otherwise be a pristine innings-gobbling profile.

Like Kowar, Lynch collided with a (metaphorical) low-hanging pipe upon entering the big leagues. The 6-foot-6 southpaw struck out just 55 in his first 68 innings with the Royals, walking 31 and racking up a whopping –1.4 WARP in just 15 starts. It wasn't just rookie adjustments, however. Lynch's prospect profile popped as he sat mid-90s throughout 2019 and 2020 with a solid slider and improving changeup. The velocity was down in the bigs, however, and we got a better look at what may be at the root of Lynch's perplexing inability to miss bats. Namely, the towering lefty seems not to have a feel for spin. While this can manifest positively in its extremity, such as with the near-pure drop of his gyro slider, it seems to make his fastball and other pitches play down. Already seen as a reliever risk, Lynch could expand his room for error by finding that extra tick or two of heat again with consistency, but the Royals' plan to get their young arms the reps needed to adjust to the bigs may mean another uneven season or two for Lynch in Kansas City.

They'll see innings filled in by Kris Bubic and Carlos Hernández, as well, who represent the extremes of the number 5–6, starter/swingman spectrum. Both players already saw time in the bullpen in addition to making double-digit starts in 2021. Bubic nibbles around the zone with his funky delivery, below-average heater and a platoon-checking changeup, but neither induces enough whiffs nor lives within the zone capably enough to earn the benefit of the doubt for upside. Hernández pumped his heater 96–99 with consistency but either drank too much from the same Gatorade bottles as Lynch and Kowar or simply located too erratically to manifest strikeouts. Presuming the latter, it was also evident that his dubious off-speed repertoire was not up to snuff yet, working a 117 DRA– in 85 ⅔ innings and striking out just 74 against 41 free passes. This is a deep, enticing system, and most of its most impressive pieces are at or on the precipice of the majors, but a collective breakthrough depends on strides from the group that stumbled out of the gate in their first looks last year.

Los Angeles Angels

The State of the System:

The Angels' system is back to its mid-2010s doldrums. We were not nostalgic for this nor for "Thinking Out Loud."

The Top Ten:

1 **Reid Detmers LHP** OFP: 55 ETA: Debuted in 2021

Born: 07/08/99 Age: 22 Bats: L Throws: L Height: 6'2" Weight: 210 lb. Origin: Round 1, 2020 Draft (#10 overall)

YEAR	TEAM	LVL	AGE	W	L	SV	G	GS	IP	H	HR	BB/9	K/9	K	GB%	BABIP	WHIP	ERA	DRA-	WARP
2021	RCT	AA	21	2	4	0	12	12	54	45	10	3.0	16.2	97	33.9%	.361	1.17	3.50	69	1.4
2021	SL	AAA	21	1	0	0	2	2	8	7	0	1.1	12.4	11	31.6%	.368	1.00	1.13	97	0.0
2021	LAA	MLB	21	1	3	0	5	5	20^{2}	26	5	4.8	8.3	19	33.3%	.328	1.79	7.40	143	-0.3
2022 DC	*LAA*	*MLB*	*22*	*7*	*7*	*0*	*22*	*22*	*113.3*	*102*	*19*	*3.8*	*10.0*	*126*	*50.8%*	*.288*	*1.33*	*4.39*	*108*	*0.5*

Comparables: Tarik Skubal, Clay Buchholz, Brian Matusz

The Report: Detmers didn't need much more than his pretty, plus-plus curve to dominate the upper minors, but he added a few ticks to his previously low-90s fastball, as well. His slider also flashed plus, showing a different breaking-ball look around 10-mph firmer than the hook. Then he got to the majors and found out the best hitters in the world are perfectly capable of squaring 94 mph as easily as 91 if it's not located well. Detmers was still able to bamboozle big-league bats with his breaking balls—and he threw his slider or curve about half the time—but he's going to need to refine his fastball command in order to put himself in spots where he can beat major-league hitters with the secondary stuff. He has a long track record of performance, both in college and the minors, and his arsenal has two potential swing-and-miss secondaries. So, we are considering his major-league struggles more of a blip. It's not nothing, though. Blips do show up on your radar, after all.

OFP: 55 / No. 3–4 starter

Variance: Low. Detmers would hardly be the first good pitching prospect to have to make some adjustments in the bigs. We think he'll make them, but his fastball is not likely to be more than an average offering, so that might limit his upside some.

Mark Barry's Fantasy Take: I've been known to have a soft spot for Angels pitchers (your guess as to why is as good as mine), but, even with that in mind, I really like Detmers. The southpaw found a couple extra ticks for his heater, helping him escape the dreaded "soft-tossing lefty" stigma. I don't think he's an ace, but he should solidify himself in the middle of the rotation fairly quickly. He's a top-50 dynasty prospect for me.

2 **Sam Bachman RHP** OFP: 55 ETA: 2023

Born: 09/30/99 Age: 22 Bats: R Throws: R Height: 6'1" Weight: 235 lb. Origin: Round 1, 2021 Draft (#9 overall)

YEAR	TEAM	LVL	AGE	W	L	SV	G	GS	IP	H	HR	BB/9	K/9	K	GB%	BABIP	WHIP	ERA	DRA-	WARP
2021	TRI	A+	21	0	2	0	5	5	14^{1}	13	1	2.5	9.4	15	65.8%	.324	1.19	3.77	109	0.0
2022 non-DC	*LAA*	*MLB*	*22*	*2*	*3*	*0*	*57*	*0*	*50*	*53*	*6*	*4.6*	*7.7*	*42*	*41.2%*	*.312*	*1.57*	*5.21*	*123*	*-0.4*

Comparables: Parker Markel, Ryan Lawlor, Henry Centeno

The Report: Across all of these lists, up and down any organization, from top-101 arms to others of note, we will write about reliever risk. Bachman has a lot of the flags that might portend a bullpen future. He's a shorter, broader righty with some effort in his delivery—although not as much as you'd think for a guy regularly hitting 100 mph. He has a theoretical changeup, but he's mostly a two-pitch guy. He also wasn't super durable in college. On the other hand, those two pitches are both potential 70-grade offerings. We don't need to say much more about the fastball than it regularly hits triple digits, but there's arm-side movement and solid present command of the pitch, as well. Bachmans's slider is a sharp, upper-80s offering he can spot for strikes or use to induce swing-and-miss out of the zone. Does he really need much more? Well, maybe. And he's "only" mid-to-upper 90s as a starter, so there might be continued temptation to try to get as much out of that fastball/slider combo as possible in the late innings.

OFP: 55 / No. 3–4 starter or second-division closer

Variance: Medium. Sure, Bachman hasn't thrown much in the pros. He could also probably pitch in a major-league pen this year. The Angels will see what they have in him as a starter, for now. The best use of Bachman might end up somewhere in between a 180-inning starter and a 60-inning, high-leverage arm.

Mark Barry's Fantasy Take:

Tell me somethin', girl
Are you happy in this modern world?
Or do you need more?
Is there somethin' else you're searchin' for?

3 Arol Vera SS   OFP: 55   ETA: 2025

Born: 09/12/02 Age: 19 Bats: S Throws: R Height: 6'2" Weight: 170 lb. Origin: International Free Agent, 2019

YEAR	TEAM	LVL	AGE	PA	R	2B	3B	HR	RBI	BB	K	SB	CS	AVG/OBP/SLG	DRC+	BABIP	BRR	FRAA	WARP
2021	ANG	ROK	18	164	24	16	3	0	17	12	39	2	2	.317/.384/.469		.426			
2021	IE	A	18	90	10	0	0	0	5	6	20	9	2	.280/.344/.280	100	.371	0.2	SS(12) 1.0, 2B(7) 0.3	0.4
2022 non-DC	*LAA*	*MLB*	*19*	*251*	*18*	*9*	*1*	*2*	*19*	*14*	*70*	*11*	*4*	*.215/.267/.291*	*50*	*.298*	*1.0*	*SS 0, 2B 0*	*-0.6*

Comparables: Hernán Pérez, Jose Salas, Adrian Marin

The Report: One of two seven-figure middle infielders from the Angels' 2019 international-free-agent class, Vera showed an impressive combination of physical projection and present production as an 18-year-old in the low minors last year. He's still lean enough that sometimes it looks like the bat is swinging him, but his fundamentals at the plate are strong, and he has a good feel for the barrel, so we would expect at least fringe power to come as he fills out and adds strength. Defensively, Vera is a potential plus shortstop capable of making the routine play look glamorous and the harder ones look easy. He's a long way from the majors, but he has enough offensive upside coupled with a good glove at a premium spot to rank him highly in a system this . . . well, Mark has you covered there.

OFP: 55 / Above-average shortstop

Variance: Extreme. Vera has little experience above the complex league, and you are banking on a lot of physical projection and offensive gains.

Mark Barry's Fantasy Take:

I'm fallin'
In all the good times, I find myself longin' for change
And in the bad times, I fear myself

4 Jordyn Adams CF   OFP: 50   ETA: 2024

Born: 10/18/99 Age: 22 Bats: R Throws: R Height: 6'2" Weight: 180 lb. Origin: Round 1, 2018 Draft (#17 overall)

YEAR	TEAM	LVL	AGE	PA	R	2B	3B	HR	RBI	BB	K	SB	CS	AVG/OBP/SLG	DRC+	BABIP	BRR	FRAA	WARP
2019	ANG	ROK	19	14	4	1	0	0	4	1	3	4	0	.538/.571/.615		.700			
2019	BUR	A	19	428	52	15	2	7	31	50	94	12	5	.250/.346/.358	109	.316	1.6	CF(73) -1.2, LF(9) 2.7, RF(8) -0.4	2.0
2019	IE	A+	19	40	7	1	1	1	1	5	14	0	1	.229/.325/.400	85	.350	0.2	CF(4) 0.4, LF(2) -0.2, RF(2) -0.3	0.1
2021	TRI	A+	21	307	37	7	2	5	27	28	116	18	4	.217/.290/.310	69	.350	2.9	CF(62) -9.9	-0.8
2022 non-DC	*LAA*	*MLB*	*22*	*251*	*20*	*9*	*1*	*4*	*21*	*19*	*89*	*4*	*3*	*.195/.263/.297*	*51*	*.299*	*0.4*	*CF 0, LF 0*	*-0.6*

Comparables: Dalton Pompey, Rymer Liriano, Aaron Hicks

The Report: One spot behind Vera, we have perhaps a cautionary tale of a highly-regarded amateur with an advanced glove at a premium spot but questions about how his bat will develop. Adams has never really gotten going in full-season ball, as he too often ends up out of sync at the plate despite good bat speed and average raw pop. He was badly overmatched at the alternate site to start the 2021 season and continued to struggle with swing-and-miss in High-A. When he did make contact, his swing could be a bit armsy and lacked the oomph to consistently drive the ball. Defensively, Adams uses his plus-plus speed to good effect in the outfield and should end up at least a plus center fielder. That kind of defense can give a prospect a little more leeway with the bat, but Adams's mechanical struggles, as well as his issues with better velocity and offspeed, are concerning.

OFP: 50 / Glove-first center fielder

Variance: High. Adams really hasn't hit above Low-A, so, as good as the defense and speed are, that's a problem.

Mark Barry's Fantasy Take:

Tell me something, boy
Aren't you tired tryin' to fill that void
Or do you need more?
Ain't it hard keepin' it so hardcore?

5 Kyren Paris MI OFP: 50 ETA: 2024

Born: 11/11/01 Age: 20 Bats: R Throws: R Height: 6'0" Weight: 165 lb. Origin: Round 2, 2019 Draft (#55 overall)

YEAR	TEAM	LVL	AGE	PA	R	2B	3B	HR	RBI	BB	K	SB	CS	AVG/OBP/SLG	DRC+	BABIP	BRR	FRAA	WARP
2019	ANG	ROK	17	13	4	1	0	0	2	3	4	0	0	.300/.462/.400		.500			
2021	IE	A	19	136	29	5	6	2	18	27	41	16	4	.274/.434/.491	98	.429	0.7	SS(17) 2.9, 2B(11) 1.2	0.8
2021	TRI	A+	19	55	6	2	1	1	6	2	20	4	0	.231/.273/.365	88	.355	-0.1	SS(9) 0.6, 2B(2) -0.0	0.1
2022 non-DC	*LAA*	*MLB*	*20*	*251*	*20*	*9*	*2*	*3*	*20*	*24*	*95*	*13*	*4*	*.191/.278/.302*	*58*	*.317*	*1.6*	*SS 1, 2B 0*	*-0.1*

Comparables: Jonathan Villar, Richard Ureña, Cole Tucker

The Report: Paris was off to a hot start in 2021 before a fractured fibula cost him two months of the season. He never quite got back to where he was pre-injury, and that, combined with the pandemic year, means the former second-round pick has missed a lot of developmental reps. Still, there's plenty to like out of what we've seen so far. Paris is twitchy at the plate with feel for contact and the ability to sting the ball gap-to-gap. He will need to clean up his approach and swing decisions, but, hopefully, that will come with more reps. Meaningful game power is far less likely to come, as Paris has a pretty level swing and not a ton of physicality. In the field, Paris has the range and hands for shortstop, but an arm better suited for second base, where he would be a plus defender.

OFP: 50 / Average middle infielder

Variance: High. Paris has limited pro reps and questions about his ultimate offensive projection that will need to be answered at higher levels.

Mark Barry's Fantasy Take:

I'm falling
In all the good times, I find myself longing for change
And in the bad times, I fear myself

6 Alexander Ramirez OF OFP: 50 ETA: 2025

Born: 08/29/02 Age: 19 Bats: R Throws: R Height: 6'2" Weight: 180 lb. Origin: International Free Agent, 2018

YEAR	TEAM	LVL	AGE	PA	R	2B	3B	HR	RBI	BB	K	SB	CS	AVG/OBP/SLG	DRC+	BABIP	BRR	FRAA	WARP
2019	DSL ANG	ROK	16	177	37	8	5	4	19	16	59	6	0	.234/.328/.429		.348			
2021	ANG	ROK	18	154	30	7	4	5	27	22	50	3	3	.276/.396/.512		.411			
2021	IE	A	18	81	4	0	1	0	4	7	34	1	1	.083/.185/.111	60	.158	0.7	RF(6) -0.6, LF(3) -0.7	-0.2
2022 non-DC	*LAA*	*MLB*	*19*	*251*	*16*	*9*	*1*	*2*	*17*	*15*	*107*	*3*	*1*	*.161/.223/.240*	*22*	*.286*	*0.3*	*CF 0, RF 0*	*-1.7*

Comparables: Leonardo Molina, Ronald Acuña Jr., Jasson Dominguez

The Report: One of the youngest players in the 2018 IFA class, Ramirez came stateside last season and flashed loud tools and a projectable frame. He's playing mostly center field now but will likely slide over to a corner, and his plus pop and arm fit the classic right-field profile well. As is common with pretty much every Angels position-player prospect in recent years, Ramirez has a noisy setup and handsy load that leads to fringe barrel control and subsequent swing-and-miss issues. It's the kind of thing that can get smoothed out as his frame gets a bit sturdier, but you have to go a ways back to find an Angels hitting prospect like this that has worked out. That's not baked into the projection, but it's in the back of our minds.

OFP: 50 / Average corner outfielder

Variance: Extreme. Ramirez has intriguing tools, but a noisy swing and questions about how his hit tool will develop means his profile has a wide range of even near-term outcomes.

Mark Barry's Fantasy Take:

I'm off the deep end, watch as I dive in
I'll never meet the ground
Crash through the surface, where they can't hurt us
We're far from the shallow now

7 Ky Bush LHP OFP: 50 ETA: 2024

Born: 11/12/99 Age: 22 Bats: L Throws: L Height: 6'6" Weight: 240 lb. Origin: Round 2, 2021 Draft (#45 overall)

YEAR	TEAM	LVL	AGE	W	L	SV	G	GS	IP	H	HR	BB/9	K/9	K	GB%	BABIP	WHIP	ERA	DRA-	WARP
2021	TRI	A+	21	0	2	0	5	5	12	14	0	3.8	15.0	20	46.4%	.500	1.58	4.50	103	0.1
2022 non-DC	*LAA*	*MLB*	*22*	*2*	*3*	*0*	*57*	*0*	*50*	*47*	*7*	*4.7*	*9.6*	*53*	*41.6%*	*.303*	*1.48*	*4.82*	*114*	*-0.2*

Comparables: Paul Clemens, Wes Helsabeck, Rafael Pineda

The Report: A tall, sturdy lefty that can run his fastball up into the mid-90s is always going to be on your draft board. Bush often struggled with control in a college career that took him from the Pac-12 to junior college and, finally, to St. Mary's College of California, where he started to put it all together during a dominant junior season. His delivery has some deception, as there's late torque, and he throws a little across his body. So, between that and his possibly related short track record of quality strike-throwing, there's reliever risk. Mid-90s heat with a potentially solid slider from the left side is a pretty good reliever, at least.

OFP: 50 / No. 4 starter or set-up man

Variance: High. There are a lot of moving parts in Bush's delivery, and he may be best suited to short relief.

Mark Barry's Fantasy Take:

In the sha-ha, sha-ha-llow
In the sha-ha-sha-la-la-la-llow
In the sha-ha, sha-ha-llow
We're far from the shallow now

8 Jack Kochanowicz RHP OFP: 45 ETA: 2025

Born: 12/22/00 Age: 21 Bats: L Throws: R Height: 6'6" Weight: 220 lb. Origin: Round 3, 2019 Draft (#92 overall)

YEAR	TEAM	LVL	AGE	W	L	SV	G	GS	IP	H	HR	BB/9	K/9	K	GB%	BABIP	WHIP	ERA	DRA-	WARP
2021	IE	A	20	4	2	0	20	18	83[1]	102	12	3.8	7.9	73	48.4%	.345	1.64	6.91	128	-0.9
2022 non-DC	*LAA*	*MLB*	*21*	*2*	*3*	*0*	*57*	*0*	*50*	*59*	*8*	*5.0*	*5.8*	*32*	*44.3%*	*.315*	*1.76*	*6.58*	*145*	*-1.0*

Comparables: Anthony Swarzak, Brock Burke, Marcus Moore

The Report: When you have a 6-foot-6, projectable, cold-weather prep arm making his full-season debut, you expect a few speed bumps, and Kochanowicz hit plenty of them in 2021. He has already filled out some since draft day and can run his fastball up into the mid-90s, although he sits more low 90s, generally. He pairs the fastball with a big-breaking, 12–6 curve and a potentially average change that shows both fade and sink. His mechanics are fairly simple, but he can lose the strike zone at times, and, at others, the stuff is strangely hittable. It might take a while for everything to come together here.

OFP: 45 / Back-end starter

Variance: High. The raw stuff suggests at least another half grade on this OFP, but Kochanowicz has struggled with both his control and command.

Mark Barry's Fantasy Take:

Oh, ha-ah-ahhhh
Ah, ha-ah-ah-ah-ah, oh, ah
Ha-ah-ah-oh-ahhhhhhh

9 Adam Seminaris LHP OFP: 45 ETA: 2024

Born: 10/19/98 Age: 23 Bats: R Throws: L Height: 6'0" Weight: 185 lb. Origin: Round 5, 2020 Draft (#141 overall)

YEAR	TEAM	LVL	AGE	W	L	SV	G	GS	IP	H	HR	BB/9	K/9	K	GB%	BABIP	WHIP	ERA	DRA-	WARP
2021	IE	A	22	4	5	0	16	14	64[1]	73	9	2.7	13.2	94	48.9%	.390	1.43	5.46	91	0.7
2021	TRI	A+	22	2	0	0	4	4	19	15	0	3.3	8.5	18	64.7%	.294	1.16	2.84	106	0.1
2022 non-DC	*LAA*	*MLB*	*23*	*2*	*2*	*0*	*57*	*0*	*50*	*50*	*6*	*3.9*	*7.9*	*43*	*44.2%*	*.302*	*1.44*	*4.55*	*110*	*-0.1*

The Report: Seminaris's report isn't that far off from what it was on the Cape in 2019. His fastball/slurvy-slider/changeup repertoire has played up due to Seminaris' impressive ability to repeat his fundamentally sound, easygoing delivery to the plate. The combination of a now-true plus pitch, his changeup, and plus command makes him one of the beter pitching prospects in this system. However, his fastball only scrapes 91, and both his slider and curve are fringe-average. The key question is: Are Seminaris's command and changeup good enough to make up for an otherwise light arsenal? Well, the answer actually might be a yes. Seminaris struck out hitters at an impressive clip last season with one potentially plus pitch and a bad fastball. How is that possible? Well, his changeup is really that good and plays up against righties, and his crossfire delivery really plays up against lefties. So, is this sustainable? Yes . . . but the variance is high for a reason.

OFP: 45 / No. 4–5 starter

Variance: High. His fastball is well below average, and changeup specialists often run into trouble in the upper minors.

Mark Barry's Fantasy Take:

I'm off the deep end, watch as I dive in
I'll never meet the ground
Crash through the surface, where they can't hurt us
We're far from the shallow now

10 Jeremiah Jackson IF OFP: 45 ETA: 2024

Born: 03/26/00 Age: 22 Bats: R Throws: R Height: 6'0" Weight: 165 lb. Origin: Round 2, 2018 Draft (#57 overall)

YEAR	TEAM	LVL	AGE	PA	R	2B	3B	HR	RBI	BB	K	SB	CS	AVG/OBP/SLG	DRC+	BABIP	BRR	FRAA	WARP
2019	ORM	ROA	19	291	47	14	2	23	60	24	96	5	1	.266/.333/.605		.315			
2021	GDD	WIN	21	61	10	1	0	3	10	2	23	0	1	.161/.213/.339		.194			
2021	IE	A	21	196	29	14	3	8	46	24	65	11	3	.263/.352/.527	101	.367	-1.3	SS(31) -1.2, 2B(9) -0.4	0.4
2022 non-DC	*LAA*	*MLB*	*22*	*251*	*21*	*11*	*1*	*5*	*23*	*19*	*100*	*6*	*2*	*.196/.264/.328*	*58*	*.322*	*0.6*	*SS 0, 2B 0*	*-0.5*

Comparables: Daniel Robertson, Dixon Machado, Nico Hoerner

The Report: The dream version of Jackson has long been a power-hitting shortstop, and he still shows plenty of plus raw pop despite a still-wiry frame. He has great hand speed, but still primarily hunts fastballs and will chase offspeed out of the zone too often. Jackson is able to do a ton of damage on contact due to the whip and loft in his swing, but running 33-percent K rates will make that unsustainable up the ladder. To be fair, Jackson never really got a chance to adjust to full-season ball in 2021 due to a quad strain that cost him more than two months. In the field, Jackson still projects as at least an average shortstop, showing a quick first step, plus range and an above-average arm. If he can even get the hit tool to below average, he likely has enough power and glove to carve out a role as a second-division regular, but that's above the 75th-percentile outcome right now.

OFP: 45 / Fifth infielder or fringe starter

Variance: High. His swing-and-miss has been an issue in the lower levels of the minors, and there is significant risk that his hit tool will fall apart as soon as Double-A, but there's a skyscraper ceiling if things start to click.

Mark Barry's Fantasy Take:

In the sha-ha, sha-ha-llow
In the sha-ha-sha-la-la-la-llow
In the sha-ha, sha-ha-llow
We're far from the shallow now

The Prospects You Meet Outside the Top Ten

Prospects on the Rise

Werner Blakely IF Born: 02/21/02 Age: 20 Bats: L Throws: R Height: 6'3" Weight: 185 lb. Origin: Round 4, 2020 Draft (#111 overall)

YEAR	TEAM	LVL	AGE	PA	R	2B	3B	HR	RBI	BB	K	SB	CS	AVG/OBP/SLG	DRC+	BABIP	BRR	FRAA	WARP
2021	ANG	ROK	19	186	22	6	0	3	19	33	69	15	2	.182/.339/.284		.308			

The Angels' 2020 fourth-round pick possesses a skinny frame and a long swing. Blakely has a lot of room for physical growth, and it seems like there is some raw power that he could unlock thanks to some natural lift and good plate coverage. The young infielder is twitchy pre-swing but calms down as the ball is delivered and clearly has an advanced eye. If it weren't for a truly abysmal end to the year, Blakely surely would have garnered more buzz.

Coleman Crow RHP Born: 12/30/00 Age: 21 Bats: R Throws: R Height: 6'0" Weight: 175 lb. Origin: Round 28, 2019 Draft (#841 overall)

YEAR	TEAM	LVL	AGE	W	L	SV	G	GS	IP	H	HR	BB/9	K/9	K	GB%	BABIP	WHIP	ERA	DRA-	WARP
2021	IE	A	20	4	3	0	13	10	62^1	68	7	4.2	9.0	62	42.2%	.332	1.56	4.19	128	-0.7
2022 non-DC	*LAA*	*MLB*	*21*	*2*	*3*	*0*	*57*	*0*	*50*	*56*	*8*	*5.1*	*6.4*	*35*	*41.7%*	*.305*	*1.70*	*6.37*	*141*	*-0.9*

An undersized, Day-Three prep righty from the 2019 draft, Crow popped up at Low-A Inland Empire touching 94 mph out of an athletic delivery. His slider will flash above average, and he has feel for a changeup, as well. He's a long way from the majors, but there's enough here, at present, to like him as a back-end starting-pitching prospect.

Robinson Pina RHP Born: 11/26/98 Age: 23 Bats: R Throws: R Height: 6'4" Weight: 180 lb. Origin: International Free Agent, 2017

YEAR	TEAM	LVL	AGE	W	L	SV	G	GS	IP	H	HR	BB/9	K/9	K	GB%	BABIP	WHIP	ERA	DRA-	WARP
2019	BUR	A	20	5	8	1	26	21	108	85	5	5.1	12.2	146	47.1%	.317	1.35	3.83	92	1.3
2021	IE	A	22	0	0	0	4	4	22^2	15	2	2.4	13.1	33	46.9%	.283	0.93	1.19	82	0.4
2021	TRI	A+	22	2	7	0	13	13	57^1	38	4	6.4	13.3	85	40.5%	.309	1.38	4.40	83	1.0
2021	RCT	AA	22	0	3	0	4	4	15^1	19	7	5.3	12.9	22	33.3%	.343	1.83	9.39	87	0.3
2022 non-DC	*LAA*	*MLB*	*23*	*2*	*3*	*0*	*57*	*0*	*50*	*44*	*7*	*6.1*	*10.5*	*58*	*42.5%*	*.295*	*1.57*	*5.16*	*115*	*-0.2*

Pina crossed three levels as a 22-year-old last season, ending the year in Double-A. His walk rates ballooned once he left Inland Empire, and he projects for maybe 40 command, at best, so those control issues weren't exactly out of character. As a starter, his fastball has merely average velocity, but Pina has a potentially plus breaker and has shown feel for a split. His command likely will force him to the bullpen fairly soon, but if the fastball ticks up a bit in shorter stints, the quality of his secondaries could work in the seventh or eighth inning.

Factors on the Farm

Orlando Martinez OF Born: 02/17/98 Age: 24 Bats: L Throws: L Height: 6'0" Weight: 185 lb. Origin: International Free Agent, 2017

YEAR	TEAM	LVL	AGE	PA	R	2B	3B	HR	RBI	BB	K	SB	CS	AVG/OBP/SLG	DRC+	BABIP	BRR	FRAA	WARP
2019	IE	A+	21	422	55	21	4	12	49	36	79	5	4	.263/.325/.434	116	.299	1.0	CF(41) 3.3, RF(21) -2.0, LF(20) 1.4	2.6
2021	GDD	WIN	23	81	5	2	2	1	4	2	14	0	1	.215/.235/.329		.250			
2021	RCT	AA	23	436	58	23	2	16	54	30	119	5	3	.258/.313/.445	94	.326	0.1	LF(57) -2.3, CF(28) -3.3, RF(15) -0.4	0.4
2022 non-DC	*LAA*	*MLB*	*24*	*251*	*23*	*11*	*1*	*5*	*25*	*15*	*73*	*1*	*2*	*.229/.281/.363*	*69*	*.308*	*0.0*	*CF 1, LF 1*	*0.0*

Comparables: Jake Cave, Gerardo Parra, Juan Lagares

Martinez continues to stay on track toward being a useful fourth outfielder. He can play all three spots and has average pop. He also has platoon issues, but, in a bench role, you can hide him from lefties more easily, and his power plays more against righties, anyway, so you will want to leverage that in a part time role. The swing-and-miss did tick up in Double-A, though, and Martinez can't really afford to see his hit tool fall short of fringe-average.

Packy Naughton LHP Born: 04/16/96 Age: 26 Bats: R Throws: L Height: 6'2" Weight: 195 lb. Origin: Round 9, 2017 Draft (#257 overall)

YEAR	TEAM	LVL	AGE	W	L	SV	G	GS	IP	H	HR	BB/9	K/9	K	GB%	BABIP	WHIP	ERA	DRA-	WARP
2019	DBT	A+	23	5	2	0	9	9	51^{1}	49	2	1.6	8.8	50	43.6%	.320	1.13	2.63	91	0.8
2019	CHA	AA	23	6	10	0	19	19	105^{2}	109	8	2.2	6.9	81	39.1%	.309	1.28	3.66	112	0.0
2021	SL	AAA	25	2	2	0	13	9	56^{2}	69	7	2.1	8.4	53	47.8%	.363	1.45	4.76	94	0.4
2021	LAA	MLB	25	0	4	0	7	5	22^{2}	27	3	5.6	4.8	12	50.6%	.308	1.81	6.35	150	-0.4
2022 DC	*LAA*	*MLB*	*26*	*2*	*2*	*0*	*17*	*3*	*25.7*	*29*	*3*	*3.3*	*6.9*	*19*	*39.9%*	*.314*	*1.50*	*5.29*	*125*	*-0.2*

Comparables: Luis Cessa, Anthony Vasquez, Tyler Wilson

The 6-foot-2, lanky lefty, who made his MLB debut in 2021, has a somewhat wacky (ha) approach on the mound. His front knee comes up as high as his hands mid-windup. There are a lot of moving parts, as Naughtom also torques the ball well behind his backside, which creates a fair amount of deception. This isn't a profile that is going to blow you away. His low-90s fastball and slider are average, at best, but his changeup is slightly above and works well when his command is on, perhaps enough so that he can be a back-end starter or swingman.

Andrew Wantz RHP Born: 10/13/95 Age: 26 Bats: R Throws: R Height: 6'4" Weight: 235 lb. Origin: Round 7, 2018 Draft (#211 overall)

YEAR	TEAM	LVL	AGE	W	L	SV	G	GS	IP	H	HR	BB/9	K/9	K	GB%	BABIP	WHIP	ERA	DRA-	WARP
2019	IE	A+	23	5	3	0	11	6	48	40	4	3.2	10.9	58	34.1%	.300	1.19	3.56	93	0.3
2019	MOB	AA	23	0	6	0	13	12	48	59	12	4.9	10.1	54	33.8%	.346	1.77	7.13	140	-0.8
2021	SL	AAA	25	1	0	0	12	5	30^{1}	22	2	1.8	8.9	30	47.5%	.256	0.92	1.78	94	0.2
2021	LAA	MLB	25	1	0	0	21	0	27^{1}	23	5	3.6	12.5	38	29.9%	.290	1.24	4.94	82	0.5
2022 DC	*LAA*	*MLB*	*26*	*2*	*2*	*0*	*44*	*0*	*38.7*	*35*	*6*	*3.8*	*9.9*	*42*	*43.9%*	*.287*	*1.33*	*4.46*	*107*	*0.0*

Comparables: Austin Brice, Ryne Stanek, J.J. Hoover

After an incredible statistical showing in Triple-A last year, Wantz got the call to the bigs and looked to be more of what his stuff profile suggests. His high-spin fastball sits 91–93 mph, touching 94, with natural cutting action, followed by a slider—his best pitch—and an average changeup. The slider is an above-average pitch, flashing plus potential with sharp cutting action that deceives hitters thanks to Wantz's new-and-improved command. However, high-spin fastball guys with low-90s velocity probably need to be starters today, and it appears the Angels have conceded that Wantz is more of an opener type or long reliever.

Top Talents 25 and Under (as of 4/1/2022):

1. Jo Adell, OF
2. Brandon Marsh, OF
3. Reid Detmers, LHP
4. Patrick Sandoval, LHP
5. Sam Bachman, RHP
6. Arol Vera, SS
7. José Suarez, LHP
8. Jordyn Adams, OF
9. Kyren Paris, IF
10. Jaime Barría, RHP

Adell didn't make it all the way back to the halcyon days of hype in 2021, but he did show marked improvement after eventually being promoted from a lengthy session launching big flies into the Salt Lake City sky. He's still struggling to make enough quality contact, but he looked more like a 22-year-old with talent attempting to make adjustments as opposed to his 2020 self, who seemed utterly lost. The odds of Adell reaching his ceiling are more distant than they appeared ahead of 2020, but a strikeout rate in the low 20-percent range is vastly more tenable and promising.

Struggles similar to Adell's in 2020 befell Marsh in his rookie sojourn, as big-league pitching made for a weighty challenge to the part-time Conan the Barbarian impersonator. A shoulder injury held him out for the first half of the season, forcing a challenging catch-up pace that Marsh was unable to match. Though he played a healthy second half, Marsh struck out more than a third of the time and struggled to provide a spark in the back half of Anaheim's season, posting a 60 DRC+

after middling numbers in Triple-A Salt Lake. He has a better minor-league track record, of course, and should benefit from a healthy offseason. In the coming season, he should provide above-average defense in the outfield and hopefully take a sophomore step forward.

Despite the Angels' hyper-aggressive pitching approach in recent drafts, their big-league staff has had some glimpses of average, homegrown arms. Sandoval is the best of the bunch, with a 92 DRA– in 87 innings built on promising peripherals and visuals only moderately undercut by the lower-back stress fracture which short-circuited his season. He is expected to be ready for spring and could help stabilize the soft underbelly of Anaheim's top-heavy rotation. Joining him in the back of the group are Suarez and Barría, who have shown a distaste for missing bats in the big leagues, rendering their otherwise-pedestrian repertoires difficult to view rosily. Suarez leaned more heavily on his curveball, helping him establish a more groundball-based profile, but that is a narrow pathway to success.

Los Angeles Dodgers

The State of the System:

The Dodgers' system continues to ebb a bit from their peak organizational depth a few years ago, but they still have enough in the pipeline to fortify more 100-plus-win major-league teams over the next couple seasons.

The Top Ten:

1 Miguel Vargas 3B OFP: 60 ETA: Late 2022/Early 2023

Born: 11/17/99 Age: 22 Bats: R Throws: R Height: 6'3" Weight: 205 lb. Origin: International Free Agent, 2017

YEAR	TEAM	LVL	AGE	PA	R	2B	3B	HR	RBI	BB	K	SB	CS	AVG/OBP/SLG	DRC+	BABIP	BRR	FRAA	WARP
2019	GL	A	19	323	53	20	2	5	45	35	43	9	1	.325/.399/.464	143	.363	-2.6	3B(59) 2.4, 1B(2) 0.3, 2B(2) 0.3	2.7
2019	RC	A+	19	236	23	18	1	2	32	20	40	4	3	.284/.353/.408	111	.341	-2.1	3B(43) -1.9, 1B(6) 0.4	0.6
2021	GL	A+	21	172	31	11	1	7	16	9	32	4	0	.314/.366/.532	121	.353	-1.1	3B(31) -1.9, 2B(2) -0.6, 1B(1) -0.0	0.6
2021	TUL	AA	21	370	67	16	1	16	60	36	57	7	1	.321/.386/.523	125	.344	1.0	3B(53) -0.4, 2B(15) -1.0, 1B(9) 0.1	2.2
2022 non-DC	*LAD*	*MLB*	*22*	*251*	*24*	*12*	*1*	*4*	*25*	*18*	*46*	*2*	*1*	*.258/.318/.383*	*89*	*.305*	*-0.1*	*3B 0, 2B 0*	*0.3*

Comparables: Miguel Andújar, Brandon Drury, Blake DeWitt

The Report: Vargas just continues to rake. After losing a year to the pandemic, he looked bigger and stronger in 2021, and his all-fields approach is now all-fields power. He always had plus raw power; it's now looking like it will be at least plus in games, and there's a chance Vargas's pop plays above his raw-power grade because of his ability to drive the ball from any part of the zone. It's easy power from a quiet setup, although his swing has a bit of length, which might limit his ability to keep hitting .300 further up the ladder. Defensively, well he is *bigger* and stronger now. His defensive tools at third remain around average—with more than enough arm for the left side—but there's still a chance that he will eventually move off the position. The Dodgers, being the Dodgers, have responded by getting him more games at second than first. Vargas is never going to have the ideal range for the keystone—or even third, for that matter—but perhaps his plus arm allows him to play a bit deeper. He is probably as athletic as Max Muncy, so this might work well enough to give Los Angeles another option to get Vargas's bat in the lineup every day. That's what we're all here for, anyway.

OFP: 60 / Classic number-three hitter, perhaps a less-classic third baseman

Variance: Medium. The bat is low variance, the defensive/positional value is high variance. Let's split the difference.

Mark Barry's Fantasy Take: Know thyself. I've come to learn that I love dudes that can make a lot of contact. Typically, when I'm fawning over a high-contact profile, however, said profile doesn't come with Vargas's power potential. And while I wouldn't read too much into raw minor-league stolen-base numbers, Vargas managed to snag 11 bags in 12 tries, an efficiency that foreshadows the potential for some success. For me, Vargas is pretty clearly a top-50 name, and he's probably closer to number 30 than 50.

2 Diego Cartaya C OFP: 60 ETA: Late 2023/Early 2024

Born: 09/07/01 Age: 20 Bats: R Throws: R Height: 6'3" Weight: 219 lb. Origin: International Free Agent, 2018

YEAR	TEAM	LVL	AGE	PA	R	2B	3B	HR	RBI	BB	K	SB	CS	AVG/OBP/SLG	DRC+	BABIP	BRR	FRAA	WARP
2019	DODM	ROK	17	150	25	10	0	3	13	11	31	1	0	.296/.353/.437		.359			
2019	DSL BAU	ROK	17	57	11	2	2	1	9	5	11	0	0	.240/.316/.420		.282			
2021	RC	A	19	137	31	6	0	10	31	18	37	0	0	.298/.409/.614	119	.353	0.5	C(31) -4.0	0.4
2022 non-DC	*LAD*	*MLB*	*20*	*251*	*23*	*10*	*0*	*6*	*25*	*19*	*81*	*0*	*0*	*.206/.277/.344*	*68*	*.289*	*-0.3*	*C -6*	*-0.6*

Comparables: Francisco Mejía, Christian Bethancourt, Christian Vázquez

The Report: Injuries limited the 20-year-old catcher to 31 games in 2021, but, when on the field, he announced his presence with authority, slashing .298/.409/.614 with 10 homers in 137 plate appearances. His 11.4 at-bats per home run are indicative of his inherent strength and natural power. Currently, that power is generated primarily to his pull side, but he has demonstrated a willingness to drive the ball to all fields. Already 6-foot-3 and 219 pounds, Cartaya exhibits solid athleticism and mobility at the catcher's position. His receptive hands, astute baseball IQ and above-average arm strength provide a suitable foundation for him to remain behind the plate long-term. If he does grow out of the position, his offensive prowess makes an everyday first-base role an alternative option. Cartaya's conditioning and durability will be key to keeping him behind the plate, where his run-producing bat would certify him as an All-Star-caliber player.

OFP: 60 / Bat-first catcher or appropriately offensive-minded first baseman

Variance: Medium. His large frame and physicality place an emphasis on his health and conditioning. Soft-tissue injuries and the nicks and bruises that come with the territory behind the plate may push him to first base to ensure his bat remains in the lineup.

Mark Barry's Fantasy Take: Unlike hoverboards, Cartaya could certainly work on water. You know, because he has power. He still strikes out a bunch, though, and there are rumblings that he might need to move out from behind the plate. If that happens, he'd have a lot less fantasy utility. You can pass for now.

Eyewitness Report: Diego Cartaya

Evaluator: Trevor Andresen
Report Date: 10/30/2021
Dates Seen: 6/8/21-6/12/21
Risk Factor: High
Physical/Health: XL 6'3 220 lb. frame. Strong, mature build capable of handling the rigors of catching

Tool	Future Grade	Report
Hit	45	Hits from an upright, slightly open stance w/ quiet hands & a leg kick load. Advance approach for a 19-year old, showing feel for the strike zone & taking aggressive swings in positive counts, though he is still getting accustomed to good spin/offspeed & can get beat on quality secondaries in-zone. Might wind up as more of a .240-.250 bat, but should come w/ strong OBP's
Power	60	Generates easy plus raw power. Gets to it in-game due to his approach & the simplicity of his swing. 30+ HR bat
Baserunning/ Speed	30	Well below-avg athleticism. Base-clogging type
Glove	45	Work in progress behind the dish. Fringy to below-avg mobility w/ stiff hands. Automated strike zone could help him become an avg defender, otherwise he's a below-avg defender at risk of moving to 1B
Arm	60	Asset w/ plus strength/accuracy

Conclusion: Defensive variance along w/ the general physical toll of catching create a good amount of risk, but there aren't many catchers capable of putting up 30 HR's annually & the bat would play at 1B should he slide down the defensive spectrum. Cartaya ultimately projects as an above-avg regular w/ a middle-of-the-order offensive profile

3 Bobby Miller RHP OFP: 55 ETA: Late 2022/Early 2023

Born: 04/05/99 Age: 23 Bats: L Throws: R Height: 6'5" Weight: 220 lb. Origin: Round 1, 2020 Draft (#29 overall)

YEAR	TEAM	LVL	AGE	W	L	SV	G	GS	IP	H	HR	BB/9	K/9	K	GB%	BABIP	WHIP	ERA	DRA-	WARP
2021	GL	A+	22	2	2	0	14	11	47	30	1	2.1	10.7	56	45.6%	.257	0.87	1.91	84	0.9
2021	TUL	AA	22	0	0	0	3	3	9^1	10	1	1.9	13.5	14	52.0%	.375	1.29	4.82	70	0.2
2022 non-DC	*LAD*	*MLB*	*23*	*2*	*2*	*0*	*57*	*0*	*50*	*48*	*6*	*3.2*	*8.0*	*44*	*46.6%*	*.292*	*1.33*	*4.19*	*102*	*0.1*

Comparables: Jesus Colome, Henry Alberto Rodriguez, Bryan Shaw

The Report: An oblique injury cost Miller six weeks of the 2021 season, but he still had plenty of time to show off his plus stuff, most notably his much-improved changeup. But let's start with his fastball, per usual. Miller can still pop it into the upper 90s, although he sits more around 95. The pitch is more of a heavy, ground-ball inducer than a bat-misser, but it's comfortably above average. His slider was his best secondary coming out of college and remains so. He'll manipulate it into more of a cutter in the upper 80s, but the plus version is a bit lower in the velo band, showing hard, late, 10–4 break. His changeup also flashes plus now, with hard, bat-missing sink and a bit of fade, as well. It's a power cambio that can bump the upper 80s, but that still gives Miller plenty of separation off his fastball. We expect him to continue to improve his feel for the changeup and get to all of the plus projection here. He works in a potentially average curveball as well as a fourth offering.

Well, that sounds like a pretty good starter, but Miller's control outpaces his command at the moment, so we haven't completely quashed the relief risk that he has carried since the draft. His delivery has some effort and features a long arm action. We also haven't seen him fully healthy or full stretched out as a pro yet. So we don't know exactly how sharp the stuff will be in the sixth or seventh inning, but it's 2022; we may never need to.

OFP: 55 / No. 3–4 starter, good bulk guy or late-inning reliever

Variance: Medium. The arsenal is major-league quality, we just need to see Miller hold up for a whole season. He could move quickly once that box is checked.

Mark Barry's Fantasy Take: Heading into 2021, I was concerned about Miller's light workloads and his lack of a great third offering. The righty was still handled with kid gloves last year, but flashed enough promise in his secondaries to get me amped about his potential ceiling. I'm scooping up Miller wherever I can this offseason, with the hope that he'll be able to pitch deeper into games in 2022–everything else is there for SP2 upside.

4 Andy Pages OF OFP: 55 ETA: Late 2023/Early 2024

Born: 12/08/00 Age: 21 Bats: R Throws: R Height: 6'1" Weight: 212 lb. Origin: International Free Agent, 2018

YEAR	TEAM	LVL	AGE	PA	R	2B	3B	HR	RBI	BB	K	SB	CS	AVG/OBP/SLG	DRC+	BABIP	BRR	FRAA	WARP
2019	OGD	ROA	18	279	57	22	2	19	55	26	79	7	6	.298/.398/.651		.364			
2021	GL	A+	20	538	96	25	1	31	88	77	132	6	3	.265/.394/.539	139	.305	1.4	RF(83) 4.4, CF(27) -5.2	4.3
2022 non-DC	*LAD*	*MLB*	*21*	*251*	*27*	*10*	*0*	*7*	*28*	*26*	*69*	*3*	*3*	*.220/.317/.379*	*88*	*.287*	*0.1*	*RF 1, CF -1*	*0.4*

Comparables: Franmil Reyes, Eloy Jiménez, Moisés Sierra

The Report: This isn't scientific, but we think the two "coolest" 70-grade tools you can have are power and arm. That's a flashy combination but also useful. They would get your attention in a world without stats. But even in a world with them, those two plus-plus grades help make Pages a very good prospect. Honestly, even big bombs aren't as cool as a baseball going 0–60 faster than a Koenigsegg on a line from right field to third base, but the plus-plus raw power is going to have the most game impact here. Pages gets his from a heady combination of plus strength and bat speed. With some refinements in his hit tool, he could be a perennial 30-home-run bat, as he's capable of generating loud contact from line to line. He does tend to sell out for that power, though, and will expand the zone too readily. That said, he jumped into High-A with limited pro reps, so some growing pains with the hit tool are not unexpected. Enough warning signs reveal themselves to make it tough to get that projection to average at present, which may limit the game power to just a single plus.

Pages is an average runner right now, but already doesn't really have the foot speed for center and will likely lose a half step or two in the coming years. He should be a perfectly adequate defender in right—with that flashy arm making runners think twice about going first-to-third—but a corner-outfield outcome does mean he will have to make some refinements to his approach and swing decisions to be a solid regular.

OFP: 55 / Above-average rightfielder

Variance: High. While Pages' strikeout rate wasn't egregious given his experience level, there are some red flags that he might struggle more with swing-and-miss as soon as Double-A./p>

Mark Barry's Fantasy Take: You may think to yourself that a 25-percent strikeout rate isn't all that bad, and you'd be right, but Pages posting that number in High-A does have me wondering if he might be a little more Diamond Dallas than Hangman Adam in the year of our lord 2022. If he irons out the whiff issues, Pages should soar up rankings lists—the power numbers have been that impressive.

5 Ryan Pepiot RHP OFP: 55 ETA: 2022

Born: 08/21/97 Age: 24 Bats: R Throws: R Height: 6'3" Weight: 215 lb. Origin: Round 3, 2019 Draft (#102 overall)

YEAR	TEAM	LVL	AGE	W	L	SV	G	GS	IP	H	HR	BB/9	K/9	K	GB%	BABIP	WHIP	ERA	DRA-	WARP
2019	GL	A	21	0	0	0	9	9	18^{1}	13	0	4.4	10.3	21	46.7%	.289	1.20	2.45	89	0.2
2021	TUL	AA	23	3	4	0	15	13	59^{2}	30	7	3.9	12.2	81	32.5%	.198	0.94	2.87	70	1.4
2021	OKC	AAA	23	2	5	0	11	9	41^{2}	54	12	4.5	9.9	46	40.6%	.350	1.80	7.13	99	0.2
2022 non-DC	*LAD*	*MLB*	*24*	*2*	*3*	*0*	*57*	*0*	*50*	*47*	*8*	*4.7*	*9.3*	*51*	*47.5%*	*.294*	*1.48*	*4.89*	*114*	*-0.2*

Comparables: Alex Colomé, Chris Flexen, Jorge López

The Report: Pepiot might have the single-best pitch in the Dodgers' system. His changeup is a potential plus-plus offering with big sink and fade. It'll be a bat-misser all the way up to the majors. And, after a 2021 season that saw him get all the way to Triple-A, he might be testing that theory early in 2022. Pepiot's rapid ascent did hit a bit of a speed bump in Oklahoma City, but the former PCL can exaggerate any weaknesses in a pitcher's game. For Pepiot, that's his command. He has plenty of fastball by changeup-artist standards, now sitting in the mid-90s with a good spin profile, but he too often carves out a lot of plate with the heater. He has mostly scrapped his curveball for a high-80s slider/cutter-type thing. It runs close enough in velocity to the change to keep hitters off-balance, but it's not really a bat-misser in shape or command. Like with Miller, there is relief risk, but that might just be "isn't a traditional 32-start, 180-inning dude" risk, as the fastball/change combo should play well enough a couple times through the order.

OFP: 55 / No. 3–4 starter, good bulk guy or late-inning reliever

Variance: Medium. Pepiot has a longer pro track record than Miller and some success in the upper minors, as well, but similar command and "relief" risks.

Mark Barry's Fantasy Take: Pepiot could be a very serviceable big-league starter, but the combination of middling velocity, spotty control and an already-present reliever risk have him starting behind the eight ball. I'll take a flier in leagues that roster 150-plus prospects, but his ceiling is admittedly pretty low.

6 Michael Busch 2B OFP: 55 ETA: Late 2022/Early 2023

Born: 11/09/97 Age: 24 Bats: L Throws: R Height: 6'1" Weight: 210 lb. Origin: Round 1, 2019 Draft (#31 overall)

YEAR	TEAM	LVL	AGE	PA	R	2B	3B	HR	RBI	BB	K	SB	CS	AVG/OBP/SLG	DRC+	BABIP	BRR	FRAA	WARP
2019	DODL	ROK	21	16	1	0	0	0	0	1	2	0	0	.077/.250/.077		.091			
2019	GL	A	21	19	4	0	0	0	2	6	3	0	0	.182/.474/.182	111	.222	0.5	2B(4) 0.2	0.2
2021	TUL	AA	23	495	84	27	1	20	67	70	129	2	3	.267/.386/.484	112	.337	0.4	2B(88) 7.2, 1B(11) -0.1	3.0
2022 non-DC	*LAD*	*MLB*	*24*	*251*	*24*	*11*	*0*	*5*	*24*	*26*	*68*	*0*	*1*	*.213/.310/.345*	*80*	*.285*	*-0.3*	*2B 2, 1B 0*	*0.4*

Comparables: Jordany Valdespin, Zach McKinstry, Kyle Seager

The Report: Busch was perfectly fine in 2021, but that felt a tad underwhelming after the big instructs reports we got in 2020. To be fair, although Busch was an advanced college bat, he had very little pro experience and almost none above instructs/short-season ball before being dropped into the upper minors. Double-A Central pitchers exploited Busch's uppercut and occasionally pull-happy swing early in the year, but he finished the campaign red hot. His profile is tilting a little more toward the three true outcomes than expected, and his power is more solid than plus, but Busch continues to project as an average second baseman and should have defensive flexibility past that—he played a fair bit of left field in college. He has some swing-and-miss and platoon issues, but the Dodgers are good at managing this kind of player, so he looks like a 60 for 450 leveraged at-bats, even if his OFP remains a half-step below that on the tools and overall performance. And again, the overall performance was perfectly fine. Busch would be a cromulent major-league second baseman for any team, offering walks, plenty of doubles and bopping 20 home runs or so, even if he only hits .250.

OFP: 55 / Above-average second baseman

Variance: Medium. Busch has a performance-over-tools profile, so you'd like to see a little bit better performance, but his pop, platoon leverage and potential defensive flexibility should make him at least a useful bench piece.

Mark Barry's Fantasy Take: WARNING: "Fun" arbitrary endpoints ahead!

Busch was included in the August 23 edition of the "Monday Morning Ten Pack" (incidentally, one of my favorite in-season columns at BP), in which Brandon Williams provided a fairly glowing report on Busch but did point to his 33-percent strikeout rate as something that would need to be cleaned up. After that fateful day, Busch slashed .364/.422/.636 in 90 trips to the plate to close out the season and struck out just 22 percent of the time. His ultimate upside will be determined by whether this was a) a hot streak or b) real improvement. Either way, Busch is a top-60 dynasty prospect for me.

7 Maddux Bruns LHP OFP: 50 ETA: 2025

Born: 06/20/02 Age: 20 Bats: L Throws: L Height: 6'2" Weight: 205 lb. Origin: Round 1, 2021 Draft (#29 overall)

The Report: Bruns was a bit of a surprise first-round pick, but he's the kind of prep project that fits well with what the Dodgers do, from a player development standpoint. His stuff is relatively advanced for a high-school arm, featuring a big, 12–6 hook and a better-than-you'd-expect change. He has touched the upper 90s as an amateur, but was more low 90s/ touching mid after signing. His delivery also features some late arm acceleration and effort that has limited his command and consistency. There is the outline of a mid-rotation starter here, but his volatility is . . . well, see below.

OFP: 50 / No. 4 starter

Variance: Extreme. Bruns is going to be a slow burn as a pitching prospect, and his profile could go a number of ways in coming seasons.

Mark Barry's Fantasy Take: I don't want to doubt the Dodgers' player development, but there's currently a little too much volatility in Bruns's profile for me to dive in headfirst. He's purely watchlist material for me right now, unless your league allows you to retroactively use stats from hurlers that shared surnames with a prospect's first name.

8 Jorbit Vivas IF OFP: 50 ETA: Late 2022/Early 2023

Born: 03/09/01 Age: 21 Bats: L Throws: R Height: 5'10" Weight: 171 lb. Origin: International Free Agent, 2017

YEAR	TEAM	LVL	AGE	PA	R	2B	3B	HR	RBI	BB	K	SB	CS	AVG/OBP/SLG	DRC+	BABIP	BRR	FRAA	WARP
2019	DODL	ROK	18	137	18	11	2	1	20	13	15	5	4	.357/.438/.513		.392			
2019	OGD	ROA	18	97	13	6	1	1	12	6	16	5	5	.286/.371/.417		.338			
2021	RC	A	20	375	73	20	4	13	73	27	42	5	3	.311/.389/.515	140	.322	-0.7	2B(38) -1.0, 3B(34) 2.6, SS(2) -0.1	3.0
2021	GL	A+	20	102	12	6	0	1	14	13	13	3	1	.318/.422/.424	121	.361	-0.7	3B(14) 0.0, 2B(9) -1.3	0.4
2022 non-DC	*LAD*	*MLB*	*21*	*251*	*22*	*10*	*1*	*3*	*23*	*15*	*41*	*6*	*3*	*.246/.307/.355*	*81*	*.286*	*0.4*	*2B 0, 3B 1*	*0.3*

Comparables: Jorge Polanco, Jose Altuve, Jeimer Candelario

The Report: The left-handed-hitting infielder has been a steady offensive machine since signing with the Dodgers as an international free agent in 2017. Now 20 years old, Vivas has a baseball acumen and gritty approach to the game that contributed to a .312/.396/.496 line across two levels in 2021. He makes a lot of contact due to his exceptional hand-eye coordination, plate awareness and professional at-bats. A slight uppercut swing and a preference to pull the baseball produced solid power, primarily to the right side of the field. His above-average athleticism, mobility and dexterity allow him to excel as an infielder, while his average arm strength and nimble footwork around the bag make second base his ideal position. Listed at 5-foot-10, Vivas plays bigger than his measurements, and the well-rounded competitor can contribute to a winning ballclub in a variety of ways. Added to the Dodgers' 40-man roster late last year, Vivas demonstrates the attributes to be an everyday, offensive-minded infielder or a key contributor as a sub.

OFP: 50 / Second-division starter or good fifth infielder

Variance: Medium. His defensive limitations cut into his opportunities to get onto the field, but his offensive capabilities and instincts for the game will make him a valuable bench asset, at the least.

Mark Barry's Fantasy Take: When I talk about loving the high-contact guys, it's usually in the mold of a Vivas, as opposed to a Vargas. While Vivas smacked 14 homers in 2021, I'm not sure if that's something that will translate as he faces more advanced pitching. He can definitely put the bat to the ball, so he'll hit for average, but his middling power is a problem, especially since I don't think he'll run. Vivas is a watchlist guy for me right now, but I'll keep an eye on his Double-A performance.

9 Eddys Leonard IF

OFP: 50 ETA: Late 2022/Early 2023

Born: 11/10/00 Age: 21 Bats: R Throws: R Height: 6'0" Weight: 160 lb. Origin: International Free Agent, 2017

YEAR	TEAM	LVL	AGE	PA	R	2B	3B	HR	RBI	BB	K	SB	CS	AVG/OBP/SLG	DRC+	BABIP	BRR	FRAA	WARP
2019	DODL	ROK	18	200	27	7	4	3	20	27	48	2	4	.280/.380/.423		.367			
2021	RC	A	20	308	59	19	2	14	57	34	74	6	2	.295/.399/.544	122	.362	-0.1	SS(32) -1.0, 2B(16) 1.2, 3B(9) 1.1	1.9
2021	GL	A+	20	184	30	10	2	8	24	17	42	3	1	.299/.375/.530	117	.360	-0.4	3B(15) -2.1, 2B(11) -1.1, CF(11) -1.1	0.4
2022 non-DC	*LAD*	*MLB*	*21*	*251*	*23*	*11*	*1*	*5*	*25*	*18*	*72*	*4*	*2*	*.230/.299/.365*	*79*	*.312*	*0.2*	*SS -1, 2B 0*	*0.1*

Comparables: Yairo Muñoz, Thairo Estrada, Jeimer Candelario

The Report: Signed by the Dodgers as a free agent in 2017, the 21-year-old Leonard broke out offensively in his third pro season last year, slashing .296/.390/.539 with 55 extra-base hits across two levels. Listed at 6-feet and 160 pounds, Leonard's twitchy athleticism and relatively flat swing generate significant backspin and lift, which helped him launch 22 home runs. His middle-of-the-field approach, gap-to-gap power and ball-striking abilities present a difficult challenge for opposing pitchers. Defensively, his receptive hands, expansive range and above-average throwing arm provide plenty of versatility. He played second base, third base, shortstop and the outfield last season, creating ample opportunities to get his bat into the lineup. Added to the Dodgers 40-man roster in November, Leonard is an intriguing super-utility prospect who is capable of contributing on both sides of the ball.

OFP: 50 / Super-utility player

Variance: Medium. His bat-to-ball and defensive skills could use further cultivation, but power and positional flexibility make him a potentially valuable contributor.

Mark Barry's Fantasy Take: Call me lazy or call me, well, fine, lazy, but every time I hear super-utility guy, I think Chris Taylor. Aside from the organizational similarities and the Swiss Army–knife skill set, Leonard's profile looks awfully similar to his multi-positional brethren. Leonard can work a walk and will hit for a little power, but, ultimately, his propensity for striking out could limit his ability to hit for average. His fantasy ceiling isn't sky high, but he's closer to the big leagues than you might think from his experience.

10 Andre Jackson RHP

OFP: 50 ETA: Debuted in 2021

Born: 05/01/96 Age: 26 Bats: R Throws: R Height: 6'3" Weight: 210 lb. Origin: Round 12, 2017 Draft (#370 overall)

YEAR	TEAM	LVL	AGE	W	L	SV	G	GS	IP	H	HR	BB/9	K/9	K	GB%	BABIP	WHIP	ERA	DRA-	WARP
2019	GL	A	23	4	1	0	10	10	48^{1}	29	1	3.5	9.3	50	46.7%	.237	0.99	2.23	95	0.5
2019	RC	A+	23	3	1	0	15	15	66^{1}	61	5	5.2	12.3	91	45.9%	.368	1.49	3.66	88	0.6
2021	TUL	AA	25	3	2	0	15	13	63^{1}	46	12	2.8	10.7	75	31.8%	.239	1.04	3.27	82	1.0
2021	OKC	AAA	25	2	3	0	6	5	26^{1}	26	6	3.1	7.9	23	35.4%	.263	1.33	5.13	99	0.1
2021	LAD	MLB	25	0	1	1	3	0	11^{2}	10	1	4.6	7.7	10	26.5%	.290	1.37	2.31	100	0.1
2022 DC	*LAD*	*MLB*	*26*	*5*	*5*	*0*	*46*	*9*	*71*	*73*	*13*	*4.4*	*7.7*	*61*	*42.4%*	*.295*	*1.53*	*5.38*	*123*	*-0.4*

Comparables: Jeremy Hefner, Shane Greene, Rafael Montero

The Report: Jackson crossed three levels of the minors last year and made it all the way to Los Angeles, where he got a few multi-inning relief outings down the stretch. He now leans heavily on a much-improved and potentially plus changeup that sits in the mid-80s with good sink and fade. He runs his fastball up to the mid-90s, but it sits more 92-ish and, despite a high slot, runs fairly true. Jackson will mix in a short, little slider occasionally, as well, but his success will rely mostly on the interplay between his fastball and change. Jackson proved himself a little home-run prone, as his strike-throwing has improved, but his command remains fringy. And when you throw the changeup that often, you are going to hang some. He has limited miles on his arm, as he mostly played outfield in college, so there could still be more here, despite Jackson already being in his mid-twenties. Just look at the rapid maturation of his cambio. Still, the most likely outcome here is something similar to how he was used by the Dodgers in 2021: following an opener or general long relief.

OFP: 50 / Bulk guy

Variance: Medium. Jackson wasn't great in Triple-A or the majors and has a fairly short track record of throwing strikes, but the Dodgers do seem to get a fair bit out of this specific kind of role.

Mark Barry's Fantasy Take: I like Jackson as a pitcher. I think he'll be very useful as a modern baseball player. I do not think he'll be all that great for fantasy unless he makes a huge leap with his command. You can pass for now.

The Prospects You Meet Outside the Top Ten

Prospects on the Rise

Alex De Jesus SS Born: 03/22/02 Age: 20 Bats: R Throws: R Height: 6'2" Weight: 170 lb. Origin: International Free Agent, 2018

YEAR	TEAM	LVL	AGE	PA	R	2B	3B	HR	RBI	BB	K	SB	CS	AVG/OBP/SLG	DRC+	BABIP	BRR	FRAA	WARP
2019	DODM	ROK	17	178	13	8	1	2	25	12	58	5	1	.276/.326/.374		.410			
2019	DSL SHO	ROK	17	63	8	5	0	1	9	8	14	0	0	.296/.381/.444		.375			
2021	RC	A	19	422	67	25	1	12	73	69	128	1	0	.268/.386/.447	106	.385	0.0	SS(75) -8.3, 3B(1) -0.0	0.8
2022 non-DC	*LAD*	*MLB*	*20*	*251*	*21*	*11*	*0*	*3*	*20*	*26*	*89*	*0*	*1*	*.198/.284/.301*	*57*	*.312*	*-0.2*	*SS -3, 3B 0*	*-0.8*

Signed by the Dodgers as an international free agent in July 2018, De Jesus is an offense-minded shortstop. He compiled a .268/.386/.447 line with 12 home runs and 25 doubles as a 19-year-old in the Low-A West last season. He is prone to swing-and-miss, as his 30-percent strikeout rate suggests, but he also generates impressive power with a neutral, middle-of-the-field approach that imparts plenty of lift and carry to the baseball. He can struggle to identify spin but is willing to work deep into counts and draws his fair share of walks. Defensively, he has average range, a solid glove, and above-average arm strength that should allow him to remain at the shortstop position for some time. He'll need to improve his pitch identification and selection versus higher-level pitching, but his power should continue to develop as he matures. He may need to shift from shortstop to third base eventually, but his run-producing offensive profile would fit the hot corner.

Peter Heubeck RHP Born: 07/22/02 Age: 19 Bats: R Throws: R Height: 6'3" Weight: 170 lb. Origin: Round 3, 2021 Draft (#101 overall)

The Dodgers doubled down on their prep project arms, taking Heubeck in the third round last year. A projectable righty out of Maryland, Heubeck has plenty of arm speed but requires a fair bit of wish-casting on both his stuff and command profile, at present. Heubeck mostly sits low 90s with a spinny fastball, and he has some feel for the curve, although he has a tendency to snap it off. The Dodgers have had plenty of success developing arms, but last year's draft class might verge towards a heat check.

Jose Ramos RF Born: 01/01/01 Age: 21 Bats: R Throws: R Height: 6'1" Weight: 200 lb. Origin: International Free Agent, 2018

YEAR	TEAM	LVL	AGE	PA	R	2B	3B	HR	RBI	BB	K	SB	CS	AVG/OBP/SLG	DRC+	BABIP	BRR	FRAA	WARP
2019	DSL BAU	ROK	18	243	34	15	0	2	27	20	46	9	3	.275/.362/.377		.335			
2021	DOD	ROK	20	68	13	6	0	3	15	7	14	1	0	.383/.456/.633		.465			
2021	RC	A	20	220	30	18	3	8	44	16	57	1	4	.313/.377/.559	108	.398	-1.6	RF(44) 3.4	1.1
2022 non-DC	*LAD*	*MLB*	*21*	*251*	*21*	*12*	*1*	*4*	*23*	*14*	*75*	*3*	*2*	*.221/.275/.340*	*64*	*.308*	*0.2*	*RF 0, CF 0*	*-0.4*

Comparables: Starling Marte, Michael Hermosillo, Brett Phillips

Signed by the Dodgers as an international free agent out of Panama in 2018, Ramos made his stateside debut last season, slashing .329/.396/.576 across two levels of the minor leagues. Listed at 6-foot-1 and 200 pounds, the right-handed-hitting outfielder utilizes his lean strength and fast-twitch athleticism to swat balls from gap to gap. His run-producing mentality is evident in his aggressive swings, which produced 38 extra-base hits in 62 games, including 11 home runs. The free-swinging Ramos struck out at a 25-percent clip while drawing a walk in eight percent of his plate appearances, although he has demonstrated a promising degree of spin recognition and pitch selection. While not much of a base-stealing threat, he runs well on the basepaths and in the outfield, where he's capable of playing all three positions but will probably settle in a corner.

Factors on the Farm

Jacob Amaya SS Born: 09/03/98 Age: 23 Bats: R Throws: R Height: 6'0" Weight: 180 lb. Origin: Round 11, 2017 Draft (#340 overall)

YEAR	TEAM	LVL	AGE	PA	R	2B	3B	HR	RBI	BB	K	SB	CS	AVG/OBP/SLG	DRC+	BABIP	BRR	FRAA	WARP
2019	GL	A	20	470	68	25	4	6	58	74	83	4	4	.262/.381/.394	132	.314	-0.1	SS(51) -4.2, 2B(49) 2.1, 3B(4) 0.1	3.0
2019	RC	A+	20	89	14	3	2	1	13	7	15	1	3	.250/.307/.375	108	.292	1.0	SS(14) -1.8, 2B(4) 1.0, 3B(1) -0.0	0.3
2021	GDD	WIN	22	67	14	3	0	3	6	13	13	1	1	.333/.463/.556		.395			
2021	TUL	AA	22	476	60	15	1	12	47	52	103	5	0	.216/.303/.343	94	.254	-0.9	SS(112) -3.8	0.7
2022 DC	*LAD*	*MLB*	*23*	*63*	*7*	*2*	*0*	*0*	*6*	*5*	*14*	*0*	*0*	*.215/.293/.318*	*66*	*.273*	*0.0*	*SS 0, 2B 0*	*0.0*

Comparables: Cristhian Adames, Didi Gregorius, Dawel Lugo

The 23-year-old infielder has a high baseball IQ and an exceptional feel for the game. He struggled to a .216/.303/.343 batting line in 2021 but provided strong defense at shortstop and can impact a game with his savvy instincts and small-ball repertoire. He stroked 12 home runs last season and could make his major league debut in 2022 as a versatile, defense-minded contributor off the bench.

Brandon Lewis CI Born: 10/23/98 Age: 23 Bats: R Throws: R Height: 6'2" Weight: 222 lb. Origin: Round 4, 2019 Draft (#131 overall)

YEAR	TEAM	LVL	AGE	PA	R	2B	3B	HR	RBI	BB	K	SB	CS	AVG/OBP/SLG	DRC+	BABIP	BRR	FRAA	WARP
2019	DODL	ROK	20	49	5	1	0	0	2	5	8	0	0	.220/.327/.244		.265			
2019	OGD	ROA	20	142	32	10	0	12	39	10	35	0	2	.369/.423/.723		.434			
2019	GL	A	20	53	9	2	0	1	5	4	15	0	0	.167/.245/.271	82	.219	-0.4	3B(9) -0.5	0.0
2021	RC	A	22	200	36	14	1	10	35	26	63	0	1	.278/.380/.550	108	.378	-0.2	3B(32) 2.6, 1B(9) 0.1	1.0
2021	GL	A+	22	234	33	7	1	20	51	14	70	2	0	.262/.321/.584	125	.288	0.3	3B(27) -1.1, 1B(24) 2.2	1.5
2022 non-DC	*LAD*	*MLB*	*23*	*251*	*25*	*10*	*0*	*8*	*28*	*16*	*89*	*0*	*0*	*.214/.276/.378*	*69*	*.308*	*-0.3*	*3B 0, 1B 1*	*-0.4*

Drafted out of UC Irvine in the fourth round of the 2019 MLB Draft, the 23-year-old Lewis is a bat-first corner infielder who slugged a combined 30 homers at two stops on the Dodgers' farm last season. He exhibits an advanced awareness and professional approach in the batter's box, fully aware of his strengths and objectives when he steps to the plate. While he could address last season's 30-percent strikeout rate, his batting average and walk rate prove that he's more than a one-dimensional slugger. He doesn't provide much defensively, but his impact bat could carry him to the big leagues as soon as next season.

James Outman CF Born: 05/14/97 Age: 25 Bats: L Throws: R Height: 6'3" Weight: 215 lb. Origin: Round 7, 2018 Draft (#224 overall)

YEAR	TEAM	LVL	AGE	PA	R	2B	3B	HR	RBI	BB	K	SB	CS	AVG/OBP/SLG	DRC+	BABIP	BRR	FRAA	WARP
2019	GL	A	22	509	59	15	4	19	56	56	128	20	10	.226/.322/.407	109	.272	-2.5	CF(93) 4.1, LF(10) -1.1, RF(10) 1.3	2.3
2021	GDD	WIN	24	83	17	7	1	3	11	15	23	2	1	.284/.422/.552		.390			
2021	GL	A+	24	304	50	12	8	9	30	45	88	21	2	.250/.385/.472	120	.349	1.4	CF(51) -6.5, RF(13) 1.6	1.4
2021	TUL	AA	24	187	40	9	1	9	24	18	51	2	2	.289/.369/.518	98	.368	0.7	CF(36) 1.6, RF(3) -0.1	0.8
2022 non-DC	*LAD*	*MLB*	*25*	*251*	*24*	*9*	*2*	*5*	*25*	*23*	*78*	*6*	*3*	*.212/.297/.357*	*74*	*.298*	*0.7*	*CF 1, RF 0*	*0.3*

Comparables: Brandon Boggs, Logan Schafer, Adam Engel

The athletic 24-year-old outfielder compiled a .266/.379/.490 line at two stops on the Dodgers' farm in 2021. He showcased a combination of power and speed, producing 18 home runs and 23 stolen bases while hitting at the top of the lineup. He can provide above-average defense at all three outfield positions, and his two-way contributions would make him a valuable fourth outfielder. His 28-percent strikeout rate leaves room for improvement, but Outman could make his big-league debut as soon as next season.

Top Talents 25 and Under (as of 4/1/2022):

1. Julio Urías, LHP
2. Gavin Lux, 2B
3. Dustin May, RHP
4. Miguel Vargas, 3B
5. Diego Cartaya, C
6. Brusdar Graterol, RHP

7. Bobby Miller, RHP
8. Andy Pages, OF
9. Ryan Pepiot, RHP
10. Michael Busch, 2B

The thinning of the Dodgers' dynasty cohort has a basis in reality but should not be overstated. L.A.'s present and future are built upon the potency of several young stars, even after the team bid adieu to Corey Seager and dealt away several other longtime top minor leaguers.

The emergent acehood of Urías was instrumental in another 100-win season for Los Doyers in 2021. His 185-plus innings and 32 starts of 2.96-ERA/3.64-DRA ball led the mighty wild-card winners. Still just 25, Urías has a claim to co-ace of the Dodgers staff alongside Walker Buehler. The rotation is also augmented by the looming return of May, who saw what appeared to be a breakout campaign cut short by Tommy John surgery in his namesake month last year. He'll likely return in the middle or back half of 2022, and, given L.A.'s rotating rotation style, he may be eased in or even work from the bullpen until 2023. Gingergaard was frozen mid-"leap" by the injury, but if he picks up where he left off, with better utilization of his fastball for bat-missing, he can help regrow another hydra head for the Dodgers.

As for Lux, he has a bit of a make-or-break campaign looming, as he has compiled nearly a full big-league season of plate appearances as a below-average bat, despite his lofty minor-league lines. With Trea Turner and Chris Taylor in the fold, Lux appears set to be the latter's understudy. He made positive strides in terms of plate discipline in 2021, as the now-24-year-old adjusted a bit better to big-league pitching, striking out less than league average and walking more, but his minor-league power has yet to materialize through his Jordan Year—perhaps it will arrive in his Griffey Year.

Graterol hasn't yet materialized as the elite bullpen arm he appeared destined to be. He has been limited partially by command issues as well as a deceptively easy-to-square-up, sinking, triple-digit fastball. At this stage, he's a 100-mph ground-ball pitcher, à la Jordan Hicks, which is certainly a route to success—but, given his health history and lagging command development, expectations must be tempered slightly.

Miami Marlins

The State of the System:

If there is, in fact, no such thing as a pitching prospect, the Marlins might have a bit of an issue.

The Top Ten:

1 Max Meyer RHP OFP: 70 ETA: 2022

Born: 03/12/99 Age: 23 Bats: L Throws: R Height: 6'0" Weight: 196 lb. Origin: Round 1, 2020 Draft (#3 overall)

YEAR	TEAM	LVL	AGE	W	L	SV	G	GS	IP	H	HR	BB/9	K/9	K	GB%	BABIP	WHIP	ERA	DRA-	WARP
2021	PNS	AA	22	6	3	0	20	20	101	84	7	3.6	10.1	113	52.7%	.304	1.23	2.41	91	1.5
2021	JAX	AAA	22	0	1	0	2	2	10	6	1	1.8	15.3	17	47.4%	.278	0.80	0.90	72	0.3
2022 non-DC	*MIA*	*MLB*	*23*	*2*	*2*	*0*	*57*	*0*	*50*	*48*	*6*	*4.2*	*8.8*	*48*	*36.1%*	*.303*	*1.44*	*4.57*	*107*	*0.0*

Comparables: Trevor Bauer, Kevin Gausman, Chad Kuhl

The Report: You have to forget everything you think about pitching prospects before dissecting what Max Meyer is. He has a live arm and possesses one of the best breaking balls in the entire sport. That he is undersized, has only two effective pitches, and his fastball control can be erratic all qualify as concerns, but those are mostly footnotes when describing the player. The question becomes: How good can a pitcher be relying solely on velocity and a 70 (or better) out-pitch? Meyer has tried to develop the Marlins' patented firm changeup, but it still lacks consistency. Maybe that comes around eventually, but does he even need it? If mid- to upper-90s heaters and high-80s sliders are all you need to get guys out, having a show-me third pitch could be useful, even if it's unnecessary. Even though he may look like an elite closer, as long as Meyer continues to miss bats, he will remain an enigmatic starter in scouting projections.

OFP:70 / Front-of-the-rotation starter or elite closer

Variance: High. He's so atypical, who knows what it will look like when he faces major leaguers.

Mark Barry's Fantasy Take: A closer in college before transitioning to the rotation, Meyer prompted some some reliever concerns heading into 2021 FYPD SZN. While I wouldn't say he's completely out of the woods in that regard, the righty dominated an aggressive Double-A assignment in his first pro season, suggesting he could probably handle at least a mid-rotation starter's workload. Seeing as how the days of 200-inning workhorses have been going the way of the dodo (or, like, literal workhorses), and even 140-ish innings from Meyer could result in 200 strikeouts, there aren't many minor-league arms I'd rather have right now. For me, that makes Meyer a top-three prospect arm.

2 Kahlil Watson SS OFP: 60 ETA: Late 2024

Born: 04/16/03 Age: 19 Bats: L Throws: R Height: 5'9" Weight: 178 lb. Origin: Round 1, 2021 Draft (#16 overall)

YEAR	TEAM	LVL	AGE	PA	R	2B	3B	HR	RBI	BB	K	SB	CS	AVG/OBP/SLG	DRC+	BABIP	BRR	FRAA	WARP
2021	MRL	ROK	18	42	13	3	2	0	5	8	7	4	1	.394/.524/.606		.500			

The Report: It came as quite a surprise when the fifth-best prospect in this year's draft fell into the laps of the Marlins picking all the way down at sixteen. As noted in his pre-draft write-up, Watson has some of the best quick-twitch actions in the class, a predilection for barreling baseballs with regularity and is beginning to grow into game power as he adds strength. Where he ends up defensively is a bit of mystery, since he can handle each infield position with aplomb, but the likelihood is that he settles somewhere up the middle by merit, or perhaps third base out of necessity. There isn't a ton of physical growth left to project since he is on the shorter side. The bulk of his development arc will focus on the refinement and consistency of his tools.

OFP: 60 / Plus regular, occasional all-star

Variance: High. His offensive ceiling is quite high. However, his overall value is predicated on that being the carrying tool. He can provide utility in other facets of the game, but the question, as always seems to be the case with young players, is: can he actually hit? His ability to make hard contact routinely helps inflate our confidence.

Mark Barry's Fantasy Take: For fantasy purposes, Watson might more appropriately be a 1(b) option on any Marlins list, and if you wanted to sneak him above Meyer, I wouldn't argue too much. That's how juicy the upside is for Watson, who could be a true five-category star . . . if he hits. And therein lies the rub. I do think Watson will hit enough to be at least a 15-homer, 25-steal contributor that won't drag you down in the batting average category.

3 Eury Perez RHP OFP: 60 ETA: Late 2023/Early 2024

Born: 04/15/03 Age: 19 Bats: R Throws: R Height: 6'8" Weight: 200 lb. Origin: International Free Agent, 2019

YEAR	TEAM	LVL	AGE	W	L	SV	G	GS	IP	H	HR	BB/9	K/9	K	GB%	BABIP	WHIP	ERA	DRA-	WARP
2021	JUP	A	18	2	3	0	15	15	56	32	2	3.4	13.2	82	36.0%	.268	0.95	1.61	78	1.2
2021	BEL	A+	18	1	2	0	5	5	22	11	5	2.0	10.6	26	37.7%	.133	0.73	2.86	92	0.3
2022 non-DC	*MIA*	*MLB*	*19*	*2*	*3*	*0*	*57*	*0*	*50*	*48*	*8*	*4.3*	*8.6*	*47*	*34.0%*	*.292*	*1.46*	*5.09*	*119*	*-0.3*

Comparables: Luis Patiño, Jacob Turner, Julio Teheran

The Report: In his first full year of professional ball, all Perez did was pitch 78 innings across two levels with 108 punch-outs and a WHIP south of one. He is a very thin 6-foot-8 but making strides to fill out his lean frame in the same mold as Sandy Alcantara, which is an interesting name to begin the comparisons. Throwing from a lower arm slot, he gets a lot of sink on his mid-90s heater. This mutes some of the downward-plane advantages he could have throwing from that height, but the pitch is still highly effective and paired with a slurvy breaking ball he has decent command of and yet another trademark Marlins firm cambio. One National League scout said, "he's a baby . . . a baby monster."

OFP: 60 / Likely No. 3 starter, with equal chances to be better or a closer

Variance: Extreme. Between having so many moving parts to his delivery and physically maturing at such a young age, there are a lot of places where this could go wrong despite all the markers that suggest how good he might be.

Mark Barry's Fantasy Take: You guys probably don't know this about me, but I have a bit of an affection for Marlins pitchers. And they just keep coming. Perez is a top-75 prospect right now, but he's young enough and tall enough to still need lots of time to refine and perfect his mechanics. That makes him the perfect type of dynasty pitcher to float on the trade market.

4 Edward Cabrera RHP OFP: 60 ETA: Debuted in 2021

Born: 04/13/98 Age: 24 Bats: R Throws: R Height: 6'5" Weight: 217 lb. Origin: International Free Agent, 2015

YEAR	TEAM	LVL	AGE	W	L	SV	G	GS	IP	H	HR	BB/9	K/9	K	GB%	BABIP	WHIP	ERA	DRA-	WARP
2019	JUP	A+	21	5	3	0	11	11	58	37	1	2.8	11.3	73	47.3%	.281	0.95	2.02	76	1.4
2019	JAX	AA	21	4	1	0	8	8	38^2	28	6	3.0	10.0	43	48.5%	.242	1.06	2.56	86	0.5
2021	JUP	A	23	0	0	0	2	2	6	4	0	0.0	16.5	11	36.4%	.364	0.67	0.00	89	0.1
2021	PNS	AA	23	2	1	0	5	5	26	19	3	2.1	11.4	33	48.3%	.296	0.96	2.77	85	0.5
2021	JAX	AAA	23	1	3	0	6	6	29^1	22	4	5.8	14.7	48	37.7%	.316	1.40	3.68	77	0.7
2021	MIA	MLB	23	0	3	0	7	7	26^1	24	6	6.5	9.6	28	40.6%	.286	1.63	5.81	107	0.1
2022 DC	*MIA*	*MLB*	*24*	*7*	*5*	*0*	*52*	*8*	*72.7*	*58*	*10*	*4.7*	*11.0*	*89*	*50.3%*	*.280*	*1.32*	*3.90*	*93*	*0.8*

Comparables: Alex Cobb, Jake Odorizzi, Tyler Mahle

The Report: For years, scouts both inside and outside of the Miami organization kept telling us to watch out for the arrival of Edward Cabrera. In 2021, we finally got the chance to see him dominate multiple levels before making his major-league debut. With that minor-league dominance came some concerns as to how it might translate to the majors, and those suspicions seemed to be validated after a rough introduction to the bigs. It boils down to fastball control: Is he capable of being confident enough in the pitch for his two main weapons—the changeup and slider—to operate off the velocity instead of being the featured attractions? Using his fastball just 39 percent of the time last year, he did not throw the heater with enough conviction to get batters off his change, which, in turn, was pummeled in the zone. Cabrera's size, delivery and pure stuff all look like future top-end starter material, but without his upper 90s velocity setting the tone, it will be difficult for him to actualize his potential.

OFP: 60 / No. 3 starter

Variance: High. At worst, with no improvements to his fastball, he can get outs and eat innings, so long as his health holds up. If, by chance, both of those question marks are alleviated, then we're talking about someone with front-line potential.

Mark Barry's Fantasy Take: If Cabrera figures out where his fastball is going (and, you know, stays healthy, because pitchers), he's going to be a stud dynasty hurler held in comparable esteem to Sixto Sánchez last year at this time. If he doesn't figure his fastball out, he'll be effective-ish in the Tyler Mahle vein, posting solid-enough seasons speckled with plenty of ERAs above 4.00.

5 Sixto Sánchez RHP OFP: 60 ETA: Debuted in 2020

Born: 07/29/98 Age: 23 Bats: R Throws: R Height: 6'0" Weight: 234 lb. Origin: International Free Agent, 2015

YEAR	TEAM	LVL	AGE	W	L	SV	G	GS	IP	H	HR	BB/9	K/9	K	GB%	BABIP	WHIP	ERA	DRA-	WARP
2019	JUP	A+	20	0	2	0	2	2	11	14	1	1.6	4.9	6	60.5%	.351	1.45	4.91	114	0.1
2019	JAX	AA	20	8	4	0	18	18	103	87	5	1.7	8.5	97	47.3%	.288	1.03	2.53	79	1.8
2020	MIA	MLB	21	3	2	0	7	7	39	36	3	2.5	7.6	33	58.0%	.303	1.21	3.46	78	0.9
2022 DC	*MIA*	*MLB*	*23*	*5*	*4*	*0*	*17*	*17*	*83.7*	*82*	*8*	*2.9*	*8.1*	*75*	*44.2%*	*.303*	*1.31*	*3.85*	*95*	*0.9*

Comparables: CC Sabathia, Randall Delgado, Julio Teheran

The Report: Sánchez is not really a prospect in any meaningful sense—he starred in the pandemic-shortened 2020 major-league season and would've taken the ball 30 times in the bigs in 2021 if he had been healthy. His 2021 season never got underway; he was delayed for weeks in spring training because of a combination of visa and COVID-testing issues, and then started experiencing shoulder issues while ramping up. He ultimately had shoulder surgery for a small tear in his posterior capsule in July. We have no specific reason to think he won't be ready to go for spring training this year, but a torn shoulder capsule is just about the most concerning medical flag a pitcher can have.

Otherwise, everything we wrote last year when we called him a potential ace still applies. In the majors in 2020, both his four-seam fastball and sinker sat in the upper 90s and hit triple digits—velocity he has shown dating back to A-ball—his changeup jumped to plus-plus, and the slider wasn't far behind. About the only knock on him on the mound is that both fastballs are shaped such that they generate weak contact instead of whiffs; he might end up as more of a variability-prone contact manager than someone who truly posts front-of-the-rotation strikeout rates.

OFP: 60 / No. 2–3 starter

Variance: Extreme in all directions. Sánchez has the same arm talent as when he was our number-four overall prospect on last year's Top 101. However, until we see what he looks like on the mound in 2022, there will be very significant concerns about injuries and diminished stuff, and, beyond that, he has a long path towards building back up to a starter's workload.

Mark Barry's Fantasy Take: Ugh. Can I say pass? No? Fine. It has become a trope to lean on the "pitching prospects will break your heart" adage, but the range of outcomes for Sánchez is about as vast as a Chloé Zhao establishing shot. There's a real chance that Sánchez is an SP1, inducing enough weak contact to post elite rate stats, even without gaudy strikeout totals. There's also a chance his shoulder injury keeps him from ever making 20 starts in a season. The latter outcome is super bleak, and I'm rooting hard against it, but it's also keeping me from paying the lofty acquisition cost to secure Sánchez's services as potentially one of the most exciting young hurlers in the game.

6 Dax Fulton LHP OFP: 60 ETA: 2023

Born: 10/16/01 Age: 20 Bats: L Throws: L Height: 6'7" Weight: 225 lb. Origin: Round 2, 2020 Draft (#40 overall)

YEAR	TEAM	LVL	AGE	W	L	SV	G	GS	IP	H	HR	BB/9	K/9	K	GB%	BABIP	WHIP	ERA	DRA-	WARP
2021	JUP	A	19	2	4	0	15	14	58^2	50	3	4.6	10.1	66	51.6%	.313	1.36	4.30	109	0.3
2021	BEL	A+	19	0	1	0	5	5	19^2	21	3	3.7	8.2	18	56.9%	.327	1.47	5.49	103	0.2
2022 non-DC	*MIA*	*MLB*	*20*	*2*	*3*	*0*	*57*	*0*	*50*	*54*	*6*	*5.4*	*6.8*	*37*	*46.0%*	*.308*	*1.68*	*5.81*	*129*	*-0.6*

Comparables: Luis Patiño, Jacob Turner, Vin Mazzaro

The Report: The second of the twin towers for your Marlins A-ball affiliates is lefty Dax Fulton, who also had an eye-opening first professional campaign. Seen by many as a potential first-round talent in 2020, Fulton slipped to the second round after undergoing Tommy John surgery during his senior year of high school. What was known then remains true now: Fulton has an ankle-breaker of a curveball and tons to dream on. His mechanics are surprisingly consistent given his 6-foot-7, 225-pound frame, and he does a great job of hiding the ball in his body and maintaining arm speed. A quick worker, his tempo and three-pitch mix keep hitters off balance and constantly guessing. The downside? The control can waver at times, which is unsurprising for anyone coming off the rust of an elbow procedure and so much down time in 2020. With continued reps to reign in some of his control issues, as well as the continued development of his body and arsenal, Fulton has as much upside as any of the other pitching prospects in this system.

OFP:60 / No. 2 or 3 starter

Variance: High. Even with the injury history, the frame and fundamentals give him a higher floor than some of his teammates.

Mark Barry's Fantasy Take: Like Perez, Fulton is super tall, which has always made it difficult for pitchers to repeate their mechanics. That the delivery looks clean, but the command sure hasn't been. That really lowers Fulton's ceiling for me, even though he could still sprinkle a season of fantasy-SP3 seasons onto his résumé. As a dynasty prospect, he's outside of the top 200.

7 Jose Salas SS OFP: 55 ETA: 2024/2025

Born: 04/26/03 Age: 19 Bats: S Throws: R Height: 6'2" Weight: 191 lb. Origin: International Free Agent, 2019

YEAR	TEAM	LVL	AGE	PA	R	2B	3B	HR	RBI	BB	K	SB	CS	AVG/OBP/SLG	DRC+	BABIP	BRR	FRAA	WARP
2021	MRL	ROK	18	107	14	10	0	1	11	11	23	8	5	.370/.458/.511		.485			
2021	JUP	A	18	123	12	4	0	1	8	11	28	6	0	.250/.333/.315	99	.325	2.1	SS(25) -2.6	0.3
2022 non-DC	*MIA*	*MLB*	*19*	*251*	*19*	*10*	*1*	*2*	*19*	*15*	*65*	*6*	*1*	*.211/.268/.296*	*53*	*.284*	*0.4*	*SS -1, 2B 0*	*-0.7*

Comparables: Carlos Correa, Jurickson Profar, Wenceel Perez

The Report: Salas was born and raised in Central Florida and played in high-level stateside showcases up to the 17U level through early 2018. His primary residence by 2019 was in Venezuela, thus he was eligible for the 2019–20 international signing period instead of the 2021 MLB Draft (where he'd still have been one of the youngest prep players in the class). By the time that draft actually happened, he was already laying waste to the Florida Complex League after playing against men as a 17-year-old for Águilas del Zulia the prior winter in Liga Venezolana de Béisbol. Just a few weeks later, he was promoted to Low-A, where he more than held his own as one of the youngest players at the level.

Salas is an extremely advanced hitter for his age from both sides of the plate; you're just not going to survive as an 18-year-old in full-season ball if that's not true. He's compact and quick to the ball from both sides, with a whippy bat. He's already flashing plus raw power, although his developing frame has not filled out to the point where he's making consistent hard contact quite yet. We believe he will get there in a few years. His defensive actions are sound, and he runs well at present, although there's the possibility he'll grow off shortstop as he continues to physically mature.

OFP: 55 / First-division infielder

Variance: High. We've been getting very strong industry feedback on Salas for some time now, and he has a lot of good building blocks for future development. Now we need to see the development.

Mark Barry's Fantasy Take: Salas has a pretty decent skill set for a teenager, but the combination of his lead time and lack of a standout tool probably keeps him as a watchlist option for now.

8 Jake Eder LHP OFP: 55 ETA: 2023

Born: 10/09/98 Age: 23 Bats: L Throws: L Height: 6'4" Weight: 215 lb. Origin: Round 4, 2020 Draft (#104 overall)

YEAR	TEAM	LVL	AGE	W	L	SV	G	GS	IP	H	HR	BB/9	K/9	K	GB%	BABIP	WHIP	ERA	DRA-	WARP
2021	PNS	AA	22	3	5	0	15	15	71^1	43	3	3.4	12.5	99	50.3%	.261	0.98	1.77	82	1.4
2022 non-DC	*MIA*	*MLB*	*23*	*2*	*2*	*0*	*57*	*0*	*50*	*43*	*6*	*4.2*	*9.8*	*54*	*26.6%*	*.289*	*1.33*	*3.90*	*95*	*0.3*

Comparables: Génesis Cabrera, Francisco Liriano, Fernando Nieve

The Report: At midseason, Eder was tracking to be in the top three on this list. After a career of inconsistency in both stuff and success at Vanderbilt, he burst onto the national-prospect scene when camp broke in May, jumping immediately to Double-A along with Meyer and matching him nearly pitch-for-pitch. Eder's velocity jumped from the low 90s to the mid-90s, and his breaking ball was settling in as plus. He was merely an additional bit of changeup development—something in which Miami player development specializes—away from being one of the best pitching prospects in the minors.

Then, in August, Eder had Tommy John surgery, which will likely cost him most or all of the 2022 season. That surgery is more common than you'd like for pitching prospects who just experienced significant velocity jumps, and the rehab will push his timeline back by more than a year. Now there are new questions about whether his the improvement in his stuff will hold over the course of a full starting campaign.

OFP: 55 / High-quality innings in some amorphous role or another

Variance: High. It'll be at least 2023, maybe even 2024, before we see whether the best version of Eder can sustain as a long-term starter.

Mark Barry's Fantasy Take: Eder's rosterability depends solely on the depth of your league and your willingness to clog up a roster spot until maybe 2023, probably 2024. If the wait-with-bated-breath approach doesn't make you too squeamish, Eder definitely has one of the highest ceilings for any minor-league injury stash.

9 Joe Mack C/DH OFP: 50 ETA: 2025

Born: 12/27/02 Age: 19 Bats: L Throws: R Height: 6'1" Weight: 210 lb. Origin: Round 1, 2021 Draft (#31 overall)

YEAR	TEAM	LVL	AGE	PA	R	2B	3B	HR	RBI	BB	K	SB	CS	AVG/OBP/SLG	DRC+	BABIP	BRR	FRAA	WARP
2021	MRL	ROK	18	75	9	1	0	1	2	20	22	0	1	.132/.373/.208		.194			

Comparables: Alberto Mineo, Bryant Aragon, Carlos Rodriguez

The Report: In a stellar class of high school catchers, Mack was considered among the very best throughout the evaluation process. Built like your standard-framed backstops, Mack received high marks for his fundamentals behind the plate and ability to work with pitchers; the kind of intangibles you rarely see in a player at that position at that age. Defensively, his tools are average to maybe slightly above. Offensively, you'll mostly find 50s, with the exception of a lofty swing that produces a ton of power from the left side. He seems to see the ball well enough to earn his share of walks but if he is going to employ a slightly conservative approach, he needs to work on the mechanics of his swing to make more consistent contact.

OFP: 50 / Starting catcher, perhaps part of a platoon

Variance: Extreme. Catchers are some of the most difficult players to project because of everything they have to do sufficiently well.

Mark Barry's Fantasy Take: Mack is a prep catcher. He's very far away. Return to the Mack in 2024 to check in on his future fantasy relevance.

10 JJ Bleday OF OFP: 45 ETA: 2023

Born: 11/10/97 Age: 24 Bats: L Throws: L Height: 6'3" Weight: 205 lb. Origin: Round 1, 2019 Draft (#4 overall)

YEAR	TEAM	LVL	AGE	PA	R	2B	3B	HR	RBI	BB	K	SB	CS	AVG/OBP/SLG	DRC+	BABIP	BRR	FRAA	WARP
2019	JUP	A+	21	151	13	8	0	3	19	11	29	0	0	.257/.311/.379	108	.306	-1.2	RF(32) -0.8	0.4
2021	MSS	WIN	23	115	20	8	2	5	24	20	23	2	0	.316/.435/.600		.373			
2021	PNS	AA	23	468	52	22	3	12	54	64	101	5	3	.212/.323/.373	103	.250	0.0	RF(38) 5.8, LF(28) 5.2, CF(23) 1.1	2.8
2022 non-DC	*MIA*	*MLB*	*24*	*251*	*23*	*11*	*1*	*4*	*24*	*24*	*61*	*0*	*1*	*.216/.297/.342*	*74*	*.275*	*-0.2*	*RF 1, CF 0*	*0.2*

Comparables: Abraham Almonte, Zoilo Almonte, Carlos Peguero

The Report: It has been tough sledding thus far in Bleday's professional career. After dominating the Cape Cod League and the SEC, he was a prudent top-five draft pick for an organization desperate to cultivate big bats. Since his selection, he has been in a constant struggle to consistently produce results that reflect his draft pedigree. Despite being regarded as an offensive-minded prospect, he has slashed just .223/.320/.373 in what amounts to one-and-a-half minor-league seasons. His swing at Vanderbilt, while far from perfect, was good enough to abuse collegiate pitching because of his double-plus raw strength. He has yet to make the necessary adjustments against better competition as a pro, and will need to re-work those mechanics for the Fish to be able to count on his future value.

OFP: 45 / Below-average regular or bench bat

Variance: Moderate. With certain tweaks, he could recapture some of the glory days and get closer to some of the lofty expectations. However, without much to offer with his legs or glove, his value is limited to whatever he can produce at the plate.

Mark Barry's Fantasy Take: Bleday was supposed to be a safe college bat, or, you know, about as safe as you could hope for. Since his fantasy value was completely hit-tool dependent, seeing a .212 average in Double-A is extremely Not What You Want. You can caveat that number a bunch with sample sizes and batted-ball luck, but if Bleday doesn't hit .270-plus, he's probably not worth much in fantasy circles.

Eyewitness Report: JJ Bleday

Evaluator: Trevor Andresen
Report Date: 11/20/2021
Dates Seen: 11/8 - 11/13 (Arizona Fall League)
Risk Factor: Medium
Physical/Health: XL 6'3" 205 lb. frame. Physical build w/ strength throughout.

Tool	Future Grade	Report
Hit	50	Hits from an open stance w/ a wide base & hands resting on his shoulder. Eliminated the noisy hand load that had given him trouble up to this point. Now employs more of a direct, "Point A to Point B" swing. Above-avg hand speed. No trouble handling velo inside. Level swing plane enables him to drive the ball from gap-gap. Consistently puts together competitive AB's. Pure hit tool plays up due to approach/walk rates.
Power	55	Generates easy plus raw power to all fields. Should get to 25-30 HR impact in-game.
Baserunning/ Speed	30	Well below-avg foot speed. Little to no value on the basepaths
Glove	50	Has seen time in all 3 outfield spots, but lacks the foot speed/instincts to handle CF. Arm strength is playable in RF (45-grade glove) but he fits most comfortably in LF.
Arm	50	Average strength. Fringy RF fit, works best in LF.

Conclusion: It was a tale of two seasons for Bleday, who struggled mightily in Double-A but made a noticeable change & looked like a completely different player in the AFL. It's a bat-only profile, but I believe he'll produce enough to profile as a regular in an outfield corner.

The Prospects You Meet Outside the Top Ten

Prospects on the Rise

Kameron Misner OF Born: 01/08/98 Age: 24 Bats: L Throws: L Height: 6'4" Weight: 218 lb. Origin: Round 1, 2019 Draft (#35 overall)

YEAR	TEAM	LVL	AGE	PA	R	2B	3B	HR	RBI	BB	K	SB	CS	AVG/OBP/SLG	DRC+	BABIP	BRR	FRAA	WARP
2019	MRL	ROK	21	38	2	2	0	0	4	9	7	3	0	.241/.421/.310		.318			
2019	CLI	A	21	158	25	7	0	2	20	21	35	8	0	.276/.380/.373	103	.357	1.3	CF(32) 6.7	1.4
2021	MSS	WIN	23	102	21	3	0	7	14	20	34	4	2	.205/.373/.513		.231			
2021	BEL	A+	23	400	58	22	3	11	56	50	119	24	2	.244/.350/.424	95	.338	-0.1	CF(38) -3.2, LF(36) -0.4, RF(7) 1.1	0.8
2021	PNS	AA	23	62	12	7	0	1	3	7	17	2	2	.309/.387/.491	87	.432	-0.6	CF(9) -1.0, LF(2) -0.0	-0.1
2022 non-DC	*TB*	*MLB*	*24*	*251*	*22*	*11*	*1*	*4*	*23*	*23*	*83*	*7*	*2*	*.213/.294/.334*	*69*	*.317*	*0.5*	*CF 2, LF 0*	*0.2*

Comparables: Derek Hill, Aaron Altherr, Drew Stubbs

The ups and downs of Misner's roller-coaster evaluation track continued into the 2021 offseason. He has gone from power-hitting college bat, to A-ball contact hitter, and most recently back to slugger in the hitter-friendly Arizona Fall League. Always one to fiddle with his swing, he is attempting to shorten his stride so he can be quicker to the ball while still maintaining the same loopy path that creates lift on impact. The physical tools are there to be an above-average corner outfielder, he just needs to find a swing that consistently works for him.

Ian Lewis 2B Born: 02/04/03 Age: 19 Bats: S Throws: R Height: 5'10" Weight: 177 lb. Origin: International Free Agent, 2019

YEAR	TEAM	LVL	AGE	PA	R	2B	3B	HR	RBI	BB	K	SB	CS	AVG/OBP/SLG	DRC+	BABIP	BRR	FRAA	WARP
2021	MRL	ROK	18	161	24	10	5	3	27	11	24	9	4	.302/.354/.497		.344			

Without jumping to conclusions way too early, the Marlins' 2019 international-free-agent class has a chance to be special. With Perez and Salas already in the top ten, and Lewis just missing, the trio will be linked for years to come. This switch-hitting Bahamian impressed at the plate with surprisingly loud contact from his 5-foot-10 frame. Raw and still getting a feel for where his natural positioning might be in the future, he seems destined to slot in comfortably at second base where his bat can play in the lineup everyday.

Yiddi Cappe SS Born: 09/17/02 Age: 19 Bats: R Throws: R Height: 6'3" Weight: 175 lb. Origin: International Free Agent, 2021

YEAR	TEAM	LVL	AGE	PA	R	2B	3B	HR	RBI	BB	K	SB	CS	AVG/OBP/SLG	DRC+	BABIP	BRR	FRAA	WARP
2021	DSL MIA	ROK	18	216	31	17	1	2	27	19	35	9	8	.270/.329/.402		.308			

Comparables: Pedro Guerrero, Daniel Bravo, Yairo Muñoz

Ultra projectable, yet extremely raw, Cappe has the furthest to go among any of the prospects discussed in the upper tier of this system. The 6-foot-3 Cuban played exclusively in the Dominican Summer League last year and hopes to make his stateside debut either this spring or in the Complex League. His long levers produce a rather lengthy swing, but he has enough quickness in his hands that some in the organization believe he can develop into a well-above-average offensive player.

Factors on the Farm

Cody Morissette 2B/3B Born: 01/16/00 Age: 22 Bats: L Throws: R Height: 6'0" Weight: 175 lb. Origin: Round 2, 2021 Draft (#52 overall)

YEAR	TEAM	LVL	AGE	PA	R	2B	3B	HR	RBI	BB	K	SB	CS	AVG/OBP/SLG	DRC+	BABIP	BRR	FRAA	WARP
2021	JUP	A	21	159	22	8	1	1	10	20	38	0	2	.204/.308/.299	94	.273	-0.4	2B(16) -1.2, 3B(14) 2.2, SS(2) -0.3	0.4
2022 non-DC	*MIA*	*MLB*	*22*	*251*	*19*	*10*	*1*	*2*	*19*	*20*	*67*	*0*	*1*	*.208/.277/.299*	*58*	*.283*	*-0.2*	*2B -1, 3B 2*	*-0.5*

Comparables: Everth Cabrera, Brandon Lowe, Jimmy Paredes

Poised for a breakout season at Boston College last spring, Morissette was beset by a lingering hand injury that caused him to miss some time and sapped some of his power. Fortunately, the book on him had mostly been written already, describing him as an offensive-minded prospect with a short lefty stroke and the versatility to play multiple positions around the diamond. His stats are unlikely to ever jump off the page, but he'll be solid in all facets of the game that can help contribute to a winning ballclub.

Kyle Nicolas RHP Born: 02/22/99 Age: 23 Bats: R Throws: R Height: 6'4" Weight: 223 lb. Origin: Round 2, 2020 Draft (#61 overall)

YEAR	TEAM	LVL	AGE	W	L	SV	G	GS	IP	H	HR	BB/9	K/9	K	GB%	BABIP	WHIP	ERA	DRA-	WARP
2021	BEL	A+	22	3	2	0	13	12	59^2	57	13	3.6	13.0	86	33.3%	.328	1.36	5.28	81	1.2
2021	PNS	AA	22	3	2	0	8	8	39^1	23	3	5.7	11.4	50	29.2%	.235	1.22	2.52	110	0.2
2022 non-DC	*PIT*	*MLB*	*23*	*2*	*3*	*0*	*57*	*0*	*50*	*49*	*9*	*5.4*	*9.9*	*54*	*43.9%*	*.304*	*1.58*	*5.70*	*126*	*-0.5*

Comparables: Rocky Coppinger, Jeff Karstens, Jordan Yamamoto

Nicolas looks the part of a mid-rotation starter but fits best as a 95-and-a-slider relief arm. "Slider" is describing two breaking balls here, as his curve and slider looks can bleed together a bit, but the best were a low-80s slurve with good depth. Nicolas has four pitches—the change shows occasional split/sink action, but is generally too firm—and a frame built to log innings, but he struggles with his control and command due to an inconsistent arm action, and he doesn't hold the 95. He could help out the Marlins bullpen quickly, though.

Peyton Burdick OF Born: 02/26/97 Age: 25 Bats: R Throws: R Height: 6'0" Weight: 205 lb. Origin: Round 3, 2019 Draft (#82 overall)

YEAR	TEAM	LVL	AGE	PA	R	2B	3B	HR	RBI	BB	K	SB	CS	AVG/OBP/SLG	DRC+	BABIP	BRR	FRAA	WARP
2019	BAT	SS	22	25	3	0	1	1	5	2	5	1	1	.318/.400/.545		.375			
2019	CLI	A	22	288	57	20	3	10	59	32	67	6	6	.307/.408/.542	132	.380	-0.4	LF(59) 11.2, RF(2) 0.4	3.1
2021	PNS	AA	24	460	71	17	2	23	52	76	135	9	5	.231/.376/.472	133	.293	0.3	CF(50) -5.1, LF(25) 0.9, RF(15) -1.2	2.7
2021	JAX	AAA	24	31	5	3	0	0	1	3	11	0	0	.143/.226/.250	77	.235	0.1	LF(3) -0.5, CF(3) -0.8, RF(1) -0.1	-0.1
2022 non-DC	*MIA*	*MLB*	*25*	*251*	*27*	*11*	*1*	*8*	*28*	*28*	*81*	*2*	*2*	*.215/.318/.390*	*91*	*.303*	*0.0*	*LF 2, CF 0*	*0.7*

Comparables: Chris Heisey, Adam Engel, Jaycob Brugman

When speaking to contacts both inside and outside of the Marlins' organization, one of the names that constantly came up was Burdick's, a third-round pick out of Wright State in 2019. Words like "animal" and "beast" were used to describe a player who had an uncanny work ethic and whose time spent in the gym was easily noticed. Not the biggest guy ever at just six feet, Burdick is inarguably well-muscled, with forearms that bare some resemblance to Popeye's. The strength shows up in his power numbers. He blasted 23 dingers in the notoriously difficult-for-hitters Double-A South, albeit with a Brutus-sized amount of strikeouts. He'll need to make more contact if he is to squeeze into the revolving door of outfield options in Miami.

Top Talents 25 and Under (as of 4/1/2022):

1. Trevor Rogers, LHP
2. Max Meyer, RHP
3. Jazz Chisholm, 2B/SS
4. Kahlil Watson, SS
5. Jesús Luzardo, LHP
6. Eury Perez, RHP
7. Edward Cabrera, RHP
8. Sixto Sánchez, RHP
9. Dax Fulton, LHP
10. Jesús Sánchez, OF

Few organizations have the concentration of youth on their roster that Miami does. Sandy Alcantara, Pablo López and Elieser Hernández are the aged vets of Miami's pitching staff, narrowly missing the cut as 26-year-olds. That leaves the emergent Rogers to take the lead on this list, even as arguably the fourth- or even fifth-most-notable member of his own rotation when everyone is healthy. After an unlucky 2020 in which DRA saw significant promise, Rogers broke out, sitting 94 and locating his changeup and slider to great effect on his low-three-quarters delivery.

Chisholm continued to play with explosiveness and verve, though his overall numbers still show significant room for improvement. With shortstop Miguel Rojas, functionally a dinosaur at 33 years of age this season, recently extended through 2023, Chisholm's route to reps should continue to be splitting time up the middle on the dirt. Jazz's tools and personality are evident for all to see, and, with experience, his performance will hopefully continue trending upward. With Rojas locked in, and Chisholm a more competent flag-bearer, Isan Díaz appears the odd man out. Though he made last year's 25 and Under and still qualifies this season, another disappointing year at the dish puts him squarely in a bench role.

Two other names of note on this list were recently among the most well-regarded pitching prospects of the past several years, but injuries and inconsistency have harried their ascent to excellence. Luzardo and Sánchez are exhilarating to watch and almost as difficult to hit, even with traits that sometimes force their fastballs to play down compared to the mph that pops up on the chyron. Luzardo may have also been among the pitchers most impacted by the sticky-stuff crackdown. His spin rates cratered in the second half of the year, after he missed a month with a fractured pinky on his pitching hand, while his velocity seemed unaltered. Miami may endeavor to have Luzardo ape some of the traits of Rogers, his taller but similarly repertoired rotation mate.

The rest of the Marlins' school of youths is impressive in its multitude, even as they all come with their warts. Jesús Sánchez showed his immense toolsiness and power, but the length of his swing is still an exploitable issue. Bryan De La Cruz checks a different set of boxes as a high-floor defender with a bunch of 45s and 50s but no knack for base stealing to ensure a role as a bench outfielder. Catchers Payton Henry and Nick Fortes collectively save Miami the hassle of calling Sandy León's agents back when they check in about re-upping a bench backstop.

Milwaukee Brewers

The State of the System:

The Brewers' system still lacks clear impact talent, but is improving overall thanks to strong recent drafts and international-free-agent classes.

The Top Ten:

1 Garrett Mitchell OF OFP: 55 ETA: 2023

Born: 09/04/98 Age: 23 Bats: L Throws: R Height: 6'3" Weight: 215 lb. Origin: Round 1, 2020 Draft (#20 overall)

YEAR	TEAM	LVL	AGE	PA	R	2B	3B	HR	RBI	BB	K	SB	CS	AVG/OBP/SLG	DRC+	BABIP	BRR	FRAA	WARP
2021	WIS	A+	22	120	33	5	2	5	20	28	30	12	1	.359/.508/.620	126	.491	0.8	CF(13) -2.5, RF(2) 0.3	0.6
2021	BLX	AA	22	148	16	1	0	3	10	18	41	5	1	.186/.291/.264	84	.247	-0.7	CF(30) 0.9, RF(2) -0.0, LF(1) -0.1	0.2
2022 non-DC	*MIL*	*MLB*	*23*	*251*	*23*	*9*	*1*	*4*	*23*	*28*	*72*	*6*	*2*	*.211/.306/.328*	*77*	*.293*	*0.5*	*CF 2, RF 1*	*0.5*

Comparables: Jackie Bradley Jr., Brandon Nimmo, Julio Borbon

The Report: Mitchell was drafted in the first round as a toolsy, high-upside college bat whose plus raw power was limited by a line-drive, contact-oriented swing. He dominated High-A last year, flashing a bit more game power, but flailed after a promotion to the former Southern League. He also suffered a knee injury in the midst of all that, but there did not seem to be much in the way of lingering effects. We don't have a ton more information on Mitchell than we had this time last year. The 70 speed and potential plus defense in center field gives him a reasonable major-league floor. The hit tool is probably at least average, which would bump that reasonable floor to good fourth outfielder or fringe starter. Unlocking even 15–20-home-run power will get Mitchell to the OFP below, but there's no evidence that is coming down the pipeline quite yet.

OFP: 55 / Above-average outfielder

Variance: High. There's some concern about Mitchell staying healthy in the long term, as he has a bit of a history of leg injuries now. That's most of the negative side of the variance—although we aren't sure the hit tool will play at higher levels, either. On the positive side, his contact ability, approach and raw pop sure fit the profile of a prospect who can make real power gains with a swing tweak or two.

Darius Austin's Fantasy Take: There's still a five-category fantasy stalwart in here. We just haven't seen the advancements we might hope for in the power department to get him there, and his Double-A stint didn't provide a ton of confidence that his hit tool will translate, either. He could still have a path to fantasy relevance in all leagues with his speed, but he won't have a real-life starting spot without both the power and the average. Now could be a great moment to buy in; he'll rocket back up dynasty rankings if he starts out hot this year.

Eyewitness Report: Garrett Mitchell

Evaluator: Nathan Graham
Report Date: 07/14/2021
Dates Seen: Multiple, June 2021
Risk Factor: High
Physical/Health: Extra-large frame, athletic build, room for additional good weight

Tool	Future Grade	Report
Hit	60	Slightly open, balanced stance with a mild load and stride; swing lacks loft, generates hard, line drives; Mitchell has a knack for contact and shows an excellent knowledge of the strike zone.
Power	40	Plus raw power plays below-average due to the way the swing is geared. Mitchell is strong enough and has plenty of bat speed to generate double digit home runs the way it is, but could produce 20-25 if the approach were to focus more on pop.
Baserunning/ Speed	70	Moves exceptionally well for someone his size, quick out of the box and accelerates down the line; 3.97 home to first clock on a dig down the line; not a prolific base stealer but will swipe the occasional base, speed geared more for taking extra bases.
Glove	60	Athleticism allows him to cover plenty of ground in the outfield; Gets good reads and takes efficient routes; will be able to play an above average center field for the foreseeable future.
Arm	50	Makes accurate throws from the outfield, above average arm strength; Arm will play average in right field and slightly above in center.

Conclusion: An exceptional athlete, Mitchell has the tools to become a plus major league starting outfielder. The speed and defense give him a high floor but if he can tap into the power just a bit there's potential for an occasional All-Star.

2 Sal Frelick OF

OFP: 55 ETA: Late 2023

Born: 04/19/00 Age: 22 Bats: L Throws: R Height: 5'9" Weight: 175 lb. Origin: Round 1, 2021 Draft (#15 overall)

YEAR	TEAM	LVL	AGE	PA	R	2B	3B	HR	RBI	BB	K	SB	CS	AVG/OBP/SLG	DRC+	BABIP	BRR	FRAA	WARP
2021	CAR	A	21	81	17	6	1	1	12	9	10	6	2	.437/.494/.592	128	.492	0.3	CF(14) 2.3	0.8
2021	WIS	A+	21	71	7	1	1	1	5	10	13	3	0	.167/.296/.267	110	.196	0.1	CF(13) 0.4	0.4
2022 non-DC	*MIL*	*MLB*	*22*	*251*	*21*	*10*	*1*	*2*	*21*	*20*	*48*	*7*	*3*	*.237/.305/.332*	*76*	*.290*	*0.6*	*CF 1*	*0.4*

Comparables: Ender Inciarte, Adam Haseley, Mallex Smith

The Report: Unlike Mitchell, Frelick doesn't have the kind of upside you'd associate with a first-round, up-the-middle college bat. A somewhat slight 5-foot-9, he's never going to hit for much power, although his approach and contact ability will make him a pesky hitter. The bat speed is only average, and we do wonder if pitchers will challenge him in the zone further up the ladder, but he will beat out some infield hits with his 70 speed, bunt his way on, take an extra base in the gap and just generally do enough offensively to be a useful table-setter. His straight-line speed covers for less-than-ideal reads and routes in center, but a fair bit of Frelick's value is tied up in him sticking at a premium position and being above average there, so that warrants continued monitoring. He had a strong pro debut post-draft last year and, outside of the small-sample 2020 season, has always performed with the bat. To an extent, Frelick is going to be a prove-it-at-every-level prospect, but so far, so good.

OFP: 55 / Above-average outfielder, top-of-the-order pest

Variance: Medium. There isn't really a carrying tool here, and if Frelick is more of a .260–.270 hitter, there may not be enough secondary skills to start.

Darius Austin's Fantasy Take: Frelick's standing is fairly similar to Mitchell's right now, except Frelick doesn't have the possibility of a higher power ceiling. Relying on stolen-base prowess to heavily support value three or four years down the line is rarely a good idea; just ask Jorge Mateo. While that might undersell the quality of his approach, Frelick really needs to steal 25–30 bags in the majors to provide genuine impact. The Brewers aren't going to place nearly as much value on that as we are, so let's hope he's an OBP machine.

3 Aaron Ashby LHP OFP: 55 ETA: Debuted in 2021

Born: 05/24/98 Age: 24 Bats: R Throws: L Height: 6'2" Weight: 181 lb. Origin: Round 4, 2018 Draft (#125 overall)

YEAR	TEAM	LVL	AGE	W	L	SV	G	GS	IP	H	HR	BB/9	K/9	K	GB%	BABIP	WHIP	ERA	DRA-	WARP
2019	WIS	A	21	3	4	0	11	10	61	47	4	4.1	11.8	80	48.9%	.319	1.23	3.54	84	1.0
2019	CAR	A+	21	2	6	0	13	13	65	54	1	4.4	7.6	55	47.3%	.286	1.32	3.46	109	0.3
2021	NAS	AAA	23	5	4	0	21	12	63^1	55	4	4.5	14.2	100	66.9%	.370	1.37	4.41	86	1.3
2021	MIL	MLB	23	3	2	1	13	4	31^2	25	4	3.4	11.1	39	61.7%	.273	1.17	4.55	84	0.6
2022 DC	*MIL*	*MLB*	*24*	*7*	*5*	*0*	*50*	*11*	*85*	*71*	*8*	*4.4*	*10.8*	*102*	*57.7%*	*.302*	*1.33*	*3.55*	*84*	*1.2*

Comparables: Will Smith, Rafael Soriano, Robinson Tejeda

The Report: Ashby pitched very well in an opener/long-relief role down the stretch for Milwaukee; his overall numbers are weighed down by a June spot start in which he didn't make it out of the first inning. His stuff profile is interesting; he threw a plus slider with some slurvy qualities more than he threw his fastball, and he largely shelved his curveball as a distinct offering. His fastball has elite velocity for a lefty—he was sitting 96–97, and these weren't exactly short bursts—but it is a low-spin, high-sink pitch. That's better than doing nothing but also unlikely to miss a lot of bats. He continued to throw an average changeup more than a fifth of the time, so he was pitching like a starter even in relief. His command profile still isn't great; he does not have a long track record of throwing strikes, and the walks need to remain manageable. But he's holding his stuff and striking out a lot of batters as a high-velocity lefty with a clear out-pitch, and that's a profile you should be very keen on, in general.

OFP: 55 / Mid-rotation starter or high-leverage reliever

Variance: Medium, mostly command related.

Darius Austin's Fantasy Take: I have suggested elsewhere that Ashby is going to be a Helium Guy in drafts this year. Among those enthusiastic enough to draft him this early on NFBC, he's around 270th off the board on average. That seems like a perfectly reasonable point to take a shot on perhaps your seventh starter in 15-teamers. If it looks more likely he'll get a rotation spot out of the gate, however, watch out; in all honesty, I think Ashby's going to end up much closer to pick 200, at the highest, even if his rotation status is murky. "High-strikeout, high-velocity, poor-command lefty" is basically Robbie Ray pre-2021, a profile that sometimes brought tremendous value and other times left you wondering why you would do that to your WHIP. You have to love a near-30-percent strikeout rate in the debut; just make sure you aren't drafting Ashby like he has already figured out the rest, especially if Milwaukee hasn't confirmed he'll start.

4 Ethan Small LHP OFP: 55 ETA: 2022

Born: 02/14/97 Age: 25 Bats: L Throws: L Height: 6'4" Weight: 215 lb. Origin: Round 1, 2019 Draft (#28 overall)

YEAR	TEAM	LVL	AGE	W	L	SV	G	GS	IP	H	HR	BB/9	K/9	K	GB%	BABIP	WHIP	ERA	DRA-	WARP
2019	BRG	ROK	22	0	0	0	2	2	3	0	0	0.0	15.0	5	50.0%	.000	0.00	0.00		
2019	WIS	A	22	0	2	0	5	5	18	11	0	2.0	15.5	31	30.3%	.333	0.83	1.00	73	0.4
2021	BLX	AA	24	2	2	0	8	8	41^1	26	1	4.6	14.6	67	39.2%	.342	1.14	1.96	83	0.8
2021	NAS	AAA	24	2	0	0	9	9	35	27	3	5.4	6.2	24	43.6%	.245	1.37	2.06	117	0.2
2022 DC	*MIL*	*MLB*	*25*	*1*	*1*	*0*	*4*	*4*	*19.3*	*18*	*2*	*5.4*	*10.1*	*21*	*46.9%*	*.312*	*1.55*	*5.22*	*114*	*0.0*

Comparables: Vidal Nuño, Jack Cassel, Billy Traber

The Report: Small's mechanics are anything but what his last name suggests, as the left-hander has a lot of moving parts. With a high-three-quarters slot and aggressive follow-through, this is a really tough delivery for hitters to pick up. Perhaps the most deceptive feature is his ability to hide the ball through his windup and bring it behind his backside, then torque his arm above his ear and fire across his body with consistency. The fastball sits low 90s and is a bit straight with some sinking action at times, but plays up thanks to the delivery. His upper-70s changeup is a plus pitch with a bottom that drops out and works beautifully in conjunction with the fastball. The third pitch is a slurvy curve that hasn't quite gotten to average yet, but Small's command is sharp enough that it could potentially play up.

OFP: 55 / No. 3–4 starter

Variance: Medium. He needs to develop that third pitch, but his delivery, command and primary 1-2 punch should remain effective at the highest level.

Darius Austin's Fantasy Take: The development of that third pitch would make Small extremely interesting. As things stand, he may not have enough to turn over a big-league lineup more than twice, but he's close enough that he should be rostered in most dynasty leagues. It might only take a couple of guys like Small and Ashby not working out for us to stop talking about how good Milwaukee is at pitching development . . . but, as of right now, you'd have to say he's in a great place to take that next step forward.

5 Joey Wiemer RF/DH OFP: 55 ETA: 2024

Born: 02/11/99 Age: 23 Bats: R Throws: R Height: 6'5" Weight: 215 lb. Origin: Round 4, 2020 Draft (#121 overall)

YEAR	TEAM	LVL	AGE	PA	R	2B	3B	HR	RBI	BB	K	SB	CS	AVG/OBP/SLG	DRC+	BABIP	BRR	FRAA	WARP
2021	CAR	A	22	320	53	11	2	13	44	45	69	22	4	.276/.391/.478	126	.326	-0.4	RF(50) 12.5, CF(23) 1.3, LF(5) 0.7	3.4
2021	WIS	A+	22	152	33	7	0	14	33	18	36	8	2	.336/.428/.719	155	.363	-0.1	RF(22) -1.1, CF(4) -1.1	1.2
2022 non-DC	*MIL*	*MLB*	*23*	*251*	*28*	*9*	*1*	*9*	*30*	*22*	*73*	*8*	*3*	*.238/.316/.414*	*95*	*.313*	*0.7*	*RF 4, CF 0*	*1.1*

Comparables: Aaron Judge, Mitch Haniger, Marcell Ozuna

The Report: The Milwaukee Brewers' 2021 Minor League Player of the Year has been a favorite of the Prospect Team since his stint on Cape Cod back in 2019. Still ridiculously twitchy, Wiemer's potential for plus-plus raw power appears to have been realized as he has bulked up a bit and adjusted his leg kick to be more of a toe tap and smooth stride to the pitcher. Wiemer's added strength has helped gear his power to all fields, compared to a more pull-side approach in college. He's now a danger from line-to-line. Perhaps most exciting, his CCBL report noted that his plate discipline was his best trait. Wiemer sees pitches at an advanced level and really waits for his favorite offerings. Wiemer also has displayed a plus-plus arm in right field, making some beaming throws, and has asserted that he is going to stick in right field. Oh, and he stole 30 bases this year. Sure, this might be a bit of recency bias. You have to really believe the hit tool will continue to play up the ladder, but we thought it was an easy 5 back on the Cape and despite a big leg kick and very noticeable uppercut. Wiemer is unlikely to repeat that kind of season this year, but the tools are very much there for him to be a good regular.

OFP: 55 / Above-average outfielder

Variance: High. He hadn't hit for that kind of power before last year, and the corner-outfield profile will put pressure on him to keep hitting bombs.

Darius Austin's Fantasy Take: If this is a good time to try to acquire Mitchell, it's arguably awful timing to go after Wiemer, who stacked a brief-but-incandescent Arizona Fall League performance on top of an utterly ludicrous regular-season line. No matter how much I try to tell people not to care about minor-league stolen base rates, especially with the new rules in place, there is no doubt that Wiemer has impact-power and -speed potential and might just be the best position player on this list for fantasy in relatively short order. I think his batting average is going to be a bit of a drag, even if the rest works, but the rest looks like it has a great chance of working.

6 Tyler Black 2B/DH OFP: 50 ETA: 2024

Born: 07/26/00 Age: 21 Bats: L Throws: R Height: 6'2" Weight: 190 lb. Origin: Round 1, 2021 Draft (#33 overall)

YEAR	TEAM	LVL	AGE	PA	R	2B	3B	HR	RBI	BB	K	SB	CS	AVG/OBP/SLG	DRC+	BABIP	BRR	FRAA	WARP
2021	CAR	A	20	103	11	4	0	0	6	20	29	3	2	.222/.388/.272	104	.346	-1.3	2B(15) -1.4	0.1
2022 non-DC	*MIL*	*MLB*	*21*	*251*	*19*	*10*	*1*	*2*	*18*	*25*	*67*	*3*	*2*	*.186/.278/.270*	*55*	*.257*	*0.1*	*2B -2*	*-0.8*

Comparables: Alvaro Gonzalez, Jagger Rusconi, Luis Mendez

The Report: Black freakin' demolished opposing pitchers at Wright State (.383/.496/.683 in his junior year with a 1.56 BB/K ratio), and while the quality of competition in the Horizon League isn't great, he did show off against SEC money in the bank, such as Vanderbilt and Tennessee, too. He was also very young for a college hitter in his class, playing his entire draft season at 20, not quite a man's man yet. When you put all that together, it's certainly not a surprise that he ended up with a team with model-heavy draft architecture like Milwaukee.

Black has excellent strike-zone judgment, a quick bat, and a knack for contact. He's the rare prospect whose average raw power shields how much game power he might hit for; he projects at least for above-average power output, on balance. He was a second baseman in college and is more likely than not to stay at the position but unlikely to be a defensive messiah. This profile isn't going to inspire anyone to burn it down, but his track record of big performance in college and aptitude for hitting is not dissimilar to Frelick's.

OFP: 50 / Offensively-minded starting second baseman

Variance: Medium. Black didn't do much other than walk after being promoted to full-season ball for the last month of the season, but gassed end-of-the-season cameos aren't particularly worrisome for college draftees.

Darius Austin's Fantasy Take: Not gonna lie, this write-up ticked a lot of boxes for me. Young relative to his competition, great eye, contact and bat speed, clear room to grow—it feels like a recipe for a hitter who is going to exceed expectations as he gets more reps. I'm not saying you should take Black in the top 10 of first-year player drafts, but I do think he should be going relatively soon after that.

7 Hedbert Perez OF   OFP: 50   ETA: 2025/2026

Born: 04/04/03 Age: 19 Bats: L Throws: L Height: 5'10" Weight: 160 lb. Origin: International Free Agent, 2019

YEAR	TEAM	LVL	AGE	PA	R	2B	3B	HR	RBI	BB	K	SB	CS	AVG/OBP/SLG	DRC+	BABIP	BRR	FRAA	WARP
2021	BRWG	ROK	18	132	19	11	0	6	21	8	34	2	0	.333/.394/.575		.425			
2021	CAR	A	18	68	5	2	0	1	7	1	25	0	0	.169/.206/.246	76	.256	-0.4	CF(16) 2.8, LF(1) -0.1	0.3
2022 non-DC	*MIL*	*MLB*	*19*	*251*	*16*	*9*	*1*	*2*	*18*	*10*	*105*	*0*	*0*	*.186/.229/.270*	*32*	*.320*	*-0.2*	*CF 2, RF 0*	*-1.2*

Comparables: Ronald Acuña Jr., Fernando Martinez, Riley Greene

The Report: Perez was a buzzy alternate-site name for the Brewers last summer and dominated the complex in his delayed pro debut last year before the 18-year-old hit a speed bump after a promotion to A-ball. At the plate, his stance includes a very interesting front foot, which is kept inside out until his stride, but, overall, it's a very calm lower half with a slight toe tap. Conversely, his upper half can be a bit twitchy, but he does relax and see the ball through the zone on pitches he does not like and shows very quick hands when he decides to swing. The big issue here is that, at times, it's a max-effort swing with a bit of an off-balanced, one-handed release. Given that Perez has been able to move the bat around the zone with a compact swing, we are really surprised at his K rate this past season. Regardless, there is still plenty more time to tell how this plays out with more game experience. We've described Perez as barrel-chested, and that remains the case. The young outfielder has a muscular core, but thin arms. It's a body to dream on, but it's one that should eventually move to a corner-outfield spot.

OFP:50 / Average outfielder

Variance: Extreme. Perez was extremely overmatched at Low-A but was just 18-years-old and is very projectable with loud tools.

Darius Austin's Fantasy Take: I don't know if the whiff-tastic debut or the woeful—albeit brief—full-season line has depressed Perez's dynasty value a ton. Those who roster him were probably already too high on the 18-year-old to consider selling at the first sign of struggles. As with all of these extremely high-variance prospects, you're not going to come out on top in the aggregate if you buy in close to the peak value, so maybe you need to wait for a slow 2022 start before striking. My gut says that he's physically gifted and young enough that he'll figure things out with more exposure. It's not hard to see him being either a top-20 dynasty prospect or sliding well outside the top 101 in a year's time.

8 Brice Turang SS   OFP: 50   ETA: 2022

Born: 11/21/99 Age: 22 Bats: L Throws: R Height: 6'0" Weight: 173 lb. Origin: Round 1, 2018 Draft (#21 overall)

YEAR	TEAM	LVL	AGE	PA	R	2B	3B	HR	RBI	BB	K	SB	CS	AVG/OBP/SLG	DRC+	BABIP	BRR	FRAA	WARP
2019	WIS	A	19	357	57	13	4	2	31	49	54	21	4	.287/.384/.376	122	.339	2.7	SS(43) 1.6, 2B(28) 0.7	2.6
2019	CAR	A+	19	207	25	6	2	1	6	34	47	9	1	.200/.338/.276	97	.268	1.6	SS(35) -2.9, 2B(5) -0.8	0.2
2021	BLX	AA	21	320	40	14	3	5	39	28	48	11	7	.264/.329/.385	107	.300	0.4	SS(71) 2.4	1.5
2021	NAS	AAA	21	176	19	7	0	1	14	32	35	9	2	.245/.381/.315	100	.315	0.1	SS(44) 2.1	0.8
2022 non-DC	*MIL*	*MLB*	*22*	*251*	*21*	*9*	*1*	*2*	*20*	*24*	*48*	*7*	*3*	*.231/.310/.321*	*74*	*.286*	*0.6*	*SS 0, 2B 0*	*0.1*

Comparables: J.P. Crawford, Tyler Pastornicky, Richard Ureña

The Report: Turang has been famous for a long time; He was an early candidate to go 1.1 in the 2018 Draft as a projectable prep shortstop with a well-rounded skill group. As early as that draft, many lost confidence in his ultimate ability to hit for power. And here we are, four years and five levels later, and the only time his slugging percentage hasn't started with a three was the time it started with a two

Turang hit the ball on the ground less in Double-A last year, which we had vaguely hoped was the key to at least gapping it more. He hit five home runs, more than doubling his career high, but didn't *really* make the hoped-for power gains. He went back to hitting the ball on the ground way more in Triple-A, and, well, he hit for even less power there, although that wasn't the "slugging starts with a two" stop (High-A in 2019, for the record). He just doesn't barrel the ball up enough, and there's no encouraging signs in his batted-ball data or anywhere else, at this point.

It's a shame, because every other skill is present. Turang makes good contact and sprays the ball well, if you ignore how hard it's hit. He has a very advanced plate approach. He's a solidly above-average shortstop who can also handle second. He's a moderate stolen-base threat. If he even could get to just 40 game power . . .

OFP: 50 / Starting shortstop without major impact

Variance: Low. He's going to play in the bigs forever because of his positive skills, but he's running out of time to get even to fringe-average pop without some sort of unexpected strength-and-swing overhaul.

Darius Austin's Fantasy Take: Turang is going to have to run quite a bit. We're in an environment in which people will desperately scramble to draft 15-steal threats, and he should be able to do that. Being able to play a good shortstop and thus stay on the field is going to help. You'll still have to draft Turang for teams that you've already stocked well with power, and you're not going to feel particularly good about it unless he starts to push those swipes into the 20–25 range on a regular basis.

9 Freddy Zamora SS OFP: 50 ETA: 2023

Born: 11/01/98 Age: 23 Bats: R Throws: R Height: 6'1" Weight: 190 lb. Origin: Round 2, 2020 Draft (#53 overall)

YEAR	TEAM	LVL	AGE	PA	R	2B	3B	HR	RBI	BB	K	SB	CS	AVG/OBP/SLG	DRC+	BABIP	BRR	FRAA	WARP
2021	CAR	A	22	321	58	13	1	5	40	45	57	9	5	.287/.396/.399	118	.344	-0.5	SS(63) 2.8	1.8
2021	WIS	A+	22	92	12	9	0	1	9	12	19	1	0	.342/.435/.494	103	.441	0.3	SS(21) -2.6	0.1
2022 non-DC	*MIL*	*MLB*	*23*	*251*	*22*	*11*	*0*	*2*	*21*	*23*	*51*	*2*	*2*	*.236/.312/.332*	*77*	*.294*	*0.0*	*SS -1*	*0.1*

Comparables: Matt Duffy, Emmanuel Burriss, Jason Donald

The Report: The 2020 second-round selection might have some room to fill out, but Zamora's profile seems pretty much set. He was already 23 years old and playing at two A-ball levels in 2021, and a lot of our lack of excitement for his ceiling is due to the fact that we think what we see now is kind of who he is, through and through. Clearly a polished hitter, the former Miami Hurricane has a good feel for hitting and has advanced bat-to-ball skills. At the plate, everything is very balanced, despite a noticeable leg kick. Zamora has an all-fields approach with good plate discipline, and it's relaxed. This has the makings of a .280- 10–15-home-run-type guy. He should stick at shortstop, where he shows clean actions and soft hands. Given the advanced tool set, look for Zamora to get pushed through that system in the next year or two.

OFP: 50 / Average contact-first shortstop

Variance: Medium. The bat should play, and he's a good defender, but the power is still a bit away.

Darius Austin's Fantasy Take: This is rather similar to Turang's outlook, from the clearly below-average power to the defensive profile. Zamora looks more likely to be capable of reaching double-digit homers in the majors, a fact that's offset by his lesser stolen-base contributions. He may well hit for more average than Turang, too, but, for now, we do have to care about steals quite a bit. We're rearranging deck chairs on the middle-infield *Titanic* here. They're both reliable-volume, low-impact MIs unless there's a significant change in outlook.

10 Jeferson Quero C/DH OFP: 50 ETA: 2025/2026

Born: 10/08/02 Age: 19 Bats: R Throws: R Height: 5'10" Weight: 165 lb. Origin: International Free Agent, 2019

YEAR	TEAM	LVL	AGE	PA	R	2B	3B	HR	RBI	BB	K	SB	CS	AVG/OBP/SLG	DRC+	BABIP	BRR	FRAA	WARP
2021	BRWB	ROK	18	83	15	5	1	2	8	12	10	4	3	.309/.434/.500		.339			

Comparables: Marcos Betancourt, Kelvin Mateo, Daniel Rams

The Report: Quero gets less attention than his 2019 J2 classmate Perez, and certainly doesn't have the projectability or the loud tool set. He's on the smaller side for a catcher and has logged a grand total of 14 games at the position. He does have an advanced hit tool and impressive contact rates and hits the ball harder than you'd think given his frame. You might have figured out by now that we will end this blurb with "check back next year," but it's likely more along the lines of "check back three years from now." Nevertheless, his potential upside as a two-way catcher is worth flagging him at the back of this list this year.

OFP: 50 / Average backstop

Variance: Extreme. This is going to be a slow burn, even if things go well, and there's a lot that can go badly for a teenaged catcher in the complex.

Darius Austin's Fantasy Take: I can do no more than to echo the advice to check back three years from now, and then some. We say don't roster prospect catchers in dynasty in almost all cases. Definitely don't roster prospect catchers who are potentially five years away.

The Prospects You Meet Outside the Top Ten

#11

Zavier Warren 3B Born: 01/08/99 Age: 23 Bats: S Throws: R Height: 6'0" Weight: 190 lb. Origin: Round 3, 2020 Draft (#92 overall)

YEAR	TEAM	LVL	AGE	PA	R	2B	3B	HR	RBI	BB	K	SB	CS	AVG/OBP/SLG	DRC+	BABIP	BRR	FRAA	WARP
2021	CAR	A	22	230	34	8	2	10	30	33	49	1	0	.251/.374/.471	125	.286	-0.8	C(17) -0.7, 3B(13) 1.3, 1B(9) 1.6	1.4
2021	WIS	A+	22	157	21	7	1	3	18	18	32	5	0	.267/.357/.400	105	.324	1.0	3B(21) 1.6, 1B(10) -0.9, C(3) -0.2	0.7
2022 non-DC	*MIL*	*MLB*	*23*	*251*	*24*	*9*	*1*	*5*	*24*	*23*	*62*	*1*	*1*	*.224/.303/.351*	*77*	*.285*	*-0.1*	*3B 1, C -3*	*-0.2*

Comparables: Brent Morel, Peter O'Brien, Danny Valencia

Okay, well, this is fun. This switch-hitting, soon-to-be-23-year-old jack-of-all-trades features an open stance in which he gets his hands up in the zone quicker than most. On pitches lower in the zone, he still has somewhat of an uppercut, but it's a quick swing, nonetheless, thanks to his really fast hands, which plays well into his all-gap-to-gap approach. Warren also sees pitches at a high level and displayed impressive patience in his first minor-league season. The hit tool and game-power tool both seem average, as he still has some holes in his swing, but he is strong and quick enough to grade out as a 5 in both.

Defensively, we absolutely love that an athlete like Warren is getting at least a chance to prove what he can do as a catcher. He is very clearly working on framing pitches, as he sometimes overdoes it, but that is a sign that the Brewers are probably trying to emphasize that part of his game. Obviously, he looks a bit twitchy back there and is a bit unpolished, but, certainly, if he fared worse at third base, he could probably profile as an offense-first catcher. Warren is a better fit at third base, with an above-average arm and average infield actions, but the catcher flex is intriguing.

#12

Eduardo Garcia SS Born: 07/10/02 Age: 19 Bats: R Throws: R Height: 6'2" Weight: 160 lb. Origin: International Free Agent, 2019

YEAR	TEAM	LVL	AGE	PA	R	2B	3B	HR	RBI	BB	K	SB	CS	AVG/OBP/SLG	DRC+	BABIP	BRR	FRAA	WARP
2019	DSL BRW	ROK	16	40	6	2	0	1	3	6	9	1	1	.313/.450/.469		.409			
2021	BRWG	ROK	18	136	24	10	3	3	24	9	40	2	2	.238/.316/.443		.329			
2021	CAR	A	18	42	8	4	0	0	7	6	13	1	0	.333/.452/.455	96	.524	0.4	SS(10) 0.5	0.2
2022 non-DC	*MIL*	*MLB*	*19*	*251*	*18*	*10*	*1*	*2*	*18*	*18*	*84*	*2*	*1*	*.186/.257/.272*	*44*	*.284*	*0.0*	*SS 0, 3B 0*	*-0.9*

The big name from the Brewers' 2018 IFA class, Garcia got his professional legs under him after a fractured ankle limited him to 10 Dominican Summer League games in 2019. He made it all the way to Low-A in his Age-18 season last year. The top line numbers all look pretty good, but Garcia's swing is a little awkward and noisy, and he often ends up out of sync. He was chasing more than you'd like, too, although that is forgivable given his age and relative lack of reps. He has some projection left, although he has a narrow frame, and he has already shown some sneaky pop, although he doesn't really have a swing geared to elevate, at present—he often looked like he was merely trying to hang with it at the plate. Garcia looks pretty nondescript on the routine plays at the six, but can flash the leather when called upon. While his arm isn't plus, it's solid enough for the left side.

#13

Joe Gray Jr. OF Born: 03/12/00 Age: 22 Bats: R Throws: R Height: 6'1" Weight: 195 lb. Origin: Round 2, 2018 Draft (#60 overall)

YEAR	TEAM	LVL	AGE	PA	R	2B	3B	HR	RBI	BB	K	SB	CS	AVG/OBP/SLG	DRC+	BABIP	BRR	FRAA	WARP
2019	RMV	ROA	19	129	19	4	1	3	9	13	36	3	2	.164/.279/.300		.208			
2021	SRR	WIN	21	70	3	1	0	1	6	10	24	1	0	.069/.229/.138		.091			
2021	CAR	A	21	231	40	15	7	12	53	33	61	12	0	.289/.407/.632	135	.361	0.3	CF(39) 2.5, RF(9) -0.2	2.0
2021	WIS	A+	21	248	32	7	2	8	37	20	70	11	3	.219/.306/.381	95	.277	1.1	CF(31) 1.1, RF(18) 1.4, LF(2) 1.6	1.2
2022 non-DC	*MIL*	*MLB*	*22*	*251*	*24*	*10*	*2*	*6*	*27*	*19*	*79*	*7*	*2*	*.219/.294/.379*	*79*	*.305*	*0.8*	*CF 2, RF 0*	*0.5*

Comparables: Michael Hermosillo, Ender Inciarte, Teoscar Hernández

A four-and-a-half-tool prospect with projection, Joe Gray Jr. might be one of those players that just needs to refine his swing a tick and, boom, you have an everyday number-two hitter type in your lineup. Of course, it's not as simple as that. The jump from Low-A to High-A proved quite difficult for the potentially exciting outfielder, exposing the issues in his offensive game. The swing is long, and, at times, the bat looks a little heavy for the 2018 second-round pick, but he has an above-average game-power projection and good plate discipline already. At times, Gray's leg kick seems to slow the rest of his swing down a bit, but it's probably something that will become less pronounced. The hit tool is clearly Gray's weakest tool, but given that he projects above average just about everywhere else and still has room to fill out, if the swing clicks, he could rocket up this list.

Prospects on the Rise

Jackson Chourio CF Born: 03/11/04 Age: 18 Bats: R Throws: R Height: 6'1" Weight: 165 lb. Origin: International Free Agent, 2021

YEAR	TEAM	LVL	AGE	PA	R	2B	3B	HR	RBI	BB	K	SB	CS	AVG/OBP/SLG	DRC+	BABIP	BRR	FRAA	WARP
2021	DSL BRW2	ROK	17	189	31	7	1	5	25	23	28	8	3	.296/.386/.447		.323			

We don't love writing up recent IFAs with only foreign-complex experience, but there's probably something to the fact that Chourio was playing winter ball as a 17-year-old. Signed as a shortstop, was playing mostly center field, and the very early days' batted-ball data looked good. He's certainly one for the watch list.

Felix Valerio IF Born: 12/26/00 Age: 21 Bats: R Throws: R Height: 5'7" Weight: 165 lb. Origin: International Free Agent, 2018

YEAR	TEAM	LVL	AGE	PA	R	2B	3B	HR	RBI	BB	K	SB	CS	AVG/OBP/SLG	DRC+	BABIP	BRR	FRAA	WARP
2019	BRG	ROK	18	178	16	13	0	0	18	17	21	16	5	.306/.376/.389		.348			
2021	CAR	A	20	377	71	24	3	6	63	54	49	27	8	.314/.430/.469	135	.354	0.7	2B(40) -4.2, SS(18) -0.5, 3B(17) 2.4	2.5
2021	WIS	A+	20	134	19	13	0	5	16	15	22	4	1	.229/.321/.466	120	.242	-0.6	2B(27) -3.8	0.3
2022 non-DC	*MIL*	*MLB*	*21*	*251*	*23*	*12*	*1*	*3*	*23*	*22*	*43*	*9*	*4*	*.240/.318/.355*	*85*	*.284*	*0.7*	*2B -3, SS 0*	*0.2*

The (listed) 5-foot-7 second baseman is really fun and might have a bit of projection left (but not much). He has a pretty max-effort swing paired with low strikeout numbers—which is always fun. His leg kick is huge, but he has truly impressive bat-to-ball skills, which keeps him in at-bats and leads to the fouling off of tough pitches, low strikeout numbers, and a high OBP. There was a noticeable jump in power for the short-statured Valerio last year, but we're not buying into it. As with a few other propsect on this list, the jump from Low-A to High-A led to some struggles, but, at just 20 years old, we think Valerio is one of those 55-hit, low-power guys that will always have a place in the majors.

Factors on the Farm

Mario Feliciano C Born: 11/20/98 Age: 23 Bats: R Throws: R Height: 6'1" Weight: 200 lb. Origin: Round 2, 2016 Draft (#75 overall)

YEAR	TEAM	LVL	AGE	PA	R	2B	3B	HR	RBI	BB	K	SB	CS	AVG/OBP/SLG	DRC+	BABIP	BRR	FRAA	WARP
2019	MAN	WIN	20	101	2	6	0	0	4	5	20	0	0	.269/.327/.333		.342			
2019	CAR	A+	20	482	62	25	4	19	81	29	139	2	1	.273/.324/.477	107	.351	-4.3	C(61) 3.4	1.8
2021	BRWG	ROK	22	29	7	3	1	0	4	1	6	0	0	.360/.448/.560		.474			
2021	NAS	AAA	22	114	12	2	0	3	19	4	26	1	0	.210/.246/.314	87	.241	0.7	C(30) 1.8	0.5
2021	MIL	MLB	22	1	1	0	0	0	0	1	0	0	0	.000/1.000/.000	110		0.1		0.0
2022 DC	*MIL*	*MLB*	*23*	*30*	*3*	*1*	*0*	*0*	*3*	*1*	*7*	*0*	*0*	*.234/.288/.381*	*76*	*.297*	*0.0*	*C 1*	*0.1*

Comparables: Gary Sánchez, Salvador Perez, Wilson Ramos

An offense-first catcher through and through, Feliciano's overall profile hasn't really changed from our previous reports. He keeps his hands high and generates power thanks to a big leg kick and max-effort swing. A shoulder injury limited last year, so this is probably not the fairest time to evaluate him, but if you want a catcher who can bring potential above-average game power at the cost of some swing-and-miss, Feliciano is your guy.

Corey Ray CF Born: 09/22/94 Age: 27 Bats: L Throws: L Height: 6'0" Weight: 196 lb. Origin: Round 1, 2016 Draft (#5 overall)

YEAR	TEAM	LVL	AGE	PA	R	2B	3B	HR	RBI	BB	K	SB	CS	AVG/OBP/SLG	DRC+	BABIP	BRR	FRAA	WARP
2019	BLX	AA	24	46	5	3	0	0	0	6	14	3	2	.250/.348/.325	83	.385	0.0	CF(10) 1.4, LF(1) -0.2	0.2
2019	SA	AAA	24	230	23	8	0	7	21	20	89	3	1	.188/.261/.329	60	.283	-0.5	CF(41) -4.3, RF(8) -1.1, LF(2) -0.3	-0.9
2021	NAS	AAA	26	157	18	11	2	6	19	10	45	2	0	.274/.325/.500	96	.358	0.5	CF(34) 5.3, RF(3) 0.1, LF(1) 0.0	1.0
2021	MIL	MLB	26	3	1	0	0	0	0	1	1	0	0	.000/.333/.000	88			RF(1) 0.0	0.0
2022 DC	*MIL*	*MLB*	*27*	*97*	*11*	*4*	*0*	*2*	*11*	*7*	*32*	*3*	*1*	*.218/.282/.383*	*71*	*.311*	*0.3*	*RF 0, LF 0*	*0.0*

Comparables: Roger Bernadina, Abraham Almonte, Ryan LaMarre

An injury-riddled season limited the former first-round pick to just 39 games in 2021. In Ray's short time on the field, however, he made improvements and solidified his projection as a useful fourth outfielder. His unpolished and somewhat-long swing has contributed to his high strikeout numbers throughout the minors. Despite this, he does generate plenty of power. Seeing more opposite-field hits and fight-em-off dribbler singles from him was a positive, but, overall, his hit tool remains below average with potentially average game power. Ray definitely has some wheels, and while the stolen-base numbers have taken a drastic dip, he is still clearly an above-average runner. Defensively, Ray is probably an average center fielder and slightly above average in left. Keep in mind, though, Ray is 27 years old. In pretty much all of our internal reports to this point, "he is what he is" was a theme. What he is is a fourth outfielder who could probably hit .245, get on base at maybe a .330 clip, and sock 15 homers.

Top Talents 25 and Under (as of 4/1/2022):

1. Freddy Peralta, RHP
2. Luis Urías, 3B/SS/2B
3. Garrett Mitchell, OF
4. Sal Frelick, OF
5. Aaron Ashby, LHP
6. Ethan Small, LHP
7. Keston Hiura, 1B
8. Joey Wiemer, OF
9. Tyler Black, 2B
10. Hedbert Perez, OF

Last year, we pleaded with the Brewers to give Peralta a shot in a genuine rotation role, working 2–3 times through the opposing batting order. Suffice it to say: opportunity given, opportunity seized. Milwaukee's ace assembly line appears to have pumped out another top-of-the-line arm having improved both utilization and raw stuff. Peralta's overhauled off-speed repertoire is now headlined by a plus slider, giving his already hard-to-handle medley added pizzazz. His strong curveball continued to give hitters trouble, as well, and helped him shake off platoon threats. The totality was 144 ⅓ innings in 27 starts, good for a 71 DRA– and a performance as a number-three starter that many clubs would joyfully take from their number one.

The slow burn on Urías is a great reminder why age-adjustments are not gospel but should never be summarily dismissed. Reaching just shy of 1,000 plate appearances across four seasons well before his 25th birthday, Urías finally turned in a season worthy of his once-lofty prospect status. Playing all three premium infield positions, Urías neither stood out nor dug a hole, which is to be expected given his middling foot speed. Fortunately, his long-heralded bat-to-ball skills manifested in quality contact, at last, with a 25-home-run campaign that drove a 107 DRC+. The pint-size power-plug gets on base at a healthy clip, seeing the ball well and delivering a pull-heavy-but-potent approach that is notable in part for how it contrasts with that of another much-heralded teammate.

We're in full on crisis mode for Hiura, who was the sixth-overall prospect ahead of the 2019 season on a rich, high-floor profile that seemed to deliver immediately with a strong debut that year. A 100 DRC+ on a .303/.368/.570 line was some caution to pump the breaks, but that same measure saw his disappointing 2020 as possibly anomalous, with a 92 DRC+ for his .212/.297/.410 line there. Nothing could rightly defend Hiura's 2021's putrefaction, however. The floating leg lift that Hiura has long utilized, with success, to track and time pitches late into their break and splash them on a line has drifted off the map. Hiura's swing resembled a pitcher's in many cases in 2021, and the results weren't massively better (53 DRC+). His inability to handle MLB velocity appears pronounced, particularly at the letters or above. To make matters worse, his defensive slide has already pushed him to primarily manning first, with mediocre foot speed placing an onerous emphasis on his production at the dish as a right-handed cold cornerer.

Minnesota Twins

The State of the System:

The Twins' system is quite deep, especially after dealing José Berríos and Nelson Cruz at the deadline, but injuries plagued a lot of their big-name prospects in 2021.

The Top Ten:

1 Austin Martin SS/OF OFP: 60 ETA: Late 2022

Born: 03/23/99 Age: 23 Bats: R Throws: R Height: 6'0" Weight: 185 lb. Origin: Round 1, 2020 Draft (#5 overall)

YEAR	TEAM	LVL	AGE	PA	R	2B	3B	HR	RBI	BB	K	SB	CS	AVG/OBP/SLG	DRC+	BABIP	BRR	FRAA	WARP
2021	NH	AA	22	250	43	10	2	2	16	37	53	9	3	.281/.424/.383	116	.368	0.8	SS(27) 1.1, CF(26) 4.5	1.9
2021	WCH	AA	22	168	24	8	0	3	19	23	30	5	1	.254/.399/.381	112	.304	1.6	CF(20) 1.0, SS(16) -2.3	0.8
2022 DC	*MIN*	*MLB*	*23*	*28*	*3*	*1*	*0*	*0*	*2*	*2*	*5*	*0*	*0*	*.216/.325/.307*	*81*	*.271*	*0.0*	*SS 0*	*0.0*

Comparables: Trayvon Robinson, Aaron Hicks, Jake Marisnick

The Report: You'd be forgiven if you started singing Peggy Lee's "Is That All There Is?" when looking at Martin's 2021 stat line. He was a legitimate candidate to go first in the 2020 draft and received the second highest bonus. Yes, power was never going to be the carrying tool, but you'd like the slugging to have started with a four this year (and his hit tool was going to be the carrying tool, so, yeah, it would have been nice if his average started with a three). Martin has a very unorthodox swing that starts with the bat head at a near-45-degree angle to the pitcher. You have to have good wrists to make that work, and he does, but it's going to limit his ability to consistently lift and drive the ball. The underlying physical tools for 6 hit and 5 power are still here, but the edges need to be smoothed. The approach is as polished as they come, though, and Martin should keep the OBP up around .400.

Martin split his time between center field and shortstop in 2021. Neither is an ideal fit, and, like his former New Hampshire teammate Jordan Groshans, he can lack the quick twitch to profile as a true up-the-middle defender. Conversely, you could credibly plug him in at seven spots, defensively. That kind of defensive flex, with what could end up an admittedly OBP-heavy .800 OPS? That will inspire a different Peggy Lee tune when he's in the lineup: "It's a good day from morning 'til night . . ."

OFP:60 / Hey, Jonathan India was worth like 3–4 wins this year.

Variance: Medium. Yeah, he still needs to hit for some pop, or major-league pitching won't nibble. Weirdly, we suspect a change of scenery might not have been the worst thing here.

Mark Barry's Fantasy Take: Admittedly, Martin's first season as a pro was a little disappointing. Five homers and the aforementioned sub-.400 slugging percentage is extremely Not What You Want when talking top-25 prospects. Still, Martin has all the tools that I covet with a dynasty prospect. His bat-to-ball skills and ability to work a walk are difficult to teach, and I'm still optimistic that he can eventually flirt with 20 homers. Fold in the positional flexibility, and I still think you're looking at a top-25 guy, even if it's not as much of a lock as it was this time last year.

2 Jordan Balazovic RHP OFP: 60 ETA: Late 2022/Early 2023

Born: 09/17/98 Age: 23 Bats: R Throws: R Height: 6'5" Weight: 215 lb. Origin: Round 5, 2016 Draft (#153 overall)

YEAR	TEAM	LVL	AGE	W	L	SV	G	GS	IP	H	HR	BB/9	K/9	K	GB%	BABIP	WHIP	ERA	DRA-	WARP
2019	CR	A	20	2	1	0	4	4	20^2	15	1	1.7	14.4	33	42.2%	.318	0.92	2.18	85	0.3
2019	FTM	A+	20	6	4	0	15	14	73	52	3	2.6	11.8	96	44.3%	.283	1.00	2.84	93	1.1
2021	WCH	AA	22	5	4	0	20	20	97	98	9	3.5	9.5	102	48.6%	.324	1.40	3.62	86	1.4
2022 DC	*MIN*	*MLB*	*23*	*0*	*0*	*0*	*3*	*3*	*14*	*14*	*1*	*3.9*	*8.4*	*13*	*48.3%*	*.303*	*1.42*	*4.56*	*111*	*0.0*

Comparables: Jake Thompson, Brad Keller, Collin Balester

The Report: Jordan Balazovic is a third-starter prospect. His fastball holds a solid-average-to-plus velo band deep into starts, and he can reach back for more. The fastball rides well, almost runs uphill to batters, and gets bad, late swings under it. Balazovic's requisite plus-projecting breaking ball takes two different forms: (1) a low-80s power curve with short, 12–6 action that sometimes he twists off, that sometimes doesn't have ideal depth, but could be a future out-pitch; (2) A slider that bleeds into the curve at the lower end of its velocity range, but can be distinguished by a bit more glove-side break. His change is too firm and lacks ideal separation off the fastball, although it can show a little sink. Balazovic has a high, inconsistent arm path, and his delivery features late acceleration with all his limbs. That can lead to general command issues or just not being on top of his pitches at the release point. The changeup isn't likely to get past "has some utility against lefties," but if he can smooth out the delivery/command issues . . . well, he's a number-three starter.

OFP: 60 / Mid-rotation starter or late-inning reliever

Variance: Medium. He isn't the first good starting-pitching prospect in this book that needs some command refinement and a changeup jump to reach his number-three starter projection, and he won't be the last.

Mark Barry's Fantasy Take: So, let me get this straight: If everything goes right with Balazovic's cambio, he *could* be a number-three starter? If not, he's probably a reliever? I'm fine with it if you have the space and want to roll the dice, but I don't know that his profile is the best use of a roster spot.

3 Joe Ryan RHP OFP: 55 ETA: Debuted in 2021

Born: 06/05/96 Age: 26 Bats: R Throws: R Height: 6'2" Weight: 205 lb. Origin: Round 7, 2018 Draft (#210 overall)

YEAR	TEAM	LVL	AGE	W	L	SV	G	GS	IP	H	HR	BB/9	K/9	K	GB%	BABIP	WHIP	ERA	DRA-	WARP
2019	BG	A	23	2	2	0	6	6	27^2	19	2	3.6	15.3	47	28.6%	.315	1.08	2.93	91	0.3
2019	CHA	A+	23	7	2	0	15	13	82^2	47	3	1.3	12.2	112	36.6%	.246	0.71	1.42	67	2.3
2019	MTG	AA	23	0	0	0	3	3	13^1	11	2	2.7	16.2	24	23.1%	.375	1.13	3.38	78	0.2
2021	STP	AAA	25	0	0	0	2	2	9	5	1	2.0	17.0	17	66.7%	.286	0.78	2.00	87	0.2
2021	DUR	AAA	25	4	3	0	12	11	57	35	8	1.6	11.8	75	32.3%	.227	0.79	3.63	87	1.1
2021	MIN	MLB	25	2	1	0	5	5	26^2	16	4	1.7	10.1	30	26.2%	.197	0.79	4.05	104	0.2
2022 DC	*MIN*	*MLB*	*26*	*10*	*7*	*0*	*27*	*27*	*143*	*115*	*20*	*2.4*	*9.7*	*154*	*39.7%*	*.263*	*1.07*	*3.00*	*82*	*2.5*

Comparables: Tyler Thornburg, Armando Galarraga, A.J. Griffin

The Report: All Ryan has done since being drafted is put up great strikeout and walk rates at every level. He does not have overwhelming velocity or spin rate, nor does he have a clear out-pitch amongst his three offspeeds. But amidst the bushel of 5s and 55s on his pitches—the curveball has been the best pitch for him in the minors, and he got a lot of whiffs with it in a small major-league sample—he has excellent command and control.

There are two data points worth mentioning here which ultimately conflict. The first is that the Rays, a very smart baseball team, traded him at midseason (along with another prospect you'll read about later on this list) for a half-season of a 41-year-old designated hitter who lingered into the latter stages of free agency the prior winter. The other is that, after going to Minnesota, Ryan had five splendid starts in the majors in which the contours of a contact-suppressing, mid-rotation starter were very apparent. How much to weigh each of those, if at all, is up to you.

OFP: 55 / Mid-rotation starter

Variance: Low, at least for a pitcher. The performance and health records here are very solid, and he has already pitched well in the majors. Conversely, the stuff really isn't present for a huge breakout.

Mark Barry's Fantasy Take: We all love Jordans. They're classic, cool and, judging by SNKRS app success rates, they're pretty hard to come by. Still, there's a lot to be said for a comfy, not typically flashy pair of Vans. They're less exciting and less exclusive, but they're also perfectly functional and capable. If a guy like Grayson Rodriguez is the pair of Jordans, Ryan is the pair of Vans. Ryan might never be a top-20 fantasy hurler, but he'll put up solid middle-of-the-rotation production to bolster fantasy staffs. Also, if you want to take this a step further, an anagram of Joe Ryan's name *almost* spells Jordan. Close, but not quite. So there's that.

4 Chase Petty RHP OFP: 55 ETA: 2025

Born: 04/04/03 Age: 19 Bats: R Throws: R Height: 6'1" Weight: 190 lb. Origin: Round 1, 2021 Draft (#26 overall)

The Report: Petty has been known to sit 99 mph with his fastball, which has repeatedly touched triple-digits in the past, and it's explosive heat. His slider is plus-plus. Everything else about his profile is a hot mess.

Sure, Petty is the kind of extremely live, extremely wild prep arm that our sabermetric forerunners tried to scare us away from. His changeup is nascent. He throws balls to the backstop too often. His delivery is violent. But that fastball and slider combination can be quite elite if he can hit his spots a little better, and the more we dig into analytics, the more we value individual elite pitches. So, if you're a team that has just the right inputs on your draft models, the young-for-his-class pitcher with the makings of two 70 pitches is going to fare quite well, isn't he?

OFP:55 / Mid-rotation starter or closer

Variance: Extreme. Petty is unrefined even for a prep arm, which is a notoriously high-variance crop to begin with.

Mark Barry's Fantasy Take: The old me would look at Petty's two pitches, violent delivery, and Ricky Vaughn (pre-glasses) command and immediately banish the prep arm to the bullpen. The new me, wise and handsome, sees two plus pitches and high velocity in a landscape where hurlers are leaning on their best offerings more than ever. The new me still thinks Petty is destined for the bullpen, but he's worth a spot on the watchlist until that picture crystallizes.

5 Royce Lewis SS OFP: 55 ETA: 2022

Born: 06/05/99 Age: 23 Bats: R Throws: R Height: 6'2" Weight: 200 lb. Origin: Round 1, 2017 Draft (#1 overall)

YEAR	TEAM	LVL	AGE	PA	R	2B	3B	HR	RBI	BB	K	SB	CS	AVG/OBP/SLG	DRC+	BABIP	BRR	FRAA	WARP
2019	SRR	WIN	20	95	21	9	0	3	20	9	22	5	1	.353/.411/.565		.443			
2019	FTM	A+	20	418	55	17	3	10	35	27	90	16	8	.238/.289/.376	101	.281	-1.9	SS(84) 3.9	1.3
2019	PNS	AA	20	148	18	9	1	2	14	11	33	6	2	.231/.291/.358	94	.287	1.6	SS(29) -2.9, 2B(1) 0.0, 3B(1) -0.0	0.5
2022 DC	*MIN*	*MLB*	*23*	*128*	*15*	*5*	*0*	*3*	*15*	*8*	*33*	*3*	*2*	*.228/.285/.366*	*78*	*.288*	*0.3*	*SS 0*	*0.2*

Comparables: Tyler Pastornicky, Ryan Mountcastle, Richard Ureña

The Report: It has been two full years since Lewis last appeared in competitive games, tearing up the Arizona Fall League after a dismal 2019 season. The confidence boost from that performance was supposed to catapult him back into the elite-prospect discussion, as was being asked to the satellite camp during the COVID-shortened 2020 season. As we say often: how a team moves a player explains far more than any quote or evaluation they provide. With the Twins beset by injury in 2020, they continuously bypassed their former first-overall pick in favor of others. With a chance to prove himself at the upper levels this past year, he tore the anterior cruciate ligament in his right knee before spring training began, leaving everyone wondering what to make of his future status. Quite frankly, we don't know if the time away can make his noisy swing and lackluster approach any worse than it was, but it certainly didn't help him figure out where his defensive home might be. In the meantime, we wait to see how he bounces back, and if he can recapture any of the flashes of past magic.

OFP: 55 / Multi-positional boom-or-bust threat

Variance: Extreme. His lost season couldn't have come at a worse time. The physical tools will eventually shuttle him to the show, his success—good or bad—will be determined by his adjustments and how he recovers from a serious knee injury.

Mark Barry's Fantasy Take: Last year, J.P. Breen labeled Lewis a "tough dynasty prospect to value" and one "impossible to acquire." And that was before Lewis tore his ACL last spring and missed the entire 2021 campaign. In theory, the skills that made Lewis a top-notch dynasty prospect are still there. In reality, we haven't seen him play in competitive games since 2019. I'm interested in scooping him up for my fantasy squad, but if another manager has stashed Lewis for this long, odds are the acquisition cost will be too rich for the gamble.

6 Matt Canterino RHP   OFP: 55   ETA: 2022 as a reliever, 2023 as a starter, either is health permitting

Born: 12/14/97 Age: 24 Bats: R Throws: R Height: 6'2" Weight: 222 lb. Origin: Round 2, 2019 Draft (#54 overall)

YEAR	TEAM	LVL	AGE	W	L	SV	G	GS	IP	H	HR	BB/9	K/9	K	GB%	BABIP	WHIP	ERA	DRA-	WARP
2019	CR	A	21	1	1	0	5	5	20	6	0	3.2	11.3	25	48.8%	.146	0.65	1.35	89	0.3
2021	CR	A+	23	1	0	0	5	5	21	10	1	1.7	18.4	43	41.9%	.300	0.67	0.86	54	0.7
2022 non-DC	*MIN*	*MLB*	*24*	*2*	*2*	*0*	*57*	*0*	*50*	*41*	*7*	*3.6*	*12.3*	*68*	*42.8%*	*.305*	*1.24*	*3.76*	*91*	*0.4*

Comparables: Jacob Barnes, Phil Coke, Anthony Castro

The Report: You might be surprised to to learn that we think Canterino has the best stuff of any Twins pitching prospect. You will be less surprised to hear that a former Rice pitcher had an injury-marred pro season. An elbow strain truncated Canterino's 2021, but as 23-inning campaigns go, it was a helluva 23 innings. From an uptempo, funky delivery, he offers three potentially above-average offerings. The fastball/slider combo is the headline act: mid-90s heat that rides up in the zone from an over-the-top slot and a razorblade 12–5 power breaker with big depth that misses plenty of lumber. The developing changeup that we heard about last summer plays as well. Canterino sells the pitch, and it shows solid split/sink action. He might remind you a little bit of James Karinchak (pre-June-2021 version), but as a potential starter. Of course, "potential" is doing a lot of work there for a pitcher that threw 23 innings last season and then missed significant time with an elbow strain.

OFP: 55 / No. 3 starter or late-inning reliever

Variance: High. There is purportedly no structural damage to Canterino's elbow, but there was significant relief risk here even before his ligaments started barking. It's Top-101 stuff, but there's very little in the way of floor at the moment.

Mark Barry's Fantasy Take: If Canterino had a better track record for health, he'd be a lot higher on this (and the top-101) list. Similarly, if my cat could talk, I'd have a talking cat. I still think Canterino is worth a speculative add, if you have a roster spot designated for churn and burn. If he pops, he'll pop quickly. If the injuries linger, then you shouldn't feel too bad about moving on.

7 Jose Miranda IF   OFP: 55   ETA: 2022

Born: 06/29/98 Age: 24 Bats: R Throws: R Height: 6'2" Weight: 210 lb. Origin: Round 2, 2016 Draft (#73 overall)

YEAR	TEAM	LVL	AGE	PA	R	2B	3B	HR	RBI	BB	K	SB	CS	AVG/OBP/SLG	DRC+	BABIP	BRR	FRAA	WARP
2019	FTM	A+	21	478	48	25	1	8	55	24	54	0	0	.248/.299/.364	116	.264	-1.5	3B(71) 0.5, 2B(35) 0.5, SS(6) 0.1	2.2
2020	CAG	WIN	22	61	10	6	0	1	8	6	10	0	0	.302/.377/.472		.349			
2021	WCH	AA	23	218	36	8	0	13	38	17	25	4	2	.345/.408/.588	148	.342	0.9	3B(15) 1.3, 1B(14) 1.0, 2B(14) 0.2	2.2
2021	STP	AAA	23	373	61	24	0	17	56	25	49	0	2	.343/.397/.563	133	.362	-2.7	3B(39) -0.9, 2B(20) 0.8, 1B(14) -0.3	2.2
2022 DC	*MIN*	*MLB*	*24*	*333*	*44*	*16*	*0*	*9*	*43*	*19*	*48*	*0*	*1*	*.266/.317/.415*	*103*	*.288*	*-0.5*	*3B 1, 2B 0*	*1.3*

Comparables: Josh Bell, Jose Altuve, Miguel Andújar

The Report: "It's all in ze wrist." So said Marcel Hilliare, Audrey Hepburn's extremely French (although the actor was German) culinary instructor in *Sabrina*. As it goes for cracking an egg, so it goes for Jose Miranda's swing. The wrists generate some pre-swing noise and induce a late hitch, but also lend him plus bat control. Despite a surfeit of extra motion—he utilizes a big leg kick, as well—there's a discernible rhythm to Miranda's swing. Hitters hit, after all, and the better ones have a clear cadence. This one sounds like it's plus.

We don't know if Miranda will continue to generate this kind of power, though. He can drive the ball authoritatively the other way, but his aggressive approach can lead to a lot of early-count ground-ball contact, and the natural inside-out of his swing mechanics doesn't emphasize the kind of consistent pull-side pop you see from most 20-plus-home-run hitters. He can turn inside on fringe offspeed or flat fastballs, but we'd expect him to be more of a 15-ish-home-run hitter when he's seeing major-league velocity in his kitchen every night.

Miranda primarily saw time at second and third base in 2021, and he's a solid, if unspectacular, fit at either spot. The hands work fine. He's not much of a runner, but his range is serviceable. His arm strength is perhaps a tick on the good side of average, but it's accurate, and he throws well on the run. It's a very average defensive profile, but at useful spots to have an average glove. Ultimately, it's about the bat, and while .340 and 30 home runs in the upper minors overstates the projection in the bat, it should have no problem carrying the profile.

OFP: 55 / Above-average infielder

Variance: Medium. We're not really convinced the game power plays to this level against night-in/night-out major-league velocity and sequencing, but if it does? Well, this projection might be low.

Mark Barry's Fantasy Take: It doesn't happen often, but Miranda is probably better as a fantasy prospect than IRL. The contact ability and plus hit tool should make for consistently high batting averages, and there's enough power for that average not to be empty. Lazy org-comp incoming: he has all the makings to be a better Luis Arraez. While that might sound like false praise, Arraez has been A Thing in deeper leagues for a while now.

Eyewitness Report: Jose Miranda

Evaluator: Nathan Graham
Report Date: 10/06/2021
Dates Seen: 9/19/21
Risk Factor: Medium
Physical/Health: Extra large frame, strong and thick build, physically mature

Tool	Future Grade	Report
Hit	60	Balanced stance, hands start high with a moderate load and leg kick; mild leverage in the swing, excellent barrel control, tracks pitches well and recognizes spin.
Power	60	Plus raw generated by above average bat speed and physical strength, advanced approach and excellent bat to ball skills help him get to it in-game; slight lift to the swing, ball jumps off the bat, able to go deep to all fields.
Baserunning/ Speed	40	Below average raw speed, lacks quickness out of the box, not a threat to steal.
Glove	50	Lacks lateral quickness and range but has good hands and show solid instincts in the field; Not flashy, but also not a liability; Versatile, can passably be plugged in at multiple positions in the infield and outfield.
Arm	50	Average arm strength from the left side of the diamond.

Conclusion: Miranda used 2020 to revamp the offensive approach, becoming more selective and working counts more to his advantage. It allowed the plus power to play in-game and made him a breakout prospect of the summer. The pop/contact ability will make up for any defensive liabilities that exist and will make him a middle of the order run producer.

8 Simeon Woods Richardson RHP OFP: 55 ETA: Late 2022/Early 2023

Born: 09/27/00 Age: 21 Bats: R Throws: R Height: 6'3" Weight: 210 lb. Origin: Round 2, 2018 Draft (#48 overall)

YEAR	TEAM	LVL	AGE	W	L	SV	G	GS	IP	H	HR	BB/9	K/9	K	GB%	BABIP	WHIP	ERA	DRA-	WARP
2019	COL	A	18	3	8	0	20	20	78^{1}	78	5	2.0	11.1	97	49.5%	.358	1.21	4.25	80	1.5
2019	DUN	A+	18	3	2	0	6	6	28^{1}	18	1	2.2	9.2	29	33.8%	.246	0.88	2.54	88	0.5
2021	NH	AA	20	2	4	0	11	11	45^{1}	42	5	5.2	13.3	67	32.4%	.359	1.50	5.76	86	0.7
2021	WCH	AA	20	1	1	0	4	3	8	6	0	9.0	11.2	10	38.1%	.316	1.75	6.75	101	0.0
2022 non-DC	*MIN*	*MLB*	*21*	*2*	*3*	*0*	*57*	*0*	*50*	*45*	*7*	*4.9*	*10.3*	*57*	*36.8%*	*.298*	*1.45*	*4.70*	*110*	*-0.1*

Comparables: Luis Severino, Ian Anderson, José Berríos

The Report: Woods Richardson has been traded twice in the three years since he was drafted in the second round by the Mets. That can cause people to look askance at a prospect's stock, but he remains mostly the same pitching prospect he has been since draft day. First the newish stuff: Woods Richardson has added a slider in the last couple of years and suffered from some wildness around the time he was going to and from the Olympics last year but, generally, has thrown strikes working off his fastball/curve combo. His fastball velocity popped his senior year of high school but has settled into an average velocity band, although he can reach back for 95-plus and pop it above the bat. His 12–6 curve plays well off the heater, although it doesn't always have true bat-missing late dive. The changeup is fringy but useful enough as another crossover look. Woods Richardson repeats his up-tempo delivery well, although his command and control projection are more average than above. He has some deception to help his spinny arsenal get on you even faster. His time on the Olympic team and changing of organizations made for an uneven 2021. Between that and a lighter workload coming off a season spent at the alternate Site, there's a bit more risk in the profile than you might prefer in an upper-minors arm.

OFP: 55 / No. 3–4 starter or set-up reliever

Variance: We're going with Medium, but we don't feel great about it after the control blip in 2021. Woods Richardson doesn't have the kind of stuff that can support a walk rate over 10 percent, gaudy strikeout numbers aside. It was also a stop-start season for him, and, if he sorts things out going forward, he remains a perfectly fine mid-rotation-starter prospect on the strength of his above-average fastball/curve combo.

Mark Barry's Fantasy Take: It feels like Woods Richardson has been around for a while, but somehow he's still just 21 years old. Something something forever young, I guess. Anyway, like the aforementioned Joe Ryan, SWR is cruising toward a career of solid, but not spectacular, production. There's even a bit of room for a bump if he can hone his command. For now, he's a top-150 guy for me, based more on floor than ceiling.

9 Jhoan Duran RHP OFP: 55 ETA: 2022, health permitting

Born: 01/08/98 Age: 24 Bats: R Throws: R Height: 6'5" Weight: 230 lb. Origin: International Free Agent, 2014

YEAR	TEAM	LVL	AGE	W	L	SV	G	GS	IP	H	HR	BB/9	K/9	K	GB%	BABIP	WHIP	ERA	DRA-	WARP
2019	FTM	A+	21	2	9	0	16	15	78	63	5	3.6	11.0	95	51.6%	.317	1.21	3.23	84	1.5
2019	PNS	AA	21	3	3	0	7	7	37	34	2	2.2	10.0	41	63.0%	.330	1.16	4.86	79	0.6
2021	STP	AAA	23	0	3	0	5	4	16	16	1	7.3	12.4	22	62.5%	.385	1.81	5.06	85	0.3
2022 DC	*MIN*	*MLB*	*24*	*0*	*0*	*0*	*3*	*3*	*12.7*	*11*	*1*	*5.2*	*10.2*	*14*	*51.6%*	*.303*	*1.47*	*4.44*	*106*	*0.1*

Comparables: José Ureña, JC Ramírez, Hunter Wood

The Report: Another Twins pitching prospect with big stuff and a balky elbow, like Canterino, Duran dealt with an elbow strain that limited him to just 16 innings last season. While he was on the mound, the stuff was as advertised: an upper-90s fastball—bumping triple digits—a power curve and a low-90s "changeup" that plays somewhere between a split and a power sinker. The injury concerns are somewhat new—he threw more than 100 innings in both 2018 and '19—but the stuff hasn't developed as much as you'd like in the interim. Perhaps that is patently unfair given the lost 2020 and 2021 game reps, but Duran will be 24 next season, with an uncertain health prognosis. His fastball certainly pops the mitt, but it can run a little true. The "splinker" can show good, late bottom or be a rather nondescript two-seam. The breaking ball can be slurvy in a good way—a big 11–5 breaker—or it can float in or ride high. His mechanics have always had arm-barn markers. These all feel like things that can be worked out with more game reps, and the outline of a mid-rotation starter or impact reliever remain, but Duran's future on the mound carries a very ominous "TBD," at present.

OFP: 55 / No. 3–4 starter or late-inning reliever

Variance: High. If Duran is healthy for 2022, we'd expect him to have some sort of meaningful MLB role, although he likely needs some consolidation/stretch time in Triple-A. That's a big "if," though, and the elbow injury might force him to the bullpen sooner than planned.

Mark Barry's Fantasy Take: First of all, not enough dudes throw splinkers, and we, as a society, don't use the word splinker enough. As it pertains to Duran's fantasy viability, however, I'm definitely more concerned about his reliever risk than that of many of his colleagues on this list. Even if he starts, he hasn't shown much by way of, uh, not walking people, so while there might be some K's, there will also be a ton of walks and, in turn, bloated rate stats. He's a top-200 guy, to be sure, but, honestly, that feels like it is mostly thanks to proximity.

10 Josh Winder RHP OFP: 50 ETA: 2022, health permitting

Born: 10/11/96 Age: 25 Bats: R Throws: R Height: 6'5" Weight: 210 lb. Origin: Round 7, 2018 Draft (#214 overall)

YEAR	TEAM	LVL	AGE	W	L	SV	G	GS	IP	H	HR	BB/9	K/9	K	GB%	BABIP	WHIP	ERA	DRA-	WARP
2019	CR	A	22	7	2	0	21	21	125^2	93	10	2.1	8.5	118	35.8%	.252	0.98	2.65	95	1.3
2021	WCH	AA	24	3	0	0	10	10	54^2	41	5	1.6	10.7	65	40.6%	.281	0.93	1.98	88	0.7
2021	STP	AAA	24	1	0	0	4	4	17^1	14	4	1.6	7.8	15	32.7%	.222	0.98	4.67	111	0.1
2022 DC	*MIN*	*MLB*	*25*	*0*	*0*	*0*	*3*	*3*	*14.3*	*14*	*2*	*2.9*	*8.1*	*13*	*35.4%*	*.294*	*1.32*	*4.33*	*109*	*0.1*

Comparables: Craig Stammen, David Buchanan, Tyler Cloyd

The Report: We weren't exaggerating about the injury issues for the Twins organization. Winder did at least manage to throw a whole 72 innings before a shoulder impingement ended his 2021 season. He's another potential mid-rotation arm with profile questions even before the injury bug bit. Winder certainly looks the part of a rotation workhouse. He's a sturdy 6-foot-5 with a relatively easy delivery. His fastball sits in the average velo band and can touch mid-90s; it gets groundballs more than it misses bats and, therefore, is more solid-average than plus. The slider and curve can bleed together at times, but both have above-average potential. The change lags behind, showing a little bit of run, but Winder struggles to turn it over consistently. You'll always cringe a bit with anything shoulder related for a pitcher, but impingements happen. Barring further issues, Winder is another fairly close-to-the-majors pitching option for a system rich in them, if not rich in healthy ones.

OFP: 50 / No. 4 starter or set-up

Variance: Medium. Winder would have likely gotten some MLB time if he had stayed healthy for the balance of 2021. But he didn't, and it was his shoulder. There's some profile risk here given the lack of an arm-side option, but we think he's more likely to be a starter than some of the arms ahead of him on this list, but less likely to be an impact reliever.

Mark Barry's Fantasy Take: Shoulders scare me, man. I don't know if there's enough upside in Winder's fantasy profile to warrant speculating on an add, but if he flashes healthy this spring, there are worse dice rolls to bet on. Don't expect ace upside, but dependable, streaming production from Winder wouldn't be surprising in the least.

The Prospects You Meet Outside the Top Ten

#11

Marco Raya RHP Born: 08/07/02 Age: 19 Bats: R Throws: R Height: 6'0" Weight: 165 lb. Origin: Round 4, 2020 Draft (#128 overall)

We pegged Raya as an "Interesting Draft Follow" last year, and while he didn't pitch at all in official games in 2021 due to a poorly timed injured-list stint, he is more than just "interesting" now. Everything has firmed up, and his low-90s fastball is now into the plus velocity range with the same bat-missing shape. Raya was an unusual prep arm, in that he had a full repertoire as an amateur. He's also listed at six-feet and has yet to throw in a professional game, so this ranking might feel aggressive, but, given the trend line so far and the fact that, despite the missed time, he will pitch almost all of 2022 as a 19-year-old, we are fine being bullish.

Prospects on the Rise

Jeferson Morales RF Born: 05/13/99 Age: 23 Bats: R Throws: R Height: 5'8" Weight: 170 lb. Origin: International Free Agent, 2016

YEAR	TEAM	LVL	AGE	PA	R	2B	3B	HR	RBI	BB	K	SB	CS	AVG/OBP/SLG	DRC+	BABIP	BRR	FRAA	WARP
2019	TWI	ROK	20	134	24	7	3	3	16	20	18	0	1	.236/.373/.436		.258			
2021	FTM	A	22	292	43	19	0	7	31	42	52	12	2	.237/.377/.407	124	.274	0.2	RF(33) 0.2, C(21) 0.4, LF(2) -0.0	1.8
2021	CR	A+	22	100	11	5	0	5	22	5	20	0	1	.301/.350/.516	116	.338	-0.2	C(9) 0.7, LF(7) -0.1, RF(2) -0.7	0.5
2022 non-DC	*MIN*	*MLB*	*23*	*251*	*23*	*11*	*0*	*5*	*24*	*20*	*58*	*6*	*3*	*.228/.305/.353*	*80*	*.287*	*0.3*	*C -1, RF 0*	*0.3*

The "outfield" here is mostly theoretical. Although he got more reps on the grass than behind the plate last year, that was mostly due to a playing-time crunch at catcher in A-ball. It's a credit to Morales that he was even able to battle out there—he's an average-ish runner—but his future is going to be behind the dish. He's a little undersized for a catcher and awkward defensively, at present, but he projects well as a receiver and has above-average arm strength. At the plate, he shows the potential for average hit and power tools. It's a strength swing without too much stiffness. He's quick inside and tracks breakers well enough given his limited pro reps. Morales is still inexperienced on both sides of the ball but is a real sleeper in a deep system who could move up this list next year with more innings behind the plate.

Cade Povich LHP Born: 04/12/00 Age: 22 Bats: L Throws: L Height: 6'3" Weight: 185 lb. Origin: Round 3, 2021 Draft (#98 overall)

YEAR	TEAM	LVL	AGE	W	L	SV	G	GS	IP	H	HR	BB/9	K/9	K	GB%	BABIP	WHIP	ERA	DRA-	WARP
2021	FTM	A	21	0	0	0	3	2	8	6	0	2.3	18.0	16	33.3%	.400	1.00	1.13	91	0.1
2022 non-DC	*MIN*	*MLB*	*22*	*2*	*3*	*0*	*57*	*0*	*50*	*47*	*8*	*4.9*	*9.3*	*51*	*50.9%*	*.297*	*1.50*	*5.09*	*117*	*-0.3*

Povich was the Twins' third-round pick last summer and appeared to be a prototypical early–Day Two college arm: good frame, strong junior season, four-pitch mix, strike thrower, low-90s fastball. Some scout somewhere probably wrote down "bulldog" in his notes. After the draft, though, Povich started popping 95s, and a tweaked slider might grant him an out-pitch among his secondaries. Is this the origin story of a mid-rotation starting pitching prospect, or just another 95-and-a-slider reliever? Tune into the Cedar Rapids Kernels next year to find out.

Louie Varland RHP Born: 12/09/97 Age: 24 Bats: L Throws: R Height: 6'1" Weight: 205 lb. Origin: Round 15, 2019 Draft (#449 overall)

YEAR	TEAM	LVL	AGE	W	L	SV	G	GS	IP	H	HR	BB/9	K/9	K	GB%	BABIP	WHIP	ERA	DRA-	WARP
2019	ELZ	ROA	21	0	1	0	3	1	8^{2}	9	1	4.2	10.4	10	32.0%	.333	1.50	2.08		
2021	FTM	A	23	4	2	0	10	8	47^{1}	41	2	3.0	14.5	76	45.7%	.379	1.20	2.09	82	1.0
2021	CR	A+	23	6	2	0	10	10	55^{2}	41	4	2.3	10.7	66	37.4%	.276	0.99	2.10	87	0.9
2022 non-DC	*MIN*	*MLB*	*24*	*2*	*3*	*0*	*57*	*0*	*50*	*50*	*7*	*3.7*	*8.7*	*48*	*37.0%*	*.306*	*1.42*	*4.85*	*114*	*-0.2*

Comparables: Aaron Civale, Yefry Ramírez, Joe Kelly

Varland did not deal with an arm injury in 2021, which puts him a leg up on most of this system. Instead, he had a bit of a breakout year, adding a few ticks to his fastball. He also offers an inconsistent slider that flashes good depth in the mid-80s and a changeup that is rather firm, at present. Varland is a control-over-command guy, firing bullets from a delivery reminiscent of a position-player convert, but if he can hold his 2021 fastball gains and refine his secondaries and command in Double-A, he should move up a tier amongst Twins arms . . . health permitting, one supposes.

Factors on the Farm

Gilberto Celestino OF Born: 02/13/99 Age: 23 Bats: R Throws: L Height: 6'0" Weight: 170 lb. Origin: International Free Agent, 2015

YEAR	TEAM	LVL	AGE	PA	R	2B	3B	HR	RBI	BB	K	SB	CS	AVG/OBP/SLG	DRC+	BABIP	BRR	FRAA	WARP
2019	CR	A	20	503	52	24	3	10	51	48	81	14	8	.276/.350/.409	125	.317	-3.3	CF(83) 4.6, RF(25) -3.5	2.7
2019	FTM	A+	20	33	6	4	0	0	3	2	4	0	0	.300/.333/.433	108	.333	0.1	CF(4) -0.9, RF(3) -0.5	0.0
2021	WCH	AA	22	96	10	5	0	2	7	11	24	0	1	.250/.344/.381	95	.328	0.1	CF(12) -0.5, RF(6) 0.3, LF(1) -0.2	0.2
2021	STP	AAA	22	211	27	13	0	5	24	24	43	4	0	.290/.384/.443	101	.356	-1.2	CF(23) -5.1, RF(17) 1.0, LF(3) 0.1	0.2
2021	MIN	MLB	22	62	7	3	0	2	3	3	14	0	0	.136/.177/.288	94	.140	-0.3	CF(22) -1.2, RF(2) 1.3, LF(1) 0.0	0.2
2022 DC	*MIN*	*MLB*	*23*	*91*	*10*	*4*	*0*	*1*	*9*	*7*	*20*	*1*	*1*	*.229/.296/.347*	*78*	*.283*	*0.1*	*CF 0*	*0.1*

Comparables: Dalton Pompey, Starling Marte, Raimel Tapia

Celestino has long been a fringe-top-10 prospect—for two different organizations now—on the strength of his glove, with the hope that his bat would develop enough to make him a regular in center field. He remains an above-average outfielder with plus speed and long strides that eat up ground in center, and he shows enough arm for right. He has always hit enough to keep us interested, but there's nothing in the offensive profile that pops. The swing has some length and features merely average bat speed. The defense isn't so good that it will carry a .260, 10-homer offensive profile, but Celestino is ready to be a fourth outfielder right now.

Cole Sands RHP Born: 07/17/97 Age: 24 Bats: R Throws: R Height: 6'3" Weight: 215 lb. Origin: Round 5, 2018 Draft (#154 overall)

YEAR	TEAM	LVL	AGE	W	L	SV	G	GS	IP	H	HR	BB/9	K/9	K	GB%	BABIP	WHIP	ERA	DRA-	WARP
2019	CR	A	21	2	1	0	8	8	41^{1}	41	0	2.4	10.7	49	40.0%	.373	1.26	3.05	89	0.6
2019	FTM	A+	21	5	2	0	9	9	52	36	4	1.2	9.2	53	36.2%	.256	0.83	2.25	87	0.9
2021	WCH	AA	23	4	2	0	19	18	80^{1}	59	6	3.9	10.8	96	40.1%	.277	1.17	2.46	78	1.5
2022 DC	*MIN*	*MLB*	*24*	*2*	*2*	*0*	*9*	*9*	*40.7*	*39*	*5*	*4.1*	*9.1*	*41*	*41.3%*	*.298*	*1.42*	*4.60*	*110*	*0.1*

Comparables: Ryan Helsley, Jarlín García, Yefry Ramírez

Sands continues to get lost a bit among the impressive pitching-prospect depth in Minnesota. He has—you'll never believe this—had some injury issues and has yet to throw 100 innings in a season. However, he features three 50-or-55 pitches and enough command to start. His 12–6 curve can flash plus depth but can also be a bit of a lazy up-and-under offering. His change projects as average with good velocity separation and some sink but has its own consistency issues. And while Sands can pop mid-90s—and the fastball has good life up—he doesn't hold his velocity well enough to call it a true plus fastball. We nitpick the stuff and durability because that's the job here, but he did throw a very good 80 innings in Double-A ,and it's not hard to see the outline of an average major-league starter in his arsenal.

Drew Strotman RHP Born: 09/03/96 Age: 25 Bats: R Throws: R Height: 6'3" Weight: 195 lb. Origin: Round 4, 2017 Draft (#109 overall)

YEAR	TEAM	LVL	AGE	W	L	SV	G	GS	IP	H	HR	BB/9	K/9	K	GB%	BABIP	WHIP	ERA	DRA-	WARP
2019	RAY	ROK	22	0	1	0	4	4	8	9	0	3.4	12.4	11	56.5%	.391	1.50	3.38		
2019	CHA	A+	22	0	2	0	5	5	16	20	3	5.1	7.3	13	43.1%	.354	1.81	5.06	103	0.2
2021	STP	AAA	24	3	3	0	12	12	54	65	9	5.0	7.0	42	42.5%	.333	1.76	7.33	117	0.3
2021	DUR	AAA	24	7	2	0	13	12	58^1	50	3	5.1	9.6	62	47.1%	.309	1.42	3.39	99	0.8
2022 DC	*MIN*	*MLB*	*25*	*2*	*2*	*0*	*18*	*4*	*34.3*	*36*	*4*	*5.2*	*7.5*	*28*	*38.2%*	*.303*	*1.63*	*5.53*	*127*	*-0.3*

Comparables: Pedro Payano, Kris Wilson, Nick Martínez

The other pitcher acquired for Nelson Cruz, Strotman has long been on our follow list, and he still has a little more fastball velocity and a deeper repertoire than Ryan. Strotman has never been a prolific strike-thrower, though, and his walk issues continued to rear their head in Triple-A last year. We can hand-wave that to an extent, given his missed development time, but a lot of that was due to Tommy John surgery, so, hey, that's a thing that happened. That fastball does sit 95 and touch 97, but we also can't tell you it's a better fastball than Ryan's 91-mph, low-release-point special, despite our fondness for our Stalker. Strotman's slider still flashes plus, and he has a useable curve and change behind it, but until he throws more good strikes with the ol' number one, he might be best suited to be a bulk- or multi-inning arm.

Because You Were Going to Ask

Keoni Cavaco SS Born: 06/02/01 Age: 21 Bats: R Throws: R Height: 6'2" Weight: 195 lb. Origin: Round 1, 2019 Draft (#13 overall)

YEAR	TEAM	LVL	AGE	PA	R	2B	3B	HR	RBI	BB	K	SB	CS	AVG/OBP/SLG	DRC+	BABIP	BRR	FRAA	WARP
2019	TWI	ROK	18	92	9	4	0	1	6	4	35	1	1	.172/.217/.253		.275			
2021	FTM	A	20	260	27	6	2	2	24	18	89	5	2	.233/.296/.301	68	.361	-0.9	SS(55) -4.7	-0.7
2022 non-DC	*MIN*	*MLB*	*21*	*251*	*17*	*9*	*1*	*2*	*18*	*13*	*97*	*2*	*1*	*.199/.249/.279*	*39*	*.328*	*0.1*	*SS -1*	*-1.1*

Comparables: Eduardo Escobar, Gavin Cecchini, Dawel Lugo

This list is quite arm-heavy despite the injuries up and down the system. Some of that is because, well, they are all good pitching prospects, Brent. Conversely, the Twins have so far struggled to develop their recent high-pick bats. Cavaco hit .233 with a sub-.100 ISO in A-ball as a 20-year-old, and that's backed up by an extreme inside-out swing and an approach designed to shoot pitches into right field. What that swing has actually accomplished is to make him late against any kind of real velocity. Cavaco struggled defensively, as well, although he has the actions and the range for the six. The profile was going to take time to develop in the best of circumstances, and certainly 2020–21 wasn't the best of circumstances for any minor leaguer trying to improve their game, but Cavaco needs, as Keanan Lamb wrote after seeing him, "a hard reset."

Aaron Sabato 1B Born: 06/04/99 Age: 23 Bats: R Throws: R Height: 6'2" Weight: 230 lb. Origin: Round 1, 2020 Draft (#27 overall)

YEAR	TEAM	LVL	AGE	PA	R	2B	3B	HR	RBI	BB	K	SB	CS	AVG/OBP/SLG	DRC+	BABIP	BRR	FRAA	WARP
2021	FTM	A	22	367	48	15	0	11	42	73	117	1	0	.189/.365/.357	110	.270	-2.2	1B(77) 4.6	1.5
2021	CR	A+	22	97	21	3	0	8	15	19	32	0	0	.253/.402/.613	120	.297	0.5	1B(20) 0.0	0.5
2022 non-DC	*MIN*	*MLB*	*23*	*251*	*25*	*10*	*0*	*6*	*25*	*32*	*88*	*0*	*0*	*.187/.302/.333*	*74*	*.280*	*-0.4*	*1B 2*	*-0.2*

Comparables: Trey Mancini, Rhys Hoskins, Gaby Sanchez

We like to say that minor-league production, whether good or bad, exists to be explained. And a .202 batting average—with a commensurate 32-percent K rate—is not good for a college corner bat in A-ball. Sabato did hit for plenty of power. That part is easy to explain: He has plus-plus raw power generated from a swing that tries to wring every bit out of his strength. And he is plenty strong. Sabato can pull outer-half fastballs over the fence when he gets extended, and he can stay back on offspeed and still hit it a long way. The problem is that there is plenty of swing-and-miss in the zone to go with the big flies due to that all-or-nothing, muscled-up swing. Sabato was better after a promotion to High-A, albeit in a small sample, but while the future projection of a three-true-outcome slugger remains, there was a little bit too much of one outcome in 2021.

Top Talents 25 and Under (as of 4/1/2022):

1. Austin Martin, IF/OF
2. Luis Arraez, 2B
3. Jordan Balazovic, RHP
4. Joe Ryan, RHP
5. Alex Kirilloff, OF/1B
6. Trevor Larnach, OF
7. Chase Petty, RHP
8. Royce Lewis, IF/OF
9. Ryan Jeffers, C
10. Matt Canterino, RHP

Plenty of sources were culpable for the shockingly disappointing 2021 Minnesota Twins, but injuries and underachievement from their top big-league-adjacent prospects is one of the first places the can should be kicked. The injury to Royce Lewis stung, of course, but it would have been easier to bear if Alex Kirilloff or Trevor Larnach had hit the ground running. Alas, both players had seasons that suggested they skipped straight to the "Variance" section in their reports, slammed their chips on the table, then watched the croupier land the ball on every "however" in the blurb. Kirilloff's struggles were suboptimal, as he hit for merely average power or a tick better, not enough to make up for his poor walk rate nor his limited glove. On the most positive end of things, when healthy, Kirilloff tore the cover off the ball when he made contact, giving the classic hope that, with better fortune and swing plane, the results could meet expectations. More troubling, Kirilloff hit the IL with a wrist sprain in early May, the same wrist that interrupted his 2019 season in Double-A. Worse still, after another month and a half, Kirilloff's season came to an end as he underwent surgery to repair a torn ligament in that wrist. A corner outfielder/ first baseman who doesn't walk is perhaps the most bat-dependent profile in the sport, and continued structural injuries to a slugger's top-hand wrist are a grim sign, even for someone just 24 years old.

Larnach's struggles were comparatively banal: the hulking would-be-slugger walked plenty, struck out too much, and didn't do nearly enough mashing. Like Kirilloff, his season came to a disappointing early end with a left-hand contusion in Triple-A St. Paul. Prior to Double-A, Larnach had always been able to out-swing his profile, making plenty of contact through the low minors, but it appears he'll need more adjustment time to bring his power out in MLB.

Arraez, by contrast, kept on plugging away, splashing contact across the diamond and getting on base at a healthy clip, to boot. He'll never hit for power, and when his BABIP is merely above average (.323 in 2021 vs. the .350s he has run in past), he's more average as a hitter than a batting-title contender. Still, his 103 DRC+ last year was right in line with the previous two years (111 in 2019, 101 in 2020), and he's easy to slot in as a positive, low-upside contributor, whether the Twins run it back or tear it down.

After a precocious 2020 debut that coincided with a Mitch Garver slump, Jeffers seemed primed for big things in 2021. Instead, a full season at the plate proved a bit more challenging for the big backstop. Still, between the impending 31-year-old Garver and the soon-to-be-25-year-old duo of Jeffers and Ben Rortvedt, Minnesota is in better shape than most clubs behind the plate.

New York Mets

The State of the System:

The Mets' system is strong at the top, but could really use their 2021 first-round pick . . . or their 2020 first- and second-round picks . . . or their 2019 second-round pick . . . or their 2018 first- and sec . . . well, you get the idea.

The Top Ten:

1 Francisco Álvarez C OFP: 70 ETA: 2023

Born: 11/19/01 Age: 20 Bats: R Throws: R Height: 5'10" Weight: 233 lb. Origin: International Free Agent, 2018

YEAR	TEAM	LVL	AGE	PA	R	2B	3B	HR	RBI	BB	K	SB	CS	AVG/OBP/SLG	DRC+	BABIP	BRR	FRAA	WARP
2019	MTS	ROK	17	31	8	4	0	2	10	4	4	0	1	.462/.548/.846		.500			
2019	KNG	ROA	17	151	24	6	0	5	16	17	33	1	1	.282/.377/.443		.344			
2021	SLU	A	19	67	12	5	0	2	12	15	7	2	2	.417/.567/.646	143	.450	0.1	C(10) -1.5	0.4
2021	BRK	A+	19	333	55	13	1	22	58	40	82	6	3	.247/.351/.538	154	.260	0.8	C(49) -7.6	2.5
2022 non-DC	*NYM*	*MLB*	*20*	*251*	*27*	*10*	*0*	*8*	*29*	*23*	*66*	*1*	*2*	*.230/.314/.399*	*92*	*.289*	*-0.1*	*C -7*	*0.2*

Comparables: Gary Sánchez, Christian Bethancourt, Giancarlo Stanton

The Report: The short pitch on Álvarez: he hits the ball as consistently hard as any player in the minors, and he's likely to stay at catcher. He has elite, high-end bat speed and generates tremendous raw *and* game power. His approach is extremely advanced for a teenager, and he wrecked both A-ball levels. His receiving and throwing aren't phenomenal, but they're enough that he's likely to stay behind the plate. A plus-hit, plus-plus-power outcome while catching 110 games a season is quite reasonable here.

The downsides, other than the usual catcher downsides, are that none of this really looks right. Álvarez is short and stout. He has an oddball batting stance, with his front foot starting very wide, almost in the bucket, and tapping again to the mesh point. He makes a very quick move to the ball and squares it up just fine, but you can see how the timing could go bad there. While he's athletic enough to play catcher, he's not a dead-bolt lock to stay there, and his lack of agility and speed would be a problem anywhere else on the diamond except first base (where he's also not a perfect fit due to his height). None of this will matter if he can hit like we think he will and be an average defender behind the dish.

OFP: 70 / The best offensive catcher in MLB

Variance: Medium. He is only barely no longer a teenage catcher. Young catching prospects are a notoriously high-risk pool of prospects, but they rarely come with this sort of offensive profile.

Mark Barry's Fantasy Take: During last year's list season, I developed a theory that dynasty catching prospects were like Highlanders—at any time, there can be only one. Right now, it's Adley Rutschman, but just a year into this experiment, Francisco Álvarez is really putting that theory to the test. Keep a close eye on the potential timing issue mentioned above. If Álvarez can't consistently hit for average, his fantasy profile looks a little more like Gary Sánchez, for better or worse. That's still a top-30-ish prospect, but perhaps not the One True Catcher just yet.

2 Brett Baty 3B OFP: 70 ETA: Late 2022/Early 2023

Born: 11/13/99 Age: 22 Bats: L Throws: R Height: 6'3" Weight: 210 lb. Origin: Round 1, 2019 Draft (#12 overall)

YEAR	TEAM	LVL	AGE	PA	R	2B	3B	HR	RBI	BB	K	SB	CS	AVG/OBP/SLG	DRC+	BABIP	BRR	FRAA	WARP
2019	MTS	ROK	19	25	5	3	0	1	8	5	6	0	0	.350/.480/.650		.462			
2019	KNG	ROA	19	186	30	12	2	6	22	24	56	0	0	.222/.339/.437		.302			
2019	BRK	SS	19	17	2	1	0	0	3	6	3	0	0	.200/.529/.300		.286			
2021	SRR	WIN	21	102	16	5	1	1	15	11	31	1	0	.292/.373/.404		.431			
2021	BRK	A+	21	209	27	14	1	7	34	24	53	4	3	.309/.397/.514	118	.402	-0.3	3B(41) 6.7, LF(3) -0.4	1.6
2021	BNG	AA	21	176	16	8	0	5	22	22	45	2	0	.272/.364/.424	91	.350	0.0	3B(24) -0.8, LF(15) 1.4	0.4
2022 non-DC	*NYM*	*MLB*	*22*	*251*	*23*	*11*	*1*	*4*	*23*	*22*	*70*	*0*	*1*	*.228/.304/.349*	*80*	*.311*	*-0.2*	*3B 1, LF 1*	*0.3*

Comparables: Jeimer Candelario, Abraham Toro, Eugenio Suárez

The Report: Speaking of plus-hit, plus-plus power outcomes . . . well, Baty actually has a shot at that one, too. He has a classic, smooth lefty swing capable of thwacking the ball to all fields nearly as high and far as Álvarez; they had the two best batting-practice rotations at the Denver Futures Game. Baty got into his game power much more in 2021 than before. Defensively, he's on track to be a capable third baseman with a plus arm and enough range for the position, although he still makes some errors born of inexperience. The Mets also gave him extensive exposure in left field as the season went on, and he runs well enough to play there, if that's the direction they choose to go.

Baty does have a demonstrable offensive hole that Álvarez does not, though. Baty hit the ball on the ground a lot last year. His swing is geared for loft and backspin, and we're fairly confident this will sort itself out in time. But if he turns out to be just okay offensively, it's probably because he is hitting way too many hard grounders on either side of second base.

OFP: 70 / All-Star third baseman or corner outfielder

Variance: Medium. We have a fair degree of confidence in Baty's hit tool playing. His power should play when he hits the ball in the air, too, but that remains an "if" until he actually does it all the time.

Mark Barry's Fantasy Take: For fantasy purposes, I prefer Baty to Álvarez. Plenty of sluggers initially struggle with the groundball, so I'm not too worried just yet about Baty's batting average. The power is real, and he's more postionally friendly than his colleague behind the dish. Baty is a top-20 dynasty prospect for me.

Eyewitness Report: Brett Baty

Evaluator: Jarrett Seidler
Report Date: 07/26/2021
Dates Seen: 5x 6/2021, 1x 7/2021
Risk Factor: Medium
Physical/Health: Big, strong frame; already significantly filled out.

Tool	Future Grade	Report
Hit	60	Would grade this a 55 on pure hit ability alone, but Baty's approach is so good for his experience level that I believe the future outcome is a half-grade higher. Classic leveraged lefty stroke that's already much better than it was when he entered pro ball two years ago (and it wasn't too bad then). Plus-plus bat speed. He does have some length to his swing given his size, and some swing-and-miss in his game because of that, though bat path optimization has helped. His approach is plus-plus in context; he has a keen eye at the plate. He's aggressive on what he thinks he can drive, and fouls off pitches in the zone he can't.
Power	70	Fairly easy plus-plus raw power; put on the best batting practice at the 2021 Futures Game. In-game, the ball can fly off his bat to all fields with excellent carry; he's clearly a strong young man, and he can drive pitches on all parts of the plate. Since 2019, he's added significant loft to his swing to get to more power at 7 PM. The one knock is that he still hits the ball on the ground a bit more than you'd like, and he's going to have to lift it even more to get to all of this potential.
Baserunning/ Speed	45	Average to fringe-average runner at present; may lose an additional step as he ages. Not a major basestealing threat, but not a huge clogger either, and has enough foot speed to play the outfield if needed.
Glove	50	All of my defensive views of him were at third base, though he's also begun to pick up reps in the outfield. I don't think he's going to be a Gold Glove candidate, and there have been some reliability questions dating back to before the draft (only fielding .931 and made a typical-looking error for me), but he showed solid range and hands on the whole.
Arm	60	Plus arm at present, plus arm strength and gets rid of the ball well. Should be well more than enough arm strength for an outfield transition if necessary.

Conclusion: If you read those grades and thought "hey, a potential 6 hit/7 power player who might stick at third sounds like a star," well, you're right. Baty is a potential building block-type player for me. Top 20 prospect in baseball.

3 Ronny Mauricio SS OFP: 60 ETA: Late 2023

Born: 04/04/01 Age: 21 Bats: S Throws: R Height: 6'3" Weight: 166 lb. Origin: International Free Agent, 2017

YEAR	TEAM	LVL	AGE	PA	R	2B	3B	HR	RBI	BB	K	SB	CS	AVG/OBP/SLG	DRC+	BABIP	BRR	FRAA	WARP
2019	COL	A	18	504	62	20	5	4	37	23	99	6	10	.268/.307/.357	97	.330	2.0	SS(106) -0.2	1.6
2021	LIC	WIN	20	94	8	5	0	2	8	3	21	1	0	.244/.277/.367		.299			
2021	BRK	A+	20	420	55	14	5	19	63	24	101	9	7	.242/.290/.449	115	.278	0.1	SS(87) 10.9	3.0
2021	BNG	AA	20	33	3	1	0	1	1	2	11	2	0	.323/.364/.452	89	.474	-0.3	SS(8) -0.4	0.0
2022 non-DC	*NYM*	*MLB*	*21*	*251*	*21*	*9*	*1*	*4*	*24*	*11*	*66*	*2*	*3*	*.227/.268/.346*	*61*	*.296*	*0.3*	*SS 1*	*-0.1*

Comparables: Chris Owings, Addison Russell, Alcides Escobar

The Report: The last time we saw Mauricio in real games, prior to last year, he was a projectable 18-year-old just trying to keep afloat in A-ball. He was able to do that due to preternatural barrel control but, at the time, wasn't really able to tap into his latent raw power. Two years later, the physical projection arrived. Likely an inch taller and 50-pounds heavier than his well-out-of-date listed height and weight, Mauricio now makes the plus-raw-power projection look a little light. His is a high-variance hit tool, though, which is the polite evaluator's way of saying we aren't convinced he can hit. His bat control covers for some of his issues with seeing and tracking spin, but it's not hard to get him off-balance if you can command your breaker a little. Double-A will be a significant test of Mauricio's offensive profile.

Despite the physical gains, if you catch Mauricio on the right day, he looks like a plus shortstop. He's rangy due to a good first step coupled with solid-average speed, and he has the kind of body control that allows him to make the spectacular play. He can be a bit more sluggish and tentative on the more routine stuff, like he's going through a checklist instead of just getting the batter out. We'd expect him to slow down a bit more as he moves through his early twenties, which might make his defensive profile fit better at third—where the aforementioned first step and plus arm give him a good shot at being above average—but, regardless, we're more confident that he will stay on the dirt than we were last year or the year before. That doesn't matter if he can't hit at least .250, though.

OFP: 60 / First-division left-side infielder

Variance: Extreme. Mauricio feels like he's more likely to be a 6 or a 3 than anything in between. The hit-tool and pitch-recognition questions suggest a very bifurcated outcome. Either he hits enough and is a good everyday guy, or he doesn't and bounces up and down off good Triple-A stretches for a few years.

Mark Barry's Fantasy Take: Last year, when it looked like he was going to hit, I was a little more bullish on Mauricio. This year, well, I guess there's still a chance, but all of the caveats above make that chance seem awfully risky. With shortstop currently overflowing with talent, I don't think that's a risk I'm taking, but I would float Mauricio on the trade block for someone with a stronger stomach and a penchant for projects.

4 Mark Vientos 3B OFP: 55 ETA: Late 2022

Born: 12/11/99 Age: 22 Bats: R Throws: R Height: 6'4" Weight: 185 lb. Origin: Round 2, 2017 Draft (#59 overall)

YEAR	TEAM	LVL	AGE	PA	R	2B	3B	HR	RBI	BB	K	SB	CS	AVG/OBP/SLG	DRC+	BABIP	BRR	FRAA	WARP
2019	COL	A	19	454	48	27	1	12	62	22	110	1	4	.255/.300/.411	111	.311	-4.9	3B(100) -2.7	1.2
2021	BNG	AA	21	306	43	16	0	22	59	26	87	0	1	.281/.346/.580	123	.327	-1.9	3B(41) -4.4, LF(12) -0.2, 1B(11) -0.1	1.1
2021	SYR	AAA	21	43	9	2	0	3	4	7	13	0	1	.278/.395/.583	110	.350	-0.1	3B(9) 1.2, LF(1) -0.1	0.3
2022 DC	*NYM*	*MLB*	*22*	*62*	*8*	*3*	*0*	*2*	*9*	*4*	*19*	*0*	*0*	*.233/.294/.426*	*86*	*.312*	*-0.1*	*SS 0, 3B 0*	*0.1*

Comparables: Miguel Andújar, Austin Riley, Brandon Drury

The Report: We often like to say that prospect development isn't linear, but Vientos has followed a pretty straight, y = x slope since he was drafted as a young prep bat with raw power but an unclear defensive home. Every year since, we have written him as an OFP 55, then tried to find a different way to say "above-average bat, below-average glove." The stat line was more than just "above average" across a strong Double-A campaign in 2021, but the underpinnings of the same profile remain. Vientos has plus raw power, but it's a strength-and-leverage swing. The contact isn't as consistently loud as you'd think given the raw slugging total, but Vientos is a potential 20-plus-home-run bat. The length and lift in his swing, coupled with merely average bat speed, can leave him vulnerable to better velocity, but he has enough of an approach and enough bat-to-ball to project an average hit tool. So that's the above-average bat covered—albeit not without some concerns about how he will fare when he's seeing better fastballs more often.

Vientos remains a below-average but passable third baseman. The Mets have started working him in the corner outfield because . . . well, he's a worse third baseman than Brett Baty. However, Vientos doesn't really have the foot speed or instincts for the outfield, and his arm, which plays average in the infield, limits him to left in the outfield. The Mets played him at first base a bit last spring, but they already have Pete Alonso, who is something like the 95th-percentile outcome for Vientos. If this all sounds kind of J.D. Davis-ish, well, that's a pretty lazy comp, but it's not inaccurate.

OFP: 55 / What if J.D. Davis was a bit better at third?

Variance: High. Despite his Double-A success, there's similar hit-tool-collapse risk to Mauricio, albeit for different reasons. Vientos's swing is more vulnerable to plus velocity, something he'll see more of as he moves up the ladder.

Mark Barry's Fantasy Take: Even though J.D. Davis has been fantasy useful over the last handful of seasons, "What if J.D. Davis, but a little worse?" is not a shiny pitch that would succeed on *Shark Tank*. Vientos is fine, but I don't know that he's much more than a corner infielder or OF5 on a good team.

5 Matt Allan RHP OFP: 55 ETA: 2025

Born: 04/17/01 Age: 21 Bats: R Throws: R Height: 6'3" Weight: 225 lb. Origin: Round 3, 2019 Draft (#89 overall)

YEAR	TEAM	LVL	AGE	W	L	SV	G	GS	IP	H	HR	BB/9	K/9	K	GB%	BABIP	WHIP	ERA	DRA-	WARP
2019	MTS	ROK	18	1	0	0	5	4	8^1	5	0	4.3	11.9	11	31.6%	.263	1.08	1.08		
2019	BRK	SS	18	0	0	0	1	1	2	5	0	4.5	13.5	3	42.9%	.714	3.00	9.00		

Comparables: Brusdar Graterol, Santos Moreno, Wilkin Ramos

The Report: Allan had Tommy John surgery in May after suffering a torn UCL ramping up for the minor-league season. He had looked very impressive in spring training, and was poised for a full breakout. The timing of the surgery will wipe out most of his 2022 season, too, and he'll end up being 22 before he sees significant full-season action.

Before the surgery (and the pandemic), he'd shown a high-spin combination of two plus pitches, a mid-90s fastball and a diving curveball. He had advanced command and pitchability for a teenager back in 2019, and the changeup was coming along. The stuff continued to improve at both the alternate site and in 2021's spring training, and if it all comes back clean after rehab, he could very quickly become one of the better pitching prospects around.

OFP: 55 / Mid-rotation starter

Variance: High. Tommy John surgery can disrupt careers more significantly than some acknowledge, and the Mets, in particular, don't have a great track record of recoveries without setbacks.

Mark Barry's Fantasy Take: A friendly reminder: Injuries are the worst, and I hate them forever. I don't think Allan needs to be on your fantasy radar until he pitches again. Using a roster spot on a guy recovering from TJS is not the most efficient use of your resources.

6 J.T. Ginn RHP

OFP: 50 ETA: Late 2022/Early 2023

Born: 05/20/99 Age: 23 Bats: R Throws: R Height: 6'2" Weight: 200 lb. Origin: Round 2, 2020 Draft (#52 overall)

YEAR	TEAM	LVL	AGE	W	L	SV	G	GS	IP	H	HR	BB/9	K/9	K	GB%	BABIP	WHIP	ERA	DRA-	WARP
2021	SLU	A	22	2	1	0	8	8	38^{2}	26	3	2.3	8.1	35	57.4%	.237	0.93	2.56	78	0.9
2021	BRK	A+	22	3	4	0	10	10	53^{1}	49	0	2.0	7.8	46	64.2%	.308	1.14	3.38	96	0.6
2022 non-DC	*NYM*	*MLB*	*23*	*2*	*3*	*0*	*57*	*0*	*50*	*53*	*4*	*3.4*	*6.4*	*35*	*43.3%*	*.305*	*1.45*	*4.65*	*110*	*-0.1*

Comparables: Spencer Howard, Kyle Kendrick, Brad Bergesen

The Report: Since he had Tommy John surgery shortly into his 2020 college season, it would be fair to consider Ginn's 92 innings last year as sort of an extended rehab assignment. The conventional wisdom is that the last thing to come back after TJ is the fastball, and Ginn didn't consistently have his pre-surgery velocity and struggled with the command of his sinker. The latter is a heavy pitch, even at 92–93, but it wasn't always down in the zone, or even in the zone. His best sinkers flash plus, but until the command and 94–95 top end show up more consistently, it's a solid-average pitch, on balance.

Behind the sinker, Ginn flashes four distinct off-speed pitches (and, if you want to split off the occasional four-seamer, it's a six-pitch arsenal). He could probably stand to trim a couple. The breaking ball is a continuum from a low-80s curve to a high-80s cutter. There's a slider in between, and they all can bleed into a glob of average pitches, flashing better. The curve was getting the most consistent swing-and-miss when we saw him, but others have seen the slider—which does show good 11–5 tilt—as the best secondary. The changeup can play off the two-seamer well, showing similar shape, but it doesn't have enough velocity separation to fool batters. The top two pitches here could end up 55–60 once he gets further away from his surgery, but until he shows above-average stuff and command more often and deeper into his outings, the projection will remain, well, average.

OFP: 50 / No. 4 starter

Variance: Medium. There's perhaps a bit more here after Ginn gets to two years post-surgery, but he also flashed more than this only in college.

Mark Barry's Fantasy Take: I'll be keeping an eye on the radar gun during Ginn's work in spring training. If his velocity creeps back, I think he's pretty interesting. He has a deep arsenal and was a pretty-buzzy name before the 2020 draft (and his 2020 TJS). And, in theory, he shouldn't be too far away.

7 Khalil Lee OF

OFP: 50 ETA: Debuted in 2021

Born: 06/26/98 Age: 24 Bats: L Throws: L Height: 5'10" Weight: 170 lb. Origin: Round 3, 2016 Draft (#103 overall)

YEAR	TEAM	LVL	AGE	PA	R	2B	3B	HR	RBI	BB	K	SB	CS	AVG/OBP/SLG	DRC+	BABIP	BRR	FRAA	WARP
2019	NWA	AA	21	546	74	21	3	8	51	65	154	53	12	.264/.363/.372	90	.374	2.7	RF(55) -5.4, CF(45) -6.1, LF(8) -0.1	0.1
2021	SYR	AAA	23	388	67	20	2	14	37	71	115	8	10	.274/.451/.500	122	.402	-0.3	RF(61) -7.7, CF(26) 6.7, LF(11) -1.0	2.0
2021	NYM	MLB	23	18	2	1	0	0	1	0	13	0	0	.056/.056/.111	41	.200		RF(11) -0.4	-0.1
2022 DC	*NYM*	*MLB*	*24*	*74*	*10*	*3*	*0*	*1*	*8*	*9*	*25*	*2*	*1*	*.209/.333/.364*	*92*	*.320*	*0.2*	*RF 0, LF 0*	*0.2*

Comparables: Michael Saunders, Nick Williams, Rey Fuentes

The Report: Lee's offensive game provides an excellent example of the difference between "plate discipline" and "pitch recognition." He is a disciplined hitter in most common ways of measuring; he doesn't expand the zone, and he walks a ton, taking ball four in 18.3 percent of his plate appearances last year in Triple-A. But while he can avoid swinging at enough balls outside the zone, he does not seem to have much ability to recognize spin, which causes a surprising amount of swing-and-miss. While he has plus raw power, he hits the ball on the ground a ton because of his swing path, and that limits his game power. And while he's a plus runner, his defense in center isn't so hot because of his routes, and his best fit is in the corners.

All that said, Lee has long had a lot of underlying talent and was a big offensive producer in Triple-A as a young player; he turned 23 during the season. He'd be a pretty good swing-change candidate for an organization which could pull that off. Is that actually the Mets?

OFP: 50 / Starting outfielder

Variance: Medium. It was High last year, but this going down really isn't great for Lee, because we're trending towards a scenario in which he's probably going to be just a second-division regular.

Mark Barry's Fantasy Take: Against my better judgment, I still like Lee. And you guessed it, it's because of the speed. It's much easier to overlook the "Yeah, but he might not hit" of it all if the potential for 30 steals is in play.

8 Alex Ramirez OF OFP: 50 ETA: 2025

Born: 01/13/03 Age: 19 Bats: R Throws: R Height: 6'3" Weight: 170 lb. Origin: International Free Agent, 2019

YEAR	TEAM	LVL	AGE	PA	R	2B	3B	HR	RBI	BB	K	SB	CS	AVG/OBP/SLG	DRC+	BABIP	BRR	FRAA	WARP
2021	SLU	A	18	334	41	15	4	5	35	23	104	16	7	.258/.326/.384	84	.376	-3.4	CF(46) 1.7, RF(22) 5.1, LF(5) -0.8	0.8
2022 non-DC	*NYM*	*MLB*	*19*	*251*	*19*	*10*	*2*	*2*	*20*	*13*	*89*	*7*	*4*	*.211/.262/.310*	*52*	*.327*	*0.9*	*CF 3, RF 3*	*0.0*

Comparables: Jasson Dominguez, Carlos Tocci, Luigi Rodriguez

The Report: Ramirez impressed enough in extended spring training last year to get an extremely aggressive promotion to Low-A in June. He proceeded to hold his own there as one of the youngest players in full-season ball; he's just a few weeks older than Jasson Dominguez from the same international-free-agent class, and their lines last year were more similar than you might've expected. As has been the case since Ramirez signed, he impressed with big bat speed and decent feel for the barrel. He's got a big, classically-projectable frame, and anytime you see a player who can make a move on the ball like Ramirez can and who has the potential to add a lot of strength, that's a high-potential scenario.

So, what's stopping him from ranking higher in a thin system? Ramirez has a noisy hand setup with some timing mechanisms, and, combined with his long levers, that leads to a longer bat path and struggles against softer stuff. While he made a fair amount of contact given his age and experience level, the hit tool is still a major mid- to long-term concern. His power is still pure projection, and he's going to need significant physical growth to maximize it. Being a roughly league-average hitter at age 18 in your first professional experience is a huge positive marker, but it's a long way from there to the majors.

OFP: 50 / Starting outfielder

Variance: Very high. There's a lot up in the air, not just about Ramirez's potential but the shape of his ultimate performance.

Mark Barry's Fantasy Take: There are things to like about Ramirez, but, ultimately, he's too far away and still has too many concerns with his hit tool. You can toss him on the watchlist, though, because, if something clicks, there's potential for significant helium.

9 Calvin Ziegler RHP OFP: 45 ETA: 2025

Born: 10/03/02 Age: 19 Bats: R Throws: R Height: 6'0" Weight: 205 lb. Origin: Round 2, 2021 Draft (#46 overall)

The Report: When you draft Kumar Rocker in the first round knowing his bonus demand is going to be north of $5 million, you have to start cutting against your bonus pool, and the Mets did precisely that in the most logical place: their next pick, second-rounder Calvin Ziegler. A hard-throwing Canadian prep arm, Ziegler signed for $700,000 less than his slot allocation, which suggests a decent-sized haircut for someone who wasn't expected to go in the first 100 picks or so.

What he can do is throw the ball hard. Standing at an even 6-feet tall, he generates a lot of power from his delivery, getting it up to 98 at times, while consistently in the low- to-mid 90s when settled in. The heater has some natural sink to it, and, like the rest of his pitches, it can be scattershot when it comes to his control. His spike curveball flashes good bat-missing potential when it's on, and his nascent changeup is distantly behind where it needs to be in order for Ziegler to be considered a starter long-term.

OFP: 45 / Emergency starter best suited for a bullpen role

Variance: Extreme. Players of his size with sudden and significant velocity gains do not have a very good track record, historically. The profile, alone, screams reliever, with the stuff faring much better in shorter stints.

Mark Barry's Fantasy Take: I'm sure Ziegler is a nice enough dude, but, in this fantasy space, uh, I'll pass.

10 Hayden Senger C OFP: 45 ETA: Late 2022/Early 2023

Born: 04/03/97 Age: 25 Bats: R Throws: R Height: 6'1" Weight: 210 lb. Origin: Round 24, 2018 Draft (#710 overall)

YEAR	TEAM	LVL	AGE	PA	R	2B	3B	HR	RBI	BB	K	SB	CS	AVG/OBP/SLG	DRC+	BABIP	BRR	FRAA	WARP
2019	COL	A	22	353	27	21	1	4	36	25	64	0	0	.230/.324/.345	116	.275	-2.7	C(69) 5.6	2.1
2021	BRK	A+	24	47	10	5	1	2	4	3	16	0	0	.302/.362/.605	90	.440	0.1	C(9) 1.4	0.2
2021	BNG	AA	24	205	23	13	1	3	10	16	62	0	0	.254/.337/.387	82	.368	-0.5	C(44) 3.9, 1B(1) 0.2	0.7
2022 non-DC	*NYM*	*MLB*	*25*	*251*	*20*	*12*	*1*	*3*	*21*	*15*	*75*	*0*	*0*	*.203/.274/.310*	*60*	*.287*	*-0.3*	*C 1, 1B 0*	*-0.1*

Comparables: Aramis Garcia, Michael McKenry, Cameron Rupp

The Report: Looking for breakouts in the Mets' system past the top prospect names quickly gets exasperating. Senger faded some at the plate down the stretch last year, and while the top-line numbers look fine for a catcher, the offensive tools are fringy. He does have above-average raw power, but some stiffness and length to the swing mean he's unlikely to get all of it into games. Senger doesn't really focus on the big fly, either. He is comfortable firing line drives the other way, and still strong enough to run into 10–15 home runs, even when he isn't trying to go for the kind of pull-side lift he will flash in batting practice.

The glove is the carrying tool here. Senger is a solid receiver that frames well at all four quadrants. While he's not going to garner more than a 20 on the run grade, he has some quick-twitch burst on defense, which shows up on tappers in front of him and getting out of the crouch on steal attempts. The transfer and arm strength aren't amazing, but he gets his throws on target in around two seconds flat. That'll play.

OFP: 45 / Fringe starter or good backup

Variance: Low. The defensive skills give him a viable path to being a good-glove backup. Conversely, there probably isn't enough offensive upside to make him a slam-dunk starter. (The Mets exposed Senger to the Rule 5 draft while protecting José Butto, who wasn't in serious contention for this list, so we're pretty sure the team doesn't think Senger is in their own Top 10.)

Mark Barry's Fantasy Take: Fringy offensive tools for a catcher? Senger is most certainly not The One.

The Prospects You Meet Outside the Top Ten

Prospects on the Rise

Dominic Hamel RHP Born: 03/02/99 Age: 23 Bats: R Throws: R Height: 6'2" Weight: 206 lb. Origin: Round 3, 2021 Draft (#81 overall)

One of the more underrated college pitchers in last year's draft, Hamel was among the NCAA leaders in strikeouts thanks to an ability to spin the ball with extreme efficiency on all of his pitches. His fastball sits in the modest 91–94 range, but he's able to locate the pitch around the zone and, especially, command it up where the spin gives it riding life. His slider and curveball can blend together sometimes, looking more like one manipulated pitch that has horizontal movement, at times, while others break straight down. He could be an interesting option in the back half of the rotation or could eat innings in a variety of different roles, as long as he continues to work on the consistency of his breaking pitches.

Jaylen Palmer CF Born: 07/31/00 Age: 21 Bats: R Throws: R Height: 6'4" Weight: 208 lb. Origin: Round 22, 2018 Draft (#650 overall)

YEAR	TEAM	LVL	AGE	PA	R	2B	3B	HR	RBI	BB	K	SB	CS	AVG/OBP/SLG	DRC+	BABIP	BRR	FRAA	WARP
2019	KNG	ROA	18	276	41	12	2	7	28	31	108	1	3	.260/.344/.413		.434			
2021	SLU	A	20	291	51	13	4	2	24	39	81	23	5	.276/.378/.386	97	.398	0.9	3B(27) -1.2, CF(17) -0.4, 2B(11) 1.6	0.9
2021	BRK	A+	20	169	28	5	2	4	15	25	65	7	1	.189/.314/.336	79	.311	1.6	CF(27) -1.8, RF(8) -0.6, 3B(4) -0.3	0.0
2022 non-DC	*NYM*	*MLB*	*21*	*251*	*19*	*10*	*1*	*2*	*19*	*23*	*92*	*5*	*3*	*.197/.277/.292*	*56*	*.320*	*0.6*	*CF 1, 3B -1*	*-0.5*

Comparables: Jeimer Candelario, Rymer Liriano, Jordan Schafer

Palmer has among the loudest tools in the Mets' system, but a passive approach can put him in bad counts, and a long swing limits his ability to make consistent contact or get his plus raw power into games. Drafted as a shortstop, Palmer spent time at second, third and all three outfield spots in 2021. His outfield reads and routes are about where you'd expect for his present level of experience, but, given more reps and refinement, his near plus-plus foot speed should make him at least an average defender out there. He's okay on the infield, as well, so defensive flexibility might pave his path to the majors, although the bat is not holding up its end, yet.

Junior Santos RHP Born: 08/16/01 Age: 20 Bats: R Throws: R Height: 6'7" Weight: 244 lb. Origin: International Free Agent, 2018

YEAR	TEAM	LVL	AGE	W	L	SV	G	GS	IP	H	HR	BB/9	K/9	K	GB%	BABIP	WHIP	ERA	DRA-	WARP
2019	KNG	ROA	17	0	5	0	14	14	40^{2}	46	4	5.5	8.0	36	30.8%	.333	1.75	5.09		
2021	SLU	A	19	6	6	0	21	16	96	108	8	3.6	7.4	79	50.0%	.339	1.52	4.59	109	0.5
2022 non-DC	*NYM*	*MLB*	*20*	*2*	*3*	*0*	*57*	*0*	*50*	*60*	*7*	*4.8*	*5.3*	*29*	*39.1%*	*.312*	*1.74*	*6.52*	*142*	*-0.9*

Comparables: Jeff D'Amico, Blake Beavan, Nate Cornejo

Santos has been a fixture in and around these lists since the Mets brought him stateside right after his 17th birthday. He spent his age-19 season in Low-A and remains both young and somewhat stagnant. Santos spent the early months of last season struggling to throw strikes before dialing back on his mid-90s sinker enough to fill up the zone. A low-80s slider and sparingly used changeup round out the arsenal. His 6-foot-7 frame is well filled out at this point, and while he could wring some more velocity out of his fairly simple delivery, that just circles us back to the throwing-strikes issue. The lower slot and underdeveloped secondaries suggest reliever long-term right now, but, given his frame and fastball, he's at least worth continuing to monitor in a system that doesn't have much lower-minors pitching depth.

Factors on the Farm

Carlos Cortes OF Born: 06/30/97 Age: 25 Bats: L Throws: S Height: 5'7" Weight: 197 lb. Origin: Round 3, 2018 Draft (#83 overall)

YEAR	TEAM	LVL	AGE	PA	R	2B	3B	HR	RBI	BB	K	SB	CS	AVG/OBP/SLG	DRC+	BABIP	BRR	FRAA	WARP
2019	STL	A+	22	526	64	26	3	11	68	52	77	6	5	.255/.336/.397	122	.281	-1.4	2B(76) -1.7, LF(1) -0.0	2.6
2021	SRR	WIN	24	67	7	2	1	0	5	10	18	0	1	.236/.358/.309		.342			
2021	BNG	AA	24	346	50	26	1	14	57	35	85	1	2	.257/.332/.487	110	.305	-1.6	LF(47) 11.1, RF(17) 0.1	2.4
2022 non-DC	*NYM*	*MLB*	*25*	*251*	*24*	*12*	*1*	*6*	*27*	*20*	*61*	*0*	*1*	*.222/.293/.374*	*80*	*.275*	*-0.2*	*2B 0, LF 3*	*0.4*

Comparables: Jordany Valdespin, Brian Anderson, Nolan Reimold

Cortes's switch-throwing has been relegated to interesting parlor trick, as he's now just a corner outfielder. The selling point on the profile—which caused the Mets to draft him twice and over-slot him as a draft-eligible sophomore—has long been the power potential, and Cortes does generate above-average raw power from a fairly compact frame and swing. He doesn't really hit the ball as consistently hard as you'd like for a power-over-hit bat, though, and, given his struggles with Double-A lefties, he's best served as a long-side platoon player. That would be fine if he was still carrying a second-baseman's glove around with him, but it's a tough fit as a pure corner-outfield bench bat.

Adam Oller RHP Born: 10/17/94 Age: 27 Bats: R Throws: R Height: 6'4" Weight: 225 lb. Origin: Round 20, 2016 Draft (#615 overall)

YEAR	TEAM	LVL	AGE	W	L	SV	G	GS	IP	H	HR	BB/9	K/9	K	GB%	BABIP	WHIP	ERA	DRA-	WARP
2019	AUG	A	24	5	6	0	17	17	87^{1}	94	5	2.7	9.6	93	44.5%	.376	1.37	4.02	94	1.0
2021	BNG	AA	26	5	3	0	15	15	76	66	8	3.4	11.3	95	47.2%	.310	1.25	4.03	84	1.3
2021	SYR	AAA	26	4	1	0	8	8	44	27	1	3.7	8.8	43	34.2%	.241	1.02	2.45	95	0.7
2022 DC	*NYM*	*MLB*	*27*	*2*	*2*	*0*	*17*	*3*	*25.7*	*25*	*4*	*4.0*	*8.5*	*24*	*40.3%*	*.300*	*1.43*	*4.93*	*113*	*0.0*

Comparables: Lucas Harrell, Pedro Villarreal, Sean Gilmartin

The fact that Oller—a 27-year-old, minor-league Rule 5 pick—is on this list is a testament to both his development last season and the relative shallowness of the Mets' system. Oller had a very strong second half once he started leaning more on a potentially average slider. He can start it in the zone consistently and show enough tilt to get whiffs, although it's not really a true bat-misser in shape. His fastball is average, and he can touch 95 early in starts. He has a serviceable change with some sink and a less-serviceable cutter. There's not an obvious relief fallback, but given how many starters the Mets tend to end up needing, and the fact that there isn't much upper-minors arm depth in this system, either, I'd expect to see Oller a fair bit in Queens in 2022. And, honestly, he has a chance to be a legitimate back-end option.

Eric Orze RHP Born: 08/21/97 Age: 24 Bats: R Throws: R Height: 6'4" Weight: 195 lb. Origin: Round 5, 2020 Draft (#150 overall)

YEAR	TEAM	LVL	AGE	W	L	SV	G	GS	IP	H	HR	BB/9	K/9	K	GB%	BABIP	WHIP	ERA	DRA-	WARP
2021	BRK	A+	23	1	2	1	13	0	20	19	2	2.7	11.7	26	41.5%	.333	1.25	4.05	76	0.4
2021	BNG	AA	23	2	0	4	11	0	17^{1}	12	2	0.5	13.0	25	52.6%	.278	0.75	2.60	83	0.3
2021	SYR	AAA	23	1	0	0	10	0	12^{1}	7	1	5.1	11.7	16	29.6%	.240	1.14	2.19	88	0.2
2022 non-DC	*NYM*	*MLB*	*24*	*2*	*2*	*0*	*57*	*0*	*50*	*45*	*7*	*3.5*	*10.1*	*56*	*36.9%*	*.300*	*1.31*	*4.16*	*99*	*0.2*

Comparables: Shawn Armstrong, Kyle McGrath, Jason Bergmann

Orze came pretty close to making this list, which is both a good sign, in that the Mets are finally getting useful senior signs, and a bad sign, in that the Mets nearly had a senior-sign reliever in their top 10. Orze has a pretty standard-issue, low-90s fastball and a usable slider, but the thing separating him from an org arm is a plus splitter. It's his out-pitch and should make him a medium- to high-leverage reliever capable against both sides of the plate. There's a pretty good argument he should've been up in July or August of last year, when the Mets desperately needed arms, but alas . . .

Top Talents 25 and Under (as of 4/1/2022):

1. Francisco Álvarez, C
2. Brett Baty, 3B/OF
3. Ronny Mauricio, SS
4. Mark Vientos, 3B/OF
5. Matt Allan, RHP
6. J.T. Ginn, RHP
7. Khalil Lee, OF
8. Alex Ramirez, OF
9. Calvin Ziegler, RHP
10. Jodan Yamamoto, RHP

The macabre state of this list is a shade misleading: six of the players vying for playing time in the everyday lineup, three of those vying for rotation spots, and the team's top two relief arms will all be between 26 and 29 years old heading into the year, so theirs is not a roster completely wizened stem to tip. But "better than grisly" is still far from "good" and, make no mistake, the Mets' age trend is no bueno.

The first non-prospect name on the list is Jordan Yamamoto, whom the Mets acquired last winter for Federico Polanco in a valiant effort to bolster their rotation depth. Unfortunately, Yamamoto is a borderline-courtesy inclusion here, as he is still working his way back from a serious shoulder injury that kept him from contributing to the pitching-starved Mets down the stretch last year. Yamamoto's velocity was never overpowering, and he dominated the minors with command over stuff before seeing those results stretched thinner at higher levels. He can still spin a decent breaking ball, it's just hard to live at 90–92 these days. Jordan Yamamoto is not only the first non-prospect name on this list, he is also the last, and, not coincidently, he is the *only* non-prospect-eligible player under 26 years old on the Mets' 40-man roster as of presstime. *Bing Bong* goes Father Time.

New York Yankees

The State of the System:

While the Yankees dealt a large chunk of their prospect cache over the last year or so, three notable breakouts at the top of the system keep them among the better farm systems in baseball.

The Top Ten:

1 Anthony Volpe SS OFP: 70 ETA: 2023

Born: 04/28/01 Age: 21 Bats: R Throws: R Height: 5'11" Weight: 180 lb. Origin: Round 1, 2019 Draft (#30 overall)

YEAR	TEAM	LVL	AGE	PA	R	2B	3B	HR	RBI	BB	K	SB	CS	AVG/OBP/SLG	DRC+	BABIP	BRR	FRAA	WARP
2019	PUL	ROA	18	150	19	7	2	2	11	23	38	6	1	.215/.349/.355		.289			
2021	TAM	A	20	257	56	18	5	12	49	51	43	21	5	.302/.455/.623	153	.331	0.4	SS(40) -1.2, 3B(3) -0.3, 2B(1) 0.1	2.3
2021	HV	A+	20	256	57	17	1	15	37	27	58	12	4	.286/.391/.587	132	.319	0.8	SS(45) 0.8, 2B(1) -0.1	1.9
2022 non-DC	*NYY*	*MLB*	*21*	*251*	*26*	*12*	*2*	*6*	*28*	*25*	*56*	*9*	*3*	*.235/.327/.405*	*98*	*.285*	*0.8*	*SS 0, 3B 0*	*1.0*

Comparables: Yairo Muñoz, Yamaico Navarro, Johan Camargo

The Report: On balance, Volpe might have had the most impressive all-around performance of any prospect in 2021. Okay, strictly speaking he wasn't all that young for A-ball, but, like everyone else, he did lose a season of game reps in 2020. He got a lot out of his pandemic year, though, tweaking his swing mechanics with former pro scout and Baseball Prospectus prospect team member, Jason Lefkowitz. As a prep prospect, Volpe was well-rounded but lacked a carrying tool or a sure-shot shortstop projection. Now he has the former, and it's game power. His swing is much steeper, and we suspect that will lead to swing-and-miss in the zone at higher levels, but he should get to all of his plus raw power in games. The hit tool will likely also play to plus on the strength of his contact profile. Plus, he'll get on-base a bunch and be an absolute terror once he's there. Volpe is only an average runner, but if one can be said to have controlled aggression on the basepaths, he has it. He's such a pest that even we were feeling sympathy pangs for the pitcher and defense having to deal with him.

While he now has a carrying tool, Volpe is still not a lock to stick at shortstop. His range is about as average as his foot speed, but he's an aggressive infielder who can make throws from anywhere in a shift and gets a lot out of a rather pedestrian defensive skill set. His arm is strong enough for any spot on the dirt, and we suspect he will be best utilized as an infield flex type.

OFP: 70 / All-Star infielder

Variance: Medium. The realistic floor of a major-league regular is still here given his broad base of skills. His power surge has upped the ceiling, but there is some risk his hit tool plays down towards average when he sees better stuff in the upper minors and, eventually, the bigs.

Mark Barry's Fantasy Take: Ah, yes. Let's fire up the old time machine, make sure the flux capacitor is fluxing and check out what I wrote about Volpe heading into last season:

"Volpe is fine."

Off to a bad start.

"If you want to tab Volpe as a future second baseman and roll the dice in leagues with at least 200 prospects, that sounds about right."

Yeah, so about that. Volpe is still just 20 years old, so he's not necessarily close to the big leagues, but he's easily one of the 15 best dynasty prospects in the game, and he's probably closer to 10 than 15. After a 27-homer and 33-steal 2021 season, the time to scoop him up at a reasonable cost has long since passed. Still, Volpe has yet to face advanced pitching, so there could be some growing pains ahead that could slightly drive down the price. If/when that happens, be ready to pounce.

2 Oswald Peraza SS OFP: 60 ETA: Late 2022/Early 2023

Born: 06/15/00 Age: 22 Bats: R Throws: R Height: 6'0" Weight: 165 lb. Origin: International Free Agent, 2016

YEAR	TEAM	LVL	AGE	PA	R	2B	3B	HR	RBI	BB	K	SB	CS	AVG/OBP/SLG	DRC+	BABIP	BRR	FRAA	WARP
2019	SI	SS	19	85	7	1	1	2	7	5	9	5	2	.241/.294/.354		.250			
2019	CSC	A	19	208	31	5	0	2	13	16	28	18	5	.273/.348/.333	108	.310	1.5	SS(44) 0.3	1.0
2021	HV	A+	21	127	20	10	0	5	16	12	24	16	1	.306/.386/.532	127	.349	1.0	SS(25) 4.9	1.4
2021	SOM	AA	21	353	51	16	2	12	40	23	82	20	8	.294/.348/.466	102	.362	-2.2	SS(69) -2.7	0.7
2021	SWB	AAA	21	31	5	0	0	1	2	2	5	2	1	.286/.323/.393	98	.304	-0.3	SS(7) 1.5	0.2
2022 DC	*NYY*	*MLB*	*22*	*195*	*24*	*7*	*0*	*3*	*23*	*12*	*46*	*8*	*3*	*.247/.302/.358*	*79*	*.312*	*0.6*	*SS 0, 2B 0*	*0.3*

Comparables: Eugenio Suárez, Junior Lake, Willi Castro

The Report: Peraza was a bit of an unexpected add to the Yankees' 40-man roster after the 2020 season. He hadn't played above Low-A and didn't hit for much power there despite good bat speed and raw pop. Well, chalk one up for Yankees baseball ops, as Peraza started lifting the ball more in 2021 on the way to a breakout season. He now whips the bat through the zone with the ideal swing plane to swat dingers, although he sacrifices some barrel control in the process and is overaggressive at times. That can lead to inconsistent contact quality, although his raw K rates aren't all that bad. Peraza is best when hunting fastballs and will swing over even fringy or below-average breaking stuff if pitchers can get it to dive below his bat path. It's going to be a bit of a balancing act to get the power into games without sacrificing too much hit, but he is a potential 20-home-run bat.

The speed-and-defense part of the equation have never been in question and were arguably the reason the Yankees sought to protect him from the Rule 5 draft to begin with. Peraza is a plus runner with a plus shortstop glove. He's rangy with good hands and actions, and while his arm doesn't have true left-side zing, he has enough arm strength for short and gets his throws out quickly and on-target from every angle.

OFP: 60 / First-division shortstop, occasional All-Star

Variance: Medium. Peraza's swing might get found out a little against better spin, but even if he's a .240 hitter, he's still probably a passable regular given the glove. There's also a high-end outcome possible if he refines his approach a bit at the upper levels.

Mark Barry's Fantasy Take: Peraza nearly hit .300 across three levels of minor-league ball in 2021, but his aggressive nature and struggles with spin have me skeptical about his ability to post plus batting averages in the big leagues. Additionally, he doesn't walk much, so if his average does dip, he'll have even fewer opportunities to really utilize his fantasy carrying tool—the speed. A .250-ish average and 20–25 steals is definitely useful (it's what Tommy Edman and Robbie Grossman did in 2021), but it's perhaps not an impact profile for fantasy.

3 Randy Vasquez RHP OFP: 55 ETA: Late 2022/Early 2023

Born: 11/03/98 Age: 23 Bats: R Throws: R Height: 6'0" Weight: 165 lb. Origin: International Free Agent, 2018

YEAR	TEAM	LVL	AGE	W	L	SV	G	GS	IP	H	HR	BB/9	K/9	K	GB%	BABIP	WHIP	ERA	DRA-	WARP
2019	PUL	ROA	20	4	1	0	11	11	54^{2}	36	6	4.6	8.7	53	44.4%	.221	1.17	3.29		
2021	TAM	A	22	3	3	0	13	11	50	35	2	4.1	10.4	58	54.7%	.262	1.16	2.34	80	1.1
2021	HV	A+	22	3	0	0	6	6	36	33	0	2.0	13.3	53	65.9%	.393	1.14	1.75	75	0.8
2021	SOM	AA	22	2	1	0	4	4	21^{1}	23	2	3.0	8.0	19	52.9%	.309	1.41	4.22	104	0.1
2022 non-DC	*NYY*	*MLB*	*23*	*2*	*3*	*0*	*57*	*0*	*50*	*51*	*5*	*4.1*	*7.7*	*42*	*49.4%*	*.309*	*1.49*	*4.68*	*111*	*-0.1*

Comparables: Dan Straily, Iván Nova, Jason Hammel

The Report: And here's a third 2021 breakout at the top of the Yankees' system. Vasquez was signed at 19 as a shorter, slighter righty. He remains a shorter, slighter righty, but the stuff is anything but light. Vasquez blitzed three full-season levels in 2021, breaking bats and K-ing names. He works off two different fastballs: a mid-90s two-seamer with big sink and run that he can get under the hands of right-handed batters, and a mid-90s four-seamer with a little bit of wiggle that he elevates effectively against lefties. Once he gets ahead, he drops a big, sweeping, low-80s power breaker. It flashes plus-plus, and he can spot it for strikes or bury it as a put-away pitch. There's a firm change that flashes average but he uses sparingly. Vasquez has two clear plus offerings—three if you want to split out the fastballs—but a tornadic delivery that is arm and upper body heavy. He repeats it well enough, but you look at the mechanics and the lack of a clear changeup, and you might think reliever. We'd give him every chance to start, even if the repertoire and frame probably aren't going to hold up for 32 starts and 180 innings. It's 2022 after all, you can leverage this profile into a very fun and dominant major-league arm. And, hey, if Vasquez does end up in the pen, we wouldn't be surprised if the fastball(s) and breaker pop enough to close.

OFP: 55 / Mid-rotation starter who you maybe limit to two times through the opposing lineup or second-division closer.

Variance: Medium. Vasquez will need to refine some things to stay out of the pen in the long term. He can overthrow the four-seamer and curve at times. The command will never be all that fine, and the changeup needs improvement to get to a useful 4.

Mark Barry's Fantasy Take: The above is right, the rules have changed so much for pitcher effectiveness, you don't really need to toss more than 150 innings to have a meaningful role in a rotation. The problem for us is that it's really difficult to pick out which guys are going to pop as two-times-through-the-order standouts. Vasquez has about as good a chance as any to be solid in this spot, but there are still enough third-pitch questions to keep him in the 150–175 range for dynasty prospects.

Eyewitness Report: Randy Vasquez

Evaluator: Jeffrey Paternostro
Report Date: 08/25/2021
Dates Seen: 8/20/21
Risk Factor: High
Delivery: Semi-wind up, full arc to low-three-quarters. Tornadic and upper body heavy, very upright at foot strike, plus arm speed. Unorthodox, but repeats well enough.

Pitch Type	Future Grade	Sitting Velocity	Peak Velocity	Report
4SFB	60	94-95	96	Four-seam is primarily used against lefties, command is average, can beat batters up in the zone, rides well.
2SFB	60	93-95	95	Borderline 70 projection here. Sink and run, bat misser, bat breaker, can get in under the hands, commands a little better than 4S which he can overthrow. still had 95 deeper in the start.
CU	60	82-83	83	Big, sweeping 10-5 power breaker, spin monster, inconsistent depth and can show as GS chase too much when he overthrows, but can spot or bury and flashes 7. changed levels/angles well with FB/CU combo. Worked back from 3-0 with two wicked breakers in a jam, but got a little lazy and lost a tick or two on it later on.
CH	40	88-89	89	Shows a little wrinkle, but very firm and kinda nothing pitch, used sparingly, sells it okay, flashed average

Conclusion: Vasquez is a smaller righty, and past that there are a lot of reliever markers here, but its at least 6/6 in short bursts and one of those might get to a 7. Reasonable shot to start if he gets the change to functional, and the top two pitches might be good enough on their own if the frame holds up. Honestly, it's a plus fastball, plus secondary with change and command questions, the performance has run him up to Double-A and that prospect usually makes the 101. Don't have a great reason to keep him off. Third starter or late inning reliever OFP.

4 Luis Gil RHP OFP: 55 ETA: Debuted in 2021

Born: 06/03/98 Age: 24 Bats: R Throws: R Height: 6'2" Weight: 185 lb. Origin: International Free Agent, 2015

YEAR	TEAM	LVL	AGE	W	L	SV	G	GS	IP	H	HR	BB/9	K/9	K	GB%	BABIP	WHIP	ERA	DRA-	WARP
2019	CSC	A	21	4	5	0	17	17	83	60	1	4.2	12.1	112	47.2%	.311	1.19	2.39	86	1.3
2019	TAM	A+	21	1	0	0	3	3	13	11	0	5.5	7.6	11	40.5%	.297	1.46	4.85	102	0.1
2021	SOM	AA	23	1	1	0	7	7	30^{2}	24	2	3.8	14.7	50	29.9%	.338	1.21	2.64	80	0.6
2021	SWB	AAA	23	4	0	1	13	10	48^{2}	35	7	5.9	12.4	67	29.1%	.275	1.38	4.81	84	1.0
2021	NYY	MLB	23	1	1	0	6	6	29^{1}	20	4	5.8	11.7	38	32.4%	.239	1.33	3.07	100	0.3
2022 DC	*NYY*	*MLB*	*24*	*7*	*5*	*0*	*53*	*9*	*85.3*	*70*	*13*	*5.6*	*11.5*	*108*	*39.5%*	*.285*	*1.44*	*4.58*	*104*	*0.5*

Comparables: Clay Buchholz, Jered Weaver, Jaime García

The Report: In *Interview with the Vampire*, Anne Rice wrote, "None of us really changes over time. We only become more fully what we are." Those are the ruminations of a world-weary Lestat and also an accurate 2021 scouting report for Luis Gil. If you ignore minor things like control and command, Gil might have the best fastball in the minors—and, frankly, one of the best in the majors—mid- to upper-90s heat with big spin, extension and vertical action. It's a pure swing-and-miss pitch on its own . .

. when it's around the zone. Gil has developed a pretty solid slider, as well. It has some slurviness to it, but it almost functions like a change of pace off the high-octane fastball, with close to 15 mph of velocity separation, at times. His actual changeup plays more like a power two-seamer, but it can also miss bats.

When Gil is repeating his delivery and throwing enough strikes, his performance looks like that of a top-line starter. The delivery, however, is even more high octane than the fastball, and he has gone through frequent bouts of wildness. Gil can lose the zone inning-to-inning or batter-to-batter. There is a ceiling for the control and command profile here, and that ceiling might be below-average, at best. The fastball is so good, it might not matter *that* much, but it's gonna matter a bit.

OFP: 55 / Bulk arm or late-inning reliever that is transcendent one day and makes you pull your hair out the next.

Variance: Low. Gil has elite fastball characteristics and two potential average-or-better secondaries backing it. He has already shown he can miss bats in the majors. He also might just be an eighth-inning guy.

Mark Barry's Fantasy Take: Gil made six starts for the Yankees in 2021 and was actually really good in some of them. The walks are a problem, though, and he hasn't been within shouting distance of even an average walk rate at any level in his professional career, which would wreak havoc on his rate stats over the course of a full season. That's a hard tightrope to walk for a starter, and it's not terribly exciting as a reliever unless saves are involved.

5 Trey Sweeney SS   OFP: 55   ETA: Late 2023/Early 2024

Born: 04/24/00 Age: 22 Bats: L Throws: R Height: 6'4" Weight: 200 lb. Origin: Round 1, 2021 Draft (#20 overall)

YEAR	TEAM	LVL	AGE	PA	R	2B	3B	HR	RBI	BB	K	SB	CS	AVG/OBP/SLG	DRC+	BABIP	BRR	FRAA	WARP
2021	TAM	A	21	129	26	4	4	6	13	18	29	3	1	.245/.357/.518	119	.280	1.3	SS(25) 0.3	0.8
2022 non-DC	*NYY*	*MLB*	*22*	*251*	*22*	*9*	*2*	*4*	*24*	*20*	*57*	*2*	*2*	*.218/.288/.349*	*74*	*.271*	*0.4*	*SS 1*	*0.3*

Comparables: Brandon Hicks, Jeremiah Jackson, Darnell Sweeney

The Report: Sweeney was a draft-model favorite. He hit .382/.522/.712 at Eastern Illinois in 2021 and hits the ball hard. Visual evaluations of his lefty swing made him less of a favorite of eye scouts, who saw him as more of a second- or third-round pick; his setup is extremely noisy with a big bat waggle, and he takes a huge leg kick. He gets to the ball very quickly once he gets going, and he had no problem hitting for power in Low-A once he entered pro ball. While his excellent plate discipline held up, he did have significant swing-and-miss, and therein lies the knock: until he proves he can get around and make appropriate contact against upper-level pitching, there are going to be questions about the hit tool and how extra everything is as he's loading up to swing. Defensively, Sweeney was drafted as a shortstop, but he's big for the position and not the world's most fleet-of-foot player, so his best long-term projection might be third base.

OFP: 55 / Above-average third baseman who can fake shortstop, walks-and-power variety

Variance: Medium. It's a weird swing, no matter how good the performance record is.

Mark Barry's Fantasy Take: I gotta be honest, swing-and-miss issues scare me a bunch, especially for a college bat that hasn't seen High-A yet. Sure, that can be a little nitpicky, as Sweeney just got drafted, but the whiffs and the lack of projected wheels are keeping him off my radar for now.

6 Jasson Dominguez CF   OFP: 55   ETA: 2025

Born: 02/07/03 Age: 19 Bats: S Throws: R Height: 5'10" Weight: 190 lb. Origin: International Free Agent, 2019

YEAR	TEAM	LVL	AGE	PA	R	2B	3B	HR	RBI	BB	K	SB	CS	AVG/OBP/SLG	DRC+	BABIP	BRR	FRAA	WARP
2021	YNK	ROK	18	27	5	0	0	0	1	6	6	2	0	.200/.407/.200		.286			
2021	TAM	A	18	214	26	9	1	5	18	21	67	7	3	.258/.346/.398	88	.371	0.2	CF(38) -4.4	0.1
2022 non-DC	*NYY*	*MLB*	*19*	*251*	*19*	*10*	*1*	*3*	*20*	*16*	*89*	*4*	*2*	*.201/.261/.296*	*50*	*.313*	*0.3*	*CF -2*	*-0.9*

Comparables: Luigi Rodriguez, Connor Scott, Jahmai Jones

The Report: We realize Yankees fans and card collectors probably aren't going to like this, but we're tapping the brakes on the hype for now. While Dominguez was 18 in a full-season league and wasn't bad, he wasn't good, either. He ran a 31-percent strikeout rate, and visual evaluations of his bat-to-ball abilities matched his Low-A struggles. His ground-ball rate eclipsed 50 percent, and the combination of not making enough contact and hitting the ball on the ground all the time is really rough for a burgeoning power prospect. Dominguez received glowing profiles and was talked about in hushed tones several years ago, but he hadn't actually played much in public before 2021. Ultimately, we have very little evidence he can put the barrel on the ball enough, no matter how famous he is.

All that said, he's a well-built, powerful player with plus-plus raw power and bat speed. His swings are very aesthetically pleasing to watch. He has a good handle on the strike zone for his age. He runs well.

The hit-tool questions certainly could be resolved with more reps. But that's true for many prospects, and the more those "generational talent" murmurs fade into our rearview, the less the label means to us presently. Right now, he's comparable in both age and demonstrated ability to a power-and-bat-speed 2021 prep prospect with major hit-tool questions (think Benny Montgomery or Jay Allen), and we're going to grade Dominguez accordingly until more evidence emerges.

OFP: 55 / Starting outfielder

Variance: Extreme. Dominguez has latent star potential, but his hit tool is an extreme question mark.

Mark Barry's Fantasy Take: For me, Dominguez is a little like an NFT. I don't really know what it is, but enough people seem to be losing their minds over NFTs that I have a little FOMO. Dominguez was supposed to be the Next Big Thing and was "okay" in his pro debut. He's already a top-30ish prospect on most dynasty lists, so there's not much room to exceed expectations. I'm probably looking to move him if I have him to try to cash in on the most recent craze. Of course, if I do, there's a non-zero chance he's a five-tool monster in a few years time. So there's that.

7 Luis Medina RHP OFP: 55 ETA: Late 2022/Early 2023

Born: 05/03/99 Age: 23 Bats: R Throws: R Height: 6'1" Weight: 175 lb. Origin: International Free Agent, 2015

YEAR	TEAM	LVL	AGE	W	L	SV	G	GS	IP	H	HR	BB/9	K/9	K	GB%	BABIP	WHIP	ERA	DRA-	WARP
2019	CSC	A	20	1	8	0	20	20	93	86	9	6.5	11.1	115	43.6%	.344	1.65	6.00	113	0.1
2019	TAM	A+	20	0	0	0	2	2	10^2	7	0	2.5	10.1	12	67.9%	.250	0.94	0.84	109	0.1
2021	HV	A+	22	2	1	0	7	7	32^2	18	4	5.2	13.8	50	50.0%	.241	1.13	2.76	79	0.6
2021	SOM	AA	22	4	3	0	15	14	73^2	65	7	5.0	10.1	83	50.5%	.314	1.44	3.67	84	1.3
2022 DC	*NYY*	*MLB*	*23*	*0*	*1*	*0*	*3*	*3*	*14.3*	*14*	*2*	*6.7*	*9.5*	*15*	*36.2%*	*.315*	*1.75*	*6.19*	*132*	*-0.1*

Comparables: Jordan Yamamoto, Matt Magill, Kyle Farnsworth

The Report: Beyond having the same first name, Medina and Gil have been linked in this system for a while now as flame-throwing prospects with high relief risk (alas, it hasn't quite worked out for Luis Rijo). The differences between the two are more than subtle, though. If anything, Medina might throw harder than Gil, sitting in the upper 90s and regularly touching 100 mph. Batters seem to get a good look at the fastball out of Medina's hand, though, and, between the below-average command and rather pedestrian life, Double-A hitters took better swings at it than you'd think. The present breaking-ball advantage goes to Medina, though. He sports a power curve in the mid-80s that routinely shows plus 12–5 break. His changeup is theoretically a split, but it tends to play on the firm side without the requisite dive. Medina has been fairly durable by pitching-prospect standards, throwing more than 100 innings in each of his last two seasons, although his delivery has moderate effort and torque. Our concern with regards to his future as a starter is his command and efficiency more than his frame and mechanics, and it probably wouldn't hurt for Medina to sit closer to triple digits in short bursts while giving lineups only one turn to time the heater.

OFP: 55 / No. 3–4 starter or late-inning reliever

Variance: Medium. Medina walks a few too many guys and is a bit more hittable than his raw stuff would suggest. He might end up in the pen by the time he's clocking regular per diems in the majors.

Mark Barry's Fantasy Take: At the risk of sounding lazy, Medina's fantasy ceiling is awfully similar to his partner in nomenclature. Medina has yet to debut, so we'll ding him a few spots for that as compared to Gil, but the same control-and-command problems exist, which keeps him out of my personal top-200 prospects.

8 Everson Pereira OF OFP: 55 ETA: Late 2023/Early 2024

Born: 04/10/01 Age: 21 Bats: R Throws: R Height: 6'0" Weight: 191 lb. Origin: International Free Agent, 2017

YEAR	TEAM	LVL	AGE	PA	R	2B	3B	HR	RBI	BB	K	SB	CS	AVG/OBP/SLG	DRC+	BABIP	BRR	FRAA	WARP
2019	SI	SS	18	74	9	3	0	1	3	4	26	3	0	.171/.216/.257		.256			
2021	TAM	A	20	83	17	5	1	5	22	10	21	4	1	.361/.446/.667	110	.457	0.5	CF(9) -0.7, LF(4) -0.6, RF(2) -0.1	0.3
2021	HV	A+	20	127	27	3	0	14	32	15	38	5	2	.259/.354/.676	129	.241	-1.0	CF(22) -2.4	0.5
2022 non-DC	*NYY*	*MLB*	*21*	*251*	*28*	*9*	*1*	*10*	*33*	*19*	*87*	*5*	*2*	*.228/.295/.424*	*89*	*.317*	*0.4*	*CF -1, LF 0*	*0.5*

Comparables: Eloy Jiménez, Manuel Margot, Victor Robles

The Report: Pereira was the Yankees' major international signing in 2017, but the hype died down for a while after he put up pedestrian numbers in the Appy League in 2018 and barely played short-season ball in 2019. He didn't make his full-season debut until mid-2021, but he lit up Low-A and earned a fairly quick promotion to High-A Hudson Valley. We saw him during his prolonged hot streak there and were fairly taken with his overall skill set. He is a good athlete with above-average speed who should be able to stick in center, which should allow him to create a big-league profile around his offensive tools. Most obvious is the plus bat speed and good loft that could get him to 20-plus homers, but we were also impressed that he keeps his swing direct and level enough to both get on top of hard stuff and stay on low breaking balls. Pereira's production tailed off near the end of the season, and his overall strikeout rate was pretty high, so he still has a lot to do in order to consolidate the strides he made last year. He also has a pretty eventful injury history for someone his age, so playing the season front to back will likely be another priority in 2022.

OFP: 55 / Above-average center fielder

Variance: High. Due to injury issues, his track record is pretty short, and he'll need to prove his strong offensive performance wasn't a blip.

Mark Barry's Fantasy Take: Even though Pereira is a bit injury prone and suffers from the occasional bout of whiff-itis, he's still pretty intriguing due to the fact that he hits the absolute bejeezus out of the ball. He probably won't run, and the strikeouts will certainly hurt his batting average, but he's also only 20 years old, can work a walk, and did I mention he tears covers off balls? I'd hesitate to push him too high, as being a three-true-outcome type isn't all that valuable without monster home-run totals, but there is a chance Pereira could get there.

9 Ken Waldichuk LHP OFP: 50 ETA: Late 2022/Early 2023

Born: 01/08/98 Age: 24 Bats: L Throws: L Height: 6'4" Weight: 220 lb. Origin: Round 5, 2019 Draft (#165 overall)

YEAR	TEAM	LVL	AGE	W	L	SV	G	GS	IP	H	HR	BB/9	K/9	K	GB%	BABIP	WHIP	ERA	DRA-	WARP
2019	PUL	ROA	21	0	2	0	10	10	29^1	19	2	2.1	15.0	49	29.3%	.304	0.89	3.68		
2021	HV	A+	23	2	0	0	7	7	30^2	12	0	3.8	16.1	55	31.1%	.267	0.82	0.00	82	0.6
2021	SOM	AA	23	4	3	0	16	14	79^1	64	13	4.3	12.3	108	36.7%	.293	1.29	4.20	87	1.2
2022 non-DC	*NYY*	*MLB*	*24*	*2*	*2*	*0*	*57*	*0*	*50*	*43*	*8*	*5.1*	*10.8*	*60*	*42.5%*	*.291*	*1.44*	*4.74*	*109*	*-0.1*

Comparables: Matt Albers, Wade Miley, Ryan Helsley

The Report: Even with all the recent changes in Yankees player development, they are still getting stuff and profile jumps from their small college arms between High-A and Double-A. Waldichuk was one of last year's beneficiaries. He didn't get the typical velocity jump—his fastball is fairly average, although it plays up some due to deception and his attack angle—but he does now have a plus-projecting slider with tight, bat-missing 1–7 action. It does get slurvy at times, though, and, in some outings, Waldichuk's change will look like his best secondary due to its good movement and big velocity separation. The likely outcome here is three 55 offerings, and he can bleed some of his stuff the second time through an order. Waldichuk has a bit of effort and torque to his delivery, as well, so he's not a clear 180-inning-a-year starter, even though his frame and stuff look the part. Given the depth of his arsenal, though, he should be a very effective utility arm for the Yankees in the Michael King sort of mold./p>

OFP: 50 / A 2020s archetypal spot starter/bulk guy/multi-inning reliever

Variance: Medium. Waldichuk already has an arsenal that can get outs given some minor refinement in the secondaries and command. "Also, he's a pitcher" applies here, but we think there's a fairly narrow range of likely outcomes.

Mark Barry's Fantasy Take: Waldichuk strikes me as a dude that's way more valuable IRL than in fantasy, and, as such, I am not keen on the gentleman's prospects in dynasty leagues.

10 Clarke Schmidt RHP OFP: 50 ETA: Debuted in 2020

Born: 02/20/96 Age: 26 Bats: R Throws: R Height: 6'1" Weight: 209 lb. Origin: Round 1, 2017 Draft (#16 overall)

YEAR	TEAM	LVL	AGE	W	L	SV	G	GS	IP	H	HR	BB/9	K/9	K	GB%	BABIP	WHIP	ERA	DRA-	WARP
2019	YAE	ROK	23	0	0	0	3	3	8^1	6	1	3.2	15.1	14	56.2%	.333	1.08	3.24		
2019	TAM	A+	23	4	5	0	13	12	63^1	59	2	3.4	9.8	69	54.6%	.333	1.31	3.84	97	0.8
2019	TRN	AA	23	2	0	0	3	3	19	14	1	0.5	9.0	19	45.1%	.260	0.79	2.37	102	0.1
2020	NYY	MLB	24	0	1	0	3	1	6^1	7	0	7.1	9.9	7	42.1%	.368	1.89	7.11	119	0.0
2021	SOM	AA	25	0	1	0	2	2	6^1	5	2	2.8	7.1	5	47.4%	.176	1.11	4.26	103	0.0
2021	SWB	AAA	25	0	1	0	6	5	25^2	25	4	2.8	11.2	32	52.9%	.318	1.29	2.10	89	0.5
2021	NYY	MLB	25	0	0	0	2	1	6^1	11	1	7.1	8.5	6	57.7%	.417	2.53	5.68	111	0.0
2022 DC	*NYY*	*MLB*	*26*	*2*	*1*	*0*	*6*	*6*	*31*	*29*	*3*	*4.0*	*8.6*	*29*	*57.4%*	*.299*	*1.41*	*4.35*	*103*	*0.2*

Comparables: Justin Haley, Jharel Cotton, Luis Cessa

The Report: A flexor strain cost Schmidt most of the 2021 season, although he avoided Tommy John surgery and got back to the majors in September. He was uncharacteristically wild once there, and his breaking ball did not have the same velocity or bite that it did pre-injury. He has always had a fair bit of reliever risk, due to his lack of a third pitch and durability concerns.

The change is still pretty firm, and we'll reiterate that he missed most of the year with an elbow injury. The 2020 version of Schmidt looked like he had a chance to start but would have a late-inning relief fallback on the strength of the breaker. The 2021 version looks more like a reliever, but, if the breaker rebounds along with his arm health, Schmidt should log effective innings for the 2022 Yankees, regardless of role.

OFP: 50 / Multi-inning fireman

Variance: Medium. There was an elbow issue, and the breaking ball took a step back, so it can't be low, per se, but Schmidt has a shot to make the Yankees' Opening Day roster.

Mark Barry's Fantasy Take: Could Schmidt be an effective big-league starter if he wasn't injured? Could Schmidt really be Schmidt if he wasn't injured? I'm hoping he pulls it together, because injuries are the worst and I'll hate them forever, but I don't have a ton of confidence that he can stay on the mound long enough to be fantasy relevant.

The Prospects You Meet Outside the Top Ten

#11

Deivi García RHP Born: 05/19/99 Age: 23 Bats: R Throws: R Height: 5'9" Weight: 163 lb. Origin: International Free Agent, 2015

YEAR	TEAM	LVL	AGE	W	L	SV	G	GS	IP	H	HR	BB/9	K/9	K	GB%	BABIP	WHIP	ERA	DRA-	WARP
2019	TAM	A+	20	0	2	0	4	4	17²	14	0	4.1	16.8	33	50.0%	.438	1.25	3.06	73	0.4
2019	TRN	AA	20	4	4	0	11	11	53²	43	2	4.4	14.6	87	40.5%	.363	1.29	3.86	77	1.1
2019	SWB	AAA	20	1	3	0	11	6	40	39	8	4.5	10.1	45	36.7%	.313	1.48	5.40	90	0.7
2020	NYY	MLB	21	3	2	0	6	6	34¹	35	6	1.6	8.7	33	34.0%	.293	1.19	4.98	111	0.2
2021	SWB	AAA	22	3	7	0	24	22	90²	102	21	6.8	9.6	97	29.9%	.333	1.88	6.85	119	0.3
2021	NYY	MLB	22	0	2	0	2	2	8¹	8	1	4.3	7.6	7	23.1%	.280	1.44	6.48	149	-0.1
2022 DC	*NYY*	*MLB*	*23*	*2*	*2*	*0*	*17*	*3*	*27.7*	*28*	*5*	*4.8*	*8.4*	*26*	*36.6%*	*.295*	*1.55*	*5.51*	*125*	*-0.2*

Comparables: Julio Teheran, Jaime Barría, Matt Wisler

García was our number-17-overall prospect one year ago coming off a strong major-league debut and upper-level dominance back in 2020. He did not make the Yankees out of camp last year, pitched poorly in a couple of early-season spot starts in the majors, and then completely imploded in Triple-A, walking almost seven batters per nine innings and giving up homers by the boatload. His arm slot drifted significantly south, and he got really slider happy. In doing so, he totally lost the fastball/curveball combo and the command and control that made him a top prospect to begin with. The proof of concept for him as a frontline pitcher already exists, but it's not going to happen as long as he's missing the zone.

Prospects on the Rise

JP Sears LHP Born: 02/19/96 Age: 26 Bats: R Throws: L Height: 5'11" Weight: 180 lb. Origin: Round 11, 2017 Draft (#333 overall)

YEAR	TEAM	LVL	AGE	W	L	SV	G	GS	IP	H	HR	BB/9	K/9	K	GB%	BABIP	WHIP	ERA	DRA-	WARP
2019	TAM	A+	23	4	4	1	13	6	48²	41	3	3.0	8.3	45	38.1%	.292	1.17	4.07	101	0.5
2021	SOM	AA	25	3	2	1	15	8	50²	45	6	3.2	12.6	71	47.5%	.351	1.24	4.09	89	0.7
2021	SWB	AAA	25	7	0	0	10	10	53¹	41	5	1.9	11.0	65	39.8%	.298	0.98	2.87	88	1.0
2022 non-DC	*NYY*	*MLB*	*26*	*2*	*2*	*0*	*57*	*0*	*50*	*45*	*7*	*3.1*	*9.0*	*50*	*40.9%*	*.286*	*1.26*	*3.90*	*96*	*0.3*

The player in the November 2017 Nick Rumbelow deal that hasn't been traded back to the Mariners—although, never count Jerry Dipoto out—Sears dominated the upper minors last year on the back of a deceptive delivery and plus command of a low-90s fastball. It's not the most exciting log line, but he is left-handed and has a solid changeup, as well. He twists off a short breaking ball a bit too much for it to be an ideal left-on-left option. There's the outline of a back-of-the-rotation starter here, but for a system with this much pitching depth, this kind of arm often gets shipped out when Brian Cashman wants to reshape the 40-man. So yeah, he hasn't been traded back to the Mariners, yet.

Alexander Vargas SS Born: 10/29/01 Age: 20 Bats: S Throws: R Height: 5'11" Weight: 148 lb. Origin: International Free Agent, 2018

YEAR	TEAM	LVL	AGE	PA	R	2B	3B	HR	RBI	BB	K	SB	CS	AVG/OBP/SLG	DRC+	BABIP	BRR	FRAA	WARP
2019	DSL NYY	ROK	17	44	6	5	2	0	2	4	6	2	3	.289/.364/.526		.333			
2019	YAE	ROK	17	173	23	5	5	1	16	14	22	13	0	.219/.301/.335		.250			
2021	YNK	ROK	19	174	37	7	1	3	26	20	40	17	8	.273/.362/.393		.349			

Comparables: Pedro Guerrero, Edgar Pineda, Gilbert Lara

The Yankees' system already doesn't lack for exciting shortstop prospects, and Vargas might be the next breakout name. He's capable of the spectacular defensive play, although his overall glovework is inconsistent. His lean frame should add power in the coming years, although he was undone at the plate by an aggressive approach too often in the complex. If we were ranking on upside alone, he'd certainly be in the top 10, but the floor here is significantly lower than Volpe's or Peraza's.

Hayden Wesneski RHP Born: 12/05/97 Age: 24 Bats: R Throws: R Height: 6'3" Weight: 210 lb. Origin: Round 6, 2019 Draft (#195 overall)

YEAR	TEAM	LVL	AGE	W	L	SV	G	GS	IP	H	HR	BB/9	K/9	K	GB%	BABIP	WHIP	ERA	DRA-	WARP
2019	PUL	ROA	21	1	1	3	18	0	28^1	32	1	1.9	9.5	30	59.1%	.356	1.34	4.76		
2021	HV	A+	23	1	1	0	7	7	36^1	24	2	2.2	11.6	47	51.9%	.293	0.91	1.49	77	0.8
2021	SOM	AA	23	8	4	0	15	15	83	76	11	2.4	10.0	92	43.6%	.305	1.18	4.01	94	0.9
2021	SWB	AAA	23	2	1	0	3	2	11	10	0	4.1	9.8	12	41.4%	.345	1.36	3.27	99	0.2
2022 non-DC	*NYY*	*MLB*	*24*	*2*	*2*	*0*	*57*	*0*	*50*	*49*	*7*	*3.4*	*8.9*	*49*	*41.7%*	*.309*	*1.38*	*4.63*	*109*	*-0.1*

Tell me if you've heard this story before: the Yankees drafted a pitcher with some interesting characteristics from a southern college, signed him for a six-figure bonus, and suddenly he was throwing harder with sharper off-speed stuff as he rose through the system. Wesneski, an under-slot 2019 sixth-rounder from Sam Houston State in Texas, bulldozed his way to Triple-A in his full-season debut off mid-90s with sink and an improved slider and changeup. The Yankees come up with this kind of development several times every year, and it's a major boon to their farm system.

Factors on the Farm

Oswaldo Cabrera IF Born: 03/01/99 Age: 23 Bats: S Throws: R Height: 5'10" Weight: 145 lb. Origin: International Free Agent, 2015

YEAR	TEAM	LVL	AGE	PA	R	2B	3B	HR	RBI	BB	K	SB	CS	AVG/OBP/SLG	DRC+	BABIP	BRR	FRAA	WARP
2019	TAM	A+	20	493	55	29	0	8	56	33	105	10	8	.260/.310/.378	103	.318	-0.4	2B(50) 8.6, 3B(43) 1.7, SS(21) -1.4	2.5
2021	SOM	AA	22	478	61	29	1	24	78	36	118	20	5	.256/.311/.492	111	.295	2.0	2B(43) -0.8, 3B(35) 4.9, SS(24) 3.9	3.1
2021	SWB	AAA	22	36	11	2	1	5	11	5	9	1	0	.500/.583/1.133	134	.625	-0.2	2B(7) 0.0, 3B(1) -0.2, SS(1) -0.2	0.2
2022 DC	*NYY*	*MLB*	*23*	*129*	*15*	*5*	*0*	*3*	*15*	*8*	*33*	*1*	*1*	*.219/.273/.362*	*66*	*.276*	*0.0*	*3B 1, 2B 0*	*-0.1*

Comparables: Enrique Hernández, Odúbel Herrera, Hernán Pérez

While he was overshadowed by his frequent double play partner Oswald Peraza in Double-A Somerset, Cabrera had his own power breakout in 2021. His swing might even be more effortful than Peraza's, featuring a huge leg lift and stomp, and his hand path can be even more all over the place. Cabrera is looking to lift and has grown into plus raw that probably won't all show up in games due to the hitchy, long, muscley swing. He has potential 20-home-run pop, though, and Cabrera can handle three infield spots, although he doesn't have the twitch or range for an everyday shortstop gig. He more than doubled his career home-run total in 2021, so we'll need to see it again in Triple-A, but if Cabrera keeps mashing, he could be a useful bench piece in the Bronx in short order.

Ron Marinaccio RHP Born: 07/01/95 Age: 27 Bats: R Throws: R Height: 6'2" Weight: 205 lb. Origin: Round 19, 2017 Draft (#572 overall)

YEAR	TEAM	LVL	AGE	W	L	SV	G	GS	IP	H	HR	BB/9	K/9	K	GB%	BABIP	WHIP	ERA	DRA-	WARP
2019	CSC	A	23	0	0	4	18	0	32^1	23	0	5.0	11.1	40	36.7%	.291	1.27	4.18	91	0.4
2021	SOM	AA	25	1	1	3	22	0	39^2	17	2	4.3	14.5	64	30.4%	.224	0.91	1.82	73	0.9
2021	SWB	AAA	25	1	0	2	18	0	26^2	18	2	2.7	13.8	41	31.6%	.291	0.97	2.36	72	0.7
2022 non-DC	*NYY*	*MLB*	*26*	*2*	*2*	*0*	*57*	*0*	*50*	*39*	*7*	*4.4*	*11.9*	*66*	*38.7%*	*.285*	*1.28*	*3.84*	*93*	*0.4*

Comparables: Zack Thornton, Giovanny Gallegos, Raynel Espinal

And here's yet another Yankees pitching prospect featuring 2021 velocity and off-speed jumps. The former Delaware Blue Hen—who didn't even get to full-season ball until his second full pro season—now pumps mid- to upper-90s heat with a plus changeup. Marinaccio obliterated the upper minors last season, and the Yanks added him to the 40-man roster. He's close enough to the majors now that he should probably start following fellow Toms River native Todd Frazier on Twitter to keep tabs on the traffic situation heading up the Garden State Parkway.

Stephen Ridings RHP Born: 08/14/95 Age: 26 Bats: R Throws: R Height: 6'8" Weight: 220 lb. Origin: Round 8, 2016 Draft (#254 overall)

YEAR	TEAM	LVL	AGE	W	L	SV	G	GS	IP	H	HR	BB/9	K/9	K	GB%	BABIP	WHIP	ERA	DRA-	WARP
2019	IDF	ROA	23	4	3	0	13	11	56^1	48	6	4.6	14.1	88	34.9%	.344	1.37	5.91		
2021	SOM	AA	25	4	0	2	14	0	19	8	0	0.9	14.2	30	37.1%	.229	0.53	0.47	84	0.3
2021	SWB	AAA	25	1	0	1	8	0	10	8	2	1.8	10.8	12	61.5%	.250	1.00	2.70	81	0.2
2021	NYY	MLB	25	0	0	0	5	0	5	4	0	3.6	12.6	7	45.5%	.400	1.20	1.80	96	0.1
2022 non-DC	*NYY*	*MLB*	*26*	*2*	*2*	*0*	*57*	*0*	*50*	*42*	*6*	*3.0*	*10.3*	*57*	*36.5%*	*.284*	*1.18*	*3.37*	*84*	*0.6*

Comparables: Arquimedes Caminero, Kam Mickolio, Ariel Hernández

Ridings is a big dude with big stuff. We often drone on in this section about 95-and-a-slider relievers. In the 2020s, those two pitches are kind of the table stakes to make a major-league bullpen. But 100 and a slider? Well, that's still going to catch our eye. Ridings sat upper 90s, touched triple digits and posted a downright-comical whiff rate on his big, diving, mid-80s slide piece during his first season as a full-time reliever. He's on the older side and dealt with an elbow issue in 2021, but, if he has no further arm pangs, Ridings could be a force in the late innings for the 2022 club.

Because You Were Going to Ask

Austin Wells C/DH Born: 07/12/99 Age: 22 Bats: L Throws: R Height: 6'2" Weight: 220 lb. Origin: Round 1, 2020 Draft (#28 overall)

YEAR	TEAM	LVL	AGE	PA	R	2B	3B	HR	RBI	BB	K	SB	CS	AVG/OBP/SLG	DRC+	BABIP	BRR	FRAA	WARP
2021	SUR	WIN	21	79	14	5	2	2	18	13	16	1	0	.344/.456/.578		.426			
2021	TAM	A	21	299	61	17	4	9	54	51	62	11	0	.258/.398/.479	122	.306	-1.6	C(47) 0.4	1.5
2021	HV	A+	21	170	21	6	1	7	22	20	55	5	0	.274/.376/.473	97	.393	0.4	C(23) 4.4	0.9
2022 non-DC	*NYY*	*MLB*	*22*	*251*	*23*	*10*	*1*	*4*	*23*	*25*	*75*	*3*	*1*	*.214/.304/.338*	*76*	*.302*	*0.2*	*C 0*	*0.4*

Comparables: Rob Brantly, Miguel Montero, Mallex Smith

The catching position and the lack of lefty power in the Yankees' lineup have been the subjects of conversation for a couple of years now, both on talk radio and on the internet equivalents of talk radio. So, when the Yanks took Wells—a left-handed batter and potential power-hitting catcher—in 2020's first round, it could have been seen as an attempt to solve two issues with one draft pick. Of course, it's never that simple; there were always defensive questions swirling around the University of Arizona backstop, and he didn't really answered them in his first professional season. He is probably athletic enough to handle first base or a corner outfield spot, but either of those options puts more pressure on his bat and makes this a more difficult big-league profile. The bat is interesting; the approach is strong, and the power is real and plays to all fields. We do have questions about his ability to consistently cover pitches above and away from his usual bat path. Wells definitely has his supporters, but there are challenges to contend with as he moves forward.

Top Talents 25 and Under (as of 4/1/2022):

1. Gleyber Torres, 2B/SS
2. Anthony Volpe, SS
3. Oswald Peraza, SS
4. Randy Vasquez, RHP
5. Luis Gil, RHP
6. Trey Sweeney, SS
7. Jasson Dominguez, OF
8. Luis Medina, RHP
9. Everson Pereira, OF
10. Ken Waldichuk, LHP

Congratulations for making it to this, the final appearance of Gleyber Torres on a 25U list. The much-debated middle infielder is a year and two months older than Adley Rutschman and will be entering his fifth big league season, still the young buck in a veteran Yankees lineup. "Volatile" would be a fair description of his performance these first few years, as Torres suffered a severe power outage in 2021, failing to eclipse the double-digit mark in home runs in 516 plate appearances two years after clubbing 38 taters in 604 PAs. Yes, it's fair to lay some culpability on the inconsistency of the baseball MLB has rouletted into games, but, as Timothy Jackson recently wrote at Baseball Prospectus, Torres has had a miserable time punishing pitchers for falling behind against him. That has coincided with his much-maligned efforts to cover the shortstop position following the departure of Didi Gregorius, an unsuccessful effort which has pushed Torres back to second base, where he's better suited. While the Yankees have promising middle infielders in the hopper, as outlined in the list above, they're surely seeking a significant external addition to ensure a swift end to their pennant drought. Surely?

Oakland Athletics

The State of the System:

The Athletics' system remains one of the shallowest in baseball despite a breakout 2020 draftee at the top.

The Top Ten:

1 Tyler Soderstrom C OFP: 60 ETA: 2024

Born: 11/24/01 Age: 20 Bats: L Throws: R Height: 6'2" Weight: 200 lb. Origin: Round 1, 2020 Draft (#26 overall)

YEAR	TEAM	LVL	AGE	PA	R	2B	3B	HR	RBI	BB	K	SB	CS	AVG/OBP/SLG	DRC+	BABIP	BRR	FRAA	WARP
2021	STK	A	19	254	39	20	1	12	49	27	61	2	1	.306/.390/.568	125	.373	-1.2	C(38) -3.6, 1B(9) -1.0	1.0
2022 non-DC	*OAK*	*MLB*	*20*	*251*	*24*	*11*	*1*	*6*	*26*	*17*	*74*	*0*	*1*	*.228/.289/.373*	*75*	*.308*	*-0.2*	*C -5, 1B -1*	*-0.4*

Comparables: Wil Myers, Francisco Mejía, Wilson Ramos

The Report: Drafted as a hit-tool-driven catcher, Soderstrom took a big step forward physically in 2021, adding quality strength and size to fill out his frame. He displays an advanced approach at the plate, consistently selecting good pitches to hit and barreling them up, and his increased physicality leads to plus power. He is still getting accustomed to advanced secondary pitches, and there will be some swing-and-miss that comes with the power, but he has shown the ability to make adjustments and projects as a 30-home-run bat.

On the defensive side of things, Soderstrom is a work in progress. His arm plays behind the dish, but his hands are below average, he has had trouble receiving premium stuff, and his ability to block balls in the dirt will come and go. The introduction of an automated strike zone would give him a chance to stick behind the plate, but given his offensive potential, it's more likely that he moves out to first base or a corner outfield spot.

OFP: 60 / First-division regular, position TBD

Variance: High. There's star upside if he can stick behind the plate, but that's a big "if," and he will really have to hit if he's limited to a corner defensively.

Darius Austin's Fantasy Take: It would be awfully fun if Soderstrom could make it to the majors with his catcher eligibility intact. We won't be able to blame the A's if they shift focus to a position that gets him 600-plus plate appearances annually and doesn't destroy his body. In all honesty, the latter might be better for fantasy, too, since it makes him more likely to reach his offensive ceiling. We're looking at a potential four-category monster at any position.

2 Nick Allen MI OFP: 55 ETA: 2022

Born: 10/08/98 Age: 23 Bats: R Throws: R Height: 5'8" Weight: 166 lb. Origin: Round 3, 2017 Draft (#81 overall)

YEAR	TEAM	LVL	AGE	PA	R	2B	3B	HR	RBI	BB	K	SB	CS	AVG/OBP/SLG	DRC+	BABIP	BRR	FRAA	WARP
2019	MSS	WIN	20	66	4	1	0	0	6	4	18	0	1	.194/.242/.210		.273			
2019	STK	A+	20	328	45	22	5	3	25	28	52	13	5	.292/.363/.434	114	.348	-3.0	SS(45) 5.2, 2B(24) -1.6	1.5
2021	MID	AA	22	229	31	9	2	6	31	18	46	8	6	.319/.374/.471	111	.381	-0.8	SS(26) -1.6, 2B(22) 3.0	1.1
2021	LV	AAA	22	151	17	8	0	0	10	11	30	4	1	.243/.302/.301	84	.308	0.8	SS(22) -2.0, 2B(14) 0.6	0.1
2022 DC	*OAK*	*MLB*	*23*	*136*	*15*	*5*	*0*	*1*	*12*	*9*	*28*	*3*	*2*	*.232/.289/.316*	*67*	*.288*	*0.3*	*SS 0*	*0.0*

Comparables: Marwin Gonzalez, Yairo Muñoz, Cristhian Adames

The Report: Allen had a fun 2021 season, which included an Olympic sojourn to win a silver medal in Tokyo. He was named the Olympic tournament's best defensive player, and he's a plus fielder at either shortstop or second base, where he has also seen substantial time up the minor-league chain. His hit tool is likely to be above average or even better, as he has hit for relatively high averages in his last two full seasons with relatively low strikeout rates, though he is not a contact outlier like Wander Franco or Nick Madrigal.

Our concerns with Allen lie more with his lack of physicality and power. His six homers in 50 games in Double-A Midland more than doubled the rest of his career total, and his power once again vanished upon his post-Olympics return to action in Triple-A. His swing is short and quick but doesn't generate much loft or high-end bat speed. He's small with limited raw power and hits the ball on the ground a lot, so there's just not a lot of projection here.

OFP: 55 / Starting middle infielder

Variance: Low. His defense and hit tool are likely to carry him to a major-league-regular outcome. His lack of power is likely to limit the upside past that.

Darius Austin's Fantasy Take: Warning: this is about to get a lot less exciting. I like Allen in the slightly irrational way one does when it feels like a guy is going to be a good ballplayer. Is this the fantasy version of the "good face"? Anyway, setting my irrational self aside for a moment, that power is a real problem. Allen should chip in some steals, but he's not a burner, and if there's a genuine possibility that he might struggle to reach double-digit homers, what you're looking at is a passable, deep-league middle infielder. The batting-average stabilization and the playing time afforded by his glove will be useful. I just doubt he's going to be more than that (but if you want to pretend with me, a good hit tool plus everyday playing time gives him the maximum opportunity to show more).

3 Zack Gelof 3B OFP: 55 ETA: 2023

Born: 10/19/99 Age: 22 Bats: R Throws: R Height: 6'3" Weight: 205 lb. Origin: Round 2, 2021 Draft (#60 overall)

YEAR	TEAM	LVL	AGE	PA	R	2B	3B	HR	RBI	BB	K	SB	CS	AVG/OBP/SLG	DRC+	BABIP	BRR	FRAA	WARP
2021	STK	A	21	145	26	8	1	7	22	19	36	11	2	.298/.393/.548	120	.366	1.5	3B(30) -6.8	0.3
2022 non-DC	*OAK*	*MLB*	*22*	*251*	*23*	*10*	*1*	*5*	*25*	*20*	*70*	*7*	*3*	*.226/.296/.355*	*78*	*.303*	*0.5*	*3B -3*	*-0.3*

Comparables: Brent Morel, Austin Riley, Paul DeJong

The Report: Gelof flashed plus raw power while at the University of Virginia, but he wasn't able to get to it frequently enough to be considered one of the top bats in his draft class. The A's plucked him in the second round, and he did nothing but hit (and hit for power) in his professional debut. His stride is a little funky, but he gets his foot down in time, displays a strong feel for the strike zone and makes consistently sound swing decisions. Refined aggression has enabled him to tap into more of his power as well, giving him 25-plus-home-run upside.

Gelof is an average athlete, though his mannerisms are a bit Hunter Pence–like and don't always look too natural. His feet can get clunky at times, but his hands and arm strength are enough to stick at third base long-term.

OFP: 55 / Solid-average everyday third baseman

Variance: Medium. Gelof lacks a true carrying tool, and the band of realistic outcomes is relatively narrow, but he offers enough to project as a well-rounded regular at third base.

Darius Austin's Fantasy Take: I told you this wasn't going to be exciting. Don't get me wrong: Gelof has the skills to be a solid third baseman or corner infielder, and his power probably gives him a more distinct fantasy tool than anything Allen possesses, unless you think Allen's going to hit for a ton of average. Batting .250 with 25 homers is also the kind of thing that Ryan McMahon does, and people mostly have interest in Ryan McMahon because of #Coors. Gelof might just be the guy you draft when you miss out on the guy you wanted.

Eyewitness Report: Zack Gelof

Evaluator: Trevor Andresen

Report Date: 09/29/2021

Dates Seen: Amateur/Pro

Risk Factor: Medium

Physical/Health: LG/XL 6'3 205 lb. frame. Well proportioned build w/ present strength

Tool	Future Grade	Report
Hit	50	SQ stance w/ a wide base & a bit of a funky stride, but gets the foot down in time to make it work. Displays solid-avg bat control & feel for the strike zone. Makes consistently sound swing decisions (intent in positive counts) & shows an ability to see/identify spin. Projecting a .250-.260 bat.
Power	55	Generates plus raw power & gets to most of it thanks to the approach/hit tool. Projecting above-avg impact. 25+ HR type.
Baserunning/ Speed	50	Avg runner w/ some athleticism, though the mannerisms are almost Hunter Pence-like.
Glove	50	The feet can get clunky at times, but the hands are solid-avg. Projects as an avg defender at the hot corner.
Arm	50	Long, funky arm action w/ avg strength & the ability to drop down & throw from different angles.

Conclusion: Gelof lacks a true carrying tool, but projects as a well-rounded solid-avg regular at 3B

4 Max Muncy SS OFP: 55 ETA: 2025

Born: 08/25/02 Age: 19 Bats: R Throws: R Height: 6'1" Weight: 180 lb. Origin: Round 1, 2021 Draft (#25 overall)

YEAR	TEAM	LVL	AGE	PA	R	2B	3B	HR	RBI	BB	K	SB	CS	AVG/OBP/SLG	DRC+	BABIP	BRR	FRAA	WARP
2021	ATH	ROK	18	34	3	0	0	0	4	3	12	1	0	.129/.206/.129		.211			

The Report: Like that Logan Allen, this Max Muncy will have to do some work to be the top result in his own Baseball-Reference searches, but the first-round prep shortstop has a broad base of tools that should at least get his name in bold text in a few years. Muncy's swing can get long, but he shows above-average bat speed and an advanced approach for a high-school hitter—all in all, the hit tool should play solid-average. He only shows average raw power, at present, but might grow into a bit more as he has room to add strength on his frame. Muncy's infield actions are good enough for an up-the-middle spot, but his footwork and range suggest he will slide over to third base in the medium term. There, his arm strength will be fine, but not a weapon. A corner-infield defensive profile puts a ceiling on his profile given that neither offensive tool projects past a 55, but Muncy does everything well enough to eventually carve out an everyday lineup spot.

OFP: 55 / Better-than-the-sum-of-his-parts third baseman

Variance: High. Muncy has no real professional track record yet and lacks a carrying tool.

Darius Austin's Fantasy Take: Do you remember the fun we used to have nominating the other Ryan Braun in auctions? (I may be showing my age. Should have picked the other Wander Francos instead.) Muncy will thus offer some entertainment in redraft leagues for a few years, before he's on most radars for anything else, but he should also be more relevant than reliever Ryan Braun. While Muncy can do a little of everything we care about in fantasy, it's—you guessed it—not the most thrilling profile. Then again, neither was Max Muncy's for a long time. You know, the other one.

5 Pedro Pineda CF OFP: 50 ETA: 2025/2026

Born: 09/06/03 Age: 18 Bats: R Throws: R Height: 6'1" Weight: 170 lb. Origin: International Free Agent, 2021

YEAR	TEAM	LVL	AGE	PA	R	2B	3B	HR	RBI	BB	K	SB	CS	AVG/OBP/SLG	DRC+	BABIP	BRR	FRAA	WARP
2021	DSL ATH	ROK	17	40	4	1	1	0	1	5	13	3	2	.200/.300/.286		.318			
2021	ATH	ROK	17	77	15	2	2	1	8	13	28	3	3	.258/.403/.403		.455			

Comparables: Luis Carlos Diaz, D'Shawn Knowles, Arturo Guerrero

The Report: The top prospect in Oakland's January 15 class last year, Pineda came stateside quickly and got a few weeks worth of at-bats in the complex. He was overmatched and chased too much but is already capable of stinging a baseball at a major-league level despite having the frame of . . . well, a 17-year-old baseball player. Pineda is projectable and should add significant upper-body strength with more time in a pro development program. He's an above-average runner, but that might not last, so the same goes for his center-field projection. He may be number-one on this list in a couple years, or not on it at all.

OFP: 50 / Starting outfielder

Variance: Extreme. Pineda's variance is akin to Travis Pastrana's double backflip in Moto X.

Darius Austin's Fantasy Take: Ah, some excitement! That there were three players between Soderstrom and Pineda on this list tells you there's no small amount of risk to go with it. That you'll have to flip to the end of this chapter to find Robert Puason also highlights how quickly a talented-but-raw, big-money international signee can plummet. If you were making an upside-only A's list, Pineda probably would be second. Holding onto his speed while adding the projected strength and developing a decent approach would put Pineda in five-category territory. It's not easy to land that backflip.

6 A.J. Puk LHP OFP: 50 ETA: Debuted in 2019

Born: 04/25/95 Age: 27 Bats: L Throws: L Height: 6'7" Weight: 248 lb. Origin: Round 1, 2016 Draft (#6 overall)

YEAR	TEAM	LVL	AGE	W	L	SV	G	GS	IP	H	HR	BB/9	K/9	K	GB%	BABIP	WHIP	ERA	DRA-	WARP
2019	STK	A+	24	0	0	0	3	3	6	5	2	6.0	13.5	9	33.3%	.300	1.50	6.00	110	0.0
2019	MID	AA	24	0	0	0	6	1	8^1	9	2	3.2	14.0	13	57.9%	.412	1.44	4.32	80	0.1
2019	LV	AAA	24	4	1	0	9	0	11	7	3	2.5	13.1	16	41.7%	.190	0.91	4.91	78	0.2
2019	OAK	MLB	24	2	0	0	10	0	11^1	10	1	4.0	10.3	13	44.8%	.321	1.32	3.18	98	0.1
2021	LV	AAA	26	2	5	1	29	4	48^2	61	12	3.5	10.7	58	39.5%	.363	1.64	6.10	91	0.4
2021	OAK	MLB	26	0	3	0	12	0	13^1	18	1	4.0	10.8	16	52.4%	.415	1.80	6.07	96	0.1
2022 DC	*OAK*	*MLB*	*27*	*2*	*2*	*4*	*44*	*0*	*38.7*	*36*	*5*	*3.7*	*9.5*	*41*	*35.0%*	*.295*	*1.34*	*4.05*	*102*	*0.1*

Comparables: Troy Cate, Scott Alexander, Jonathan Holder

The Report: Puk turns 27 in late April, his entire MLB experience consists of 22 bad relief outings, and he has severe health concerns, so it's a testament to his arm talent and our priors that he's even still on here. Let's start with the good: he still sits in the mid-to-high 90s in some outings, and he can throw a distinct, high-rising fastball and diving sinker. His slider remains a true out-pitch with which he can bury lefties and back-foot righties. The stuff has risen and fallen based on whether he's healthy or not, but he had it all the way back at times in 2021.

The major questions for the tall lefty are medical and role-based. He missed all of 2018 and some of 2019 after Tommy John surgery, all of 2020 after shoulder surgery, and parts of 2021 with bicep problems. He ended up pitching 62 innings last year without ever throwing more than four innings or 65 pitches in an appearance, and he wasn't particularly effective in Triple-A or the majors. By the end of the season, Oakland treated him as an up-and-down relief arm. He needs to improve his durability, consistency and command to return to regular starting work, and the sand is running thin in the hourglass. But it's not totally gone yet.

OFP: 50 / High-leverage reliever

Variance: Extreme. Puk was one of the top pitching prospects in baseball just two years ago, when he seemed fully back from Tommy John, and the stuff is still there. While his 75th-percentile outcome might only be high-leverage relief now, his 85th or 90th still looks like a front-of-the-rotation starter, because you can't teach high 90s with that slider.

Darius Austin's Fantasy Take: I don't mind using a roster spot on Puk for another season, since acquiring him should cost almost nothing, and, if there's still a glimmer of front-line upside, you take it. If next season offers no positive signs, however, that faint hope is probably extinguished—and it's extremely faint in the first place. It's more likely that he becomes a high-strikeout reliever, and even more likely that he remains maddeningly inconsistent and bounces back and forth until his options are exhausted.

7 Colin Peluse RHP OFP: 50 ETA: Late 2022/Early 2023

Born: 06/11/98 Age: 24 Bats: R Throws: R Height: 6'3" Weight: 230 lb. Origin: Round 9, 2019 Draft (#284 overall)

YEAR	TEAM	LVL	AGE	W	L	SV	G	GS	IP	H	HR	BB/9	K/9	K	GB%	BABIP	WHIP	ERA	DRA-	WARP
2019	VER	SS	21	2	1	0	8	5	24	21	1	2.3	9.7	26	50.7%	.303	1.13	2.25		
2021	LAN	A+	23	7	3	0	18	15	86	82	10	2.3	9.6	92	36.2%	.314	1.21	3.66	105	0.6
2021	MID	AA	23	2	0	0	3	3	15	9	1	2.4	10.2	17	22.2%	.229	0.87	1.80	98	0.1
2022 non-DC	*OAK*	*MLB*	*24*	*2*	*3*	*0*	*57*	*0*	*50*	*52*	*8*	*3.3*	*7.4*	*40*	*29.4%*	*.295*	*1.42*	*5.09*	*122*	*-0.4*

Comparables: Dillon Peters, Gabriel Ynoa, Trent Thornton

The Report: Last year we wrote that, "Peluse should move fast if the instructs performance carries over." One hundred solid innings later, he finished the 2021 season in Double-A having posted a 26 percent strikeout rate. His process was pretty simple: get ahead with an above-average fastball that regularly pops 95, and then get batters to swing over his mid-80s slider. The slide piece is not a true plus bat-misser, mostly due to inconsistency in its shape and command, but the better ones flash plus two-plane action. Peluse looks the part of a starting pitcher, but the delivery is up-tempo with a glove tap, and he doesn't always repeat everything as well as you'd like. There's not really a third pitch here either, and while we are certainly relaxing our standards for starting-pitching prospects, Peluse's top two offerings aren't the kind of dominant duo that make a starter on their own.

OFP: 50 / No. 4 starter or seventh-inning arm

Variance: Medium. The stuff is advanced enough that we don't foresee too many speed bumps in the minors, but there isn't quite enough to project impact in the majors, either.

Darius Austin's Fantasy Take: If Peluse's slider was nastier, one could imagine him being the latest Huascar Ynoa and dominating with two pitches. Since he lacks both that elite offering and a third pitch, I don't see the fantasy upside. Monitor the development of both, but otherwise wait and see if he's a worthy streamer when he arrives.

8 Jeff Criswell RHP OFP: 50 ETA: Late 2023

Born: 03/10/99 Age: 23 Bats: R Throws: R Height: 6'4" Weight: 225 lb. Origin: Round 2, 2020 Draft (#58 overall)

YEAR	TEAM	LVL	AGE	W	L	SV	G	GS	IP	H	HR	BB/9	K/9	K	GB%	BABIP	WHIP	ERA	DRA-	WARP
2021	LAN	A+	22	0	0	0	5	5	12	9	1	3.0	9.0	12	54.5%	.250	1.08	4.50	95	0.2
2022 non-DC	*OAK*	*MLB*	*23*	*2*	*3*	*0*	*57*	*0*	*50*	*53*	*7*	*4.6*	*7.0*	*39*	*39.2%*	*.304*	*1.59*	*5.57*	*126*	*-0.5*

Comparables: Jake Newberry, Reynaldo López, Frankie Rodriguez

The Report: Criswell only threw 12 innings in the 2021 minor-league season. He missed three months with an unspecified injury and struggled with his command and secondaries in his brief late-season return. His fastball velocity was down a tick, as well, although it still sat in the above-average range. His slider has been a potential plus pitch in the recent past, but he had a fairly scattershot feel for both that and the changeup. It was more a lost season for developmental purposes than anything damning to the long-term projection, but given that his delivery already had reliever markers, it might accelerate a move to the pen.

OFP: 50 / No. 4 starter or seventh-inning arm

Variance: Medium. Criswell hasn't had a regular, full season of reps since his sophomore year with Michigan, which makes things murky.

Darius Austin's Fantasy Take: Reliever indicators plus a lost season is not the stuff that dynasty dreams are made of. If Criswell gets back in the rotation every fifth day and resumes throwing strikes the way he apparently was in 2020, you can start to think about rostering him.

9 Brayan Buelvas OF OFP: 45 ETA: Late 2024 or 2025

Born: 06/08/02 Age: 20 Bats: R Throws: R Height: 5'11" Weight: 155 lb. Origin: International Free Agent, 2018

YEAR	TEAM	LVL	AGE	PA	R	2B	3B	HR	RBI	BB	K	SB	CS	AVG/OBP/SLG	DRC+	BABIP	BRR	FRAA	WARP
2019	DSL ATH	ROK	17	88	4	5	1	0	14	8	14	4	4	.244/.330/.333		.297			
2019	ASGR	ROK	17	186	26	10	7	3	27	22	46	12	5	.300/.392/.506		.402			
2021	STK	A	19	392	54	11	4	16	50	37	95	17	7	.219/.306/.412	106	.253	-3.4	LF(32) -1.8, CF(32) -2.4, RF(23) -1.0	0.9
2022 non-DC	*OAK*	*MLB*	*20*	*251*	*21*	*9*	*1*	*5*	*23*	*16*	*71*	*8*	*5*	*.203/.265/.325*	*58*	*.270*	*1.0*	*CF 0, LF 0*	*-0.4*

Comparables: Dilson Herrera, Delino DeShields, Victor Robles

The Report: A buzzy name from the alternate site and instructs in 2020, the 19-year-old Buelvas generally kept his head above water during a somewhat-aggressive Low-A assignment in 2021. He has grown into more over-the-fence pop but is too often a mistake hitter who is overmatched by anything off-speed. He's a plus runner to go with the plus raw power and has a shot to stick in center field, but his pitch recognition and swing decisions will have to improve as he moves up the organizational ladder. His power/speed combo and ability to play all three outfield spots make him an ideal bench outfielder, even if the bat doesn't play fully to projection, but these kind of approach issues can also cause a prospect to stall out in the upper minors.

OFP: 45 / Good fourth outfielder or fringe starter

Variance: High. Buelvas has the tool set to be an everyday outfielder, but his issues with anything that isn't a fastball will limit his hit-tool projection unless here is marked improvement.

Darius Austin's Fantasy Take: This is a long time to wait for a player who might be sitting just to the right side of starting caliber, at best. The skill set is appealing if Buelvas can get the power and speed into games, but you're probably not going to know whether he will have a decent chance of doing that until he has a decent sample at Double-A, at least. It's fine to file Buelvas away on the watchlist for a while.

10 Lawrence Butler 1B OFP: 45 ETA: 2024

Born: 07/10/00 Age: 21 Bats: L Throws: R Height: 6'3" Weight: 210 lb. Origin: Round 6, 2018 Draft (#173 overall)

YEAR	TEAM	LVL	AGE	PA	R	2B	3B	HR	RBI	BB	K	SB	CS	AVG/OBP/SLG	DRC+	BABIP	BRR	FRAA	WARP
2019	VER	SS	18	221	20	5	2	4	22	26	90	1	0	.177/.276/.286		.300			
2021	STK	A	20	396	62	20	4	17	67	55	131	26	4	.263/.364/.499	104	.370	0.6	1B(47) -2.3, LF(25) 0.1, CF(11) 0.2	1.2
2021	LAN	A+	20	54	14	4	0	2	8	4	15	3	1	.340/.389/.540	95	.455	-0.5	1B(6) 2.0, RF(6) -0.6, CF(1) 0.2	0.2
2022 non-DC	*OAK*	*MLB*	*21*	*251*	*23*	*10*	*1*	*6*	*25*	*22*	*90*	*6*	*2*	*.208/.281/.346*	*67*	*.314*	*0.5*	*1B 0, LF 0*	*-0.3*

The Report: Standing at 6-foot-3 and 210 pounds with a tapered build, Butler certainly looks the part. There's rhythm and looseness to his swing, and his frame enables him to generate easy plus power to all fields. He handles velocity well and can punish mistake breaking balls, but he can get beat with quality secondaries, especially when behind in the count. There is 30-home-run potential here, but it will likely come with batting averages in the .230–.240 range. He's athletic enough to handle a corner-outfield spot, at least on a part-time basis, but fits most comfortably at first base.

OFP: 45 / Strong side of a 1B/LF platoon or power bench bat

Variance: High. There's significant risk/variance given the hit tool and where he falls on the defensive spectrum, but there should be enough juice for a major-league contribution of some sort.

Darius Austin's Fantasy Take: Power-first, corner outfield or first base, could potentially put a big dent in your average . . . yeah, I can see Butler doing a reasonable Seth Brown impression for the A's in a few years' time. If you're in the kind of league where it was justifiable to roster Seth Brown before this season, go ahead. Otherwise, it's another wait and see: if he hits .240 and at least starts against every righty, there's a pretty functional fantasy profile here. Most leagues don't warrant rostering likely part-timers this far in advance.

The Prospects You Meet Outside the Top Ten

Prospects on the Rise

Denzel Clarke OF Born: 05/01/00 Age: 22 Bats: R Throws: R Height: 6'5" Weight: 220 lb. Origin: Round 4, 2021 Draft (#127 overall)

A Canadian prep outfielder who starred at Cal State Northridge, Clarke has an impressive potential power/speed combo and a pretty swing, but there are questions about his hit tool and pitch recognition that will have to be answered in the pros. If you want to heavily weight upside, Clarke's isn't that far off names high up in the Athletics' top 10.

CJ Rodriguez C Born: 07/07/00 Age: 21 Bats: R Throws: R Height: 5'10" Weight: 200 lb. Origin: Round 5, 2021 Draft (#158 overall)

YEAR	TEAM	LVL	AGE	PA	R	2B	3B	HR	RBI	BB	K	SB	CS	AVG/OBP/SLG	DRC+	BABIP	BRR	FRAA	WARP
2021	STK	A	20	86	5	2	0	1	4	4	13	0	0	.160/.198/.222	104	.176	-0.1	C(20) 1.4	0.4
2022 non-DC	*OAK*	*MLB*	*21*	*251*	*19*	*9*	*1*	*2*	*20*	*13*	*57*	*0*	*1*	*.220/.267/.304*	*56*	*.281*	*-0.2*	*C -1*	*-0.4*

Oakland's fifth-round pick from last year got off to a slow professional start, but that can mostly be chalked up to a long season and a lot of games behind the plate, as the approach and swing looked fine, even if the results weren't there. It's a glove first profile, but Rodriguez should hit enough to be a good backup or fringe regular.

Factrs on the Farm

Luis Barrera OF Born: 11/15/95 Age: 26 Bats: L Throws: L Height: 6'0" Weight: 195 lb. Origin: International Free Agent, 2012

YEAR	TEAM	LVL	AGE	PA	R	2B	3B	HR	RBI	BB	K	SB	CS	AVG/OBP/SLG	DRC+	BABIP	BRR	FRAA	WARP
2019	MID	AA	23	240	35	9	11	4	24	12	48	9	7	.321/.357/.513	121	.393	-0.2	CF(36) -5.8, RF(14) 2.9, LF(1) -0.1	1.1
2021	LV	AAA	25	386	53	16	6	4	37	39	67	10	2	.276/.348/.393	92	.328	3.7	CF(37) -3.6, RF(33) -0.6, LF(28) -3.2	0.5
2021	OAK	MLB	25	8	1	0	0	0	0	0	2	0	0	.250/.250/.250	84	.333	0.2	LF(2) -0.2, RF(2) -0.1, CF(1) 0.0	0.0
2022 DC	*OAK*	*MLB*	*26*	*155*	*16*	*6*	*2*	*1*	*16*	*11*	*33*	*3*	*2*	*.244/.302/.351*	*77*	*.308*	*0.5*	*CF 0, LF -1*	*0.1*

Comparables: Lorenzo Cain, Scott Van Slyke, Ezequiel Carrera

Barrera has felt like a Factor on the Farm type for his entire minor-league career. He's built like Clyde Wynant, and most of his slugging will come from triples he slashes into the gap. He can fly on the bases or the grass, which gives him the flexibility to play any outfield spot. The lack of any real power limits Barrera to a bench role, but his speed and glove make him a useful extra outfielder.

Daulton Jefferies RHP Born: 08/02/95 Age: 26 Bats: L Throws: R Height: 6'0" Weight: 182 lb. Origin: Round 1, 2016 Draft (#37 overall)

YEAR	TEAM	LVL	AGE	W	L	SV	G	GS	IP	H	HR	BB/9	K/9	K	GB%	BABIP	WHIP	ERA	DRA-	WARP
2019	STK	A+	23	1	0	0	5	3	15	10	1	1.2	12.6	21	44.1%	.273	0.80	2.40	76	0.2
2019	MID	AA	23	1	2	0	21	12	64	63	7	1.0	10.1	72	41.0%	.329	1.09	3.66	71	1.2
2020	OAK	MLB	24	0	1	0	1	1	2	5	2	9.0	4.5	1	30.0%	.375	3.50	22.50	133	0.0
2021	LV	AAA	25	5	1	0	15	15	77	90	13	1.3	7.9	68	42.4%	.326	1.31	4.91	103	0.2
2021	OAK	MLB	25	1	0	0	5	1	15	11	1	2.4	4.8	8	44.4%	.227	1.00	3.60	124	-0.1
2022 DC	*OAK*	*MLB*	*26*	*6*	*5*	*0*	*40*	*12*	*86.3*	*89*	*11*	*2.0*	*6.3*	*60*	*55.1%*	*.288*	*1.26*	*4.00*	*105*	*0.3*

Comparables: Aaron Slegers, Mitch Talbot, Luis Mendoza

Jeffries' 92 innings in 2021 were a professional high, and they were effective innings, to boot. His season did end with an elbow-nerve issue, so the future health/durability/role continues to be a bit opaque. Jeffries works primarily off a 93-ish mph sinker he can throw for good strikes but shows more run than sink. His power change has both fade and sink and works well off the fastball, and a curveball gives him an average right-on-right option, although it can have more sweep than depth. If we thought he could ever stay healthy for a season, he'd be in the top 10 as an average-starter/bulk type, given the advanced command of an average arsenal, but he's 26, and those 92 innings are a professional high.

Because You Were Going to Ask

Austin Beck OF Born: 11/21/98 Age: 23 Bats: R Throws: R Height: 6'1" Weight: 200 lb. Origin: Round 1, 2017 Draft (#6 overall)

YEAR	TEAM	LVL	AGE	PA	R	2B	3B	HR	RBI	BB	K	SB	CS	AVG/OBP/SLG	DRC+	BABIP	BRR	FRAA	WARP
2019	STK	A+	20	367	40	22	4	8	49	24	126	2	2	.251/.302/.411	72	.372	0.1	CF(69) 0.0, RF(10) 2.8	0.3
2021	MSS	WIN	22	60	9	2	0	0	9	5	23	1	1	.170/.233/.208		.281			
2021	LAN	A+	22	269	20	12	2	7	33	15	91	3	1	.202/.253/.351	73	.281	-0.3	CF(37) -6.4, RF(15) -0.8, LF(9) 0.4	-0.6
2022 non-DC	*OAK*	*MLB*	*23*	*251*	*19*	*11*	*1*	*4*	*22*	*13*	*89*	*1*	*2*	*.197/.245/.311*	*44*	*.297*	*0.0*	*CF -1, RF 0*	*-1.0*

Beck has just never made enough contact as a pro to let his plus raw power play in games. He dealt with injuries in both 2019 and 2021, but he's 23 and coming off a season in which he posted a 34-percent K rate in High-A. He has a long and lofted swing that is too often late on average velocity, and he hasn't grown as much into his lean frame as you'd have expected back on draft day. The flipside of that is Beck's still an above-average runner with a shot to stick in center field, but none of that really comes into play until and unless he hits.

Robert Puason SS Born: 09/11/02 Age: 19 Bats: S Throws: R Height: 6'3" Weight: 165 lb. Origin: International Free Agent, 2019

YEAR	TEAM	LVL	AGE	PA	R	2B	3B	HR	RBI	BB	K	SB	CS	AVG/OBP/SLG	DRC+	BABIP	BRR	FRAA	WARP
2021	STK	A	18	337	43	12	1	3	27	24	139	3	1	.215/.282/.291	55	.383	2.2	SS(91) -0.7	-0.7
2022 non-DC	*OAK*	*MLB*	*19*	*251*	*16*	*9*	*0*	*2*	*17*	*13*	*115*	*0*	*1*	*.171/.224/.245*	*22*	*.323*	*-0.2*	*SS 0*	*-1.7*

Comparables: Wander Franco, Fernando Tatis Jr., Ruddy Giron

Quite simply, Puason got bullied as a physically immature 18-year-old in Low-A last year. He lacks the physicality to impact the baseball, and his swing-happy approach and questionable pitch-recognition ability result in consistently poor swing decisions and a significant amount of swing-and-miss. His raw power is likely is likely to jump two, maybe three full grades as he continues to fill out, theoretically enabling him to make a higher quality of contact, but he'll still need to improve his ability to barrel the baseball for that to matter.

Puason's plus arm plays at shortstop, but his hands and actions are inconsistent in games, and his glove likely plays more average to slightly above than something that can truly carry the profile. Puason played all but a handful of games as an 18-year old last year, so the performance does have to be taken with a grain of salt, but it will take a significant amount of development for him to even project as a utility bench piece.

Top Talents 25 and Under (as of 4/1/2022):

1. Tyler Soderstrom, C/1B/DH
2. Nick Allen, SS
3. Zack Gelof, 3B
4. Max Muncy, SS
5. Pedro Pineda, OF
6. A.J. Puk, LHP
7. Colin Peluse, RHP
8. Jeff Criswell, RHP
9. Brayan Buelvas, OF
10. Lawrence Butler, OF/1B

The Athletics of the past few years have had a core that would be the envy of all but a handful of clubs, but their pinchpenny ways ensured that Matt Olson, Matt Chapman and Mark "Matt" Canha would make their departures from The Bay before payrolls increased. That's a shame for Oakland fans, who were treated to a genuine force of a club and several exceptional players for most of the past few years. Oakland's entire roster, and, frankly, the organizational depth writ large, is older than might be expected. None of their current non-prospect 40-man players will be under the age of 26 by Opening Day, though that could easily change with some post-lockout trades.

Philadelphia Phillies

The State of the System:

The Phillies' system is awash in high-upside arms and bats, but the floor is lava.

The Top Ten:

1 **Mick Abel RHP** OFP: 60 ETA: Late 2024 or 2025

Born: 08/18/01 Age: 20 Bats: R Throws: R Height: 6'5" Weight: 190 lb. Origin: Round 1, 2020 Draft (#15 overall)

YEAR	TEAM	LVL	AGE	W	L	SV	G	GS	IP	H	HR	BB/9	K/9	K	GB%	BABIP	WHIP	ERA	DRA-	WARP
2021	CLR	A	19	1	3	0	14	14	44^2	27	5	5.4	13.3	66	40.0%	.259	1.21	4.43	78	1.0
2022 non-DC	*PHI*	*MLB*	*20*	*2*	*3*	*0*	*57*	*0*	*50*	*47*	*8*	*6.2*	*9.3*	*51*	*41.2%*	*.291*	*1.62*	*5.64*	*126*	*-0.5*

Comparables: Luis Ortiz, Todd Van Poppel, Scott Kazmir

The Report: The top prep arm in the 2020 draft had a bit of an uneven pro debut, but his stuff was exactly as advertised. Abel's fastball sat mid-90s, with more in the tank on occasion, and featured a plus-flashing slider along with a developing curve and change to round out the repertoire. He could end up with something like a 70/60/50/50 pitch mix, and, if the command gets to above-average, that's a front-line arm. Abel has a sturdy frame and a good delivery already, with more room to fill out in his twenties. The Phillies managed the 19-year-old's workload conservatively, giving him extra rest and slowly ramping up his pitch count. Nevertheless, he dealt with a minor shoulder injury that truncated his season further. This shouldn't be a long-term issue, but Abel will need to prove he can hold up for something approaching a full prospect workload in the coming seasons. There's plenty of runway for him to do that still, and we likely haven't seen the best yet.

OFP: 60 / No. 3 starter

Variance: High. There's an alternate scenario in which Abel doesn't get hurt, gets stretched out more, runs off six or seven dominant Low-A starts to end the season and is one of the five or so best pitching prospects in baseball. That didn't happen. What actually happened is he threw 40 innings and got hurt. So, yeah, he's high variance—for both good and for ill—going forward.

Darius Austin's Fantasy Take: Abel is unquestionably . . . able to be a fantasy anchor from a talent perspective. The lead time is lengthy, though, and the potential variance in his fantasy standing might be even greater than his real-life uncertainty. The shoulder issue and his distance from the majors make him a better target for teams that can afford to be patient. I'm also not convinced his strikeout potential is all that impressive as long as his heater is comfortably his best pitch, and that really does put a lot of pressure on him generating volume.

2 **Andrew Painter RHP** OFP: 55 ETA: 2025/2026

Born: 04/10/03 Age: 19 Bats: R Throws: R Height: 6'7" Weight: 215 lb. Origin: Round 1, 2021 Draft (#13 overall)

YEAR	TEAM	LVL	AGE	W	L	SV	G	GS	IP	H	HR	BB/9	K/9	K	GB%	BABIP	WHIP	ERA	DRA-	WARP
2021	PHI	ROK	18	0	0	0	4	4	6	4	0	0.0	18.0	12	88.9%	.444	0.67	0.00		

The Report: The Phillies came back for another projectable prep righty in the 2021 draft. Painter is even bigger than Abel, standing 6-foot-8 with plenty of present strength and future projection. He sits in the mid-90s with his fastball and touched 100 in instructs and has easy and relatively clean mechanics given his size. The heater can run a little true, but given how tall Painter is—and how tall he stays through his delivery—he still gets decent plane on the pitch despite a three-quarters slot. His breaking ball is somewhere between a slider and curve, but slurvy seems like too much of a pejorative, although he can struggle to command the pitch at times. The rest of the arsenal, past the fastball, isn't as advanced as Abel's—and he will futz around with a wider variety of offerings and delivery timings—but Painter is also a year behind Abel developmentally.

OFP: 55 / No. 3–4 starter

Variance: High. Well, Painter hasn't had an arm injury, but he is a recent prep pick with limited pro experience and is a projection/development bet for everything past the fastball. There's a front-of-the-rotation outcome here, as well, though. So, yeah, he's high variance—for both good and for ill—going forward.

Darius Austin's Fantasy Take: If you can't afford to wait for Abel, Painter isn't helping you much. The picture is all a little fuzzier, but I wouldn't be surprised if he ends up becoming the more coveted fantasy arm on the basis of strikeout potential. That still requires some significant arsenal development and enough nominative determinism to make sure the fastball doesn't get torched by advanced hitters. We're probably not going to find out for a half-decade.

3 Bryson Stott IF   OFP: 55   ETA: 2022, as needed

Born: 10/06/97 Age: 24 Bats: L Throws: R Height: 6'3" Weight: 200 lb. Origin: Round 1, 2019 Draft (#14 overall)

YEAR	TEAM	LVL	AGE	PA	R	2B	3B	HR	RBI	BB	K	SB	CS	AVG/OBP/SLG	DRC+	BABIP	BRR	FRAA	WARP
2019	PHE	ROK	21	11	3	1	1	1	3	2	0	0	0	.667/.727/1.333		.625			
2019	WIL	SS	21	182	27	8	2	5	24	22	39	5	3	.274/.370/.446		.336			
2021	PEJ	WIN	23	119	20	7	1	2	31	24	14	5	3	.318/.445/.489		.333			
2021	JS	A+	23	95	18	4	0	5	10	22	22	3	2	.288/.453/.548	134	.348	1.5	SS(16) -0.0, 2B(6) 0.1	0.8
2021	REA	AA	23	351	49	22	2	10	36	35	78	6	2	.301/.368/.481	109	.368	1.9	SS(71) -3.5, 3B(5) 1.5, 2B(4) 1.0	1.6
2021	LHV	AAA	23	41	4	0	0	1	3	8	8	1	0	.303/.439/.394	111	.375	1.4	SS(10) -2.4	0.1
2022 DC	*PHI*	*MLB*	*24*	*99*	*12*	*4*	*0*	*1*	*10*	*9*	*24*	*0*	*1*	*.240/.319/.361*	*86*	*.312*	*0.0*	*SS -1*	*0.1*

Comparables: JT Riddle, Jed Lowrie, Danny Espinosa

The Report: The strength of this Phillies system—as much as there is one—is the potential for high-end, tools-based outcomes. Stott, on the other hand, is more of a Steady Eddie. But everywhere he's gone, from the Mountain West Conference all the way up to Triple-A, he has hit. Now, it's not a bad tool chest. There just aren't a lot of bells and whistles. It's four drawers, matte gray, but no assembly required. Nothing here is clearly plus. Nothing here is below average. Stott is a patient hitter who works the opposing pitcher before unleashing a pretty—and pretty effective—left-handed swing. He often gets deep enough in counts that he can be susceptible to better offspeed, but he should end up a solid-average hitter. The raw power is solid to average, as well, although he doesn't consistently get it into games due to more of a gap-to-gap approach. Stott's athletic tools are average, and the arm is a better fit for second base, but he makes enough plays at shortstop that he can remain an option there for now. He is best deployed all over the infield, and his defensive flexibility, along with his potential for an above-average bat, makes him a productive and reliable piece of any organization.

OFP: 55 / Above-average infielder

Variance: Low. The hit tool doesn't come with a lifetime warranty like the tool chest, but Stott should be a useful regular for a good long while.

Darius Austin's Fantasy Take: For those who need their impact served almost immediately, Stott fits the bill far better. Yes, "impact" might be overselling things. Stott is fairly close to being the type of multi-positional infield option who is useful unless your league is too shallow to afford rostering someone without truly plus contributions in any category. It's too soon to anoint him the next Josh Rojas, but I'm getting that kind of vibe.

Eyewitness Report: Bryson Stott

Evaluator: Trevor Andresen
Report Date: 11/16/2021
Dates Seen: 11/8 - 11/13 (Arizona Fall League)
Risk Factor: Medium
Physical/Health: LG/XL 6'3" 200 lb. frame. Average, well-proportioned build

Tool	Future Grade	Report
Hit	55	Open, upright stance w/ a toe-tap load. Loose, easy left-handed stroke capable of working gap-gap. Above-average bat control w/ a strong feel for the strike zone. Puts together consistent, high quality at-bats & isn't afraid to work deep counts, though he can get passive at times & the frequency of 2-strike counts leaves him susceptible to some swing-and-miss on quality spin/offpseed
Power	50	Generates solid to above-average raw power and has started to tap into it more in-game Continued refinements in pitch selection (being selectively aggressive in positive counts) should lead to 20 HR power
Baserunning/ Speed	50	Solid-avg runner. Consistent 4.16-4.22 run times
Glove	50	Athleticism plays on the dirt. Average lateral range, but comes in on the ball nicely. Fluid actions w/ consistent hands. Average defender w/ strong instincts who will dominate the routine play
Arm	50	Average raw strength w/ a long arm action. Accurate. Instincts help it play at SS

Conclusion: While Stott lacks a true carrying tool, he is a well-rounded player & projects as an above-avg regular at a premium position

4 **Griff McGarry RHP** OFP: 55 ETA: Late 2023

Born: 06/08/99 Age: 23 Bats: R Throws: R Height: 6'2" Weight: 190 lb. Origin: Round 5, 2021 Draft (#145 overall)

YEAR	TEAM	LVL	AGE	W	L	SV	G	GS	IP	H	HR	BB/9	K/9	K	GB%	BABIP	WHIP	ERA	DRA-	WARP
2021	CLR	A	22	0	0	1	5	1	11	6	0	5.7	18.0	22	52.9%	.353	1.18	3.27	84	0.2
2021	JS	A+	22	1	0	0	3	3	13^{1}	7	0	4.7	14.2	21	34.6%	.269	1.05	2.70	98	0.1
2022 non-DC	*PHI*	*MLB*	*23*	*2*	*3*	*0*	*57*	*0*	*50*	*43*	*7*	*6.1*	*11.5*	*64*	*40.8%*	*.307*	*1.56*	*5.09*	*113*	*-0.2*

The Report: Now back to your regularly scheduled high-upside arms. This one is a . . . uh . . . hmm . . . let me double check my notes. Yeah, okay. This one is a fifth-round college senior who didn't post a BB/9 under eight in four years at the University of Virginia. So, not your traditional projectable prep pitcher or major college performer. Something changed for McGarry in his pro debut, though. Okay, the walk rate was still pretty high, but it was more manageable given the bat-missing stuff he showed. His fastball sat in the mid-90s, touching higher. He utilized both a four-seam and two-seam, and the two-seam can move—and be used—like a changeup (although he flashed a proper change, as well). McGarry throws two different breaking balls, with the curve ahead of the slider at this point, showing plus potential with sharp, two-plane break. Given his short track record of even fringy control and command, his profile contains a lot of reliever risk. However, like the top two arms on the Phillies' list, there is a very plausible high-end outcome with McGarry. You just have to squint a little harder.

OFP: 55 / No. 3–4 starter or late-inning reliever

Variance: High. Limited pro track record. Limited strike-throwing track record.

Darius Austin's Fantasy Take: I'll say one thing for this list: if you're rostering players based on pitching upside, alone, you're in heaven. McGarry is older and college experienced, so we shouldn't have to wait so long to find out if he's a reliever, and that upside, alone, might be enough to make him your last pick in first-year player drafts in 400-plus-prospect leagues. Then you can drop him after a month if he goes back to his college walk rates.

5 **Johan Rojas CF** OFP: 55 ETA: 2024

Born: 08/14/00 Age: 21 Bats: R Throws: R Height: 6'1" Weight: 165 lb. Origin: International Free Agent, 2018

YEAR	TEAM	LVL	AGE	PA	R	2B	3B	HR	RBI	BB	K	SB	CS	AVG/OBP/SLG	DRC+	BABIP	BRR	FRAA	WARP
2019	PHW	ROK	18	84	13	6	5	0	4	9	12	3	2	.311/.393/.527		.371			
2019	WIL	SS	18	172	17	5	6	2	11	5	29	11	4	.244/.273/.384		.284			
2021	CLR	A	20	351	51	15	3	7	38	26	69	25	6	.240/.305/.374	100	.283	3.4	CF(66) 11.1, RF(10) -0.7, LF(1) 0.5	2.6
2021	JS	A+	20	74	16	3	1	3	11	7	8	8	3	.344/.419/.563	139	.352	2.5	CF(14) 2.8, LF(2) -0.3, RF(1) -0.0	1.1
2022 non-DC	*PHI*	*MLB*	*21*	*251*	*21*	*10*	*1*	*3*	*22*	*14*	*56*	*11*	*5*	*.233/.284/.340*	*69*	*.291*	*1.2*	*CF 3, RF 0*	*0.4*

Comparables: Victor Robles, Manuel Margot, Albert Almora Jr.

The Report: "Can Johan Rojas Hit"—the greatest thread in the history of BP Slack, locked by Craig Goldstein after 12,239 comments of heated debate.

Craig also hates it when we write about our process, so we will spare you a detailed rundown of the schism in the BP Prospect Team about Rojas's hit tool and stick to the report. Rojas broke out in 2019 in the dearly departed New York-Penn League, flashing four and a half out of five tools. His approach was certainly aggressive even then—we wrote, "He's aggressive and the swing can get noisy generally or choppy against off-speed stuff, so the hit tool will take some time to develop." We are still in the developmental phase here, and Rojas still struggles with spin moving down and away. His K rate wasn't egregious, and he was better after his promotion to High-A—and his time in Low-A Clearwater was marked by injury and COVID-19 pauses. If the hit tool even gets to average, he can be a solid major-league regular, because that is the half tool above. As for the other four tools: Rojas has excellent bat speed and generates plus raw power despite a shorter, stockier frame. He's a 70-grade runner whose foot speed is ahead of his routes but is a potential above-average defender in center. He flashes a strong arm, as well. But ultimately, the question remains: Can Johan Rojas hit?

OFP: 55 / Above-average center fielder

Variance: High. If you ask us, this hit tool could end about 100 different ways: 1) Rojas hits .200 2) Rojas hits .201 3) Rojas hits .20 . . .

Darius Austin's Fantasy Take: So you're not satisfied with only pitching prospects who have a wide range of potential outcomes? Let Rojas address that on the hitting side. He's fast, he has a quick bat, he could fill up all five categories. There's just that little problem of whether he can actually hit. If he can hit enough to not flame out in the majors, he could be at least a four-category type with a pedestrian average. He certainly wouldn't be the first ultra-toolsy prospect to fall by the wayside because he couldn't quite find the last piece in the puzzle, but if you prefer your lower-ranked prospects to have a lofty ceiling, you aren't going to find many better candidates than Rojas.

6 Ethan Wilson RF OFP: 50 ETA: 2024

Born: 11/07/99 Age: 22 Bats: L Throws: L Height: 6'1" Weight: 210 lb. Origin: Round 2, 2021 Draft (#49 overall)

YEAR	TEAM	LVL	AGE	PA	R	2B	3B	HR	RBI	BB	K	SB	CS	AVG/OBP/SLG	DRC+	BABIP	BRR	FRAA	WARP
2021	CLR	A	21	117	15	4	2	3	17	10	25	2	2	.215/.282/.374	101	.253	0.5	RF(9) -0.4, LF(7) -0.4, CF(6) -1.1	0.3
2022 non-DC	*PHI*	*MLB*	*22*	*251*	*20*	*9*	*1*	*3*	*22*	*16*	*66*	*3*	*3*	*.222/.277/.327*	*64*	*.295*	*0.4*	*LF 0, RF 1*	*-0.3*

Comparables: Ryan Reed, Brett Siddall, Michael Beltre

The Report: Wilson had an absolutely monster season his freshman year at South Alabama. His sophomore year was truncated by the pandemic, and his junior year was merely quite good and marred by some foot issues. The Phillies are betting his bat will bounce back, as Wilson has shown a potential plus hit/power combo in the past coupled with a very strong approach at the plate. He has serious whip and barrel control, so it's certainly possible he is a Brobdingnagian bat once again in 2022, although he didn't exactly sear the ball in Clearwater. The rest of the blurb is that Wilson a below-average defender in a corner-outfield spot, probably left field. So the plus hit/power combo will have to show up in the pros.

OFP: 50 / Average corner outfielder

Variance: High. Wilson has potential impact offensive tools, but not a lot else to carry the profile if they end up not so impactful.

Darius Austin's Fantasy Take: An obvious better-in-fantasy-than-reality type, Wilson was rather disappointing in his debut for a college bat in Low-A, but then it's fair to say he hasn't had the smoothest developmental path over the last few years. I think he's going to move back up the rankings quite quickly if he hits out of the gate this season and, thus, despite the debut, is thus worth adding anywhere 300-ish prospects are rostered. He's a potential OBP boon in addition to his average and power contributions.

7 Luis García MI OFP: 50 ETA: 2024

Born: 10/01/00 Age: 21 Bats: S Throws: R Height: 5'11" Weight: 170 lb. Origin: International Free Agent, 2017

YEAR	TEAM	LVL	AGE	PA	R	2B	3B	HR	RBI	BB	K	SB	CS	AVG/OBP/SLG	DRC+	BABIP	BRR	FRAA	WARP
2019	LWD	A	18	524	36	14	3	4	36	44	132	9	8	.186/.261/.255	76	.247	-4.1	SS(72) -0.5, 2B(55) -5.6	-1.0
2021	CLR	A	20	395	57	16	5	11	42	54	93	11	6	.246/.356/.423	113	.307	-0.8	SS(57) -0.9, 2B(30) -1.8	1.4
2021	JS	A+	20	70	6	2	0	2	8	10	19	4	0	.224/.333/.362	105	.289	0.6	SS(11) -0.7, 2B(4) -0.4	0.2
2022 non-DC	*PHI*	*MLB*	*21*	*251*	*20*	*9*	*1*	*3*	*21*	*21*	*70*	*5*	*3*	*.202/.276/.307*	*58*	*.275*	*0.5*	*SS 0, 2B -1*	*-0.5*

Comparables: Dawel Lugo, Cole Tucker, Chris Owings

The Report: Repeating a level can be seen as a black mark on one's prospect profile. For García though, it was a pleasant reset. As a 20-year-old, he was perfectly age appropriate for A-ball the second time around, and he erased the unpleasant reports from his first pass at the level as a teenager in 2019. That was an extremely aggressive assignment, and while García flashed some strong defensive tools and a bit of bat-to-ball skill, he simply wasn't physically ready to see that level of pitching night in and night out. He has potentially average game power now with some whippy bat speed. He still struggled a bit with his contact profile, but he has shown more at the plate and remains a strong up-the-middle defender.

OFP: 50 / Everyday middle infielder

Variance: High. There's some hit-tool projection to go along with his physical gains. However, while .240 in A-ball is better than .180, there's still significant risk that he won't hit enough to be a regular.

Darius Austin's Fantasy Take: This is a pretty fringy profile for me, especially as García struggled to post either impressive steal totals or a decent success rate despite the favorable rule changes at Low-A. Perhaps he's a reasonable, late-round, middle-infield fall-back option who can give you a bit of pop. He's only going to get to that if he can prove he can play every day, though.

8 Logan O'Hoppe C

OFP: 50 ETA: Late 2023

Born: 02/09/00 Age: 22 Bats: R Throws: R Height: 6'2" Weight: 185 lb. Origin: Round 23, 2018 Draft (#677 overall)

YEAR	TEAM	LVL	AGE	PA	R	2B	3B	HR	RBI	BB	K	SB	CS	AVG/OBP/SLG	DRC+	BABIP	BRR	FRAA	WARP
2019	ADE	WIN	19	109	17	5	0	5	18	18	23	1	1	.258/.389/.483		.295			
2019	WIL	SS	19	177	20	12	2	5	26	12	49	3	0	.216/.266/.407		.270			
2021	PEJ	WIN	21	100	19	8	0	3	17	21	15	3	1	.299/.440/.519		.328			
2021	JS	A+	21	358	43	17	2	13	48	30	63	6	3	.270/.335/.459	124	.294	0.2	C(60) 3.2	2.4
2021	REA	AA	21	57	6	1	0	3	7	1	9	0	0	.296/.333/.481	109	.310	-0.3	C(11) -0.5	0.2
2022 non-DC	*PHI*	*MLB*	*22*	*251*	*24*	*10*	*1*	*5*	*26*	*14*	*52*	*2*	*1*	*.245/.297/.377*	*83*	*.292*	*0.0*	*C -2*	*0.4*

Comparables: Pablo Sandoval, Wilson Ramos, Salvador Perez

The Report: Cold-weather prep prospects can be a bit of a slow burn. Cold-weather catching prospects can be the Queensland pitch-drop experiment. Well, O'Hoppe found a bit of fluidity in his prospect profile in 2021. He added some good weight and strength, bumping his raw pop from average to above. He also started getting it into games more often while playing in the not-particularly-friendly confines of the Jersey Shore. He's a bit of a mistake hitter at present, and better stuff in the upper minors will test his hit tool, but there's enough thunder in his bat now to keep his offensive line within a shout of the major-league mean. Combine that with a solid-enough catcher glove—the receiving is developing apace, and he's an average thrower and blocker—and you have a potential regular behind the plate. It's not the most exciting profile as catching prospects go—especially in 2022, when we have a bumper crop—but O'Hoppe offers a broad base of skills with the possibility of further offensive projection to come.

OFP: 50 / Average catcher

Variance: High. O'Hoppe remains immutably a cold-weather catching prospect. There's risk on both the offensive and defensive sides of the skill set. He also offers enough power projection that, if he does refine the hit tool, he's potentially an above-average catcher.

Darius Austin's Fantasy Take: There's enough power here that O'Hoppe might be one of the cluster of functional backstops in the late rounds a few years down the line. With the high variance and the dynasty catcher of it all, it's time to hop along to the next name.

9 Matt Vierling 1B

OFP: 50 ETA: Debuted in 2021

Born: 09/16/96 Age: 25 Bats: R Throws: R Height: 6'3" Weight: 205 lb. Origin: Round 5, 2018 Draft (#137 overall)

YEAR	TEAM	LVL	AGE	PA	R	2B	3B	HR	RBI	BB	K	SB	CS	AVG/OBP/SLG	DRC+	BABIP	BRR	FRAA	WARP
2019	CLR	A+	22	483	41	23	2	5	41	34	94	22	5	.232/.297/.329	95	.279	-2.0	LF(53) 0.5, CF(24) 0.5, RF(22) -2.2	0.9
2021	REA	AA	24	102	16	6	1	6	16	12	18	5	1	.345/.422/.644	136	.369	-0.1	CF(15) -1.0, RF(10) 4.5	1.1
2021	LHV	AAA	24	236	25	6	1	5	31	24	46	5	1	.248/.331/.359	99	.291	-0.8	LF(20) 2.5, RF(17) -1.6, 3B(11) 1.8	1.0
2021	PHI	MLB	24	77	11	3	1	2	6	4	20	2	0	.324/.364/.479	92	.420	-0.4	1B(9) 0.5, CF(8) -0.6, LF(7) 0.1	0.1
2022 DC	*PHI*	*MLB*	*25*	*468*	*56*	*19*	*1*	*9*	*53*	*33*	*103*	*10*	*4*	*.233/.297/.355*	*75*	*.287*	*0.6*	*LF 1, CF 0*	*0.2*

Comparables: Brian Anderson, Gaby Sanchez, Pablo Reyes

The Report: The sabermetric revolution in some ways just quantified and codified old, received scouting wisdom. The most obvious example of this is catcher framing. We also learned that hitting the ball very hard—in scouting terms: "it just sounds different"—is good. Matt Vierling hits the ball very hard. That's good.

A few years ago at BP Mets Day, Mets executive Sandy Alderson related a story about infielder Eric Campbell. As Alderson's story goes, the Mets kept giving Campbell shots on the major-league squad because the data they had said he hit the ball quite hard. They thought he was perhaps just unlucky. The punchline to the anecdote is that they had exit velocity, but not launch angle yet. Matt Vierling hits the ball on the ground more often than Eric Campbell.

Vierling's swing is nice and level and generates loud contact from a fairly short stroke, but if you didn't have access to his Baseball Savant page, you'd see a 24-year-old probable corner outfielder who has really only hit in Reading. One of the other things we've learned in the last decade or so is that players with some latent bat-to-ball, a good approach and the ability to hit the ball hard can have power breakouts in their mid-twenties. That's not a compelling philosophy for prospect evaluation, but it is worth keeping in mind.

OFP: 50 / Second-division starter or good fourth outfielder

Variance: On one level, Vierling has pretty low variance. He has hit in the upper minors, seen some major-league time and has the kind of bat-to-ball skills and ability to stand in center field—among other places—that portend a significant major-league career, albeit not as a starter. However, you'd be forgiven for thinking there is a good-regular outcome here if he just starts lifting the ball a little more.

Darius Austin's Fantasy Take: Vierling has already arrived, and the Phillies have an extremely questionable outfield depth chart after Bryce Harper, so there's at least theoretical opportunity until the lockout ends. Vierling is also part of the questionable portion of that chart, and there's not enough to carry a fantasy profile here unless that power breakout becomes a reality. If you're in an "at-bats alone are valuable" situation, like an NL-only, he's going to get some ABs, regardless.

10 Símon Muzziotti OF

OFP: 50 ETA: Late 2022/Early 2023

Born: 12/27/98 Age: 23 Bats: L Throws: L Height: 6'1" Weight: 175 lb. Origin: International Free Agent, 2015

YEAR	TEAM	LVL	AGE	PA	R	2B	3B	HR	RBI	BB	K	SB	CS	AVG/OBP/SLG	DRC+	BABIP	BRR	FRAA	WARP
2019	CLR	A+	20	465	52	21	3	3	28	32	60	21	12	.287/.337/.372	115	.327	1.9	CF(80) 0.1, RF(16) 0.6, LF(6) 1.5	2.7
2021	PEJ	WIN	22	83	10	1	0	0	13	15	13	3	3	.254/.398/.269		.315			
2021	LHV	AAA	22	32	2	0	0	0	2	5	4	2	0	.200/.333/.200	110	.238	0.9	LF(5) 0.4, CF(3) -0.1	0.3
2022 non-DC	*PHI*	*MLB*	*23*	*251*	*20*	*10*	*1*	*2*	*20*	*16*	*40*	*9*	*4*	*.241/.295/.324*	*70*	*.284*	*0.8*	*CF 1, RF 0*	*0.1*

Comparables: Trayvon Robinson, Raimel Tapia, Ender Inciarte

The Report: Muzziotti was limited to 20 games in 2021 due to visa issues. In those 20 games, he hit zero home runs. Then he went to the launching pad of the Arizona Fall League . . . and hit zero home runs. So, the lack of power is still a concern. It is also what's keeping him this low in a relatively shallow system, as everything else in the profile pops. Muzziotti is a good glove in center field with plus run and arm grades supporting the underlying reads and routes. He has a penchant for contact, although we haven't seen his aggressive approach tested against upper-minors pitching for any length of time. The likely outcome remains a speed-and-defense fringe starter or good bench outfielder, but we have two mostly lost seasons to contend with, obscuring the projection a bit.

OFP: 50 / Glove-first center fielder who bats at the bottom of the order

Variance: High. Prospects with this little useable game power often find their ability to hit for average and get on base sorely tested in the higher levels of the minors.

Darius Austin's Fantasy Take: If you're going to hit for this little power, then you have to be Ben Revere to carry significant fantasy utility. I doubt Muzziotti is going to hit for as much average as Revere, and he's definitely not going to run as much, so, once again, we're in NL-only or extremely deep mixed territory, where carrying fourth outfielders who might give you a steal now and then is a viable strategy.

The Prospects You Meet Outside the Top Ten

Prospects on the Rise

Jamari Baylor MI Born: 08/25/00 Age: 21 Bats: R Throws: R Height: 5'11" Weight: 190 lb. Origin: Round 3, 2019 Draft (#91 overall)

YEAR	TEAM	LVL	AGE	PA	R	2B	3B	HR	RBI	BB	K	SB	CS	AVG/OBP/SLG	DRC+	BABIP	BRR	FRAA	WARP
2021	PHI	ROK	20	110	24	8	1	5	16	18	33	11	5	.303/.436/.584		.431			
2021	CLR	A	20	59	5	1	0	0	5	1	27	1	0	.214/.254/.232	54	.414	0.5	2B(8) 1.6, SS(7) -1.1	0.0
2022 non-DC	*PHI*	*MLB*	*21*	*251*	*16*	*9*	*0*	*2*	*18*	*12*	*122*	*3*	*1*	*.177/.228/.258*	*27*	*.355*	*0.1*	*SS 0, 2B 1*	*-1.4*

A third-round prep shortstop drafted in 2019, Baylor improved on the defensive end last season while showing off an intriguing power/speed combo offensively. He's likely to end up somewhere up the middle, but there remain hit-tool questions; he struggled badly with swing-and-miss after his late-season promotion to full-season ball.

Hao Yu Lee 2B Born: 02/03/03 Age: 19 Bats: R Throws: R Height: 5'10" Weight: 190 lb. Origin: International Free Agent, 2021

YEAR	TEAM	LVL	AGE	PA	R	2B	3B	HR	RBI	BB	K	SB	CS	AVG/OBP/SLG	DRC+	BABIP	BRR	FRAA	WARP
2021	PHI	ROK	18	25	9	2	2	1	5	3	5	0	0	.364/.440/.773		.438			

Signed out of Taiwan in June, Lee only briefly played stateside in the complex. Even in that brief Florida Complex League cameo, he showed an ability to hit and hit for power; he also has a strong international track record of performance. He profiles as a bat-first second baseman.

Erik Miller LHP Born: 02/13/98 Age: 24 Bats: L Throws: L Height: 6'5" Weight: 240 lb. Origin: Round 4, 2019 Draft (#120 overall)

YEAR	TEAM	LVL	AGE	W	L	SV	G	GS	IP	H	HR	BB/9	K/9	K	GB%	BABIP	WHIP	ERA	DRA-	WARP
2019	WIL	SS	21	0	0	0	6	4	20	13	0	3.2	13.1	29	52.2%	.289	1.00	0.90		
2019	LWD	A	21	1	0	0	3	2	13	10	0	4.2	11.8	17	29.0%	.323	1.23	2.08	81	0.2
2022 non-DC	*PHI*	*MLB*	*24*	*2*	*3*	*0*	*57*	*0*	*50*	*50*	*9*	*6.6*	*10.4*	*57*	*47.2%*	*.322*	*1.75*	*6.33*	*134*	*-0.7*

Comparables: Chris Haney, Caleb Smith, Radhames Liz

Miller battled injuries in 2021, but his stuff is as good as that of some of the arms on the top half of the Phillies' top 10. He can ramp his fastball up into the upper 90s. He has a potentially above-average slider and a promising changeup. His fastball has played more in the average velocity range in longer stints, but he also hasn't had too many longer stints because of the injuries. Given that Miller is going to be 24 this season and that his fastball/slider combo is potentially plus in short bursts, he is also more likely to end up a reliever than the arms on the top half of the top 10.

Factors on the Farm

Hans Crouse RHP Born: 09/15/98 Age: 23 Bats: L Throws: R Height: 6'4" Weight: 180 lb. Origin: Round 2, 2017 Draft (#66 overall)

YEAR	TEAM	LVL	AGE	W	L	SV	G	GS	IP	H	HR	BB/9	K/9	K	GB%	BABIP	WHIP	ERA	DRA-	WARP
2019	HIC	A	20	6	1	0	19	19	87^{2}	86	12	2.0	7.8	76	31.3%	.296	1.20	4.41	109	0.3
2021	FRI	AA	22	3	2	0	13	13	51	27	5	3.4	9.5	54	35.0%	.191	0.90	3.35	94	0.5
2021	REA	AA	22	2	2	0	6	6	29^{2}	24	3	3.6	11.5	38	28.6%	.313	1.21	2.73	89	0.4
2021	PHI	MLB	22	0	2	0	2	2	7	4	2	9.0	2.6	2	17.4%	.100	1.57	5.14	156	-0.1
2022 DC	*PHI*	*MLB*	*23*	*5*	*6*	*0*	*36*	*14*	*77.7*	*77*	*14*	*4.6*	*8.8*	*76*	*36.0%*	*.296*	*1.51*	*5.49*	*125*	*-0.4*

Comparables: Aaron Sanchez, Doug Waechter, Chase De Jong

Acquired from the Rangers along with Ian Kennedy and Kyle Gibson, Crouse still has the same herky-jerky, high-effort delivery, but his fastball—now a sinker—sits more in the average velocity band than the mid-90s-and-up he has flashed in the past. His changeup has developed into an above-average pitch with power sink and fade. His breaking ball is a sweepy power slider now. Crouse still misses bats. The delivery still limits his command profile, and he's ready to be a multi-inning reliever or back-end spot starter in 2022.

Francisco Morales RHP Born: 10/27/99 Age: 22 Bats: R Throws: R Height: 6'4" Weight: 185 lb. Origin: International Free Agent, 2016

YEAR	TEAM	LVL	AGE	W	L	SV	G	GS	IP	H	HR	BB/9	K/9	K	GB%	BABIP	WHIP	ERA	DRA-	WARP
2019	LWD	A	19	1	8	1	27	15	96^{2}	82	8	4.3	12.0	129	44.5%	.325	1.32	3.82	82	1.7
2021	REA	AA	21	4	13	0	22	20	83	76	11	6.5	11.9	110	40.8%	.323	1.64	6.94	84	1.4
2021	LHV	AAA	21	0	1	0	2	2	8^{2}	6	0	7.3	7.3	7	44.0%	.240	1.50	0.00	114	0.1
2022 DC	*PHI*	*MLB*	*22*	*1*	*2*	*0*	*6*	*6*	*25.7*	*24*	*4*	*6.5*	*9.3*	*26*	*40.1%*	*.297*	*1.68*	*5.79*	*127*	*-0.2*

Comparables: Aaron Sanchez, Steve Karsay, Cristian Javier

Morales was in consideration for the Top 101 list the past couple of seasons, and, in 2021, was in consideration for the Because You Were Going to Ask "superlative" on this list. But really, start-to-start in 2021, he might have fit into either category. In the good outings, he showed enough command of mid-90s heat and his plus-or-better slider. In the bad outings, he completely lost the plate, and a cursory look at his game logs will tell you there was more bad than good, with just about nothing in between. Morales doesn't have the smoothest or most-athletic delivery, and he struggles to repeat it. He doesn't really have a third pitch, so he will need to find some fastball command to make it as a reliever, which is now the likely outcome.

Dominic Pipkin RHP Born: 11/05/99 Age: 22 Bats: R Throws: R Height: 6'4" Weight: 160 lb. Origin: Round 9, 2018 Draft (#257 overall)

YEAR	TEAM	LVL	AGE	W	L	SV	G	GS	IP	H	HR	BB/9	K/9	K	GB%	BABIP	WHIP	ERA	DRA-	WARP
2019	LWD	A	19	3	4	1	24	12	71²	71	4	5.7	5.5	44	47.0%	.298	1.62	5.15	157	-1.6
2021	JS	A+	21	4	3	0	16	12	58	58	6	4.2	9.9	64	44.0%	.340	1.47	4.97	96	0.6
2022 non-DC	*PHI*	*MLB*	*22*	*2*	*3*	*0*	*57*	*0*	*50*	*53*	*7*	*5.8*	*7.0*	*38*	*35.5%*	*.301*	*1.71*	*6.02*	*132*	*-0.6*

As a projectable Cali prep righty, Pipkin got significantly over slot as a ninth-round pick in the 2018 draft. He remains on the lean side but can ramp his fastball up to 98, and it sits mid-90s. He's probably not a starter long-term, and his mid-80s slider isn't quite sharp enough or consistent enough, at present, for him to be a 95-and-a-slider guy. He has more of a changeup than that profile suggests, though, and he has made enough improvement as a pro to stay stretched out a little longer. Pipkin could move quickly in relief, especially if his fastball is seeing the upper end of his range more often in short bursts, and the bullpen is the betting favorite on the Futures market here, anyway.

Top Talents 25 and Under (as of 4/1/2021):

1. Alec Bohm, 3B
2. Mick Abel, RHP
3. Andrew Painter, RHP
4. Bryson Stott, IF
5. Griff McGarry, RHP
6. Johan Rojas, OF
7. Ethan Wilson, OF
8. Luis García, IF
9. Logan O'Hoppe, C
10. Matt Vierling, OF

Many clubs simply lack many players who even qualify for a 25U list, which can mean little, such as for a club with plenty of mid-prime players, or a lot, for a team with either an aging or unimpressive roster. The Phillies are regrettably somewhat of a third option, with elements of a top-tier core led by a few genuine stars, a roster reliant on a thin first line of talent that utterly lacks for quality depth, and a multitude of young players who could qualify as that next wave, if only they had met their original potential.

Despite his disappointing sophomore campaign, Bohm retains the most promise and import of this group to Philly's present and phuture. The towering third baseman took a step backwards in 2021, pounding the ball into the ground with regularity and proving correspondingly incapable of accessing almost any of his excellent natural power. His .095 ISO was completely unacceptable given the physical tools he has displayed. Compounding concerns, he was a poor mark with the glove at the hot corner, struggling with inconsistency in his footwork and arm accuracy. Bohm has often drawn comparisons to Rhys Hoskins due to his bat-first profile and rather dubious defensive home, but Hoskins hit well from the jump. Bohm, of course, has the defense of youth—he'll be 25 for most of the 2022 season—but the expectation has been that Bohm's refinement would come eventually, the projection bearing out the potential. That time must come soon.

Pittsburgh Pirates

The State of the System:

A big-time draft class and some recent trades—along with a few breakouts here and there—have given the Pirates the strongest system in baseball. Just don't ask us anything else about this team.

The Top Ten:

1 **Oneil Cruz SS** OFP: 70 ETA: Debuted in 2021

Born: 10/04/98 Age: 23 Bats: L Throws: R Height: 6'7" Weight: 210 lb. Origin: International Free Agent, 2015

YEAR	TEAM	LVL	AGE	PA	R	2B	3B	HR	RBI	BB	K	SB	CS	AVG/OBP/SLG	DRC+	BABIP	BRR	FRAA	WARP
2019	PIR	ROK	20	11	0	1	0	0	1	1	1	1	0	.600/.636/.700		.667			
2019	BRD	A+	20	145	21	6	1	7	16	8	38	7	3	.301/.345/.515	115	.374	0.7	SS(35) 2.5	0.9
2019	ALT	AA	20	136	14	8	3	1	17	15	35	3	1	.269/.346/.412	93	.365	1.7	SS(35) 3.2	0.9
2021	ALT	AA	22	273	51	15	5	12	40	20	64	18	3	.292/.346/.536	120	.349	2.6	SS(54) -1.7	1.6
2021	IND	AAA	22	29	11	1	0	5	7	8	5	1	0	.524/.655/1.286	147	.545	0.0	SS(5) 1.1	0.3
2021	PIT	MLB	22	9	2	0	0	1	3	0	4	0	0	.333/.333/.667	82	.500		SS(2) -0.7	-0.1
2022 DC	*PIT*	*MLB*	*23*	*288*	*32*	*12*	*2*	*10*	*36*	*20*	*86*	*5*	*3*	*.253/.312/.441*	*96*	*.340*	*0.6*	*SS 1*	*1.1*

Comparables: Nick Franklin, Jonathan Villar, Cole Tucker

The Report: Three years ago we wrote: "Could he actually stick at short? If you assume he 'only' ends up being something like 6-foot-7 and 220 pounds, he'd be by far the biggest real shortstop in MLB history, but he might still be light and nimble enough for it to work." Well, Cruz is now listed at 6-foot-7 and 210 pounds. That's probably an inch and 30 pounds light, and he's still a solid defensive shortstop. It's a bizarre prospect profile, defensively, but Cruz makes it work and is capable of plus play in the field while showing off a true left-side arm.

At the plate, he continues to look like a perennial 30-home-run bat. He has true 80 raw pop, just easy power, housed in a pretty, rotational swing with plus-plus bat speed. Cruz can hit them out of the stadium in batting practice at less than full effort. There will always be swing-and-miss issues given just how long his levers are. Cruz is a high-ball hitter given his size and swing plane and can end up lunging or flailing against soft stuff or spin down in the zone. He has a solid approach, though, and the amplitude of his contact profile should allow his hit tool to play to average, even if he's striking out close to 30 percent of the time in the majors. In 2018, we thought he might end up in right field, now it looks like he will stick somewhere on the left side of the infield. The power bat plays anywhere.

Cruz was involved in a fatal motor-vehicle accident in the Dominican Republic in the 2020–21 offseason, and we did not rank him in last year's book over uncertainty about his availability at press time.

OFP: 70 / Middle-of-the-order hitter, pretty good defensive infielder

Variance: Medium. Cruz debuted in the majors at the end of last season and promptly hit a home run that was in the top one percent of exit velocity for all of major-league baseball. We're still not sure about his hit tool or ultimate positional home, but, on pure upside, Cruz belongs with the top prospects in the game. He did deal with an arm injury in 2021 that cost him six weeks, but he hit just as well upon his return.

Darius Austin's Fantasy Take: Cruz's debut was about as loud as it could be, given its brevity. That both highlights his tremendous power upside and creates the risk of significant small-sample helium. Redraft players aren't having to invest too heavily in him at the moment, as he is barely being drafted inside the top 250. For the homer potential, I think that's worth the shot; he should be a significant contributor in that category for the foreseeable future. His batting average may well be a drag, particularly in the early going, and I doubt it'll ever be sustainably helpful. He'll chip in a few steals, too, while he's still in his early twenties. You'll never be short of Statcast highlights.

2 Henry Davis C OFP: 70 ETA: 2022 or 2023

Born: 09/21/99 Age: 22 Bats: R Throws: R Height: 6'2" Weight: 210 lb. Origin: Round 1, 2021 Draft (#1 overall)

YEAR	TEAM	LVL	AGE	PA	R	2B	3B	HR	RBI	BB	K	SB	CS	AVG/OBP/SLG	DRC+	BABIP	BRR	FRAA	WARP
2022 non-DC	*PIT*	*MLB*	*22*	*251*	*21*	*9*	*1*	*4*	*23*	*20*	*76*	*3*	*2*	*.198/.273/.319*	*61*	*.275*	*0.2*	*C -4*	*-0.5*

The Report: Davis might not have been the top overall talent in the 2021 draft, but he was certainly the best college hitter and has a chance to stick at a premium defensive position. Despite an unusual setup and swing, he hit the ball about as hard as anyone in the NCAA. Davis has plus bat speed and strength, and he knows which pitches to try to drive. Both his hit and power tools have plus potential, and his pop could end up a tick above that. That offensive profile plays anywhere, but, at catcher, it has serious roster impact. Davis has the frame and arm to stick behind the plate, but his receiving isn't yet at a level where most major-league teams would be comfortable rolling him out as a five-day-a-week backstop. That's a teachable skill—and one that might be rendered obsolete in the coming years with an Automatic Ball-Strike system—but Davis's bat may advance quickly enough that the Pirates explore other ways to get it into their major-league lineup.

OFP: 70 / All-Star . . . catcher?

Variance: Medium. Davis was the most advanced bat of the 2021 draft class. If he didn't need development behind the plate, he could be in the majors by the end of this season. As it stands, the Pirates will need to figure out how to balance his near-term impact offensive potential with his potential long-term positional value.

Darius Austin's Fantasy Take: We can largely dispense with the usual fantasy-catcher warnings here since Davis's bat is so close to being ready. There's probably still an outcome in which his defensive development gets in the way of Davis realizing his full offensive potential and frustratingly delays his arrival, but the likelihood is that he'll be at least a good four-category fantasy contributor wherever he plays, with the potential to be great.

3 Nick Gonzales 2B OFP: 60 ETA: 2023

Born: 05/27/99 Age: 23 Bats: R Throws: R Height: 5'10" Weight: 195 lb. Origin: Round 1, 2020 Draft (#7 overall)

YEAR	TEAM	LVL	AGE	PA	R	2B	3B	HR	RBI	BB	K	SB	CS	AVG/OBP/SLG	DRC+	BABIP	BRR	FRAA	WARP
2021	PEJ	WIN	22	87	18	4	1	2	13	13	14	4	0	.380/.483/.549		.446			
2021	GBO	A+	22	369	53	23	4	18	54	40	101	7	2	.302/.385/.565	112	.388	-3.4	2B(73) -0.8, SS(1) -0.0	1.2
2022 non-DC	*PIT*	*MLB*	*23*	*251*	*23*	*11*	*1*	*5*	*25*	*20*	*82*	*1*	*1*	*.231/.299/.368*	*80*	*.337*	*0.0*	*2B -1, SS 0*	*0.1*

Comparables: Brandon Lowe, Cory Spangenberg, Chris Taylor

The Report: Gonzales was an unusually uncontroversial top-10 pick for an undersized, second-base-only prospect. This is because he was seen as a high-floor, high-ceiling offensive talent. One professional season in, and it has been "so far, so good" on that front. Greensboro is generally considered a hitter-friendly environment, but Gonzales has skills in the batter's box that would play anywhere. His bat speed is absolutely elite, allowing for consistent hard contact and more power than you might expect from his frame. It isn't often he lets a high fastball past him, and he'll lace liners all over the park (and often over the fence). He is a little vulnerable to good breaking stuff down-and-away, which fuels a K rate that would probably strike many as surprisingly high. His swing path seems more suited to driving the high, hard stuff, so it will be interesting to see if he needs to make adjustments in the upper levels. He makes the plays at second and gets around the bases okay, but the lion's share of the loot will come from the bat.

OFP: 60 / First-division, bat-first second baseman

Variance: Medium. There's slight swing-and-miss concern, but he mitigates it with a good approach and high quality of contact.

Darius Austin's Fantasy Take: I'm sure I'm not alone in enjoying the usage of both "bat-first" and "high-floor" when interpreting a prospect report from a fantasy perspective. I wouldn't go overboard on Gonzales's ceiling in fantasy. I think there's some risk that he doesn't hit for quite as much power as standard roto players would want, and we won't know for certain how Gonzales will adjust to truly advanced pitching until he sees it. There still aren't many prospects likely to contribute as much in batting average, and there's five-category potential here, even if the average is the only one that stands out.

Eyewitness Report: Nick Gonzales

Evaluator: Ben Spanier
Report Date: 08/31/2021
Dates Seen: several
Risk Factor: Low
Physical/Health: Fairly stocky frame, strength present, minimal physical projection.

Tool	Future Grade	Report
Hit	60	Strong hands, gets the bat head out extremely quickly, barrel control is sufficient given his other abilities. Hits to all fields and is a line drive machine. Hits fastballs, doesn't miss much up in the zone. Has shown more swing and miss than expected, often on good hard breaking pitches down and away. This is a potential concern but for me is mitigated by excellent quality of contact and general ability to lay off pitches out of the zone.
Power	55	Elite bat speed and has swing path conducive to slug, quick enough to drive good velo located up. Probably more doubles power given frame but will hit a decent number of homers as well. Hits the ball very hard, pop should come as he refines his approach.
Baserunning/ Speed	50	Average runner, not a difference maker on the bases.
Glove	50	Perfectly decent defender at second, good instincts but lacks the range necessary to take some of the more difficult chances.
Arm	50	Adequate for the keystone, don't see it playing anywhere else. Mostly throws sidearm and haven't seen him make throws from that many angles.

Conclusion: Bat-first middle-infield profile. Second base only but gifted enough offensively to be a very good everyday player there.

4 Liover Peguero SS OFP: 60 ETA: 2024

Born: 12/31/00 Age: 21 Bats: R Throws: R Height: 6'1" Weight: 200 lb. Origin: International Free Agent, 2017

YEAR	TEAM	LVL	AGE	PA	R	2B	3B	HR	RBI	BB	K	SB	CS	AVG/OBP/SLG	DRC+	BABIP	BRR	FRAA	WARP
2019	MIS	ROA	18	156	34	7	3	5	27	12	34	8	1	.364/.410/.559		.448			
2019	HIL	SS	18	93	13	4	2	0	11	8	17	3	1	.262/.333/.357		.328			
2021	GBO	A+	20	417	67	19	2	14	45	33	105	28	6	.270/.332/.444	96	.337	-0.6	SS(86) 8.1	1.7
2022 non-DC	*PIT*	*MLB*	*21*	*251*	*21*	*10*	*1*	*4*	*22*	*15*	*73*	*8*	*3*	*.223/.277/.332*	*64*	*.307*	*0.7*	*SS 3*	*0.2*

Comparables: Amed Rosario, Anderson Tejeda, Thairo Estrada

The Report: The discussion over whether the present-day Pirates "won" a trade always seems to veer into murky territory of a more philosophical nature. Taking that into account, the Buccos do seem to have done fairly well, value-wise, on the original Starling Marte trade. Peguero was the lead piece in the January 2020 deal, at the time a 19-year-old yet to play full-season ball. His profile has developed quite well since, even if his numbers don't quite jump off the page. His High-A stats may pale in comparison to Gonzales's, but it is worth bearing in mind that Peguero is 18-months younger and plays a position higher up the defensive spectrum. An excellent athlete with plus speed, he possesses a variety of tools that should prove useful as the Pirates try to fit him into their future plans. He has the ability to play a very good shortstop, with a quick first step allowing him to cover a lot of ground and superior upper-body actions that beget quick transfers and slick tags. Additionally, his arm plays from all angles, and he shows an exciting level of awareness and élan. If, for whatever reason, it doesn't happen at the six, we tend to think that he could handle a move to one of the other infield spots or even, perhaps, to the outfield grass. The efficacy of all of this is, of course, dependent on further development with the bat, which is not quite a certainty. His swing is loose and natural, creating a promising quality of barrel control that lets him cover pitches in all quadrants. He also has room for growth on the power side, as his bat speed is very good, and there is still some projection left in his frame. There are mechanical inconsistencies and questions about how well he will hit high-quality breaking stuff, but given his age, level and performance, Peguero deserves the benefit of the doubt.

OFP: 60 / High-level offensive production from a premium position

Variance: High. Hit-tool uncertainties remain, but he has a lot of skills on both sides of the ball that could make him a very valuable player.

Darius Austin's Fantasy Take: This is a fun system, isn't it? Speaking of five-category potential, I think Peguero's might be louder than Gonzales's—it just comes with a whole lot more uncertainty. While it could all collapse along with the hit tool at higher levels, he carries more potential to vault up prospect rankings than most given his broad base of skills, athleticism, room to grow and that obvious stolen-base upside. He's already a top-101 prospect, but if you're in the market for those who might make the jump to the top 20, Peguero is high on my list.

Eyewitness Report: Liover Peguero

Evaluator: Ben Spanier

Report Date: 08/09/2021

Dates Seen: several late June-early August

Risk Factor: High

Physical/Health: Long legs, high waist, thick lower half, relatively slim through the shoulders, limited physical projection. athletic, has a rhythm to his movements.

Tool	Future Grade	Report
Hit	55	By far the highest-variance tool in the profile, and the one that will determine the trajectory of his career. Has at times exhibited the barrel control necessary to square up pitches on both halves and can use the whole field when so inclined. Has bouts of inconsistency though; swing can become grooved and power-centric and he sometimes struggles to pick up spin. Hand movement isn't always efficient so with mechanical refinement he could get more out of his natural hand-eye coordination.
Power	55	Very good bat speed and significant lower half strength create more power than might generally be expected from someone with his frame. I don't see as much physical projection as some others, so for me that slightly hampers this future grade.
Baserunning/ Speed	60	Plus at present, obviously could go down a tick as he ages and body evolves. Aware and opportunistic on the bases, has some steals and will take the extra bag.
Glove	60	I may be the high person here, but I think he has a very good chance to stick at short. Has a really good first step and excellent upper body actions that allow him to make a wide variety of plays look simple. Has a quick transfer and slick tag, lower body movements not always quite as smooth. Proficient coming and and moving laterally. Shows good awareness and energy.
Arm	60	Am I being slightly generous here? On pure strength maybe, but he really uses this tool well. He makes throws from every angle necessary, whether it's overhand from the deep hole or sidearm after coming in on a ball.

Conclusion: Could be a star shortstop with these tools, could also be an up-and-down 3B/COF with swing-and-miss issues. Could be worse if everything collapses. He's a 20-year-old who has been decent in High-A, so I tend to see an at least an above-average starter here, but there is a lot of variance.

5 Roansy Contreras RHP OFP: 55 ETA: Debuted in 2021

Born: 11/07/99 Age: 22 Bats: R Throws: R Height: 6'0" Weight: 175 lb. Origin: International Free Agent, 2016

YEAR	TEAM	LVL	AGE	W	L	SV	G	GS	IP	H	HR	BB/9	K/9	K	GB%	BABIP	WHIP	ERA	DRA-	WARP
2019	CSC	A	19	12	5	0	24	24	132[1]	105	10	2.4	7.7	113	39.9%	.256	1.07	3.33	101	1.0
2021	ALT	AA	21	3	2	0	12	12	54[1]	37	5	2.0	12.6	76	48.4%	.267	0.90	2.65	83	0.9
2021	PIT	MLB	21	0	0	0	1	1	3	3	0	3.0	12.0	4	57.1%	.429	1.33	0.00	84	0.1
2022 DC	*PIT*	*MLB*	*22*	*1*	*1*	*0*	*6*	*6*	*29*	*26*	*3*	*3.1*	*8.8*	*28*	*44.2%*	*.290*	*1.26*	*3.81*	*95*	*0.3*

Comparables: Alex Cobb, Rafael Soriano, Wade Davis

The Report: Contreras was the breakout prospect from last offseason's Jameson Taillon deal. We had him as the best prospect in the trade, at the time, but if you preferred the proximity of Miguel Yajure or the upside of Maikol Escotto, that was certainly defensible. Yajure struggled with injuries last year. Escotto flashed intriguing tools, but struggled at the plate. Contreras went from a command-and-pitch-mix, backend-starter profile with an average fastball to sitting mid-90s with ride and showing two potential above-average breakers. He dominated Double-A before missing most of the summer with a forearm strain, but he made it back on the mound and all the way to the majors in September, throwing three scoreless innings the last week of the season. Contreras is an undersized righty, and there's some effort for him to squeeze out the plus velocity, but he generally repeats his delivery well. He has a full, four-pitch mix. The mid-80s slider with late, two-plane action is his best secondary offering, but his curve can flash above average, as well, and his change shows promising split/sink action. Contreras doesn't have a long track record of this level of stuff or professional performance, and any forearm strain is always going to register somewhere above "slightly concerning." Those caveats aside, he looked like an almost-major-league-ready mid-rotation starter in 2021.

OFP: 55 / No. 3–4 starter

Variance: Medium. Contreras has a four-pitch arsenal that merely needs refinement, not augmentation. But he is coming off a season in which he threw only 75 innings between the minors, majors and fall ball, and sometimes these pop-up-stuff guys give a bit back the next season.

Darius Austin's Fantasy Take: Contreras already made his debut, possesses what looks like a big-league-ready arsenal, and it doesn't take much of a leap to think he might be the best starting pitcher Pittsburgh currently has available. If the opportunity doesn't arrive right away, then it will do so soon, health permitting. As long as the spring goes well (whenever spring might be), he's a worthy late-round option in deeper leagues and should be worth at least streaming in shallower formats.

6 Quinn Priester RHP OFP: 55 ETA: Late 2023/Early 2024

Born: 09/16/00 Age: 21 Bats: R Throws: R Height: 6'3" Weight: 210 lb. Origin: Round 1, 2019 Draft (#18 overall)

YEAR	TEAM	LVL	AGE	W	L	SV	G	GS	IP	H	HR	BB/9	K/9	K	GB%	BABIP	WHIP	ERA	DRA-	WARP
2019	PIR	ROK	18	1	1	0	8	7	32^{2}	29	1	2.8	10.2	37	57.3%	.322	1.19	3.03		
2019	WV	SS	18	0	0	0	1	1	4	3	0	9.0	9.0	4	90.0%	.300	1.75	4.50		
2021	GBO	A+	20	7	4	0	20	20	97^{2}	82	8	3.6	9.0	98	53.7%	.285	1.24	3.04	85	1.6
2022 non-DC	*PIT*	*MLB*	*21*	*2*	*3*	*0*	*57*	*0*	*50*	*53*	*6*	*4.7*	*7.5*	*41*	*36.1%*	*.310*	*1.58*	*5.31*	*121*	*-0.4*

Comparables: Shairon Martis, Ricky Bones, Sidney Ponson

The Report: Despite performing reasonably well as a 20-year-old in High-A, Priester left an ambient feeling of disappointment behind after the 2021 season. Again, he was fairly effective, but how he got it done was not expected and not necessarily encouraging. Prior to his full season debut, Priester was generally perceived as a high-octane power pitcher who sat upper 90s with his fastball and paired it with a dangerous curve. In 2021, he generally sat low-to-mid 90s and often relied on armside run and sink to produce soft contact. The curve is still a potential plus pitch, featuring a pretty 11–5 shape and sharp downward action. He does throw it consistently for strikes, and when he commands it down and away, it is a legitimate swing-and-miss weapon. The change is so-so, at present, and, if we're talking about third-pitch candidates, we actually find his recently hatched slider more interesting. Generally thrown in the mid-to-upper 80s, it features short, tight, almost cutter-ish break. The different shape and in-between speed seem to play well off the fastball and curve when he has both breakers working and located. Priester is still a good pitching prospect, though it might be prudent to let go of the ace expectations and accept that a mid-rotation outcome is more likely.

OFP: 55 / Mid-rotation arm

Variance: Medium. Command gains and further development of his secondaries are still necessary. We're also interested to see where his velocity is next season.

Darius Austin's Fantasy Take: This is not particularly where we hoped Priester's career might head after he was drafted. That disappointment might take the shine off enough to make him a solid buy-low candidate, as long as you're not counting on getting ace-like production. As things currently stand, he seems . . . fine. We all need fine, unless we're in six-team leagues. No one's hyped up about it. You can always pray that he comes out next year sitting 97 with a fully-formed third offering.

7 Bubba Chandler RHP OFP: 55 ETA: 2025

Born: 09/14/02 Age: 19 Bats: S Throws: R Height: 6'3" Weight: 200 lb. Origin: Round 3, 2021 Draft (#72 overall)

The Report: The Pirates went well over-slot to sign Chandler away from a two-sport commitment at Clemson last year. He was a two-way player in high school, and the Pirates gave him some reps as a designated hitter and shortstop in the Florida Complex League, but his near- and long-term future is on the mound. For a prep prospect that didn't fully focus on pitching or even baseball, Chandler has a surprisingly deep arsenal, showing four pitches with a potential plus fastball leading the way. His delivery is athletic, but he battled consistency issues as an amateur. Given his arm speed and feel for the secondaries, we wouldn't be shocked if Chandler breaks out in a professional player-development system once he focuses solely on his mound work.

OFP: 55 / No. 3–4 starter

Variance: High. Chandler is a bit of a mystery box given his premium athletic tools and limited pro reps.

Darius Austin's Fantasy Take: While the depth of Chandler's arsenal is encouraging as far as his development goes, it's still likely to be an awfully long time before he's approaching the majors. He's definitely one of those players to monitor closely, since he could shoot up rankings rapidly if focusing on pitching alone proves to be significantly beneficial. He's a watchlist guy, unless your league's at least 250-prospects deep and you're in a position to be patient.

8 Lonnie White Jr. OF OFP: 55 ETA: 2025

Born: 12/31/02 Age: 19 Bats: R Throws: R Height: 6'3" Weight: 212 lb. Origin: Round 2, 2021 Draft (#64 overall)

YEAR	TEAM	LVL	AGE	PA	R	2B	3B	HR	RBI	BB	K	SB	CS	AVG/OBP/SLG	DRC+	BABIP	BRR	FRAA	WARP
2021	PIRB	ROK	18	33	6	2	0	2	5	2	14	0	0	.258/.303/.516		.400			

The Report: White also had a strong football commitment—he was slated to play wide receiver for Penn State—but the Pirates inked him for above slot, as well. He is a prototypical prep corner-outfield prospect—although he has the speed to stick in center, for now. He shows above-average bat speed and is incredibly strong for his age, but his swing has some length, stiffness and loft. There are long-term hit-tool and positional questions—White's likely to add more good weight to his frame and slide over to right field full time. But, like with Chandler, the Pirates were able to move their bonus pool around to get a first-round-quality prospect later in the draft, and White has impact power potential.

OFP: 55 / Above-average outfielder

Variance: High. White has 33 professional plate appearances and struck out in almost half of them. You absolutely should not scout that stat line, but this is a high-variance profile in both directions.

Darius Austin's Fantasy Take: This system just keeps on going, doesn't it? At present, White obviously has both the power and speed we're looking for in fantasy, and the power looks to be significant enough to carry a starting fantasy outfield profile, even if the speed falls off as he fills out. Once again, the lead time is fairly lengthy, but if you love to bet on athleticism and strength, White is your guy.

9 Anthony Solometo LHP OFP: 55 ETA: 2025

Born: 12/02/02 Age: 19 Bats: L Throws: L Height: 6'5" Weight: 220 lb. Origin: Round 2, 2021 Draft (#37 overall)

The Report: Featuring a delivery that is half Madison Bumgarner and half MacKenzie Gore, Solometo is a funkier lefty than Gang of Four. The tall, long-limbed southpaw has some room left to fill out, but also already has a sturdy, starter's frame. His unusual delivery is a concern for some evaluators—the BP Prospect Team included—but, so far, he hasn't had issues corralling his big leg kick or long arm action. His stuff is advanced for a cold-weather prep arm, as he features a potentially plus fastball/slider combo. His delivery can make his pitches tough to pick up, too, but you do wonder about his long-term durability, role and command profile given those mechanics.

OFP: 55 / No. 3–4 starter or late-inning reliever

Variance: High. Solometo is a cold-weather prep arm who hasn't thrown a professional pitch yet, so he's a high-variance profile even before you consider the unusual delivery.

Darius Austin's Fantasy Take: Evoking MacKenzie Gore's name isn't likely to make many fantasy-prospect hounds jump for joy at this point. I can easily see Solometo being a deceptive fantasy stalwart who sparks annual arguments because his peripherals aren't as gaudy as his results. Since we haven't actually seen his delivery in pro ball yet, let alone had a chance to determine how it'll hold up, I think it's fine to wait and see how he fares in regular competition.

10 Endy Rodriguez C OFP: 55 ETA: 2024

Born: 05/26/00 Age: 22 Bats: S Throws: R Height: 6'0" Weight: 170 lb. Origin: International Free Agent, 2018

YEAR	TEAM	LVL	AGE	PA	R	2B	3B	HR	RBI	BB	K	SB	CS	AVG/OBP/SLG	DRC+	BABIP	BRR	FRAA	WARP
2019	DSL MET1	ROK	19	35	5	4	0	2	8	5	5	0	0	.296/.457/.667		.300			
2019	MTS	ROK	19	90	14	10	1	0	6	10	13	4	0	.293/.393/.453		.349			
2021	BRD	A	21	434	73	25	6	15	73	50	77	2	0	.294/.380/.512	130	.333	-2.3	C(54) -1.5, 1B(18) -1.7, LF(4) -1.2	2.1
2022 non-DC	*PIT*	*MLB*	*22*	*251*	*24*	*11*	*2*	*5*	*26*	*19*	*51*	*1*	*1*	*.242/.305/.382*	*86*	*.289*	*0.0*	*C -4, 1B -1*	*0.1*

Comparables: Kennys Vargas, Salvador Perez, Wilin Rosario

The Report: The Mets inserted themselves into last offseason's Joe Musgrove deal to snag Joey Lucchesi from the Padres and sent a complex-league catcher, Endy Rodriguez, to the Pirates to sweeten the overall prospect package. It seemed like a nice bit of business at the time, but, a year later, Lucchesi is rehabbing from Tommy John surgery, while Rodriguez posted a near-.900 OPS in Low-A Bradenton. His batting line was pretty legit, as he has above-average bat speed and the barrel control to hit the ball hard just about anywhere in the zone. He was perhaps a touch on the older side for A-ball, and is physically mature, but both offensive tools could get to 55.

Perhaps one of the reasons Rodriguez is being brought along a bit slower—outside of, you know, the pandemic year—is his work behind the plate is well behind his performance at it. He has a cannon of an arm, but his receiving is noisy, and he graded out as a below-average receiver relative to the average A-ball catcher on the metrics. He saw a fair bit of time at first base and DH, and a bit in left field, as well. That isn't an unusual tactic for managing the workload of a young catcher while still getting his bat reps, but this seems to be more a case of preparing Rodriguez to play at other positions further up the ladder. To echo our Henry Davis comment, though, receiving is a teachable skill, and one that might be rendered obsolete in the coming years with an ABS system.

OFP: 55 / The exactly 75th-percentile outcome is a solid, starting, bat-first catcher

Variance: High. There's certainly offensive risk for any prospect that's a little old for A-ball and only played in A-ball. But ultimately, how his defense behind the plate develops will determine his eventual outcome. Rodriguez may hit enough to carry a corner spot, but real impact will only come if he stays a catcher at least a few days a week.

Darius Austin's Fantasy Take: It's nice that we have another potential bat-first catcher on the list here. That bat isn't comparable to Davis's, however, and, as long as the Pirates are slow-playing Rodriguez to either help him figure out catcher or see where else he might be able to stand on the field, I wouldn't use a roster spot on him outside of a very deep dynasty.

The Prospects You Meet Outside the Top Ten

#11

Matt Fraizer OF Born: 01/12/98 Age: 24 Bats: L Throws: R Height: 6'3" Weight: 217 lb. Origin: Round 3, 2019 Draft (#95 overall)

YEAR	TEAM	LVL	AGE	PA	R	2B	3B	HR	RBI	BB	K	SB	CS	AVG/OBP/SLG	DRC+	BABIP	BRR	FRAA	WARP
2019	WV	SS	21	171	20	5	1	0	15	14	38	5	3	.221/.287/.266		.288			
2021	GBO	A+	23	350	64	14	3	20	50	43	74	14	6	.314/.401/.578	130	.357	-1.2	LF(36) 1.9, CF(29) 5.0, RF(3) -0.0	2.9
2021	ALT	AA	23	149	20	12	3	3	18	13	34	1	2	.288/.356/.492	101	.361	-0.2	CF(31) -0.9, RF(1) 0.1	0.4
2022 non-DC	*PIT*	*MLB*	*24*	*251*	*25*	*11*	*1*	*6*	*26*	*20*	*64*	*4*	*3*	*.246/.314/.391*	*89*	*.318*	*0.3*	*CF 1, LF 1*	*0.8*

Comparables: Billy Burns, Greg Allen, Bryan Reynolds

A 2019 college third-rounder who has turned into an overaged and underrated prospect due to the lost 2020 season, Fraizer did nothing but perform in 2021, slashing .314/.401/.578 with 20 homers in 350 High-A plate appearances and managing .288/.356/.492 in 149 PA following a promotion to Double-A Altoona. Fraizer split his time relatively evenly between left and center while in Greensboro, but, after the promotion, played center field almost exclusively. At a listed 6-foot-3 and more than 200 pounds, he may eventually grow off the more-premium defensive spot, but, for now, he has the range and the arm for anywhere in the outfield. A lot of his success at the plate is the result of a strong approach, particularly his selectivity and an ability to foul off difficult pitches and extend at-bats. His pop comes from a swing path geared for power and a bat quick enough to get around and hammer balls inside. Although it's not the highest upside profile in the world, as long as Fraizer continues to perform offensively, he could be a major-league regular in the outfield.

#12

Brennan Malone RHP Born: 09/08/00 Age: 21 Bats: R Throws: R Height: 6'4" Weight: 205 lb. Origin: Round 1, 2019 Draft (#33 overall)

YEAR	TEAM	LVL	AGE	W	L	SV	G	GS	IP	H	HR	BB/9	K/9	K	GB%	BABIP	WHIP	ERA	DRA-	WARP
2019	DIA	ROK	18	1	2	0	6	3	7	4	0	6.4	9.0	7	33.3%	.222	1.29	5.14		
2019	HIL	SS	18	0	0	0	1	0	1	0	0	0.0	9.0	1	50.0%	.000	0.00	0.00		
2021	PIRG	ROK	20	0	0	0	6	5	10^{1}	7	1	4.4	12.2	14	60.9%	.273	1.16	5.23		
2022 non-DC	*PIT*	*MLB*	*21*	*2*	*3*	*0*	*57*	*0*	*50*	*55*	*8*	*6.8*	*7.6*	*42*	*42.8%*	*.316*	*1.88*	*7.13*	*149*	*-1.1*

Malone dealt with a blister issue early in the 2021 season and never really got stretched out before going down with a lat injury. His mid-90s fastball was more low 90s when he did pitch, but, really, it was just a lost season. He still has mid-rotation upside, assuming his fastball comes back and his breaking balls continue to project to above average, but Malone has thrown just 22 professional innings over three seasons. Most of that is bad luck rather than real durability concerns, but, until we see him back on a mound for something resembling a full season, we will have to ratchet down the fringe-101-prospect OFP from last season and tick up the risks.

#13

Cal Mitchell RF Born: 03/08/99 Age: 23 Bats: L Throws: L Height: 6'0" Weight: 205 lb. Origin: Round 2, 2017 Draft (#50 overall)

YEAR	TEAM	LVL	AGE	PA	R	2B	3B	HR	RBI	BB	K	SB	CS	AVG/OBP/SLG	DRC+	BABIP	BRR	FRAA	WARP
2019	BRD	A+	20	493	54	21	2	15	64	32	142	1	1	.251/.304/.406	94	.328	-0.4	RF(111) -1.7	0.9
2021	ALT	AA	22	419	43	19	1	12	61	24	71	6	7	.280/.330/.429	111	.313	-0.4	RF(92) -2.3, LF(5) -0.2	1.6
2022 non-DC	*PIT*	*MLB*	*23*	*251*	*24*	*10*	*0*	*6*	*27*	*13*	*52*	*1*	*1*	*.253/.301/.388*	*83*	*.302*	*-0.2*	*RF 1, LF 0*	*0.2*

Comparables: Jesse Winker, David Dahl, Tyler O'Neill

Mitchell made our Top 101 before the 2019 season on the strength of a plus-hit/plus-power projection and strong production in A-ball as a 19-year-old. Three years on, his plus raw power still hasn't turned into plus game power. He still takes an impressive batting practice and shows flashes in games, but his stroke can get a little armsy, and he doesn't really sell out for the pull-side lift. Overall, his swing just looks right once he lets those hands go, though, and can cover just about everything in the zone. Mitchell can look a little rough left-on-left, but he will battle and has a good two-strike approach, generally. Defensively, he's a better fit for left field than right, due to his merely average arm, but he runs well and is a savvy outfielder, so he should be at least solid-average there. We're still waiting for that power breakout three years on, but we're content to keep waiting, even with the corner defensive profile and occasional platoon issues. We think Mitchell still ends up a regular.

#14

Carmen Mlodzinski RHP Born: 02/19/99 Age: 23 Bats: R Throws: R Height: 6'2" Weight: 232 lb. Origin: Round 1, 2020 Draft (#31 overall)

YEAR	TEAM	LVL	AGE	W	L	SV	G	GS	IP	H	HR	BB/9	K/9	K	GB%	BABIP	WHIP	ERA	DRA-	WARP
2021	GBO	A+	22	2	3	0	14	14	50^{1}	45	7	3.6	11.4	64	43.3%	.317	1.29	3.93	81	0.9
2022 non-DC	*PIT*	*MLB*	*23*	*2*	*3*	*0*	*57*	*0*	*50*	*49*	*7*	*4.8*	*8.4*	*46*	*39.4%*	*.297*	*1.52*	*5.09*	*119*	*-0.3*

Comparables: Kameron Loe, Danny Duffy, Francis Beltran

When healthy, Mlodzinksi was a fairly successful High-A starter in 2021. Still, there are reliever markers here that leave him lower in the rankings than a recent first-ish-round college arm generally would be. His delivery is abrupt, and he's basically a two-pitch guy, though the two pitches are both pretty interesting. The fastball is a heavy 92–94 with hard, arm-side bore that generates plenty of soft contact, especially against same-sided hitters. He pairs his number one with a low- to mid-80s slider with varying characteristics; we've seen it big and sweeping, and we've seen it plus with depth and sharp, tight break. Generally, his plan of attack seems to be to pound the fastball in and the slider away to righties, and we have questions about how this will play (against lefties, especially) at the higher levels.

#15

Rodolfo Castro 2B Born: 05/21/99 Age: 23 Bats: S Throws: R Height: 6'0" Weight: 205 lb. Origin: International Free Agent, 2015

YEAR	TEAM	LVL	AGE	PA	R	2B	3B	HR	RBI	BB	K	SB	CS	AVG/OBP/SLG	DRC+	BABIP	BRR	FRAA	WARP
2019	GBO	A	20	246	33	13	2	14	46	18	68	6	5	.242/.306/.516	128	.271	2.0	2B(34) -0.1, SS(17) -0.6, 3B(7) 0.6	1.8
2019	BRD	A+	20	215	26	13	1	5	27	13	54	1	0	.243/.288/.391	98	.308	0.8	2B(37) 2.6, SS(16) -1.6, 3B(4) -0.2	0.7
2021	TOR	WIN	22	109	15	6	2	1	8	22	26	2	1	.235/.394/.388		.322			
2021	ALT	AA	22	312	43	14	1	12	47	19	72	7	4	.242/.295/.425	105	.278	0.9	3B(44) 2.1, 2B(24) 2.6, SS(4) -0.3	1.7
2021	IND	AAA	22	38	7	4	0	3	8	3	11	0	0	.286/.342/.657	107	.333	1.1	3B(4) -0.1, SS(3) -0.3, 2B(1) -0.1	0.2
2021	PIT	MLB	22	93	9	2	0	5	8	6	27	0	0	.198/.258/.395	90	.222	-0.2	2B(20) -2.1, 3B(5) 0.8	0.1
2022 DC	*PIT*	*MLB*	*23*	*198*	*20*	*9*	*1*	*6*	*23*	*11*	*52*	*2*	*1*	*.220/.273/.389*	*74*	*.273*	*0.1*	*2B 0, 3B 0*	*0.0*

Comparables: Jorge Polanco, Hernán Pérez, Yolmer Sánchez

Castro was added to the Pirates' 40-man after the 2020 season, so, despite being in Double-A for most of 2021, he did get a few major-league stints when Pittsburgh needed a fill-in infielder. He was mostly overmatched, especially against righties, but he showed legitimate plus power and the ability to play a few infield spots. His setup and load can be a little busy, but Castro shows plus bat speed and the ability to generate much louder contact than his rather-generously listed 6-foot frame suggests. He does tend to be overly aggressive early in counts, and you can get him off balance with spin. And despite being a switch hitter, he has consistently struggled with righties in his pro career. Castro is a better third baseman than second baseman, he's not quite as rangy as you'd like as the latter. He could probably even handle shortstop in an emergency. You can squint and see a second-division starter if he refines his approach a bit more in the upper minors and gets more of his power into games, but, given his platoon and approach issues, Castro is more likely to end up a very useful bench piece.

#16

Miguel Yajure RHP Born: 05/01/98 Age: 24 Bats: R Throws: R Height: 6'1" Weight: 220 lb. Origin: International Free Agent, 2015

YEAR	TEAM	LVL	AGE	W	L	SV	G	GS	IP	H	HR	BB/9	K/9	K	GB%	BABIP	WHIP	ERA	DRA-	WARP
2019	TAM	A+	21	8	6	0	22	18	127^2	110	5	2.0	8.6	122	54.8%	.301	1.08	2.26	102	1.4
2019	TRN	AA	21	1	0	0	2	2	11	9	0	1.6	9.0	11	35.5%	.290	1.00	0.82	111	0.0
2020	NYY	MLB	22	0	0	0	3	0	7	3	1	6.4	10.3	8	40.0%	.143	1.14	1.29	96	0.1
2021	IND	AAA	23	2	3	0	9	9	43^2	33	6	2.7	8.2	40	45.4%	.239	1.05	3.09	99	0.6
2021	PIT	MLB	23	0	2	0	4	3	15	17	6	4.2	6.6	11	34.7%	.256	1.60	8.40	122	0.0
2022 DC	*PIT*	*MLB*	*24*	*6*	*5*	*0*	*46*	*9*	*73*	*71*	*10*	*3.4*	*7.7*	*62*	*29.9%*	*.291*	*1.35*	*4.36*	*105*	*0.2*

Comparables: Jaime Navarro, Jason Hammel, Iván Nova

A forearm injury cost Yajure most of the 2021 season. The injury also may have cost him a tick or so on his fastball when he did pitch, and both minor- and major-league hitters were able to take him deep a fair bit more than you'd prefer. Yajure has a deep arsenal, showing six distinct pitches, but the best remains a hard, sinking change that comes in almost as firm as his fastball(s). That's fine for the changeup, which dips below bats, but makes it easier to time his low-90s fastball. Yajure will work a couple of fringy breaking balls in, as well, and, if healthy and if the fastball bounces back, he should be a useful spot starter or long reliever.

Prospects on the Rise

Maikol Escotto SS Born: 06/04/02 Age: 20 Bats: R Throws: R Height: 5'11" Weight: 180 lb. Origin: International Free Agent, 2018

YEAR	TEAM	LVL	AGE	PA	R	2B	3B	HR	RBI	BB	K	SB	CS	AVG/OBP/SLG	DRC+	BABIP	BRR	FRAA	WARP
2019	DSL NYY	ROK	17	218	47	11	4	8	26	32	57	13	3	.315/.429/.552		.422			
2021	BRD	A	19	381	61	13	1	7	38	54	116	22	5	.234/.354/.347	89	.343	1.0	SS(77) -0.0, 2B(10) -2.3	0.6
2022 non-DC	*PIT*	*MLB*	*20*	*251*	*20*	*9*	*0*	*3*	*19*	*22*	*85*	*7*	*3*	*.195/.274/.286*	*53*	*.298*	*0.6*	*SS 0, 2B -1*	*-0.6*

Comparables: Willi Castro, Junior Lake, Dilson Herrera

Escotto was a buzzy name in the Yankees' system last offseason before he was dealt to the Pirates. He seemed to confirm those reports with a strong start in A-ball. Escotto showed big-time bat speed and power potential but was an aggressive swinger and tended to expand the zone more than he should, belying his high walk rate. That, coupled with perhaps the rigors of his first full pro season, led to some offensive struggles down the stretch. Escotto is a smooth defender with a shot to stick at shortstop and the offensive upside to potentially survive a move down the defensive spectrum, but his profile at the plate is high risk until his swing decisions improve.

Jared Jones RHP Born: 08/06/01 Age: 20 Bats: L Throws: R Height: 6'1" Weight: 180 lb. Origin: Round 2, 2020 Draft (#44 overall)

YEAR	TEAM	LVL	AGE	W	L	SV	G	GS	IP	H	HR	BB/9	K/9	K	GB%	BABIP	WHIP	ERA	DRA-	WARP
2021	BRD	A	19	3	6	0	18	15	66	63	6	4.6	14.0	103	45.5%	.385	1.47	4.64	79	1.4
2022 non-DC	*PIT*	*MLB*	*20*	*2*	*3*	*0*	*57*	*0*	*50*	*49*	*7*	*5.5*	*9.4*	*51*	*41.6%*	*.306*	*1.59*	*5.41*	*123*	*-0.4*

Comparables: Luis Patiño, Willie Banks, Chad Gaudin

The Pirates' second-round pick in 2020, Jones flashed a big fastball and potentially above-average curve as a teenager in A-ball. His heater sometimes betrayed a fairly wide velocity range, but he regularly sat mid-90s and touched higher. It's a lively pitch, as well. His curve shows good 12–6 action and put away hitters in A-ball. His delivery is inconsistent, leading to occasional bouts of wildness and general issues with fastball command. He'll need to iron that out and improve one or both of the changeup and slider to stick in a rotation long-term, but there are building blocks here for a good starting-pitching prospect.

Luis Ortiz RHP Born: 01/27/99 Age: 23 Bats: R Throws: R Height: 6'2" Weight: 163 lb. Origin: International Free Agent, 2018

YEAR	TEAM	LVL	AGE	W	L	SV	G	GS	IP	H	HR	BB/9	K/9	K	GB%	BABIP	WHIP	ERA	DRA-	WARP
2019	BRS	ROA	20	2	2	0	11	11	50^{2}	48	4	4.3	6.6	37	48.4%	.284	1.42	4.09		
2021	BRD	A	22	5	3	0	22	19	87^{1}	82	5	2.9	11.6	113	51.3%	.344	1.26	3.09	89	1.4
2022 non-DC	*PIT*	*MLB*	*23*	*2*	*3*	*0*	*57*	*0*	*50*	*52*	*6*	*4.0*	*7.8*	*43*	*41.5%*	*.312*	*1.50*	*5.02*	*117*	*-0.3*

Signed at 19 for a five-figure bonus, Ortiz dominated Low-A last season on the strength of his mid-90s fastball and big-breaking, sweepy slider. His high-80s change will occasionally show enough power fade to have some utility, while, conversely, the slider's shape and, especially, depth can be inconsistent. Ortiz is an older power arm with some effort in his delivery, so perhaps he just ends up a 95-and-a-slider middle reliever. But he throws strikes, and his secondaries are intriguing, so there's no harm in letting him pitch in the High-A Greensboro (and hopefully Double-A Altoona) rotation this season.

Factors on the Farm

Max Kranick RHP Born: 07/21/97 Age: 24 Bats: R Throws: R Height: 6'3" Weight: 210 lb. Origin: Round 11, 2016 Draft (#345 overall)

YEAR	TEAM	LVL	AGE	W	L	SV	G	GS	IP	H	HR	BB/9	K/9	K	GB%	BABIP	WHIP	ERA	DRA-	WARP
2019	BRD	A+	21	6	7	0	20	20	109^{1}	100	11	2.5	6.4	78	41.9%	.276	1.19	3.79	111	0.7
2021	ALT	AA	23	1	0	0	3	3	15^{2}	14	2	1.1	9.2	16	38.6%	.286	1.02	4.02	107	0.1
2021	IND	AAA	23	4	4	0	12	12	54^{1}	53	6	2.7	7.5	45	35.1%	.292	1.27	4.14	104	0.6
2021	PIT	MLB	23	2	3	0	9	9	38^{2}	47	4	4.4	7.4	32	32.3%	.352	1.71	6.28	129	-0.3
2022 DC	*PIT*	*MLB*	*24*	*6*	*7*	*0*	*33*	*19*	*92.3*	*99*	*15*	*3.4*	*7.0*	*72*	*33.5%*	*.302*	*1.45*	*5.17*	*121*	*-0.3*

Comparables: Reynaldo López, Anthony Swarzak, Kyle Drabek

Kranick got knocked around in his major-league debut, making nine starts and never pitching into the sixth inning. He has never really had bat-missing stuff, and he got punished in the zone in the majors; he nibbled a bit too much in response, leading to a walk-rate bump, as well. His fastball sits mid-90s, and his slurvy breaking ball and cutter-ish slider do have average potential, but his command of all three pitches was lacking in his first shot at the bigs. Perhaps he'd be better deployed in short bursts as a fastball/breaking ball(s) reliever.

Tucupita Marcano UT Born: 09/16/99 Age: 22 Bats: L Throws: R Height: 6'0" Weight: 170 lb. Origin: International Free Agent, 2016

YEAR	TEAM	LVL	AGE	PA	R	2B	3B	HR	RBI	BB	K	SB	CS	AVG/OBP/SLG	DRC+	BABIP	BRR	FRAA	WARP
2019	FW	A	19	504	55	19	3	2	45	35	45	15	16	.270/.323/.337	107	.293	-4.6	3B(42) -2.0, SS(40) -5.2, 2B(32) 0.6	0.8
2021	IND	AAA	21	210	29	4	1	1	12	26	33	8	1	.230/.325/.279	97	.275	-1.4	2B(34) 0.9, LF(7) 0.9, 3B(4) -0.8	0.5
2021	ELP	AAA	21	202	31	7	2	6	27	27	26	4	4	.273/.366/.442	112	.287	-0.8	LF(12) -1.0, 2B(11) 1.6, SS(11) -0.6	0.9
2021	SD	MLB	21	50	7	1	0	0	3	6	9	0	1	.182/.280/.205	90	.229	0.5	2B(8) 0.9, LF(4) -0.3, RF(4) -0.5	0.2
2022 DC	*PIT*	*MLB*	*22*	*67*	*6*	*2*	*0*	*0*	*6*	*6*	*9*	*1*	*1*	*.230/.306/.320*	*73*	*.264*	*0.1*	*2B 0*	*0.0*

Comparables: Richard Ureña, Luis Sardinas, José Peraza

The Padres' system had been mostly emptied out by the time the Pirates dealt Adam Frazier to them at the deadline, but Marcano was a bit of a strange choice for the top piece in that trade. You could see the Bucs figuring he's a Frazier replacement in the medium term, given his defensive flexibility. Marcano has always shown some bat-to-ball and on-base ability in the minors, as well, but he doesn't have the kind of pop or contact profile that will keep major-league pitchers from challenging him. His speed—although he's never been a great base stealer—and defensive flexibility should make him a useful piece on a major-league bench, but, given his lack of oomph on offense, it's tough to see a starting role for him.

Travis Swaggerty CF Born: 08/19/97 Age: 24 Bats: L Throws: L Height: 5'11" Weight: 200 lb. Origin: Round 1, 2018 Draft (#10 overall)

YEAR	TEAM	LVL	AGE	PA	R	2B	3B	HR	RBI	BB	K	SB	CS	AVG/OBP/SLG	DRC+	BABIP	BRR	FRAA	WARP
2019	BRD	A+	21	524	79	20	3	9	40	57	116	23	8	.265/.347/.381	110	.334	1.8	CF(121) 6.8	3.3
2021	IND	AAA	23	48	6	0	0	3	7	6	8	3	0	.220/.333/.439	128	.200	0.2	CF(9) 2.3	0.6
2022 non-DC	*PIT*	*MLB*	*24*	*251*	*23*	*9*	*1*	*5*	*24*	*22*	*64*	*5*	*3*	*.223/.296/.347*	*74*	*.287*	*0.4*	*CF 3*	*0.5*

Comparables: Brett Jackson, Luis Liberato, Ben Gamel

Swaggerty missed most of the 2021 season after dislocating his shoulder on a dive back into first base in an early-season Triple-A game. He has revamped his swing to try to tap into more power, which has been a missing part of his game as a prospect. He showed more pop towards the end of the 2019 season and even for the first two weeks of 2021, but that's not a long track record, and we've thrown a serious shoulder injury into the pile, as well. Assuming Swaggerty comes back healthy in 2022, he could certainly be in line for some playing time with the big club. As with every significant 2021 prospect injury, though, we now have very little recent information about what exactly that major-league role will look like.

Because You Were Going to Ask

Tahnaj Thomas RHP Born: 06/16/99 Age: 23 Bats: R Throws: R Height: 6'4" Weight: 190 lb. Origin: International Free Agent, 2016

YEAR	TEAM	LVL	AGE	W	L	SV	G	GS	IP	H	HR	BB/9	K/9	K	GB%	BABIP	WHIP	ERA	DRA-	WARP
2019	BRS	ROA	20	2	3	0	12	12	48[1]	40	5	2.6	11.0	59	41.6%	.292	1.12	3.17		
2021	GBO	A+	22	3	3	0	16	16	60[2]	61	13	5.2	9.2	62	35.2%	.289	1.58	5.19	113	0.0
2022 non-DC	*PIT*	*MLB*	*23*	*2*	*3*	*0*	*57*	*0*	*50*	*56*	*9*	*5.9*	*7.4*	*41*	*42.3%*	*.311*	*1.78*	*6.90*	*149*	*-1.1*

Comparables: Chase De Jong, Brian Reith, Dennis Tankersley

Thomas had a rough year at High-A Greensboro; everybody knows it, so we'll try not to belabor the point. He began the season throwing upper 90s and flashed a promising breaking ball with a massive speed deficit. By midsummer, the stuff was diminished, and he spent some time on the shelf. His stuff ticked up when he returned, but then the command was an issue. He was left off the 40-man and unprotected from the Rule 5 draft. The pandemic non-season disrupted a lot of development schedules, and Thomas could still emerge as a future power reliever if he tweaks some things and harnesses what could still be a pair of plus pitches.

Top Talents 25 and Under (as of 4/1/2022):

1. Ke'Bryan Hayes, 3B
2. Oneil Cruz, SS
3. Henry Davis, C
4. Nick Gonzales, IF
5. Liover Peguero, SS
6. Roansy Contreras, RHP
7. Quinn Priester, RHP
8. Mitch Keller, RHP
9. Anthony Solamento, RHP
10. Lonnie White Jr., OF

The Buccos now have their two best hopes for homegrown stars up on their big-league roster in Hayes and Cruz, who could make a genuinely exceptional left side of the infield for the next half-decade or more. Hayes struggled through a wrist injury last year that hampered him for much of the season and cost him more than half the year in game time. His offense looked diminished from his 2020 taster, but it's fair to expect both improvement and health to proffer better results in 2022. If Hayes settles in as a league-average bat with Gold Glove defense, that's a magnificent building block, though he'll need to play a healthy full season before getting his hands measured for a bust.

Keller clips within the cutoff by a few days, but it's not entirely clear whether the next step in his development will ever come. His velocity remained a tick down from his adrenaline-fueled debut season, and his secondaries dropped a grade, correspondingly. Fortunately, Keller was healthy for nearly all of 2021 after missing much of the COVID-shortened 2020 with a muscle strain in his torso. The halting first 170 innings of Keller's career haven't matched his formerly lofty pedigree, but there is still hope that he can reclaim his potential, particularly in a Pirates rotation that can't help but offer reps. Much like fellow 25-and-under-er Bryse Wilson, however, the clock is ticking on this once-promising arm to both rediscover his peak stuff and the key to missing bats along with it.

San Diego Padres

The State of the System:

Boy, that (de)escalated quickly.

The Top Ten:

1 CJ Abrams SS OFP: 70 ETA: 2022

Born: 10/03/00 Age: 21 Bats: L Throws: R Height: 6'2" Weight: 185 lb. Origin: Round 1, 2019 Draft (#6 overall)

YEAR	TEAM	LVL	AGE	PA	R	2B	3B	HR	RBI	BB	K	SB	CS	AVG/OBP/SLG	DRC+	BABIP	BRR	FRAA	WARP
2019	SD1	ROK	18	156	40	12	8	3	22	10	14	14	6	.401/.442/.662		.425			
2019	FW	A	18	9	1	1	0	0	0	1	0	1	0	.250/.333/.375	110	.250	0.1	SS(1) 0.1	0.1
2021	SA	AA	20	183	26	14	0	2	23	15	36	13	2	.296/.363/.420	104	.365	2.7	SS(33) -0.6, 2B(6) -0.5	0.8
2022 non-DC	*SD*	*MLB*	*21*	*251*	*20*	*11*	*1*	*2*	*21*	*17*	*58*	*13*	*4*	*.231/.291/.330*	*71*	*.297*	*1.1*	*SS 0, 2B 0*	*0.1*

Comparables: J.P. Crawford, Gavin Lux, Richard Ureña

The Report: Abrams has one of the most advanced hit tools in the minors; he's a career .343 hitter. He has a fairly compact and sweet lefty swing, getting to the ball quickly with innate bat-to-ball ability. He's an 80 runner, so anything hit on the ground is a potential infield single. We have little doubt that he is going to hit for a good average as long as he continues to swing at good pitches. Defensively, he has a shot to stick at shortstop, pending the disposition of Fernando Tatis Jr.'s future position; he also has experience at second base and, given his speed, would certainly profile in center, as well.

The one skill-related question is his future power output. If Abrams had even a solid-average power projection, he might be the best prospect in the game. But he doesn't—his batted ball data just doesn't show a lot of hard-hit balls—and we've heard from scouts who are fairly out on him based on 2021 game action because they just don't see any power projection actualizing. For now, we're middling it and holding the line on a fringe-average future output, but we are going to have to see it show up in games pretty soon.

Abrams was on his way to the Futures Game, and possibly even a major-league call-up, when he broke his left leg and sprained his medial collateral ligament in a basepath collision in July. The Padres put him on the Arizona Fall League roster in October, but he never got into a game due to a shoulder injury. While we expect him to be absolutely fine by the time spring rolls around, the missed reps are a concern.

OFP: 70 / All-Star shortstop or second baseman

Variance: Medium. Health and future power output are the only nitpicks.

Mark Barry's Fantasy Take: The range of fantasy outcomes is wide for Abrams, but his elite speed should keep the floor pretty high. If any power comes, we're looking at a dude who can be a perennial first rounder in most redraft leagues. If it doesn't, Abrams should still challenge for the league lead in steals with regular playing time. Obviously, both are super-useful fantasy options, which justifies his spot as a no-doubt, top-10 dynasty prospect.

2 Robert Hassell III OF OFP: 60 ETA: 2024

Born: 08/15/01 Age: 20 Bats: L Throws: L Height: 6'2" Weight: 195 lb. Origin: Round 1, 2020 Draft (#8 overall)

YEAR	TEAM	LVL	AGE	PA	R	2B	3B	HR	RBI	BB	K	SB	CS	AVG/OBP/SLG	DRC+	BABIP	BRR	FRAA	WARP
2021	LE	A	19	429	77	31	3	7	65	57	74	31	6	.323/.415/.482	125	.385	3.1	CF(84) -3.8, RF(2) -0.1	2.9
2021	FW	A+	19	87	10	2	1	4	11	9	25	3	0	.205/.287/.410	102	.245	-0.3	CF(16) -0.9	0.2
2022 non-DC	*SD*	*MLB*	*20*	*251*	*22*	*11*	*1*	*3*	*22*	*21*	*58*	*9*	*3*	*.231/.301/.343*	*76*	*.295*	*0.8*	*CF 1, RF 0*	*0.3*

Comparables: Alex Verdugo, Colby Rasmus, Manuel Margot

The Report: Considered by many to be the top prep bat in the 2020 draft class, Hassell did little to alter those opinions throughout his professional debut last year. Lean and wiry with a skinny lower half, Hassell generates above-average bat speed and showcases plus bat control from the left side of the plate. His approach can turn passive, at times, but he has an advanced feel for the strike zone and rarely expands. The next step will be continuing to hone in on his plan of attack within the zone, singling out pitches to hit in favorable counts. It's primarily gap power at present, but his hit tool and approach, in addition to physical maturity, should lead to fringe-average game power at maturity. He's a solid-average runner with good instincts on the bases, but his reads and jumps are inconsistent, and he will need further refinement to profile as an average defender in center field.

OFP: 60 / First-division regular

Variance: Medium. The bat should be enough to play everyday, regardless of position, but he will need to stick in center field to reach his ceiling as a first-division regular.

Mark Barry's Fantasy Take: BOB-BY BAR-RELS (clap, clap, clapclapclap)!

Hassell hit the ground running in his first taste of pro ball this season, doing nothing to quell my Diet Michael Brantley comp from a year ago. His struggles in High-A (mostly the strikeouts) were a little more concerning—so maybe Michael Brantley Zero? Is that worse? New Michael Brantley? Michael Brantley 2?

Anyway, Hassell is a clear top-25 dynasty prospect with batting average and OBP as the carrying categories.

Eyewitness Report: Robert Hassell III

Evaluator: Trevor Andresen

Report Date: 08/05/2021

Dates Seen: 5/11/21-5/16/21. 6/8/21-6/13/21, 7/27/21-8/1/21

Risk Factor: Medium

Physical/Health: 6'2 195 lb. frame w/ a lean, wiry build & skinny lower half.

Tool	Future Grade	Report
Hit	60	Above-average bat speed w/ plus bat control. Patient, almost passive approach at times, but has an advanced feel for the strike zone w/ little chase & the ability to both recognize & react to spin. The last step will be continuing to hone in on his approach within the zone & singling out pitches he can drive into the gaps, but the framework is there for a .270-.280 bat.
Power	50	Primarily gap-gap power at present, but the hit tool/approach in addition to physical maturity should lead to 15-20 HR power.
Baserunning/ Speed	50	Solid-average runner w/ good instincts on the bases.
Glove	50	Average overall package in CF. His routes are fine, but the reads/jumps are inconsistent & he lacks the pure speed to make up for it. He also has a tendency to coast towards the ball & gets too nonchalant at times. Real shot to stick in CF, but further development is required & will likely slide to a corner in deference to a stronger defender on a championship caliber team.
Arm	50	Average strength & accuracy. Works in CF, but might limit him to LF if he is forced to move to a corner.

Conclusion: Above-average regular w/ a hit tool-driven profile. Occasional all-star type if he's able to stick in CF.

3 Luis Campusano C   OFP: 60   ETA: Debuted in 2020

Born: 09/29/98 Age: 23 Bats: R Throws: R Height: 5'11" Weight: 232 lb. Origin: Round 2, 2017 Draft (#39 overall)

YEAR	TEAM	LVL	AGE	PA	R	2B	3B	HR	RBI	BB	K	SB	CS	AVG/OBP/SLG	DRC+	BABIP	BRR	FRAA	WARP
2019	LE	A+	20	487	63	31	1	15	81	52	57	0	0	.325/.396/.509	148	.340	-3.1	C(77) 5.2, 1B(2) 0.0	4.5
2020	SD	MLB	21	4	2	0	0	1	1	0	2	0	0	.333/.500/1.333	103		0.0		0.0
2021	ELP	AAA	22	326	47	21	3	15	45	27	66	1	0	.295/.365/.541	111	.335	-0.8	C(62) 1.8, 1B(3) -0.1	1.7
2021	SD	MLB	22	38	0	0	0	0	1	4	11	0	0	.088/.184/.088	76	.130	-1.3	C(9) -0.4	-0.1
2022 DC	*SD*	*MLB*	*23*	*30*	*3*	*1*	*0*	*0*	*3*	*2*	*6*	*0*	*0*	*.241/.309/.397*	*89*	*.291*	*0.0*	*C 0*	*0.1*

Comparables: Salvador Perez, Wilson Ramos, Pablo Sandoval

The Report: Campusano spent the first month of the 2021 season on the Padres' bench and then had a nice consolidation season as a 22-year-old in Triple-A after his late-2020/early-2021 major-league run. He has a potential plus hit tool that has manifested in healthy batting averages at all minor-league levels. His eye and approach are well refined, and he barrels the baseball up for solid contact. His power is getting to above average as more balls, which were previously falling in the gaps, get over the fence, although he was in a juiced power environment in Triple-A last season.

Defensively, he has a strong arm, which is one of the most-visible and least-important parts of catching, although he has posted below-par caught-stealing rates so far. He is improving as a receiver; his framing metrics have been a bit above average in the minors and a bit below average in his limited major-league action, which lines up with the eyeball test.

In October 2020, Campusano was charged with felony marijuana possession during a traffic stop near his home in Georgia. Charges were dropped six months later for lack of probable cause on the traffic stop. It is, in a single word, horseshit that overzealous prosecutors could charge someone—especially a young person of color—with a felony for possession of less than three ounces of weed, especially off a bad traffic stop.

OFP: 60 / First-division catcher

Variance: Medium. Campusano has had success all the way up and down the minor leagues and has already seen major-league time.

Mark Barry's Fantasy Take: It's typically tough to rank fantasy catchers. The turnover in the top 10 behind the dish on a year-to-year basis is wild, which leads me to severely devalue backstops in one-catcher formats. Campusano is a good hitter—he's never been below a .275 average at any level (minimum 60 plate appearances), and he's adding some game power to his output. As far as dynasty catching prospects go, Campusano is a good one, but being a good dynasty prospect at catcher is less valuable than at pretty much any other position.

4 MacKenzie Gore LHP   OFP: 55   ETA: 2022? Never?

Born: 02/24/99 Age: 23 Bats: L Throws: L Height: 6'2" Weight: 197 lb. Origin: Round 1, 2017 Draft (#3 overall)

YEAR	TEAM	LVL	AGE	W	L	SV	G	GS	IP	H	HR	BB/9	K/9	K	GB%	BABIP	WHIP	ERA	DRA-	WARP
2019	LE	A+	20	7	1	0	15	15	79^1	36	4	2.3	12.5	110	36.5%	.212	0.71	1.02	77	1.3
2019	AMA	AA	20	2	1	0	5	5	21^2	20	3	3.3	10.4	25	44.6%	.321	1.29	4.15	83	0.3
2021	PAD	ROK	22	1	0	0	3	3	16^1	13	0	2.2	12.1	22	45.9%	.351	1.04	1.65		
2021	SA	AA	22	0	0	0	2	2	9	6	0	8.0	16.0	16	47.1%	.353	1.56	3.00	92	0.1
2021	ELP	AAA	22	0	2	0	6	6	20	24	3	5.4	8.1	18	46.2%	.339	1.80	5.85	105	0.0
2022 DC	*SD*	*MLB*	*23*	*1*	*1*	*0*	*6*	*6*	*29*	*27*	*4*	*5.0*	*9.7*	*31*	*42.0%*	*.300*	*1.50*	*4.97*	*114*	*0.0*

Comparables: Robb Nen, Luiz Gohara, Carlos Martínez

The Report: Last year in this space we wrote about "industry scuttlebutt" that Gore was having command and mechanical problems. To make a long, muddled story digestible: In late summer 2020, we started hearing major chatter that Gore had lost the strike zone. Because San Diego was not in the alternate-site data/video share, and Gore never threw in front of opposing scouts or the public after summer camp, we were not able to fully report that out at the time, and the Padres, themselves, were tight-lipped about it. But the industry was pretty convinced something was up, and Gore's lack of a 2020 promotion, despite desperate organizational need, gave us some inferential confirmation, enough to fade him both on this list and the Top 101. Dennis Lin of *The Athletic* contemporaneously confirmed with Gore, himself, that the lefty had issues ramping up and with his mechanics in 2020.

Fast-forward to 2021. Gore—who, in 2018–19, showed potential for four plus pitches—came out in spring training, and then Triple-A, ineffective with diminished stuff. Worse, he frequently lost the strike zone. After a month and a half of struggles in El Paso, the Padres pulled him back to the complex. When he started pitching in front of outside observers again two months later, he barely looked like the same pitcher, mechanically; he had severely shortened his arm path and leg kick, quickening his whole delivery. He pitched nine more games, spread across three levels and the Arizona Fall League, and was no more successful at throwing consistent strikes with his new motion. Depending on precisely which outing you saw, you could come away thinking he was back to the old MacKenzie Gore, thinking he was done, or anything in between.

Any future projection or comp here is a pure dart throw.

OFP: 55 / We guess we have to put a number on this

Variance: Extreme. Do I need to explain this one further?

Mark Barry's Fantasy Take: When a team opts to sign *2021 Jake Arrieta* after he was waived by the *2021 Cubs* rather than promote a former top prospect and future ace, well, it's not good. Maybe I'll miss out on a Gore discount since the bloom seems to be off the rose, but I'm out on the lefty until he flashes any signs of consistency.

5 James Wood CF   OFP: 55   ETA: 2025

Born: 09/17/02 Age: 19 Bats: L Throws: R Height: 6'7" Weight: 240 lb. Origin: Round 2, 2021 Draft (#62 overall)

YEAR	TEAM	LVL	AGE	PA	R	2B	3B	HR	RBI	BB	K	SB	CS	AVG/OBP/SLG	DRC+	BABIP	BRR	FRAA	WARP
2021	PAD	ROK	18	101	18	5	0	3	22	13	32	10	0	.372/.465/.535		.569			

Comparables: Jairo Mendez, Dalton Pompey, Devon Torrence

The Report: Wood was a showcase phenom before his draft season at IMG Academy. He has a swing that comps best to one of those optical illusions that can either be a vase or two people kissing—it's awkward or easy depending on how you look at it—but that generates an elite contact profile, nonetheless. He's only going to get stronger, too, as, even at a listed 240 pounds, he's a lean 6-foot-7. That means Wood will likely grow off center field but into enough power that it doesn't matter. Swing-and-miss will be a recurring ding on the profile—it's hard to be short to the ball at that size, and the swing does often look awkward—and those concerns were only exacerbated last year with a down spring season. Everything was copacetic on the back fields of Arizona, though, and Wood is a scout's favorite who doesn't lack for ceiling.

OFP: 55 / Above-average outfielder

Variance: Extreme. The prep-season struggles are concerning, but IMG plays one of the toughest schedules in the country. The upside in the tools is obvious. Check back again next year.

Mark Barry's Fantasy Take: The athletic package sounds great, it really does. And we've recently seen big, tall dudes have success, from Aaron Judge to Oneil Cruz. Still, since 1871 (yep, that's right) only 10 guys 6-foot-7 or taller have swatted 10 or more homers in a career. Two of them were pitchers. So, while the eventual profile is tantalizing, I'd approach Wood with all of the grains of salt, as being that big and that talented is a rare combination.

6 Jackson Merrill SS   OFP: 55   ETA: 2025/2026

Born: 04/19/03 Age: 19 Bats: L Throws: R Height: 6'3" Weight: 195 lb. Origin: Round 1, 2021 Draft (#27 overall)

YEAR	TEAM	LVL	AGE	PA	R	2B	3B	HR	RBI	BB	K	SB	CS	AVG/OBP/SLG	DRC+	BABIP	BRR	FRAA	WARP
2021	PAD	ROK	18	120	19	7	2	0	10	10	27	5	1	.280/.339/.383		.370			

Comparables: Luis Guillorme, Adrian Valerio, Nelson Molina

The Report: Merrill was a true out-of-nowhere pop-up last spring. We first heard his name in May, when a scout flagged for us that upper-level decision-makers were coming in on a Maryland shortstop nobody had on public lists (we thought we might get a few of these late-risers given the realities of pandemic scouting). Within weeks, the word circulated around, and Merrill was on everyone's lists as a prospect likely to be taken in the first couple of rounds. He ended up going late in the first round for a below-slot deal. If there was ever a team president or GM willing to sign off on a first-round pick who nobody had heard of two months earlier, it's A.J. Preller.

Merrill has a great-looking swing and bat path that hint at the potential for an above-average-to-plus hit projection, although his relatively low level of competition and his late jump in development means that's way more projection than we're usually comfortable making for prospects. His power also projects to above average given his projectable frame and ability to make hard contact. Merrill is currently a shortstop, and his actions are fine there, but, given the expectations for his projectable body, his long-term defensive home might be first base.

OFP: 55 / Starting third baseman or shortstop

Variance: High. We have a very limited track record on Merrill.

Mark Barry's Fantasy Take: Prep shortstops that could be cold corner pros are definitely not my jam. Merrill could be the exception that proves this rule, I guess, as dudes with his kind of background and emergence don't come around all that often. Toss him on the watchlist, for now, and be ready to pounce if he starts making noise in the spring.

7 Reiss Knehr RHP OFP: 45 ETA: Debuted in 2021

Born: 11/03/96 Age: 25 Bats: L Throws: R Height: 6'2" Weight: 205 lb. Origin: Round 20, 2018 Draft (#591 overall)

YEAR	TEAM	LVL	AGE	W	L	SV	G	GS	IP	H	HR	BB/9	K/9	K	GB%	BABIP	WHIP	ERA	DRA-	WARP
2019	LE	A+	22	3	5	1	17	12	66[1]	71	11	3.8	11.3	83	43.5%	.347	1.49	5.43	94	0.4
2021	SA	AA	24	6	1	0	11	11	55[1]	41	4	3.6	7.5	46	43.7%	.253	1.14	3.90	107	0.1
2021	ELP	AAA	24	0	2	1	8	5	20[1]	15	3	4.0	8.9	20	51.9%	.250	1.18	2.66	91	0.2
2021	SD	MLB	24	1	2	0	12	5	29	23	2	6.2	6.2	20	34.5%	.247	1.48	4.97	120	0.0
2022 DC	*SD*	*MLB*	*25*	*3*	*3*	*0*	*32*	*3*	*38.7*	*40*	*6*	*5.1*	*7.8*	*33*	*41.6%*	*.299*	*1.60*	*5.68*	*126*	*-0.3*

Comparables: Tyler Cravy, Kip Gross, Brock Stewart

The Report: A two-way player at Fordham, Knehr has struggled to consistently throw enough strikes in the pros, but his combination of a high-spin fastball that can regularly scrape 95 and a firm power change with late fade meant he didn't have to be too fine in the upper minors to be successful. That didn't work quite as well in the majors, as Knehr's lively fastball was getting swings-and-misses almost as often as his secondaries—he occasionally throws a cutter and slider, as well. In 2021, the cutter looked like it might emerge as the above-average secondary, but it was hit about as hard as any pitch in the majors last year. Knehr's delivery is upright and up-tempo with arm effort, so he fits best in the pen, but hopefully he will soon have enough command and a right-on-right offering that allows him to throw multiple innings.

OFP: 45 / Utility arm

Variance: Medium. Knehr needs to iron out the control and command before he can be more than an up-and-down pen-arm option, but the fastball/change combo flashed above-average quality.

Mark Barry's Fantasy Take: I think we saw the Padres' plan for Knehr in 2021, when they used him occasionally as an opener but mostly as an option out of the pen. If he gets multiple innings, he could be rosterable in NL-only leagues, but, otherwise, I'm passing.

8 Ethan Elliott LHP OFP: 45 ETA: 2023

Born: 04/28/97 Age: 25 Bats: L Throws: L Height: 6'3" Weight: 180 lb. Origin: Round 10, 2019 Draft (#293 overall)

YEAR	TEAM	LVL	AGE	W	L	SV	G	GS	IP	H	HR	BB/9	K/9	K	GB%	BABIP	WHIP	ERA	DRA-	WARP
2019	TRI	SS	22	0	0	0	12	12	35[2]	27	3	1.0	9.6	38	52.1%	.264	0.87	1.77		
2021	FW	A+	24	2	1	0	12	12	58	43	13	2.0	11.0	71	35.5%	.234	0.97	2.95	85	1.1
2021	SA	AA	24	0	1	0	3	3	12[2]	16	1	4.3	11.4	16	31.6%	.405	1.74	3.55	115	0.0
2022 non-DC	*SD*	*MLB*	*25*	*2*	*3*	*0*	*57*	*0*	*50*	*50*	*8*	*3.6*	*7.8*	*43*	*42.0%*	*.290*	*1.40*	*4.97*	*116*	*-0.2*

Comparables: Vidal Nuño, Dereck Rodríguez, Dillon Peters

The Report: Elliot is the kind of soft-tossing lefty with a good change that we generally value more as an aesthetic experience at the ballpark—this cohort usually works quickly and throws strikes—than within the list-making process, but here we are. Elliot works off a bit of deception and advanced command of a fastball that generally sits around 90 mph. His best secondary is the aforementioned change piece, a low-80s straight change with just enough fade and just enough velocity separation to keep righties (and the occasional lefty) off balance. It doesn't really have the kind of bat-missing shape to merit plus projection, but it could be a solid-average pitch. Elliot rounds out his arsenal with a short slider, around 80 mph, which can come at a tricky angle for lefties when he's locating it down and out of the zone. He also hit the injured list shortly after a midseason promotion to Double-A and never returned.

OFP: 45 / No. 4–5 starter

Variance: Medium. The building blocks are all here for a back-end starter, and the stuff is reasonably advanced, but this is also the kind of profile that can hit a speed bump in the upper minors. There's also the fact that he missed half the 2021 season with the always encouraging "unspecified issue."

Mark Barry's Fantasy Take: There's a chance Elliott could "crafty lefty" his way to the back end of the rotation, but, even then, he's likely a streaming option that you'd only use on an emergency basis.

9 Euribiel Angeles IF   OFP: 45   ETA: 2024

Born: 05/11/02 Age: 20 Bats: R Throws: R Height: 5'11" Weight: 175 lb. Origin: International Free Agent, 2018

YEAR	TEAM	LVL	AGE	PA	R	2B	3B	HR	RBI	BB	K	SB	CS	AVG/OBP/SLG	DRC+	BABIP	BRR	FRAA	WARP
2019	DSL PAD	ROK	17	198	28	9	2	0	26	15	19	17	9	.301/.359/.376		.325			
2021	LE	A	19	405	65	22	6	3	56	32	61	18	6	.343/.397/.461	117	.399	1.3	SS(41) 0.2, 2B(28) -1.2, 3B(14) -0.9	2.0
2021	FW	A+	19	86	12	4	0	1	8	8	16	1	1	.264/.369/.361	104	.327	1.6	3B(9) 0.4, SS(8) 0.8, 2B(1) 0.1	0.6
2022 non-DC	*SD*	*MLB*	*20*	*251*	*20*	*10*	*1*	*1*	*20*	*15*	*51*	*7*	*4*	*.250/.302/.338*	*74*	*.313*	*0.7*	*SS 1, 2B 0*	*0.2*

The Report: One of the youngest players at both of the levels he appeared at in 2021, Angeles performed on paper and passed the eye test, as well. He utilizes a short, simple swing with above-average bat control and strong strike-zone awareness to overcome his lack of raw impact, but he will need to continue to hone in on pitch selection as advanced pitchers will challenge him in the zone more frequently. Just an average runner, Angeles displays smooth, fluid actions on the dirt and shows the ability to slow the game down. He lacks the lateral range and quickness to make him a slam dunk to stick at shortstop, but his above-average arm and reliable hands are capable of playing anywhere on the dirt.

OFP: 45 / Good utility infielder or second-division regular.

Variance: Medium. There isn't huge upside here, but his raw bat control and defensive versatility give him a high probability of turning in major-league value.

Mark Barry's Fantasy Take: You could argue that Angeles might be the third-best fantasy prospect in this system . . . and the second-best Angeles in the division. He hasn't faced advanced-level arms yet, but, so far, he has managed to steal a bunch of bases and make a bunch of contact.

10 Justin Lange RHP   OFP: 45   ETA: 2025

Born: 09/11/01 Age: 20 Bats: R Throws: R Height: 6'4" Weight: 220 lb. Origin: Round 1, 2020 Draft (#34 overall)

YEAR	TEAM	LVL	AGE	W	L	SV	G	GS	IP	H	HR	BB/9	K/9	K	GB%	BABIP	WHIP	ERA	DRA-	WARP
2021	PAD	ROK	19	0	3	0	9	9	22	18	1	6.1	11.9	29	44.4%	.321	1.50	6.95		

The Report: Lange was a pop-up velocity guy in the 2020 draft after filling out more of his 6-foot-4 frame. The fastball backslid into the low 90s in 2021, and while he had advanced feel for a changeup for a prep arm, he didn't have a noteworthy breaking ball. Lange uses a low-80s slider, which hasn't come along as far as you would have hoped after a year of pro instruction. His lower slot and the arm effort in the delivery might mark him for the pen, anyway, but he has at least had a track record of throwing harder than this in the recent past.

OFP: 45 / Back-end starter or medium-leverage relief

Variance: High. Lange still has some projection left and flashed plus-or-better velocity in 2020, but he remains a long-term project as a pitching prospect.

Mark Barry's Fantasy Take: Lange is still pretty much exclusively projection, but, at least this time around, he has some minor-league strikeouts to dream on, as well. The command is, let's be generous, not good, so there's still a long way to go before projection becomes reality and a long way to go before you need to put him on your fantasy radar.

The Prospects You Meet Outside the Top Ten

Prospects on the Rise

Victor Acosta SS Born: 06/10/04 Age: 18 Bats: S Throws: R Height: 5'11" Weight: 170 lb. Origin: International Free Agent, 2021

YEAR	TEAM	LVL	AGE	PA	R	2B	3B	HR	RBI	BB	K	SB	CS	AVG/OBP/SLG	DRC+	BABIP	BRR	FRAA	WARP
2021	DSL PAD	ROK	17	240	45	12	5	5	31	38	45	26	7	.285/.431/.484		.345			

Comparables: Pedro Guerrero, Geral Silva, Emerson Jimenez

A switch-hitting shortstop signed in the 2020–21 international-free-agent period for $1.8 million, Acosta posted the kind of speed and approach numbers that mean he's probably already rostered in your dynasty league. However, he looked overmatched in instructs, albeit while facing more-advanced competition than in your typical October on the backfields, and he isn't likely to be a shortstop for long. He has enough bat speed for us to put him in this section in an otherwise-shallow system and to unhelpfully tell you to check back in with us in a year.

Robert Gasser LHP Born: 05/31/99 Age: 23 Bats: L Throws: L Height: 6'1" Weight: 190 lb. Origin: Round 2, 2021 Draft (#71 overall)

YEAR	TEAM	LVL	AGE	W	L	SV	G	GS	IP	H	HR	BB/9	K/9	K	GB%	BABIP	WHIP	ERA	DRA-	WARP
2021	LE	A	22	0	0	0	5	5	14	11	1	1.3	8.4	13	52.8%	.286	0.93	1.29	110	0.0
2022 non-DC	*SD*	*MLB*	*23*	*2*	*3*	*0*	*57*	*0*	*50*	*52*	*7*	*4.0*	*7.0*	*38*	*45.7%*	*.297*	*1.49*	*5.15*	*117*	*-0.3*

Comparables: Pedro Hernandez, Tyler Alexander, Leo Crawford

Gasser works from a simple, easy delivery with a short arm action and low-three-quarters release. He repeats his operation well and creates deception that helps his raw stuff play up. He'll run his fastball up to 94, sitting comfortably in the 90–93 range with run, sink and strong command. His low-80s slider is his best secondary, flashing above-average with 10–4 tilt at its best. He also works in a low- to mid-80s changeup with slight fade and depth, giving him a solid third offering. He doesn't have huge upside, but the ingredients are present for a pitchability/command back-end starter.

Brandon Valenzuela C Born: 10/02/00 Age: 21 Bats: S Throws: R Height: 6'0" Weight: 170 lb. Origin: International Free Agent, 2017

YEAR	TEAM	LVL	AGE	PA	R	2B	3B	HR	RBI	BB	K	SB	CS	AVG/OBP/SLG	DRC+	BABIP	BRR	FRAA	WARP
2019	SD1	ROK	18	183	21	4	1	0	20	34	32	0	0	.248/.399/.290		.316			
2021	LE	A	20	378	50	21	3	6	62	44	80	3	2	.307/.389/.444	114	.386	-0.8	C(49) 10.8, 1B(19) 0.8	2.7
2021	FW	A+	20	65	4	1	0	1	7	15	20	1	0	.245/.415/.327	98	.379	-0.2	C(14) -1.4	0.0
2022 non-DC	*SD*	*MLB*	*21*	*251*	*21*	*10*	*1*	*2*	*20*	*22*	*68*	*0*	*1*	*.219/.294/.315*	*66*	*.301*	*-0.2*	*C -1, 1B 0*	*-0.3*

Comparables: Rafael Marchan, William Contreras, Francisco Mejía

Valenzuela is a physical, 6-foot, 200-pound, switch-hitting catcher with average bat speed and a level swing plane from both sides of the plate, limiting the utility of his raw impact. He puts together quality at-bats on a consistent basis but is primarily a fastball hitter who suffered from the lack of a 2020 season and is still learning to handle quality spin. He's surprisingly athletic and mobile behind the plate given his size, but his hands and receiving ability are more fringy to below-average. His field-general presence gives him a chance to profile as a backup catcher, especially with automated strike zones on on horizon.

Factors on the Farm

Jonny Homza C Born: 06/13/99 Age: 23 Bats: R Throws: R Height: 6'0" Weight: 185 lb. Origin: Round 5, 2017 Draft (#138 overall)

YEAR	TEAM	LVL	AGE	PA	R	2B	3B	HR	RBI	BB	K	SB	CS	AVG/OBP/SLG	DRC+	BABIP	BRR	FRAA	WARP
2019	AKL	WIN	20	143	24	5	1	5	21	12	35	2	0	.287/.352/.457		.360			
2019	TRI	SS	20	211	18	14	1	0	13	21	62	2	0	.216/.313/.303		.325			
2021	FW	A+	22	368	52	17	3	6	43	42	116	8	5	.218/.329/.349	87	.321	-4.3	C(44) 3.6, 3B(8) -0.7, 1B(3) -0.4	0.3
2022 non-DC	*SD*	*MLB*	*23*	*251*	*19*	*10*	*1*	*3*	*20*	*20*	*84*	*1*	*1*	*.191/.270/.289*	*52*	*.290*	*0.0*	*C 0, 3B 0*	*-0.6*

Homza is a prep shortstop who converted to catcher, and the defensive transition is going well, as his frame is starting to grow into the position, and his sneaky twitch helps him behind the plate. At the dish, Homza shows off a good approach and the ability to sting the ball into the gaps. That, coupled with his defensive flexibility beyond being just a backstop, should make him a very useful bench piece in the majors if he can hit a little bit more than he has shown so far.

Eguy Rosario IF Born: 08/25/99 Age: 22 Bats: R Throws: R Height: 5'9" Weight: 150 lb. Origin: International Free Agent, 2015

YEAR	TEAM	LVL	AGE	PA	R	2B	3B	HR	RBI	BB	K	SB	CS	AVG/OBP/SLG	DRC+	BABIP	BRR	FRAA	WARP
2019	LE	A+	19	512	60	25	8	7	72	37	103	21	9	.278/.331/.412	105	.338	0.7	3B(69) -1.8, SS(20) -0.2, 2B(15) -0.6	1.4
2020	MAR	WIN	20	112	18	6	2	0	14	7	13	8	0	.327/.393/.429		.368			
2021	PEJ	WIN	21	73	9	3	0	1	12	8	13	2	2	.250/.342/.344		.300			
2021	SA	AA	21	481	65	31	3	12	61	49	109	30	14	.281/.360/.455	110	.349	-4.6	SS(69) -3.3, 2B(38) 4.2, 3B(7) 0.6	1.7
2022 non-DC	*SD*	*MLB*	*22*	*251*	*22*	*12*	*1*	*4*	*23*	*19*	*58*	*8*	*5*	*.230/.297/.351*	*75*	*.292*	*0.8*	*SS -1, 3B 0*	*0.1*

Comparables: Jorge Polanco, Cheslor Cuthbert, Wilmer Flores

One of the few interesting (and healthy) bats left in the Padres' upper minors, Rosario profiles best as a good fifth infielder. He has the ability to play an average shortstop and an arm that is far enough above average for third base. At the plate, his loose right-handed stroke generates average raw power, but he doesn't always pick the right pitch to try to drive, which might limit both his hit and power tools to fringe- or below-average, making it hard to pencil him into a lineup every day.

Kevin Kopps RHP Born: 03/02/97 Age: 25 Bats: R Throws: R Height: 6'0" Weight: 200 lb. Origin: Round 3, 2021 Draft (#99 overall)

YEAR	TEAM	LVL	AGE	W	L	SV	G	GS	IP	H	HR	BB/9	K/9	K	GB%	BABIP	WHIP	ERA	DRA-	WARP
2021	FW	A+	24	1	0	3	8	0	8	2	0	4.5	11.2	10	60.0%	.133	0.75	0.00	97	0.1
2022 non-DC	*SD*	*MLB*	*25*	*2*	*3*	*0*	*57*	*0*	*50*	*47*	*7*	*5.2*	*9.5*	*53*	*36.0%*	*.304*	*1.53*	*5.17*	*114*	*-0.2*

Your favorite college baseball writer's favorite player, Kopps was absolutely dominant as a sixth-year senior for the Arkansas Razorbacks in 2021, before the Padres popped him in the third round of the draft. The Golden Spikes winner doesn't have the kind of eye-popping fastball you'd associate with a college reliever who struck out nearly 40 percent of the batters he faced—Kopps sits in the low-90s—but he does have a present plus, mid-80s cutter with big-time late depth. That should be enough to get him to the majors quickly, albeit in a lower-leverage role than he had in Arkansas.

Top Talents 25 and Under (as of 4/1/2022):

1. Fernando Tatis Jr., SS/OF
2. CJ Abrams, SS
3. Robert Hassell III, OF
4. Trent Grisham, OF
5. Luis Campusano, C
6. MacKenzie Gore, LHP
7. Adrian Morejon, LHP
8. Jackson Merrill, SS
9. James Wood, OF
10. Reiss Knehr, RHP

Few clubs concluded 2021 as disappointingly as the Padres. Despite their shortfall last season, this remains an impressive collective of young talent, headlined by one of the sport's brightest young stars.

Fernando Tatis Jr. signed a 14-year contract extension ahead of last season, then promptly tore his left shoulder labrum in early April. A premature end to the 22-year-old wunderkind's season seemed likely, yet Tatis managed not only to gut it out for 130 games, but to perform at an MVP-caliber pace while on the field. He spent roughly one-fifth of his games in the outfield, where his athleticism would surely translate comfortably, and where his body might sustain more consistently. Defensively, he has not quite locked it in at shortstop, though he hits and runs well enough to help a team no matter what position he plays, just as long as he stays in the lineup.

Unfortunately for the Dads, Grisham saw his 2020 power surge slip back to more average numbers last year. A series of mostly non-structural lower-body injuries may have played a role in his slugging backslide, as they kept him off the field for nearly a month. Still, he looks like an average big-league regular with the potential for some seasons of slightly more.

Sadly, the Thomas Edward John surgery he underwent in April of 2021 means we won't see Morejon until a few months into 2022, at best, particularly if San Diego still harbors goals of working the nearly 23-year-old into a starting role. More likely, if things are hewing slightly closer to plan for the Padres, they'll take this opportunity to ease Morejon in with bullpen work, revisiting the rotation in 2023, if at all. A healthy Morejon has three above-average pitches and is easy to envision slotting in well in the back of a contending bullpen, but the continued opportunities for more keep slipping away due to health, even with a pitcher as young as Morejon.

San Francisco Giants

The State of the System:

The Giants' organization is peaking along with the major-league roster. Although there is a limited amount of immediate help, it is a deep and balanced system with potential impact talent towards the top.

The Top Ten:

1 Marco Luciano SS OFP: 70 ETA: 2024

Born: 09/10/01 Age: 20 Bats: R Throws: R Height: 6'2" Weight: 178 lb. Origin: International Free Agent, 2018

YEAR	TEAM	LVL	AGE	PA	R	2B	3B	HR	RBI	BB	K	SB	CS	AVG/OBP/SLG	DRC+	BABIP	BRR	FRAA	WARP
2019	GIO	ROK	17	178	46	9	2	10	38	27	39	8	6	.322/.438/.616		.378			
2019	SK	SS	17	38	6	4	0	0	4	5	6	1	0	.212/.316/.333		.259			
2021	SCO	WIN	19	87	7	0	0	3	13	11	28	0	1	.253/.356/.373		.364			
2021	SJ	A	19	308	52	14	3	18	57	38	68	5	5	.278/.373/.556	129	.309	-0.9	SS(60) -0.1	1.9
2021	EUG	A+	19	145	16	3	2	1	14	10	54	1	0	.217/.283/.295	69	.351	-0.1	SS(29) -1.2	-0.3
2022 non-DC	*SF*	*MLB*	*20*	*251*	*22*	*9*	*1*	*5*	*24*	*18*	*77*	*3*	*2*	*.209/.273/.338*	*64*	*.288*	*0.3*	*SS 0*	*-0.2*

Comparables: Jonathan Villar, Gleyber Torres, Richard Ureña

The Report: Luciano entered 2021 as a top-10 prospect in the game despite having accrued only 38 plate appearances above Rookie ball, creating sky-high expectations. He tore up Low-A pitching to start the year, flashing a rare plus-hit/plus-power combination with a non-zero chance of sticking at shortstop, but scuffled after a late-season promotion to High-A and carried some of those struggles into the Arizona Fall League, as well. Failure is often an important part of the development process and was to be expected given the challenging assignments Luciano was given as a 19-year-old, which makes his statistical performance down the stretch less concerning. There's still plus-plus power potential, but he will need to continue to adjust to advanced secondaries and pitch sequencing.

On the defensive side of the ball, Luciano displays reliable hands and has plenty of arm for the left side of the infield, but his feet are heavy and will likely force him over to third base sooner rather than later.

OFP: 70 / All-Star third baseman

Variance: Medium. A slide down the defensive spectrum places more pressure on his bat, but it's still a special, middle-of-the-order offensive profile.

Darius Austin's Fantasy Take: As if we needed it, Luciano's struggles are a reminder that even the most-talented prospects can struggle sometimes. I wouldn't read too much more into it than that. If he hasn't made any more strides after another few hundred plate appearances at High-A, I'll do more than raise an eyebrow. He remains an elite four-category threat with truly monstrous home-run potential.

Eyewitness Report: Marco Luciano

Evaluator: Trevor Andresen

Report Date: 07/28/2021

Dates Seen: 5/25/21-5/30/21

Risk Factor: Medium

Physical/Health: LG 6'2 210 lb. frame that is still filling out. Likely to add another 10-15 lbs. before all is said & done.

Tool	Future Grade	Report
Hit	60	Upright, slightly open stance w/ good rhythm. Natural load w/ plus bat speed & a slightly uphill swing plane. Approach & pitch selection are very advanced for a 19-year-old, showing a strong feel for the strike zone & taking good swings in positive counts. Recognizes spin/offspeed & will punish mistakes. There will be some swing/miss as a trade-off for the power, but it still looks like a .270-.280 bat w/ high walk rates.
Power	70	Generates easy plus-plus raw power to all fields w/ a chance to grow into 80-grade raw at physical maturity. Combined w/ the hit tool/approach/swing plane it's easy to see a 30+ HR bat.
Baserunning/ Speed	40	Below-average runner at present & will likely lose at least a step as he continues to age.
Glove	50	Hands/feet work at SS for now (albeit as a 40/45 glove due to range) but the athleticism is trending downward & he will all but certainly lose a step as he continues to mature. Future 40-grade defender at SS, but should maintain enough agility to turn in average defense at 3B.
Arm	55	Above-average strength w/ accuracy to match. Fits on the left side of the infield.

Conclusion: Impact, middle-of-the-order run producer w/ a rare hit/power combination & polish beyond his years. Perennial all star type, even if he moves down the defensive spectrum.

2 Luis Matos OF   OFP: 60   ETA: 2024

Born: 01/28/02 Age: 20 Bats: R Throws: R Height: 5'11" Weight: 160 lb. Origin: International Free Agent, 2018

YEAR	TEAM	LVL	AGE	PA	R	2B	3B	HR	RBI	BB	K	SB	CS	AVG/OBP/SLG	DRC+	BABIP	BRR	FRAA	WARP
2019	DSL GIA	ROK	17	270	60	24	2	7	47	19	30	20	2	.362/.430/.570		.386			
2019	GIO	ROK	17	20	5	1	0	0	1	1	1	1	1	.438/.550/.500		.467			
2021	SJ	A	19	491	84	35	1	15	86	28	61	21	5	.313/.358/.494	129	.332	1.2	CF(86) -4.7, RF(14) -2.9, LF(4) 0.0	3.0
2022 non-DC	*SF*	*MLB*	*20*	*251*	*22*	*12*	*0*	*4*	*24*	*11*	*45*	*8*	*2*	*.253/.292/.365*	*76*	*.298*	*0.5*	*CF -1, RF 0*	*0.0*

Comparables: Manuel Margot, Victor Robles, Trayvon Robinson

The Report: You could argue that Matos had a more-impressive full-season debut than Luciano, hitting for both average and power while showing the ability to handle a premium defensive position. Despite his small-ish frame, Matos generates plus bat speed and an incredible amount of torque from his swing, which leads to plus power potential. Matos is a free swinger by nature, and his swing decisions will need to be cleaned up as he continues to climb, but he possesses plus bat-to-ball skills and could realistically wind up with an above-average-or-better hit tool, as well.

He's athletic enough to stick in center field long-term, although he's more of an average defender who might move to a corner in deference to a stronger glove. Still, the arm should play at all three spots and help him add value on the defensive side of the ball.

OFP: 60 / First-division outfielder

Variance: High. Plus bat control, plus power and a center-field fit create a skyscraper ceiling, but the swing-happy approach adds significant hit-tool variance and extends the range of potential outcomes.

Darius Austin's Fantasy Take: We're into a run of volatile hit-tool outcomes that are going to do an awful lot to determine fantasy relevance. You can argue that Matos is the safest, given his athleticism and stolen-base upside, and also that he has the most variance, since we haven't seen him play above Low-A San Jose. I predict that there will be strong arguments for Matos in the top five of fantasy lists in a year or two, and that his five-category potential may even send him above Luciano. I'd get in now, if you can.

3 Joey Bart C OFP: 60 ETA: Debuted in 2020

Born: 12/15/96 Age: 25 Bats: R Throws: R Height: 6'2" Weight: 238 lb. Origin: Round 1, 2018 Draft (#2 overall)

YEAR	TEAM	LVL	AGE	PA	R	2B	3B	HR	RBI	BB	K	SB	CS	AVG/OBP/SLG	DRC+	BABIP	BRR	FRAA	WARP
2019	SJ	A+	22	251	37	10	2	12	37	14	50	5	2	.265/.315/.479	121	.291	0.5	C(50) -1.7	1.3
2019	RIC	AA	22	87	9	4	1	4	11	7	21	0	2	.316/.368/.544	104	.382	-1.0	C(15) 0.4	0.3
2020	SF	MLB	23	111	15	5	2	0	7	3	41	0	0	.233/.288/.320	62	.387	-0.1	C(32) 2.8	0.1
2021	SAC	AAA	24	279	37	15	0	10	46	21	82	0	0	.294/.358/.472	92	.398	-1.5	C(63) 8.8	1.4
2021	SF	MLB	24	6	1	0	0	0	1	0	2	0	0	.333/.333/.333	96	.500	0.1	C(1) -0.1	0.0
2022 DC	*SF*	*MLB*	*25*	*318*	*33*	*13*	*1*	*9*	*37*	*17*	*102*	*1*	*1*	*.223/.279/.375*	*74*	*.307*	*-0.2*	*C 6*	*1.0*

Comparables: Chris Iannetta, Yasmani Grandal, Buster Posey

The Report: Bart has just sort of floated along as a very good, but not elite, catching prospect since his draft day in 2018. A lot of that isn't his fault. Minor injuries in 2019 and '21, coupled with his lost 2020 season, meant he has never really had the kind of sustained dominance with the bat you would have expected to see from an advanced college power hitter. A quad strain cost him time last year, but, when on the field in Triple-A, he posted a more-than-acceptable line for a backstop. Bart is a big, strong lad that is out there looking to lift and is capable of knocking 20-plus home runs, even in a 110-to-120-game starting-catcher season. If you ignore his 2020 season entirely, this looks like a normal, if a bit conservative, track for a top catching prospect.

The 2020 season did happen, though, and his swing-and-miss issues continued last year, even in the upper minors. That hulking power-hitter's stroke can get a bit stiff and a bit grooved, and the outcomes can be boom-or-bust. Bart is a good defensive catcher—a potential above-average catch, frame and throw guy—so he only needs a handful of booms to be a major leaguer, but we've never been fully convinced by his hit tool, even coming out of college, and he wouldn't be the first top catching prospect to hit .230 or so once he saw major-league pitching. We do wonder how he will handle better velocity over the long haul, but with Buster Posey's retirement, we'll find out soon.

OFP: 60 / First-division catcher

Variance: Medium. Bart's profile hasn't really changed across his pro career, but he hasn't actualized the profile yet. Young Catcher Offensive Stagnation Syndrome (trademark, John Sickels) is real.

Darius Austin's Fantasy Take: We all know that top catching prospects can take a while to give us what we're looking for in fantasy, if they ever do at all. Buster Posey's retirement means that we can stop worrying about Bart's playing time, but I just don't know how much of a difference-maker he really is with the bat—especially if his hit tool is a cut below average in the bigs. I sense that his dynasty stock has at least adjusted somewhat to compensate for the possibility that he's a good power contributor for the position and little else.

4 Jairo Pomares OF OFP: 55 ETA: 2024

Born: 08/04/00 Age: 21 Bats: L Throws: R Height: 6'1" Weight: 185 lb. Origin: International Free Agent, 2018

YEAR	TEAM	LVL	AGE	PA	R	2B	3B	HR	RBI	BB	K	SB	CS	AVG/OBP/SLG	DRC+	BABIP	BRR	FRAA	WARP
2019	GIB	ROK	18	167	17	10	4	3	33	10	26	5	3	.368/.401/.542		.422			
2019	SK	SS	18	62	7	3	0	0	4	1	17	0	0	.207/.258/.259		.293			
2021	SJ	A	20	224	45	22	0	14	44	15	54	0	0	.372/.429/.693	138	.448	-0.7	RF(26) -2.3, LF(3) -1.0	1.4
2021	EUG	A+	20	104	13	5	1	6	15	1	33	1	0	.262/.269/.505	107	.328	0.4	LF(22) -1.7	0.3
2022 non-DC	*SF*	*MLB*	*21*	*251*	*25*	*12*	*1*	*8*	*29*	*11*	*79*	*1*	*1*	*.247/.291/.413*	*85*	*.339*	*-0.1*	*RF -1, LF 0*	*0.2*

Comparables: Alex Kirilloff, David Dahl, Ryan Kalish

The Report: It wasn't going to be easy to stand out on a San Jose team that included Marco Luciano and Luis Matos, but Pomares's slash line was downright eye-popping. The 40-home-run pace he set in the former Cal League overstates his power projection (it is the Cal League, after all), as his swing isn't geared for true 70-grade pop, but it's easy plus given how hard he hits the ball. His approach is aggressive, and while Pomares didn't see many pitches in Low-A he couldn't sting, his freewheeling ways at the plate got a little exposed after a promotion, although the power was still there. Given his hand-eye and bat speed, with refinement and adjustment he could have a plus hit tool, as well, although that is going to be more volatile. Pomares split time in the outfield corners in 2021 and has enough arm for right and enough foot speed to be solid defensively in either. His bat is what is going to carry his profile, though, and while he has shown some ability to be selective at times, his value is very much going to be linked to how often and how hard he can put bat to ball.

OFP: 55 / Above-average corner outfielder

Variance: High. This is more a risk profile than a variance profile, as the hit tool and approach will be tested in the upper minors.

Darius Austin's Fantasy Take: Once again, the hit-tool development is going to determine a lot here. He doesn't have a ton of speed, and a plus walk rate looks unlikely, so we're counting on significant refinement from an approach that generated a 33:1 K/BB ratio at High-A. I'm getting Avisaíl García vibes with a little more homer pop. That plays if the average is .270, not so much if it's .230.

5 Kyle Harrison LHP OFP: 55 ETA: Late 2024

Born: 08/12/01 Age: 20 Bats: R Throws: L Height: 6'2" Weight: 200 lb. Origin: Round 3, 2020 Draft (#85 overall)

YEAR	TEAM	LVL	AGE	W	L	SV	G	GS	IP	H	HR	BB/9	K/9	K	GB%	BABIP	WHIP	ERA	DRA-	WARP
2021	SJ	A	19	4	3	0	23	23	98^{2}	86	3	4.7	14.3	157	49.1%	.393	1.40	3.19	82	1.6
2022 non-DC	*SF*	*MLB*	*20*	*2*	*3*	*0*	*57*	*0*	*50*	*46*	*6*	*5.5*	*9.7*	*54*	*48.2%*	*.302*	*1.54*	*4.95*	*113*	*-0.2*

Comparables: Julio Teheran, Luiz Gohara, Jacob Turner

The Report: Harrison was widely seen as a pitchability starter heading into the 2020 draft, but his stuff ticked up during instructs that fall, and he maintained his newfound velocity throughout his professional debut in 2021. As a result, the southpaw now comfortably sits in the 92–94 range, routinely running it up to 96 with life in the zone. His changeup has taken a step forward, and his added power has turned his sweeping slider into a legitimate swing-and-miss offering, as well. His innate feel for pitching is still present, but now he has the power stuff to come right at hitters and challenge them in the zone. The only real question mark is his command, which can be erratic and will ultimately dictate his future role.

OFP: 55 / Mid-rotation starter or high-leverage reliever

Variance: High. It is very difficult to stick in the rotation while running walk rates north of 10 percent. He has shown flashes but will need to live in and around the zone more consistently to avoid a move to the bullpen.

Darius Austin's Fantasy Take: A lefty who can hit 96 with life? That'll play. There's a considerable chance that Harrison never throws enough strikes to make it as a starter, but I think the strikeout potential is huge, and the unusual delivery is going to keep hitters off balance all the way up the ladder. A lot has already changed since Harrison was drafted, and I'm willing to bet on his command coming around with time. If Robbie Ray can learn to just throw strikes . . .

6 Will Bednar RHP OFP: 55 ETA: Late 2023/Early 2024

Born: 06/13/00 Age: 22 Bats: R Throws: R Height: 6'2" Weight: 229 lb. Origin: Round 1, 2021 Draft (#14 overall)

YEAR	TEAM	LVL	AGE	W	L	SV	G	GS	IP	H	HR	BB/9	K/9	K	GB%	BABIP	WHIP	ERA	DRA-	WARP
2022 non-DC	*SF*	*MLB*	*22*	*2*	*3*	*0*	*57*	*0*	*50*	*57*	*7*	*4.3*	*6.3*	*34*	*39.3%*	*.310*	*1.63*	*5.92*	*135*	*-0.7*

Comparables: Felipe Lira, Bryan Rekar, Bill Champion

The Report: Whatever happens in the pros, Bednar will never have to buy a drink in Starkville again. The ace of Mississippi State's College World Series Champions pitched his way up draft boards with big performances in big games. His stuff isn't as big, but Bednar is a real . . . sigh . . . bulldog on the mound, going right after hitters with a fastball he can run into the mid-90s and a potentially plus slider, with advanced command of both. His heater can sit in more of an average velo band, and his changeup might not get past a 40 offering, so there's some reliever risk—and, indeed, Bednar started the last two seasons in the Mississippi State bullpen. He has the build of a mid-rotation stalwart, now the stuff and stamina just have to prove out their part of the projection.

OFP: 55 / No. 3–4 starter

Variance: Medium. I doubt the low minors will be any more difficult than the SEC for Bednar, but his profile and arsenal will be tested once he hits Double-A. Given his limited starting experience, though, there could be more in the tank once he's in a professional development program.

Darius Austin's Fantasy Take: I have a feeling that Bednar is going to be a fairly reliable fantasy starter in San Francisco three or four years down the line. I'd also really like to see him turn over professional lineups and develop that change before I get too excited. He should go in all first-year player drafts, just not in the first round.

7 Camilo Doval RHP OFP: 55 ETA: Debuted in 2021

Born: 07/04/97 Age: 25 Bats: R Throws: R Height: 6'2" Weight: 185 lb. Origin: International Free Agent, 2015

YEAR	TEAM	LVL	AGE	W	L	SV	G	GS	IP	H	HR	BB/9	K/9	K	GB%	BABIP	WHIP	ERA	DRA-	WARP
2019	SJ	A+	21	3	5	0	45	0	56^1	41	2	5.4	12.8	80	52.4%	.315	1.33	3.83	75	1.0
2021	SAC	AAA	23	3	0	1	28	0	30^2	28	3	7.0	12.9	44	50.7%	.362	1.70	4.99	86	0.4
2021	SF	MLB	23	5	1	3	29	0	27	19	4	3.0	12.3	37	50.0%	.259	1.04	3.00	73	0.6
2022 DC	*SF*	*MLB*	*24*	*3*	*3*	*5*	*67*	*0*	*58*	*46*	*6*	*5.3*	*11.4*	*74*	*51.1%*	*.294*	*1.39*	*3.92*	*94*	*0.4*

Comparables: Bryan Shaw, Trevor Gott, Jorge Julio

The Report: Camilo Doval threw only 27 innings in the majors in 2021 and, thus, is still eligible for this list. Camilio Doval is likely a present late-inning reliever and, thus, is annoying to rank. He's a very modern reliever, leaning heavily on a mid-80s power slider to get swings-and-misses. His fastball command isn't good, but when you throw 98-plus with high spin, you don't have to be all that fine with your location. His track record of throwing enough strikes starts in, like, September 2021, however, if his major-league performance is taken at face value, Doval is an eighth-inning guy without quite enough command to be a sure-shot closer. Would you take that over Will Bednar, who has some reliever markers himself? We don't have a good answer, although we obviously have made a decision. This profile also does tend to burn hot and fast, so Doval might be a frustrating middle reliever by the time Bednar gets the call, anyway.

OFP: 55 / High-end set-up arm or second-division closer

Variance: Low. He's a major-league reliever now, a pretty good one, too. This profile can have weirdly fine margins, where, if he loses a little more command, or the slider isn't quite as sharp, suddenly he's a little too hittable or a little too wild for the late innings.

Darius Austin's Fantasy Take: Unlike most of the future relievers we're going to tell you not to bother rostering, Doval is already in the majors, and he was closing out games for the Giants at the end of the season. I very much doubt that his 2022 ADP bakes in the risks highlighted above or the alternative options on the roster (Jake McGee and Tyler Rogers had 44 saves between them in 2021). That said, the strikeouts will be there, he's technically the incumbent, and, if your league counts holds, you're not going to lose much if he isn't the capital-C closer all year.

8 Patrick Bailey C OFP: 55 ETA: Late 2023/Early 2024

Born: 05/29/99 Age: 23 Bats: S Throws: R Height: 6'1" Weight: 210 lb. Origin: Round 1, 2020 Draft (#13 overall)

YEAR	TEAM	LVL	AGE	PA	R	2B	3B	HR	RBI	BB	K	SB	CS	AVG/OBP/SLG	DRC+	BABIP	BRR	FRAA	WARP
2021	SJ	A	22	207	45	16	0	7	24	28	47	1	1	.322/.415/.531	122	.403	0.8	C(39) 18.6	3.0
2021	EUG	A+	22	155	13	9	0	2	15	18	43	6	0	.185/.290/.296	84	.256	0.8	C(25) 6.3, 1B(4) -0.0	0.8
2022 non-DC	*SF*	*MLB*	*23*	*251*	*21*	*12*	*0*	*3*	*22*	*21*	*76*	*2*	*1*	*.215/.288/.324*	*64*	*.306*	*-0.1*	*C 7, 1B 0*	*0.7*

Comparables: Francisco Cervelli, Bruce Maxwell, Martín Maldonado

The Report: The other Giants catching prospect, Bailey had a successful full-season debut in 2021, in which he showed all the building blocks to be a two-way starting catcher in the majors. His offensive contribution will lean power over hit, although his bat-to-ball improved over the course of the year, as he refined his approach and made better swing decisions. Bailey generates plus raw power from both sides from a fairly simple swing, and that should play as 20-home-run pop in games, although he may sacrifice some batting average to get to it. Defensively, Bailey is a solid receiver and blocker with an above-average arm.

OFP: 55 / Above-average catcher

Variance: Medium. Bailey did struggle upon moving up a level, and you'd have expected an Atlantic Coast Conference catcher with an advanced bat to handle the low minors, so we don't know if we have enough info on his offensive projection yet. He might have a longer development path than you'd expect for a college bat, even a catcher.

Darius Austin's Fantasy Take: Bailey's profile doesn't sound a whole lot different from Bart's for fantasy, except Bailey is further off and has more work to do with the bat, judging by that High-A showing. You probably know how we feel about hanging on to non-premium catching prospects with extended lead times by now. I wouldn't be surprised if the switch-hitting Bailey ultimately hits for more average than Bart, but that's more than offset by proximity and current levels of development.

9 Heliot Ramos CF OFP: 50 ETA: 2022, as needed

Born: 09/07/99 Age: 22 Bats: R Throws: R Height: 6'1" Weight: 188 lb. Origin: Round 1, 2017 Draft (#19 overall)

YEAR	TEAM	LVL	AGE	PA	R	2B	3B	HR	RBI	BB	K	SB	CS	AVG/OBP/SLG	DRC+	BABIP	BRR	FRAA	WARP
2019	SAN	WIN	19	72	9	2	0	1	6	5	23	1	1	.185/.250/.262		.262			
2019	SCO	WIN	19	72	9	2	0	1	6	5	23	1	1	.185/.250/.262		.262			
2019	SJ	A+	19	338	51	18	0	13	40	32	85	6	7	.306/.385/.500	120	.385	-0.5	CF(71) -5.5	1.3
2019	RIC	AA	19	106	13	6	1	3	15	10	33	2	3	.242/.321/.421	85	.339	-1.4	CF(19) -1.4	-0.1
2021	RIC	AA	21	266	36	14	1	10	26	27	73	7	2	.237/.323/.432	104	.301	0.0	CF(58) -3.2	0.7
2021	SAC	AAA	21	229	30	11	2	4	30	15	65	8	2	.272/.323/.399	78	.375	2.9	CF(32) -2.4, RF(17) 1.2	0.3
2022 DC	*SF*	*MLB*	*22*	*63*	*6*	*2*	*0*	*1*	*7*	*4*	*20*	*0*	*1*	*.229/.292/.367*	*77*	*.326*	*0.1*	*CF 0*	*0.0*

Comparables: Manuel Margot, Avisaíl García, Carlos Tocci

The Report: Despite not turning 22 until the last days of the 2021 season, it feels like Ramos has gone through multiple lifetimes as a prospect already, or perhaps just one long roller-coaster ride. He hit a bit of a dip last season, as his approach got overly aggressive against more advanced arms and he found he couldn't just uppercut piss missiles anymore. Ramos takes a mighty rip and has plus bat speed and raw power, but he can get long, which means you can get in his kitchen with good velocity or get him to pull off on breakers down and away. That's not a great combination for a prospect who is going to need an above-average hit-and-power combination to carry an eventual corner-outfield profile—although he is still playing mostly center. Given Ramos's age and relative lack of upper-minors experience, we won't call last season a disaster or anything—and his dip in this Top 10 is, at least in part, due to breakouts around him—but he is looking less like an obvious future regular nowadays.

OFP: 50 / Average corner outfielder

Variance: Medium. We've seen the hit-tool concerns manifest now, but, given that Ramos can at least stand in all three outfield spots and mash lefties some, he has a path to being a useful bench piece, even if he doesn't hit enough to be an everyday outfielder. And perhaps another year in Triple-A will refine his approach enough that his offensive tools pop once again. It wouldn't be the first time that happened for him.

Darius Austin's Fantasy Take: The specter of potential short-side platoon duty isn't what any fantasy player wanted to see in Ramos's write-up. For an organization that now prizes versatility as much as the Giants, it's handy that he can still play all three outfield spots, but we want Ramos to be starting in one of those every day. Don't give up on Ramos if you roster him—he's still very young and still has the fantasy-relevant tools we got excited about in the first place. We can start to worry if the outlook is the same this time next year.

10 Matt Mikulski LHP OFP: 50 ETA: 2024

Born: 05/08/99 Age: 23 Bats: L Throws: L Height: 6'4" Weight: 205 lb. Origin: Round 2, 2021 Draft (#50 overall)

The Report: A velocity bump in the spring of 2021 moved Mikulski from an interesting priority senior sign to a seven-figure second-round pick. The extra octane on his now-mid-90s fastball sharpened up his breakers, and Mikulski has always had an advanced change. His older draft age and the level of competition in the Atlantic 10 may put a little bit of a damper on his stock, but you can only beat who you face, and it's hard to do better than 16 K/9 outside of the Rookie mode in *MLB The Show*. He has a short track record of this kind of stuff, though, and Mikulski had to tweak his mechanics to be much more up-tempo and high-effort to get the velocity jump, and it's unclear how (or if) that will play out as a starter long-term.

OFP: 50 / No. 4 starter

Variance: Medium. We honestly don't know how efficient Mikulski will be in the pros with that delivery, but what he showed his senior year at Fordham certainly had at least number-three-starter potential.

Darius Austin's Fantasy Take: It will be revealing to see Mikulski against some more age-appropriate competition. He doesn't need to be on rosters, unless your league goes 300-plus-prospects deep, but I think he's one of the more interesting watchlist pitchers for 2022, and he won't last long on the waiver wire if this proves at all sustainable.

The Prospects You Meet Outside the Top Ten

#11

Carson Ragsdale RHP Born: 05/25/98 Age: 24 Bats: R Throws: R Height: 6'8" Weight: 225 lb. Origin: Round 4, 2020 Draft (#116 overall)

YEAR	TEAM	LVL	AGE	W	L	SV	G	GS	IP	H	HR	BB/9	K/9	K	GB%	BABIP	WHIP	ERA	DRA-	WARP
2021	SJ	A	23	8	6	0	24	24	113^{2}	107	13	3.6	13.2	167	37.3%	.360	1.34	4.43	116	-0.5
2022 non-DC	*SF*	*MLB*	*24*	*2*	*3*	*0*	*57*	*0*	*50*	*47*	*8*	*4.3*	*8.5*	*47*	*46.2%*	*.284*	*1.43*	*4.80*	*113*	*-0.2*

Ragsdale impressed in 2021 in what was essentially his first full year as a starting pitcher, even if the entirety of his age-23 season was spent facing Low-A hitters. He'll flash mid-rotation stuff, sitting 92–94 with bat-missing life and snapping off a 12–6 breaker that tunnels nicely off his fastball, but he lacks a true third offering and is more control over command due to his long limbs. Add in the October 2018 Tommy John surgery under his belt, and there's a good bit of variance in his profile. He's tracking like a role 50, but whether that is a number-four starter or a late-inning bullpen piece remains to be seen.

#12

Ryan Murphy RHP Born: 10/08/99 Age: 22 Bats: R Throws: R Height: 6'1" Weight: 190 lb. Origin: Round 5, 2020 Draft (#144 overall)

YEAR	TEAM	LVL	AGE	W	L	SV	G	GS	IP	H	HR	BB/9	K/9	K	GB%	BABIP	WHIP	ERA	DRA-	WARP
2021	SJ	A	21	4	2	0	15	15	76	59	11	2.1	13.7	116	43.9%	.318	1.01	2.96	78	1.4
2021	EUG	A+	21	2	2	0	6	6	31^{1}	13	1	2.3	13.8	48	42.4%	.207	0.67	1.44	97	0.3
2022 non-DC	*SF*	*MLB*	*22*	*2*	*2*	*0*	*57*	*0*	*50*	*42*	*7*	*3.2*	*9.7*	*54*	*47.5%*	*.277*	*1.21*	*3.59*	*90*	*0.4*

A fifth-round selection out of Le Moyne College in 2020, Murphy dominated Low-A hitters in his debut last year and managed to perform even better after a late-season promotion to High-A. His stuff doesn't immediately jump off the page, sitting in the low 90s with two solid-average breaking balls, but his fastball has swing-and-miss characteristics, and he pounds the zone with above-average control. The floor is more encouraging than the ceiling here, but Murphy has the look of a back-end starter and should continue to move quickly.

Prospects on the Rise

Nick Swiney LHP Born: 02/12/99 Age: 23 Bats: R Throws: L Height: 6'3" Weight: 185 lb. Origin: Round 2, 2020 Draft (#67 overall)

YEAR	TEAM	LVL	AGE	W	L	SV	G	GS	IP	H	HR	BB/9	K/9	K	GB%	BABIP	WHIP	ERA	DRA-	WARP
2021	GNTB	ROK	22	0	0	0	5	5	8	7	0	6.7	18.0	16	50.0%	.500	1.63	1.13		
2021	SJ	A	22	0	0	0	7	7	24^{1}	16	0	4.4	15.5	42	45.8%	.333	1.15	0.74	85	0.4
2022 non-DC	*SF*	*MLB*	*23*	*2*	*3*	*0*	*57*	*0*	*50*	*46*	*7*	*5.3*	*10.9*	*60*	*34.3%*	*.311*	*1.52*	*5.12*	*116*	*-0.2*

Comparables: Jon Lester, Tim Davis, Cristian Javier

The Giants' second-round pick in the 2020 draft missed most of the 2021 season with a concussion, but, when on the mound, dominated Low-A on the strength of an advanced curve and change. Both pitches have a chance to be above-average, and he leans on them over a fringy fastball. Swiney's delivery is a little hitchy and a little stiff, and while that makes his stuff harder to square, it also makes his control a bit scattershot. His arsenal should overwhelm A-ball, but without more consistent strike-throwing, Swiney will struggle to fulfill his back-end starter projection.

Diego Rincones RF Born: 06/14/99 Age: 23 Bats: R Throws: R Height: 6'0" Weight: 175 lb. Origin: International Free Agent, 2015

YEAR	TEAM	LVL	AGE	PA	R	2B	3B	HR	RBI	BB	K	SB	CS	AVG/OBP/SLG	DRC+	BABIP	BRR	FRAA	WARP
2019	AUG	A	20	442	48	25	4	5	57	27	56	0	0	.295/.346/.415	119	.327	-1.6	RF(45) -4.3, LF(39) -1.6	1.5
2019	SJ	A+	20	88	14	4	0	2	8	11	8	0	0	.247/.375/.384	133	.254	-0.5	LF(15) -0.4	0.5
2020	MAR	WIN	21	85	12	7	0	2	25	5	9	1	1	.342/.412/.513		.369			
2021	MAR	WIN	22	187	30	8	0	4	30	13	10	0	0	.335/.412/.460		.333			
2021	EUG	A+	22	107	15	6	0	5	15	10	19	0	0	.300/.385/.533	123	.328	-0.2	LF(21) -2.1	0.4
2021	RIC	AA	22	213	31	8	1	10	33	16	37	1	0	.290/.373/.505	125	.314	-0.5	RF(34) -4.5	0.8
2022 non-DC	*SF*	*MLB*	*23*	*251*	*25*	*10*	*1*	*5*	*26*	*16*	*47*	*0*	*0*	*.245/.310/.381*	*86*	*.286*	*-0.3*	*RF -1, LF 0*	*0.2*

The Giants didn't protect Rincones in the Rule 5 draft—uh, whenever that happens—but he's not the ideal profile to carry on a major-league roster for a year. He's limited to a corner outfield spot and not much of an asset there defensively. He only has 51 games above A-ball. He swings really freaking hard, and he swings a lot.

Look, they don't put us in charge of a pro-scouting department for a lot of reasons, but we'd be tempted to swing hard on Rincones ourselves. As the old saying goes, swing hard in case you hit it, and he hits it a lot. He has premium bat speed and unleashes controlled violence. And it *is* controlled; he can hang back on breaking stuff and still square it and get bat to ball wherever you put your fastball. Rincones really needs to have an above-average hit-and-power tool to even be viable as a fringe regular, and asking him to do that while jumping from Double-A to the majors is a lot. It's much easier to ask that of a right-handed reliever sitting 97 and flashing a plus slider. And yet . . .

Randy Rodriguez RHP Born: 09/05/99 Age: 22 Bats: R Throws: R Height: 6'0" Weight: 166 lb. Origin: International Free Agent, 2017

YEAR	TEAM	LVL	AGE	W	L	SV	G	GS	IP	H	HR	BB/9	K/9	K	GB%	BABIP	WHIP	ERA	DRA-	WARP
2019	GIB	ROK	19	2	6	2	16	0	25	26	1	5.8	10.4	29	51.4%	.368	1.68	5.40		
2021	SJ	A	21	6	3	2	32	0	62	44	0	3.3	14.7	101	36.2%	.346	1.08	1.74	88	0.8
2022 non-DC	*SF*	*MLB*	*22*	*2*	*2*	*0*	*57*	*0*	*50*	*43*	*7*	*4.5*	*10.1*	*56*	*44.9%*	*.288*	*1.38*	*4.43*	*105*	*0.0*

Comparables: José Domínguez, Scott Strickland, David Robertson

Rodriguez enjoyed a breakout full-season debut in 2021. He sits in the mid-90s, flashes a plus slider and throws strikes at an average clip, giving him the look of a medium- to high-leverage bullpen arm. He'll also show feel for a changeup, which, combined with his athletic delivery, control and the fact that he was often used as a multi-inning reliever, make it reasonable to wonder what it would look like if you stretched him out as a starter.

Factors on the Farm

Kervin Castro RHP Born: 02/07/99 Age: 23 Bats: R Throws: R Height: 6'0" Weight: 185 lb. Origin: International Free Agent, 2015

YEAR	TEAM	LVL	AGE	W	L	SV	G	GS	IP	H	HR	BB/9	K/9	K	GB%	BABIP	WHIP	ERA	DRA-	WARP
2019	SK	SS	20	5	3	0	14	14	67^2	52	2	1.7	8.1	61	48.9%	.267	0.96	2.66		
2021	SAC	AAA	22	6	1	1	30	0	44	31	3	4.5	12.3	60	38.4%	.292	1.20	2.86	76	0.8
2021	SF	MLB	22	1	1	0	10	0	13^1	13	0	2.7	8.8	13	35.9%	.342	1.28	0.00	99	0.1
2022 DC	*SF*	*MLB*	*23*	*6*	*4*	*0*	*50*	*6*	*58*	*51*	*8*	*4.3*	*9.8*	*63*	*49.8%*	*.288*	*1.36*	*4.23*	*102*	*0.2*

Comparables: Miguel Diaz, Dan Miceli, Jason Bergmann

Despite having never pitched above the (old) Northwest League prior to last season, Castro dominate Triple-A after a relief conversion and earned a September call-up in which he tossed 13 scoreless innings. The short-and-stocky righty's fastball velocity sits around average for a reliever, but the pitch rides uphill to hitters, getting consistent late swings under it. He pairs it with a downer 12–6 curve around 80 mph, making him a very newfangled pitching prospect, but one that should miss enough bats to work in at least middle relief and possibly even a setup role.

R.J. Dabovich RHP Born: 01/11/99 Age: 23 Bats: R Throws: R Height: 6'3" Weight: 208 lb. Origin: Round 4, 2020 Draft (#114 overall)

YEAR	TEAM	LVL	AGE	W	L	SV	G	GS	IP	H	HR	BB/9	K/9	K	GB%	BABIP	WHIP	ERA	DRA-	WARP
2021	EUG	A+	22	0	0	4	11	0	12^2	2	2	4.3	19.9	28	33.3%	.000	0.63	1.42	70	0.3
2021	RIC	AA	22	1	1	6	20	0	19^2	13	1	3.2	15.6	34	25.6%	.316	1.02	3.66	90	0.3
2022 non-DC	*SF*	*MLB*	*23*	*2*	*2*	*0*	*57*	*0*	*50*	*38*	*8*	*4.6*	*13.2*	*73*	*43.0%*	*.292*	*1.29*	*3.95*	*94*	*0.4*

Dabovich struck out just a smidge less than half the batters he faced in 2021. He doesn't have blow-away, late-inning stuff, but it's an easy plus fastball/slider combo, with the latter showing true swing-and-miss dive in the low 80s. He might not have quite enough control and command to make you feel all that comfortable if he comes into a one-run game in the seventh, but the slide piece should get him out of trouble more often than not, and Dabovich is ready to get major-league hitters out now.

Sammy Long LHP Born: 07/08/95 Age: 26 Bats: L Throws: L Height: 6'1" Weight: 185 lb. Origin: Round 18, 2016 Draft (#540 overall)

YEAR	TEAM	LVL	AGE	W	L	SV	G	GS	IP	H	HR	BB/9	K/9	K	GB%	BABIP	WHIP	ERA	DRA-	WARP
2019	KAN	A	23	8	5	0	30	15	97	73	7	2.6	10.4	112	39.5%	.277	1.04	3.06	77	2.0
2021	RIC	AA	25	0	1	0	4	4	15	12	0	2.4	13.2	22	41.2%	.353	1.07	3.00	89	0.2
2021	SAC	AAA	25	1	0	0	11	3	26^{1}	16	2	3.1	10.6	31	45.2%	.233	0.95	2.05	84	0.4
2021	SF	MLB	25	2	1	0	12	5	40^{2}	37	5	3.3	8.4	38	39.2%	.278	1.28	5.53	99	0.4
2022 DC	*SF*	*MLB*	*26*	*5*	*5*	*0*	*34*	*12*	*71*	*66*	*9*	*3.4*	*8.6*	*67*	*45.8%*	*.287*	*1.30*	*4.11*	*102*	*0.4*

Comparables: Nate Karns, Caleb Smith, Spencer Turnbull

Long had a very unusual path to the big leagues. Developed as a sidearmer by the Rays and then cut, he switched to a more traditional slot and added some velocity while studying to be an EMT. He caught the attention of the White Sox but was cut again during the pandemic year. He blitzed three levels for the Giants in 2021 before making the majors. Long's stuff isn't going to light up your scouting report. He can run it up to 94, but the fastball is average and a little bit too hittable. He throws a solid 1–7 curve and and average straight change most of the time, and they are effective enough. He's an ideal utility arm, able to be an opener, a swingman or a five-and-dive starter.

Because You Were Going to Ask

Hunter Bishop OF Born: 06/25/98 Age: 24 Bats: L Throws: R Height: 6'5" Weight: 210 lb. Origin: Round 1, 2019 Draft (#10 overall)

YEAR	TEAM	LVL	AGE	PA	R	2B	3B	HR	RBI	BB	K	SB	CS	AVG/OBP/SLG	DRC+	BABIP	BRR	FRAA	WARP
2019	GIO	ROK	21	29	4	3	0	1	3	9	11	2	0	.250/.483/.550		.500			
2019	SK	SS	21	117	21	1	1	4	9	29	28	5	2	.224/.427/.400		.278			
2021	GNTB	ROK	23	32	5	1	0	0	3	5	10	1	1	.160/.313/.200		.250			
2022 non-DC	*SF*	*MLB*	*24*	*251*	*18*	*10*	*1*	*2*	*19*	*19*	*103*	*4*	*2*	*.173/.249/.267*	*42*	*.300*	*0.3*	*CF 0, LF 0*	*-1.0*

Comparables: Scott Cousins, Matt Angle, Cord Phelps

Bishop scuffled a bit in the pros in 2019 after a record-breaking junior season for Arizona State. The reports from the alternate site in 2020 were fine but focused more on his improving defense. The question with Bishop was if he would hit enough to get his impressive raw power into games. We don't really have any additional clarity now, as Bishop dealt with a shoulder strain for most of 2021 and then struck out 40 percent of the time in the Arizona Fall League, where he looked like a player that had missed a ton of reps. He'll turn 24 this season and doesn't really have any tangible experience in full-season ball. A healthy Bishop could hit and move quickly, but given the outstanding questions about the bat and the fairly significant injury, we need to know what we don't know.

Luis Toribio IF Born: 09/28/00 Age: 21 Bats: L Throws: R Height: 6'1" Weight: 185 lb. Origin: International Free Agent, 2017

YEAR	TEAM	LVL	AGE	PA	R	2B	3B	HR	RBI	BB	K	SB	CS	AVG/OBP/SLG	DRC+	BABIP	BRR	FRAA	WARP
2019	GIO	ROK	18	234	45	15	3	3	33	45	54	4	5	.297/.436/.459		.400			
2019	SK	SS	18	13	2	1	0	0	0	2	5	0	0	.273/.385/.364		.500			
2021	SJ	A	20	408	59	20	1	7	39	63	113	2	1	.229/.351/.356	94	.320	0.0	1B(47) -5.2, 3B(29) -1.3	0.1
2022 non-DC	*SF*	*MLB*	*21*	*251*	*20*	*10*	*0*	*2*	*19*	*25*	*84*	*1*	*1*	*.192/.279/.282*	*54*	*.295*	*-0.1*	*3B -1, 1B -2*	*-1.2*

Comparables: Carson Kelly, Chris Carter, Jeimer Candelario

Toribio took a step backwards in 2021, seeing both his athleticism and offensive production regress. Now, instead of a third baseman with power and feel to hit, he looks more like an undersized first baseman lacking the pitch recognition and selection to get to his plus raw power. It's not time to give up on him completely, but he's tracking more like an organizational piece rather than a major-league contributor.

Will Wilson SS Born: 07/21/98 Age: 23 Bats: R Throws: R Height: 6'0" Weight: 184 lb. Origin: Round 1, 2019 Draft (#15 overall)

YEAR	TEAM	LVL	AGE	PA	R	2B	3B	HR	RBI	BB	K	SB	CS	AVG/OBP/SLG	DRC+	BABIP	BRR	FRAA	WARP
2019	ORM	ROA	20	204	23	10	3	5	18	14	47	0	0	.275/.328/.439		.343			
2021	SCO	WIN	22	74	9	3	0	2	8	6	19	0	0	.164/.243/.299		.196			
2021	EUG	A+	22	224	37	14	2	10	26	24	56	7	1	.251/.339/.497	110	.298	0.8	SS(42) -2.0, 2B(4) -0.4	0.8
2021	RIC	AA	22	221	20	8	0	5	22	22	81	1	0	.189/.281/.306	68	.291	-0.6	SS(48) -6.8, 3B(3) -0.1	-0.9
2022 non-DC	*SF*	*MLB*	*23*	*251*	*21*	*10*	*1*	*5*	*23*	*20*	*85*	*0*	*1*	*.197/.269/.324*	*59*	*.288*	*-0.2*	*SS -4, 2B 0*	*-0.8*

Comparables: Chris Taylor, Mark Reynolds, Pedro Florimón

Wilson is here because he's not really a top-10 name or a Factor on the Farm after seeing his hit tool collapse in his first taste of the upper minors. This overstates his drop, and, if pressed, we'd tell you he's an OFP 50 and the 13th-best prospect in this system. But he was also the kind of prospect that was going to need to hit at every level, given his lack of a carrying tool. The reports from Eugene early in the season were about what you'd expect given his collection of polished, potentially average tools playing against High-A competition, so it's not panic stations yet, but Wilson is going to need to hit second time around in Richmond.

Top Talents 25 and Under (as of 4/1/2022):

1. Logan Webb, RHP
2. Marco Luciano, SS
3. Luis Matos, OF
4. Joey Bart, C
5. Jairo Pomares, OF
6. Kyle Harrison, LHP
7. Will Bednar, RHP
8. Camilo Doval, RHP
9. Patrick Bailey, C
10. Heliot Ramos, OF

The venerable Giants roster had a well-documented resurgence in 2021, but the Giants have not gotten any younger since last we checked in on them. San Francisco has more 30-year-olds in their infield than the Pirates have on their 40-man roster, a fact I'm sure Pirates general manager Ben Cherington would share with pride, while not a single fan of the orange and black would want to trade places.

When you are the 24-year-old ace of MLB's most surprising juggernaut, you get to stand upon the shoulders of this list of talented Giants. Webb found little success in his first two big-league stints, but completely overhauled his repertoire for 2021 to a medley of extreme (and extremely effective) offerings. He ditched his four-seam predominantly in favor of a heavy sinker, improved his changeup into what video games make forkballs look like, and finished his shoulder-strain shortened season with two seven-plus-inning masterpieces in San Francisco's epic Division Series matchup with the Dodgers. Webb's history has been blemished by missed time—Tommy John surgery early in his pro career, then an 80-game suspension for performance-enhancing drugs potentially tied to efforts to recover from that injury. Several years and many mechanical tweaks later, Webb is the unlikely ace of the Bay.

Seattle Mariners

The State of the System:

The Mariners' system remains elite at the top, but graduations have cut out some of its depth.

The Top Ten:

1 **Julio Rodríguez OF** OFP: 70 ETA: Early 2022
Born: 12/29/00 Age: 21 Bats: R Throws: R Height: 6'3" Weight: 180 lb. Origin: International Free Agent, 2017

YEAR	TEAM	LVL	AGE	PA	R	2B	3B	HR	RBI	BB	K	SB	CS	AVG/OBP/SLG	DRC+	BABIP	BRR	FRAA	WARP
2019	PEJ	WIN	18	63	7	4	0	0	10	8	10	4	1	.288/.397/.365		.349			
2019	WV	A	18	295	50	20	1	10	50	20	66	1	3	.293/.359/.490	124	.353	0.3	RF(40) 4.2, CF(23) -0.1	2.2
2019	MOD	A+	18	72	13	6	3	2	19	5	10	0	0	.462/.514/.738	134	.528	0.7	CF(13) -3.3, RF(3) -0.4	0.2
2020	ESC	WIN	19	64	4	1	1	0	7	6	16	3	0	.196/.297/.250		.275			
2021	EVE	A+	20	134	29	8	2	6	21	14	29	5	1	.325/.410/.581	114	.390	0.6	RF(19) 1.8, LF(1) -0.1, CF(1) -0.2	0.8
2021	ARK	AA	20	206	35	11	0	7	26	29	37	16	4	.362/.461/.546	125	.431	0.9	RF(20) 4.0, CF(12) -0.6, LF(9) -0.9	1.6
2022 DC	*SEA*	*MLB*	*21*	*63*	*8*	*2*	*0*	*1*	*8*	*5*	*14*	*0*	*1*	*.263/.333/.415*	*108*	*.327*	*0.1*	*RF 1*	*0.4*

Comparables: Giancarlo Stanton, Eloy Jiménez, Domingo Santana

The Report: Signed as one of the top projectable power hitters in his international-free-agent class back in 2017, Rodríguez has developed into one of the best all-around bats in the minors. The massive 21-year-old covers the plate preternaturally well, with quicksilver wrists that help him adjust to offspeed and get the barrel to most locations on the plate. When he makes contact, his exit velocities already sit on par with the hardest hitters in the majors, and his approach allows him to drive the ball with power to all fields. Rodríguez dominated High-A for the first month of the 2021 season before joining the Dominican Republic's Olympic team and starring on their bronze-medal-winning club. He returned stateside to head straight to Double-A, where he walked 14.1 percent of the time and continued to dominate more experienced pitching. Improved physicality with an emphasis on speed and flexibility appeared to yield benefits, as Rodríguez stole 21 bases in 26 attempts across the two levels while frequently beating out infield singles and stretching singles into doubles. Defensively, he'll still be stretched if asked to man center field but should be average or a tick above in a corner. His arm is plenty strong for right, and he moves with fluidity not always prevalent in players his size. Add in his emotional maturity and significant leadership role within the Mariners organization already, and you have a prospect with an exceedingly high likelihood, given his age, of becoming an immediate impact player.

OFP: 70 / All-Star outfielder

Variance: Low. The nearest thing to a nit to pick is hoping to see more power and elevation, but, given that his home park in Double-A Arkansas was the hardest park to go yard from in all of MiLB, he should be just fine. He'll hit enough to be an excellent corner outfield bat, at least, but whether or not his improved speed and range translate and sustain will be tested.

Mark Barry's Fantasy Take: Last year, I tried to get cute with nitpicks for Rodríguez, saying he wouldn't really run all that much. Then he went and swiped 21 bases almost certainly to spite me personally. This dude is the best hitter in the minor leagues and pretty clearly the top dynasty prospect in the game.

2 Noelvi Marte SS OFP: 70 ETA: 2024

Born: 10/16/01 Age: 20 Bats: R Throws: R Height: 6'1" Weight: 181 lb. Origin: International Free Agent, 2018

YEAR	TEAM	LVL	AGE	PA	R	2B	3B	HR	RBI	BB	K	SB	CS	AVG/OBP/SLG	DRC+	BABIP	BRR	FRAA	WARP
2019	DSL SEA	ROK	17	299	56	18	4	9	54	29	55	17	7	.309/.371/.511		.351			
2021	MOD	A	19	478	87	24	2	17	69	58	106	23	7	.271/.368/.462	123	.326	4.1	SS(92) -1.1	3.1
2021	EVE	A+	19	33	4	4	0	0	2	2	11	1	0	.290/.333/.419	95	.450	0.4	SS(7) 0.9	0.2
2022 non-DC	*SEA*	*MLB*	*20*	*251*	*23*	*10*	*0*	*5*	*25*	*19*	*69*	*8*	*3*	*.222/.288/.351*	*73*	*.294*	*0.6*	*SS 1*	*0.2*

Comparables: Jonathan Villar, Richard Ureña, Carlos Correa

The Report: Marte made his stateside and full-season debut in one fell swoop in 2021 and more than held his own despite some struggles with pitch recognition and swing decisions. He did improve his approach against spin as the year wore on, and he has more than enough bat speed to rip plus velocity. His power is mostly pull side at present, but Marte should grow into more all-fields pop and is a potential 30-home-run hitter in the majors. He's already merely an average runner and was inconsistent in the field, so his likely long-term landing spot is third base, where his plus arm plays and his hands and range will be just fine. He has oodles of offensive upside, but Marte does need to refine how he attacks pitchers and improve against offspeed. This isn't uncommon for a teenager debuting in full-season ball, but it does increase the risk in the profile.

OFP: 70 / All-Star third baseman

Variance: High. There will be pressure on the hit tool as Marte moves up the ladder, especially if and when he slides down the defensive spectrum.

Mark Barry's Fantasy Take: I am infinitely befuddled by prospects like Marte. I totally understand the tantalizing power/speed/athleticism combo, and I fully get that he's already produced enough (even at a low level) to be considered a top-10 dynasty prospect in the industry. Still, I'm so scared by hit-tool concerns in the lower levels. Sure, he's still young for his levels, and he could certainly figure it out, but I'm just skeptical enough to not want to pay the sticker price.

3 George Kirby RHP OFP: 70 ETA: Late 2022

Born: 02/04/98 Age: 24 Bats: R Throws: R Height: 6'4" Weight: 215 lb. Origin: Round 1, 2019 Draft (#20 overall)

YEAR	TEAM	LVL	AGE	W	L	SV	G	GS	IP	H	HR	BB/9	K/9	K	GB%	BABIP	WHIP	ERA	DRA-	WARP
2019	EVE	SS	21	0	0	0	9	8	23	24	1	0.0	9.8	25	45.3%	.365	1.04	2.35		
2021	EVE	A+	23	4	2	0	9	9	41^{2}	33	1	1.7	11.2	52	58.3%	.317	0.98	2.38	83	0.7
2021	ARK	AA	23	1	1	0	6	6	26	25	0	2.4	9.7	28	48.6%	.338	1.23	2.77	83	0.4
2022 DC	*SEA*	*MLB*	*24*	*2*	*1*	*0*	*6*	*6*	*32.3*	*32*	*3*	*3.2*	*7.8*	*27*	*34.2%*	*.299*	*1.36*	*4.24*	*106*	*0.2*

Comparables: Cal Quantrill, Andrew Suárez, Rogelio Armenteros

The Report: The calling card for Kirby since his college days has been superlative command, with a walkless streak that spanned two calendar years thanks to 2020's shutdown. He added significant muscle throughout his frame prior to 2021 and got a correlating significant bump in his velocity. Kirby did not throw a pitch south of 95 mph all year, working 95–98 in most of his outings with a few triple-digit offerings. The 6-foot-4 righty mixes in a firm slider and changeup, both of which are comfortably average and flash plus at times, augmented by his exceptional command. His curveball hews a little lower, but all four pitches are located effectively to push his profile forward. Kirby's delivery has a take-and-bake simplicity that is reflected in his high-caliber command, and, given the strides he has made with his stuff, there's very little in his repertoire to suggest he'll be anything less than an above-average rotation arm and perhaps one who can top a rotation.

OFP: 70 / No. 2 Starter

Variance: Medium. Kirby's still a pitcher, let's not go too crazy, but every component is solid and he has easily handled every assignment thus far. He missed a month in the middle of last season with "shoulder fatigue" before returning and heading straight to Double-A, where he scarcely missed a beat. If Kirby had a longer leash in 2021, it'd be easier to envision him spending much of 2022 with Seattle, but he'll likely still be limited on innings after throwing just shy of 70 last year.

Mark Barry's Fantasy Take: I love guys that throw strikes, generally. When those plus-control dudes add, like, five miles per hour to their heaters, well, that just sends me over the moon. In my estimation, Grayson Rodriguez and Shane Baz are the two best dynasty pitching prospects, but Kirby really isn't all that far off, and he might be closer to number one than number four.

4 Emerson Hancock RHP OFP: 60 ETA: 2023

Born: 05/31/99 Age: 23 Bats: R Throws: R Height: 6'4" Weight: 213 lb. Origin: Round 1, 2020 Draft (#6 overall)

YEAR	TEAM	LVL	AGE	W	L	SV	G	GS	IP	H	HR	BB/9	K/9	K	GB%	BABIP	WHIP	ERA	DRA-	WARP
2021	EVE	A+	22	2	0	0	9	9	31	19	1	3.8	8.7	30	57.0%	.231	1.03	2.32	100	0.2
2021	ARK	AA	22	1	1	0	3	3	13^2	10	0	2.6	8.6	13	36.8%	.263	1.02	3.29	95	0.1
2022 non-DC	*SEA*	*MLB*	*23*	*2*	*3*	*0*	*57*	*0*	*50*	*52*	*6*	*4.7*	*6.8*	*37*	*48.4%*	*.299*	*1.57*	*5.29*	*121*	*-0.4*

Comparables: Jeff Hoffman, Reynaldo López, Rocky Coppinger

The Report: Despite strong results in his 12 starts last year, Hancock's 2021 highlighted many of the same issues he has faced for years. He's had durability concerns stretching back to his shortened college seasons and uncertainty about his pitch shapes for just as long. The 6-foot-4 righty looks the part of a prototypical starter, though his low-three-quarters release makes for more run and sink on his fastball than ride. That heater typically sits 93–96, however he did not always sustain that velocity deep into starts, as he struggled to build up his workload across multiple shutdowns for arm fatigue throughout the season. At his best, Hancock has two secondaries that tend towards plus—a firm slider that dives under the table and a fading changeup that bites with similar late intensity. He commands all his pitches well, albeit not quite to George Kirby's level.

Seattle was emphasizing fastball development for Hancock when healthy, with multiple outings that intentionally utilized the pitch exclusively, likely artificially limiting his strikeout totals to some degree. At times, it seemed as though Hancock was experimenting with a cut fastball, as well, but the brevity of his coursework last year made it difficult to track his progression.

OFP: 60 / No. 3 starter

Variance: High. Seattle has been ultra cautious with Hancock while developing his physicality to handle a starter's workload, but, at some point, we need to see a full season of the pitcher, not just glimpses.

Mark Barry's Fantasy Take: Pitchers are scary, we know this. But the red flags for Hancock seem brighter than most. He's more pedigree than production right now, so that probably makes him better trade bait than a trade target.

5 Harry Ford C/DH OFP: 55 ETA: 2025

Born: 02/21/03 Age: 19 Bats: R Throws: R Height: 5'10" Weight: 200 lb. Origin: Round 1, 2021 Draft (#12 overall)

YEAR	TEAM	LVL	AGE	PA	R	2B	3B	HR	RBI	BB	K	SB	CS	AVG/OBP/SLG	DRC+	BABIP	BRR	FRAA	WARP
2021	MRN	ROK	18	65	12	7	0	3	10	9	14	3	0	.291/.400/.582		.342			

Comparables: Marcos Betancourt, Maikel Hernandez, Daniel Rams

The Report: God help us, we are in on a prep catcher. Ford is a catch-and-hit backstop with big-power upside, as his lightning-quick wrists generate seriously hard contact from a short and stout frame. Ford certainly looks the part of a catcher, and while he's not a clear plus defender, all aspects of his defensive game project to at least average. Most of the recent ("recent") successful prep backstops moved off the position quickly (Wil Myers, Neil Walker). Most of the current top prep catching prospects might do so soon enough (Tyler Soderstrom, MJ Melendez). Ford is certainly a good enough athlete to move to the outfield to get his bat in the lineup more often—or, alternatively, to accelerate his timetable to the majors—but a potential plus-hit/plus-power starting-catcher outcome might be worth the longer wait.

OFP: 55 / Above-average catcher

Variance: High. The bat is very good for an outfield prospect, but it could be special for a catching prospect. He has the defensive projection to stay behind the plate, but catchers are weird, and the grind of getting from here to the majors can take a toll on the bat.

Mark Barry's Fantasy Take: On a post-draft episode of the award-winning* TINO podcast (*do not fact check this), I admitted my inability to discern the actual difference between bat-speed guys. Harry Ford, though, has a noticeably fast bat. If you're going to roster catching prospects, roster ones that are hitters first. Ford's just outside the top-100, for me.

6 Matt Brash RHP

OFP: 55 ETA: Called up in 2021 but did not appear in a game

Born: 05/12/98 Age: 24 Bats: R Throws: R Height: 6'1" Weight: 170 lb. Origin: Round 4, 2019 Draft (#113 overall)

YEAR	TEAM	LVL	AGE	W	L	SV	G	GS	IP	H	HR	BB/9	K/9	K	GB%	BABIP	WHIP	ERA	DRA-	WARP
2021	EVE	A+	23	3	2	1	10	9	42^{1}	31	3	5.3	13.2	62	51.1%	.315	1.32	2.55	92	0.5
2021	ARK	AA	23	3	2	0	10	10	55	32	3	3.8	13.1	80	45.4%	.252	1.00	2.13	78	1.0
2022 DC	*SEA*	*MLB*	*24*	*3*	*3*	*0*	*11*	*11*	*51*	*45*	*6*	*5.3*	*10.5*	*59*	*46.1%*	*.300*	*1.48*	*4.56*	*105*	*0.3*

Comparables: Mike Busby, Yordano Ventura, Robbie Ross Jr.

The Report: A Wiffle-ball slider and a velocity spike after being acquired from San Diego at the 2020 deadline made Brash one of the most dominant pitchers in the minors in 2021, getting the Pitching Ninja treatment even before his ultimately unutilized late-season call-up as Seattle made its final playoff push. Brash's highlight reel somewhat belies his occasionally inconsistent package, particularly where command is concerned, but when you've got three bat-missing pitches (four-seamer, slider and changeup), sit 96–98 and strike out more than a third of the batters you face, there's substance behind the style. Brash's moneymaker is his high-spin slider, which he can vary to feature more sweep (typically to righties) or drop (for lefties), and Brash has shown the confidence to throw the pitch in all counts, at times with greater comfort and command than his fastball. Though he's listed at 6-foot-1 and might barely scrape that, Brash is sturdily built and generates a flat angle of approach on his running heater that helps it work at the top of the zone. Though Brash was often able to work himself out of trouble with his brilliant stuff, his double-digit walk percentages will put him in position to struggle at times, possibly limiting him to a fireman role if he can't curtail the walks enough to clear five innings long-term.

OFP: 55 / No. 3 starter or multi-inning relief ace

Variance: Medium. As a late-blooming Canadian arm from a small school, Brash has, essentially, one year of a track record as this caliber of pitcher. There's slight violence in his delivery, which makes a pitcher of his size a bit scarier, but it's easy to see him at least in the back of a bullpen as soon as this year.

Mark Barry's Fantasy Take: Brash doesn't have a very long pro track record, so I'm not willing to call him a high-volume walk guy just yet, but if he doesn't get stingier with the free passes, he's going to be a nightmare for your rate stats. There's a non-zero chance he scrapes up against a fantasy SP2, but I think his best role might be the ninth inning.

7 Brandon Williamson LHP

OFP: 55 ETA: Late 2022

Born: 04/02/98 Age: 24 Bats: R Throws: L Height: 6'6" Weight: 210 lb. Origin: Round 2, 2019 Draft (#59 overall)

YEAR	TEAM	LVL	AGE	W	L	SV	G	GS	IP	H	HR	BB/9	K/9	K	GB%	BABIP	WHIP	ERA	DRA-	WARP
2019	EVE	SS	21	0	0	0	10	9	15^{1}	9	0	2.9	14.7	25	55.2%	.310	0.91	2.35		
2021	EVE	A+	23	2	1	0	6	6	31	21	4	2.9	17.1	59	44.2%	.354	1.00	3.19	77	0.6
2021	ARK	AA	23	2	5	0	13	13	67^{1}	62	7	3.1	12.6	94	36.6%	.353	1.26	3.48	77	1.3
2022 non-DC	*SEA*	*MLB*	*24*	*2*	*2*	*0*	*57*	*0*	*50*	*44*	*7*	*3.9*	*10.7*	*59*	*45.0%*	*.299*	*1.33*	*4.42*	*104*	*0.1*

Comparables: Eric Lauer, Seth Maness, Shaun Marcum

The Report: Despite having the prototypical size and frame of a workhorse, this 6-foot-6 southpaw dealt with lower body/torso injuries at Texas Christian University, including surgery to repair torn labrums in both hips. That, plus a proclivity to see his stuff fade around the fourth or fifth inning, has tempered expectations for the long-levered lefty. His 2021 season was a significant step in the right direction on that front, however, as Williamson made 19 starts between High-A and Double-A and struck out 153 batters in 98 ⅓ innings while walking just 8 percent. His high-three-quarters delivery augments the deception he can create due to his size, which helps his low-90s fastball play up significantly. That pitch pairs extremely well with a plus 12–6 curveball that is Williamson's out-pitch. He locates the curve consistently at or near the bottom of the zone with enough bite to beat both lefties and righties. At times, Williamson will turn to a slider, as well, which has more sweep but comes in the low 80s, and he rounds out his arsenal with a passable mid-80s changeup that has short, late drop. Williamson's delivery is low effort and fosters solid control, particularly of his secondaries. His pro development has focused on improving his physicality to sustain a starter's workload. That said, he can still fade at times over the course of an outing, disrupting his starter-projection ceiling despite an otherwise well-rounded profile.

OFP: 55 / No. 3 starter but at a 150-inning pace instead of 180-plus

Variance: Medium. Despite his success, Williamson only pitched past the sixth inning once in his 2021 campaign, and his struggles with health and durability remain fairly recent. Williamson is likely to beat Kirby, and perhaps even Brash, to a big league start, but his long-term future depends on if his stuff looks the same over pitches 61–100 as it does over pitches 0–60.

Mark Barry's Fantasy Take: I'm not overly confident that Williamson will be able to provide the bulk necessary to be a high-end fantasy starter. Luckily for him, the days of 200-plus-inning workhorses have gone the way of the super-skinny jean. If you can roster the southpaw as a potential three-to-four-inning guy each time out, I'm a fan. If he carries a starter's premium, I'm less interested.

8 Alberto Rodriguez RF OFP: 50 ETA: Late 2023/Early 2024

Born: 10/06/00 Age: 21 Bats: L Throws: L Height: 5'11" Weight: 180 lb. Origin: International Free Agent, 2017

YEAR	TEAM	LVL	AGE	PA	R	2B	3B	HR	RBI	BB	K	SB	CS	AVG/OBP/SLG	DRC+	BABIP	BRR	FRAA	WARP
2019	BLU	ROK	18	195	19	13	1	2	29	19	32	13	2	.301/.364/.422		.352			
2021	MOD	A	20	431	75	30	5	10	63	51	95	13	7	.295/.383/.484	120	.367	-3.9	RF(75) 15.9, LF(5) -0.5, CF(2) -0.4	3.5
2021	EVE	A+	20	28	5	1	0	0	2	2	7	2	0	.208/.321/.250	104	.294	-0.1	LF(3) -0.1, RF(3) -0.2	0.1
2022 non-DC	*SEA*	*MLB*	*21*	*251*	*21*	*12*	*1*	*3*	*22*	*19*	*65*	*8*	*3*	*.226/.293/.342*	*72*	*.299*	*0.7*	*RF 3, LF 0*	*0.2*

Comparables: Gregory Polanco, Alex Kirilloff, Marcell Ozuna

The Report: At age 20 last year, this squat, 5-foot-11, lefty corner outfielder had an impressive offensive season in Low-A, highlighted by a strong approach leading to loud exit velocities. After coming over from Toronto at the 2020 trade deadline, Rodriguez's conditioning improved significantly, with better flexibility and torque noticeable in the swing. His toe-tap load feeds into a high-effort stroke that maximizes impact and has thus far not sacrificed contact, but he may be exposed on the outer half and/or by lefties at higher levels. Rodriguez had success hunting pitches over the middle and on the inner half of the plate that he could handle and eschewing those he couldn't. His confidence and enthusiasm is evident on the field and throughout the game, and his patience at the plate allows him to get on base at a healthy clip if pitchers don't come to him and can't locate on the outer half. Average speed and range in the outfield alongside an above-average arm will keep Rodriguez in either corner outfield spot, but puts pressure on him to continue progressing offensively with a frame that is already reasonably built out.

OFP: 50 / Average regular in an outfield corner

Variance: High. The odds of Rodriguez matriculating to MLB as more than a platoon bat are longer than you'd like and represent the suspect depth of Seattle's system on the position player side. But 20-year-olds who hit in Low-A are not a dime a dozen.

Mark Barry's Fantasy Take: "Long odds of being better than a platoon bat" is not a phrase that I love to associate with my dynasty farm system. Throw Rodriguez on the watchlist for performing as one of the youngest guys in Low-A, but you can wait to see more before rostering him.

9 Gabriel Gonzalez OF OFP: 50 ETA: 2025

Born: 01/04/04 Age: 18 Bats: R Throws: R Height: 5'10" Weight: 165 lb. Origin: International Free Agent, 2021

YEAR	TEAM	LVL	AGE	PA	R	2B	3B	HR	RBI	BB	K	SB	CS	AVG/OBP/SLG	DRC+	BABIP	BRR	FRAA	WARP
2021	DSL SEA	ROK	17	221	39	15	4	7	36	21	35	9	3	.287/.371/.521		.311			

Comparables: Christian Capellan, Cesar Colmenares, Kenneth Bautista

The Report: Seattle's modus operandi for all J2 international-amateur signees has been to start them in the Dominican Summer League for a season, no matter their perceived maturity or advancement. While there's merit to such an approach, it makes appraising the performance and development of the organization's top signees particularly challenging for their first year or two. In the case of Gonzalez, the 5-foot-11 outfielder has a bat-over-glove profile and should be a reasonable tri-positional outfielder with above-average speed that will ultimately scale down as he adds strength. Fortunately, Gonzalez has at least the early look of a balanced, potent hitter, with a powerful swing despite his size. Drawing conclusions off DSL stats is a fool's errand, but he was appropriately dominant to merit monitoring, and the 18-year-old could see affiliated ball by midseason or perhaps skip the Arizona Complex League entirely to offer a more well-defined profile.

OFP: 50 / Average right fielder

Variance: Extreme. Gonzalez did what he should against inferior competition, and though he'd hardly be the first DSL star to sputter, his pedigree and performance make him an 18-year-old worth keeping tabs on.

Mark Barry's Fantasy Take: This is the type of profile that I like to add immediately based on an exciting DSL debut. There's rarely ever a premium to be paid, and, if things work out, you're looking at the next Noelvi Marte-esque helium. If not, you can churn the roster spot in search of the next pop up.

10 Adam Macko LHP

OFP: 50 ETA: 2024

Born: 12/30/00 Age: 21 Bats: L Throws: L Height: 6'0" Weight: 170 lb. Origin: Round 7, 2019 Draft (#216 overall)

YEAR	TEAM	LVL	AGE	W	L	SV	G	GS	IP	H	HR	BB/9	K/9	K	GB%	BABIP	WHIP	ERA	DRA-	WARP
2019	MAR	ROK	18	0	3	0	8	2	21^1	19	1	4.6	13.1	31	48.0%	.375	1.41	3.38		
2021	MOD	A	20	2	2	0	9	9	33^1	29	1	5.7	15.1	56	36.8%	.373	1.50	4.59	104	0.1
2022 non-DC	*SEA*	*MLB*	*21*	*2*	*3*	*0*	*57*	*0*	*50*	*46*	*8*	*6.1*	*9.9*	*55*	*35.3%*	*.298*	*1.61*	*5.49*	*122*	*-0.4*

Comparables: Henry Owens, Jose Rodriguez, Wilson Alvarez

The Report: Baseball-Reference lists two Slovakian-born players in its big-league database: Jack Quinn—a fascinating, early 20th-century star whose birth name was certainly not Jack Quinn and was only maybe born in the part of the Austro-Hungarian Empire that is now Slovakia—and Elmer Valo—whose Czechoslovakian birth and subsequent route to fame as a clean-living, max-effort outfielder made him a fan favorite in the 1940s and '50s. Macko, who moved from Slovakia to Ireland, then on to Alberta, Canada, seeks to be the third member of that club and the first to grace the field in more than half a century. His pathway is built on a plus-plus curveball, as the 6-foot southpaw has cranked his high-spin, sweeping breaker into a superior bat-misser. Sitting in the upper 80s in high school when drafted, Macko has added significant strength and his fastball now averages 92–95, topping out at 98, with strong backspin that induces plenty of swing-and-miss. He struck out 36.1 percent of hitters last year while walking 13.5 percent, showcasing the present limitations of his higher-effort delivery, and was slowed by non-structural shoulder soreness. Two plus pitches and dominating older hitters at the age of 20 is the shine, while the rub is the need for better health and command, as well as improvements to his mediocre slider and changeup to keep platoon bats honest at higher levels.

OFP: 50 / No. 4 starter or high-octane lefty reliever

Variance: Extreme. One could make the case (and we did) for Macko as a prospect on the verge of a breakout, if health allows, as few players were as unhittable at any level. Conversely, he's an undersized lefty who struggled to stay on the mound last year while trying to throw harder than he ever has. We're two healthy seasons away from having genuine confidence in Macko as a starter, but the framework is there.

Mark Barry's Fantasy Take: Honestly, I want to see Macko succeed so he can join the illustrious list of famous, Slovakian-born ballplayers. I don't really want him for my dynasty rotation, however. Shout out to Elmer Valo.

The Prospects You Meet Outside the Top Ten

Prospects on the Rise

Edwin Arroyo IF Born: 08/25/03 Age: 18 Bats: S Throws: S Height: 6'0" Weight: 175 lb. Origin: Round 2, 2021 Draft (#48 overall)

YEAR	TEAM	LVL	AGE	PA	R	2B	3B	HR	RBI	BB	K	SB	CS	AVG/OBP/SLG	DRC+	BABIP	BRR	FRAA	WARP
2021	RA12	WIN	17	65	6	3	0	0	2	6	14	1	0	.250/.333/.304		.333			
2021	MRN	ROK	17	86	16	2	0	2	10	10	26	4	1	.211/.337/.324		.295			

Comparables: Hector Nieves, Luis Ortiz, Emir Velasquez

A switch-hitting (and switch-throwing) infielder, Arroyo was the Mariners' second-round pick last summer. Young for his draft class, Arroyo is mostly a line-drive hitter, at present, although he has started to add some thump, from the right side at least. A smooth defender, he has a good chance to stick at shortstop, but his offensive tools might be more of a slow burn.

Victor Labrada CF Born: 01/16/00 Age: 22 Bats: L Throws: L Height: 5'9" Weight: 165 lb. Origin: International Free Agent, 2021

YEAR	TEAM	LVL	AGE	PA	R	2B	3B	HR	RBI	BB	K	SB	CS	AVG/OBP/SLG	DRC+	BABIP	BRR	FRAA	WARP
2021	MOD	A	21	243	44	16	3	1	28	34	60	22	9	.294/.407/.418	104	.408	-0.4	CF(46) -8.5	0.2
2021	EVE	A+	21	227	35	7	3	6	27	19	63	10	6	.246/.314/.399	90	.324	0.6	CF(42) -6.0, RF(4) 0.4, LF(2) -0.7	0.0
2022 non-DC	*SEA*	*MLB*	*22*	*251*	*20*	*10*	*1*	*2*	*20*	*20*	*76*	*10*	*6*	*.214/.285/.310*	*61*	*.309*	*1.2*	*CF -3, RF 0*	*-0.5*

Comparables: Mallex Smith, Michael Hermosillo, Ender Inciarte

Signed out of Cuba in last year's . . . uh, J15 class, Labrada is a quick-footed outfielder who can handle all three outfield spots and uses his plus speed to take an extra base whenever he shoots one into the gap. He has mostly doubles power and, given his small frame, isn't likely to grow into much more. That limits the upside in his profile, but Labrada might slash, walk and field his way into becoming an average outfielder, although a bench role looks far more likely, at present.

Levi Stoudt RHP Born: 12/04/97 Age: 24 Bats: R Throws: R Height: 6'1" Weight: 195 lb. Origin: Round 3, 2019 Draft (#97 overall)

YEAR	TEAM	LVL	AGE	W	L	SV	G	GS	IP	H	HR	BB/9	K/9	K	GB%	BABIP	WHIP	ERA	DRA-	WARP
2021	EVE	A+	23	6	1	0	12	12	64	47	6	4.1	9.4	67	43.6%	.261	1.19	3.52	101	0.4
2021	ARK	AA	23	1	2	0	3	3	17^{2}	14	2	4.1	9.7	19	31.9%	.267	1.25	2.55	114	0.0
2022 non-DC	*SEA*	*MLB*	*24*	*2*	*3*	*0*	*57*	*0*	*50*	*53*	*8*	*5.3*	*8.1*	*45*	*39.1%*	*.310*	*1.66*	*6.24*	*136*	*-0.8*

Comparables: Cole Irvin, Mike Wright Jr., Luke French

Since the day he was drafted in 2019, this third-rounder from Lehigh University has been seen as likely to move to the bullpen. That could still be the case, but, as a starter last year, Stoudt has held his velocity well, albeit with some shortcomings on his command. Typically 93–95, though clipping 98–99 when rearing back a few times per game, Stoudt has an aesthetically pleasing split-change that runs around 80–82 and is his out-pitch. His profile resembles that of several other arms on this list—plus stuff but questions about his results and/or rotation future—but, as a college signee from 2019, Stoudt will already be 24 for all of 2022. Because of his struggles with command and the high degree of effort in his delivery, it seems likely he will ultimately settle in as a bullpen arm in the bigs, despite his curveball making strides in 2021, as well. Unless Stoudt's location improves, he'll be limited to, albeit likely still effective in, short bursts.

Factors on the Farm

Zach DeLoach OF Born: 08/18/98 Age: 23 Bats: L Throws: R Height: 6'1" Weight: 205 lb. Origin: Round 2, 2020 Draft (#43 overall)

YEAR	TEAM	LVL	AGE	PA	R	2B	3B	HR	RBI	BB	K	SB	CS	AVG/OBP/SLG	DRC+	BABIP	BRR	FRAA	WARP
2021	EVE	A+	22	285	56	23	2	9	37	32	63	6	3	.313/.400/.530	113	.390	0.3	RF(31) 0.7, LF(23) 1.4	1.6
2021	ARK	AA	22	216	28	10	2	5	22	28	58	1	2	.227/.338/.384	98	.303	-0.1	RF(26) 3.1, LF(17) 2.6	1.1
2022 non-DC	*SEA*	*MLB*	*23*	*251*	*23*	*12*	*1*	*4*	*24*	*22*	*69*	*1*	*1*	*.224/.300/.353*	*75*	*.303*	*-0.1*	*RF 0, LF 1*	*0.0*

Comparables: Adam Eaton, Anthony Santander, Domonic Brown

After two unremarkable seasons at Texas A&M, DeLoach hit his way into the top two rounds of the 2020 draft on the strength of a strong Cape Cod League performance and a blisteringly hot start to his junior year in the SEC. He kept hitting in High-A to start 2021, showing off a well-rounded offensive game with good contact rates, plenty of doubles and a willingness to work a walk. He didn't show ideal home-run power for a corner outfielder but had enough else going for him at the plate to wave off talk of his being a tweener, for a bit. A promotion to Double-A saw his contact rate and power tank, as upper-minors arms could put him away when he got deeper in counts. DeLoach is a perfectly fine corner outfielder but is limited to a less defensively valuable spot, so he will have to show a bit more in Double-A this time around if he's going to hit his way past a bench-outfielder projection.

Connor Phillips RHP Born: 05/04/01 Age: 21 Bats: R Throws: R Height: 6'2" Weight: 190 lb. Origin: Round 2, 2020 Draft (#64 overall)

YEAR	TEAM	LVL	AGE	W	L	SV	G	GS	IP	H	HR	BB/9	K/9	K	GB%	BABIP	WHIP	ERA	DRA-	WARP
2021	MOD	A	20	7	3	0	16	16	72	62	1	5.5	13.0	104	41.2%	.361	1.47	4.75	95	0.6
2022 non-DC	*SEA*	*MLB*	*21*	*2*	*3*	*0*	*57*	*0*	*50*	*49*	*7*	*6.3*	*9.5*	*52*	*32.4%*	*.310*	*1.70*	*5.87*	*127*	*-0.5*

Comparables: Tyler Clippard, Kyle Ryan, Triston McKenzie

If you crafted a prospect to make certain people salivate and others red in the face with rage at Kids These Days and The State Of The Game, he might look a lot like Phillips. The 64th-overall pick in the 2020 draft, Phillips was a JUCO product from McLennan Community College in Texas and is as three-true as they outcome. In 2021, it was mostly K or BB for the righty with a mid-90s-backspin-four-seam/tight-12-6-curveball combo that misses bats or the plate and rarely anything in between. His motion resembles the trend of several analytics-attuned arms, with a shorter arm action/circle that bursts into a high-effort, compact, over-the-top release. He won't turn 21 until May and, last year, reached High-A, where he should start this season, making any improvements to his command both plausible and worth monitoring, but, as of right now, he has reliever risk oozing from every pore.

Juan Then RHP Born: 02/07/00 Age: 22 Bats: R Throws: R Height: 6'1" Weight: 175 lb. Origin: International Free Agent, 2016

YEAR	TEAM	LVL	AGE	W	L	SV	G	GS	IP	H	HR	BB/9	K/9	K	GB%	BABIP	WHIP	ERA	DRA-	WARP
2019	MAR	ROK	19	0	0	0	1	0	2	2	0	0.0	9.0	2	20.0%	.400	1.00	0.00		
2019	EVE	SS	19	0	3	0	7	6	30[1]	24	1	2.7	9.5	32	34.6%	.299	1.09	3.56		
2019	WV	A	19	1	2	0	3	3	16	7	1	2.3	7.9	14	29.3%	.150	0.69	2.25	93	0.2
2021	EVE	A+	21	2	5	0	14	14	54[1]	68	12	3.1	9.8	59	47.1%	.354	1.60	6.46	100	0.4
2022 non-DC	*SEA*	*MLB*	*22*	*2*	*3*	*0*	*57*	*0*	*50*	*54*	*8*	*4.0*	*6.8*	*37*	*45.8%*	*.303*	*1.54*	*5.59*	*129*	*-0.6*

Comparables: Reynaldo López, Chris Flexen, Elieser Hernandez

One imagines that, when they added him to the 40-man roster after the 2020 season, the Mariners hoped Then would have made more progress towards a major-league role by now than he has, as his option clock is ticking. He did get treated with the same kind of kid gloves as the rest of the Mariners low-minors pitching prospects last year and dealt with an injury, as well. Although, it's tough to work deep into games when you are getting hit as hard as Then was. He has a high-effort delivery with an arm action best described as a purposeful yank. That leads to both control and command issues for his mid-90s heater. His curve and change both still flash, but, given that he can ramp his heater up towards triple digits in short bursts, it might be time for Then to head to the pen to try to accelerate his major-league timetable and mitigate some of his command issues.

Top Talents 25 and Under (as of 4/1/2022):

1. Julio Rodríguez, OF
2. Jarred Kelenic, OF
3. Logan Gilbert, RHP
4. Noelvi Marte, SS
5. George Kirby, RHP
6. Emerson Hancock, RHP
7. Harry Ford, C
8. Abraham Toro, 3B/2B
9. Matt Brash, RHP
10. Cal Raleigh, C

Not many teams have more players eligible for the 25-and-Under ranking on their roster than Seattle, and several of those players should be building blocks for years to come. Others, however, are a bit difficult to place. Kelenic's nightmarish first couple months in the majors abated by the end, as a Tacoma refresher and a happy medium between the stance he'd excelled with in 2019 and the over-crouched version he brought into 2021 led to a strong September/October during Seattle's surprising playoff hunt. If you believe that final month harbingers smooth sailing going forward for the ultra-polished 22-year-old, you'd be well within your rights, but those miserable first few months happened and can't be cast out entirely. There are noo sure things under the sun, at least not immediately.

Kelenic's call-up-mate, Gilbert, had his own bouts with inconsistency, though he ultimately proved more capable in his initial exposure. Gilbert was essentially a league-average pitcher in his first 120-odd innings, with a 96 DRA– and both healthy strikeout (25.4 percent) and walk (5.6 percent) rates. He did it all while essentially just throwing fastballs and, more specifically, while throwing fastballs mostly over the heart of the plate. That could be cause for concern—Gilbert has great extension and a solid heater, but he needs more comfort with his offspeed to succeed. More optimistically, if he can be that effective with atypically middling control and only one primary pitch, there's plenty of potential yet untapped. Don't expect any massive off-speed revelations from Big Bert, but greater usage, alone, seems inevitable.

With Toro begins the uncertainty that is Seattle's young array. The controversial midseason acquisition played what critics everywhere are calling "too much" second base given the trilingual switch-hitter's mechanical movements in the field, but, with Kyle Seager officially retired, the 25-year-old could slot in as a likely league-average third baseman. Seattle's intent to add offensive talent, however, seems liable to include a post-lockout infield addition, which would shift Toro into a platoon/utility role alongside Adam Frazier.

Then we get into the uncertain post-prospects. Raleigh is the emblem-bearer but is joined by outfielder Taylor Trammell, first baseman Evan White and impossibly still-eligible lefty pitcher Justus Sheffield. Raleigh's debut was grisly for a bat-first backstop. While his framing and glove work seemed sound, teams ran on him without much fear. It'd be easier to name catching prospects who came up and struggled to hit than those who slugged from the jump, but Raleigh looked lost at the plate by the end of the season. In all likelihood, Trammell is once again in need of a change of scenery given the prospects in front of and looming behind him. He got a somewhat-unexpected run as Seattle's center fielder at the season's outset and showed his immense raw power but didn't make nearly enough contact, otherwise. White was once seen as a high-floor 1B/ OF type who would rack up Gold Gloves, but it's unclear if he can stay healthy or make enough contact to be eligible for any more trophies. Sheffield's stuff abandoned him, and he missed much of last season with a forearm strain after what had been a promising 2020, but, if his stuff returns, he still could make for a back-end starter when healthy.

Lastly, we come to two players whose roles are unclear due to Seattle's present roster state, but who could easily be more impactful big leaguers than the more-heralded series of names in the previous paragraph. Luis Torrens is a catcher(?) whose abysmal first couple months in the majors, on both sides of the ball, got him sent down to Triple-A Tacoma. When he returned a month later, his swing was simplified, and he looked to be a potent weak-side platoon bat, with the tiny caveat that Seattle ceased playing him at catcher. The Mariners have claimed that Torrens remains a catcher in their eyes, which is the absolute defining point for whether he could track forward on a Stephen Vogt trajectory or fall into Quad-A obscurity with haste. As for Andrés Muñoz, he seemed likely to be a high-leverage reliever prior to having Tommy John surgery in 2019. The 23-year-old returned for one inning in the final game of 2021, sat 99–101, and showed no reason to expect less moving forward at full health into 2022.

St. Louis Cardinals

The State of the System:

There were lots of ups and downs last year among the names below, which leaves the organization about where it was: a little-below-median system with some depth issues.

The Top Ten:

1 Jordan Walker 3B   OFP: 70   ETA: 2024

Born: 05/22/02 Age: 20 Bats: R Throws: R Height: 6'5" Weight: 220 lb. Origin: Round 1, 2020 Draft (#21 overall)

YEAR	TEAM	LVL	AGE	PA	R	2B	3B	HR	RBI	BB	K	SB	CS	AVG/OBP/SLG	DRC+	BABIP	BRR	FRAA	WARP
2021	PMB	A	19	122	24	11	1	6	21	18	21	1	0	.374/.475/.687	145	.419	-0.3	3B(22) -3.6	0.6
2021	PEO	A+	19	244	39	14	3	8	27	15	66	13	2	.292/.344/.487	101	.382	-0.5	3B(54) -3.6	0.4
2022 non-DC	*STL*	*MLB*	*20*	*251*	*24*	*12*	*1*	*5*	*26*	*16*	*69*	*5*	*2*	*.243/.300/.390*	*86*	*.321*	*0.4*	*3B -3*	*0.0*

Comparables: Josh Vitters, Rafael Devers, Blake DeWitt

The Report: So, what exactly is the argument against Jordan Walker as one of the top prospects in baseball? We don't know if we bump up against the Sagan Standard (extraordinary claims require extraordinary evidence) for a former first-round pick who hit .317/.388/.548 between two A-ball levels and won't turn 20 until May, but there is nothing ordinary about Jordan Walker, anyway. He hits the ball as hard as anyone in the minors. His contact rates were perfectly fine given his age and experience level. Despite some long levers in his swing, he has above-average bat speed, an advanced approach and doesn't expand. Walker doesn't sell out for dingers and is fine driving the ball the other way when the pitch calls for it. He's not a mere corner slugger, he has a chance to have a plus hit tool.

And if Walker does hit .280, well, a lot of his prodigious raw power is going to get into games. He still has room to fill out and turn his plus-plus raw power into true elite pop. It is showing up more as doubles than true over-the-fence power right now, but 14 bombs in 82 games, given the leagues and parks he was playing in, is nothing to sneeze at. We want to see his approach and swing tested in the upper minors, of course, but the offensive upside here is as high as that of any hitter in the minors. His 2021 doesn't look all that different from Julio Rodríguez's 2019, for one example, and Walker had a better season, both statistically and per his underlying batted-ball and swing data, than Marco Luciano.

We do have to talk about his defensive profile, although his is an impact bat anywhere on the diamond. Walker is presently fine at third base. He's also already on the larger side for a left-side infielder. It's an XL frame, and he's likely to add more physicality as he enters his twenties. That might get him to 40 home runs a season, it's also likely to make him a left fielder or first baseman. But, to quote Tommy Lee Jones in *The Fugitive*, "I don't care."

OFP: 70 / Frequent All-Star, maybe at third, maybe in an outfield corner, maybe even at first

Variance: Medium. We're really confident in the bat. We'll be more confident when he does this in Double-A and we get a better feel for his ultimate defensive home.

Mark Barry's Fantasy Take: It's hard to think of a prospect that improved his stock more in 2021 than Walker. As one of the youngest guys drafted in last year's first round, Walker had a fantasy profile that was mostly speculation—there was power, but maybe nothing else. Fast forward to the present day, and he's one of the very best dynasty prospects in baseball, having proven that he can make enough contact (at least at the lower levels) to be a plus contributor in four categories. That plays wherever he ends up defensively.

Eyewitness Report: Jordan Walker

Evaluator: Nathan Graham
Report Date: 08/23/2021
Dates Seen: 8/4-8/6/21
Risk Factor: High
Physical/Health: XXL Frame, tall and athletic build with growth and strength potential remaining.

Tool	Future Grade	Report
Hit	60	Slightly open, upright stance, stays balanced, quiet pre-swing; above average bat speed that has some natural loft; Rare approach for a young hitter, shows excellent pitch recognition and rarely expands the zone, will attack when ahead and hit the ball with authority but also shows the ability to take outside pitches opposite field.
Power	70	Current plus raw power will increase to double plus with physical maturity; power generated by natural strength and plus bat speed; Hits to all fields, still learning how to make it play in-game but will be a future run producer.
Baserunning/ Speed	40	Current average raw foot speed, 4.35 clock home to first, long strides; will play down to below average with physical maturity.
Glove	50	Average hands and range make him a adequate defender currently, not flashy but gets the job done; Has the tools to handle a move to 1B or LF if needed in the future.
Arm	50	Accurate arm with enough strength to handle the left side of the diamond.

Conclusion: Future impact bat that will anchor a lineup with his plus contact/power tools. His eventual landing spot defensively doesn't matter, the bat will carry the profile.

2 Nolan Gorman 3B/2B OFP: 60 ETA: 2022, as needed

Born: 05/10/00 Age: 22 Bats: L Throws: R Height: 6'1" Weight: 210 lb. Origin: Round 1, 2018 Draft (#19 overall)

YEAR	TEAM	LVL	AGE	PA	R	2B	3B	HR	RBI	BB	K	SB	CS	AVG/OBP/SLG	DRC+	BABIP	BRR	FRAA	WARP
2019	PEO	A	19	282	41	14	3	10	41	32	79	2	0	.241/.344/.448	117	.312	0.4	3B(51) 8.3	2.4
2019	PMB	A+	19	230	24	16	3	5	21	13	73	0	1	.256/.304/.428	87	.365	-1.9	3B(49) -6.6	-0.6
2021	SPR	AA	21	195	26	6	0	11	27	18	52	4	0	.288/.354/.508	114	.351	0.5	3B(23) -0.6, 2B(16) 2.0	1.1
2021	MEM	AAA	21	328	45	14	1	14	48	20	63	3	0	.274/.320/.465	109	.301	0.2	2B(61) 8.2, 3B(9) 0.4	2.2
2022 DC	*STL*	*MLB*	*22*	*64*	*7*	*2*	*0*	*2*	*7*	*4*	*17*	*0*	*0*	*.250/.304/.418*	*92*	*.318*	*0.0*	*3B 0, 2B 1*	*0.2*

Comparables: Miguel Andújar, Blake DeWitt, Jorge Polanco

The Report: Suddenly, it's a bit tougher to stand out as a former first-round prep third baseman in the Cardinals' system. Gorman started taking grounders at the keystone last spring—there's another Nolan entrenched at the hot corner in St. Louis—and he's . . . playable there. He's not the rangiest middle infielder but is still around an average runner and moves well enough. He looks fine on the double-play pivot, and the left-side-quality arm is a weapon as a second baseman. Gorman has a bit of a Brian Dozier build, and we'd expect he could play Dozier-quality defense at second.

The whole point of moving him to second is to get his bat in the lineup, and it's progressing fine. Unlike Walker, who has more of a traditional power-hitter's swing, Gorman can look like he's taking a two-strike emergency hack, at times. He creates big whip and separation, and while it doesn't look pretty, he can also flick it 400 feet to dead center. Gorman doesn't always create ideal contact doing this, and his batted-ball profile notably tanked a bit in Triple-A. That said, when he does lift the ball, it goes far. There might be a little less hit-and-power projection here than with Walker, but Gorman is just about ready to be an above-average regular.

OFP: 60 / First-division regular, bat-first second baseman

Variance: Medium. Like Walker, Gorman doesn't consistently get to his game power yet. Unlike Walker, he has less time to start consistently lifting the ball before he's expected to swing a major-league stick.

Mark Barry's Fantasy Take: Honestly, not much has changed in Gorman's fantasy projection—aside from his potential move to the keystone. He's still a good bet for 25–30 homers annually, and he could definitely chip in some seasons hitting .270-plus with some batted-ball luck. Walker's ceiling is higher, but Gorman's power and proximity place him firmly in the top-20 prospect range, as well.

3 Matthew Liberatore LHP OFP: 55 ETA: 2022

Born: 11/06/99 Age: 22 Bats: L Throws: L Height: 6'4" Weight: 200 lb. Origin: Round 1, 2018 Draft (#16 overall)

YEAR	TEAM	LVL	AGE	W	L	SV	G	GS	IP	H	HR	BB/9	K/9	K	GB%	BABIP	WHIP	ERA	DRA-	WARP
2019	BG	A	19	6	2	0	16	15	78^{1}	70	2	3.6	8.7	76	55.7%	.312	1.29	3.10	96	0.8
2021	MEM	AAA	21	9	9	0	22	18	124^{2}	123	19	2.4	8.9	123	38.3%	.308	1.25	4.04	104	1.4
2022 non-DC	*STL*	*MLB*	*22*	*2*	*3*	*0*	*57*	*0*	*50*	*51*	*7*	*3.4*	*7.2*	*39*	*42.3%*	*.295*	*1.41*	*4.69*	*111*	*-0.1*

Comparables: Zach Duke, Iván Nova, Chris Volstad

The Report: Dig into the back of your closet, find your favorite flannel and beanie. Maybe give *24 Hour Revenge Therapy* a spin. That should put you in the right frame of mind to read about Liberatore, who is a throwback to your favorite '90s pitching prospect. Hitting 95 on the gun isn't as impressive nowadays as it was during the first Clinton administration, and, given Liberatore's three-quarters slot and the lack of vertical action on the heater, it doesn't really miss bats, although he moves it around well and gets a lot of weak grounders. A firm slider has emerged as his swing-and-miss pitch, and it can sit upper 80s with late, two-plane action when he gets it down in the zone. It's plus-flashing, although the shape and depth can be inconsistent. There's a little, slow, 12–6 curve he'll pop in every once in a while and a firm-ish change that can feature a bit of a wandering slot. Nothing here is obviously plus—although the slider might get there—but Liberatore keeps everything down, gets groundballs and misses enough bats to profile as a solid, mid-rotation starter. We're loath to get this precise with it, but he seems like the type of arm that gives you a 3.60 ERA and eight strikeouts per nine just about every season and is perpetually a little underrated.

OFP: 55 / No. 3–4 starter

Variance: Low. Liberatore scuffled a bit early last season after jumping to Triple-A as a 21-year-old, but he found more success as he found his slider and pitched himself into a major-league-rotation candidate down the stretch. He doesn't have a ton of upside beyond number-three starter given his pitch mix, but he's likely to have some rotation utility given his command and pitchability.

Mark Barry's Fantasy Take: Who else got strong Marco Gonzales vibes from reading that write-up?

[Taps earpiece]

What's that? I used that comp last season, too? Ok, what about, well—nope, still Marco Gonzales. In reality, that's not a bad outcome to hang on anyone, and, if Liberatore keeps the ball in the yard, he'll be a healthy fantasy contributor, providing enough volume to bolster your rates.

4 Alec Burleson OF OFP: 55 ETA: Late 2022

Born: 11/25/98 Age: 23 Bats: L Throws: L Height: 6'2" Weight: 212 lb. Origin: Round 2, 2020 Draft (#70 overall)

YEAR	TEAM	LVL	AGE	PA	R	2B	3B	HR	RBI	BB	K	SB	CS	AVG/OBP/SLG	DRC+	BABIP	BRR	FRAA	WARP
2021	PEO	A+	22	49	8	1	0	4	10	6	15	1	0	.286/.367/.595	121	.333	-0.3	LF(7) 0.1, RF(3) -0.4	0.2
2021	SPR	AA	22	282	34	10	0	14	44	19	59	2	0	.288/.333/.488	113	.321	-0.7	RF(54) -1.9, 1B(1) -0.1, LF(1) 0.0	1.0
2021	MEM	AAA	22	172	19	7	0	4	22	17	27	0	1	.234/.310/.357	106	.260	-0.4	LF(21) -4.2, RF(18) 3.0	0.5
2022 non-DC	*STL*	*MLB*	*23*	*251*	*24*	*9*	*0*	*6*	*27*	*17*	*57*	*0*	*0*	*.242/.297/.377*	*80*	*.294*	*-0.3*	*RF 1, LF 0*	*0.1*

Comparables: Billy McKinney, Eddie Rosario, Michael Conforto

The Report: Burleson's was about as good a debut as you could hope for from a smaller-college, bat-first profile. Burleson scorched High-A and Double-A before finally scuffling a bit in Triple-A Memphis last year. A two-way player at East Carolina University, Burleson's singular focus on hitting last year paid off quickly, as he has already gotten far more of his above-average raw power into games than he did in college. It's not the prettiest swing, he's a little muscly and always looking to lift. Burleson is going to need to strike a balance between his hit and power tools, and his aggressive approach can put him in bad spots or keep him off the bases a bit too much, but he has shown both plus-hit and plus-power projections at various points. He is going to have to get to at least 55 in both to be a starter, as he's limited defensively. He has seen time at both outfield corners, but despite the pitching background, his arm is a better fit for left. He might end up seeing some time at first base, as well.

OFP: 55 / Solid-average corner bat

Variance: Medium. He doesn't really have a ton of upside past solid regular given his defensive limitations, but Burleson's power spike, combined with his latent contact ability, means he's likely to be at least a useful fringe regular or good bench bat.

Mark Barry's Fantasy Take: When Burleson hits 30 homers for, oh, let's say the Diamondbacks, it will look too obvious, in retrospect. The Cardinals have a knack for developing (and subsequently trading) outfielders who don't necessarily fit their team needs. Burleson could suffer a similar fate. He's an OF4 type that doesn't really have a clear path at the moment.

5 Joshua Baez CF OFP: 55 ETA: 2025

Born: 06/28/03 Age: 19 Bats: R Throws: R Height: 6'4" Weight: 220 lb. Origin: Round 2, 2021 Draft (#54 overall)

YEAR	TEAM	LVL	AGE	PA	R	2B	3B	HR	RBI	BB	K	SB	CS	AVG/OBP/SLG	DRC+	BABIP	BRR	FRAA	WARP
2021	CAR	ROK	18	95	18	3	1	2	8	14	28	5	0	.158/.305/.303		.208			

Comparables: Marlin Almonte, Frank Tolentino, Eudy Pina

The Report: Baez is a big, over-slot, cold-weather prep bat with plenty of developmental room to grow. A two-way player in high school, Baez had mid-90s heat on the mound, which will serve him well in his eventual professional role as a bopping right fielder. His steep swing with plus bat speed generates huge raw power to all fields, but a slow spring against New England prep competition mellowed his stock some after a big showcase season in 2020. He started his pro career in center field, but an extra-large frame that should fill out more as he ages will likely force him to a corner. His power will play there. His arm will play there. Now he just needs to settle in as a full-time hitter and figure out the rest. We can make it sound so easy . . .

OFP: 55 / Above-average right fielder

Variance: Extreme. If something clicks here, Baez could be a top-50 prospect in a year or two. He's also a cold-weather prep bat that was on the interstate in his first look at professional pitching. Check back in a couple years.

Mark Barry's Fantasy Take: "If something clicks" is the key point for Baez's fantasy prospects. Sometimes, it can take awhile for cold-weather high schoolers to heat up, but when it happens, it happens fast. If you have an available spot on your minor-league roster, I'd recommend taking a flier on Baez, hoping for a quick stock rise in his second year as a pro. He's probably a top-175 guy in most formats, even as is.

6 Michael McGreevy RHP OFP: 50 ETA: Late 2023/Early 2024

Born: 07/08/00 Age: 21 Bats: R Throws: R Height: 6'4" Weight: 215 lb. Origin: Round 1, 2021 Draft (#18 overall)

YEAR	TEAM	LVL	AGE	W	L	SV	G	GS	IP	H	HR	BB/9	K/9	K	GB%	BABIP	WHIP	ERA	DRA-	WARP
2021	PMB	A	20	0	0	0	5	5	6	10	1	1.5	6.0	4	75.0%	.391	1.83	9.00	111	0.0
2022 non-DC	*STL*	*MLB*	*21*	*2*	*3*	*0*	*57*	*0*	*50*	*57*	*6*	*4.3*	*5.8*	*32*	*44.7%*	*.312*	*1.64*	*5.89*	*132*	*-0.7*

Comparables: Shane Watson, Tommy Romero, Ruben Mejia

The Report: The other Missouri team found their own pop-up arm to take in the first round of last year's draft. Unlike Frank Mozzicato, McGreevy was an advanced college arm who had crushed the Big West his freshman and (abbreviated) sophomore seasons. However, he did it with a four-pitch mix and command, as opposed to dominant stuff. A velocity spike into the low 90s (touching higher) his junior season made McGreevy a first-round pick, albeit slightly under-slot. Like Baez, he's a very analytics-friendly pick, and *The Ringer*'s Michael Baumann recently noted the trend toward taking pitchers that could already throw good strikes and trying to get them to just throw harder. McGreevy's velocity was inconsistent post-draft, he doesn't really have a secondary out-pitch, and there's reason to be concerned that he will be a little too hittable further up the ladder. He's a little more of a project than your typical first-round college pick, but given the advanced strike-throwing, any developmental gains could have a multiplicative effect. Do you want to bet against the Cardinals' Devil Magic?

OFP: 50 / No. 4 starter

Variance: Medium. McGreevy was more of a supplemental/early-second-round pick on our big board, but even that carried a realistic floor of a back-end starter or swingman. If he can hold or build on his velocity gains, he could take a big step forward in 2022.

Mark Barry's Fantasy Take: I really like the new strategy of teams targeting dudes who throw strikes. Seems simple enough, but with the rise of drastic developmental improvements in velocity, now is a better time than ever to draft based on control. If an uptick in velo doesn't come, then McGreevy is a back-end starter, probably relegated to streaming status in fantasy leagues. If he can blend some heat with his strikability (sure, let's go with that phrasing), there's a chance he shoots up prospect lists in a George Kirby–esque manner.

7 Juan Yepez 1B OFP: 50 ETA: 2022

Born: 02/19/98 Age: 24 Bats: R Throws: R Height: 6'1" Weight: 200 lb. Origin: International Free Agent, 2014

YEAR	TEAM	LVL	AGE	PA	R	2B	3B	HR	RBI	BB	K	SB	CS	AVG/OBP/SLG	DRC+	BABIP	BRR	FRAA	WARP
2019	PEO	A	21	101	14	7	0	4	13	11	24	2	1	.284/.366/.500	109	.344	-0.3	3B(11) 0.2, 1B(6) 0.4, RF(2) 0.4	0.4
2019	PMB	A+	21	115	16	4	0	4	20	10	21	1	0	.275/.351/.431	121	.312	-0.4	RF(22) -0.3, 3B(5) 0.6, 1B(4) -0.1	0.6
2019	SPR	AA	21	59	8	2	0	2	10	5	14	0	0	.231/.288/.385	85	.263	0.3	LF(12) -1.5, 1B(5) -0.0, 3B(1) -0.0	-0.1
2021	GDD	WIN	23	103	15	8	0	7	26	12	18	1	0	.302/.388/.640		.297			
2021	SPR	AA	23	77	11	4	0	5	14	9	13	0	0	.270/.387/.571	128	.267	-0.7	1B(7) -0.4, LF(5) -0.9, 3B(4) 0.1	0.3
2021	MEM	AAA	23	357	56	25	0	22	63	42	69	1	3	.289/.382/.589	146	.304	-0.2	1B(60) -2.6, 3B(11) -0.6, LF(9) -0.7	2.3
2022 DC	*STL*	*MLB*	*24*	*205*	*25*	*10*	*0*	*6*	*23*	*17*	*49*	*1*	*1*	*.243/.316/.415*	*100*	*.294*	*-0.2*	*1B 0, 3B 0*	*0.5*

Comparables: José Osuna, Avisaíl García, Jeimer Candelario

The Report: Yepez took a giant leap forward in 2021, improving his approach and discipline while simultaneously getting to more of his plus-plus raw power into games. While light-tower power will always be his carrying tool, he is a legitimate hitter who is selectively aggressive in the zone, fights with two strikes and can manipulate the barrel when fooled. Put it all together, and Yepez looks like a potential .260–.270 bat with 30 home runs. Unfortunately, that's about where his value ends, as Yepez is a well-below-average athlete with a fringy arm. That not only limits him to first base, but makes him a poor defender there, as well.

OFP: 50 / Average regular somewhere at the bottom of the defensive spectrum

Variance: Medium. His defensive limitations place significant pressure on his bat and could easily relegate him to Quad-A territory once his athleticism begins to regress, but he'll be ready to compete for a major-league role this spring.

Mark Barry's Fantasy Take: It wouldn't surprise me to learn that Yepez is planning a roadtrip with Nelson Cruz and Kyle Schwarber to lobby decision-makers for a universal designated hitter. The 23-year-old developed a bit of a cult following in dynasty circles last season, mashing 27 dingers spread over 111 games in Double- and Triple-A, but he is also charitably listed as a "first baseman." Factor in the giant, Paul Goldschmidt–sized cloud hanging over the cold corner for the next three seasons, and you're looking at a very narrow path to playing time for Yepez in St. Louis. Yepez makes enough contact to believe that he'll hit when he's up, but regular reps could be hard to find. If his road was more clear, he'd probably be the number-three fantasy prospect on this list.

8 Masyn Winn SS

Born: 03/21/02 Age: 20 Bats: R Throws: R Height: 5'11" Weight: 180 lb. Origin: Round 2, 2020 Draft (#54 overall)

YEAR	TEAM	LVL	AGE	PA	R	2B	3B	HR	RBI	BB	K	SB	CS	AVG/OBP/SLG	DRC+	BABIP	BRR	FRAA	WARP
2021	PMB	A	19	284	50	15	3	3	34	40	60	16	2	.262/.370/.388	108	.331	3.8	SS(55) 6.5	2.0
2021	PEO	A+	19	154	26	4	2	2	10	6	40	16	3	.209/.240/.304	87	.274	0.7	SS(31) 1.3	0.4
2022 non-DC	*STL*	*MLB*	*20*	*251*	*19*	*10*	*2*	*2*	*20*	*18*	*65*	*12*	*3*	*.220/.282/.316*	*63*	*.297*	*1.2*	*SS 3, 1B 0*	*0.2*

Comparables: Ketel Marte, Tyler Pastornicky, Jonathan Villar

The Report: Winn was drafted as an intriguing two-way development project capable of throwing 95 mph in the top half of an inning and hitting it out at 100 mph in the bottom half. Winn's focus was mostly on the position-player side in 2021, and he had an all-in-all successful full-season debut. His defensive tools are the most-advanced part of his profile so far: quick-twitch motions, plus speed and, of course, a top-of-the-scale arm. His actual infield actions will need further development, but everything is in place for him to mature into a plus shortstop. At the plate, Winn has above-average bat speed but a raw approach—not particularly worrisome for a 19-year-old that saw High-A time. He may grow into more raw power, but his current projection looks more like an average hitter who socks some doubles and plays a good shortstop. That's a nice prospect, but the two-way possibilities are what tantalize here. Winn had one mound outing towards the end of the year, but, otherwise, his pitching has been limited to side work. There is so much unknown here, and we are mostly just ranking him as the present shortstop prospect for now.

OFP: 50 / Average shortstop, maybe with some relief utility

Variance: Extreme. To be honest, we still don't have a good handle on these types of prospects, especially one coming from the prep ranks rather than college. Shohei Ohtani? Really good at both. We got that one. With Winn, he still needs hit-tool development and defensive reps and, at some point, will be expected to work on his secondaries at the same time. That's a lot of bandwidth and could easily lead to stagnation or regression in either role. That said, if it comes together enough that he's a useful major-league shortstop and pitcher. Well, that's really good.

Mark Barry's Fantasy Take: It has been an interesting development path so far for Winn, and it really doesn't look like that is going to change. Since we don't really have a frame of reference for how he'll be brought along, it's hard to know exactly how to value a guy like this. Sometimes you get an Ohtani, sometimes you get Christian Bethancourt. I'm intrigued by the skill set enough to have Winn as a top-100 fantasy prospect, but I literally have no idea what to expect.

9 Iván Herrera C OFP: 50 ETA: 2023

Born: 06/01/00 Age: 22 Bats: R Throws: R Height: 5'11" Weight: 220 lb. Origin: International Free Agent, 2016

YEAR	TEAM	LVL	AGE	PA	R	2B	3B	HR	RBI	BB	K	SB	CS	AVG/OBP/SLG	DRC+	BABIP	BRR	FRAA	WARP
2019	PEO	A	19	291	41	10	0	8	42	35	56	1	1	.286/.381/.423	127	.337	0.0	C(64) -5.4	1.2
2019	PMB	A+	19	65	7	0	0	1	5	5	16	0	0	.276/.338/.328	90	.357	-1.0	C(18) -0.5	0.0
2021	SPR	AA	21	437	50	13	0	17	63	60	96	2	3	.231/.346/.408	106	.261	-1.7	C(71) 4.3	2.1
2022 DC	*STL*	*MLB*	*22*	*30*	*3*	*1*	*0*	*0*	*2*	*2*	*6*	*0*	*0*	*.223/.308/.349*	*83*	*.273*	*0.0*	*C 0*	*0.0*

Comparables: Christian Bethancourt, Wilson Ramos, Salvador Perez

The Report: We often write, around these parts, that player development is not linear. Catcher development is definitely not linear. Catchers, dear readers, are weird. Herrera scuffled in his first extended look at Double-A. His bat, which previously showed some punch while being short to the ball, looked a little long and a little slow, at times. He did start to hit for more game power, but that came at a cost to his hit tool, and Herrera still struggles against better spin. Defensively, everything is proceeding apace. He's a fine receiver for his age and experience level, and more reps should smooth out the rough edges to produce an average glove back there. He shows above-average arm strength, but his actions and release can make that play down some when trying to control the running game. We are managing our expectations down a little bit now. Is that entirely fair after a missed season of reps? Well, just like we missed some 2020 breakouts, it's possible we missed some prospects stagnating, as well. Or, perhaps, catchers are just weird.

OFP: 50 / Second-division catcher

Variance: Medium. You are hoping for something like average tools across the board here, but that leaves very little margin for error anywhere, and the hit tool is already starting to look fringier.

Mark Barry's Fantasy Take: Herrera is a perfectly cromulent catching prospect. You do not need to go out of your way to acquire perfectly cromulent catching prospects in dynasty leagues.

10 Brendan Donovan IF OFP: 50 ETA: 2022

Born: 01/16/97 Age: 25 Bats: L Throws: R Height: 6'1" Weight: 195 lb. Origin: Round 7, 2018 Draft (#213 overall)

YEAR	TEAM	LVL	AGE	PA	R	2B	3B	HR	RBI	BB	K	SB	CS	AVG/OBP/SLG	DRC+	BABIP	BRR	FRAA	WARP
2019	PEO	A	22	480	70	26	3	8	53	63	91	4	2	.266/.377/.405	122	.322	1.1	2B(101) -5.0	2.3
2021	GDD	WIN	24	64	10	5	0	2	8	10	8	2	1	.308/.422/.519		.326			
2021	PEO	A+	24	109	15	6	0	2	13	10	15	7	1	.295/.385/.421	118	.333	0.0	2B(22) -1.5, 3B(1) 0.3, LF(1) -0.0	0.5
2021	SPR	AA	24	219	35	10	1	4	28	25	39	8	5	.319/.411/.449	117	.379	-1.3	3B(18) 0.6, LF(14) -1.5, SS(9) 0.5	1.0
2021	MEM	AAA	24	131	23	5	0	6	25	15	23	4	2	.288/.389/.495	123	.313	0.7	1B(17) -3.0, 3B(12) -1.3, 2B(2) -0.5	0.3
2022 DC	*STL*	*MLB*	*25*	*133*	*14*	*6*	*0*	*2*	*12*	*11*	*25*	*1*	*1*	*.245/.326/.361*	*88*	*.293*	*0.0*	*2B 0, RF 1*	*0.3*

Comparables: Vimael Machín, Scott Sizemore, Jake Cronenworth

The Report: Well here he is, right on schedule, your 24-year-old, seventh-round college bat that is going to outplay this ranking. We could make a joke about how he fits the meme of "We have Tommy Edman at home," and that's probably true. We don't like false precision, but we know how this goes: Donovan will be a pesky, 103 DRC+ hitter who can stand at six different spots—although he won't offer Edman's true above-average defensive utility at most of them. He will hit exactly 13 home runs, and at least one of them will be backbreaking for your favorite team. His arm's a little short for the premium defensive spots on the left side of the dirt, but the Cardinals don't really need him there, anyway. His bat speed doesn't really portend a .300 hitter, but he's hitterish enough and strong enough and will foul off enough junk to hit .273, especially if he doesn't see too many good lefties. Donovan will no doubt be merrily on his way to a 2.4 WARP season, while Michael McGreevy is sitting 91, or Masyn Winn is whiffing too much, or Iván Herrera is still struggling to take that next step. We will learn nothing, and we will do this again next year with Mike Antico or whoever.

OFP: 50 / Good super utility or second-division starter

Variance: Low. He doesn't have enough power or glove to really be a first-division, everyday guy, but Donovan is likely to have a seven-year career of some sort.

Mark Barry's Fantasy Take: Donovan also swiped 19 bags as a minor leaguer in 2022, so, yeah, the Tommy Edman thing checks out for fantasy, too.

The Prospects You Meet Outside the Top Ten

Prospects on the Rise

Tink Hence RHP Born: 08/06/02 Age: 19 Bats: R Throws: R Height: 6'1" Weight: 175 lb. Origin: Round 2, 2020 Draft (#63 overall)

YEAR	TEAM	LVL	AGE	W	L	SV	G	GS	IP	H	HR	BB/9	K/9	K	GB%	BABIP	WHIP	ERA	DRA-	WARP
2021	CAR	ROK	18	0	1	1	8	1	8	11	1	3.4	15.7	14	31.8%	.476	1.75	9.00		

The Cardinals were very cautious with Hence, giving him only a handful of short complex outings. Out of sight can mean out of mind—and off the list—for a non-elite prep arm, but while we'd prefer to have more information on him than we do, by all accounts, he has is the same mid-90s heat and potential plus curve in the arsenal that he had. But Hence is a shorter, slimmer righty, and eight short outings won't quell the durability concerns that kept him out of the first round. If he has a more-normal teenaged-pitching-prospect workload next season, we suspect he will rise back into the top 10.

Austin Love RHP Born: 01/26/99 Age: 23 Bats: R Throws: R Height: 6'3" Weight: 232 lb. Origin: Round 3, 2021 Draft (#90 overall)

YEAR	TEAM	LVL	AGE	W	L	SV	G	GS	IP	H	HR	BB/9	K/9	K	GB%	BABIP	WHIP	ERA	DRA-	WARP
2022 non-DC	*STL*	*MLB*	*23*	*2*	*3*	*0*	*57*	*0*	*50*	*49*	*7*	*4.7*	*9.0*	*50*	*42.2%*	*.303*	*1.51*	*5.21*	*121*	*-0.4*

Comparables: Jarett Miller, Aaron Civale, Charle Rosario

The Cardinals' third-round pick last summer, Love can be a bit of a polarizing prospect. Deception in his delivery makes his mid-90s fastball play up, and the pitch features sink, as well. The mid-80s slider is average, and there's a changeup with some potential, as well. Whether you think he has enough to start or not is where the disagreements begin. We think he's more likely than not to be a reliever, but if he does more than just flash upper 90s in short bursts, that's a pretty good reliever.

Gordon Graceffo RHP Born: 03/17/00 Age: 22 Bats: R Throws: R Height: 6'4" Weight: 210 lb. Origin: Round 5, 2021 Draft (#151 overall)

YEAR	TEAM	LVL	AGE	W	L	SV	G	GS	IP	H	HR	BB/9	K/9	K	GB%	BABIP	WHIP	ERA	DRA-	WARP
2021	PMB	A	21	1	0	1	11	1	26	28	1	3.1	12.8	37	63.2%	.403	1.42	1.73	87	0.4
2022 non-DC	*STL*	*MLB*	*22*	*2*	*3*	*0*	*57*	*0*	*50*	*50*	*5*	*4.3*	*7.9*	*44*	*36.4%*	*.306*	*1.49*	*4.79*	*112*	*-0.1*

St. Louis always seems to have interesting mid-round college arms knocking about. Their version of this in 2020, Ian Bedell, was buzzy before he went under the knife for Tommy John surgery last May. Like Love, Graceffo, the Cardinals' fifth-round pick last year, features mid-90s heat and an advanced secondary, in his case his changeup. Graceffo has a fairly simple delivery and a sturdy frame with a bit of a projection left. He will have to find a consistent breaking ball, but given his present tool kit and the cold-weather profile, Graceffo could have a bit more than just a back-end projection a year from now.

Factors on the Farm

Andre Pallante RHP Born: 09/18/98 Age: 23 Bats: R Throws: R Height: 6'0" Weight: 203 lb. Origin: Round 4, 2019 Draft (#125 overall)

YEAR	TEAM	LVL	AGE	W	L	SV	G	GS	IP	H	HR	BB/9	K/9	K	GB%	BABIP	WHIP	ERA	DRA-	WARP
2019	SC	SS	20	1	0	0	11	9	35^{2}	27	2	2.8	9.6	38	46.2%	.281	1.07	2.78		
2021	SPR	AA	22	4	7	0	21	21	94^{1}	102	8	4.0	7.8	82	60.3%	.331	1.53	3.82	109	0.1
2022 non-DC	*STL*	*MLB*	*23*	*2*	*3*	*0*	*57*	*0*	*50*	*55*	*5*	*4.8*	*6.3*	*34*	*43.7%*	*.310*	*1.63*	*5.32*	*122*	*-0.4*

The Cardinals' fourth-round pick in 2019, Pallante features a mid-90s fastball that can touch higher and a potentially plus 12–6 curve along with a slider look, as well. He's also a shorter, stockier righty with a delivery-and-command profile that fits best in the bullpen, but that fastball/breaker combo could have late-inning utility soon.

Delvin Pérez SS Born: 11/24/98 Age: 23 Bats: R Throws: R Height: 6'3" Weight: 175 lb. Origin: Round 1, 2016 Draft (#23 overall)

YEAR	TEAM	LVL	AGE	PA	R	2B	3B	HR	RBI	BB	K	SB	CS	AVG/OBP/SLG	DRC+	BABIP	BRR	FRAA	WARP
2019	PEO	A	20	506	64	17	3	1	30	27	117	22	9	.269/.329/.325	89	.359	2.1	SS(112) -1.3	1.0
2021	SPR	AA	22	423	62	9	4	4	23	28	98	24	8	.265/.322/.339	89	.344	-0.1	SS(97) 5.2	1.2
2022 non-DC	*STL*	*MLB*	*23*	*251*	*19*	*8*	*1*	*1*	*19*	*13*	*70*	*7*	*4*	*.232/.283/.307*	*59*	*.326*	*0.7*	*SS 1*	*-0.2*

We do think Pérez will play in the majors and probably in fairly short order. That's his only real qualification to be listed here. We suppose we could have just as easily written a bit about Conner Capel, who could be a useful bench outfielder, or Freddy Pacheco, newly added to the 40-man, and his power fastball/slider combo. We're not even all that inclined to write one of our philosophical jags here. We don't think there is a greater lesson in the path Delvin Pérez has taken from 1.1 candidate shortly before his draft year in 2016 to fifth-infielder candidate for 2022. He never really developed enough physicality to consistently drive the ball, and it still kind of looks like the bat is swinging him, at times. He has some feel to hit, though, he's a plus runner and is still a good glove at the six. He will play in the majors, and that is his only real qualification to be listed here.

Connor Thomas LHP Born: 05/29/98 Age: 24 Bats: L Throws: L Height: 5'11" Weight: 173 lb. Origin: Round 5, 2019 Draft (#155 overall)

YEAR	TEAM	LVL	AGE	W	L	SV	G	GS	IP	H	HR	BB/9	K/9	K	GB%	BABIP	WHIP	ERA	DRA-	WARP
2019	SC	SS	21	2	0	0	5	2	15^2	17	0	0.6	9.8	17	49.0%	.362	1.15	4.02		
2019	PEO	A	21	2	1	1	10	2	27^1	25	2	3.0	6.3	19	65.1%	.284	1.24	3.62	103	0.2
2021	SPR	AA	23	0	2	0	4	4	20^1	26	5	1.3	10.6	24	58.6%	.396	1.43	4.87	101	0.1
2021	MEM	AAA	23	6	4	1	22	14	101^2	108	11	2.7	8.1	92	60.1%	.326	1.36	3.10	104	1.2
2022 non-DC	*STL*	*MLB*	*24*	*2*	*3*	*0*	*57*	*0*	*50*	*53*	*5*	*3.2*	*6.9*	*38*	*48.9%*	*.312*	*1.44*	*4.79*	*113*	*-0.2*

Comparables: Walker Lockett, David Phelps, Rogelio Armenteros

The soft-tossing lefty that keeps it away from the fat part of the barrel is a more-recent Cardinals type, but they leaned into it with gusto in the 2021 major-league rotation. Thomas is not the kind of prospect we find generally endearing, but we have to admit, he's got something. The fastball is only around 90, but is usually located well, and the slider can be a swing-and-miss pitch to both lefties and righties. He has a useable change to keep righties honest. He's a short, little lefty who works fast with a slinky, compact delivery and gets a lot of groundballs. And, to be honest, there are worse strategies than getting them to hit it where Nolan Arenado is. Thomas is ready to be a useful back-end starter for the 2022 Cardinals. He's not the kind of guy you plan on having in your Opening Day rotation, but you end up not minding all that much when he takes 10–15 starts as a fill in.

Becuse You Were Going To Ask

Zack Thompson LHP Born: 10/28/97 Age: 24 Bats: L Throws: L Height: 6'2" Weight: 215 lb. Origin: Round 1, 2019 Draft (#19 overall)

YEAR	TEAM	LVL	AGE	W	L	SV	G	GS	IP	H	HR	BB/9	K/9	K	GB%	BABIP	WHIP	ERA	DRA-	WARP
2019	CAR	ROK	21	0	0	0	2	2	2	3	0	0.0	18.0	4	66.7%	.500	1.50	0.00		
2019	PMB	A+	21	0	0	0	11	0	13^1	16	0	2.7	12.8	19	48.6%	.471	1.50	4.05	80	0.3
2021	MEM	AAA	23	2	10	2	22	19	93	114	18	5.5	7.9	82	38.3%	.343	1.84	7.06	131	-0.2
2022 non-DC	*STL*	*MLB*	*24*	*2*	*3*	*0*	*57*	*0*	*50*	*55*	*8*	*5.1*	*7.1*	*39*	*48.3%*	*.308*	*1.67*	*6.04*	*134*	*-0.7*

Comparables: David Huff, Chase De Jong, Chris Beck

As long as we're running through our Prospect Team maxims, here's another: On-field production, whether good or bad, exists to be explained. There's not much sugar-coating you can do with a 7-plus ERA and walk rate over 12 percent, though; in that case, the results speak for themselves. Thompson's velocity was all over the place in 2021. At times, he leaned more on a flat, fringy cutter/slider-type thing over his previously plus-flashing curve, which looked more average in 2021. Even in the AFL, where his stuff looked more like you'd have hoped, he still didn't throw strikes. If you were inclined to explain some of this away, you could note that, between the lost 2020 season and his limited 2019 post-draft reps, Thompson really hadn't pitched much in real professional games and was dropped into Triple-A to fend for himself. But, he really should have had enough to fend for himself. Thompson's long arm action and up-tempo delivery aren't super-repeatable and are the main culprits for his scattershot control and command. His mid-rotation upside is still in there somewhere—if you caught him on the right day, or even the right inning, he'd show 96 and that pretty plus curve—but he's looking more like a reliever or back-end starter. .

Top Talents 25 and Under (as of 4/1/2022):

1. Jordan Walker, 3B
2. Dylan Carlson, OF
3. Nolan Gorman, 3B
4. Matthew Liberatore, LHP
5. Lars Nootbar, OF
6. Alec Burleson, OF
7. Joshua Baez, OF
8. Michael McGreevey, RHP
9. Juan Yepez, IF/OF
10. Génesis Cabrera, LHP

The rip-roaring playoff push from St. Louis came in large part courtesy of the Cardinals' potent young outfield. Carlson will play 2022 at just 23 years old, having blossomed into an above-average, switch-hitting, tri-positional outfielder, as expected, with a 101 DRC+ and room to continue improving. He does everything fairly well already, high-praise for such a young player, particularly as his jack-of-all-trades/master-of-none profile took time to calibrate in a slow 2020 debut.

A surprisingly strong first taste of the bigs came to fruition in 2021 for Nootbar, who earned the honor of starting 2021 in Triple-A Memphis, cracking the bigs with St. Louis for 58 productive games, making the playoff roster, then still getting sent to the Arizona Fall League for more reps. Things went about as well as could be expected for the unfathomably Dutch youngster, and his excellent speed showed well as he looked the part as a plus-gloved fourth-outfielder type. Nootbar still shows better speed underway than at acceleration, which may hinder his base-stealing totals and, ultimately, his upside.

It was a coin flip between Cabrera and his north-pawed fireballing counterpart Jordan Hicks for the 10th spot on this list, but Cabrera gets the nod for his solid 71 appearances in 2021. The lefty always seemed destined for the bullpen, and, in his age-24 season, we saw Cabrera sit 98 and make for many an uneasy at-bat. His control is not so much pinpoint as it is hoping he doesn't miss everything and accidentally send a ball out to North Pointe, but many clubs could do, and are doing, far worse when it comes to a lefty out of the bullpen.

By contrast, Hicks was barely able to get on the mound at all in 2021, though he worked with a casual, 101-plus-average fastball before being shut down with elbow inflammation. The Cardinals' former relief ace is expected back at full bore this spring, with St. Louis reportedly making the intriguing choice to work him back in as a starter. The sinking/horizontal movement profile on Hicks' heater ensures he'll always induce more contact than expected given the eye-popping velocity, but perhaps that will play better over five innings. Hicks hasn't made a start that lasted more than one inning since 2017, but the experiment will certainly be fascinating to track.

Tampa Bay Rays

The State of the System:

The Rays don't have the best system in baseball anymore—graduating Wander Franco has a lot to do with that, as did trading a fair bit of their prospect depth—but they're still a very strong organization with ready-now help for the big club at the top.

The Top Ten:

1 Shane Baz RHP OFP: 70 ETA: Debuted in 2021

Born: 06/17/99 Age: 23 Bats: R Throws: R Height: 6'2" Weight: 190 lb. Origin: Round 1, 2017 Draft (#12 overall)

YEAR	TEAM	LVL	AGE	W	L	SV	G	GS	IP	H	HR	BB/9	K/9	K	GB%	BABIP	WHIP	ERA	DRA-	WARP
2019	BG	A	20	3	2	0	17	17	81^{1}	63	5	4.1	9.6	87	37.1%	.280	1.23	2.99	85	1.3
2021	MTG	AA	22	2	4	0	7	7	32^{2}	22	3	0.6	13.5	49	44.8%	.297	0.73	2.48	76	0.7
2021	DUR	AAA	22	3	0	0	10	10	46	28	6	2.2	12.5	64	39.8%	.242	0.85	1.76	79	1.1
2021	TB	MLB	22	2	0	0	3	3	13^{1}	6	3	2.0	12.1	18	39.3%	.120	0.68	2.03	91	0.2
2022 DC	*TB*	*MLB*	*23*	*9*	*6*	*0*	*25*	*25*	*129.3*	*103*	*19*	*3.0*	*10.3*	*148*	*26.7%*	*.268*	*1.13*	*3.10*	*80*	*2.4*

Comparables: Chris Archer, Jeremy Hellickson, Ubaldo Jiménez

The Report: Baz had an out-and-out valedictory 2021, blowing the doors off both levels of the high-minors en route to a silver medal in the Olympics and a spot in Tampa Bay's playoff rotation. The factors that were supposed to introduce bullpen risk—a shorter arm path, an infrequently used changeup, a past history of wandering command—just don't seem like substantive present concerns. At least not after he showed off an elite fastball/slider mix that also included occasional curves and changes while throwing strikes at every level he pitched at.

Baz can sit as high as the upper 90s and touch triple digits with the heat, as a starter. He gets great extension with good spin, and he already throws one of the flattest high fastballs in the majors. His fastball has every characteristic needed to call it an 8 pitch. It doesn't stop there, either; he now has a more firmly distinct hard slider (the slider has been his best secondary offering for years), separated out from his two-plane curveball. Both induced elite whiff rates, albeit in small samples. His changeup remains sparsely used at present but still has the makings of a plus pitch due to arm-side fade; if it gets better, watch out.

OFP: 70 / Top-of-the-rotation starter

Variance: Low. Yeah, we're calling a pitcher low variance. It's razor close between Baz and Baltimore's Grayson Rodriguez for the title of best pitching prospect in the game.

Mark Barry's Fantasy Take: Baz is awesome. I'm not sure what else you need from me. He's either the best or the second-best dynasty pitching prospect, and the only question remaining is how deep the Rays will let him get into games. He's gonna strike guys out.

2 Vidal Bruján IF/OF

OFP: 55 ETA: Debuted in 2021

Born: 02/09/98 Age: 24 Bats: S Throws: R Height: 5'10" Weight: 180 lb. Origin: International Free Agent, 2014

YEAR	TEAM	LVL	AGE	PA	R	2B	3B	HR	RBI	BB	K	SB	CS	AVG/OBP/SLG	DRC+	BABIP	BRR	FRAA	WARP
2019	SRR	WIN	21	100	12	3	4	2	10	15	17	4	5	.256/.380/.463		.297			
2019	CHA	A+	21	196	28	8	3	1	15	17	26	24	5	.290/.357/.386	121	.333	5.8	2B(29) 1.5, SS(14) 1.0	1.9
2019	MTG	AA	21	233	28	9	4	3	25	20	35	24	8	.266/.336/.391	112	.304	-1.7	2B(33) 3.0, SS(15) 0.8	1.5
2020	TOR	WIN	22	75	14	2	1	0	5	11	10	10	3	.254/.373/.317		.302			
2021	TOR	WIN	23	69	7	2	1	0	3	6	11	8	3	.206/.275/.270		.250			
2021	DUR	AAA	23	441	77	31	1	12	56	49	68	44	8	.262/.345/.440	116	.290	2.7	2B(29) 0.1, LF(24) 2.8, SS(16) 2.6	2.7
2021	TB	MLB	23	26	3	0	0	0	2	0	8	1	0	.077/.077/.077	82	.111	0.2	2B(4) 0.7, RF(2) 0.0, LF(1) -0.0	0.1
2022 DC	*TB*	*MLB*	*24*	*350*	*44*	*16*	*2*	*6*	*37*	*29*	*61*	*23*	*8*	*.245/.313/.369*	*85*	*.288*	*2.2*	*2B 1, LF 0*	*0.8*

Comparables: Jose Altuve, Hanser Alberto, Hernán Pérez

The Report: Bruján has had a pretty stable prospect profile for nearly half a decade now. He makes a lot of contact and controls the strike zone well beyond his pure bat-to-ball ability. He's a plus-plus runner who was fine at second base but was always going to end up with a bit of positional flexibility—and he played at six different spots in 2021. Bruján has traded off some quality of contact for a bit more pop, which is a fair-enough swap as he was never that likely to be a .300 hitter, anyway. He has always been a bit better from the left side than the right, but the Rays' roster is built on the team's ability to leverage the strengths of players like this. Bruján can fill in defensively just about anywhere, sit against tougher lefties, and wind and Wendle his way to above-average seasons, even if and when his slash line looks somewhat pedestrian.

OFP: 55 / That Rays guy

Variance: Low. Bruján had a brief and rather unspectacular major-league debut, but he should be a solid contributor as soon as 2022. He has little left to prove in the minors.

Mark Barry's Fantasy Take: I'm not sure Triple-A provides much of a challenge for Bruján anymore, especially after he flashed some pop for the first time in his career. He doesn't *need* to hit homers to be a fantasy stud, mind you, as that sweet, sweet speed is obviously the carrying tool. Even 12–15 dingers could elevate Bruján to elite status.

3 Josh Lowe OF

OFP: 55 ETA: Debuted in 2021

Born: 02/02/98 Age: 24 Bats: L Throws: R Height: 6'4" Weight: 205 lb. Origin: Round 1, 2016 Draft (#13 overall)

YEAR	TEAM	LVL	AGE	PA	R	2B	3B	HR	RBI	BB	K	SB	CS	AVG/OBP/SLG	DRC+	BABIP	BRR	FRAA	WARP
2019	MTG	AA	21	519	70	23	4	18	62	59	132	30	9	.252/.341/.442	110	.316	4.2	CF(110) -7.5, RF(9) 5.2, LF(1) -0.2	2.8
2021	DUR	AAA	23	470	76	28	2	22	78	61	123	26	0	.291/.381/.535	119	.361	4.5	CF(55) -5.9, RF(38) 1.7, LF(11) 2.5	2.9
2021	TB	MLB	23	2	0	0	0	0	0	1	0	1	0	1.000/1.000/1.000	96	1.000	0.1	LF(1) -0.0, RF(1) -0.1	0.0
2022 DC	*TB*	*MLB*	*24*	*60*	*7*	*2*	*0*	*1*	*8*	*6*	*17*	*1*	*1*	*.235/.316/.399*	*87*	*.318*	*0.1*	*CF 0*	*0.1*

Comparables: Trayvon Robinson, Austin Meadows, Carlos González

The Report: We often talk about physical projection with prep prospects. Well, Lowe has projected. He wasn't exactly a stick figure when he was drafted as a prep third baseman, but he has added significant good weight without losing much in the way of twitch or straight-line speed. That means his move to center field has gone quite well, and he should be an above-average defender there while still having that hot-corner arm in the holster. At the plate, Lowe has continued to add game power. He's a strong kid with above-average bat speed and an uppercut that can be vicious at times. His swing can get long, and he has shown swing-and-miss in the zone against both lefties and righties—although left-on-left spin is the more notable sticking point. Lowe projects as a power-over-hit outfielder with some platoon issues, but his speed and defense in center field give him more ways to contribute, even if he hits .250 or has to sit twice a week against southpaws.

OFP: 55 / Above-average center fielder, pop-and-leather version

Variance: Medium. Lowe has more strict-platoon risk than Bruján, but he's the long side of the platoon, at least, and his advanced glove in center gives him a fourth-outfielder fallback if the hit tool slides a little more in the majors against righties, as well.

Mark Barry's Fantasy Take: I mean, it would be nice if Lowe struck out a little less, sure. But at a certain point, it feels a little greedy to ask more of a dude that hit .291 with 22 homers, a 13-percent walk rate, and 26 steals in 26 tries. The extra Ks will hurt his batting average at the next level, but Lowe is a stud and slots in around the top 25 or 30 for dynasty prospects.

4 Taj Bradley RHP OFP: 55 ETA: 2023

Born: 03/20/01 Age: 21 Bats: R Throws: R Height: 6'2" Weight: 190 lb. Origin: Round 5, 2018 Draft (#150 overall)

YEAR	TEAM	LVL	AGE	W	L	SV	G	GS	IP	H	HR	BB/9	K/9	K	GB%	BABIP	WHIP	ERA	DRA-	WARP
2019	PRN	ROA	18	2	5	0	12	11	51	42	4	3.4	10.1	57	38.0%	.286	1.20	3.18		
2021	CSC	A	20	9	3	0	15	14	66^{2}	37	4	2.7	10.9	81	50.3%	.237	0.85	1.76	79	1.4
2021	BG	A+	20	3	0	0	8	8	36^{2}	28	4	2.7	10.3	42	47.4%	.267	1.06	1.96	85	0.6
2022 non-DC	*TB*	*MLB*	*21*	*2*	*3*	*0*	*57*	*0*	*50*	*49*	*7*	*4.1*	*8.1*	*45*	*36.1%*	*.298*	*1.46*	*4.81*	*114*	*-0.2*

Comparables: Lorenzo Barcelo, Jonathan Pettibone, Chris Volstad

The Report: After two solid-yet-unspectacular pre-pandemic seasons, Bradley spent 2020 growing physically, increasing his velocity, and tightening up his secondaries. That work paid dividends, as he held opposing hitters to a .181 average over two levels as a 20-year-old last year. Lean and with a quick arm, he sits comfortably in the mid-90s with the heater. Working up in the zone, he pairs it well with his breaking pitches, and both have potential to generate plenty of swing-and-miss. His upper-80s slider has good depth and features devastating late break. Bradley has also added a much-improved 12–6 curve, giving him the potential for three plus offerings.

OFP: 55 / No. 3 starter

Variance: High. He's still not old enough to legally buy a beer and has yet to face more-advanced hitters in the upper minors. However, there's a chance we're a bit low with our projection, and Bradley is the next in line to be the ace of the Rays' staff.

Mark Barry's Fantasy Take: At this point, we all know that dynasty pitchers are inherently risky, but Bradley is the platonic ideal of the type of prospect I like to gamble on. He has the frame, the mix, and there's a ton of room to improve upon his already sparkling production. Of course, there's a chance it doesn't work out—such is life when talking pitching prospects—but Bradley is still far enough away that you likely won't have to pay a premium to acquire him.

5 Greg Jones SS OFP: 55 ETA: 2023

Born: 03/07/98 Age: 24 Bats: S Throws: R Height: 6'2" Weight: 175 lb. Origin: Round 1, 2019 Draft (#22 overall)

YEAR	TEAM	LVL	AGE	PA	R	2B	3B	HR	RBI	BB	K	SB	CS	AVG/OBP/SLG	DRC+	BABIP	BRR	FRAA	WARP
2019	HV	SS	21	218	39	13	4	1	24	22	56	19	8	.335/.413/.461		.467			
2021	BG	A+	23	257	48	7	3	13	38	29	75	27	2	.291/.389/.527	122	.383	1.7	SS(50) 1.4	1.8
2021	MTG	AA	23	60	8	1	1	1	2	4	21	7	0	.185/.267/.296	70	.281	0.3	SS(15) -0.9	-0.1
2022 non-DC	*TB*	*MLB*	*24*	*251*	*22*	*9*	*1*	*5*	*24*	*19*	*83*	*14*	*4*	*.209/.283/.337*	*68*	*.304*	*1.4*	*SS 0*	*0.1*

Comparables: JaCoby Jones, JT Riddle, Wilmer Difo

The Report: A quad strain delayed the start of Jones's 2021 campaign, but, once on the field, he started to flash the kind of over-the-fence power that had been the sole missing tool in his bag. Most of his pop comes from the right side, where he muscles up and generates more hard contact, and it's still more sneaky pop than clearly above-average thump. Jones can fall in love with his power stroke a little too much, even with two strikes, and that lift-heavy approach got exposed more after his promotion to Double-A. In the upper minors, he's going to have to strike a little more of a balance there to keep his contact rate and quality where it needs to be.

Jones continues to play shortstop exclusively, and, while his first-step quickness, overall range and arm are all fine fits there, his hands and actions can be a little mechanical and awkward at times. You watch the way he covers ground on pop-ups and flares, and you think the plus-plus speed might play better in center field, although he hasn't played there since his Cape Cod League days.

OFP: 55 / Solid regular somewhere (maybe several somewheres) up the middle

Variance: Medium. Jones's first foray into the upper minors had an awful lot of swing-and-miss, and the ultimate power and defensive projections here are still a bit of a moving target.

Mark Barry's Fantasy Take: Rule changes have made it much harder to glean information from minor-league steals, but high volume and high efficiency is still a great foundation for future success. Last year, Jones attempted 36 steals with a 94-percent success rate. He also added some power to an otherwise lacking profile, although it came with a fair amount of swing-and-miss. All of the tools are there for Jones to be a fantasy star. At this point, he just needs to find the right balance.

6 Curtis Mead 3B OFP: 55 ETA: 2023

Born: 10/26/00 Age: 21 Bats: R Throws: R Height: 6'2" Weight: 171 lb. Origin: International Free Agent, 2018

YEAR	TEAM	LVL	AGE	PA	R	2B	3B	HR	RBI	BB	K	SB	CS	AVG/OBP/SLG	DRC+	BABIP	BRR	FRAA	WARP
2019	ADE	WIN	18	151	21	6	0	6	18	12	24	5	1	.309/.373/.485		.340			
2019	PHE	ROK	18	175	26	12	2	4	19	13	23	4	3	.285/.351/.462		.313			
2020	ADE	WIN	19	76	11	7	0	3	12	3	13	2	0	.347/.382/.569		.393			
2021	SCO	WIN	20	90	16	5	2	3	11	4	13	1	1	.313/.360/.530		.343			
2021	CSC	A	20	211	36	21	1	7	35	15	30	9	2	.356/.408/.586	134	.391	-1.0	3B(25) -0.6, 1B(15) 2.2	1.5
2021	BG	A+	20	233	38	15	1	7	32	19	38	2	2	.282/.348/.466	119	.309	0.4	3B(43) 1.1, 1B(3) 0.1	1.4
2022 non-DC	*TB*	*MLB*	*21*	*251*	*23*	*14*	*1*	*4*	*25*	*14*	*49*	*3*	*2*	*.259/.309/.393*	*88*	*.311*	*0.1*	*3B 0, 1B 1*	*0.4*

Comparables: Enrique Hernández, Miguel Sanó, Wilmer Flores

The Report: Mead has had a knack for hard contact ever since his teenage days, when he was competing against much older competition in the Australian Baseball League. He held his own during his first stateside stint with the Phillies but has blossomed since being acquired by Tampa after the 2019 season. Mead was especially locked in during 2021, compiling an OPS of .911 over three levels. Offensively, he has a natural clock at the plate and shows the ability to square up most offerings with high exit velocities. He controls the zone well, and his walk rate should increase as he gains experience. His swing isn't geared for power, but Mead should sit in the 20–25-home-run range with plenty of doubles at his peak. In the field, he has been a versatile defender spending time at multiple infield positions but is likely to eventually settle into a first-base/corner-outfield role.

OFP: 55 / Starting first baseman with some corner flex

Variance: High. The bat will carry him to Tampa, but it will be tough for him to stick in a full-time role if the power doesn't develop. If it does, it's not hard to imagine Mead becoming a Trey Mancini–type middle-of-the-order run producer for the Rays.

Mark Barry's Fantasy Take: We're cultured and smart (mostly), we should be able to acknowledge that two things can be true at once. If Mead turns into Mancini, that's a really nice outcome, and one that's pretty valuable in fantasy circles. Still, it's a replicable skill set, so while a nice, crisp Mead can often be refreshing, there are a lot of other options that should slake that thirst.

7 Seth Johnson RHP OFP: 55 ETA: Late 2023/Early 2024

Born: 09/19/98 Age: 23 Bats: R Throws: R Height: 6'1" Weight: 200 lb. Origin: Round 1, 2019 Draft (#40 overall)

YEAR	TEAM	LVL	AGE	W	L	SV	G	GS	IP	H	HR	BB/9	K/9	K	GB%	BABIP	WHIP	ERA	DRA-	WARP
2019	RAY	ROK	20	0	0	0	5	5	10	7	0	1.8	6.3	7	43.3%	.233	0.90	0.00		
2019	PRN	ROA	20	0	1	0	4	4	7	10	0	1.3	11.6	9	40.0%	.500	1.57	5.14		
2021	CSC	A	22	6	6	0	23	16	93^2	86	7	3.2	11.0	115	48.0%	.336	1.27	2.88	89	1.4
2022 non-DC	*TB*	*MLB*	*23*	*2*	*3*	*0*	*57*	*0*	*50*	*52*	*7*	*4.2*	*7.5*	*41*	*37.9%*	*.307*	*1.53*	*5.17*	*120*	*-0.4*

Comparables: Jose Mercedes, Dan Straily, Joe Musgrove

The Report: Johnson is a recent convert to pitching, not that you'd know it from his first full year in the pros. Working primarily off an easy mid-90s fastball that can touch higher and shows explosive life up in the zone, Johnson dominated A-ball lineups in 2021. Yes, he was old for his level, but we just have to bake the Rays' conservative pitcher tracks in at this point, and the stuff is the stuff. Backing the potential plus-plus fastball is a full suite of secondaries. The slider shows the most promise, at present—firm with short, late tilt—but he has a feel for a 12–6 curve, as well. His changeup lags behind, but, all in all, it's an advanced arsenal considering Johnson wasn't a full-time pitcher until his junior year. The delivery is pretty easy and repeatable, although his control is ahead of his command, at present.

OFP: 55 / No. 3–4 starter who probably ends up a good bulk guy in this organization

Variance: Medium. There's positive variance here given his relative lack of mound experience, but he also needs to refine his command and round out a more-consistent arsenal to stay a starter (or the Rays' equivalent thereof).

Mark Barry's Fantasy Take: Johnson's rise to relevance on the mound has been impressive. That said, his late start to pitching, paired with the Rays Of It All, will likely limit his fantasy usefulness. Despite his age, I think he's still far away, so I'm not all that interested.

8 Xavier Edwards 2B/3B OFP: 55 ETA: 2022

Born: 08/09/99 Age: 22 Bats: S Throws: R Height: 5'10" Weight: 175 lb. Origin: Round 1, 2018 Draft (#38 overall)

YEAR	TEAM	LVL	AGE	PA	R	2B	3B	HR	RBI	BB	K	SB	CS	AVG/OBP/SLG	DRC+	BABIP	BRR	FRAA	WARP
2019	FW	A	19	344	44	13	4	1	30	30	35	20	9	.336/.392/.414	127	.371	0.2	2B(51) 3.3, SS(21) 3.1	2.9
2019	LE	A+	19	217	32	5	4	0	13	14	19	14	2	.301/.349/.367	121	.331	3.4	2B(36) 1.1, SS(9) -1.1	1.6
2021	MTG	AA	21	337	40	13	3	0	27	36	42	19	11	.302/.377/.368	110	.348	-1.2	2B(55) -1.1, 3B(22) 1.7	1.3
2022 non-DC	*TB*	*MLB*	*22*	*251*	*21*	*9*	*1*	*1*	*19*	*19*	*34*	*11*	*4*	*.260/.320/.333*	*81*	*.301*	*0.9*	*2B 0, SS 0*	*0.5*

Comparables: Odúbel Herrera, Jonathan Villar, Thairo Estrada

The Report: Edwards was going to be a low-power prospect no matter what, but he's actually settling in as a 20-power player instead of the 30- or 40-power player we'd previously hoped for, and that knicks his profile substantially. Ewards had just 16 extra-base hits in 79 games at Double-A and has only one career homer in 1,093 professional plate appearances. He has an advanced approach and makes a ton of contact, but his batted-ball data is pretty terrible, and there's a limit to how many ground-ball singles a prospect can reasonably be expected to leg out.

Defensively, Edwards played mostly at second last season, as shortstop is now firmly in his rearview mirror. He has picked up third base as a secondary position and is fast enough to play the outfield; he has 70 straight-line speed, perhaps 80 on his best days. But he has been an inefficient baserunner and only stole 19 bags last year with a mediocre success rate. Because he's a Rays prospect, expect his versatility and positives to be leveraged more heavily than with most teams.

OFP: 55 / Dunk-and-run multi-positional regular

Variance: Medium. The speed and defensive versatility make him a likely bench piece, even if things don't totally work out offensively, but the extreme lack of power is limiting.

Mark Barry's Fantasy Take: If Edwards isn't going to hit for *any* power, he's going to need to be way more efficient at stealing bases. Snagging 19 bags in just 79 games is pretty solid; getting thrown out 11 times is, uh, not. Even with the steals, Edwards looks Mallex Smith-y, at best, which is a tough ceiling to strive for in most fantasy prospects.

9 Heriberto Hernandez OF OFP: 55 ETA: 2023

Born: 12/16/99 Age: 22 Bats: R Throws: R Height: 6'1" Weight: 195 lb. Origin: International Free Agent, 2017

YEAR	TEAM	LVL	AGE	PA	R	2B	3B	HR	RBI	BB	K	SB	CS	AVG/OBP/SLG	DRC+	BABIP	BRR	FRAA	WARP
2019	RAN	ROK	19	224	42	17	4	11	48	27	57	3	3	.344/.433/.646		.440			
2019	SPO	SS	19	10	4	0	0	0	1	2	3	3	0	.375/.500/.375		.600			
2021	CSC	A	21	320	57	15	0	12	44	49	90	7	4	.252/.381/.453	113	.325	0.2	LF(54) -2.0, RF(12) -0.1	1.4
2022 non-DC	*TB*	*MLB*	*22*	*251*	*23*	*10*	*0*	*5*	*23*	*24*	*84*	*3*	*2*	*.197/.286/.322*	*67*	*.290*	*0.1*	*LF 1, RF 0*	*-0.2*

Comparables: Michael Hermosillo, Mallex Smith, Josh Reddick

The Report: Hernandez had gained a lot of buzz coming into 2021, nominally as a hit-and-power catching prospect, based on complex performances of all types (Dominican complex, Arizona complex, prospect-development camp in the Rangers' system). We remained skeptical until he showed up in full-season ball, and one reason for that skepticism was quickly confirmed: Hernandez was never *really* a catching prospect, and he didn't catch a single game in 2021, playing more in left field than anywhere else.

The hard-hitting part mostly panned out in his initial debut, though. He has a very quick, simple stroke and generates a lot of bat speed, so he has substantial raw power, and he's getting most of it into games already. His hit tool needs some work; despite a good approach, he's swinging and missing too much. Or put another way, against more-advanced pitching than he'd previously seen, his average dipped to mere mortal levels instead of his complex dominance. Given that he is already sliding down the defensive spectrum, his bat is going to have to carry everything else, so there's pressure to *really* hit here.

OFP: 55 / Hard-hitting corner outfielder

Variance: Medium. We do kind of need to see him hit for average in a full-season league to really get the hype train rolling.

Mark Barry's Fantasy Take: I actually like Hernandez more after his defensive move from behind the plate. He's turning into a bit of a three-true-outcome slugger, which is fine, but it's not what we dreamed on when the Rays brought him in from Texas. As of now, I'd have him in the top-175 or so, but cleaning up even some of the swing-and-miss would skyrocket Hernandez up dynasty lists.

10 Cole Wilcox RHP OFP: 55 ETA: 2025 or so

Born: 07/14/99 Age: 22 Bats: R Throws: R Height: 6'5" Weight: 232 lb. Origin: Round 3, 2020 Draft (#80 overall)

YEAR	TEAM	LVL	AGE	W	L	SV	G	GS	IP	H	HR	BB/9	K/9	K	GB%	BABIP	WHIP	ERA	DRA-	WARP
2021	CSC	A	21	1	0	0	10	10	44¹	33	1	1.0	10.6	52	61.7%	.281	0.86	2.03	80	0.9
2022 non-DC	*TB*	*MLB*	*22*	*2*	*2*	*0*	*57*	*0*	*50*	*51*	*5*	*2.8*	*7.0*	*38*	*37.1%*	*.300*	*1.34*	*4.14*	*103*	*0.1*

Comparables: Matt Garza, Garrett Richards, Fernando Romero

The Report: Wilcox was showing the kind of plus stuff that would have had him far higher on this list, but he then went under the knife for Tommy John surgery in September. His delivery has always had some stiffness to it—whether that's the culprit for the elbow injury or not is out of our areas of expertise—but Wilcox flashed three potential plus pitches when he was on the mound last year. His fastball is a power sinker in the mid-90s that gets plenty of groundballs. Deeper in counts, he will use a power slider which can get a little sweepy, but when it's sharp, with good tilt, it's an easy plus bat-misser. Wilcox also has a mid-80s sinking change which is very advanced, and he will use it to both righties and lefties. It's mid-rotation-or-better stuff with an ideal starter's frame, but, unfortunately, we won't see him back on the mound until 2023.

OFP: 55 / No. 3–4 starter or late-inning reliever

Variance: Extreme. We're in the early days post surgery, and while Tommy John is sadly common, recovery is not always routine. Wilcox also has limited pro reps in the low minors—the Rays are notoriously conservative with pitching prospect tracks—so there's a lot of uncertainty here. He has top-of-the-rotation upside if he comes back with the stuff intact, though.

Mark Barry's Fantasy Take: I don't really like to stash Tommy John guys on my minor-league rosters. I think there are almost always better ways to fill a roster spot. Still, Wilcox's stuff and pedigree should keep him on the periphery of fantasy managers' minds. You just won't have to make a move on him for at least a year.

The Prospects You Meet Outside the Top Ten

#11

Carson Williams SS Born: 06/25/03 Age: 19 Bats: R Throws: R Height: 6'2" Weight: 180 lb. Origin: Round 1, 2021 Draft (#28 overall)

YEAR	TEAM	LVL	AGE	PA	R	2B	3B	HR	RBI	BB	K	SB	CS	AVG/OBP/SLG	DRC+	BABIP	BRR	FRAA	WARP
2021	RAY	ROK	18	47	8	4	1	0	8	6	13	2	2	.282/.404/.436		.423			

Williams is a bit of a blank canvas. A two-way player in high school who some scouts liked better on the mound, he was drafted by an organization more willing than most to try developing him there, as well. Williams wanted to be bat-only, though, and, so far, he has been a position player despite being a bit of a divisive prospect as an amateur due to hit-tool questions. He's likely to grow off shortstop and slide over to third. He already hits the ball hard and should grow into more power with the right kind of swing to tap into any burgeoning pop.

#12

Nick Bitsko RHP Born: 06/16/02 Age: 20 Bats: R Throws: R Height: 6'4" Weight: 225 lb. Origin: Round 1, 2020 Draft (#24 overall)

Bitsko didn't pitch in an official game last season after undergoing labrum surgery in December 2020; we expect him to make his pro debut in 2022. He hasn't really pitched much since he was a high-school sophomore: he reclassified up in the draft a year, then the pandemic wiped out his junior-turned-senior year, then he got hurt. He rose in the draft partially by posting videos to his social media that portrayed a high-velocity (up to 98 and change), high-spin, excellent-vertical-approach fastball, which is about as 2020s as it gets. He also had two interesting breaking balls and a nascent changeup. We'll see what this all looks like on a pro mound this year, hopefully.

#13

Blake Hunt C Born: 11/10/98 Age: 23 Bats: R Throws: R Height: 6'3" Weight: 215 lb. Origin: Round 2, 2017 Draft (#69 overall)

YEAR	TEAM	LVL	AGE	PA	R	2B	3B	HR	RBI	BB	K	SB	CS	AVG/OBP/SLG	DRC+	BABIP	BRR	FRAA	WARP
2019	FW	A	20	376	40	21	3	5	39	35	67	4	1	.255/.331/.381	114	.303	-4.6	C(77) 16.1, 1B(9) -0.5	3.0
2021	BG	A+	22	257	41	15	2	9	41	26	79	1	0	.225/.307/.427	92	.298	-0.1	C(50) 9.7	1.4
2021	MTG	AA	22	63	5	2	0	0	0	6	25	0	0	.125/.210/.161	58	.226	0.8	C(17) -0.2	0.0
2022 non-DC	*TB*	*MLB*	*23*	*251*	*20*	*11*	*1*	*3*	*21*	*19*	*83*	*0*	*1*	*.194/.263/.306*	*51*	*.287*	*-0.2*	*C 3, 1B 0*	*-0.2*

Comparables: Lou Marson, Derek Norris, Danny Jansen

If there's ever going to be a Rule 5 draft this offseason, Hunt will be available in it, as the Rays simply couldn't protect all their good prospects. The toast of 2020 Padres instructs arrived in the Blake Snell deal before last season, and his performance in High-A more closely resembled his pre-2020 track—low batting average, too much swing-and-miss—than the whispered-about gains from behind closed doors. Hunt has a lot of potential as a power-hitting catcher down the road, and catcher developmental paths are especially non-linear, but it's hard to see how a team would be able to carry a player who hit .225 in A-ball unless they are outwardly tanking. Which, hey, several teams are, right?

Prospects on the Rise

Carlos Colmenarez SS/DH Born: 11/15/03 Age: 18 Bats: L Throws: R Height: 5'10" Weight: 170 lb. Origin: International Free Agent, 2021

YEAR	TEAM	LVL	AGE	PA	R	2B	3B	HR	RBI	BB	K	SB	CS	AVG/OBP/SLG	DRC+	BABIP	BRR	FRAA	WARP
2021	DSL TB1	ROK	17	114	7	2	1	0	12	8	30	7	6	.247/.319/.289		.338			

Comparables: Adrian Valerio, Yordys Valdes, Yonathan Mendoza

Colmenarez was one of the top international-free-agent prospects in the January 2021 class. His top-line stats in the Dominican Summer League weren't particularly noteworthy, but the batted-ball data was good for his age. He's also a potential plus defender, but this could go a number of ways in upcoming editions of this list. There also just isn't a lot of evidence this was a "bad" season, even if Colmenarez might now be available in your dynasty league.

Sandy Gaston RHP Born: 12/16/01 Age: 20 Bats: R Throws: R Height: 6'3" Weight: 200 lb. Origin: International Free Agent, 2018

YEAR	TEAM	LVL	AGE	W	L	SV	G	GS	IP	H	HR	BB/9	K/9	K	GB%	BABIP	WHIP	ERA	DRA-	WARP
2019	RAY	ROK	17	1	2	0	11	6	27	23	1	9.0	10.3	31	55.1%	.324	1.85	6.00		
2021	RAY	ROK	19	1	0	0	7	3	19^2	7	1	5.9	14.6	32	58.6%	.214	1.02	3.20		
2021	CSC	A	19	2	1	0	7	7	30^1	22	2	6.5	11.3	38	47.1%	.294	1.45	3.86	95	0.4
2022 non-DC	*TB*	*MLB*	*20*	*2*	*3*	*0*	*57*	*0*	*50*	*51*	*8*	*7.2*	*8.7*	*48*	*48.2%*	*.306*	*1.82*	*6.42*	*136*	*-0.8*

Comparables: Nate Cornejo, Taijuan Walker, Julio Teheran

We like to say that minor-league production exists primarily to be explained. That is to say, the stat line isn't necessarily representative of the prospect. In Gaston's case though, the 2021 line gives you a pretty good at-a-glance look at what he is. The 19-year-old is already pumping upper-90s heat and has a low-80s power curve with big 11–5 tilt. That's going to overwhelm low-minors hitters if it's even close to the zone. As you may have gathered from his six walks per nine (not nice), it's not near the zone enough. His control issues and lack of much changeup projection will tab Gaston for the bullpen sooner rather than later, but it's true late-inning stuff if he can wrangle a few more strikes with the fastball and more consistent command of the curve.

Cooper Kinney 2B Born: 01/27/03 Age: 19 Bats: L Throws: R Height: 6'3" Weight: 200 lb. Origin: Round 1, 2021 Draft (#34 overall)

YEAR	TEAM	LVL	AGE	PA	R	2B	3B	HR	RBI	BB	K	SB	CS	AVG/OBP/SLG	DRC+	BABIP	BRR	FRAA	WARP
2021	RAY	ROK	18	47	9	1	1	0	5	10	9	2	0	.286/.468/.371		.385			

The Rays' Comp-A pick was announced as a second baseman, is already playing some third base and might end up at first. He has a slugger's frame, though, and a chance to grow into enough power to carry the cold corner. Kinney also already has an advanced approach for his age and level.

Factors on the Farm

Calvin Faucher RHP Born: 09/22/95 Age: 26 Bats: R Throws: R Height: 6'1" Weight: 190 lb. Origin: Round 10, 2017 Draft (#286 overall)

YEAR	TEAM	LVL	AGE	W	L	SV	G	GS	IP	H	HR	BB/9	K/9	K	GB%	BABIP	WHIP	ERA	DRA-	WARP
2019	FTM	A+	23	3	2	2	34	0	55	59	2	3.6	10.0	61	51.3%	.375	1.47	4.42	101	0.6
2021	WCH	AA	25	1	1	1	19	0	30^{2}	39	6	7.0	12.3	42	47.1%	.423	2.05	7.04	118	-0.1
2021	DUR	AAA	25	0	0	0	11	3	20^{1}	14	1	3.1	11.5	26	37.0%	.289	1.03	1.77	83	0.4
2022 non-DC	*TB*	*MLB*	*26*	*2*	*3*	*0*	*57*	*0*	*50*	*49*	*6*	*5.1*	*9.2*	*50*	*34.3%*	*.307*	*1.55*	*5.17*	*117*	*-0.3*

Comparables: Jose Ortega, Ryan Meisinger, Lisalverto Bonilla

Faucher came along with Nelson Cruz from Minnesota, and you'd be forgiven for forgetting that. He was a 25-year-old reliever who didn't have a great track record of throwing strikes. Faucher threw a lot more strikes with the Rays, though, and now you have to consider his lively 95-plus fastball and potentially plus-plus curve late-inning weapons. His track record of passable control is short, and his mechanics don't really suggest any kind of long-term command profile, yet he'll no doubt be mowing down batters in next year's Division Series.

Tommy Romero RHP Born: 07/08/97 Age: 24 Bats: R Throws: R Height: 6'2" Weight: 225 lb. Origin: Round 15, 2017 Draft (#453 overall)

YEAR	TEAM	LVL	AGE	W	L	SV	G	GS	IP	H	HR	BB/9	K/9	K	GB%	BABIP	WHIP	ERA	DRA-	WARP
2019	CHA	A+	21	12	4	0	23	18	119^{1}	86	4	2.7	7.8	103	34.4%	.260	1.02	1.89	89	2.0
2019	MTG	AA	21	1	0	0	1	1	6	7	1	3.0	1.5	1	31.8%	.286	1.50	7.50	147	-0.1
2021	MTG	AA	23	1	0	0	11	9	48	36	3	1.9	14.1	75	37.1%	.324	0.96	1.88	75	1.1
2021	DUR	AAA	23	7	2	0	12	12	62^{1}	39	7	3.0	10.1	70	34.4%	.224	0.96	3.18	92	1.1
2022 non-DC	*TB*	*MLB*	*24*	*2*	*2*	*0*	*57*	*0*	*50*	*44*	*7*	*3.5*	*9.1*	*50*	*35.2%*	*.280*	*1.28*	*3.96*	*97*	*0.3*

Comparables: Steve Johnson, Alex Cobb, Johnny Cueto

Set your Rays arm clock for noon and watch Romero pump low-90s fastballs by upper-minors hitters. He dominated Double- and Triple-A without a clear above-average secondary—his slider has good shape, but his command often limits it to a glove-side chase pitch—but the swings tell you all you need to know about how good the fastball plays now: late swings, swings under balls at the top of the zone and just plenty of whiffs, generally. He may not have enough off-speed stuff for a traditional starter's role, but Romero is a perfect fit to follow Tampa Bay's low-arm-slot, left-handed opener *du jour*.

Austin Shenton 3B Born: 01/22/98 Age: 24 Bats: L Throws: R Height: 6'0" Weight: 205 lb. Origin: Round 5, 2019 Draft (#156 overall)

YEAR	TEAM	LVL	AGE	PA	R	2B	3B	HR	RBI	BB	K	SB	CS	AVG/OBP/SLG	DRC+	BABIP	BRR	FRAA	WARP
2019	EVE	SS	21	92	16	10	1	2	16	8	15	0	0	.367/.446/.595		.429			
2019	WV	A	21	134	13	7	1	5	20	11	29	0	0	.252/.328/.454	105	.291	-0.8	2B(8) -1.4, 3B(7) 0.2, LF(6) -0.7	0.2
2021	EVE	A+	23	273	55	24	3	11	53	41	62	1	0	.295/.418/.576	124	.362	-0.1	3B(41) 1.8, 1B(12) -0.2, 2B(3) -0.2	1.7
2021	ARK	AA	23	48	6	5	0	1	8	4	10	0	0	.326/.396/.512	104	.406	-0.8	3B(7) 0.9, 1B(3) -0.2	0.1
2021	MTG	AA	23	51	5	3	0	2	9	2	15	0	0	.271/.294/.458	79	.344	-0.1	1B(1) -0.1	0.0
2022 non-DC	*TB*	*MLB*	*24*	*251*	*25*	*13*	*1*	*6*	*26*	*21*	*68*	*0*	*0*	*.233/.310/.385*	*86*	*.308*	*-0.3*	*3B 0, 2B 0*	*0.3*

Tampa Bay's return for Diego Castillo at the deadline, Shenton is certainly Rays-y. He has no clear defensive home—his best fit is probably first, but he has seen time at second, third and the outfield corners. He gets on base and will smack some doubles but doesn't have ideal power for a corner bat—although that's more an issue against lefties, so you can platoon him and leverage his medium pop against righties. Shenton will no doubt give the Rays several 110 DRC+ seasons in which he gets 400 at-bats, mostly in a long-side platoon while playing four different spots, and will have one random, 27-home-run season in there. He will then be traded for a Triple-A reliever with good pitch-type characteristics who will produce a few seasons like Diego Castillo, who will then get . . . well, you get it by now.

Because You Were Going To Ask

Brendan McKay DH Born: 12/18/95 Age: 26 Bats: L Throws: L Height: 6'2" Weight: 220 lb. Origin: Round 1, 2017 Draft (#4 overall)

YEAR	TEAM	LVL	AGE	PA	R	2B	3B	HR	RBI	BB	K	SB	CS	AVG/OBP/SLG	DRC+	BABIP	BRR	FRAA	WARP
2019	MTG	AA	23	90	8	2	0	0	8	7	27	0	1	.167/.256/.192	77	.245	0.3	P(8) 0.6	0.1
2019	DUR	AAA	23	78	11	2	0	5	11	10	24	1	0	.239/.346/.493	95	.289	-0.6	P(7) -0.2	0.1
2019	TB	MLB	23	11	2	0	0	1	1	1	2	0	0	.200/.273/.500	51	.143	-0.1	P(13) -0.1	0.0
2021	DUR	AAA	25	25	1	0	0	0	1	3	8	0	0	.091/.200/.091	90	.143	-0.1		0.0

Comparables: Christian Walker, Casey Gillaspie, Ryan O'Hearn

YEAR	TEAM	LVL	AGE	W	L	SV	G	GS	IP	H	HR	BB/9	K/9	K	GB%	BABIP	WHIP	ERA	DRA-	WARP
2019	MTG	AA	23	3	0	0	8	7	41^{2}	25	2	1.9	13.4	62	40.5%	.280	0.82	1.30	58	1.2
2019	DUR	AAA	23	3	0	0	7	6	32	17	1	2.5	11.2	40	45.1%	.232	0.81	0.84	78	0.8
2019	TB	MLB	23	2	4	0	13	11	49	53	8	2.9	10.3	56	35.4%	.333	1.41	5.14	108	0.3
2021	MTG	AA	25	0	2	0	3	3	7	10	5	5.1	10.3	8	20.8%	.263	2.00	12.86	111	0.0
2022 DC	*TB*	*MLB*	*26*	*5*	*3*	*0*	*35*	*6*	*55*	*51*	*8*	*3.2*	*9.2*	*56*	*37.1%*	*.293*	*1.30*	*4.19*	*104*	*0.3*

Comparables: Robbie Ray, Brian Flynn, Travis Wood

As recently as two years ago, McKay seemed a sure-shot number-three starter. That was a little underwhelming, given his college career and potential two-way stardom, but still a fine outcome for most any prospect. He spent most of 2020 and 2021 battling shoulder and elbow injuries—there's actually no such thing as a sure-shot pitcher—and had thoracic outlet surgery in November, which is about the worst news you can get on a pitcher. While he once had an obvious hitting fallback as a first-round-quality first baseman at Louisville, he has hit only .209/.336/.343 spread across a season's worth of playing time in the minors; perhaps he'd flourish if he gave the bat more attention.

Top Talents 25 and Under (as of 4/1/2022):

1. Wander Franco, SS
2. Shane Baz, RHP
3. Shane McClanahan, LHP
4. Luis Patiño, RHP
5. Vidal Bruján, IF
6. Josh Lowe, OF
7. Taj Bradley, RHP
8. Greg Jones, SS
9. Curtis Mead, 3B/1B
10. Seth Johnson, RHP

Sometimes a consensus forms around a player so talented that, when addressing them, there is almost an instinct to edge contrarian, to see something that others do not. That's not inherently bad—the nature of scouting is one of challenging assumptions and biases over and over, attempting to find an edge. But few players are as pared-down, efficient and polished like the Heason Sphere as Wander Franco. After an extraordinary degree of hype for such a young player, MLB fans were finally treated to Franco in the Show, and they saw much of what was promised: an above-average hitter, runner and defender at the most important defensive position that does not demand a crouch. In less than half a season at the age of 20, Franco established himself as a force for the best team in the AL East, and inspired the Rays to extend him the longest and richest contract in club history. Players who debut this young and this well do not always finish their careers on freight trains to Cooperstown, but many of them do just that.

Two other youthful members of the AL East's defending champions should help make up a formidable starting rotation alongside Shane Baz, as McClanahan and Patiño delivered eye-popping heat as starters, even for this day and age. Both players were held back significantly by Tampa's typical restraint in allowing their pitchers to work through the order numerous times. Those restrictions are unlikely to fully loosen, but we should see some level of expansion in role for both players with another year of distance from the shortened 2020 campaign.

Due to Tyler Glasnow's injury, which will cost him most or all of 2022, McClanahan is the de facto ace of Tampa's staff, a heavy burden for a southpaw in his sophomore campaign. Patiño could shoulder some of that load, but, at just 22 years of age, he'll need to continue honing his electric repertoire into something that can fuel Tampa for 5-plus innings at a time and extinguish opposing hitters.

Texas Rangers

The State of the System:

The Rangers got the top arm in the draft and saw a couple of internal pitching breakouts along the way. They added even more prospect depth with the Joey Gallo trade, but, somehow, they don't feel quite as upside-laden as in past versions of these rankings. Maybe they've changed, or maybe we've changed.

The Top Ten:

1 Jack Leiter RHP OFP: 70 ETA: Late 2022

Born: 04/21/00 Age: 22 Bats: R Throws: R Height: 6'1" Weight: 205 lb. Origin: Round 1, 2021 Draft (#2 overall)

The Report: The son of former All-Star lefty and current MLB Network personality Al Leiter, Jack initially rose to prominence as a first-round talent in the 2019 draft out of a Morristown, New Jersey, prep school. He had a near-unbreakable commitment to Vanderbilt—his family is wealthy, and he was going to be age-eligible for the 2021 draft—and fell to a courtesy/backup late pick by the Yankees. From the moment he stepped on campus, he was a sensation, only interrupted by a global pandemic.

While he has been tagged as a minimally projectable player since high school, he has, in fact, already gained significant velocity from his prep days; he was 91–96 for us as a high-school senior and was more often in the mid-90s and scraped 98 at Vandy in 2021. He has a lively, rising heater. His curveball has long graded out as a future plus-plus pitch with strong, two-plane break, and his sweeping slider jumped in college and has out-pitch potential of its own now. His changeup flashes above-average, too, although he rarely had to use it as an amateur player. His fastball and both breaking balls showed strong characteristics, and Leiter is known to work on modern pitch design and training.

OFP: 70 / No. 2 starter

Variance: Medium. It's going to be awfully tempting for the Rangers, suddenly pushing their window open, to get Leiter to the majors quickly. If he starts off 2022 hot, he could easily be the first 2021 draftee to the Show.

Mark Barry's Fantasy Take: We can quibble about the TINSTAAPP of it all, but from pedigree to stuff to frame, Leiter has pretty much everything you'd want in that unicorn, top-level-starter profile. He's a top-10 prospect arm for me right now, and I think he has one of the highest floors in the minors—with plenty of ceiling, to boot.

2 Josh Jung 3B OFP: 60 ETA: 2022, as needed

Born: 02/12/98 Age: 24 Bats: R Throws: R Height: 6'2" Weight: 214 lb. Origin: Round 1, 2019 Draft (#8 overall)

YEAR	TEAM	LVL	AGE	PA	R	2B	3B	HR	RBI	BB	K	SB	CS	AVG/OBP/SLG	DRC+	BABIP	BRR	FRAA	WARP
2019	RAN	ROK	21	19	5	1	1	1	5	2	3	0	0	.588/.632/.941		.692			
2019	HIC	A	21	179	18	13	0	1	23	16	29	4	1	.287/.363/.389	109	.341	0.9	3B(35) 2.7	1.1
2021	FRI	AA	23	186	25	8	1	10	40	13	42	2	2	.308/.366/.544	114	.356	-1.9	3B(32) 0.2	0.7
2021	RR	AAA	23	156	29	14	0	9	21	18	34	0	0	.348/.436/.652	125	.413	-0.4	3B(24) 1.3	1.1
2022 non-DC	*TEX*	*MLB*	*24*	*251*	*25*	*12*	*0*	*6*	*27*	*18*	*60*	*1*	*1*	*.248/.313/.398*	*91*	*.308*	*-0.2*	*3B 1*	*0.5*

Comparables: Matt Chapman, Brent Morel, Ryan Braun

The Report: We got positive reports on Jung's bat from the alternate site in 2020 but needed to see the supposedly burgeoning game power in . . . well, games. That was delayed by Jung's foot surgery at the end of spring training, but he made up for lost time by absolutely blistering upper-minors pitching over the summer. Jung's swing is certainly more geared for power now, which can lead to him getting a little too long at times, but his balance and bat control suggest at least a solid-average hit tool, which should allow just about all of his plus raw power to play in games. Defensively, Jung is perfectly adequate at third base. He has become a little thicker and has never been the rangiest at the hot corner, but he aggressively attacks groundballs and has a good enough first step to be an average glove. His arm is also average but accurate.

OFP: 60 / First-division third baseman

Variance: Medium. We think there is some risk that major-league arms will find some holes in his tweaked and now-occasionally-violent swing, but Jung is ready to test that theory.

Mark Barry's Fantasy Take: There were some rumblings last spring about Jung getting a chance to lock down the hot corner in Arlington, but a stress fracture (and a terrible big-league team) all but extinguished his chances for a 2021 debut. Dude rebounded with a line of .326/.398/.592 with 22 homers in 342 trips to the plate, spread out across two levels. Leiter has tremendous upside on the mound, but, for me, Jung is the best fantasy prospect in the organization, and it's not all that close. If he's not a top-10 dynasty prospect right now, well, hopefully your list goes up to 11.

3 Justin Foscue 2B OFP: 60 ETA: 2023

Born: 03/02/99 Age: 23 Bats: R Throws: R Height: 6'0" Weight: 205 lb. Origin: Round 1, 2020 Draft (#14 overall)

YEAR	TEAM	LVL	AGE	PA	R	2B	3B	HR	RBI	BB	K	SB	CS	AVG/OBP/SLG	DRC+	BABIP	BRR	FRAA	WARP
2021	SUR	WIN	22	89	15	4	0	5	14	15	23	3	1	.257/.416/.529		.310			
2021	HIC	A+	22	150	34	11	1	14	35	16	39	1	1	.296/.407/.736	127	.315	0.7	2B(29) -0.2	1.0
2021	FRI	AA	22	104	14	7	0	2	13	8	29	0	1	.247/.317/.387	84	.333	-1.6	2B(24) -0.7	-0.1
2022 non-DC	*TEX*	*MLB*	*23*	*251*	*25*	*12*	*1*	*7*	*28*	*18*	*70*	*0*	*1*	*.221/.294/.385*	*80*	*.285*	*-0.3*	*2B -1*	*0.2*

Comparables: Brandon Lowe, Cory Spangenberg, Chris Taylor

The Report: So far, so good for Foscue, who is living up to his billing as an advanced college bat despite struggling a bit following a late-season promotion to Double-A Frisco. He absolutely torched High-A with Hickory, most notably homering in eight straight games back in late July. His excellent approach and his penchant for hitting the ball very hard very often is a dynamic combination that goes a ways toward making up for the deficiencies in his overall game. He's not a big-time athlete, and he is already limited to second base, so he'll need the aforementioned hitting ability to stick in the bigs. We saw him cover breaking balls down and away pretty well during our Low-A look, but he struggled a bit upon exposure to the more-advanced stuff, and his strikeout rate runs a little higher than one might like. Still, his track record and innate ability point toward a very good everyday player.

OFP: 60 / First-division starter who creates most of his value with his bat.

Variance: Low. He'll need to hit, but most available evidence indicates that he will.

Mark Barry's Fantasy Take: I'm always a little wary of "second basemen" that really need to hit to be viable. Well, maybe not always, let's say post–Keston Hiura. If Foscue doesn't hit, his defense isn't going to keep him in the lineup, which limits the opportunity for volume, which limits his usefulness for your fantasy team. Despite the Jon Dowd–esque numbers from High-A, Foscue never really excelled at avoiding strikeouts, which is alarming as he climbs the organizational ladder. Based on promise and pedigree, he's still a top-101 prospect, but he's a top-101 prospect I'd look to move on from.

4 Cole Winn RHP OFP: 55 ETA: Late 2022

Born: 11/25/99 Age: 22 Bats: R Throws: R Height: 6'2" Weight: 190 lb. Origin: Round 1, 2018 Draft (#15 overall)

YEAR	TEAM	LVL	AGE	W	L	SV	G	GS	IP	H	HR	BB/9	K/9	K	GB%	BABIP	WHIP	ERA	DRA-	WARP
2019	HIC	A	19	4	4	0	18	18	68^2	59	5	5.1	8.5	65	46.6%	.292	1.43	4.46	114	0.1
2021	FRI	AA	21	3	3	0	19	19	78	38	6	3.0	11.2	97	36.7%	.198	0.82	2.31	84	1.2
2021	RR	AAA	21	1	0	0	2	2	8	5	1	5.6	11.2	10	30.0%	.211	1.25	3.38	101	0.0
2022 non-DC	*TEX*	*MLB*	*22*	*2*	*3*	*0*	*57*	*0*	*50*	*46*	*7*	*4.8*	*8.8*	*48*	*36.5%*	*.284*	*1.46*	*4.72*	*112*	*-0.1*

Comparables: Ben Howard, Nathan Eovaldi, Cristian Javier

The Report: At the alternate site in 2020, Winn smoothed out the control issues that plagued him early in his pro career, and his four-pitch arsenal played up commensurately in the upper minors in 2021. Everything here is at least average, with a fastball that sits 93–94 but can touch higher and a potentially above-average change backing it. The cambio is the best present pitch in his arsenal, and Winn is comfortable throwing it whenever and to whomever. It can be a little firm, but he sells it well, and it usually has enough late dip to miss bats, but a lack of consistency in shape and movement keeps it from having a true plus outcome, at present. His curve and his slider offer two different breaking-ball looks, with the curve showing more depth, and the slider more glove-side run. As with the change, neither is consistent enough to have true major-league swing-and-miss outcomes, but Winn is able to lean on all his secondaries to make the fastball play up late in counts, and the change could develop into that plus out-pitch. He is control-over-command, at present, but, really, everything here is just at the refinement stage now. We don't know if there is a true high-side rotation outcome here—although this kind of profile only really needs one pitch jump to play up—but Winn should be a rotation stalwart in Arlington in short order.

OFP: 55 / No. 3–4 starter

Variance: Medium. While we do wonder if Winn will end up with a true swing-and-miss offering, there's enough in his pitch mix that—outside of normal pitching health risks, which are never "low"—he should be some sort of major-league starter.

Mark Barry's Fantasy Take: If Leiter has the floor *and* the ceiling, Winn has the floor. Maybe said floor is a little lower than Leiter's—perhaps, like, on the third floor, whereas Leiter's is on, say, the seventh floor. But for their ceilings, Winn's might be on, say the sixth floor . . . okay, so I've lost the thread on this metaphor.

Winn's pitch mix is enough for a mid-rotation starter, but injury and workload concerns could keep him in the realm of the streaming options long-term.

5 Ezequiel Duran 2B/SS OFP: 55 ETA: Late 2023

Born: 05/22/99 Age: 23 Bats: R Throws: R Height: 5'11" Weight: 185 lb. Origin: International Free Agent, 2017

YEAR	TEAM	LVL	AGE	PA	R	2B	3B	HR	RBI	BB	K	SB	CS	AVG/OBP/SLG	DRC+	BABIP	BRR	FRAA	WARP
2019	SI	SS	20	277	49	12	4	13	37	25	77	11	4	.256/.329/.496		.314			
2021	SUR	WIN	22	78	16	7	4	3	12	5	9	0	2	.278/.333/.611		.283			
2021	HIC	A+	22	174	25	7	0	7	31	12	59	7	2	.229/.287/.408	81	.309	-0.9	SS(25) 2.3, 2B(4) 0.3, 3B(3) -0.2	0.3
2021	HV	A+	22	297	42	15	6	12	48	28	71	12	7	.290/.374/.533	124	.354	-2.2	2B(42) 7.4, SS(16) -1.9	2.0
2022 non-DC	*TEX*	*MLB*	*23*	*251*	*22*	*10*	*1*	*4*	*24*	*16*	*76*	*6*	*3*	*.219/.282/.345*	*67*	*.305*	*0.7*	*2B 3, SS 0*	*0.2*

Comparables: César Hernández, Breyvic Valera, Jimmy Paredes

The Report: Duran is too good a prospect to be a personal cheeseball, but he has long been a personal cheeseball all the same. We worried that the lost year might impact his development, but he went to High-A and basically had the Ezequiel Duran season, which fits well into our old format.

The Good: He continued to hit for significant pop. The "real 60 power" is now real 70 power.

The Bad: His swing remains unorthodox, and his approach aggressive. Duran does enough damage on contact to keep his slash line respectable, but that might not be the case further up the ladder. This is more a swing-decision issue than a pure bat-to-ball issue—although he does not get cheated up there—so it's perhaps more fixable, but we've been told we tend to get too attached to this profile, even when there is evidence that whiffs will be a problem.

Defensively, Duran saw a fair amount of time at shortstop once he wasn't sharing an infield with Oswald Peraza, but he is a better fit at second or even third—where he played most of his games in the Arizona Fall League. He's not quite rangy enough for the six, but his arm is good enough for the left side, and he is potentially plus at the keystone. Duran's ability to move around on the dirt will make it easier to get his power bat into the lineup, now we just need to see the stick perform at higher levels.

OFP: 55 / Slugging infielder with positional flex

Variance: High. We really need to see him in Double-A before fully buying in on a 30-home-run outcome here, but if Duran does keep hitting for power, he's a potential first-division starter wherever he ends up on the dirt.

Mark Barry's Fantasy Take: Until Duran gets his propensity for striking out, uh, out of his system, he'll continue his trajectory as a useful option at the keystone, but one from which you always want a little more.

6 Owen White RHP OFP: 55 ETA: 2023

Born: 08/09/99 Age: 22 Bats: R Throws: R Height: 6'3" Weight: 199 lb. Origin: Round 2, 2018 Draft (#55 overall)

YEAR	TEAM	LVL	AGE	W	L	SV	G	GS	IP	H	HR	BB/9	K/9	K	GB%	BABIP	WHIP	ERA	DRA-	WARP
2021	SUR	WIN	21	5	0	0	6	6	28[1]	20	1	4.1	9.2	29	39.4%	.271	1.16	1.91		
2021	DE	A	21	3	1	0	8	8	33[1]	25	2	3.2	14.6	54	41.2%	.348	1.11	3.24	68	0.9
2022 non-DC	*TEX*	*MLB*	*22*	*2*	*3*	*0*	*57*	*0*	*50*	*48*	*8*	*4.7*	*9.9*	*54*	*37.1%*	*.305*	*1.48*	*5.09*	*117*	*-0.3*

The Report: It took White three years to make his professional debut following Tommy John surgery and a fractured hand, but he made a strong first impression in Low-A and carried that success into the Arizona Fall League. The physical right-hander works 93–95, touching 96 with above-average command and bat-missing life in the zone. His mid-80s slider is a true put-away offering with hard, late, two-plane break, and he rounds out his arsenal with a 12–6 curveball and usable changeup.

OFP: 55 / No. 3–4 Starter

Variance: High. His injury history, and the accompanying workload management it required, elevate the risk, but White looks the part of a strong mid-rotation starter.

Mark Barry's Fantasy Take: A couple of things: 1) White struck out pretty much everybody with Low-A Down East, fanning 40 percent of opposing hitters, however 2) He only tossed 35 ⅓ innings and has a history of injuries. So basically, he's a pitching prospect. If there's a silver lining to White's most recent bout with injuries, it's that a broken hand is a little more fluky than a typical pitcher injury. All that is stopping White from mid-rotation status is a consistent workload.

Eyewitness Report: Owen White

Evaluator: Trevor Andresen

Report Date: 11/16/2021

Dates Seen: 11/8 - 11/13 (Arizona Fall League)

Risk Factor: High

Delivery: XL 6'3" 200 lb. frame. Mature, physical build. Pitches from a slow, controlled delivery w/ a H3/4 release. Repeats it well enough to project above-average control

Pitch Type	Future Grade	Sitting Velocity	Peak Velocity	Report
Fastball	60	93-95	96	Above-avg command. Good life helps it generate swing-and-miss in the zone
Slider	60	83-86	87	Consistent plus offering w/ hard, late two-plane break. Future put away offering
Curveball	50	78-82	83	12/6 shape. Feel for it. Average third offering
Changeup	45	85-87	88	Firm w/ some arm side fade. Usable fourth offering

Conclusion: Injury history (Tommy John in 2019, broken hand in 2021) and the accompanied workload management required elevate the risk, but White looks the part of a strong #3 starter

7 Josh H. Smith SS OFP: 50 ETA: 2023

Born: 08/07/97 Age: 24 Bats: L Throws: R Height: 5'10" Weight: 172 lb. Origin: Round 2, 2019 Draft (#67 overall)

YEAR	TEAM	LVL	AGE	PA	R	2B	3B	HR	RBI	BB	K	SB	CS	AVG/OBP/SLG	DRC+	BABIP	BRR	FRAA	WARP
2019	SI	SS	21	141	17	6	1	3	15	25	17	6	3	.324/.450/.477		.355			
2021	TAM	A	23	50	15	0	0	6	15	7	6	5	0	.333/.480/.795	138	.259	1.1	SS(7) -0.4, 2B(1) -0.0	0.4
2021	HIC	A+	23	49	10	3	0	1	7	2	9	2	0	.295/.367/.432	105	.353	-0.1	SS(9) 1.0	0.3
2021	HV	A+	23	125	29	12	3	3	9	16	27	12	3	.320/.435/.583	109	.411	-0.3	SS(23) 3.6	0.8
2021	FRI	AA	23	127	12	5	0	3	10	18	20	7	2	.294/.425/.431	124	.338	-0.1	SS(30) -1.8	0.6
2022 non-DC	*TEX*	*MLB*	*24*	*251*	*25*	*11*	*1*	*5*	*25*	*22*	*47*	*8*	*3*	*.240/.327/.376*	*93*	*.283*	*0.6*	*SS 1, 2B 0*	*0.9*

Comparables: Jake Cronenworth, Wilmer Difo, JT Riddle

The Report: Smith is small-framed, bereft of projectability, and his tools aren't loud, but he has just enough of everything to make it work. He very well might be irritating the fans of the Rangers' NL West opponents very soon. Smith was also a bit overaged for High-A in 2021, and he performed accordingly. To his credit, he kept it going after a midseason trade and promotion to Double-A. He takes a surprisingly aggressive and power-oriented cut at the plate, and has enough barrel control and approach that he still makes a lot of contact and taps into some sneaky pop. He can also run a bit and has the ability to contribute either up the middle or, potentially, as a broader utility profile, though his arm might be slightly fringy for an everyday shortstop.

OFP: 50 / Utility option or complementary lineup piece

Variance: Low. We suppose there might be some hit-tool risk, but, really, he is what he is and he brings what he brings.

Mark Barry's Fantasy Take: (Don't say David Eckstein. Don't say David Eckstein. Don't say David Eckstein.)

Actually, you know who Smith really reminds me of? Fine, nevermind. There are a lot of things that the former second-rounder does well, but without any standout tools, it's easy to see him fall into a utility role upon major-league call up. He's worth a speculative add in AL-only formats, but I don't think he'll be overly helpful in mixed leagues.

8 Glenn Otto RHP OFP: 50 ETA: Debuted in 2021

Born: 03/11/96 Age: 26 Bats: R Throws: R Height: 6'3" Weight: 240 lb. Origin: Round 5, 2017 Draft (#152 overall)

YEAR	TEAM	LVL	AGE	W	L	SV	G	GS	IP	H	HR	BB/9	K/9	K	GB%	BABIP	WHIP	ERA	DRA-	WARP
2019	TAM	A+	23	3	3	0	14	12	56^1	54	1	5.3	10.9	68	44.4%	.376	1.54	3.20	88	1.0
2021	SOM	AA	25	6	3	0	11	10	65^1	46	6	1.9	14.2	103	38.1%	.315	0.92	3.17	86	1.0
2021	SWB	AAA	25	1	0	0	2	2	10^1	14	0	2.6	10.5	12	33.3%	.424	1.65	4.35	104	0.1
2021	RR	AAA	25	2	1	0	4	4	20	13	0	3.2	8.6	19	49.0%	.255	1.00	2.70	100	0.1
2021	TEX	MLB	25	0	3	0	6	6	23^1	32	2	3.1	10.8	28	43.8%	.429	1.71	9.26	99	0.2
2022 DC	*TEX*	*MLB*	*26*	*4*	*4*	*0*	*16*	*16*	*66.3*	*61*	*9*	*3.6*	*9.0*	*66*	*51.2%*	*.291*	*1.33*	*4.12*	*101*	*0.5*

Comparables: Spencer Turnbull, Matt Andriese, Tyler Duffey

The Report: Every year, the Yankees have a college arm develop a new slider and tear up the minors out of nowhere. This year, it was Otto, who had barely pitched as a pro due to injuries after a heavy workload at Rice. (Tell us if you've heard that one before.) Mid-pop-up, he was sent to Texas with Smith and Duran in the Joey Gallo trade, and he made his major-league debut at the end of August after an excellent minor-league campaign in which both his stuff and command jumped.

Otto threw his fastball or slider nearly 85 percent of the time last year, so it's pretty safe to say he's close to a two-pitch guy, at present. He can get his fastball up to 95–96 but more often lives in the low 90s than the mid-90s, and the pitch does not have particularly notable spin or movement; it got waffled pretty good in the majors. The slider is his out-offering, at present, a hard plus sweeper around 80 mph which gets ample swings-and-misses. He also throws a curveball and changeup less frequently.

OFP: 50 / No. 4 starter or set-up reliever

Variance: High. Otto has a sketchy health history, and his pitch mix is pretty close to 95-and-a-slider, so he certainly could end up as a reliever. However, his rate stats as a starter in the high minors were great, and his command profile came together last year.

Mark Barry's Fantasy Take: Otto debuted last year and sacrificed his 2021 campaign to the BABIP gods. Despite a decent strikeout rate, he worked in the zone a little too much and paid for it dearly when he couldn't miss bats. His two-pitch mix leads me to believe he'll be a reliever, but if he can miss a few more bats, a back-end-rotation guy isn't out of the question. And if I'm being honest, I'm hoping for the latter, so I can praise his good starts with: "You go, Glenn Otto."

9 Aaron Zavala RF/DH OFP: 50 ETA: Late 2023/Early 2024

Born: 06/23/00 Age: 22 Bats: L Throws: R Height: 6'0" Weight: 193 lb. Origin: Round 2, 2021 Draft (#38 overall)

YEAR	TEAM	LVL	AGE	PA	R	2B	3B	HR	RBI	BB	K	SB	CS	AVG/OBP/SLG	DRC+	BABIP	BRR	FRAA	WARP
2021	RAN	ROK	21	26	5	1	0	0	2	3	7	2	0	.273/.385/.318		.400			
2021	DE	A	21	67	13	4	0	1	7	10	13	7	0	.302/.433/.434	122	.375	-0.2	RF(10) -1.3, LF(1) 0.4	0.3
2022 non-DC	*TEX*	*MLB*	*22*	*251*	*20*	*10*	*1*	*2*	*20*	*20*	*66*	*11*	*2*	*.210/.284/.307*	*65*	*.283*	*0.8*	*RF 0, LF 0*	*-0.3*

The Report: A big-time college performer with the bat for the Oregon Ducks, Zavala showed a keen eye and plus bat-to-ball skills throughout his time in Eugene. He added some physicality and pop his junior year, but he has a fairly direct stroke without a ton of lift. He does have plenty of bat speed and stings the ball hard, but it remains to be seen how much over-the-fence power he'll show with wood bats. He has enough gap power to keep professional pitchers honest, though, and Zavala is a pesky contact guy who will foul off your better breakers when he's behind. So, we think, given the overall eye and approach, he should continue to run high OBPs, even if he's more a 10–15-home-run and 30-double guy. That's not a special bat, given his defensive limitations—he played all four corners in college and mostly right field in the pros—but it's about time for the . . . sigh . . . early 2000s to become a popular retro aesthetic, and Zavala could easily have been drafted by Moneyball-era Billy Beane.

OFP: 50 / Moneyball leadoff hitter

Variance: Medium. Given his lack of positional/defensive value, Zavala is going to have to hit (and walk) his way up the ladder. He's an advanced college bat, though, and looked the part in his pro debut. He's also the kind of hitter that is a good swing-maximization candidate, but we can't project that until we at least start to see signs.

Mark Barry's Fantasy Take: If I was personally required to provide a hot-ish take for this system, it would be that Zavala might be the third-most-intriguing dynasty prospect. I'm a sucker for the dudes that get on base, and Zavala has developed a knack for making a bunch of contact in addition to drawing walks. He tapped into a little more power in his final collegiate season, so there's an outside chance for contribution in five categories. He's under-the-radar enough that you shouldn't have to rush out and acquire the Oregon Duck, but toss him on the watchlist and pounce if he's popping dingers this spring.

10 A.J. Alexy RHP

OFP: 50 ETA: Debuted in 2021

Born: 04/21/98 Age: 24 Bats: R Throws: R Height: 6'4" Weight: 195 lb. Origin: Round 11, 2016 Draft (#341 overall)

YEAR	TEAM	LVL	AGE	W	L	SV	G	GS	IP	H	HR	BB/9	K/9	K	GB%	BABIP	WHIP	ERA	DRA-	WARP
2019	DE	A+	21	0	3	0	5	5	19¹	14	1	6.1	10.7	23	34.0%	.289	1.40	5.12	111	0.1
2021	FRI	AA	23	3	1	0	13	7	50¹	30	4	3.8	10.2	57	44.8%	.232	1.01	1.61	93	0.5
2021	RR	AAA	23	0	0	0	3	3	14²	9	2	3.7	11.7	19	46.9%	.233	1.02	1.84	91	0.1
2021	TEX	MLB	23	3	1	0	5	4	23	13	4	6.7	6.7	17	24.2%	.155	1.30	4.70	144	-0.3
2022 DC	*TEX*	*MLB*	*24*	*5*	*5*	*0*	*34*	*12*	*76.3*	*69*	*12*	*5.7*	*8.8*	*74*	*49.4%*	*.277*	*1.54*	*5.09*	*118*	*-0.2*

Comparables: Matt Moore, Chad Durbin, Alex Cobb

The Report: After missing most of 2019 with a lat injury and then, obviously, all of 2020, Alexy was a bit of a wild card for 2021. Like Winn, he came out and dominated the upper minors with a four-pitch mix, but you have to squint a little harder here to see the major-league out-pitch. His fastball is fine if a bit nondescript—perhaps even too hittable at 93–94—although his compact and funky arm action can lend a bit of deception. Alexy also leans heavily on a slurvy, low-80s slider and an average changeup, which can have more fade than depth and a little less velocity separation than you'd like. He will also sprinkle in a slower curve with more of a 12–6 shape. Alexy struggled to throw strikes during his late-season call up, and that has been a long-standing problem to varying degrees during his pro career. His delivery is fairly simple and stretch-only, but the aforementioned arm stroke can be inconsistent. You can deal with a few extra walks when you are missing enough bats, but his current repertoire makes that a bit of a tightrope act.

OFP: 50 / No. 4 starter

Variance: Medium. After two good major-league starts, Alexy's control and command nosedived. He's never going to be super fine in that regard, but he will need to run walk rates closer to average, both to allow him to work deeper as a starter and because he doesn't really have the arsenal to pitch his way out of jams consistently.

Mark Barry's Fantasy Take: Alexy, show me a righty that can notch a strikeout or two, but won't stop walking guys.

The Prospects You Meet Outside the Top Ten

#11

Evan Carter CF Born: 08/29/02 Age: 19 Bats: L Throws: R Height: 6'4" Weight: 190 lb. Origin: Round 2, 2020 Draft (#50 overall)

YEAR	TEAM	LVL	AGE	PA	R	2B	3B	HR	RBI	BB	K	SB	CS	AVG/OBP/SLG	DRC+	BABIP	BRR	FRAA	WARP
2021	DE	A	18	146	22	8	1	2	12	34	28	12	4	.236/.438/.387	121	.299	-2.0	CF(30) -4.0	0.4
2022 non-DC	*TEX*	*MLB*	*19*	*251*	*21*	*10*	*1*	*2*	*19*	*31*	*65*	*10*	*5*	*.195/.306/.294*	*70*	*.267*	*0.9*	*CF -3*	*-0.3*

Comparables: Justin Upton, Ronald Acuña Jr., Mike Trout

If you had asked us before Memorial Day last year, we'd have expected Carter to be in the top three on this list. The reports out of 2020 instructs and 2021 spring training were so strong that he was trending towards our Midseason Top 50 list and would've easily slotted into an updated Top 101. Instead, he injured his back in mid-June, ultimately missed the rest of the season with a stress fracture and had a setback that took him out of instructs, as well. Before that, he'd shown almost extremely strong plate discipline for his age, walking 23.3 percent of the time as an 18-year-old at Low-A. Carter has a beautiful lefty swing leveraged for loft and power that his projectable frame should provide later on. The only two real questions here are health—recurring back issues for a teenager are an enormous red flag—and hit tool; we just haven't seen enough of his ability to hit pro pitching yet. He's a candidate for a huge jump up our lists if he can conquer those two issues.

#12

Ronny Henriquez RHP Born: 06/20/00 Age: 22 Bats: R Throws: R Height: 5'10" Weight: 155 lb. Origin: International Free Agent, 2017

YEAR	TEAM	LVL	AGE	W	L	SV	G	GS	IP	H	HR	BB/9	K/9	K	GB%	BABIP	WHIP	ERA	DRA-	WARP
2019	HIC	A	19	6	6	0	21	19	82	91	6	3.0	10.9	99	36.8%	.385	1.44	4.50	96	0.8
2021	HIC	A+	21	1	3	0	5	5	24	13	2	3.0	10.1	27	42.4%	.193	0.88	3.75	94	0.3
2021	FRI	AA	21	4	4	0	16	11	69^{2}	65	15	2.2	10.1	78	43.6%	.279	1.18	5.04	76	1.4
2022 non-DC	*TEX*	*MLB*	*22*	*2*	*3*	*0*	*57*	*0*	*50*	*51*	*7*	*3.4*	*7.8*	*43*	*40.0%*	*.298*	*1.40*	*4.64*	*115*	*-0.2*

Comparables: Daniel Norris, Brad Keller, Iván Nova

Despite 2021 season in which he racked up strikeouts at two levels, Henriquez didn't exactly quell concerns that he's a reliever long-term. He still has a lively fastball that can touch the mid-90s and comes from an awkward angle for hitters given his height. His breaking ball is a slider that flashes above-average depth but can run down the barrel more than miss bats, at times. His power change is his best secondary and flashes plus when he pulls the string on it, but it can also be flat and inviting. Henriquez is on the shorter and slighter side—we'd be surprised if he's actually 5-foot-10—and might not hold up over 160 innings, or whatever we are calling a starter's workload nowadays. His command projection isn't going to get much past average, either, but given his age and limited pro reps, it's worth keeping him stretched out for another year to see if some breaking-ball and command gains can move his projection up into the 3–4 starter range.

Prospects on the Rise

Jose Acuna RHP Born: 10/20/02 Age: 19 Bats: R Throws: R Height: 6'2" Weight: 175 lb. Origin: International Free Agent, 2019

He isn't a generational talent like his older brother Ronald, but the younger Acuña has the tools to make himself into a contributor at the big-league level. The 19-year-old got off to a slow start in his full-season debut but picked it up in time for the dog days, all-in-all slashing .266/.345/.404 with 12 homers and 44 stolen bases for Low-A Down East. He is quite obviously short of his listed 6-feet, but his substantial build, quick bat and strong hands produce more pop than you might otherwise expect. Acuña knows that and will take big cuts early in the count, though he also covers the plate well and shows the ability to adjust to breaking stuff when necessary. The speed and athleticism are there for him to remain up the middle, but he may end up better suited for second base than shortstop.

Tekoah Roby RHP Born: 09/18/01 Age: 20 Bats: R Throws: R Height: 6'1" Weight: 185 lb. Origin: Round 3, 2020 Draft (#86 overall)

YEAR	TEAM	LVL	AGE	W	L	SV	G	GS	IP	H	HR	BB/9	K/9	K	GB%	BABIP	WHIP	ERA	DRA-	WARP
2021	DE	A	19	2	2	0	6	6	22	14	1	2.9	14.3	35	46.7%	.295	0.95	2.45	68	0.6
2022 non-DC	*TEX*	*MLB*	*20*	*2*	*3*	*0*	*57*	*0*	*50*	*47*	*7*	*4.5*	*8.9*	*49*	*39.3%*	*.292*	*1.44*	*4.68*	*111*	*-0.1*

Roby barely pitched in 2021, making six mostly abbreviated but good starts in Low-A with slightly diminished stuff before missing the rest of the season with an elbow sprain. That's a pretty concerning diagnosis for a teenage pitcher, but he was back on the mound during fall instructs. Roby was throwing in the low 90s with an interesting curveball before he got hurt; his arm path had noticeably shortened up since his amateur days. There are scouts who like the foundational pieces here quite a lot, and he's worth keeping an eye on.

Trevor Hauver 2B/LF Born: 11/20/98 Age: 23 Bats: L Throws: R Height: 6'0" Weight: 205 lb. Origin: Round 3, 2020 Draft (#99 overall)

YEAR	TEAM	LVL	AGE	PA	R	2B	3B	HR	RBI	BB	K	SB	CS	AVG/OBP/SLG	DRC+	BABIP	BRR	FRAA	WARP
2021	TAM	A	22	299	48	17	2	9	49	64	78	2	0	.288/.445/.498	124	.393	-0.7	2B(56) 2.3, 3B(1) -0.0	1.8
2021	HIC	A+	22	143	20	4	0	6	21	20	47	0	0	.246/.357/.426	92	.348	-1.3	LF(18) -2.2, 2B(12) -0.4	-0.1
2022 non-DC	*TEX*	*MLB*	*23*	*251*	*23*	*10*	*1*	*4*	*23*	*30*	*77*	*0*	*0*	*.209/.311/.329*	*75*	*.302*	*-0.3*	*2B 0, LF -1*	*0.0*

Comparables: DJ Stewart, Jordan Luplow, Travis Buck

Hauver has an excellent approach, very good bat-to-ball ability, and a developing power stroke from the left side. So, what's the issue? He doesn't really have a position. He's listed at exactly 6-feet, is squarely built and generally splits his time between second base and left field. Thus far, he has performed like a solid-but-unspectacular college bat, but there is upside there. It's a tough profile, but Hauver is gifted enough offensively that he might just make it work.

Factors on the Farm

Sam Huff 1B Born: 01/14/98 Age: 24 Bats: R Throws: R Height: 6'5" Weight: 240 lb. Origin: Round 7, 2016 Draft (#219 overall)

YEAR	TEAM	LVL	AGE	PA	R	2B	3B	HR	RBI	BB	K	SB	CS	AVG/OBP/SLG	DRC+	BABIP	BRR	FRAA	WARP
2019	HIC	A	21	114	22	5	0	15	29	6	37	4	1	.333/.368/.796	188	.375	-0.2	C(14) -0.6	1.4
2019	DE	A+	21	405	49	17	2	13	43	27	117	2	5	.262/.326/.425	99	.347	-3.0	C(51) 3.6, 1B(4) 0.1	1.3
2020	TEX	MLB	22	33	5	3	0	3	4	2	11	0	0	.355/.394/.742	96	.471	-0.7	C(10) -1.0	-0.1
2021	RAN	ROK	23	33	6	2	0	3	6	3	11	0	0	.276/.364/.655		.333			
2021	FRI	AA	23	191	24	5	0	10	23	16	77	0	0	.237/.309/.439	70	.360	-0.1	1B(34) -0.8	-0.3
2021	RR	AAA	23	25	4	1	0	3	7	2	9	0	0	.273/.320/.727	90	.273	0.0	1B(4) -0.5	0.0
2022 DC	*TEX*	*MLB*	*24*	*221*	*25*	*8*	*0*	*10*	*28*	*14*	*84*	*1*	*1*	*.220/.279/.419*	*81*	*.314*	*-0.1*	*C -4*	*-0.1*

Comparables: Nick Evans, Mark Trumbo, José Osuna

We're keeping the catcher label up there—for now—but make no mistake, Huff did not don the tools of ignorance in 2021 due to recurring knee injuries, only playing first and DH-ing. While the Rangers claim he'll return behind the plate in 2022, knee problems are an extreme concern for a catching prospect. Adding to our concern: after a promising and unexpected 2020 MLB debut, Huff spent most of his healthy time in 2021 struggling mightily to even make contact in Double-A. While he has always had something of an all-or-nothing power profile, hitting .237 and striking out more than 36 percent of the time in the former Texas League is leaning way more towards "nothing." We're only a season off Huff ranking near the top of this list, but it's a season in which the bottom fell out on both his offensive and defensive projections.

Ricky Vanasco RHP Born: 10/13/98 Age: 23 Bats: R Throws: R Height: 6'3" Weight: 180 lb. Origin: Round 15, 2017 Draft (#464 overall)

YEAR	TEAM	LVL	AGE	W	L	SV	G	GS	IP	H	HR	BB/9	K/9	K	GB%	BABIP	WHIP	ERA	DRA-	WARP
2019	SPO	SS	20	3	1	0	9	9	39	23	2	5.1	13.6	59	50.0%	.292	1.15	1.85		
2019	HIC	A	20	0	0	0	2	2	10^{2}	5	0	2.5	13.5	16	47.4%	.263	0.75	1.69	86	0.2

Comparables: Andrew Brown, Jordan Hicks, Ethan Hankins

Vanasco was added to the 40-man roster in November despite being barely more than a year out from Tommy John surgery and having throw only ten innings in full-season ball to going under the knife. He was one of the big breakouts at the Rangers' alternate site in 2020, flashing triple-digit heat and a potentially plus breaker, and, given his age and the option clock that's now ticking, Texas might be best served to move him into a quicker-moving relief role once he's fully ready to go in 2022.

Yerry Rodriguez RHP Born: 10/15/97 Age: 24 Bats: R Throws: R Height: 6'2" Weight: 198 lb. Origin: International Free Agent, 2015

YEAR	TEAM	LVL	AGE	W	L	SV	G	GS	IP	H	HR	BB/9	K/9	K	GB%	BABIP	WHIP	ERA	DRA-	WARP
2019	HIC	A	21	7	3	0	13	13	73^{2}	45	5	2.6	10.4	85	45.3%	.241	0.90	2.08	86	1.1
2021	FRI	AA	23	1	1	0	14	14	51^{1}	38	3	3.7	11.0	63	41.9%	.289	1.15	2.63	96	0.4
2021	RR	AAA	23	3	3	0	13	4	30^{1}	37	5	3.6	11.0	37	48.9%	.386	1.62	8.01	88	0.3
2022 DC	*TEX*	*MLB*	*24*	*0*	*0*	*0*	*3*	*3*	*13.3*	*13*	*1*	*4.1*	*9.0*	*13*	*37.7%*	*.298*	*1.42*	*4.45*	*109*	*0.0*

Comparables: Hunter Wood, Ryan Helsley, John Gant

You can see the outline here of a three-pitch guy with enough command to be an average rotation piece, so Rodriguez isn't that far off Alexy and Henriquez as a pitching prospect. However, he misses the list proper because he has struggled with command and feel for his secondaries, a high-spin power curve and a low-80s change. Triple-A hitters, especially, punished him for his mistakes, and, in some ways, he feels even more reliever-ish than Henriquez despite something closer to a starter's frame. He might be able to wring a more consistent 95–96 from his fastball in short bursts, and, in that scenario, he would only need the curveball to develop further. The Rangers used him in multi-inning relief after his promotion to Triple-A Round Rock. That was probably more for innings management, but it might also be a preview of his role to come.

Top Talents 25 and Under (as of 4/1/2022):

1. Jack Leiter, RHP
2. Josh Jung, 3B
3. Justin Foscue, IF
4. Spencer Howard, RHP
5. Cole Winn, RHP
6. Ezequiel Duran, 2B

7. Owen White, RHP
8. Josh H. Smith, SS
9. Glenn Otto, RHP
10. Dennis Santana, RHP

Texas has put the cart before the horse in modern baseball's conventional wisdom this winter, spending big to attract stars while their roster and farm system lack much luster. When a club's roster is full of 25–28-year-olds and lacks star power, however, why shouldn't the denizens of Dallas–Fort Worth—the fourth-largest metro area in the United States by population—spend big to create a possible core of contention? Though Rookie of the Year finalist Adolis García will play next year at 29 and is more than a year older than Corey Seager, plenty members of Texas's lineup and rotation have the opportunity to improve with experience and aging.

Howard's first two tastes of MLB were disappointing given the caliber of his stuff and his promising pedigree, and, in some ways, his rate numbers obscure further questions. With 21 games started and 25 total appearances, the last and only time Howard pitched through the fifth inning in MLB was August of 2020, when he worked five innings exactly. Not once since—between piggybacking, stretching out from the short season and injury, and his transition from Philadelphia to Texas—has Howard pitch more than four innings on the dot in an outing. Given those (sometimes) intentional guard rails, one might have expected better results than a below-average 22.7-percent strikeout rate and higher-than-average 11.8-percent walk rate in 2021. Howard was probably not as bad (110 DRA–) as his base results showed (58 ERA+), however he leaned heavily on his four-seam without appearing to get fully acclimated on any of his off-speed stuff. He'll still be 25 for most of 2021 and gets movement in nearly every direction with his amuse-bouche of offerings, but what once looked like a mid-rotation profile has hit big-league road bumps.

In the bullpen, the Rangers have been treated to a reinvigoration of Santana's raw stuff, with results still pending. Injuries have weighed down his once-airy ceiling, but the former Dodgers farmhand got his fastball back up to sitting mid-to-upper 90s in bullpen work between Los Angeles and Texas last year. The trouble now is figuring out how to maximize his repertoire, which features a high-spin sinker, notably a poorly optimized pitch. Even as we enter 2022, we can't disregard pitchers who sit 95–96 with a solid slider and a workable changeup with a solid velocity gap. That's ultimately a solid bullpen piece with a high-leverage tool kit, the type of player whose development could go a long way toward improving Texas's circumstances in the short and long term.

Toronto Blue Jays

The State of the System:

When you've recently developed Bo Bichette and Vladimir Guerrero Jr., you are entitled to a bit of a grace period from the Baseball Prospectus Prospect Team. However, you might not want to use it up too quickly.

The Top Ten:

1 Gabriel Moreno C OFP: 60 ETA: Late 2022/Early 2023

Born: 02/14/00 Age: 22 Bats: R Throws: R Height: 5'11" Weight: 160 lb. Origin: International Free Agent, 2016

YEAR	TEAM	LVL	AGE	PA	R	2B	3B	HR	RBI	BB	K	SB	CS	AVG/OBP/SLG	DRC+	BABIP	BRR	FRAA	WARP
2019	LAN	A	19	341	47	17	5	12	52	22	38	7	1	.280/.337/.485	130	.282	1.1	C(54) -0.6	2.3
2020	LAR	WIN	20	70	12	5	0	1	11	11	6	1	0	.373/.471/.508		.404			
2021	MSS	WIN	21	100	16	11	0	1	18	13	13	0	0	.329/.410/.494		.370			
2021	LAR	WIN	21	73	11	0	1	1	8	11	11	2	0	.279/.397/.361		.327			
2021	NH	AA	21	145	29	9	1	8	45	14	22	1	2	.373/.441/.651	147	.398	0.6	C(27) -2.9, 3B(1) -0.1	1.1
2022 DC	*TOR*	*MLB*	*22*	*31*	*4*	*1*	*0*	*1*	*4*	*2*	*5*	*0*	*0*	*.258/.317/.431*	*102*	*.285*	*0.0*	*C 0*	*0.1*

Comparables: Salvador Perez, Wilson Ramos, Rowdy Tellez

The Report: We don't scout the stat line, but if you hit .370 with power, you will at least have our attention. Moreno missed time with a groin injury and then a thumb fracture in 2021, but, when he was on the field, he laid waste to Double-A East pitching. Moreno is a little jittery in his setup, and his bat ends up nearly horizontal when everything starts moving, but he generates the kind of bat speed best captured at 1000 fps. In other words, blink and you will miss the line drive. Despite the violence in the swing, Moreno moves the barrel around the zone well, and while he's aggressive, he didn't really see too many pitches he couldn't drive in 2021. That might get undone to an extent in the majors—no, we don't think he's a .370 hitter in the bigs—but .300 is certainly in play, and Moreno hits the ball hard enough and lifts it enough to pop 20-ish bombs. That's an obscene batting line for a catcher. In fact, it sounds pretty similar to the future Hall of Famer that just hung up the tools of ignorance.

But no, we don't comp Hall of Famers, either, and, behind the plate, Moreno really needed those missing 2021 reps. He sets a good target and is flexible, but his receiving is rough—it's all arms and, at times, stiff and stabby. Receiving is a teachable skill—and might be removed from the catching curriculum soon, anyway—but Moreno's is the kind of below-average catching profile teams are loath to run out there five days a week right now. The Jays were planning to give Moreno reps elsewhere, perhaps to accelerate the time table on his bat. Third base seemed a possibility, and he's a fringe runner, at present, which might be enough for him to man a corner outfield spot, as well. Ultimately though, how much and how well he can catch will determine whether Moreno is an All-Star or just a good regular. The bat should have no problem holding up its end of the bargain.

OFP: 60 / First-division catcher that sees time around the diamond on off-days

Variance: High. We think his offensive breakout is mostly real, but it was only 30-ish games of it (50-ish if you want to toss in fall ball). We also think his defensive issues are mostly real, but they might not matter by the time he's ready to be an everyday guy.

Mark Barry's Fantasy Take: Last year, J.P. Breen outlined the case for Moreno to post top-10 fantasy catcher seasons blending solid batting averages and some power with a great Toronto lineup. Moreno's video-game numbers in 2021 (let's say Sega's Sports Talk Baseball, still the GOAT, don't @ me) only added fuel to that flame. The bar is super-low behind the plate for fantasy backstops, but Moreno could be one of the better ones, even without big power.

Eyewitness Report: Gabriel Moreno

Evaluator: Trevor Andresen
Report Date: 11/25/2021
Dates Seen: 11/8 - 11/13 (Arizona Fall League)
Risk Factor: Medium
Physical/Health: LG/XL 5'11" 200 lb. frame. Thick build that will need to be monitored/maintained.

Tool	Future Grade	Report
Hit	55	Wide base w/ a rhythmic leg kick & noisy hand load, but displays plus bat control & has a knack for finding the barrel. Shows feel for the strike zone, though he was prone to expanding & chasing advanced spin. Willing to give him the benefit of the doubt due to missed reps this season.
Power	55	Doesn't show it off in BP, but generates above-average raw power & should get to all of it in-game due to his feel for contact.
Baserunning/ Speed	40	Fringy runner at present w/ surprising athleticism, though it will likely regress quickly as he ages.
Glove	50	Fringy receiver w/ hands that can get noisy at times. Quick out of his crouch & moves well laterally, resulting in above-avg blocking ability. Also saw time at 3B & didn't look bad per se, but it wasn't enough to seriously consider a move from behind the plate.
Arm	60	True plus arm behind the plate, routinely clocking sub-1.90 pop times w/ a quick release & accurate arm.

Conclusion: There's a low offensive bar to clear for those who can catch & Moreno offers enough on both sides of the ball to turn in All Star level production.

2 Jordan Groshans IF OFP: 55 ETA: Late 2022/Early 2023

Born: 11/10/99 Age: 22 Bats: R Throws: R Height: 6'3" Weight: 205 lb. Origin: Round 1, 2018 Draft (#12 overall)

YEAR	TEAM	LVL	AGE	PA	R	2B	3B	HR	RBI	BB	K	SB	CS	AVG/OBP/SLG	DRC+	BABIP	BRR	FRAA	WARP
2019	LAN	A	19	96	12	6	0	2	13	13	21	1	1	.337/.427/.482	121	.433	0.0	SS(20) -1.5	0.4
2021	NH	AA	21	316	46	23	0	7	40	34	61	0	0	.291/.367/.450	118	.347	-1.2	SS(43) -1.9, 3B(21) -0.6, 1B(1) -0.1	1.3
2022 DC	*TOR*	*MLB*	*22*	*63*	*7*	*3*	*0*	*1*	*7*	*5*	*13*	*0*	*0*	*.243/.312/.360*	*82*	*.299*	*-0.1*	*3B 0*	*0.0*

Comparables: Junior Lake, Nick Franklin, Corey Seager

The Report: After a foot injury limited him to just 23 games in 2019, you could argue that no prospect was hurt as much by the lost 2020 reps as Groshans. The only problem with that is he was perfectly fine during an aggressive Double-A assignment in 2021. He got out of the gate a little slowly, but as the weather turned warmer—well, as warm as it gets in Manchester—Groshans heated up. He's hitterish at the plate, a little busy and only shows average bat speed, but he makes consistent solid contact and marries it to an advanced approach—although you can get him on the front foot in hitter's counts. His contact is more solid than loud, and his above-average raw power plays more average in games. He can drive the ball to both gaps, it's just not quite as much oomph as you'd prefer.

That's especially true if Groshans has to move off shortstop. He's a little plodding there, at present, although a plus arm will cover for some range issues, and he gets clothesline carry on the move. He's a better fit at third, where he'd be above average given his good first step and hands, but we expect him to move around the dirt. Groshans has a collection of average-to-above tools but may lack a true carrying skill if his raw power doesn't get into games more, and there's a notable lack of twitch both in the field and at the plate. At the same time, there is no real weakness in his game, either, and his balanced skill set gives him a number of ways to help a major-league team.

OFP: 55 / Above-average infielder, position to be determined (perhaps day-by-day)

Variance: Medium. Despite the lack of game time—and you can have durability concerns at this point—Groshans is an advanced player on both sides of the ball. He has some tweener-ish infield characteristics, and you are still betting on some game-power development. If it comes, he's a true plus regular, but he might fall into the "good fifth infielder" bucket just as readily.

Mark Barry's Fantasy Take: Even if none of his tools are especially loud, I still like Groshans quite a bit as a fantasy fixture. I think Groshans could produce a little like Gleyber Torres the big leaguer, if not Gleyber Torres the exciting prospect: decent average, decent power and aided by a good lineup. He probably won't run. Groshans is flirting with the top-25 for me.

3 Orelvis Martinez SS OFP: 55 ETA: 2024

Born: 11/19/01 Age: 20 Bats: R Throws: R Height: 6'1" Weight: 188 lb. Origin: International Free Agent, 2018

YEAR	TEAM	LVL	AGE	PA	R	2B	3B	HR	RBI	BB	K	SB	CS	AVG/OBP/SLG	DRC+	BABIP	BRR	FRAA	WARP
2019	BLU	ROK	17	163	20	8	5	7	32	14	29	2	0	.275/.352/.549		.296			
2021	DUN	A	19	326	49	22	2	19	68	33	85	4	1	.279/.369/.572	130	.333	-1.8	SS(46) -5.2, 3B(12) 0.1	1.5
2021	VAN	A+	19	125	17	4	0	9	19	10	28	0	1	.214/.282/.491	125	.197	-0.4	SS(19) -1.1, 3B(6) -0.5	0.6
2022 non-DC	*TOR*	*MLB*	*20*	*251*	*27*	*11*	*1*	*9*	*31*	*16*	*73*	*0*	*1*	*.230/.290/.416*	*86*	*.294*	*-0.2*	*SS -2, 3B 0*	*0.2*

Comparables: Carlos Correa, Richard Ureña, Ketel Marte

The Report: If you were going to map out the ideal development path for your big, seven-figure, international-free-agent shortstop, slugging .550 in A-ball would certainly be on the flowchart. Despite the lost 2020 season—albeit one in which we got strong instructs reports on him—Martinez dropped right into full-season in 2021 and started bashing baseballs. He already has a sturdy upper body with room to add more good strength. He generates plus bat speed with lift and can pull even outer-half fastballs with authority as a teenager. His hit tool lags behind, as he had particular issues with offspeed after his promotion to High-A, but Martinez's issue can be more quality of contact than pure swing-and-miss, and his underlying approach and swing give us confidence that he'll be at least a .260–.270 hitter.

Sliding from shortstop to third base might not be on that Platonic-IFA path, but it's hardly uncommon. There's a trade off for those physical gains, after all. The problem is Martinez's actions are rough, and while he flashes above-average arm strength, his throws lack the kind of clothesline carry you want from third base, and they can be scattershot, generally. He's perhaps a better fit for the outfield but may not have the foot speed for center. His bat will play just about anywhere, but his defensive profile might end up testing that theory.

OFP: 55 / Middle-of-the-order hitter, position TBD

Variance: High. If Martinez can develop as a left-side infielder, we believe in the bat enough to cast him as a plus regular. There's the risk that he ends up in, like, left field, though, and he still has work to do with the stick when facing better off-speed pitches.

Mark Barry's Fantasy Take: Martinez's defensive home will carry a lot of his fantasy value. If he stays on the dirt, he'll be more than useful. If he shifts to the outfield, well, his numbers are a little easier to replicate. Still, although it feels like he has been around forever, Martinez is just 19 years old, so he'll have lots of time to refine his approach at the plate. He's a top-50 name, for sure, but I'd be apprehensive to push him much higher than that, personally.

4 Nate Pearson RHP OFP: 55 ETA: Debuted in 2020

Born: 08/20/96 Age: 25 Bats: R Throws: R Height: 6'6" Weight: 250 lb. Origin: Round 1, 2017 Draft (#28 overall)

YEAR	TEAM	LVL	AGE	W	L	SV	G	GS	IP	H	HR	BB/9	K/9	K	GB%	BABIP	WHIP	ERA	DRA-	WARP
2019	DUN	A+	22	3	0	0	6	6	21	10	2	1.3	15.0	35	35.1%	.229	0.62	0.86	68	0.6
2019	NH	AA	22	1	4	0	16	16	62²	41	4	3.0	9.9	69	38.8%	.250	0.99	2.59	86	0.9
2019	BUF	AAA	22	1	0	0	3	3	18	12	2	1.5	7.5	15	44.0%	.208	0.83	3.00	90	0.3
2020	TOR	MLB	23	1	0	0	5	4	18	14	5	6.5	8.0	16	38.5%	.191	1.50	6.00	124	0.0
2021	BUF	AAA	24	1	3	0	12	6	30²	21	4	3.8	12.9	44	36.8%	.266	1.11	4.40	91	0.6
2021	TOR	MLB	24	1	1	0	12	1	15	14	2	7.2	12.0	20	41.0%	.324	1.73	4.20	102	0.1
2022 DC	*TOR*	*MLB*	*25*	*7*	*6*	*0*	*30*	*19*	*99*	*84*	*15*	*4.6*	*11.1*	*122*	*49.2%*	*.292*	*1.36*	*4.19*	*98*	*0.7*

Comparables: Tyler Clippard, Jon Rauch, Lucas Sims

The Report: Pearson would be a good candidate for our "The Good/The Bad" format here. The good part is the same as it ever was: He flashes elite velocity and a 70 slider. His changeup and curveball will both at least flash above average on a median day. His command can profile well, when he's sharp. The bad parts are that the changeup, curveball and command are all inconsistent; in particular, Pearson has struggled to locate his fastball at his top velocities when starting. He also has a very long series of injuries dating back to high school and missed large chunks of the 2021 season with shoulder and groin issues. He underwent hernia surgery shortly before press time.

If you're thinking, "this sounds like a reliever," well, it kinda does, and that's largely what's driving his fall in our prospect rankings. Here's the thing, though: going back to short-burst showcase appearances in the 2018 Arizona Fall League and 2019 Futures Game, when he was one of the top starting-pitching prospects in the game, his stuff has always looked *best* in relief. He has been pretty consistently able to stay 98–101 out of the pen, touching as high as 104, and he's only consistently 95–99 as a starter. His slider is a more consistent plus-plus offering when he can just air it out, and relief work largely lets him ditch his inconsistent curve and change. His upside in the rotation—it's still two 7 pitches and some others that flash average—is so high that the Blue Jays have continued to let him develop as a starter, and we don't want to rule that out entirely, but he's 25 now. At some point, the temptation to just let him go once through the order and air it out might be too much.

OFP: 55 / First-division closer or some type of amorphous limited-innings role

Variance: High. We're still not entirely sure what role he's going to fit into on a staff, and there are both health and command risks.

Mark Barry's Fantasy Take: So, here's the thing. I'm out on Pearson as a starting pitcher. His fastball/slider combo can definitely be breathtaking more often than not, but his durability issues and bouts of spotty control over the course of multiple innings leave me cold on nabbing the righty as a starter. It's true that Pearson could be a dominant closer, but I don't really think that's the going rate for a former top-tier prospect. If you can score Pearson at closer prices, that's great. If not, well, see the second sentence.

5 Gunnar Hoglund RHP OFP: 55 ETA: 2024

Born: 12/17/99 Age: 22 Bats: L Throws: R Height: 6'4" Weight: 220 lb. Origin: Round 1, 2021 Draft (#19 overall)

The Report: On the cusp of being among the first 10 picks in last year's draft, mentioned not far behind the likes of Jack Leiter and Kumar Rocker, Hoglund had his stellar junior season cut by Tommy John surgery. The 6-foot-4 righty from Ole Miss has the ideal starter's build, a three-pitch mix with some of the best command in the class and is thought to have clean, repeatable mechanics. The injury definitely softened his stock, fairly or unfairly, and he was the perfect fit for the Jays, who were looking to add quality college arms that wouldn't take too long to join their young core in Toronto. Because of the timing of his surgery, Hoglund is unlikely to step into any meaningful game action until the second half of the 2022 season. However, don't be surprised—barring any setbacks or additional rust—if he becomes a quick mover in their system beginning in 2023.

OFP: 55 / Mid-rotation starter

Variance: Medium. While elbow injuries are always scary at face value, if we can assume he'll bounce back to normal form after rehab, we are talking about an excellent strike-thrower who was just scraping the surface of his potential before the blowout. Worst case scenario? He becomes a command/control type vital to any pitching staff.

Mark Barry's Fantasy Take: Hoglund was pretty interesting heading into the 2021 Mississippi State season. He's still interesting, but Tommy John surgery will keep him out until late 2022, at the earliest, so I don't think you need to rush out and plant your Hoglund flag in all but the deepest leagues.

6 Ricky Tiedemann LHP OFP: 50 ETA: Late 2023, more likely 2024

Born: 08/18/02 Age: 19 Bats: L Throws: L Height: 6'4" Weight: 220 lb. Origin: Round 3, 2021 Draft (#91 overall)

The Report: Instead of heading to college after not being selected in the shortened, five-round version of the 2020 draft, Tiedemann bet on himself and opted to go the JUCO route so he could be eligible in 2021. That foresight allowed him to add some strength, a few ticks in velocity and get plucked in the third round. He has some typical control issues which require polish, and which you can find on just about any physically advanced 19-year-old. Reports last fall indicated he had added another velo jump to his fastball, which is now sitting in the mid-to-upper 90s from his low-90s band as a prepster. If the same levels of physical development occur over the next two seasons, you could see him in the big leagues before he's legally allowed to consume alcohol (in the United States, at least).

OFP: 50 / Starter tools with maybe reliever control

Variance: High. The glimpses, especially after the draft, have been impressive when they've flashed. This could go a number of directions, including upwards from this modest OFP. As it is with most young hurlers: will he throw enough strikes?

Mark Barry's Fantasy Take: For now, Tiedemann is just a project. He's an intriguing project, no doubt, but he'll need some time to refine his command before he needs to be on your radar.

7 Kevin Smith 3B OFP: 50 ETA: Debuted in 2021

Born: 07/04/96 Age: 26 Bats: R Throws: R Height: 6'0" Weight: 190 lb. Origin: Round 4, 2017 Draft (#129 overall)

YEAR	TEAM	LVL	AGE	PA	R	2B	3B	HR	RBI	BB	K	SB	CS	AVG/OBP/SLG	DRC+	BABIP	BRR	FRAA	WARP
2019	SCO	WIN	22	67	3	2	1	0	0	3	38	1	0	.095/.149/.159		.240			
2019	NH	AA	22	468	49	22	2	19	61	29	151	11	6	.209/.263/.402	89	.269	1.7	SS(87) 0.7, 3B(18) -1.4, 2B(5) -0.8	1.0
2021	BUF	AAA	24	410	65	27	4	21	69	46	97	18	3	.285/.370/.561	130	.333	0.6	SS(66) 6.3, 3B(17) 2.1, LF(4) 0.2	3.5
2021	TOR	MLB	24	36	2	0	0	1	1	3	11	0	0	.094/.194/.188	87	.100	0.5	3B(14) -0.5, 1B(1) -0.0, LF(1) -0.2	0.0
2022 DC	*TOR*	*MLB*	*25*	*284*	*40*	*13*	*1*	*12*	*42*	*22*	*77*	*6*	*3*	*.238/.305/.447*	*99*	*.291*	*0.5*	*3B 0, 2B -1*	*0.9*

Comparables: Erik González, Chris Nelson, Pat Valaika

The Report: Smith has had a roller-coaster ride as a prospect. After a breakout 2018 that saw him as a fringe 101 candidate, a bad swing change tanked his contact rate in 2019. There were positive indications on his new new (new old?) swing from the 2020 alternate site, and 2021 looked more like 2018 in output. Smith's current stroke is still geared for power, pretty steep and sometimes a bit long, but he taps into his strength well without being too stiff. His bat speed is on the fringe side, though, and he can be late on better velocity. It's power-over-hit, but the power is playing.

Smith played five different positions in 2021, and while he was still primarily penciled in at shortstop, his arm is a little light for the left side, lacking the kind of zip you'd want, even when he is set and able to rear back. His hands and actions are fine for the infield, otherwise, and his value is going to be in his positional flexibility, anyway.

OFP: 50 / Four- or five-day-a-week starter playing here and there

Variance: Low. There is still some risk that Smith just strikes out a bit too much against major-league stuff to be really viable, but his speed, pop and versatility should make him a useful player at the end of the bench, even if he doesn't hit a ton.

Mark Barry's Fantasy Take: Don't make too much of small samples. Don't make too much of small samples. Don't make too much of small samples. Look, I know that it was only 36 trips to the plate, but Smith looked pretty overmatched in his first taste, mustering just three hits against 11 strikeouts. His power might play, but he also might not hit, so his positional flexibility would only be helpful in all-in onlies. Still, you're going to want Smith on the watchlist in case he becomes a Quad-A success story.

8 Samad Taylor UT OFP: 50 ETA: Late 2022/Early 2023

Born: 07/11/98 Age: 23 Bats: R Throws: R Height: 5'10" Weight: 160 lb. Origin: Round 10, 2016 Draft (#302 overall)

YEAR	TEAM	LVL	AGE	PA	R	2B	3B	HR	RBI	BB	K	SB	CS	AVG/OBP/SLG	DRC+	BABIP	BRR	FRAA	WARP
2019	DUN	A+	20	384	48	20	3	7	38	49	107	26	10	.216/.325/.364	99	.292	2.7	2B(91) -2.2, 3B(13) -0.1, SS(4) 0.4	1.2
2020	CAN	WIN	21	105	11	5	0	2	15	12	21	3	0	.244/.333/.367		.290			
2021	NH	AA	22	374	69	17	1	16	52	42	110	30	8	.294/.385/.503	116	.394	2.4	2B(34) -1.8, LF(22) -1.4, 3B(14) -0.4	1.7
2022 non-DC	*TOR*	*MLB*	*23*	*251*	*24*	*10*	*1*	*6*	*25*	*23*	*79*	*12*	*5*	*.209/.293/.354*	*75*	*.293*	*1.3*	*2B -2, 3B 0*	*0.0*

Comparables: Enrique Hernández, Odúbel Herrera, Jorge Polanco

The Report: Taylor nearly doubled his career minor-league home-run total in 2021, and it wasn't too hard to suss out why. He has a big leg kick now (with a bit off a pause/hang) before whipping the barrel through the zone with the intent to lift. It's impressive pop for his size, and, while his swing does create holes, Taylor has very strong wrists to allow that pop to play line-to-line. The trade off for that kind of hard contact is swing-and-miss. He sacrifices balance and bat control for the bat speed and launch angle, and while he tracks offspeed all right, the nature of his approach means he has to commit early. The median projection here is something like .240–.250 with 15–20 home runs.

Taylor is a plus runner, aggressive on the base paths and capable of holding down multiple spots on the dirt or grass. His best pure fit is second base, where he is potentially plus, but his value is going to come from moving around and providing some speed and pop, as long as he can make enough contact. That last is yet to be determined.

OFP: 50 / Super-utility with pop

Variance: High. His hit tool is going to be the determinant here, and it's a high-variance hit tool given the hang/stomp/lift (and corresponding Double-A K rate).

Mark Barry's Fantasy Take: I'm getting strong, strong Rougned Odor vibes from Taylor's reports. That's not the worst thing in the world, as Odor had several highly productive fantasy seasons. On the other hand, he also flirted with the Mendoza Line more than he didn't, which can be awfully infuriating for fantasy managers. Taylor might be a top-200 guy right now, and, if not, he's pretty close.

9 Irv Carter RHP OFP: 50 ETA: 2025

Born: 10/09/02 Age: 19 Bats: R Throws: R Height: 6'4" Weight: 210 lb. Origin: Round 5, 2021 Draft (#152 overall)

The Report: They don't come much more physically mature out of high school than the Jays' fifth-rounder out of south Florida. The 6-foot-4, 210-pound righty was a teammate of Phillies first-round pick Andrew Painter; they would often piggyback starts to shut down teams. His extra-high leg kick helps propel his stout lower half forward down the mound, where he consistently lives in the mid-90s with life. A bulldog of a competitor, he has excellent mound presence, and you can tell he loves challenging hitters. His secondary pitches are a bit behind the rest of his profile, perhaps due to all the moving parts of his delivery. A refinement and simplification could be just the thing he needs to regain his status as a future starter.

OFP: 50 / Back-end starter, possible middle-innings reliever

Variance: Extreme. The track record for high schoolers with inconsistent deliveries who make willful changes mid-at-bat to "throw off the batter's timing" is that they tend to do more harm than good during early development.

Mark Barry's Fantasy Take: Prep righties, amirite? There are things to like with Carter's profile, but he's pretty far away. I don't really know if his ceiling, as currently constructed, is fantasy relevant.

10 Otto Lopez UT OFP: 50 ETA: Debuted in 2021

Born: 10/01/98 Age: 23 Bats: R Throws: R Height: 5'10" Weight: 160 lb. Origin: International Free Agent, 2016

YEAR	TEAM	LVL	AGE	PA	R	2B	3B	HR	RBI	BB	K	SB	CS	AVG/OBP/SLG	DRC+	BABIP	BRR	FRAA	WARP
2019	LAN	A	20	492	61	20	5	5	50	34	63	20	15	.324/.371/.425	124	.365	-1.0	SS(82) -3.1, 2B(19) 3.3, LF(11) -0.3	2.8
2020	ESC	WIN	21	66	6	4	0	0	2	6	10	3	1	.254/.333/.322		.306			
2021	GIG	WIN	22	69	9	2	0	1	4	4	12	1	0	.231/.275/.308		.269			
2021	NH	AA	22	314	52	24	1	3	39	28	62	7	3	.331/.398/.457	109	.412	0.4	2B(43) -3.4, CF(17) 4.0, LF(3) 2.6	1.8
2021	BUF	AAA	22	194	36	8	3	2	25	13	26	15	1	.289/.347/.405	101	.324	3.3	2B(15) -0.3, LF(15) 3.0, SS(10) -0.5	1.1
2021	TOR	MLB	22	1	0	0	0	0	0	0	1	0	0	.000/.000/.000	87				0.0
2022 DC	*TOR*	*MLB*	*23*	*266*	*32*	*12*	*1*	*2*	*28*	*17*	*51*	*7*	*4*	*.265/.318/.360*	*87*	*.324*	*0.5*	*2B 0, SS 0*	*0.7*

Comparables: Jose Altuve, Eugenio Suárez, César Hernández

The Report: Another in the Blue Jays' long line of "not ideal shortstop" prospects, Lopez arguably has the most advanced hit tool of the group. His swing is geared for contact and is quite level and lacking oomph, but he moves the bat around well, stays on top of the high fastball and hits the ball where it's pitched. He's a high-end plus runner with enough foot speed for center field, and while he's not a true shortstop, he has a left-side-quality arm. His over-the-fence power is going to stay in the single digits, so that makes it difficult to rubber-stamp a clear starting role, but Lopez could play any of six positions and allow you to flex your lineup a bit while being a spark plug in the bottom third of the order.

OFP: 50 / The hit-over-power version of this super-utility profile

Variance: Low. Lopez will hit enough, run enough and keep enough gloves in his locker to help your major-league club. He is in some ways a little more useful than Smith or Taylor but also lacks their upside since he has not shown much in the way of game power.

Mark Barry's Fantasy Take: Despite having next to no power, Lopez might be the best fantasy candidate of the Smith, Taylor and Lopez Positional-Flexibility Triangle. I have more confidence in Lopez's ability to get the bat to the ball, and while he doesn't hit a lot of homers, he was very efficient on the bases, snagging 15 bags in 16 tries over 43 Triple-A games. Lopez could be a high-average/high-steal fantasy weapon, and while you'd like to see a few dingers, they're not completely necessary for Lopez's fantasy success.

The Prospects You Meet Outside the Top Ten

Prospects on the Rise

Sebastian Espino LF Born: 05/29/00 Age: 22 Bats: R Throws: R Height: 6'2" Weight: 176 lb. Origin: International Free Agent, 2016

YEAR	TEAM	LVL	AGE	PA	R	2B	3B	HR	RBI	BB	K	SB	CS	AVG/OBP/SLG	DRC+	BABIP	BRR	FRAA	WARP
2019	KNG	ROA	19	202	26	7	1	2	12	12	61	3	2	.251/.303/.332		.363			
2021	VAN	A+	21	259	38	15	5	8	47	23	71	2	4	.295/.358/.511	103	.386	0.1	LF(33) -2.7, 3B(18) -1.8	0.5
2022 non-DC	*TOR*	*MLB*	*22*	*251*	*21*	*10*	*2*	*4*	*23*	*16*	*86*	*2*	*3*	*.223/.280/.342*	*67*	*.338*	*0.4*	*LF 1, 3B 0*	*-0.2*

Plucked from the Mets' system in the minor-league Rule 5 draft and having never played above the Appy League, Espino's 2021 performance at High-A Vancouver was pretty impressive. No longer a slick-fielding shortstop, he's playing a lot of left field these days, but he has added some power with room to add more. His swing decisions need work, but his bat might be good enough to carve out a role as a regular given his positional flexibility—a recurring theme at this point—but it could all come undone in Double-A, too.

Leo Jimenez MI Born: 05/17/01 Age: 21 Bats: R Throws: R Height: 5'11" Weight: 160 lb. Origin: International Free Agent, 2017

YEAR	TEAM	LVL	AGE	PA	R	2B	3B	HR	RBI	BB	K	SB	CS	AVG/OBP/SLG	DRC+	BABIP	BRR	FRAA	WARP
2019	BLU	ROA	18	245	34	13	2	0	22	21	42	2	1	.298/.377/.377		.368			
2021	DUN	A	20	242	35	8	0	1	19	51	35	4	1	.315/.517/.381	145	.388	-0.7	SS(37) -4.4, 2B(12) 0.6	1.6
2022 non-DC	*TOR*	*MLB*	*21*	*251*	*23*	*9*	*0*	*1*	*19*	*31*	*53*	*0*	*1*	*.217/.343/.300*	*85*	*.282*	*-0.2*	*SS -2, 2B 0*	*0.2*

Comparables: Luis Rengifo, Luis Urías, Hernán Pérez

There is little doubt about Jimenez's defensive ability, it is among the best in the organization. He shows plus instincts, hands, range and above-average arm strength. His overall smoothness in the field stands out watching him play. Offensively, he is adept at controlling the zone and has plus bat-to-ball ability. In other words, he's a tough out. You'll have to dream on the power, it is 3 raw currently with virtually no in-game utility and concern about how much exit velocity he can generate on the balls he does put in play. Jimenez was added to the 40-man roster in November on the strength of his glove, his youth, and his overall body projection. At his peak, he could be a plus glove at shortstop with strong on-base skills to buoy the offensive profile.

Kendry Rojas LHP Born: 11/26/02 Age: 19 Bats: L Throws: L Height: 6'2" Weight: 190 lb. Origin: International Free Agent, 2020

YEAR	TEAM	LVL	AGE	W	L	SV	G	GS	IP	H	HR	BB/9	K/9	K	GB%	BABIP	WHIP	ERA	DRA-	WARP
2021	BLU	ROK	18	0	0	0	8	4	23^2	14	1	1.9	14.8	39	44.2%	.310	0.80	2.28		

Signed out of Cuba in 2020, Rojas was the best arm for the Blue Jays in the complex level last year. A projectable 6-foot-4, he shows present pitchability with his 89–91-mph fastball that features good ride and strong control. The slider is his go-to pitch, with late sharpness that he can spin with consistency and for strikes or chase, in and out of the zone. He did not feature a changeup, which can limit his overall upside and projection, but an 18-year-old lefty with his present stuff is well worth keeping eyes on.

Factors on the Farm

Hagen Danner C Born: 09/30/98 Age: 23 Bats: R Throws: R Height: 6'2" Weight: 210 lb. Origin: Round 2, 2017 Draft (#61 overall)

YEAR	TEAM	LVL	AGE	W	L	SV	G	GS	IP	H	HR	BB/9	K/9	K	GB%	BABIP	WHIP	ERA	DRA-	WARP
2021	VAN	A+	22	2	1	3	25	0	35^2	21	2	3.0	10.6	42	35.4%	.232	0.93	2.02	92	0.4

As an amateur, Danner had potential on the mound and at the plate. Toronto let him develop as a catcher after selecting him in the second round in 2017. Well, hitting is hard, and hitting as a catcher is even more difficult, so he went back to the bump in 2021 and pitched well, gradually improving as the season progressed. He really got on radars during fall instructs, touching 100 and showing a hard 90–92 slider that was getting empty swings. With only 35 career minor-league innings, Danner needs added reps and experience, but with how electric he was last fall, the Jays had no choice but to add him to the major league 40-man roster in November.

Adrian Hernandez RHP Born: 01/22/00 Age: 22 Bats: R Throws: R Height: 5'10" Weight: 168 lb. Origin: International Free Agent, 2017

YEAR	TEAM	LVL	AGE	W	L	SV	G	GS	IP	H	HR	BB/9	K/9	K	GB%	BABIP	WHIP	ERA	DRA-	WARP
2019	BLU	ROK	19	3	2	1	16	0	21^1	28	1	3.4	6.3	15	29.3%	.370	1.69	8.02		
2020	MOC	WIN	20	1	0	0	20	0	25^2	14	0	7.0	11.9	34	39.2%	.275	1.32	2.45		
2021	DUN	A	21	0	1	3	9	1	18	13	1	7.5	18.5	37	50.0%	.414	1.56	4.50	79	0.4
2021	VAN	A+	21	3	1	0	12	0	28^2	12	2	2.5	13.8	44	28.3%	.196	0.70	1.88	84	0.5
2021	NH	AA	21	0	0	4	10	1	15^2	5	2	3.4	15.5	27	44.0%	.130	0.70	2.30	76	0.3
2022 non-DC	*TOR*	*MLB*	*22*	*2*	*2*	*0*	*57*	*0*	*50*	*40*	*7*	*5.2*	*12.2*	*68*	*50.8%*	*.296*	*1.40*	*4.47*	*104*	*0.1*

Hernandez torched three levels in 2021, putting up video-game K rates on the back of a plus changeup which can look almost like a breaking ball at times. He manipulates the pitch well, and it has more than 10 mph of separation off his average fastball. Hernandez is a bit of a trick-pitch guy, but he can run the heater up to 95, and the change is a hell of a trick. That's not a traditional late-inning profile, and he doesn't have the longest track record of throwing strikes, but he could be a useful bullpen piece as soon as this season.

Yosver Zulueta RHP Born: 01/23/98 Age: 24 Bats: R Throws: R Height: 6'1" Weight: 190 lb. Origin: International Free Agent, 2019

YEAR	TEAM	LVL	AGE	W	L	SV	G	GS	IP	H	HR	BB/9	K/9	K	GB%	BABIP	WHIP	ERA	DRA-	WARP
2022 non-DC	*TOR*	*MLB*	*24*	*2*	*3*	*0*	*57*	*0*	*50*	*52*	*7*	*4.8*	*7.7*	*42*	*45.9%*	*.302*	*1.57*	*5.48*	*125*	*-0.5*

During spring training last season, we started hearing industry murmurs that Zulueta—who had Tommy John surgery shortly after signing out of Cuba in 2019 and had not yet pitched professionally—was suddenly sitting high 90s with a wipeout breaking ball on the backfields of Florida. They were the sort of hushed tones which often precede a huge prospect breakout; we heard the same kind of spring buzz with Elly de la Cruz in the Reds' system, for example, and he's now a name everyone knows. The Zulueta secret got out a bit when he made a cameo on the major-league side and, well, he was indeed up to the high 90s with a wipeout breaker (it would've gotten out more if the game was televised or had Statcast data). He was one of our top follows entering the minor-league season, but he proceeded to blow out his knee on a fielding play on literally the first batter he faced in Low-A and missed the entire rest of the year. We thus have very little hard data to go on, but pay close attention early in 2022, because he has a *very* live arm.

Top Talents 25 and Under (as of 4/1/2021):

1. Vladimir Guerrero Jr., 1B
2. Bo Bichette, SS
3. Gabriel Moreno, C
4. Jordan Groshans, SS
5. Orelvis Martinez, SS/3B
6. Alek Manoah, RHP
7. Nate Pearson, RHP
8. Gunnar Hoglund, RHP
9. Ricky Tiedemann, LHP
10. Alejandro Kirk, C

Having modeled the MLB snowbird plan so well that, apparently against all attachment to reality, a division rival wants to emulate it, Toronto must confront an offseason in which near the best they could do is hope for a repeat of last winter. Marcus Semien, Robbie Ray and Steven Matz may be gone, but the best news for Toronto is old news, which is young news. Vladito turns 23 in March, while Bichette will be just 24. Ben Carsley wrote in August that Toronto was primed to be MLB's next juggernaut, and those two are at the core of it, combining for 10.4 WARP in 2021. No other team can boast two superstars of their youth and eminence; Guerrero and Bichette are younger than Adley Rutschman, yet they combined for the most WARP of any two position player teammates in MLB in 2021, save for Guerrero and Semien.

On those sturdy rocks, Toronto must build higher to eclipse the AL East's peculiar Cerberus of New York, Tampa Bay and Boston. Manoah was a pleasant surprise after reports that his stuff had backed up, making up, in part, for Pearson's odyssey of a season. This is a system notably thin on upper-minors pitching depth, making Manoah's 93 DRA– in 111 ⅔ innings particularly useful, particularly if that sort of competence can track forward for 30 starts this year. Toronto's lineup should again be one of the league's best, all they need from their pitching staff is a chance.

Kirk should help that lineup shine, though he might not be the best aide to an uneven pitching staff behind the plate. Much the same contact monster he has always been, Kirk ran a 125 DRC+ with plenty of quality contact and double-digit walk rates last year despite batted-ball luck that lagged behind. His excellent work at the plate was particularly impressive given that his season suffered a near-three-month layoff due to a flexor strain in his non-throwing arm. The Blue Jays traded away one bat-first backstop in Riley Adams and, yet, still have Kirk and Moreno likely to be big-league ready in 2022, as well as Danny Jansen and Reese McGuire. Someone else is getting bumped off the ice floe.

Washington Nationals

The State of the System:

The Nationals' system is no longer the worst in baseball. All it cost them was Trea Turner and Max Scherzer (okay, the Cade Cavalli breakout helped, too).

The Top Ten:

1 Cade Cavalli RHP OFP: 70 ETA: 2022

Born: 08/14/98 Age: 23 Bats: R Throws: R Height: 6'4" Weight: 230 lb. Origin: Round 1, 2020 Draft (#22 overall)

YEAR	TEAM	LVL	AGE	W	L	SV	G	GS	IP	H	HR	BB/9	K/9	K	GB%	BABIP	WHIP	ERA	DRA-	WARP
2021	WIL	A+	22	3	1	0	7	7	40^2	24	1	2.7	15.7	71	49.3%	.329	0.89	1.77	63	1.2
2021	HBG	AA	22	3	3	0	11	11	58	39	2	5.4	12.4	80	38.3%	.296	1.28	2.79	80	1.1
2021	ROC	AAA	22	1	5	0	6	6	24^2	33	2	4.7	8.8	24	52.5%	.397	1.86	7.30	109	0.2
2022 non-DC	*WAS*	*MLB*	*23*	*2*	*2*	*0*	*57*	*0*	*50*	*45*	*6*	*4.9*	*10.1*	*56*	*44.9%*	*.302*	*1.45*	*4.59*	*104*	*0.1*

Comparables: Clay Buchholz, John Gant, Jason Hammel

The Report: After his first two seasons in college were heavily weighed down by command and injury issues, Cavalli started trending up for the Collegiate National Team the summer before his draft year. He carried that into four starts in the heavily-truncated 2020 NCAA season and was one of the most intriguing arms in that year's draft. The always risk-tolerant Nationals took the chance, and, so far, it's paying off huge; Cavalli quickly shot through the minors in his pro debut, disposing of High-A and Double-A with relative ease and finishing his first season at Triple-A.

Cavalli is one of the hardest-throwing starting pitchers in the minors, capable of holding mid- to high-90s velocity and regularly touching triple digits. It's lively heat he can blow past hitters up in the zone, and he commands the pitch better than you'd think given his past walk rates. He has two distinct breaking pitches, a slider and a curve, which dot the 80s, and both project to plus. His changeup is improving with increased reps and should end up average or better. While he does not have a long history of throwing consistent strikes, he did show vastly improved command this year. If one of the breaking pitches can step forward as a true out-pitch, and he holds these gains, the sky's the limit.

OFP: 70 / No. 2 starter

Variance: High. We switched this section from "Risk" to "Variance" in part because of prospects like Cavalli, who, if things continue coming together, could even exceed these expectations. If the command keeps coming together and he stays healthy, Cavalli is one of the few pitchers in the minors who could conceivably be an ace.

Darius Austin's Fantasy Take: Cavalli is a top-10 fantasy pitching prospect on the back of this rapid rise, and you can make the case for top five. He has high-strikeout upside, and we should get a look at him in the big leagues this season. His WHIP could be a little dicey early on if he's still battling command issues, but when you see front-line-starter upside and elite -reliever fallback, you should probably stop worrying about TINSTAAP and start focusing on the potential.

2 Keibert Ruiz C   OFP: 60   ETA: Debuted in 2020

Born: 07/20/98   Age: 23   Bats: S   Throws: R   Height: 6'0"   Weight: 225 lb.   Origin: International Free Agent, 2015

YEAR	TEAM	LVL	AGE	PA	R	2B	3B	HR	RBI	BB	K	SB	CS	AVG/OBP/SLG	DRC+	BABIP	BRR	FRAA	WARP
2019	TUL	AA	20	310	33	9	0	4	25	28	21	0	0	.254/.329/.330	127	.261	-4.0	C(61) 4.5	2.2
2019	OKC	AAA	20	40	6	0	0	2	9	2	1	0	0	.316/.350/.474	118	.286	0.6	C(9) -1.4	0.2
2020	LAD	MLB	21	8	1	0	0	1	1	0	3	0	0	.250/.250/.625	86	.250		C(2) 0.3	0.0
2021	ROC	AAA	22	85	11	6	0	5	14	7	6	0	0	.308/.365/.577	135	.284	-1.3	C(19) 0.5	0.6
2021	OKC	AAA	22	231	39	18	0	16	45	23	27	0	0	.311/.381/.631	140	.293	-1.0	C(44) 2.6	2.2
2021	WAS	MLB	22	89	9	3	0	2	14	6	4	0	0	.284/.348/.395	119	.280	-0.6	C(21) 0.5	0.6
2021	LAD	MLB	22	7	1	0	0	1	1	0	5	0	0	.143/.143/.571	83			C(2) 0.0	0.0
2022 DC	*WAS*	*MLB*	*23*	*344*	*44*	*14*	*0*	*10*	*51*	*25*	*37*	*0*	*0*	*.265/.328/.417*	*101*	*.273*	*-0.6*	*C 0*	*1.6*

Comparables: Christian Bethancourt, Ketel Marte, Freddie Freeman

The Report: This will be the fifth and final season we rank Ruiz in the Top 101. He goes out with a bang, quite literally, finally marrying his raw power with his plus bat-to-ball skills and slugging over .600 in Triple-A. Most of his power comes from the left side of the plate, where he has a more-pronounced leg kick and more pull and launch in his swing. From the right side, he looks to work more gap-to-gap, but Ruiz is an effective hitter, either way. His plus bat-to-ball ability showed up immediately with the Nats. Once he gets more comfortable attacking major-league pitching, we'd expect his game power to play in the 15–20-home-run range, but merely average bat speed might limit his ability to get to more than that. Defensively, Ruiz is an above-average receiver who throws well enough to keep the running game from being too much of an issue, although his arm strength is on the fringy side.

OFP: 60 / First-division catcher

Variance: Low. Ruiz doesn't have a particularly long track record of being this good a hitter (and it's not like we think he's going to slug .600 going forward), and he has had issues with an overaggressive approach in the past, so there's some risk that a book will get out on him in the majors.

Darius Austin's Fantasy Take: Ruiz's fantasy value has taken a tumultuous journey similar to his real-life development process. In addition to his uneven performance over the years, the playing time obstacle of Dodgers catcher Will Smith factored heavily into depressing his stock as he approached the bigs. Now that he's in Washington, Ruiz looks like he'll get the playing time while being one of the safer batting-average options at the position, purely based on how good his strikeout rate is. He remains a cut below the premium names unless he can show more game power in the bigs; insert your own caveat about young dynasty catchers here.

3 Brady House SS   OFP: 60   ETA: 2024

Born: 06/04/03   Age: 19   Bats: R   Throws: R   Height: 6'4"   Weight: 215 lb.   Origin: Round 1, 2021 Draft (#11 overall)

YEAR	TEAM	LVL	AGE	PA	R	2B	3B	HR	RBI	BB	K	SB	CS	AVG/OBP/SLG	DRC+	BABIP	BRR	FRAA	WARP
2021	NAT	ROK	18	66	14	3	0	4	12	7	13	0	0	.322/.394/.576		.357			

Comparables: Pedro Guerrero, Daniel Bravo, Yairo Muñoz

The Report: During the year-plus between the 2020 and 2021 MLB drafts, House's draft stock was tumultuous. He was lauded as an underclassmen, but the summer before his senior year was—shall we say—underwhelming. His loud tools, originally showcased on both the mound and in the field, looked sluggish. His power-hitting swing was reduced to a stiff operation, as if his feet were stuck in freshly poured concrete. A refreshing winter off must have done wonders, because, by the time spring rolled around, he was back to being the player that had previously been mentioned as a high-first-round pick.

There was more fluidity in his setup inside the box, and House found rhythm and tempo against quality pitching while exploding through the ball. His actions in the field seemed much more dynamic, too, bringing back the question of whether he can stick at shortstop long-term or might grow into a third baseman (having abandoned pitching, altogether). He carried his strong pre-draft performance to the Florida Complex League, where he mashed like you'd want a player of his ilk to mash./p>

OFP: 60 / Plus regular, occasional All-Star

Variance: Medium. All the markers are there for House to perhaps be a significant player with tools on both sides of the ball and the athleticism to handle whatever is thrown his direction.

Darius Austin's Fantasy Take: Although House isn't going to crack the top three when it comes to first-year-player-draft shortstops, his monster raw power and athleticism likely make him the next-best thing. The development of his hit tool will determine whether he contributes in three or four categories, and there's a long way to go before we find out how that plays against advanced pitching, or whether physical development limits his fluidity. He's an easy top-101 fantasy prospect, regardless.

4 Jackson Rutledge RHP

OFP: 55 ETA: Somewhere between 2023 and 2025

Born: 04/01/99 Age: 23 Bats: R Throws: R Height: 6'8" Weight: 245 lb. Origin: Round 1, 2019 Draft (#17 overall)

YEAR	TEAM	LVL	AGE	W	L	SV	G	GS	IP	H	HR	BB/9	K/9	K	GB%	BABIP	WHIP	ERA	DRA-	WARP
2019	NAT	ROK	20	0	0	0	1	1	1	4	0	9.0	18.0	2	80.0%	.800	5.00	27.00		
2019	AUB	SS	20	0	0	0	3	3	9	4	2	3.0	6.0	6	41.7%	.091	0.78	3.00		
2019	HAG	A	20	2	0	0	6	6	27^{1}	14	0	3.6	10.2	31	44.4%	.222	0.91	2.30	95	0.3
2021	FBG	A	22	1	2	0	7	7	22	20	1	3.7	10.6	26	49.2%	.317	1.32	5.32	84	0.4
2021	WIL	A+	22	0	3	0	4	4	10^{2}	17	0	7.6	8.4	10	39.5%	.447	2.44	12.66	107	0.0
2022 non-DC	*WAS*	*MLB*	*23*	*2*	*3*	*0*	*57*	*0*	*50*	*56*	*7*	*5.7*	*7.6*	*42*	*43.1%*	*.319*	*1.75*	*6.46*	*139*	*-0.8*

Comparables: Raúl Alcántara, Elieser Hernandez, Jo-Jo Reyes

The Report: Rutledge has yet to really get going since his first-round selection in 2019. He got alternate site time in 2020, but a rotator cuff strain in 2021 limited him to 26 mostly ineffective innings. When he was on the mound, his stuff looked like that of a former first-round pick. His upper-90s fastball still pops the mitt, although it's not in the zone as often as you'd like. Rutledge backs up the sharp cheddar with two breaking balls. His slider has the clearer plus projection, it's a power breaker with 11–5 tilt, but his curve has made some progress. The hook has more depth but can get slurvy and bleed into the slider when it's on the firmer side. Rutledge's change needs the most work, at present. He slows his arm on it but still manages to fire it up there in the low 90s, creating suboptimal separation off the heater.

That arsenal certainly has promise, but his main issue remains control and command. Rutledge is a massive human, and, despite his simple delivery, his combination of a short arm action and a weirdly easy tempo tends to create timing issues and commensurate wildness. The upside here remains as high as Cavalli's, but Rutledge is only a few months younger, and his durability and command issues create far more reliever risk.

OFP: 55 / No. 3 starter or late-inning reliever

Variance: Extreme. You want risk factors? We got risk factors. You have a shoulder injury. You have an as-of-yet-unclear third pitch. You have command-and-control issues. You have a soon-to-be-23-year-old who hasn't made it out of A-ball. You have top-of-the-rotation upside, but you also might just have an oft-injured middle reliever.

Darius Austin's Fantasy Take: I know I just told you to focus on the potential with Cavalli, but Rutledge's report reads a lot like Cavalli's with a bunch of red flags tossed in. I'd still prefer to take a shot on Rutledge's incredibly lofty ceiling rather than a reliable-but-uninspiring back-end hurler. However, given that he seems a lot less likely to reach that upside, and the floor is lower, feel free to just keep Rutledge on the watchlist until he's closer/healthier, unless at least 200-plus prospects are rostered in your league.

5 Cole Henry RHP

OFP: 50 ETA: 2024

Born: 07/15/99 Age: 22 Bats: R Throws: R Height: 6'4" Weight: 215 lb. Origin: Round 2, 2020 Draft (#55 overall)

YEAR	TEAM	LVL	AGE	W	L	SV	G	GS	IP	H	HR	BB/9	K/9	K	GB%	BABIP	WHIP	ERA	DRA-	WARP
2021	WIL	A+	21	3	3	0	9	8	43	23	3	2.3	13.2	63	46.4%	.247	0.79	1.88	74	1.0
2022 non-DC	*WAS*	*MLB*	*22*	*2*	*2*	*0*	*57*	*0*	*50*	*42*	*6*	*3.7*	*10.1*	*55*	*43.4%*	*.285*	*1.26*	*3.73*	*92*	*0.4*

Comparables: Johnny Cueto, Daniel Hudson, Justin Masterson

The Report: Henry got off to a hot start in his abbreviated 2020 season and might have gone even higher in the draft with an uninterrupted campaign. His 2021 was more of the same: dominating High-A in another truncated season, this time limited due to elbow soreness. He is developing a bit of a sketchy track record with his arm, but, when on the mound, he gave us little with which to quibble. Henry has an above-average fastball/curveball combo, pairing mid-90s heat with a low-80s 11–6 breaker with good depth. The hook is particularly potent against lefties, as he can work it backdoor or back-foot, and makes up for a well-below-average changeup, at present.

To move from likely reliever to mid-rotation starter, Henry needs to get a full season under his belt—he hasn't built up enough to consistently hold that mid-90s deep into starts—and improve his changeup, but the curveball should make him a useful arm in any role.

OFP: 50 / No. 4 starter or set-up reliever

Variance: High. We still don't really have a feel for what Henry is as a pitching prospect due to the arm injury. It was also not his first arm injury, so you get some extra health risk sprinkled in with the relief risk. He's also certainly capable of bumping up that OFP with a full, healthy campaign and more consistency with the fastball and change.

Darius Austin's Fantasy Take: I love the insane strikeout rate. I don't love the questionable third pitch and arm track record. I think you can make the case for Henry over Rutledge in fantasy, given the former's more-impressive performance on the field and obvious strikeout potential. I still want to see more consistency over longer outings before I draw much of a distinction between the two.

6 Daylen Lile DH

OFP: 50 ETA: 2025

Born: 11/30/02 Age: 19 Bats: L Throws: R Height: 6'0" Weight: 195 lb. Origin: Round 2, 2021 Draft (#47 overall)

YEAR	TEAM	LVL	AGE	PA	R	2B	3B	HR	RBI	BB	K	SB	CS	AVG/OBP/SLG	DRC+	BABIP	BRR	FRAA	WARP
2021	NAT	ROK	18	80	16	2	0	0	10	15	20	2	1	.219/.363/.250		.311			

Comparables: Kyle Orr, Jaquez Williams, Jonnathan Valdez

The Report: If you like aesthetically pleasing swings, you'll enjoy Lile's. The lefty-hitting, righty-throwing outfielder has a quick trigger that allows him to pull the ball with ferocity. With that high energy, it's impressive to see him stay balanced through contact without overswinging. He just needs to develop more of an all-fields approach. You'd expect someone that swings as hard as he does to strike out a lot, yet, during his tour of the complex league after the draft, he managed a .363 on-base percentage, albeit with limited offensive output. He'll need to get stronger to become a well-rounded hitter, since his other tools, like his speed and arm, aren't likely to get much better.

OFP: 50 / Bat-first corner outfielder

Variance: High. He'll need to hit. That's it. That's the tweet. And although he managed a decent strikeout-to-walk ratio, he'll need to make more contact and more hard contact to succeed long-term.

Darius Austin's Fantasy Take: Is there a world in which Lile is a boring, late-round stabilizer five or six years down the line? Sure. Is there a world in which I want to wait five or six years for Josh Harrison to be reincarnated? There is not. If Lile can transfer his high-effort swing into actual over-the-fence power and avoid it having an impact on his average, we might be talking. For now, he looks like empty average, and I'm not too sure about the average.

7 Gerardo Carrillo RHP

OFP: 50 ETA: Late 2022/Early 2023

Born: 09/13/98 Age: 23 Bats: R Throws: R Height: 5'10" Weight: 170 lb. Origin: International Free Agent, 2016

YEAR	TEAM	LVL	AGE	W	L	SV	G	GS	IP	H	HR	BB/9	K/9	K	GB%	BABIP	WHIP	ERA	DRA-	WARP
2019	RC	A+	20	5	9	0	23	21	86	87	3	5.3	9.0	86	54.2%	.339	1.60	5.44	125	-1.0
2021	TUL	AA	22	3	2	0	15	14	59^1	49	9	4.4	10.6	70	48.7%	.280	1.31	4.25	83	0.9
2021	HBG	AA	22	0	5	0	8	8	37	40	5	5.1	9.2	38	49.1%	.330	1.65	5.59	108	0.1
2022 DC	*WAS*	*MLB*	*23*	*2*	*2*	*0*	*17*	*3*	*25.7*	*25*	*3*	*5.2*	*7.9*	*22*	*38.4%*	*.298*	*1.57*	*5.24*	*118*	*-0.1*

Comparables: Aaron Sanchez, Blake Beavan, Jimmy Haynes

The Report: Obviously Ruiz and Josiah Gray were the top-line names in the Scherzer/Turner return, but Carrillo is a potentially meaningful major-league piece, as well. He filled out a bit more last year, but his velocity as a starter has settled in around 93 mph, although he can touch higher. The fastball has decent spin but more run than sink. Carillo's slider sits in the high 80s with good tilt, and, because it sits in the same velocity band as the change, it can be a tough read for lefties and is a swing-and-miss offering right-on-right. The change itself flashes some power sink and fade but is firm and can play too close to the fastball. A slurvy, if high spin, curveball rounds out the arsenal.

Carillo feels like he would have been a good fit for the Dodgers in a Victor González–type role as a once-through-the-lineup long man who could five-and-dive if need be or air it out for an inning late in games. The Nats tend to have more traditional pitcher roles, and Carillo's below-average command would limit him to more of a back-end rotation piece as a traditional starter.

OFP: 50 / No. 4 starter or good bulk guy

Variance: Medium. Carillo has a pretty advanced repertoire and at least missed bats at Double-A. However, unless his command improves, he's likely a reliever.

Darius Austin's Fantasy Take: Carrillo is likely to be more immediately fantasy-relevant than most here, in the sense that you may well see him providing major-league stats within the next year, and less fantasy-relevant for the same reason that he'll be contributing sooner: his command. His lack of improvement there puts him on a relief track that will hasten his arrival while limiting his fantasy ceiling to that of a high-strikeout bullpen arm who might get some holds.

8 Aldo Ramirez RHP OFP: 50 ETA: 2024

Born: 05/06/01 Age: 21 Bats: R Throws: R Height: 6'0" Weight: 191 lb. Origin: International Free Agent, 2018

YEAR	TEAM	LVL	AGE	W	L	SV	G	GS	IP	H	HR	BB/9	K/9	K	GB%	BABIP	WHIP	ERA	DRA-	WARP
2019	LOW	SS	18	2	3	0	14	13	61^2	59	5	2.3	9.2	63	47.8%	.309	1.22	3.94		
2021	NAT	ROK	20	1	1	0	4	2	7^2	9	0	4.7	3.5	3	51.9%	.333	1.70	8.22		
2021	SAL	A	20	1	1	0	8	8	31	27	1	2.3	9.3	32	54.4%	.292	1.13	2.03	90	0.4
2022 non-DC	*WAS*	*MLB*	*21*	*2*	*3*	*0*	*57*	*0*	*50*	*56*	*6*	*4.1*	*6.1*	*34*	*40.7%*	*.308*	*1.58*	*5.50*	*125*	*-0.5*

Comparables: Brandon League, Chris Tillman, José Ureña

The Report: Ramirez is yet another interesting arm the Nats added at last year's trade deadline. He could even be a couple of spots higher here if not for elbow tendinitis that limited him to just 38 innings in 2021. We've always liked his profile, even in the Penn League, when he sat just a tick or two over 90 mph and didn't have much of a changeup. Ramirez had some pitchability and feel for spin, and, if the stuff got better, he already had the tools on the mound to get a lot out of an improved arsenal. Well, the fastball is now sitting around 93 and touching higher, and there's some weight to the pitch that gets him groundballs. His change is a bit firm, still, but improving, with enough fade to keep lefties honest. And the curve is still pretty good. It doesn't always have true bat-missing shape or velocity, but he commands it well, and the best ones in the upper 70s flash plus. Ramirez is a short, stocky righty and mostly offers a collection of potentially average stuff, an easy and repeatable delivery and some feel to pitch, but, when and if he's healthy again, he might have the best chance of this tier of arms to be an actual once-every-fifth-day back-end starter.

OFP: 50 / No. 4 starter

Variance: High. He's an undersized righty with a elbow that was recently barking, limited pro innings and the need for secondary refinement. He also doesn't have the obvious relief fallback of Henry, Carillo or Joan Adon.

Darius Austin's Fantasy Take: If you're going to roster back-end starters, do it when they're close. I will confess to being mildly intrigued by the improvements Ramirez has made. Call me when he's sitting 95 and a couple of levels higher, and we'll talk.

9 Joan Adon RHP OFP: 50 ETA: Debuted in 2021

Born: 08/12/98 Age: 23 Bats: R Throws: R Height: 6'2" Weight: 242 lb. Origin: International Free Agent, 2016

YEAR	TEAM	LVL	AGE	W	L	SV	G	GS	IP	H	HR	BB/9	K/9	K	GB%	BABIP	WHIP	ERA	DRA-	WARP
2019	HAG	A	20	11	3	0	22	21	105	93	8	3.8	7.7	90	45.6%	.286	1.30	3.86	120	-0.2
2021	WIL	A+	22	6	4	0	17	17	87	77	7	3.3	9.4	91	46.1%	.299	1.25	4.97	87	1.3
2021	HBG	AA	22	1	2	0	3	3	14	15	1	3.2	15.4	24	37.1%	.412	1.43	6.43	79	0.3
2021	WAS	MLB	22	0	0	0	1	1	5^1	6	1	5.1	15.2	9	72.7%	.500	1.69	3.38		
2022 DC	*WAS*	*MLB*	*23*	*2*	*1*	*0*	*17*	*3*	*25.7*	*24*	*3*	*4.5*	*9.0*	*25*	*43.4%*	*.293*	*1.43*	*4.60*	*106*	*0.1*

Comparables: Michael Fulmer, Alex Cobb, Joe Ross

The Report: Adon was a bit of a surprise call-up for a game-162 start with playoff implications against the Red Sox, but his power stuff immediately played in the majors. His fastball sits 95 and touches higher with some two-seam action. He pairs it with a mid-80s slider with good depth. His change-up is better than your typical, high-effort, 95-and-a-slider arm, showing bat-missing split action when Adon gets on top of it. He just doesn't get on top of it enough to project him past a late-inning relief role. Even if the cambio were more consistent, his delivery suggests he's best off airing it out in the late innings, but it is late-inning stuff.

OFP: 50 / Set-up man

Variance: Medium. Perhaps another organization could get 100 good innings out of Adon in a bulk or once-through-a-lineup relief role. The Nats have tended to be fairly traditional with their pitching roles, and Adon might just be best off as an eighth-inning guy, anyway. He still has command-and-control risk, but Adon has generally thrown enough strikes that he should be a useful middle reliever, even if he ends up a bit too inconsistent for the higher-leverage spots.

Darius Austin's Fantasy Take: Adon's debut was fun. Not many pitchers can say they out-duelled Chris Sale in their first outing. Don't take anything else away from that one start. He might be a useful strikeouts-and-holds guy at some point down the line, and that's the point at which he should be rostered, not a moment sooner. If the Rays trade for him, then, naturally, he'll be the bulk guy you're always picking up for cheap wins.

10 **Andry Lara** **RHP** OFP: 50 ETA: 2025 perhaps

Born: 01/06/03 Age: 19 Bats: R Throws: R Height: 6'4" Weight: 180 lb. Origin: International Free Agent, 2019

YEAR	TEAM	LVL	AGE	W	L	SV	G	GS	IP	H	HR	BB/9	K/9	K	GB%	BABIP	WHIP	ERA	DRA-	WARP
2021	NAT	ROK	18	3	2	0	9	7	39^{2}	35	5	2.9	10.7	47	46.7%	.300	1.21	4.54		
2021	FBG	A	18	0	1	0	2	2	8^{2}	6	2	8.3	5.2	5	20.0%	.174	1.62	5.19	162	-0.2
2022 non-DC	*WAS*	*MLB*	*19*	*2*	*3*	*0*	*57*	*0*	*50*	*63*	*10*	*8.0*	*6.3*	*35*	*45.7%*	*.323*	*2.15*	*9.02*	*174*	*-1.8*

Comparables: Brailin Rodriguez, Rainiery Rodriguez, Edgar Sanchez

The Report: Lara was a buzzy name in the Nationals' complex last year and finally made his pro debut in 2021 with uneven results. He's a projectable 6-foot-4 and already sits around 93—for a few innings, at least. His fastball command is crude, and he can have issues repeating his arm stroke and, generally, could use a more streamlined delivery that uses his lower half more. The average fastball is mostly pure arm strength, at present. Lara's low-80s curve is advanced for an 18-year-old, showing good 11–6 action at its best. It can also show slower and humpier, or firmer, but also slurvier with more glove-side run. If he can more consistently show the Goldilocks-approved hook, he might end up with an above-average breaker. He theoretically has a changeup, as well, but it's a long way from utility. Though he has now had some pro reps, we don't know that we know that much more about Lara then we did in the black box of 2020. That doesn't mean his stock is down, we just know what we don't know.

OFP: 50 / No. 4 starter

Variance: Extreme. Lara really could use another league, a short-season-type level with more hands-on development work, but we expect that, given the shape of the minors and the Nats' generally aggressive assignments, he will have to play catch-up in full-season this year. He retains breakout potential, of course, but the long-term starter profile is mostly theoretical, at the moment.

Darius Austin's Fantasy Take: Ooooh, mystery prospect! Not knowing much more about Lara than we did after a totally lost season feels about right for this archetype. You know the one: teenager you've never heard of suddenly snapped up in all your deep dynasties, held on rosters for three years while everyone waits for them to get pro experience, cast aside when they realize it's going to take three or four more seasons before we know whether they'll be anything at all. Every now and then, one of these guys suddenly explodes in pro ball and you've got something—even if it's just an overhyped trade chip. It's usually not worth using the roster spot to take that gamble.

The Prospects You Meet Outside the Top Ten

Prospects on the Rise

Yasel Antuna **SS** Born: 10/26/99 Age: 22 Bats: S Throws: R Height: 6'0" Weight: 195 lb. Origin: International Free Agent, 2016

YEAR	TEAM	LVL	AGE	PA	R	2B	3B	HR	RBI	BB	K	SB	CS	AVG/OBP/SLG	DRC+	BABIP	BRR	FRAA	WARP
2021	WIL	A+	21	457	55	26	1	12	65	46	100	4	4	.227/.307/.385	100	.270	-2.5	SS(96) -16.1	-0.4
2022 non-DC	*WAS*	*MLB*	*22*	*251*	*21*	*11*	*0*	*4*	*23*	*18*	*64*	*2*	*3*	*.215/.279/.331*	*63*	*.279*	*0.1*	*SS -6*	*-0.9*

Comparables: Eduardo Escobar, Danny Santana, Eugenio Suárez

The "Prospects on the Rise" section is generally used to mark players we think will be top-10 prospects at some point. Antuna has already made Nats top-10 lists. Generally, the names here will have had good seasons. Antuna really didn't. Now, given the shape of the Washington organization, he might make a top 10 again, so allow us to try to paint a picture of how. The switch-hitting infielder has plus bat speed and can lift the ball from the left side. Unfortunately, he tries to do that a little too much, and his maxing-out-at-Topgolf stroke means he will often pull off against slower stuff. From the right side, he's a little more level with a little less stomp and lift, but an overaggressive approach hurts him even there. There's enough latent power here to keep an eye on, and, while he's a little rough at shortstop, he can make most of the "Likely"-bucket plays. His arm strength and throwing issues mean he's a better fit for second.

Ricardo Méndez CF Born: 01/24/00 Age: 22 Bats: L Throws: L Height: 5'10" Weight: 185 lb. Origin: International Free Agent, 2016

YEAR	TEAM	LVL	AGE	PA	R	2B	3B	HR	RBI	BB	K	SB	CS	AVG/OBP/SLG	DRC+	BABIP	BRR	FRAA	WARP
2019	AUB	SS	19	149	21	4	0	1	8	16	25	5	8	.264/.349/.318		.314			
2019	HAG	A	19	81	11	1	1	0	5	8	20	5	0	.194/.284/.236	94	.269	1.2	LF(19) -1.9, CF(1) -0.0	0.1
2021	FBG	A	21	255	32	16	3	3	34	22	65	9	3	.289/.353/.427	98	.388	-1.3	RF(33) -5.2, LF(13) 4.6, CF(7) -0.9	0.5
2021	WIL	A+	21	110	19	11	1	2	18	6	29	2	3	.284/.321/.471	91	.375	-2.7	CF(21) -4.0, LF(2) -0.1, RF(2) -0.5	-0.4
2022 non-DC	*WAS*	*MLB*	*22*	*251*	*19*	*12*	*1*	*2*	*21*	*15*	*75*	*6*	*4*	*.226/.276/.327*	*62*	*.322*	*0.6*	*LF 1, CF -1*	*-0.4*

Now a more traditional prospect on the rise. Mendez was signed for $600,000 in the same international-free-agent class as Antuna. His hit tool is far more advanced. He has exceptional hand-eye and barrel control that allows him to make late swing decisions against offspeed, and he has enough bat speed to handle 95 mph. It's a bit of an oddball swing, it can look defensive at times and very opposite-field heavy. Mendez is strong enough to sting pitches, though, even if he might not even scrape 10 home runs due to how level he is at the point of contact. He's an above-average runner and smooth enough on the grass to be an average center fielder. It's not the most exciting profile, but Mendez is a potential second-division starter or good fourth outfielder and has the kind of skill set that lends itself to a power breakout at some point, although we wouldn't put very high odds on that.

Roismar Quintana RF Born: 02/06/03 Age: 19 Bats: R Throws: R Height: 6'1" Weight: 175 lb. Origin: International Free Agent, 2019

A highly ranked Venezuelan outfielder from the same 2019 IFA class as Lara, Quintana missed out on complex-side reps this year due to injury, but, during his brief time on the field, looked and mashed the part of a power-hitting corner outfielder. The lost development time could mean another year in extended spring training and at the complex, but, given that he won't turn 19 until February, patience is a reasonable virtue here.

Factors on the Farm

Matt Cronin LHP Born: 09/20/97 Age: 24 Bats: L Throws: L Height: 6'2" Weight: 195 lb. Origin: Round 4, 2019 Draft (#123 overall)

YEAR	TEAM	LVL	AGE	W	L	SV	G	GS	IP	H	HR	BB/9	K/9	K	GB%	BABIP	WHIP	ERA	DRA-	WARP
2019	HAG	A	21	0	0	1	17	0	22	11	1	4.5	16.8	41	12.5%	.333	1.00	0.82	61	0.6
2021	WIL	A+	23	2	0	4	10	0	14^{2}	8	0	3.1	17.2	28	28.6%	.381	0.89	1.23	79	0.3
2021	HBG	AA	23	0	1	0	10	0	11^{1}	9	2	7.9	14.3	18	21.7%	.333	1.68	5.56	84	0.2
2022 non-DC	*WAS*	*MLB*	*24*	*2*	*3*	*0*	*57*	*0*	*50*	*40*	*9*	*5.7*	*13.3*	*73*	*42.2%*	*.302*	*1.45*	*4.94*	*110*	*-0.1*

Comparables: Keith Butler, James Norwood, Miles Mikolas

Well, at least the trades pushed Cronin out of the top 10. The former Arkansas closer made the main list the last two years by virtue of being a close-to-ready, high-spin, fastball/curveball type with command and health questions. He remains all that after posting a couple dozen dominant-but-walk-filled innings in High-A and Double-A in between injured-list stints. He's still a likely future set-up type as soon as this year.

Drew Millas C Born: 01/15/98 Age: 24 Bats: S Throws: R Height: 6'2" Weight: 205 lb. Origin: Round 7, 2019 Draft (#224 overall)

YEAR	TEAM	LVL	AGE	PA	R	2B	3B	HR	RBI	BB	K	SB	CS	AVG/OBP/SLG	DRC+	BABIP	BRR	FRAA	WARP
2021	SUR	WIN	23	64	8	1	0	1	5	13	4	3	1	.196/.359/.275		.196			
2021	WIL	A+	23	118	15	4	0	0	20	13	14	5	1	.284/.373/.324	119	.326	0.4	C(20) -0.4	0.6
2021	LAN	A+	23	266	34	12	1	3	28	41	39	10	2	.255/.372/.359	125	.293	0.0	C(50) 2.7	1.8
2022 non-DC	*WAS*	*MLB*	*24*	*251*	*21*	*10*	*0*	*2*	*20*	*24*	*45*	*4*	*2*	*.231/.313/.313*	*74*	*.281*	*0.1*	*C -1*	*0.3*

Comparables: Omar Narváez, Tony Cruz, Andrew Knapp

Millas is a defensive whiz in the making, and you know, if we're leading off with that, the scouting report on the bat is going to look like this: both his hit tool and power projection are fringy despite a good approach and some bat-to-ball ability. At least his glove and arm project as comfortably plus. He also has a logistical problem in that he was the third-best catching prospect the Nationals got at the trade deadline, and the first two are already established in the majors—Riley Adams aged off this list on service time but easily would've made the top 10—so Millas has a long road to a job.

Dustin Saenz LHP Born: 06/02/99 Age: 23 Bats: L Throws: L Height: 5'11" Weight: 190 lb. Origin: Round 4, 2021 Draft (#112 overall)

YEAR	TEAM	LVL	AGE	W	L	SV	G	GS	IP	H	HR	BB/9	K/9	K	GB%	BABIP	WHIP	ERA	DRA-	WARP
2021	FBG	A	22	1	0	0	5	1	11¹	14	0	3.2	9.5	12	65.7%	.400	1.59	4.76	93	0.1
2022 non-DC	*WAS*	*MLB*	*23*	*2*	*3*	*0*	*57*	*0*	*50*	*52*	*6*	*4.7*	*6.9*	*38*	*40.5%*	*.304*	*1.58*	*5.37*	*121*	*-0.4*

The Nats' fourth-round pick out of Texas A&M, Saenz is a four-pitch lefty whose fastball/slider combo gives him a chance to be a useful major-league pen arm. He, hypothetically, has enough changeup to start for a bit, and it's worth keeping him stretched out for 2022 we suppose, but his solid-average fastball should play above that in short bursts. His slider needs some refinement, it can be a bit sweepy and a long breaker, but it could give him a second above-average pitch as a lefty reliever capable of giving you some length. He could also move quickly if Washington elects to move him to the bullpen sooner rather than later.

Top Talents 25 and Under (as of 4/1/2022):

1. Juan Soto, OF
2. Cade Cavalli, RHP
3. Josiah Gray, RHP
4. Keibert Ruiz, C
5. Brady House, SS
6. Luis García, 2B
7. Carter Kieboom, 3B
8. Victor Robles, OF
9. Jackson Rutledge, RHP
10. Riley Adams, C

It's difficult to cultivate a proper metaphor outlining the gap between the number-one player on this list and the number-two name, much less numbers five, eight and beyond. He's younger than every other player on this 25-and-Under list except García and Rutledge, and he'll be among the first three names mentioned 50 years from now when people discuss the superstars of this era. He's Juan Soto, a near-perfect hitter.

Despite a disappointingly wild debut season, Gray missed bats in his first 70-odd innings and won't always give up a homer on every fourth fly ball. Gray's elevated walk rate was anomalous to his career pace, seemingly more a consequence of inexperience and attempting to nibble rather than mechanical disarray. Both of his breaking balls were bat-missers, and while his high-spin fastball ended up over the fence a few too many times, he sat 94–95 and put together multiple starts indicative of the high-floor rotation arm he has grown to project to. It is possible he is Washington's only healthy starter of even remote quality right now, though hopefully Stephen Strasburg will return to form in 2022.

García, Kieboom, and Robles each received early big-league debuts and have responded by putting on a showcase in just how hard it is to be a quality MLB player, no matter your tools or pedigree. For García, in fairness, his minor-league numbers and profile might have told you as much for the player he has been through his age-20 and -21 seasons. A free swinger of the highest order, García's line has thus far looked like Ryon Healy's without the power, and he has added troubling defensive lapses, to boot. His frigid first few months dragged down a slightly improved line after some Triple-A mashing, and he did appear more comfortable at the plate as the season advanced. García's adjustments at the big-league level could easily raise the average, but the 21-year-old must find more power in his stocky frame, as it's harder to envision him taking a huge leap with the glove or on the bases.

Kieboom's stalled development has been more jarring, given his track record and long-time reputation as a high-floor, left-side infielder with a knack for contact and the frame for pop. The 23-year-old wasn't so far off in 2021, with 90 DRC+ and a double-digit walk rate, but he has been deeply unable to punish pitches within the zone. Like his fellow young slow starters, he has received halting playing time, with just 414 plate appearances on his big-league ledger, but you have to play well to merit reps, and Kieboom simply has not earned it, even on a club that brought Alcides Escobar back to the majors last July.

Sadly, to riff on Digital Underground, *all around the diamond, same song*. Robles was, unlike the other two names above, a quality big leaguer at one point, with a passable bat and lightning speed enabling his sublime center-field defense during the 2019 season. Two years later, Robles will be entering arbitration for the first time, his 25th birthday looms this May, and there is not a whiff of the game power that he showed in his age-22 campaign. It's possible his right-ankle sprain last May had a lingering effect, as none of his defensive traits shone as brightly, his speed was merely great instead of elite and a lack of fortitude in his drive leg could explain some offensive deflation. We're running out of generous interpretations, however, as the player once assumed to be Washington's next great star struggles to put together a month of quality to match his incomparable left fielder.

Like Gray and Ruiz, Adams was a midseason acquisition, a tower shield of a backstop whom the Blue Jays forked over for 11 games of Brad Hand literally doing his worst. Likely a bat-first backup, Adams is, nonetheless, in a great spot to complement Ruiz, particularly if robo umps matriculate with any pace to MLB. The 2017 third-rounder showed the good and the bad, struggling with strikeouts in a third of his plate appearances in the bigs in 2021, but elevating well when he did make contact to maximize his thump-or-slump profile.

The Top 101 Dynasty Prospects

by Ben Carsley, Jesse Roche and Bret Sayre

As always, there are a few list-specific disclaimers to go over before we jump in. These rankings are for fantasy purposes only, and they do not directly take into account things like an outfielder's ability to stick in center or a catcher's pop time. That being said, those factors matter indirectly, as they affect a player's ability to either stay in the lineup or maintain eligibility. Additionally, we factor in home parks and organizational strengths, just as when we are talking about a major-league player. We can't pretend that these prospects operate in a vacuum, unaffected by park factors. Of course, there's no guarantee that they will reach the majors with their current organization, so, while it is reflected, it's not a heavy ranking factor. Most importantly, the intention of this list is to balance the upside, probability and proximity of these players to an active fantasy lineup.

Within the list below, you'll find important information about each prospect, including their potential fantasy value (in dollars) at their peak and the risk factor associated with reaching their projected output. Also, you will find a fantasy overview, which summarizes the number of categories in which each player will be useful, along with any that carry impact. For this exercise, we defined "impact" as having the potential to be top-25 players in a given category. For instance, impact in home runs roughly equates to the potential to hit 30, impact in steals is 20, and impact for strikeouts is the potential to punch out 200. Then, you'll see a realistic ceiling and floor for each prospect, purely in terms of rotisserie value. Each player's ceiling is labeled as "Locked In" because, well, that's what it might look like if they are. Each player's realistic floor is "Locked Out" for reasons you can likely guess. Just remember that these are prospects, so everyone's actual floor is someone you'll either never roster in a fantasy league or will get burned by over and over until you finally learn to stop touching the stove. The comments are brief because we've already written fantasy-specific comments on each of these players in the individual top-10 lists.

Previous Rank correlates to where repeat entrants placed on the 2021 version of the list. The "NR" key means the player was not ranked last year, "N/A" means they were not eligible, "HM" means they received an honorable mention. Ages listed are as of 4/1/2022.

With all that said, and without further ado, please enjoy responsibly.

1. Julio Rodríguez, OF, Seattle Mariners

Age: 21.25, **Previous Rank:** 2

Potential Earnings: $35+

Risk Factor: Low

Fantasy Overview: Five-category contributor; impact potential in AVG, R, HR, RBI

Fantasy Impact ETA: Early 2022

Locked In: It would (apparently) be reckless to say Juan Soto, so let's just go with J.D. Martinez's peak and call it a day.

Locked Out: A .270 average and 30 bombs would still make him a solid OF2.

2. Bobby Witt Jr., SS/3B, Kansas City Royals

Age: 21.79, **Previous Rank:** 13

Potential Earnings: $35+

Risk Factor: Low

Fantasy Overview: Five-category contributor; impact potential in R, HR, RBI, SB

Fantasy Impact ETA: Early 2022

Locked In: What if José Ramírez had a normal-sized face?

Locked Out: Yoán Moncada is such a tease, isn't he?

3. Spencer Torkelson, 1B/3B, Detroit Tigers

Age: 22.59, **Previous Rank:** 6

Potential Earnings: $30–35

Risk Factor: Low

Fantasy Overview: Four-category contributor; impact potential in AVG, R, HR, RBI

Fantasy Impact ETA: Early 2022

Locked In: Freddie Freeman doesn't feel out of reach.

Locked Out: Ninety percent of José Abreu, but without the undervaluation.

4. Riley Greene, OF, Detroit Tigers

Age: 21.51, **Previous Rank:** 44

Potential Earnings: $25–30

Risk Factor: Low

Fantasy Overview: Five-category contributor; impact potential in AVG, R, HR, RBI

Fantasy Impact ETA: Early 2022

Locked In: A 30–20 outfielder

Locked Out: Randy Arozarena, probably

5. CJ Abrams, SS/2B, San Diego Padres

Age: 21.49, **Previous Rank:** 8

Potential Earnings: $30–35

Risk Factor: Medium

Fantasy Overview: Five-category contributor; impact potential in AVG, R, SB

Fantasy Impact ETA: 2023

Locked In: A José Reyes-type first-rounder

Locked Out: Still runs a lot, but it's more Myles Straw-ish than you want

6. Noelvi Marte, SS, Seattle Mariners

Age: 20.46, **Previous Rank:** 40

Potential Earnings: $30–35

Risk Factor: Medium

Fantasy Overview: Five-category contributor; impact potential in R, HR, SB

Fantasy Impact ETA: 2023

Locked In: What if Bobby Witt Jr. played for a more nihilistic fan base?

Locked Out: Dustin Ackley, Danny Hultzen, Evan White, etc.

7. Adley Rutschman, C, Baltimore Orioles

Age: 24.15, **Previous Rank:** 10

Potential Earnings: $20–25

Risk Factor: Low

Fantasy Overview: Four-category contributor; impact potential in AVG, HR

Fantasy Impact ETA: Early 2022

Locked In: Imagine getting genuinely excited for a fantasy catcher.

Locked Out: Imagine ever getting excited about a catching prospect again.

8. Marco Luciano, SS, San Francisco Giants

Age: 20.56, **Previous Rank:** 7

Potential Earnings: $30–35

Risk Factor: High

Fantasy Overview: Four-category contributor; impact potential in R, HR, RBI

Fantasy Impact ETA: 2023

Locked In: Miguel Tejada, adjusted for inflation

Locked Out: Pretty close to Eduardo Escobar

9. Brennen Davis, OF, Chicago Cubs

Age: 22.41, **Previous Rank:** 37

Potential Earnings: $25–30

Risk Factor: Medium

Fantasy Overview: Five-category contributor; impact potential in R, HR, RBI

Fantasy Impact ETA: Mid-2022

Locked In: A five-category OF1

Locked Out: The better version of Ian Happ

10. Shane Baz, RHP, Tampa Bay Rays

Age: 22.79, **Previous Rank:** 55

Potential Earnings: $25–30

Risk Factor: Medium

Fantasy Overview: Four-category contributor; impact potential in W, ERA, WHIP, K

Fantasy Impact ETA: Now

Locked In: An ace without the bulk, à la Brandon Woodruff

Locked Out: A high-strikeout SP3

11. Anthony Volpe, SS, New York Yankees

Age: 20.92, **Previous Rank:** NR

Potential Earnings: $25–30

Risk Factor: Medium

Fantasy Overview: Five-category contributor; impact potential in AVG, R, HR, SB

Fantasy Impact ETA: 2023

Locked In: Javier Báez seems apt

Locked Out: Faster Didi Gregorius, perhaps

12. Grayson Rodriguez, RHP, Baltimore Orioles

Age: 22.37, **Previous Rank:** 63

Potential Earnings: $25–30

Risk Factor: Medium

Fantasy Overview: Four-category contributor; impact potential in W, ERA, K

Fantasy Impact ETA: Mid-2022

Locked In: The number-one-overall fantasy starter by 2024

Locked Out: He's still an Orioles pitching prospect . . .

13. Josh Jung, 3B, Texas Rangers

Age: 24.13, **Previous Rank:** 49

Potential Earnings: $20–25

Risk Factor: Low

Fantasy Overview: Four-category contributor; impact potential in AVG, HR, RBI

Fantasy Impact ETA: Early 2022

Locked In: Younger Justin Turner

Locked Out: Older Matt Duffy

14. Alek Thomas, OF, Arizona Diamondbacks

Age: 21.92, **Previous Rank:** 32

Potential Earnings: $20–25

Risk Factor: Low

Fantasy Overview: Five-category contributor; impact potential in AVG, R

Fantasy Impact ETA: Mid-2022

Locked In: Prime Adam Eaton was really good!

Locked Out: Off-Prime Adam Eaton was basically an OF5

15. Corbin Carroll, OF, Arizona Diamondbacks

Age: 21.61, **Previous Rank:** 21

Potential Earnings: $30–35

Risk Factor: High

Fantasy Overview: Five-category contributor; impact potential in AVG, R, SB

Fantasy Impact ETA: 2023

Locked In: Remember how much fun Carl Crawford was?

Locked Out: Another reason to be wary of major shoulder injuries

16. Luis Matos, OF, San Francisco Giants

Age: 20.17, **Previous Rank:** 54

Potential Earnings: $30–35

Risk Factor: High

Fantasy Overview: Five-category contributor; impact potential in AVG, R, SB

Fantasy Impact ETA: 2023

Locked In: Starling Marte with a touch more OBP

Locked Out: Sorry, we meant Bubba Starling.

17. Seiya Suzuki, OF, Free Agent

Age: 27.62, **Previous Rank:** N/A

Potential Earnings: $20–25

Risk Factor: Low

Fantasy Overview: Four-category contributor; impact potential in AVG, HR, RBI

Fantasy Impact ETA: Now

Locked In: Yordan Alvarez, the outfielder

Locked Out: Jared Walsh, the outfielder

18. Oneil Cruz, SS, Pittsburgh Pirates

Age: 23.49, **Previous Rank:** 77

Potential Earnings: $20–25

Risk Factor: Medium

Fantasy Overview: Four-category contributor; impact potential in HR, RBI

Fantasy Impact ETA: Now

Locked In: XXL Paul DeJong, both in size and results

Locked Out: A more athletic but no less strikeout-prone Will Middlebrooks

19. Jordan Walker, 3B, St. Louis Cardinals

Age: 19.86, **Previous Rank:** NR

Potential Earnings: $25–30

Risk Factor: High

Fantasy Overview: Four-category contributor; impact potential in HR, RBI

Fantasy Impact ETA: 2023

Locked In: 35 dingers at the hot corner

Locked Out: 30 dingers at the cold corner

20. Triston Casas, 1B, Boston Red Sox

Age: 22.21, **Previous Rank:** 47

Potential Earnings: $20–25

Risk Factor: Medium

Fantasy Overview: Four-category contributor; impact potential in HR, RBI

Fantasy Impact ETA: Mid-2022

Locked In: Paul Goldschmidt minus the steals

Locked Out: Eric Hosmer minus the steals

21. Zac Veen, OF, Colorado Rockies

Age: 20.30, **Previous Rank:** 34

Potential Earnings: $25–30

Risk Factor: High

Fantasy Overview: Five-category contributor; impact potential in HR, R, RBI

Fantasy Impact ETA: 2023

Locked In: Blue-state spoonerism rates

Locked Out: Red-state spoonerism rates

22. Robert Hassell III, OF, San Diego Padres

Age: 20.63, **Previous Rank:** 86

Potential Earnings: $20–25

Risk Factor: Medium

Fantasy Overview: Five-category contributor; impact potential in AVG, R

Fantasy Impact ETA: 2023

Locked In: Michael Brantley (h/t Mark Barry)

Locked Out: Diet Michael Brantley (h/t Mary Berry)

23. Nolan Gorman, 2B/3B, St. Louis Cardinals

Age: 21.89, **Previous Rank:** 41

Potential Earnings: $20–25

Risk Factor: Medium

Fantasy Overview: Three-category contributor; impact potential in HR, RBI

Fantasy Impact ETA: Mid-2022

Locked In: Less athletic Jorge Polanco

Locked Out: More athletic Jonathan Schoop

24. Nick Gonzales, 2B, Pittsburgh Pirates

Age: 22.84, **Previous Rank:** 30

Potential Earnings: $20–25

Risk Factor: Medium

Fantasy Overview: Four-category contributor; impact potential in AVG, R

Fantasy Impact ETA: Late 2022

Locked In: Is a Dustin Pedroia comp too obvious?

Locked Out: Is a Kevin Newman comp too obvious?

25. Vidal Bruján, OF/2B/SS, Tampa Bay Rays

Age: 24.14, **Previous Rank:** 29

Potential Earnings: $20–25

Risk Factor: Medium

Fantasy Overview: Four-category contributor; impact potential in R, SB

Fantasy Impact ETA: Now-ish? It's the Rays . . .

Locked In: Peak Jonathan Villar is more of a compliment than you'd think.

Locked Out: Fancy Dog Leury García

26. George Valera, OF, Cleveland Guardians

Age: 21.38, **Previous Rank:** 28

Potential Earnings: $20–25

Risk Factor: Medium

Fantasy Overview: Four-category contributor; impact potential in HR, RBI

Fantasy Impact ETA: 2023

Locked In: J.D. Drew was a damn fine player.

Locked Out: Can a swing still be pretty mid-strikeout?

27. Nick Yorke, 2B, Boston Red Sox

Age: 19.99, **Previous Rank:** NR

Potential Earnings: $20–25

Risk Factor: Medium

Fantasy Overview: Four-category contributor; impact potential in AVG, R

Fantasy Impact ETA: 2023

Locked In: The stat line that just made Jonathan India the Rookie of the Year

Locked Out: What if Joey Wendel wasn't versatile?

28. Brett Baty, 3B/OF, New York Mets

Age: 22.38, **Previous Rank:** 98

Potential Earnings: $20–25

Risk Factor: Medium

Fantasy Overview: Four-category contributor; impact potential in HR, RBI

Fantasy Impact ETA: Late 2022

Locked In: Peak Kyle Seager

Locked Out: Peak Tyler Naquin

29. Francisco Álvarez, C, New York Mets

Age: 20.36, **Previous Rank:** HM

Potential Earnings: $25–30

Risk Factor: High

Fantasy Overview: Four-category contributor; impact potential in HR

Fantasy Impact ETA: 2023

Locked In: Somewhere between Todd Hundley and Carlos Delgado

Locked Out: A smaller Evan Gattis

30. Tyler Soderstrom, C/1B, Oakland Athletics

Age: 20.35, **Previous Rank:** NR

Potential Earnings: $25–30

Risk Factor: High

Fantasy Overview: Four-category contributor; impact potential in AVG, HR

Fantasy Impact ETA: 2023

Locked In: A really good hitter for a catcher

Locked Out: A rather pedestrian hitter for a left fielder

31. Marcelo Mayer, SS, Boston Red Sox

Age: 19.30, **Previous Rank:** N/A

Potential Earnings: $25–30

Risk Factor: High

Fantasy Overview: Four-category contributor; impact potential in AVG, R, HR

Fantasy Impact ETA: 2024

Locked In: The Next Marco Luciano

Locked Out: The Next Marco Scutaro

32. Jasson Dominguez, OF, New York Yankees

Age: 19.15, **Previous Rank:** 26

Potential Earnings: $25–30

Risk Factor: High

Fantasy Overview: Five-category contributor; impact potential in HR, RBI, R

Fantasy Impact ETA: 2024

Locked In: Tyler O'Neill, forearms and all

Locked Out: Will be remembered most for stealing Aaron Judge's glove or something

33. Max Meyer, RHP, Miami Marlins

Age: 23.05, **Previous Rank:** 71

Potential Earnings: $20–25

Risk Factor: Medium

Fantasy Overview: Four-category contributor; impact potential in ERA, K

Fantasy Impact ETA: Mid-2022

Locked In: 2021 Freddy Peralta

Locked Out: 2021 Tanner Houck

34. Oswald Peraza, SS, New York Yankees

Age: 21.79, **Previous Rank:** NR

Potential Earnings: $20–25

Risk Factor: Medium

Fantasy Overview: Four-category contributor; impact potential in R, SB

Fantasy Impact ETA: Late 2022

Locked In: Jean Segura!

Locked Out: Alcides Escobar :(

35. Orelvis Martinez, SS/3B, Toronto Blue Jays

Age: 20.36, **Previous Rank:** 76

Potential Earnings: $20–25

Risk Factor: Medium

Fantasy Overview: Four-category contributor; impact potential in HR, RBI

Fantasy Impact ETA: 2023

Locked In: A ton of power from third base

Locked Out: A solid source of power from left field

36. George Kirby, RHP, Seattle Mariners

Age: 24.14, **Previous Rank:** 100

Potential Earnings: $20–25

Risk Factor: Medium

Fantasy Overview: Four-category contributor; impact potential in ERA, WHIP

Fantasy Impact ETA: Mid-2022

Locked In: Right-handed Julio Urías

Locked Out: Right-handed John Means

37. Josh Lowe, OF, Tampa Bay Rays

Age: 24.16, **Previous Rank:** 99

Potential Earnings: $15–20

Risk Factor: Low

Fantasy Overview: Four-category contributor; impact potential in HR, SB

Fantasy Impact ETA: Early 2022

Locked In: Brandon Lowe

Locked Out: Josh Sale

38. Aaron Ashby, LHP, Milwaukee Brewers

Age: 23.85, **Previous Rank:** NR

Potential Earnings: $20–25

Risk Factor: Medium

Fantasy Overview: Four-category contributor; impact potential in W, ERA, K

Fantasy Impact ETA: Now

Locked In: Off-peak Robbie Ray

Locked Out: Off-peak Andrew Miller

39. Kahlil Watson, SS, Miami Marlins

Age: 18.96, **Previous Rank:** N/A

Potential Earnings: $25–30

Risk Factor: High

Fantasy Overview: Five-category contributor; impact potential in R, HR

Fantasy Impact ETA: 2024

Locked In: A perennial top-five shortstop

Locked Out: A perennial post-hype sleeper

40. Austin Martin, OF/SS, Minnesota Twins

Age: 23.02, **Previous Rank:** 22

Potential Earnings: $20–25

Risk Factor: Medium

Fantasy Overview: Four-category contributor; impact potential in AVG, R

Fantasy Impact ETA: Mid-2022

Locked In: The best version of Dansby Swanson is still in play.

Locked Out: Unfortunately, so is Dustin Ackley.

41. Jordan Lawlar, SS, Arizona Diamondbacks

Age: 19.70, **Previous Rank:** N/A

Potential Earnings: $25–30

Risk Factor: High

Fantasy Overview: Five-category contributor; impact potential in R, SB

Fantasy Impact ETA: 2024

Locked In: A decent Trea Turner facsimile

Locked Out: When was the last time you thought about Felipe López?

42. Jack Leiter, RHP, Texas Rangers

Age: 21.94, **Previous Rank:** N/A

Potential Earnings: $25–30

Risk Factor: High

Fantasy Overview: Four-category contributor; impact potential in W, ERA, WHIP, K

Fantasy Impact ETA: 2023

Locked In: A high-strikeout SP2 whom Twitter randos still manage to call a bust

Locked Out: He's still a Rangers pitching prospect . . .

43. Nick Pratto, 1B, Kansas City Royals

Age: 23.48, **Previous Rank:** NR

Potential Earnings: $15–20

Risk Factor: Low

Fantasy Overview: Three-category contributor; impact potential in HR, RBI

Fantasy Impact ETA: Mid-2022

Locked In: A really good corner infielder in mixed leagues

Locked Out: A pretty good corner infielder in AL-only leagues

44. Michael Harris II, OF, Atlanta Braves

Age: 21.06, **Previous Rank:** NR

Potential Earnings: $20–25

Risk Factor: Medium

Fantasy Overview: Five-category contributor; impact potential in R, AVG

Fantasy Impact ETA: Late 2022

Locked In: A steady, 20–20 OF3

Locked Out: We'd never overrate a toolsy Braves outfielder. No, siree.

45. Miguel Vargas, 3B/2B/1B, Los Angeles Dodgers

Age: 22.37, **Previous Rank:** HM

Potential Earnings: $20–25

Risk Factor: Medium

Fantasy Overview: Four-category contributor; impact potential in AVG, RBI

Fantasy Impact ETA: Late 2022

Locked In: Are we the only ones getting Max Muncy vibes?

Locked Out: Are we the only ones getting Matt Beaty vibes?

46. Cade Cavalli, RHP, Washington Nationals

Age: 23.63, **Previous Rank:** NR

Potential Earnings: $20–25

Risk Factor: Medium

Fantasy Overview: Four-category contributor; impact potential in W, K

Fantasy Impact ETA: Late 2022

Locked In: A top-10 dynasty prospect at this time next year

Locked Out: Health-deferred into 2026 or so

47. Brayan Rocchio, SS/2B/3B, Cleveland Guardians

Age: 21.21, **Previous Rank:** 89

Potential Earnings: $20–25

Risk Factor: Medium

Fantasy Overview: Five-category contributor; impact potential in R, AVG

Fantasy Impact ETA: Late 2022

Locked In: A well-rounded and versatile piece à la Jake Cronenworth

Locked Out: All too César Hernández-ish to get that worked up about

48. Hunter Greene, RHP, Cincinnati Reds

Age: 22.65, **Previous Rank:** 101

Potential Earnings: $20–25

Risk Factor: Medium

Fantasy Overview: Four-category contributor; impact potential in WHIP, K

Fantasy Impact ETA: Mid-2022

Locked In: Early Nate Eovaldi

Locked Out: Modern Jordan Hicks

49. Reid Detmers, LHP, Los Angeles Angels

Age: 22.73, **Previous Rank:** NR

Potential Earnings: $15–20

Risk Factor: Medium

Fantasy Overview: Four-category contributor; impact potential in W, K

Fantasy Impact ETA: Now

Locked In: A healthy Eduardo Rodríguez in a better ballpark

Locked Out: It's a bit too soon for an Andrew Heaney relaunch, no?

50. Jose Miranda, 3B/UT, Minnesota Twins

Age: 23.75, **Previous Rank:** NR

Potential Earnings: $15–20

Risk Factor: Medium

Fantasy Overview: Four-category contributor; impact potential in AVG, R

Fantasy Impact ETA: Mid-2022

Locked In: Super Saiyan Luis Arraez

Locked Out: Well, err, 110 percent of Luis Arraez

51. Brady House, SS, Washington Nationals

Age: 18.82, **Previous Rank:** N/A

Potential Earnings: $20–25

Risk Factor: High

Fantasy Overview: Four-category contributor; impact potential in HR, RBI

Fantasy Impact ETA: 2024

Locked In: A center-hall colonial with great lighting

Locked Out: A winnebago that can begrudgingly make it from Rochester to DC

52. Sixto Sánchez, RHP, Miami Marlins

Age: 23.67, **Previous Rank:** 14

Potential Earnings: $20–25

Risk Factor: High

Fantasy Overview: Four-category contributor; impact potential in ERA, WHIP

Fantasy Impact ETA: Now

Locked In: A 150-inning starter

Locked Out: A 70-grade David Roth namedrop in 2031

53. Daniel Espino, RHP, Cleveland Guardians

Age: 21.24, **Previous Rank:** NR

Potential Earnings: $20–25

Risk Factor: High

Fantasy Overview: Four-category contributor; impact potential in ERA, K

Fantasy Impact ETA: 2023

Locked In: In Guardians pitching prospects we trust

Locked Out: Giovanny Gallegos feels about right

54. Gabriel Moreno, C, Toronto Blue Jays

Age: 22.13, **Previous Rank:** NR

Potential Earnings: $15–20

Risk Factor: Medium

Fantasy Overview: Four-category contributor; impact potential in AVG

Fantasy Impact ETA: Mid-2022

Locked In: Almost Buster Posey

Locked Out: A hopefully healthier Travis d'Arnaud

55. Jhonkensy Noel, 3B/1B, Cleveland Guardians

Age: 20.71, **Previous Rank:** NR

Potential Earnings: $20–25

Risk Factor: High

Fantasy Overview: Three-category contributor; impact potential in HR, RBI

Fantasy Impact ETA: 2023

Locked In: What Miguel Sanó was supposed to be

Locked Out: What Miguel Sanó currently is

56. Henry Davis, C, Pittsburgh Pirates

Age: 22.53, **Previous Rank:** N/A

Potential Earnings: $15–20

Risk Factor: Medium

Fantasy Overview: Four-category contributor; impact potential in R, HR

Fantasy Impact ETA: 2023

Locked In: Those good Wil Myers seasons

Locked Out: Most Wil Myers seasons

57. Jordan Groshans, SS/3B, Toronto Blue Jays

Age: 22.39, **Previous Rank:** 43

Potential Earnings: $15–20

Risk Factor: Medium

Fantasy Overview: Four-category contributor; impact potential in AVG, RBI

Fantasy Impact ETA: Mid-2022

Locked In: Jorge Polanco, minus the bags

Locked Out: Luis Urías

58. Cristian Hernandez, SS, Chicago Cubs

Age: 18.30, **Previous Rank:** NR

Potential Earnings: $25–30

Risk Factor: Extreme

Fantasy Overview: Five-category contributor; impact potential in R, SB

Fantasy Impact ETA: 2025

Locked In: The best player in the history of baseball

Locked Out: Never makes it past Double-A

59. Royce Lewis, SS, Minnesota Twins

Age: 22.82, **Previous Rank:** 19

Potential Earnings: $20–25

Risk Factor: High

Fantasy Overview: Four-category contributor; impact potential in AVG, R

Fantasy Impact ETA: 2023

Locked In: Dansby Swanson

Locked Out: Mickey Moniak

60. Liover Peguero, SS, Pittsburgh Pirates

Age: 21.25, **Previous Rank:** NR

Potential Earnings: $15–20

Risk Factor: Medium

Fantasy Overview: Five-category contributor; impact potential in R, SB

Fantasy Impact ETA: 2023

Locked In: Where C.J. Abrams ranks now, in a year

Locked Out: Where Xavier Edwards ranks now, in a year

61. Nick Lodolo, LHP, Cincinnati Reds

Age: 24.15, **Previous Rank:** 79

Potential Earnings: $15–20

Risk Factor: Medium

Fantasy Overview: Four-category contributor; impact potential in W

Fantasy Impact ETA: Mid-2022

Locked In: A starter capable of sporadic SP2 seasons, à la Sean Manaea

Locked Out: Fancy Dog Wade Miley

62. Hedbert Perez, OF, Milwaukee Brewers

Age: 18.99, **Previous Rank:** NR

Potential Earnings: $25–30

Risk Factor: Extreme

Fantasy Overview: Four-category contributor; impact potential in R, HR, RBI

Fantasy Impact ETA: 2024

Locked In: The lottery ticket that convinces you to keep playing the lottery

Locked Out: Most lottery tickets

63. Reginald Preciado, SS/3B, Chicago Cubs

Age: 18.87, **Previous Rank:** NR

Potential Earnings: $20–25

Risk Factor: High

Fantasy Overview: Four-category contributor; impact potential in HR, RBI

Fantasy Impact ETA: 2024

Locked In: 85 percent of Corey Seager

Locked Out: 85 percent of Kyle Seager

64. Michael Busch, 2B/1B, Los Angeles Dodgers

Age: 24.15, **Previous Rank:** NR

Potential Earnings: $15–20

Risk Factor: Medium

Fantasy Overview: Three-category contributor; impact potential in R, HR

Fantasy Impact ETA: Mid-2022

Locked In: What we thought Willie Calhoun could be

Locked Out: What Willie Calhoun is

65. Gunnar Henderson, SS/3B, Baltimore Orioles

Age: 20.75, **Previous Rank:** NR

Potential Earnings: $15–20

Risk Factor: Medium

Fantasy Overview: Four-category contributor; impact potential in HR, RBI

Fantasy Impact ETA: 2023

Locked In: Prime J.J. Hardy feels lazy, and yet . . .

Locked Out: Willy Adames: Rays Edition

66. Austin Wells, C, New York Yankees

Age: 22.72, **Previous Rank:** NR

Potential Earnings: $15–20

Risk Factor: Medium

Fantasy Overview: Four-category contributor

Fantasy Impact ETA: 2023

Locked In: Mike Napoli through the looking glass

Locked Out: A tweener without a true position

67. Joe Ryan, RHP, Minnesota Twins

Age: 25.82, **Previous Rank:** NR

Potential Earnings: $10–15

Risk Factor: Low

Fantasy Overview: Three-category contributor; impact potential in W

Fantasy Impact ETA: Now

Locked In: A late-blooming SP3

Locked Out: Two more first names than out-pitches

68. Pedro Leon, SS/OF, Houston Astros

Age: 23.84, **Previous Rank:** NR

Potential Earnings: $15–20

Risk Factor: Medium

Fantasy Overview: Four-category contributor; impact potential in R, SB

Fantasy Impact ETA: Mid-2022

Locked In: What we want Amed Rosario to be

Locked Out: Niko Goodrum

69. MJ Melendez, C, Kansas City Royals

Age: 23.34, **Previous Rank:** NR

Potential Earnings: $15–20

Risk Factor: Medium

Fantasy Overview: Three-category contributor; impact potential in HR

Fantasy Impact ETA: Mid-2022

Locked In: Drop Gary Sánchez into Kauffman Stadium, gently

Locked Out: Drop Welington Castillo into Kauffman Stadium, less gently

70. Andy Pages, OF, Los Angeles Dodgers

Age: 21.31, **Previous Rank:** NR

Potential Earnings: $15–20

Risk Factor: Medium

Fantasy Overview: Three-category contributor; impact potential in HR, RBI

Fantasy Impact ETA: 2023

Locked In: Mitch Haniger

Locked Out: Remember DJ Peters?

71. Coby Mayo, 3B, Baltimore Orioles

Age: 20.31, **Previous Rank:** NR

Potential Earnings: $20–25

Risk Factor: High

Fantasy Overview: Four-category contributor; impact potential in HR, RBI

Fantasy Impact ETA: 2024

Locked In: Hellmann's

Locked Out: Miracle Whip

72. Keibert Ruiz, C, Washington Nationals

Age: 23.69, **Previous Rank:** NR

Potential Earnings: $10–15

Risk Factor: Low

Fantasy Overview: Three-category contributor; impact potential in AVG

Fantasy Impact ETA: Now

Locked In: A .280-average, 15-homer catcher

Locked Out: A .270-average, 10-homer catcher

73. Matt McLain, SS, Cincinnati Reds

Age: 22.65, **Previous Rank:** N/A

Potential Earnings: $15–20

Risk Factor: Medium

Fantasy Overview: Five-category contributor; impact potential in R

Fantasy Impact ETA: 2023

Locked In: A top-12 shortstop with a vengeance

Locked Out: Kelly Gruber

74. Eury Perez, RHP, Miami Marlins

Age: 18.96, **Previous Rank:** NR

Potential Earnings: $20–25

Risk Factor: High

Fantasy Overview: Four-category contributor; impact potential in ERA, WHIP

Fantasy Impact ETA: 2024

Locked In: An extremely tall SP3

Locked Out: An extremely tall set-up man

75. Owen Caissie, OF, Chicago Cubs

Age: 19.73, **Previous Rank:** NR

Potential Earnings: $20–25

Risk Factor: High

Fantasy Overview: Four-category contributor; impact potential in HR, RBI

Fantasy Impact ETA: 2024

Locked In: Kyle Schwarber with better defense

Locked Out: Josh Naylor with better defense

76. Colton Cowser, OF, Baltimore Orioles

Age: 22.03, **Previous Rank:** N/A

Potential Earnings: $20–25

Risk Factor: High

Fantasy Overview: Five-category contributor; impact potential in AVG, R

Fantasy Impact ETA: 2023

Locked In: Alex Verdugo with Old Bay Seasoning

Locked Out: Old man Nick Markakis

77. Jarren Duran, Boston Red Sox

Age: 25.57, **Previous Rank:** HM

Potential Earnings: $10–15

Risk Factor: Low

Fantasy Overview: Four-category contributor; impact potential in R, SB

Fantasy Impact ETA: Now

Locked In: Brett Gardner with more power

Locked Out: Kevin Kiermaier with worse defense

78. Edward Cabrera, RHP, Miami Marlins

Age: 23.96, **Previous Rank:** 85

Potential Earnings: $15–20

Risk Factor: Medium

Fantasy Overview: Four-category contributor; impact potential in ERA, K

Fantasy Impact ETA: Now

Locked In: The Platonic ideal of an SP3

Locked Out: The Platonic ideal of a streamer

79. Bobby Miller, RHP, Los Angeles Dodgers

Age: 22.99, **Previous Rank:** NR

Potential Earnings: $20–25

Risk Factor: High

Fantasy Overview: Four-category contributor; impact potential in W, ERA, K

Fantasy Impact ETA: 2023

Locked In: 2021 Nate Eovaldi

Locked Out: Brusdar Graterol is still worth rostering in deeper leagues

80. JJ Bleday, OF, Miami Marlins

Age: 24.39, **Previous Rank:** 39

Potential Earnings: $15–20

Risk Factor: Medium

Fantasy Overview: Four-category contributor; impact potential in HR, RBI

Fantasy Impact ETA: Mid-2022

Locked In: Median Michael Conforto

Locked Out: Median Stephen Piscotty

81. Nate Pearson, RHP, Toronto Blue Jays

Age: 25.61, **Previous Rank:** 24

Potential Earnings: $20–25

Risk Factor: High

Fantasy Overview: Four-category contributor; impact potential in ERA, K

Fantasy Impact ETA: Now

Locked In: Healthy

Locked Out: Hurt

82. Roansy Contreras, RHP, Pittsburgh Pirates

Age: 22.40, **Previous Rank:** NR

Potential Earnings: $15–20

Risk Factor: Medium

Fantasy Overview: Four-category contributor; impact potential in ERA, WHIP

Fantasy Impact ETA: Now

Locked In: A cromulent SP5 who won't net you many wins

Locked Out: A solid streamer who won't net you many wins

83. Emerson Hancock, RHP, Seattle Mariners

Age: 22.83, **Previous Rank:** 91

Potential Earnings: $15–20

Risk Factor: Medium

Fantasy Overview: Four-category contributor; impact potential in W, ERA

Fantasy Impact ETA: 2023

Locked In: A 190-inning Chris Bassitt

Locked Out: A matchups guy in mixed leagues

84. Justin Foscue, 2B, Texas Rangers

Age: 23.08, **Previous Rank:** NR

Potential Earnings: $15–20

Risk Factor: Medium

Fantasy Overview: Four-category contributor; impact potential in HR, RBI

Fantasy Impact ETA: Late 2022

Locked In: Mike Moustakas

Locked Out: An all-or-nothing, short-side platoon infielder

85. Joey Wiemer, OF, Milwaukee Brewers

Age: 23.14, **Previous Rank:** NR

Potential Earnings: $20–25

Risk Factor: High

Fantasy Overview: Four-category contributor; impact potential in HR, RBI, SB

Fantasy Impact ETA: 2023

Locked In: Did you enjoy Adolis García's season?

Locked Out: Haha, we said Wiemer

86. Jeremy Peña, SS, Houston Astros

Age: 24.52, **Previous Rank:** NR

Potential Earnings: $10–15

Risk Factor: Low

Fantasy Overview: Five-category contributor; impact potential in R

Fantasy Impact ETA: Early 2022

Locked In: A down-ballot ROY candidate

Locked Out: Losing paying time to Aledmys Díaz

87. Elly De La Cruz, 3B/SS, Cincinnati Reds

Age: 20.22, **Previous Rank:** NR

Potential Earnings: $20–25

Risk Factor: High

Fantasy Overview: Four-category contributor; impact potential in HR, RBI, SB

Fantasy Impact ETA: 2024

Locked In: What if Noelvi Marte had a much worse approach?

Locked Out: Louisville's third-largest renewable resource

88. Bryson Stott, SS/2B/3B, Philadelphia Phillies

Age: 24.48, **Previous Rank:** HM

Potential Earnings: $10–15

Risk Factor: Low

Fantasy Overview: Four-category contributor; impact potential in R

Fantasy Impact ETA: Early 2022

Locked In: Almost a top-12 shortstop

Locked Out: Late-career Jean Segura

89. Garrett Mitchell, OF, Milwaukee Brewers

Age: 23.57, **Previous Rank:** 57

Potential Earnings: $20–25

Risk Factor: High

Fantasy Overview: Five-category contributor; impact potential in AVG, R, SB

Fantasy Impact ETA: Late 2022

Locked In: A 15-homer, 25-steal OF2

Locked Out: He's a Brewers first-round pick, so, stung by a scorpion?

90. Tyler Freeman, SS/3B/2B, Cleveland Guardians

Age: 22.86, **Previous Rank:** HM

Potential Earnings: $10–15

Risk Factor: Low

Fantasy Overview: Three-category contributor; impact potential in AVG, R

Fantasy Impact ETA: Mid-2022

Locked In: Hope you like Adam Frazier

Locked Out: Hope you really like Adam Frazier

91. James Triantos, 2B/SS, Chicago Cubs

Age: 19.17, **Previous Rank:** N/A

Potential Earnings: $20–25

Risk Factor: High

Fantasy Overview: Four-category contributor; impact potential in AVG, R

Fantasy Impact ETA: 2024

Locked In: A top-25 prospect at this time next year

Locked Out: Ryan McMahon outside of Coors

92. Blaze Jordan, 3B/1B, Boston Red Sox

Age: 19.28, **Previous Rank:** NR

Potential Earnings: $20–25

Risk Factor: High

Fantasy Overview: Four-category contributor; impact potential in HR, RBI

Fantasy Impact ETA: 2024

Locked In: Ryan Mountcastle, maybe?

Locked Out: 2 Bobby 2 Dalbec

93. Greg Jones, SS, Tampa Bay Rays

Age: 24.06, **Previous Rank:** 88

Potential Earnings: $15–20

Risk Factor: Medium

Fantasy Overview: Four-category contributor; impact potential in R, SB

Fantasy Impact ETA: Late 2022

Locked In: Tommy Edman

Locked Out: A spare part

94. Everson Pereira, OF, New York Yankees

Age: 20.97, **Previous Rank:** NR

Potential Earnings: $20–25

Risk Factor: High

Fantasy Overview: Four-category contributor; impact potential in HR, RBI

Fantasy Impact ETA: 2023

Locked In: Healthy Aaron Hicks

Locked Out: Late-career Mike Cameron

95. Quinn Priester, RHP, Pittsburgh Pirates

Age: 21.54, **Previous Rank:** NR

Potential Earnings: $15–20

Risk Factor: Medium

Fantasy Overview: Four-category contributor; impact potential in W, ERA

Fantasy Impact ETA: 2023

Locked In: Another Joe Musgrove to trade

Locked Out: Another Mitch Keller to hold

96. Sal Frelick, OF, Milwaukee Brewers

Age: 21.95, **Previous Rank:** N/A

Potential Earnings: $15–20

Risk Factor: Medium

Fantasy Overview: Three-category contributor; impact potential in AVG, R, SB

Fantasy Impact ETA: 2023

Locked In: Faster Raimel Tapia

Locked Out: Slower Mallex Smith

97. Curtis Mead, 3B/1B, Tampa Bay Rays

Age: 21.43, **Previous Rank:** NR

Potential Earnings: $15–20

Risk Factor: Medium

Fantasy Overview: Four-category contributor; impact potential in HR, RBI

Fantasy Impact ETA: 2023

Locked In: Trey Mancini with 80 percent of the playing time

Locked Out: Righty Mitch Moreland

98. Jay Allen II, OF, Cincinnati Reds

Age: 19.36, **Previous Rank:** N/A

Potential Earnings: $20–25

Risk Factor: High

Fantasy Overview: Five-category contributor; impact potential in R, SB

Fantasy Impact ETA: 2024

Locked In: Somewhere around good Tommy Pham

Locked Out: Somewhere around median Raimel Tapia

99. Luis Gil, RHP, New York Yankees

Age: 23.83, **Previous Rank:** NR

Potential Earnings: $10–15

Risk Factor: Low

Fantasy Overview: Four-category contributor; impact potential in ERA, K

Fantasy Impact ETA: Now

Locked In: Worth the hit to your WHIP

Locked Out: A streamer when on the road

100. Jairo Pomares, OF, San Francisco Giants

Age: 21.66, **Previous Rank:** NR

Potential Earnings: $15–20

Risk Factor: Medium

Fantasy Overview: Four-category contributor; impact potential in HR, RBI

Fantasy Impact ETA: 2023

Locked In: A pretty empty 30 homers

Locked Out: A pretty empty 10 homers

101. Benny Montgomery, OF, Colorado Rockies

Age: 19.56, **Previous Rank:** N/A

Potential Earnings: $20–25

Risk Factor: Extreme

Fantasy Overview: Four-category contributor; impact potential in HR, RBI, SB

Fantasy Impact ETA: 2024

Locked In: Kyle Tucker

Locked Out: Preston Tucker

Honorable Mention (in alphabetical order): Mick Abel, RHP, Philadelphia Phillies; Kevin Alcantara, OF, Chicago Cubs; Jose Barrero, SS, Cincinnati Reds; Joey Bart, C, San Francisco Giants; Taj Bradley, RHP, Tampa Bay Rays; Pete Crow-Armstrong, OF, Chicago Cubs; Camilo Doval, RHP, San Francisco Giants; Harry Ford, C, Seattle Mariners; MacKenize Gore, LHP, San Diego Padres; D.L. Hall, LHP, Baltimore Orioles; Dustin Harris, 1B/3B, Texas Rangers; Kyle Harrison, LHP, San Francisco Giants; Drey Jameson, RHP, Arizona Diamondbacks; Jackson Jobe, RHP, Detroit Tigers; Ronny Mauricio, SS, New York Mets; Colson Montgomery, SS, Chicago White Sox; Kyle Muller, LHP, Atlanta Braves; Geraldo Perdomo, SS, Arizona Diamondbacks; Heliot Ramos, OF, San Francisco Giants; Ezequiel Tovar, SS, Colorado Rockies; Mark Vientos, 3B/OF/1B, New York Mets; Drew Waters, OF, Atlanta Braves; Cole Winn, RHP, Texas Rangers; James Wood, OF, San Diego Padres

The Top 50 Fantasy Prospects For 2022 Only

by Mike Gianella

Whether you're a newcomer to fantasy baseball or a seasoned veteran, one of the biggest challenges you face every season is trying to parse prospect lists and figure out how to apply them to your league. While the quality and quantity of information available is unprecedented, most of this information is geared toward the real kind of baseball and not the fantasy variety. This is a good thing, overall, but it also means you must make your own rough mental calculations about issues like how much to downgrade a prospect because of his good defense, which is irrelevant to fantasy, or what kind of weight to put on a catcher's value.

If you only play in redraft leagues, an additional set of challenges makes this exercise even more arduous. How much value should be placed on a prospect's proximity to the majors versus his ceiling? If a top-10-overall prospect has a slim chance of making the majors this year but could be an immediate impact player when he arrives, how do you account for this in your valuation?

The list below is designed specifically for players in one-and-done leagues. Beyond the obvious fact that prospects who are clearly two or more years away aren't listed, you'll also see more rookies who clearly aren't top prospects but have a clear opportunity for playing time in 2021 as we go to press. Your primary goal is to win your league now, not to have a great prospect on your reserve list for six months.

Of course, this list wouldn't exist without the amazing work the Baseball Prospectus Prospect Team churns out every year, especially their essential top-10 lists. Their diligent research and top-flight writing are a significant starting point for what you see below. But it is exactly that, a jumping-off point, not a final say in these one-and-done rankings.

One final note: these rankings assume a standard 5×5 roto, 15-team, mixed league with moderate reserve lists. Your mileage may vary depending on what format your league uses. Nevertheless, we believe the list below is an excellent resource for your league or leagues, and, at the very least, a solid jumping-off point for your own research and preparation.

1. Bobby Witt Jr., SS, Kansas City Royals

It's fair to argue that Witt's average draft position or salary-cap draft price will be too high this spring, but, in terms of the combination of talent, opportunity and how his skill set dovetails with his fantasy value, Witt is the no-doubt number-one player on this list. He's not even particularly risky, as the questions surrounding his short-term future center around slight contact issues and where he winds up on defense. Witt's an immediate 20–20 candidate with a .260 AVG, and his ceiling is higher than that. Yes, even in 2022.

2. Seiya Suzuki, OF, Free Agent

Suzuki is a polished, nine-year veteran of Japanese baseball and, as a 27-year-old, is relatively young for a foreign import. He crushed 38 bombs last year, is a career .309 hitter, and, while those numbers won't all translate to the other side of the Pacific, Suzuki's the sort of player whose skills will translate well to the major-league version of the game. He'd be number-one on this list if not for the lockout and the risk that he might decide to stay in Japan for another season, particularly if it drags on well past scheduled Opening Day.

3. Shane Baz, RHP, Tampa Bay Rays

Low-risk pitching prospects are unicorns, but that's exactly what Baz is. He blew the doors off across three levels in 2021, including an impressive three-start stint for the Rays in September. The biggest question about Baz revolves around whether the Rays impose a strict innings cap, or if they take the training wheels off and let Baz pitch 170–180 innings. The dude can pitch, and, no matter how the wins shake out, you're buying into a lot of strikeouts with, at worst, slightly above-average rate stats.

4. Oneil Cruz, SS, Pittsburgh Pirates

There are long-term questions about Cruz's future as a shortstop (due to his size, not his abilities), but, for 2022 at least, you'll be drafting 30-home-run potential from a shortstop-eligible player. Cruz's swing-and-miss issues push his value down in points leagues, but, in roto formats, that will only hurt him if it costs him a starting job, and we don't believe it will. Cruz's loud contact will play in any park—even in cavernous PNC in Pittsburgh—and, while a bad lineup around him and a lack of significant steals potential keeps him from pushing too high up the ranks, Cruz still has the potential to be a top-15 shortstop this year.

5. Spencer Torkelson, 1B, Detroit Tigers

The third-base experiment is over, but that doesn't matter to Tork's fantasy managers. What does matter is the easy power that will play anywhere, even in Detroit's cavernous home ballpark, and gives Torkelson 30-plus-home-run potential. He's not just a thumper, either. Torkelson's a good hitter who displays patience beyond his years, controls the strike zone and goes the other way, when required. He struggled a little bit in Triple-A last year, and it's possible he will struggle against major-league pitching initially, as well, particularly from a contact perspective. Torkelson loses a little bit from a ranking perspective only because first base is a little bit deeper than some of the other positions on the diamond.

6. Camilo Doval, RHP, San Francisco Giants

There's risk with any closer, and, with Doval, the added risk comes from the facts that he doesn't possess an elite arm, has some command questions and has had exactly one month in his professional career in which he has consistently thrown strikes. But it looks like Doval has the job entering the season, his strikeout potential is high, and he pitches for one of the best teams in baseball. In leagues that don't use holds, move Doval down a few slots, but in deep mixed leagues and mono formats, Doval will maintain value even if he isn't the closer.

7. Keibert Ruiz, C, Washington Nationals

He's not the best catching prospect on this list—heck, he isn't even the best catching prospect in the greater DC metro area—but Ruiz gets the short-term nod over Adley Rutschman because, unlike his Baltimore counterpart, he's guaranteed an opportunity from the opening bell. Ruiz certainly isn't a slouch who is here simply because of opportunity. He's as safe of a batting-average play as you'll find behind the dish, with a .260 floor, and while there are questions about how much his power will play in the majors, 15–20 home runs is a reasonable expectation.

8. Joe Ryan, RHP, Minnesota Twins

Don't mistake this lofty ranking of Ryan for a full-throated endorsement or the belief that he has "future ace" written all over him. But, unlike most of the starting pitchers ranked below Ryan on this list, he has already debuted in the majors and shown us he can succeed as a starter. Ryan's excellent command and control more than make up for above-average-but-not-great stuff and sets his floor as a back-end starting pitcher. But Ryan could also be an SP3 and pitching in a weak division against softer opponents certainly helps his cause.

9. Adley Rutschman, C, Baltimore Orioles

We have moved from the question of "if" to "when" with Rutschman. Even if he isn't up on Opening Day, he should spend most of 2022 as the Orioles' starting catcher. Growing pains on offense are quite possible as Rutschman adjusts against major-league pitching, but, even if he doesn't hit the ground running, there's potential for 15–20 home runs with a solid batting average. He is ranked this high on a short-term list because of his position. Rutschman could immediately be a top-10 catcher, which makes him worth grabbing in every format, and he certainly has the talent to exceed his 2022 expectations.

10. Julio Rodríguez, OF, Seattle Mariners

Figuring out what the "penalty" should be for an elite prospect, who will probably be up at some point in 2022 but won't be up on Opening Day, is always a challenging (and somewhat aggravating) exercise in the case of a future stud like Rodríguez. But he's the best offensive prospect in the game and has put up video-game numbers since his promotion to High-A in late

2019, posting a ludicrous .368/.454/.593 slash line in 412 plate appearances in High- and Double-A. He also added the speed to his game many were hoping would materialize given his skill set, swiping 21 bases across two levels. Even half a season of Rodríguez would be worth an early reserve stash in most formats, which makes him worth this ranking just inside the top 10.

11. Josh Jung, 3B, Texas Rangers

Jung's combined Double-A and Triple-A line speaks to a player who could step right into the Rangers' Opening Day lineup and not miss a beat. He adjusted his swing for power, which could lead to higher strikeout totals and a lower batting average against major-league pitching, but, even with some slippage, a .260–.270 average isn't an unrealistic expectation. Jung's short-term challenge is a suddenly crowded Texas infield following the signings of Marcus Semien and Corey Seager. Jung should still reach the majors in 2022, but the signings give the Rangers the luxury of giving Jung a little more time to bake in the minors.

12. Riley Greene, OF, Detroit Tigers

It is perhaps even less likely that Greene graces the Tigers' Opening Day roster than it is for his teammate Torkelson, but Greene's potential for 15–20 steals gives him a bit more of a long-term ceiling in roto formats. Whether that ceiling is realized in 2022 is an open question. His strikeout rate is higher than you'd like for a prospect whose value centers around his bat, and he struggled with in-the-zone breakers at Triple-A. Long-term, we could be looking at a future All-Star outfielder, but the possibility that he has some struggles out of the gate tempers the short-term expectations.

13. Jarren Duran, OF, Boston Red Sox

Duran's a great example of a prospect whose relatively advanced age (25) and lower ranking on traditional prospect lists (81 on the BP 101) will lead to him being overlooked in some circles. Add to this his underwhelming major-league debut last year, and Duran could be a sneaky sleeper in redraft leagues. Duran has a little pop but will rise or fall based on how much his speed carries him in fantasy. While a high on-base percentage would be optimal, a .310 OBP or so as a regular could be enough to make Duran an elite base stealer.

14. Aaron Ashby, LHP, Milwaukee Brewers

Ashby might not start 2022 in the Brewers' rotation, but he'll start at some point for Milwaukee and will stick in the rotation if his command holds. That's a considerable "if" to be sure, but Ashby's high-velocity and high-strikeout profile make him a ceiling pick worth stashing in almost any format. He is one of the riskier names in our top 20; there's the distinct possibility that his control disappears entirely, and that his high-90s sinking heater that doesn't fool hitters into swinging as much as it needs to.

15. Vidal Bruján, 2B/OF, Tampa Bay Rays

Brujan added a little power to his game last year, but if you're drafting him in 2022, it's because of his potentially game-breaking speed. He stole 40-plus bases in the minors for the second consecutive year last year, and it's encouraging that his speed translated into results almost seamlessly from the low minors to the high minors. He doesn't have a lock on a starting job heading into 2022, but the Rays have been molding Bruján into a super-utility type, and it's not difficult to envision him falling into the Joey Wendle job description and getting 450–500 plate appearances as a "backup." The risk is stagnation and the struggles rookies frequently have trying to fit into a non-starting role, but his steals ceiling makes Bruján oh so tantalizing anyway.

16. Jose Miranda, 3B, Minnesota Twins

Miranda's one of those prospects for whom you need to look past the real life ranking (he's "only" seventh on BP's Twins top 10, for Pete's sake) and consider his potential fantasy impact. He went from barely a blip on the radar to a potential impact bat thanks to a sudden power surge that saw him swat 30 home runs between two minor-league levels in 2021. He's blocked at third base by Josh Donaldson but can play second capably and will battle Luis Arraez for time there. He's unlikely to swat another 30 home runs in the majors, but a good batting average and 15–20 home runs aren't out of the question if Miranda does break camp with the Twins.

17. Joey Bart, C, San Francisco Giants

Buster Posey's retirement means that the opportunity is there for Bart, and Bart's defense gives him the inside track to be the Giants' starting backstop in 2022. His batting line at Triple-A last year was fine but also feels underwhelming given Bart's draft standing and pedigree. Bart's raw power could make him a 20-home-run hitter right out of the gate; whether he can come close to Rutschman in 2022 depends on if Bart can get past the contact issues that have dogged him throughout his professional career.

18. Jeremy Peña, SS, Houston Astros

When and if Peña gets an opportunity drives his short-term ranking as much as anything else. If the Astros really have moved on from Carlos Correa, there's a real possibility that Peña will be up for good by May, if not sooner, and will take over as the Astros' starting shortstop. His minor-league resume is limited, and his power surge was limited to a mere 133 plate appearances after Peña returned from a wrist injury, but, even if Peña's power boost is illusory, he still has the potential to be one of those sneaky, 15–15 shortstops with a decent batting average who quietly pushes a lot of your fantasy squads to a championship.

19. Jose Barrero, SS, Cincinnati Reds

Whether you believe Barrero is an underrated sleeper or appropriately rated depends on if you believe more in his strong minor-league campaign in 2021 or his abysmal 124 major-league plate appearances in 2020 and '21. Barrero will go as far as his ability to make contact will take him, but that's still a big question, and, while he's only 23 years old, it means that, on a short-term ranking list like this one, he can only be pushed so high. If it all materializes, we could be looking at a 20–25-home-run, impact bat who chips in a few steals, but those swing-and-miss issues aren't trivial.

20. Reid Detmers, LHP, Los Angeles Angels

Detmers was a polished college pitcher who dominated the minors across 13 starts, earned a promotion to the Angels in early August and then promptly fizzled out, getting dominated by big-league hitters. That's nothing to be worried about long-term—getting buzzed by the best hitters in the world during your first go-round is the norm not the exception—but it does lead to questions about when Detmers will make his 2022 debut and how that looks. He still has number-two-starter ceiling, but he could be more of a four or five this year, and might not have an inside track on one of the Angels' first five spots in April.

21. Bryson Stott, SS, Philadelphia Phillies

Stott's biggest attribute is his floor. While that might sound like damning him with an awful lot of faint praise, in deeper leagues, you need players like this to show up, provide steady production and push you to a pennant. The question for 2022 is when Stott will make his entrance. He could probably step in on Opening Day without missing a beat, but a midseason call up is more likely. Stott's favorable home venue will help his stock, although he might need to abandon his gap-to-gap approach for more power once he reaches Philadelphia.

22. MJ Melendez, C, Kansas City Royals

The Royals are so impressed with Melendez's bat and the strides he made in 2021 that there is talk that he could move to another position on the diamond to get his bat into the major-league lineup. That's bad if you invested heavily in Melendez in dynasty, but, in redraft leagues, that could give you the best of both worlds in 2022: a catcher-eligible power bat who won't get worn down or see his playing time capped due to the rigors of the position. There are some big ifs attached to this potential move, and it might not even materialize, but the fact that the Royals are even considering it tells you how much they believe in his hit tool and speaks to a potential opportunity sooner rather than later.

23. Alek Thomas, OF, Arizona Diamondbacks

Thomas could crack the Diamondbacks' Opening Day lineup, but he's more likely to be a midseason callup, instead. That's the primary reason he's so relatively low on this list, as his fantasy profile is quite favorable thanks to a great minor-league season in 2021 that his scouting profile backs up. Thomas is a leadoff candidate for the Diamondbacks when he does find his way to Arizona. His power will play up immediately, but there's some risk of both a fall in batting average and his speed not translating well for fantasy and stolen bases.

24. Josh Lowe, OF, Tampa Bay Rays

Lowe might appear to be blocked on the Rays' depth chart and ticketed for Triple-A to start 2022, but Kevin Kiermaier and Manuel Margot aren't exactly the sort of obstacles that should make you lose sleep at night if you invest. Lowe crushed minor-league pitching last year and has 20–20 potential right out of the gate. There's some swing-and-miss that leads to moderate or higher batting-average risk, but his glove in center gives Lowe a shot to be what we hoped Kiermaier would be much earlier in his career, with perhaps a little more pop thrown in for good measure.

25. Steven Kwan, OF, Cleveland Guardians

Kwan is a sabermetric darling among the prospect set: a high-average, high-OBP hitter who knows the strike zone like a 10-year veteran and will provide plenty of sneaky value that the casual fan won't notice or care about. The problem is that there isn't enough power or speed for Kwan to be more than a mid-tier outfielder, at best, unless he's a .300-plus hitter, which is much easier said than done in the 2022 iteration of a game, in which pitchers are tougher than ever. Opportunity is on Kwan's side in a soft Guardians outfield, and, in deep formats, he's a fine risk as fourth or fifth outfielder.

26. Nick Pratto, 1B, Kansas City Royals

Pratto will only go as far as his bat will carry him, but when that bat is potentially good for 30-plus home runs, that'll play. The concerns here are that his batting average could be ugly, and his defense is ordinary enough that any kind of slippage on offense will put Pratto in the dreaded Quad-A category. Opportunity is knocking if the Royals are willing to eat the remaining $10.5 million on Carlos Santana's contract, but, even if they don't, we're guessing Pratto's first crack at major-league pitching comes sooner rather than later.

27. Juan Yepez, "1B", St. Louis Cardinals

Without a universal designated hitter, ranking Yepez on a list like this would be incredibly challenging, even if he wasn't blocked by perennial All-Star Paul Goldschmidt. Yepez's iron glove limited him to first base and, even there, made him a poor defensive option. With the universal DH, Yepez will suddenly have a golden opportunity, and there's a good chance he will wins that job sooner rather than later. His power is legitimate, and, unlike some minor league mashers who fit this profile, Yepez has decent contact skills, to boot.

28. Kyle Isbel, OF, Kansas City Royals

There's an excellent chance that Isbel will be the Royals' Opening Day right fielder for the second year in a row and, unlike in 2021, an even-more-excellent chance that he sticks. That's most of the appeal in Isbel, as his ceiling isn't particularly impressive, and he's a deep-league special. The modest power he showed in Triple-A isn't likely to translate to the majors, so Isbel will need to keep most of the 22 steals he racked up last year to provide value. Even considering all these negatives, a 10–20 campaign would make Isbel quite useful.

29. Nate Pearson, RHP, Toronto Blue Jays

The stuff that we all loved and made many of us gush about Nate Pearson the prospect? Still there. But his results thus far in the majors and his health profile firmly plant Pearson in the high-risk category and probably put him on the path to future reliever. The great news is his fastball can hit triple-digits in that role, and his plus slider is more than enough in short 20–25-pitch bursts. The Blue Jays still haven't given up on him as a starter, which means this ranking is pure guesswork. The presence of Jordan Romano as closer means that Pearson will almost *have* to make his way back into the rotation to deliver any sort of useful fantasy results in 2022.

30. Nolan Gorman, 2B, St. Louis Cardinals

Gorman's just about ready for his big-league debut. How soon he arrives is contingent upon how willing the Cardinals are to move Tommy Edman into a super-sub role, and how quickly they do it. Gorman is one of those prospects who could struggle out of the gate due to a less-than-ideal approach at the dish, but his power projection is strong, and a high home-run ceiling from a middle infielder is appealing, even if it is attached to a .240-ish batting average.

31. Triston Casas, 1B, Boston Red Sox

If we believed Casas was a lock to grace the Red Sox' roster in 2022, he'd rank quite a few spots higher on this list. But while Casas performed admirably at Double-A as a 21-year-old, he didn't show the thump you'd like to see from a guy with a 6-foot-4, 250 pound frame and his sort of power projection. If Casas does make the Red Sox, he might be more underwhelming in the short term than you'd expect; even if his batting average is fine, it might only be tied to a 10–15-home-run player. The Sox could continue to be aggressive and grant Casas a midseason promotion, but it's entirely possible they just give him a full year in Triple-A to develop.

32. Grayson Rodriguez, RHP, Baltimore Orioles

On long-term lists, it's a close call between Rodriguez and Shane Baz for best pitching prospect in the game. On a list like this, it's tough to balance when Rodriguez might get called up and what his performance could look like when he does. There's a scenario in which Rodriguez is up in late April and blows the doors off and another in which he posts an ERA in the mid-fours and struggles out of the gate. Given his skill set, the former scenario is far more likely, but this ranking recognizes the reality that most pitching prospects don't excel in their rookie seasons.

33. Hunter Greene, RHP, Cincinnati Reds

Greene's fastball makes the young Aroldis Chapman's heater look slow by comparison. This isn't goofy scouting hyperbole; Greene has been clocked at 104 miles per hour. He hits triple-digits on the gun with regularity and even features a slider that's a plus offering. But there are a lot of questions about whether Greene will ever find a successful third pitch and enough consistency with health and command to survive as a starter in the majors. This is the year the rubber hits the road, and, even if Greene isn't up on Opening Day, he'll be a fun gamble to take, with tons of strikeout upside, even if everything else doesn't materialize right away.

34. Roansy Contreras, RHP, Pittsburgh Pirates

On a weak Pirates team, the opportunity is certainly there for Contreras to stake his claim to a rotation spot and hit the ground running. But it's that weak Pirates team that also tamps down Contreras's ranking somewhat. The wins most likely won't be there, and, while the park should help Contreras's ERA, the defense behind him will probably give some of that back. Contreras's performance breakout seems legitimate, and his stuff grades well, but, given his health and durability issues in 2021, Pittsburgh will likely be conservative with Contreras's innings in 2022.

35. Edward Cabrera, RHP, Miami Marlins

On ceiling alone, Cabrera would easily be ranked higher on this list, perhaps even in the top 10. It wasn't the fact that Cabrera struggled last year, but the shape of those struggles that led to significant concerns about his future. He couldn't command the fastball in the zone, allowing hitters to sit on his secondary offerings and hit Cabrera hard. His fastball is an upper-90s pitch with movement, so if Cabrera can solve his command issues this spring, he's an easy Rookie of the Year candidate. If not, he's a back-end starter who is capable of eating innings if he stays healthy.

36. Brennan Davis, OF, Chicago Cubs

If the Cubs decide to be aggressive with Davis, there's a chance he will get significant playing time in the majors this year. With the Cubs on a retooling path in the near term, there's no real need for them to be aggressive with Davis. This is the conundrum in trying to value Davis, a toolsy and talented outfielder who could hit 30-plus home runs in his prime with a little speed thrown in for good measure. This ranking assumes Davis's eventual promotion comes in the second half of 2022, if things go well for him in Triple-A. The Cubs' patchwork outfield means it's wide open should Davis really excel and force the issue.

37. Jose Siri, OF, Houston Astros

As a 26-year-old rookie outfielder with mammoth swing-and-miss issues, Siri could be a complete bust who crashes and burns and maybe doesn't even get an opportunity for the Astros at all. But his fantasy ceiling is a 25–30 player who hits for just enough batting average that you're willing to overlook the weeks when he offers less than nothing on your fantasy roster. Siri will battle Chas McCormick for the starting center-field job this spring, and, while McCormick is the safer bet, Siri is a name to keep an eye on, even if he isn't the starter out of camp.

38. Glenn Otto, RHP, Texas Rangers

Otto went from being an unknown organizational arm to a pop-up prospect thanks to the development of a slider and, then, quickly found his way to the majors after the Rangers acquired him in the Joey Gallo deal. As good as the slider was, Otto got pounded in six major-league starts. He'll need a third pitch to realize his ceiling as a number-four starter. There is opportunity for Otto to make the Rangers' Opening Day roster, but he might be better off putting the finishing touches on his game in Triple-A and refining a third (and maybe fourth) pitch.

39. Gabriel Moreno, C, Toronto Blue Jays

The huge strides Moreno made in his offensive game were front and center when he was able to take the field in 2021, but the big guy missed time with groin and thumb injuries and was limited to 159 plate appearances. He's not going to replicate his ludicrous 2021 line in the majors, but even if he's "only" a .280 hitter with 20-home-run pop, that'll play behind the dish. What he needs are reps, and while there's an easy path for Moreno to find his way to a starting role in Toronto, the Jays have the luxury of letting Moreno spend most or all of 2022 in the minors, as needed.

40. Nick Lodolo, LHP, Cincinnati Reds

Don't let the 69 professional innings temper your near-term enthusiasm. Lodolo is a polished college arm who throws three pitches for strikes, locates very well and would probably be a solid starter for the Reds right out of the gate. Health and durability are why Lodolo ranks this low, as a shoulder strain is what kept those innings down and led to questions about his durability and ability to pitch enough innings to survive as a starting pitcher. He's a must-stash in redraft leagues but also an arm you can't be afraid to cut at the first sign of health trouble in non-keeper formats.

41. Luis Gil, RHP, New York Yankees

Gil's fastball is arguably one of the best in baseball, but command-and-control issues persist and continue to make many wonder if it will ever work out for him as a starting pitcher. If he could develop even average control, Gil is talented enough to be a league-average starter with the fantasy benefit of a high-strikeout ceiling. That's a huge if, though, and pitchers like this tend to wind up as bulk relievers or late-inning arms. In AL-only or deep mixed leagues, that could make Gil useful as a high-whiff arm, but he's going to need to stick as a starter to be worth using in most formats.

42. Sixto Sánchez, RHP, Miami Marlins

Sanchez could be anything from a frontline ace to out for the season due to injury in 2022, and neither outcome would be shocking. However, the more pessimistic outcome is usually what happens in cases like this. That's a shame, because, when healthy, Sánchez throws two different fastballs in the upper 90s with regularity, has a plus-plus change and a slider that is also a plus pitch. He might never be a big strikeout arm because of the way he pitches, but, even then, his approach and stuff lead to plenty of weak contact and good results. Even with such a high ceiling, it's difficult, if not impossible, to rank a pitcher with such short-term injury concerns any higher than this, even one with as much talent as Sixto.

43. Max Meyer, RHP, Miami Marlins

Not many two-pitch pitchers can succeed, let alone thrive, as a starting pitcher, but if there's anyone who might be able to do it, it's Meyer. His mid- to upper-90s fastball and high-80s slider are so good that they could be enough, and, even if they aren't and Meyer is "only" a mid-tier starter, he's going to generate plenty of strikeouts, regardless. Beyond how the development of a third pitch goes, the other short-term question is how many innings Meyer will be allowed to pitch—in the majors or otherwise—in 2022. He'll be up at some point this year, but Miami might handle him with kid gloves, at first.

44. Seth Beer, DH, Arizona Diamondbacks

The probable addition of the DH to the National League certainly gives Beer a boost, but, even so, his ceiling is moderate at best. Beer's fantasy value is going to be tied heavily to how much he can translate his raw power into game action, something he didn't do particularly well at hitter-friendly Triple-A Reno last year. A .270 average with 15 home runs from a DH-only isn't playable in standard or shallow formats and isn't even particularly exciting outside of NL-only. Beer dislocated his left shoulder in his lone non-DH appearance in the majors in 2021 and is questionable for Opening Day at this writing. He makes this list mostly because the opportunity is clearly there.

45. Matt Brash, RHP, Seattle Mariners

Brash cemented his long-term value for the Mariners last year with a stellar 97 ⅓ innings split between High-A and Double-A. That's mostly why Brash is ranked so low on this list, as, while there's a chance he could be in the majors at some point in 2022, that ETA could be anywhere between mid-May and "sorry, not this year." Right now, he's a fastball/slider pitcher who needs a third pitch if he's going to be more than a mid-rotation arm, at best, and an excellent relief arm, at worst. He also still needs some command improvement before his inevitable promotion.

46. Nolan Jones, 3B, Cleveland Guardians

Jones's prospect stock has fallen, but this list is as much about opportunity as it is about talent, and Jones is likely to get a crack at the Guardians' starting lineup at some point in 2022. Third base is blocked by José Ramírez (I hear that guy is pretty good), but Cleveland moved Jones to right field late in 2021, and the outfield offers plenty of opportunity for Jones to break through. He has already been branded with the three-true-outcomes label, but a 25–30-home-run season with a .240 average is playable if Jones can get there. In OBP formats, Jones's walk rate gives him a little bit of a boost.

47. Sammy Long, LHP, San Francisco Giants

This one is all about the opportunity, but, right now, Long is on the outside looking in, waiting for an injury or ineffectiveness from one of the Giants' front five before he can crack the rotation. His stuff is average, but Long can throw three pitches for strikes. It helps that he pitches for a very good team in a good pitcher's park. It's all about opportunity for a pitcher like this, but, despite his advanced age and lack of prospect pedigree, Long will provide fantasy value at some point in 2022.

48. CJ Abrams, SS, San Diego Padres

Abrams broke his leg and sprained his medial collateral ligament last July and then was unable to play in the Arizona Fall League due to a shoulder injury. These injuries aren't a long-term concern, but they do push back the timetable for a player with a mere 183 plate appearances in the high minors. Abrams' power projects as below-average, at best, but he has such a good hit tool and so much speed that it hardly matters, if he maintains his current contact profile. Abrams is a future stolen-base league leader who could hit .300 in his best seasons; a mid-year call up could give you 15–20 steals in 2022.

49. George Kirby, RHP, Seattle Mariners

Kirby bulked up before the 2021 season began, resulting in a big velocity jump to go along with his stellar command. This gives him a mid-90s fastball to go with a solid slider and changeup. Kirby also keeps the ball in the yard, with only one home run allowed in 68 ⅔ innings. He's near the bottom of this list only because the Mariners have played it safe; Kirby is likely to spend most, if not all, of 2022 in the minors, and, even if he does get promoted, he's likely to be up against a strict innings cap. He's still worth a stash in leagues with reserve lists, as he'll be one of the bigger FAAB buys this year in leagues where he's available if/when he does get the call.

50. Anthony Volpe, SS, New York Yankees

We try to avoid putting players who haven't played an inning above High-A ball on lists like this—even toward the bottom—but we'd be remiss if we didn't include at least one dynamic player who checks off all the juicy fantasy boxes (power, speed, average) and has already exceeded expectations. The most likely scenario is Volpe does just fine between Double-A and Triple-A in 2022, but, even if there's only a two-percent chance he blows the doors off in the first half and forces the Yankees' hand, Volpe is worth your last reserve pick, even in redraft formats.

—Mike Gianella is an author of Baseball Prospectus.

Thanks to Jesse Roche and Bret Sayre for their assistance.

Top-100 First-Year Player Rankings for Dynasty Drafts

by Jesse Roche and Bret Sayre

Before we dive into the rankings, let's explore the landscape of First-Year Player Drafts (FYPDs) and how to approach this year's class. Much has changed for this draft class since we last opined on its quality in July:

> "The top of this draft class is kinda garbage tbh"
> "This draft class is really bad"
> —Bret Sayre, still bitter that Peyton Stovall went undrafted.
>
> Let's get this out of the way at the start. This draft class lacks the high-end fantasy talent we have seen in recent classes. There is no Spencer Torkelson. No Andrew Vaughn, Bobby Witt Jr., CJ Abrams, or Adley Rutschman. (And, no, Henry Davis is not the same fantasy prospect as Rutschman.) Simply, this class doesn't have that clear-cut top tier.
>
> Still, things change, and present evaluations may not fully capture the upside of some of these prospects, especially given the dearth of information from yet another strange, somewhat closer to normal, season.

It may have been harsh, but the fantasy outlook for this class was bleak. Well, things *have* changed. First, and most importantly, Seiya Suzuki is likely to sign shortly after the conclusion of the MLB lockout. Meanwhile, several prospects had impressive pro debuts and forced reexamination of their outlooks. Finally, the influx of presumed international-free-agent signees strengthens the class throughout. Now, this "garbage" draft class looks a whole lot better, with intriguing depth. Still, this class does pale in comparison to those of years past and to those to come (looking at you, 2023 FYPD class).

How to Approach FYPDs

Before you look at the list (and you probably already have), some important caveats:

- These rankings are for long-term fantasy leagues only.
- These rankings only include players likely designated as prospects in most dynasty formats. For our purposes, this means a player must not have exceeded 130 at-bats or 50 innings pitched in the majors.
- These rankings only include players selected in the 2021 MLB First-Year Player Draft or international free agents signed after the 2021 MLB season began.
- These rankings also include reported and anticipated signees in the international signing period beginning on January 15, 2022.
- These rankings account for a 16-team dynasty league with a standard, 5×5 scoring format, in which players can be kept forever without contracts/salaries.
- Home park, and other circumstantial information like it, matters but probably not as much as you think, since players move and variables change over the long term.
- The further down this list you venture, the larger the tiers become.
- "Rank" refers to rank on the Top 500 Dynasty Prospects.

It may go without saying, but before and during any draft, including a FYPD, you must:

1. **Understand your league scoring.** Player values change across league formats. Most FYPD rankings are developed for standard 5×5 dynasty leagues. (Per the above, we explicitly note that ours are.) For different formats, we adjust our rankings. (There are small tweaks within our Top-500 Dynasty OBP Rankings.)
2. **Understand your league size.** Meanwhile, how many prospects your league rosters should influence how you approach your draft. For example, you may choose to target high-ceiling prospects in shallow leagues and high-floor prospects in deep leagues. You may not be willing to wait for international free agents to develop in leagues where you are actively burning and churning through prospects throughout the season.
3. **Understand your league-mates and be flexible.** As with any draft, rankings are useful guides, but they are not gospel. Read the draft room, player predilections and draft trends. It is all about squeezing the most value out of your selections. If that means slightly reaching for a coveted player who is likely to be taken before your next pick, do it. Get your guys! Be prepared and willing to deviate from rankings to account for your league.

In this year's FYPD, after Suzuki, the top of the class is weak. (As we will repeatedly acknowledge.) Thus, it is a good year for late picks. Many emerging prospects (James Triantos, Jay Allen II, James Wood, etc.) likely will fall to the back end of the first round in most leagues. Given the skepticism regarding international prospects (discussed below), you can also find underrated, high-upside players (Roderick Arias, Cristhian Vaquero, Ricardo Cabrera, etc.) well outside the first round. In deeper formats (300-plus prospects), there a wealth of talent is likely to fall to the later rounds, at which point it is a prime time to target the lesser-known, but talented, international free agents.

At the same time, be mindful of roster construction moving forward into the season. If your league rosters fewer than than 200 prospects, you may not want to use your later picks to aggressively target players who are likely to debut at the Complex level in July. Back-end roster flexibility is often vital when you seek to burn and churn through pop-up prospects to find the next breakout. Borderline players unlikely to play until midseason should remain watchlist options in such leagues.

Finally, just because this class is weaker than most does not mean it is without value. Do not trade away all your picks because the class is weak. Each class has gems hiding in plain sight. Picks also provide flexibility, speculative uncertainty and, well, excitement until the selection is made. Many owners desire picks for this reason. Plus, drafting is part of the fun! Who knows if you'll uncover the next Nick Yorke!

Dynasty Valuation of MLB Draftees

As noted in July, the global pandemic has created more uncertainty—if you can ever use such a term with prospects—regarding this draft class than others in recent years. There is simply less data or track record to support emerging prospects. Still, prospect outlooks can change rapidly. Even after brief, one-to-two-month professional debuts, prospects turned heads and subtly changed reports. Consequently, our rankings look quite different from July.

This MLB draft class is weak overall, but that weakness really shows in the dearth of high-upside college players. When a catcher offers the most fantasy upside among college bats, it is bad. In particular, this college class lacks power bats who profile as impact MLB players (other than Henry Davis). Indeed, most of the well-regarded college hitters have uncertain power projections or concerning swing-and-miss issues. Meanwhile, college pitching (other than Jack Leiter) carries more risk than in recent years. Be it track-record concerns (Gavin Williams), injury recovery (Gunnar Hoglund), command (Ryan Cusick) and third-pitch (Will Bednar) issues or both (Sam Bachman), this group of college arms is questionable. At the same time, the prep class, while solid, lacks prospects with projectable elite tools at the top.

That said, this class did enjoy some strong professional debuts. Where this class does thrive (if anywhere) is in its depth. Just do not approach this class like prior years or years to come. (The 2023 FYPD class is going to be a good one!)

Dynasty Valuation of International Signees

The international signing period began on January 15 (delayed from July 2 by the pandemic). Typically, the vast majority of high-profile international signees are 16- and 17-year-old prospects. Meanwhile, each class often includes a handful of more-established, under-25-years-old international players who are still subject to international signing pools (e.g., Yoán Moncada in 2015 and Luis Robert in 2017). This year, notable established international players include Cubans Oscar Colás and César Prieto, who signed with the White Sox and Orioles, respectively.

The valuation of international free agents seems to fluctuate year to year. Certainly, some years include the standout 16-year-old prospect who comes with unreasonable expectations (such as Jasson Dominguez and Kevin Maitan). However, most years, these extremely young, raw prospects receive inconsistent press and reports that understandably change dramatically over a short period. Further, these prospects do not debut until midseason—normally in the Dominican Summer League—and likely do not arrive in the majors for five years.

It is hard to wait.

Indeed, Bret Sayre once wrote about ranking Kevin Maitan at 13th overall in 2017 (notably lower than others in the industry): "Since I started making these lists, I haven't even had a true J2 signee inside the top 25, so putting one this high is a bit of a statement I guess." Bret learned a lesson that year.

Below is a table with first-year-player-draft rankings of these players over the years:

Year	Players (Rank)
2021	Wilman Diaz (14), Carlos Colmenarez (15), Cristian Hernandez (25), *Pedro Leon (30), *Yoelkis Céspedes (31)
2020	Jasson Dominguez (4), Erick Peña (13), Robert Puason (19), Luis Rodriguez (32), Bayron Lora (44)
2019	*Victor Victor Mesa (3), *J.P. Martinez (13), Marco Luciano (27), Noelvi Marte (43), Diego Cartaya (47)
2018	*Luis Robert (3), Wander Franco (27), *Adolis García (33), *Jose Barrero (34), Ronny Mauricio (47)
2017	*Lourdes Gurriel Jr. (8), *Yuli Gurriel (11), Kevin Maitan (13), *Adrian Morejon (17), *Jorge Oña (18), *Norge Ruiz (32), *Randy Arozarena (33)
2016	*Yoán Moncada (1), *Eddy Martinez (11), *Yusniel Díaz (15), *Yadier Álvarez (23), Vladimir Guerrero Jr. (27), Lucius Fox (36)
*Established international player	

Of course, selecting a "true J2 signee" (an untested, 16-year-old prospect) is a gamble. It is a risk that some dynasty players won't take. Yet, it is hard to ignore that the top-four players in the Top 500 Dynasty Rankings are all former true J2 signees. In fact, none of those players were even considered potential star fantasy players at the time of signing. Too often, dynasty players either get caught up in chasing the next big thing or scared away due to recent disappointing performances from such high-profile signees.

After that epic 2015–16 class, however, industry perspectives began to shift toward these young prospects. Following the Maitan flop, two straight classes were rich in talent, producing the likes of Wander Franco, Julio Rodríguez, Noelvi Marte and Marco Luciano, among others. Then, along came Jasson Dominguez and . . . the global pandemic. The impact of the pandemic on these 16- and 17-year-old international prospects cannot be understated. Most, if not all, of these prospects remained abroad, unable to physically train with team personnel. (Coaching via Zoom is, well, not ideal.) Likely due in large part to the pandemic, the 2019–20 and 2020–21 international classes have disappointed in their brief professional debuts. As such, industry perspectives appear to be shifting away from these true J2 signees.

This ebb and flow of dynasty valuation is important to remember ahead of any FYPD. It is vital to recall the successes of years past. Below is a table illustrating notable players in each international class since 2015:

Signing Year	Notable Players
1/15/2021	Pedro Leon, Cristian Hernandez
7/2/2019	Jasson Dominguez, Reginald Preciado
7/2/2018	Noelvi Marte, Marco Luciano, Luis Matos, Francisco Álvarez, Orelvis Martinez, Kevin Alcantara
7/2/2017	Wander Franco, Luis Robert, Julio Rodríguez, George Valera, Everson Pereira, Ronny Mauricio
7/2/2016	Randy Arozarena, Lourdes Gurriel Jr., Luis García, Gabriel Arias
7/2/2015	Fernando Tatis Jr., Juan Soto, Vladimir Guerrero Jr., Yoán Moncada, Andrés Giménez, Leody Taveras, Cristian Pache

Some years have fallen flat. (Looking at you, Kevin Maitan and the 2016 class!) However, most years have included several big hits. Given the recent struggles noted above, this upcoming class has fallen under the radar. Now, for what feels like the first time since 2017, players from this class may actually be undervalued.

Still, most international free agents likely should be watchlist fodder in most leagues (200-or-fewer prospects). For deeper leagues, these young prospects are excellent mid- to late-round targets and stashes.

Concluding Thoughts

Indeed, this FYPD class no longer warrants the ire of Bret:

> "The class is better than I initially thought, but we still don't know as much about who the best long-term fantasy players are going to be, and it'll take another full season to really shake out. I'm also still sour about Peyton Stovall."

So basically: ¯_(ツ)_/¯

With all that said, and without further ado, please enjoy responsibly.

(Ages listed as of 4/1/2022)

Top 50

1. Seiya Suzuki, OF, Free Agent, Age: 27.62, Rank: 17

2. Marcelo Mayer, SS, Boston Red Sox, Age: 19.30, Rank: 31

3. Kahlil Watson, SS, Miami Marlins, Age: 18.96, Rank: 39

4. Jordan Lawlar, SS, Arizona Diamondbacks, Age: 19.70, Rank: 41

5. Jack Leiter, RHP, Texas Rangers, Age: 21.94, Rank: 42

Suzuki, who is arguably the top hitter in Nippon Professional Baseball (NPB), has been posted. Unfortunately, the MLB lockout has delayed his inevitable signing. Once he signs, and regardless of team, he immediately ascends to the top of this FYPD class.

Suzuki has been a force in NPB since 2016 and most recently posted a .317/.433/.636 slash line with 38 home runs. Notably, he has also thrived on the international stage, including a starring turn in the 2019 WBSC's Premier 12. At the plate, Suzuki is a disciplined and patient hitter with plus raw power and solid bat-to-ball ability. PECOTA's median projections are bullish on his immediate stateside production (.273/.382/.498 and 138 DRC+) and extrapolate to 26 home runs, 81 runs, and 86 runs batted in over 600 plate appearances.

Further, Suzuki is in the middle of his prime at just 27 years old and is likely to provide years of production. Once he arrives, he will immediately profile as a middle-of-the-order hitter with high-end four-category production. As such, he should sit atop draft boards for both rebuilding and win-now teams.

That said, it is understandable to be cautious. The recent track record for hitters from NPB has been less than stellar, including Shogo Akiyama and Yoshi Tsutsugo. Meanwhile, some may compare the Korea Baseball Organization (KBO) to NPB and note the struggles of Ha-Seong Kim and Byung Ho Park. Yet, the quality of competition in NPB is far superior to that of the KBO. Furthermore, Suzuki is the most highly regarded hitter to make the transition to MLB from from NPB (or the KBO) since Hideki Matsui. (Yes, that includes Shohei Ohtani.)

No, seriously, Suzuki remains wildly underrated throughout the industry. Projection systems, including PECOTA, are all bullish on his immediate production. In fact, after his posting, we discussed his ranking among all prospects, and Bret Sayre suggested that Suzuki "might need to be in the Top 10." He is that good.

Don't be afraid to take the leap for Suzuki!

A trio of prep shortstops headline this class after Suzuki. Marcelo Mayer possesses a picturesque left-handed swing, an advanced plate approach and burgeoning power from his projectable 6-foot-3 frame. While he lacks much speed, his bat is potentially special—so special, in fact, that some have compared him to Corey Seager. Next up, Watson may have the most fantasy upside in this class, with a lightning-fast bat, big power potential and high-end athleticism. If you like what you've seen from Jazz Chisholm Jr., you'll like Watson, another lefty hitter with similar offensive upside. Rounding out this group, Jordan Lawlar is the most likely to provide five-category production with plus-plus speed and solid pop. Questions regarding his spring swing-and-miss issues and recovery from surgery to repair a shoulder injury suffered in his second pro game make him a slightly riskier proposition than his peers.

Finally, Jack Leiter, the son of former major-league pitcher Al, is an established, successful college arm with a modern, analytically driven approach. His repertoire is headlined by a lively, mid-90s fastball with extension and carry. Behind his heater, he has three promising secondaries (curveball, slider and changeup) that flash above average or better, but all require refinement. His size (6-feet tall), occasionally shaky command and inconsistent secondaries are causes for some concern. However, Leiter is polished with proximity and massive strikeout upside.

Top 51–100

6. Brady House, SS, Washington Nationals, Age: 18.82, Rank: 51

7. Henry Davis, C, Pittsburgh Pirates, Age: 22.53, Rank: 56

8. Matt McLain, SS, Cincinnati Reds, Age 22.65, Rank: 73

9. Colton Cowser, OF, Baltimore Orioles, Age: 22.03, Rank: 76

10. James Triantos, 2B/SS, Chicago Cubs, Age: 19.17, Rank: 91

11. Sal Frelick, O F, Milwaukee Brewers, Age: 21.95, Rank: 96

12. Jay Allen II, OF, Cincinnati Reds, Age: 19.36, Rank: 98

Brady House is built like a house. (No, this will never get old!) He has a large frame, with broad shoulders, which already generates massive raw power. A strong spring and an impressive-but-brief debut in the Florida Complex League have lessened concerns regarding his athleticism and hit tool. Ultimately, power is House's calling card. His present raw power, bat speed, strength and frame combine to make him the premier power bat in this class.

As stated above, this draft class is relatively weak, in large part due to the dearth of high-upside college hitters. Henry Davis, the first-overall pick in the 2021 amateur draft, headlines the college crop with a well-rounded blend of contact ability, raw power and plate discipline. However, his unorthodox setup, level swing and position (catcher) likely limit his fantasy ceiling. Matt McLain is a prototypical, high-floor college hitter who "doesn't really have a projectable plus tool in the shed." (Basically, the yearly Bret Sayre pet prospect.) These types are often underrated in fantasy (e.g., Jonathan India). Despite lacking a carrying tool, McLain should move quickly with an advanced approach and enough power and speed to develop into a 15-home-run, 20-stolen-base threat. Colton Cowser can hit—that much is undisputed. His bat-to-ball ability and plate discipline are exceptional, and both were on display in his debut (19:22 strikeout-to-walk ratio and 5.8-percent swinging-strike rate in Low-A). How much power and speed he'll provide, however, is uncertain. Sal Frelick profiles as a high-contact tablesetter with plus-plus speed and aggressive baserunning, but he lacks much power, which is further limited by a slap-and-dash approach. Even if he barely scraps double-digit home runs, he should hit for a solid average with plenty of runs and stolen bases.

While the college bats leave much to be desired, many prep bats opened eyes in their debuts. James Triantos (.327/.376/.594) and Jay Allen II (.328/.440/.557) both shone in the Arizona Complex League (ACL). Triantos is a bat-first infielder with an unclear future position, but, boy, he can rake. Although he lacks size or projection, he taps into every last ounce of his raw power by utilizing a seemingly all-or-nothing swing. Despite his epic hacks, he consistently maintains high-end contact rates due to elite bat-to-ball skills. As Triantos faces more advanced arms, his aggressive swing and approach will certainly be tested, but, so far, so good. Allen, a three-sport star in high school, seamlessly transitioned to pro ball with unexpected ease, flashing five-category upside. He displayed plus-plus bat speed and an advanced, disciplined approach with nominal swing-and-miss. As he fills out his 6-foot-3 frame, Allen will likely develop even more power, enough to flirt with 30 home runs. Plus, Allen is an aggressive, instinctual baserunner despite average speed, and he should provide some stolen-base value, even if he slows down.

Top 101–150

13. Benny Montgomery, OF, Colorado Rockies, Age: 19.56, Rank: 101
14. Jackson Jobe, RHP, Detroit Tigers, Age: 19.67, Rank: 105
15. Roderick Arias, SS, New York Yankees, Age: 17.56
16. Cristhian Vaquero, OF, Washington Nationals, Age: 17.55
17. Harry Ford, C, Seattle Mariners, Age: 19.11, Rank: 114
18. James Wood, OF, San Diego Padres, Age: 19.54, Rank: 115
19. Colson Montgomery, SS, Chicago White Sox, Age: 20.09, Rank: 120
20. Trey Sweeney, SS, New York Yankees, Age: 21.93, Rank: 131
21. Gavin Williams, RHP, Cleveland Guardians, Age: 22.68, Rank: 137

Here come the high-upside, extreme-risk prospects!

Benny Montgomery is now a Rockies prospect, which is both a blessing (the Rockies!) and a curse (well, the Rockies). Few in this class possess his fantasy upside. Already, Montgomery has plus speed and sizable raw power, and his immensely projectable 6-foot-4 frame portends even more. As the Prospect Team notes, however, he has "a hitchy swing that begins with an odd hand-cock and glides through the zone with an unusually flat bat path," which limits his ability to tap into his power in games. Indeed, Montgomery managed just one extra-base hit (.043 ISO) in his brief debut at the complex. Still, he has tools to dream on, even if we may not see them in the majors for a long time (again, we're talking about the Rockies).

There Is No Such Thing As A Pitching Prospect ("TINSTAAPP") is a well-known mantra, yet it arguably applies with equal weight to catchers (TINSTAACP needs to be a thing). Such warnings about these extreme-risk positional demographics apply with even more force for prep prospects such as Jackson Jobe and Harry Ford. Without risk, though, there is no reward. Jobe already boasts a mid-90s fastball and a high-spin slider and has a precocious feel for a changeup despite being a relative neophyte at pitching. Meanwhile, Ford possesses electric bat speed, solid power potential and uncommon high-end speed for a catcher. Both Jobe and Ford very well may be top-50 dynasty prospects (or better) this time next year, or, well, there is no such thing as a . . .

Switch-hitters Roderick Arias and Cristhian Vaquero headline an underrated international class as potential five-tool, impact prospects. Arias has repeatedly performed in games, showcasing a potentially advanced hit tool from both sides of the plate with promising contact ability and swing decisions. Further, he has flashed both power, particularly from the right side, and speed, and his athletic, projectable frame indicates five-category upside. Vaquero received the highest bonus in the international class ($4.9 million) for good reason, as he arguably possesses the highest ceiling of anyone in this class. His athletic 6-foot-3 frame oozes projectability with present plus speed and burgeoning power. New to switch hitting, his right-handed swing remains a work in progress, but he flashes a feel for hitting. If everything clicks, Vaquero could be what we all hoped Kristian Robinson would become. As with all 16-year-old prospects, both Arias and Vaquero could develop any number of ways, and how their bats will perform in pro ball remains an open question.

James Wood is a large human. The 6-foot-7 slugger engenders comparisons to the similarly-sized Aaron Judge with understandably massive raw-power potential. Like Judge, Wood will also always have swing-and-miss in his profile. Regardless, he flashes enough bat-to-ball ability to allow for such an aggressive comparison, including a 75-percent contact rate at the complex. In addition to the obvious power, Wood has some present speed and athleticism, enough that, in tandem with solid instincts, the combination allowed him to go a perfect 10-for-10 in stolen bases in his debut. This part of his profile is not likely to age well as he fills out further, but that athleticism does make him stand apart from other gargantuan power bats.

Speaking of rose-colored-glasses comparisons, Colson Montgomery has repeatedly been compared to Corey Seager. (To hell with managing expectations for these young prospects!) Montgomery does have one of the best potential combinations of present hitting ability and power projection emanating from his 6-foot-4 frame. In fact, he had the second-highest contact rate (85 percent) among hitters with 100-plus plate appearances in the Arizona Complex League. How much power he'll ultimately get to in games is unclear (and he managed zero home runs in the ACL), but those rose-colored glasses see potential for 25-plus home runs and a solid average.

Trey Sweeney is yet another relatively untested, small-school standout. In July, we noted that he possessed "a desirable blend of a patient approach, high contact, and outstanding exit velocities." While he flashed an advanced approach during his debut in Low-A (.245/.357/.518), he struggled to regularly make hard contact (25.6 percent hard-hit rate). The long-term concern is how his noisy pre-swing load will impact his hit tool.

A Cleveland pitching prospect, you say? Gavin Williams landed in an organization that is adept at developing pitching and brought with him a ready-made, three-pitch arsenal, including a mid- to upper-90s fastball and two potentially above-average breaking balls. His command and control took huge steps forward last year, and his mechanics and athleticism bode well for future strike-throwing. So what's not to like? Williams's lengthy injury history, limited track record and rudimentary changeup cast some doubt on his ability to stick in the rotation for the long term.

Top 151–200

22. Sam Bachman, RHP, Los Angeles Angels, Age: 22.50, Rank: 152
23. Ricardo Cabrera, SS, Cincinnati Reds, Age: 17.42
24. Connor Norby, 2B, Baltimore Orioles, Age: 21.81, Rank: 167
25. Joshua Baez, OF, St. Louis Cardinals, Age: 18.76, Rank: 170
26. Gunnar Hoglund, RHP, Toronto Blue Jays, Age: 22.29, Rank: 173
27. Carson Williams, SS, Tampa Bay Rays, Age: 18.76, Rank: 181
28. Will Bednar, RHP, San Francisco Giants, Age: 21.80, Rank: 183
29. Oscar Colás, OF, Chicago White Sox, Age: 23.54
30. Andrew Painter, RHP, Philadelphia Phillies, Age: 18.97, Rank: 198

As noted at the start, college pitching carries more risk than in recent years. Sam Bachman, the ninth-overall pick in last year's amateur draft, arguably has the best two-pitch mix in this class, with a lively, mid- to upper-90s fastball and an upper-80s power slider. His violent, low-slot delivery, checkered injury history and rudimentary changeup create a lot of relief risk, however. That said, Bachman has massive strikeout upside if he can stick in the rotation, with a legitimate late-inning-relief fallback. On the topic of risk, Gunnar Hoglund is recovering from Tommy John surgery. Prior to his injury, he enjoyed a dominant spring, showcasing exceptional command of a solid-yet-unspectacular, three-pitch mix. Unlike Bachman, Hoglund has little relief risk, with an ideal starter's frame, command and enough stuff to turn a lineup over. Finally, Will Bednar, the star of the College World Series for Mississippi State, is "a real . . . sigh . . . bulldog on the mound." (It is too good not to reappropriate!) His advanced command of a low- to mid-90s fastball and mid-80s slider allowed him to bully opposing lineups throughout the year. However, he rarely utilizes his curveball or changeup, and the development of an impact third pitch is a high priority.

Following Arias and Vaquero, above, there is a substantial tier drop within the international class. Ricardo Cabrera lacks the same dynamic upside of those two, but he does everything well. Offensively, he has a quick, compact swing that utilizes the whole field with emerging power and above-average athleticism. On the other hand, Oscar Colás does one thing very well: power. The muscular lefty slugger, once known as the "Cuban Ohtani," has plus bat speed, a powerful bat, and a cannon for an arm. However, the last time Colás played regularly was in 2019 in the Japanese minor leagues, where he hit .302/.350/.516 before a brief seven-game run in NPB (.278/.381/.444). Understandably, there are legitimate questions about his hit tool. For what it's worth, his short track record in Cuba showed more promise than Yoelkis Céspedes's. Plus, Colás has remade his body and reportedly now flashes above-average run times (he's unlikely to provide stolen bases, though). Still, he is a power prospect first and foremost, and that power will most certainly play if his hit tool approaches average.

The Prospect Team compared Connor Norby to Terrin Vavra recently, which certainly does not engender much excitement. Piling on, the Orioles have moved the left-field wall in Campden Yards back thirty feet. For a prospect with limited power to start, such a change to his future park hurts. Of course, as we state above, "[h]ome park, and other circumstantial information like it, matters but probably not as much as you think, since players move and variables change over the long term." Luckily, Norby's hit tool drives his profile, anyway. Norby has superb plate discipline, a patient approach and uses the whole field. He also has enough sneaky pop and speed to project as a potential 15–15 player.

Joshua Baez and Carson Williams are two of the youngest players from the 2021 MLB draft class, having turned 18 years old just three days apart in late June. Baez had one of the worst pro debuts in this class, hitting just .158/.305/.303 in the Florida Complex League. Given his youth and pre-draft tendency to swing and miss, this early performance is not necessarily unexpected. If anything, it may actually be a little encouraging. Baez displayed solid athleticism, enough to steal bases and provide hope that he could stick in center. Even if he slows, he has immense power upside with a large, 6-foot-4 frame, plus bat speed and a swing designed to park it. Meanwhile, as the Prospect Team notes, "Williams is a bit of a blank canvas" as a former two-way player with an inconsistent hit tool. That uncertainty will likely cause him to fall in many FYPDs. Don't let it happen. He has intriguing power-speed potential with a projectable and athletic 6-foot-2 frame. (Plus, he is a Bret Sayre guy!)

Andrew Painter is a large and projectable, 6-foot-7, prep pitching prospect with a huge fastball that touched 100 mph in instructs and inconsistent secondaries. The sky's the limit, but there is no floor here. But, if and when Painter arrives in the majors, expect lots and lots of Bob Ross gifs.

Top 201–250

31. Won-Bin Cho, OF, St. Louis Cardinals, Age: 18.60
32. Lazaro Montes, OF, Seattle Mariners, Age: 17.44
33. Zack Gelof, 3B, Oakland Athletics, Age: 22.45, Rank: 213
34. Alex Binelas, 3B/1B, Boston Red Sox, Age: 21.84, Rank: 218
35. Lonnie White Jr., OF, Pittsburgh Pirates, Age: 19.25, Rank: 224
36. Diego Benitez, SS, Atlanta, Age: 17.36
37. Max Muncy, SS, Oakland Athletics, Age: 19.60, Rank: 233
38. Aaron Zavala, OF, Texas Rangers, Age: 21.77, Rank: 239
39. Tyler Black, 2B, Milwaukee Brewers, Age: 21.68, Rank: 241
40. William Bergolla Jr., SS, Philadelphia Phillies, Age: 17.44

The next tier of international prospects does not lack intriguing upside. Headlining this tier is Won-Bin Cho and his eye-popping raw power, including a 485-foot home run and 115-mph exit velocity with aluminum bats during the National Power Showcase at Globe Life Field in November 2020. The Korean prospect was a late addition to this international class, having only removed his name from the KBO draft last August. While his signing bonus ($500,000) is less than others in this class, he has just as much upside. In addition to the power, Cho has an easy, smooth swing and an athletic, 6-foot-2 frame with enough speed to potentially stick in center field. The open questions, though, are how much he'll hit and get to that power in games. Another left-handed international slugger, Lazaro Montes draws comparisons to a young Yordan Alvarez. Montes does share some similarities as a big (6-foot-4), left-handed slugger from Cuba with advanced barrel control, a feel for hitting and massive power potential. Unlike Alvarez, though, Montes has enough athleticism to likely stick in the field. When Alvarez comps are bandied about—no matter how optimistic—you need to listen.

Inconsistent college prospects Zack Gelof and Alex Binelas both enjoyed standout professional debuts. In fact, Gelof even received a brief, three-game run in Triple-A to finish the season (the Triple-A season lasted an additional two weeks). Prior to that upper-minors taste, he torched Low-A (.298/.393/.548), launching nearly as many home runs (7) in half as many at-bats as during his junior year at Virginia (9). Notably, Gelof tapped into more of his plus raw power, reminiscent of his loud (but truncated) 2020 campaign. His wide base and short stride does likely limit his long-term ability to tap into his power, but it offsets some underlying contact issues. Gelof can also chip in some steals, despite average athleticism, due to strong instincts and a long track record of success (84-for-98 across all levels).

Like Gelof, Binelas made quick work of Low-A (.314/.379/.636), showcasing the easy, all-fields raw power that made him a potential top-10 pick after his impressive freshman season with Louisville. A broken hand in 2020 limited him to just two games, then a dreadfully slow start and lots of whiffs in 2021 sunk his draft stock, causing him to fall to the third round. Indeed, Binelas continued to swing-and-miss even in that stellar debut (17 percent swinging strikes). Still, he managed to knock 28 *home runs* across just 86 games between college and his debut. Now with the Red Sox as part of the Hunter Renfroe trade, Binelas does project similarly to Bobby Dalbec as a streaky, power-hitting corner infielder with serious whiff issues.

Lonnie White Jr. and Max Muncy exemplify the wide range of potential outcomes within this prep MLB draft class. The former is a raw, tooled-up outfielder with a muscular, 6-foot-3 frame and present plus speed. In fact, White had a commitment to play both baseball and football (wide receiver) for Penn State; that is the type of elite athlete we're talking about. His hit tool is high variance, however, and his "swing has some length, stiffness and loft." As such, he has struggled with swing-and-miss, particularly against more advanced arms. Regardless, White has a potential power/speed combo that few possess. On the other hand, Muncy has more limited upside, and "neither offensive tool projects past a 55." Yet, he should make the most of his ability with an advanced approach looking to do damage and solid bat speed. Given his name and his organization, he'll certainly be compared to a certain MLB hitter. Hopefully, he doesn't become most notable for mistaken picks during fantasy drafts. (Be sure to always check before you pick!)

Atlanta is officially back as an unencumbered player on the international scene after several years of sanctions arising from the 2017 scandal. Diego Benitez, the prize of their international signings, is a bat-first infielder with a fluid, quick swing and a well-built frame that promises future power. Meanwhile, the division-rival Phillies also made a splash, signing William Bergolla Jr., the tooled-up son of a former big leaguer. While his wiry, narrow frame (listed at just 5-foot-11 and 165 pounds) does not portend a ton of power, he has advanced contact ability, a compact line-drive stroke and plus speed. Further, Bergolla has the type of well-regarded instincts and "baseball IQ" that often come with growing up around the game.

Aaron Zavala (.392/.526/.628) and Tyler Black (.383/.496/.683) had loud college seasons and understandably saw their draft stock soar. These types of draft prospects—with either limited track record (Zavala) or questionable competition (Black)—are endemic in this pandemic era and very well could boom or bust. Both are known for excellent plate discipline and bat-to-ball skills. Zavala offers less power projection with an approach geared for hard, gap-to-gap contact, but "he should continue to run high OBPs even, if he's more a 10–15-home-run and 30-double guy." In other words, something akin to late-career Michael Brantley. Black has a more-projectable, 6-foot-2 frame with average raw power that he should get to (and then some) in games. His powerless debut (.222/.388/.272) undersells how much juice is in that bat.

Top 251–300

41. Dyan Jorge, SS, Colorado Rockies, Age: 19.03
42. Ty Madden, RHP, Detroit Tigers, Age: 22.11, Rank: 256
43. Anthony Gutierrez, OF, Texas Rangers, Age: 17.35
44. Ryan Cusick, RHP, Atlanta, Age: 22.38, Rank: 266
45. Chase Petty, RHP, Minnesota Twins, Age: 18.99, Rank: 268
46. Jackson Merrill, SS, San Diego Padres, Age: 18.95, Rank: 269
47. Ethan Wilson, OF, Philadelphia Phillies, Age: 22.40, Rank: 274
48. Frank Mozzicato, LHP, Kansas City Royals, Age: 18.78, Rank: 275
49. Bubba Chandler, RHP/SS, Pittsburgh Pirates, Age: 19.54, Rank: 284
50. Ryan Reckley, SS, San Francisco Giants, Age: 17.57

For some dynasty leagues (200–250 prospects rostered), we've reached a point in these rankings at which many of these prospects should be watchlist targets. For others, we soldier on!

This may already sound like a broken record, but this international class is a whole lot of fun. Dyan Jorge has speed for days to go with an uber-athletic, 6-foot-3 frame and plus bat speed that hint at power gains. Despite gaining eligibility last year, he waited to sign until this period opened and received the third-highest bonus ($2.8 million). That figure speaks to his immense upside, though his bat receives mixed reviews. Anthony Gutierrez has a prototypical, athletic, 6-foot-3 frame with broad shoulders and a narrow waist. (Describing prospects often feels like objectifying them.) Already, he flashes a picture-perfect stroke and, as he fills out, should develop sizable power. Finally, Ryan Reckley is next in a recent influx of high-upside prospects from the Bahamas. The switch-hitting potential tablesetter is best known for his plus-or-better speed and penchant to steal, but he also has a quick bat with surprising pop.

Once again, college pitching in this class carries more risk than in recent years, and both Ty Madden and Ryan Cusick are prime examples. The workhorse ace of the University of Texas, Madden carried plenty of buzz during the draft process, but inconsistent fastball velocity (normally mid-90s) and a two-pitch-heavy repertoire (fastball, slider) caused him to fall. He flashes a serviceable changeup and a show-me curveball but too infrequently in both cases. At his best, Madden looks the part of a potential mid-rotation arm, and pro instruction may elicit more consistent, less Madden-ing performance. Meanwhile, Cusick already has two plus-to-plus-plus offerings in his upper-90s fastball and low-80s power curveball, and Low-A hitters stood no chance (50.7-percent strikeout rate!). While his command is subpar, his stuff is so good that he may be able to get by with just two pitches and a scattershot strike-throwing approach. Call Cusick a discount Sam Bachman, with a similar, but more likely, late-inning fallback.

Another group of prospects often better left for deeper formats are the non-elite prep hitters, pitchers and, well, whatever Bubba Chandler is going to be. Chase Petty carries the most upside and risk of this group, and the Prospect Team described his outlook best: "Petty has been known to sit 99 mph with his fastball, which has repeatedly touched triple-digits in the past, and it's explosive heat. His slider is plus-plus. *Everything else about his profile is a hot mess*." (Emphasis added.) This type of profile normally goes the way of Tyler Kolek or Riley Pint. We can keep dreaming, though! Jackson Merrill and Frank Mozzicato are pop-up prep prospects with 6-foot-3 frames to dream on, and each requires a fair bit of projection. Merrill boasts a pretty swing, some solid present pop and makes plenty of contact—including an 81-percent contact rate in the Arizona Complex League. It all adds up to a potential above-average hit and raw-power projection if everything clicks. Mozzicato is a more traditional pitching prospect with advanced command and a standout, high-spin curveball. Nevertheless, he requires a lot of velocity gains (he's mostly upper 80s, at present) and third-pitch development to project as an impact fantasy arm. The same could have been said about Reid Detmers not long ago. Finally, Bubba Chandler is a premium athlete and two-way player who is likely best suited to pitch—he has a potential plus fastball and three secondaries—but he spent his brief debut focused on hitting. As we said in July, "[t]hat uncertainty makes his fantasy profile more challenging, somewhat similar to Masyn Winn before him, but betting on natural ability is smart when you're outside of the top tiers."

Ethan Wilson is a power-hitting corner-outfield prospect with a sound approach who hasn't actually hit for meaningful power since his dynamic freshman year for South Alabama (.346/.453/.686). That includes his poor debut in Low-A (.215/.282/.374), in which his maximum exit velocity topped out at 105.5 mph, and his chase rate was an unseemly 40.1 percent. That was certainly not the performance of a player once thought to be a potential plus-hit and -power bat. As such, Wilson may go under the radar in FYPDs. Whether that makes him a sleeper or a trap pick, however, is unclear.

Top 301-350

51. Cooper Kinney, 2B, Tampa Bay Rays, Age: 19.18, Rank: 302

52. Jordan Wicks, LHP, Chicago Cubs, Age: 22.58, Rank: 304

53. Jonathan Mejia, SS, St. Louis Cardinals, Age: 16.97

54. Ryan Bliss, SS, Arizona Diamondbacks, Age: 22.30, Rank: 314

55. Michael McGreevy, RHP, St. Louis Cardinals, Age: 21.73, Rank: 318

56. Denzel Clarke, OF, Oakland Athletics, Age: 21.91, Rank: 319

57. Peyton Wilson, 2B, Kansas City Royals, Age: 22.41, Rank: 322

58. Kyle Manzardo, 1B, Tampa Bay Rays, Age: 21.70, Rank: 326

59. Javier Osorio, SS, Detroit Tigers, Age: 17.00

60. Matt Mikulski, LHP, San Francisco Giants, Age: 22.89, Rank: 332

61. Yasser Mercedes, OF, Minnesota Twins, Age: 17.37

62. Jose Torres, SS, Cincinnati Reds, Age: 22.51, Rank: 342

As we approach the end of a larger overall tier (normally around 200–350 overall), the talent pool shows more warts. There are the "but the kid can hit" Rays prospects: Cooper Kinney and Kyle Manzardo. Both display advanced plate discipline and bat-to-ball skills, but they may end up as atypical first basemen without much game power. Next, we have the first-round college control artists with so-so stuff: Jordan Wicks and Michael McGreevy. For both, you're hoping for post-draft velocity gains or breaking-ball development. Then, there are the lower-upside-but-advanced international signees with a potential carrying tool: Jonathan Mejia (hit), Javier Osorio (electric bat speed) and Yasser Mercedes (power). Finally, we have the higher-risk college prospects with underrated upside. This group includes diminutive second-base prospects with surprising pop (Ryan Bliss and Peyton Wilson), power/speed bats with serious hit-tool questions (Denzel Clarke and Jose Torres) and a volatile college arm with big stuff but a limited track record and questionable command (Matt Mikulski).

Top 351-400

63. Yendry Rojas, SS, San Diego Padres, Age: 17.18
64. Anthony Solometo, LHP, Pittsburgh Pirates, Age: 19.33, Rank: 356
65. Ky Bush, LHP, Los Angeles Angels, Age: 22.38, Rank: 364
66. Daylen Lile, OF, Washington Nationals, Age: 19.33, Rank: 365
67. Wes Kath, 3B, Chicago White Sox, Age: 19.66, Rank: 366
68. Braylin Tavera, OF, Baltimore Orioles, Age: 17.11
69. Simon Juan, OF, New York Mets, Age: 16.71
70. Johan Barrios, SS, Milwaukee Brewers, Age: 17.23
71. Izaac Pacheco, SS, Detroit Tigers, Age: 19.37, Rank: 382
72. Edwin Arroyo, SS/2B, Seattle Mariners, Age: 18.60, Rank: 390
73. Tony Blanco Jr., OF, Pittsburgh Pirates, Age: 16.88
74. Adan Sanchez, 3B, Chicago Cubs, Age: 16.85

From here on out, the overall tier is expansive and extends well beyond the Top-500 prospects. As such, the difference between the 63rd prospect (Yendry Rojas) and even a prospect listed within the Honorable Mentions is somewhat nominal. That said, this sub-tier is basically a “best of the rest” tier dominated by high-upside international free agents and prep prospects.

Rojas is truly on the edge of two tiers as a bat-first infielder with a dynamic, left-handed swing and a well-built, muscular frame. Outside of his bat, however, he leaves a lot to be desired, and it is unclear where he fits best defensively. Behind him within this tier, fellow international free agents Braylin Tavera, Simon Juan and Johan Barrios all have athletic, projectable frames but more uncertain hit-tool projections due to less-refined swing mechanics. For example, Juan’s current swing is stiff and upright with little lower-body involvement. Meanwhile, Tony Blanco Jr. and Adan Sanchez are potential plus-or-better power bats likely limited to a corner defensively. The former is already 6-foot-5 with the most present raw power in the class and receives comps to Franmil Reyes.

Among the prep prospects within this tier, Anthony Solometo may actually have the most upside. His projectable, 6-foot-5 frame, funky mechanics and solid command of a promising fastball/slider combo are reminiscent of a young Madison Bumgarner. Daylen Lile, Wes Kath and Izaac Pacheco were trendy names pre- and post-draft, but poor, small-sample debuts have sunk their perceived value. Lile can hit, with a gorgeous, left-handed swing and advanced bat-to-ball ability. It is unclear if he can do much of anything else, though. Kath and Pacheco have big frames and present power with more to come but also concerning contact issues. Finally, Edwin Arroyo is a raw switch-hitter (and thrower!) with some power/speed upside and a higher floor than most prep bats due to his defensive acumen.

Despite being the lone college prospect in this tier, Ky Bush remains pretty raw. The 6-foot-6 lefty only recently experienced a velocity bump into the mid-90s and is still working on developing his secondaries and command. Yet, Bush made a lot of progress over a short time, and his fastball/slider combo misses bats.

Top 401-450

75. César Prieto, 2B, Baltimore Orioles, 22.89
76. Griff McGarry, RHP, Philadelphia Phillies, Age: 22.81, Rank: 410
77. Christian Franklin, OF, Chicago Cubs, Age: 22.33, Rank: 411
78. Jaden Hill, RHP, Colorado Rockies, Age: 22.27, Rank: 416
79. Corey Rosier, OF, San Diego Padres, Age: 22.56, Rank: 420
80. Noah Miller, SS, Minnesota Twins, Age: 19.38, Rank: 422
81. Adrian Del Castillo, C, Arizona Diamondbacks, Age: 22.51, Rank: 428
82. Maddux Bruns, LHP, Los Angeles Dodgers, Age: 19.78, Rank: 431
83. Ben Kudrna, RHP, Kansas City Royals, Age: 19.17, Rank: 437
84. Nelson Rada, OF, Los Angeles Angels, Age: 16.60
85. Tyler Whitaker, OF, Houston Astros, Age: 19.66, Rank: 446
86. Reed Trimble, OF, Baltimore Orioles, Age: 21.82, Rank: 447

César Prieto is a small (5-foot-8), pesky hitter with elite contact skills. His stats from the Cuban National Series, included a miniscule 3.1-percent strikeout rate in 2020–21 at just 21 years old. While Prieto lacks much power or speed, he still can carve out a useful fantasy role akin to Luis Arraez. On the rebuilding Orioles, he may arrive quickly and receive a long look.

Griff McGarry and Jaden Hill both have some of the best pure stuff in this class. The former has a four-pitch mix, headlined by a potentially plus-or-better fastball that sits 94–96 mph (primarily two-seam) with big arm-side run. In addition to his heater, McGarry has two high-spin breaking balls in the low- and mid-80s and a promising mid-80s changeup with depth. The issue, however, is his well-below-average command and control, which resulted in a staggering 21-percent walk rate during his junior year and an "improved" 14-percent walk rate in his debut. If McGarry can harness his stuff, he will be a huge riser this year. Meanwhile, Hill is recovering from Tommy John surgery and was drafted by, gulp, the Rockies. Risk abounds, but he has flashed an upper-90s fastball and two potentially plus secondaries.

Christian Franklin and Adrian Del Castillo both carried some pre-draft hype, but disappointing junior campaigns and limited upsides have dampened their long-term outlook. Franklin is a stout, muscular corner outfielder with no projection remaining and a three-true-outcomes profile without a ton of power. Del Castillo is a bat-first "catcher" with a well-regarded hit tool who will likely move off the position eventually and really needs to tap into more raw power to be an impact player.

If you scout the stat line, then Corey Rosier immediately jumps out. He arguably had the best debut of this draft class, hitting .390/.461/.585 with 13 stolen bases in Low-A. If that is not enough, he was also the centerpiece in the trade that sent Adam Frazier to the Mariners. Not all of his performance is smoke and mirrors. Rosier is a high-contact, disciplined hitter with a quick, compact stroke and above-average speed. There is not a lot of pop in his bat, though, and the quality of his contact is too often poor. Regardless, he looks a lot like a fourth outfielder who could surprise, which is quite a find in the 12th round.

Quick hits time! Noah Miller has been aptly described by MLB Pipeline as "a less physical version of his brother Owen." In other words, he has a hit-tool-driven profile without much power or speed. Maddux Bruns and Ben Kudrna are typical, late-first/early-second-round, projectable-framed prep arms with some present velocity and promising secondaries. Nelson Rada is better known for his center-field glove, but he also has a smooth, leveraged swing with emerging power. Both Tyler Whitaker (big power and some speed) and Reed Trimble (big speed and some power) have big-time tools, but there are serious doubts whether either will actually hit.

Top 451-500

87. Samuel Muñoz, 3B, Los Angeles Dodgers, Age: 17.53
88. Alexis Hernandez, SS, Chicago Cubs, Age: 17.26
89. Yordany De Los Santos, SS, Pittsburgh Pirates, Age: 17.12
90. Niko Kavadas, 1B, Boston Red Sox, Age: 23.43, Rank: 466
91. Joe Mack, C, Miami Marlins, Age: 19.26, Rank: 467
92. Ricky Tiedemann, LHP, Toronto Blue Jays, Age: 19.62, Rank: 469
93. Tyler McDonough, OF/2B, Boston Red Sox, Age: 22.99, Rank: 472
94. Jhonny Severino, SS, Milwaukee Brewers, Age: 17.39
95. Freili Encarnacion, SS, Boston Red Sox, Age: 17.18
96. Abdias De La Cruz, SS, Arizona Diamondbacks, Age: 17.41
97. Cody Morissette, 2B/3B/SS, Miami Marlins, Age: 22.21, Rank: 490
98. Ryan Holgate, OF, St. Louis Cardinals, Age: 21.81, Rank: 493
99. Dylan Smith, RHP, Detroit Tigers, Age: 21.84, Rank: 495
100. Jaison Chourio, OF, Cleveland Guardians, Age: 16.86

This deep into a FYPD class, it is often best to bet on upside more than anything. This is the case even in 30-team leagues in which high-floor prospects carry more value. Nevertheless, "floor," at this point in a draft, is nonexistent. Consequently, this final tier is heavy on international prospects with promising offensive tools, such as hitting ability (Samuel Muñoz and Jaison Chourio), power (Yordany De Los Santos, Jhonny Severino, and Freili Encarnacion) and speed (Alexis Hernandez and Abdias De La Cruz). Among the college prospects, we find power-only bats (Niko Kavadas and Ryan Holgate), hit-tool-only bats (Tyler McDonough and Cody Morissette), and a potentially control-oriented number-five starter with a deep-but-underwhelming arsenal (Dylan Smith). On the prep side, Joe Mack is a standard prep catcher with hit-tool variance and power potential. Then, there is Ricky Tiedemann, who went the non-standard route of a JUCO in order to be eligible for the draft and saw an uptick in velocity. Since then, he has reportedly gained even more velocity and sits in the mid-to-upper 90s.

Honorable Mentions (Alphabetical Order)

Leandro Arias, SS, Baltimore Orioles, Age: 17.15
Michael Arroyo, SS, Seattle Mariners, Age: 17.41
Cooper Bowman, 2B, New York Yankees, Age: 22.18
Wes Clarke, C/1B, Milwaukee Brewers, Age: 22.46
Jose De Jesus, OF, Texas Rangers, Age: 17.13
Randy De Jesus, OF, Los Angeles Angels, Age: 17.13
Max Ferguson, 2B/UT, Houston Astros, Age: 22.60
Jake Fox, 2B/SS/3B, Cleveland Guardians, Age: 19.13
Robert Gasser, LHP, San Diego Padres, Age: 22.83
Martin Gonzales, SS, Seattle Mariners, Age: 17.51
Erick Hernandez, OF, Chicago White Sox, Age: 17.21
Luis Meza, C, Toronto Blue Jays, Age: 17.46
Matheu Nelson, C, Cincinnati Reds, Age: 23.21
Doug Nikhazy, LHP, Cleveland Guardians, Age: 22.64
Ryan Spikes, 2B/3B, Tampa Bay Rays, Age: 19.05
Jarlin Susana, RHP, San Diego Padres, Age: 18.02
Justice Thompson, OF, Cincinnati Reds, Age: 21.73
Jordan Viars, OF/1B, Philadelphia Phillies, Age: 18.70
Luke Waddell, SS/2B/3B, Atlanta, Age: 23.71
T.J. White, OF, Washington Nationals, Age: 18.69

—Jesse Roche and Bret Sayre are authors of Baseball Prospectus.

Team Codes

CODE	TEAM	LG	AFF	NAME
ABD	Aberdeen	A+ E	Orioles	IronBirds
ABQ	Albuquerque	AAA W	Rockies	Isotopes
ADE	Adelaide	ABL	-	Giants
AGS	Aguascalientes	MEX	-	Rieleros
AGU	Aguilas	LIDOM	-	Aguilas
AKL	Auckland	ABL	-	Tuatara
AKR	Akron	AA NE	Guardians	RubberDucks
ALT	Altoona	AA NE	Pirates	Curve
AMA	Amarillo	AA C	D-backs	Sod Poodles
ANG	ACL Angels	ACL	Angels	ACL Angels
ANG	AZL Angels	AZL	Angels	AZL Angels
ARA	Aragua	LVBP	Tigres	Tigres
ARI	Arizona	NL	-	D-backs
ARK	Arkansas	AA C	Mariners	Travelers
ASGO	AZL Athletics Gold	AZL	Athletics	AZL Athletics Gold
ASGR	AZL Athletics Green	AZL	Athletics	AZL Athletics Green
ASH	Asheville	A+ E	Astros	Tourists
AST	FCL Astros	FCL	Astros	FCL Astros
AST	GCL Astros	GCL	Astros	GCL Astros
ATH	ACL Athletics	ACL	Athletics	ACL Athletics
ATL	Atlanta	NL	-	Braves
AUB	Auburn	NYP	Nationals	Doubledays
AUG	Augusta	A E	Braves	GreenJackets
BAL	Baltimore	AL	-	Orioles
BAT	Batavia	NYP	Marlins	Muckdogs
BEL	Beloit	A+ C	Marlins	Snappers
BG	Bowling Green	A+ E	Rays	Hot Rods
BIL	Billings	PIO	Reds	Mustangs
BIR	Birmingham	AA S	White Sox	Barons
BLU	Bluefield	APP	Blue Jays	Blue Jays
BLU	FCL Blue Jays	FCL	Blue Jays	FCL Blue Jays
BLU	GCL Blue Jays	GCL	Blue Jays	GCL Blue Jays
BLX	Biloxi	AA S	Brewers	Shuckers
BNG	Binghamton	AA NE	Mets	Rumble Ponies
BOI	Boise	NWL	Rockies	Hawks
BOS	Boston	AL	-	Red Sox
BOW	Bowie	AA NE	Orioles	Baysox
BRA	FCL Braves	FCL	Braves	FCL Braves
BRA	GCL Braves	GCL	Braves	GCL Braves
BRB	AZL Brewers Blue	AZL	Brewers	AZL Brewers Blue
BRD	Bradenton	A SE	Pirates	Marauders
BRG	AZL Brewers	AZL	Brewers	AZL Brewers

CODE	TEAM	LG	AFF	NAME
	Gold			Gold
BRI	Brisbane	ABL	Bandits	Bandits
BRK	Brooklyn	A+ E	Mets	Cyclones
BRS	Bristol	APP	Pirates	Pirates
BRWB	ACL Brewers Blue	ACL	Brewers	ACL Brewers Blue
BRWG	ACL Brewers Gold	ACL	Brewers	ACL Brewers Gold
BUF	Buffalo	AAA E	Blue Jays	Bisons
BUR	Burlington	MID	Angels	Bees
BUR	Burlington	APP	Royals	Royals
CAG	Caguas	PWL	Caguas	Caguas
CAM	Campeche	MEX	-	Piratas
CAN	Canberra	ABL	Cavalry	Cavalry
CAR	Carolina	A E	Brewers	Mudcats
CAR	FCL Cardinals	FCL	Cardinals	FCL Cardinals
CAR	GCL Cardinals	GCL	Cardinals	GCL Cardinals
CAR	Carolina	PWL	Carolina	Carolina
CAR	Caracas	LVBP	Leones	Leones
CC	Corpus Christi	AA C	Astros	Hooks
CHA	Charlotte	INT	White Sox	Knights
CHA	Charlotte	FSL	Rays	Stone Crabs
CHA	Chattanooga	AA S	Reds	Lookouts
CHC	Chi Cubs	NL	-	Cubs
CIN	Cincinnati	NL	-	Reds
CLE	Cleveland	AL	-	Guardians
CLI	Clinton	MID	Marlins	LumberKings
CLR	Clearwater	A SE	Phillies	Threshers
CLT	Charlotte	AAA E	White Sox	Knights
COL	Colombia	CS	-	Colombia
COL	Colorado	NL	-	Rockies
COL	Columbia	A E	Royals	Fireflies
COL	Columbus	AAA E	Guardians	Clippers
CON	Connecticut	NYP	Tigers	Tigers
CR	Cedar Rapids	A+ C	Twins	Kernels
CSC	Charleston	A E	Rays	RiverDogs
CUB	ACL Cubs	ACL	Cubs	ACL Cubs
CUB1	AZL Cubs 1	AZL	Cubs	AZL Cubs 1
CUB2	AZL Cubs 2	AZL	Cubs	AZL Cubs 2
CUBB	AZL Cubs Blue	AZL	Cubs	AZL Cubs Blue
CUBR	AZL Cubs Red	AZL	Cubs	AZL Cubs Red
CUL	Culiacan	LMP	-	Culiacan
CHW	Chi White Sox	AL	-	White Sox
DAN	Danville	APP	Braves	Braves

CODE	TEAM	LG	AFF	NAME
DAY	Dayton	A+ C	Reds	Dragons
DBT	Daytona	A SE	Reds	Tortugas
DE	Down East	A E	Rangers	Wood Ducks
DEL	Delmarva	A E	Orioles	Shorebirds
DET	Detroit	AL	-	Tigers
DIA	ACL D-backs	ACL	D-backs	ACL D-backs
DIA	AZL D-backs	AZL	D-backs	AZL D-backs
DOD	ACL Dodgers	ACL	Dodgers	ACL Dodgers
DOD1	AZL Dodgers 1	AZL	Dodgers	AZL Dodgers 1
DOD2	AZL Dodgers 2	AZL	Dodgers	AZL Dodgers 2
DODL	AZL Dodgers Lasorda	AZL	Dodgers	AZL Dodgers Lasorda
DODM	AZL Dodgers Mota	AZL	Dodgers	AZL Dodgers Mota
DR	Dom. Rep.	CS	-	Dom. Rep.
DSL ANG	DSL Angels	DSL	Angels	DSL Angels
DSL AST	DSL Astros	DSL	Astros	DSL Astros
DSL ATH	DSL Athletics	DSL	Athletics	DSL Athletics
DSL BAU	DSL Dodgers Bautista	DSL	Dodgers	DSL Dodgers Bautista
DSL BLJ	DSL Blue Jays	DSL	Blue Jays	DSL Blue Jays
DSL BRA	DSL Braves	DSL	Braves	DSL Braves
DSL BRW	DSL Brewers	DSL	Brewers	DSL Brewers
DSL BRW1	DSL Brewers1	DSL	Brewers	DSL Brewers1
DSL BRW2	DSL Brewers2	DSL	Brewers	DSL Brewers2
DSL CARB	DSL Cardinals Blue	DSL	Cardinals	DSL Cardinals Blue
DSL CARR	DSL Cardinals Red	DSL	Cardinals	DSL Cardinals Red
DSL COL	DSL Colorado	DSL	Rockies	DSL Colorado
DSL COOP	DSL MIL/TOR	DSL	DSL MIL/TOR	DSL MIL/TOR
DSL COOP	DSL Guardians/ Brewers	DSL	DSL Guardians/ Brewers	DSL Guardians/ Brewers
DSL CUB1	DSL Cubs1	DSL	Cubs	DSL Cubs1
DSL CUB2	DSL Cubs2	DSL	Cubs	DSL Cubs2
DSL CUBB	DSL Cubs Blue	DSL	Cubs	DSL Cubs Blue
DSL CUBR	DSL Cubs Red	DSL	Cubs	DSL Cubs Red
DSL DB1	DSL D-backs1	DSL	D-backs	DSL D-backs1
DSL DB2	DSL D-backs2	DSL	D-backs	DSL D-backs2
DSL GIA	DSL Giants	DSL	Giants	DSL Giants
DSL GIA	DSL Giants1	DSL	Giants	DSL Giants1
DSL	DSL Giants Black	DSL	Giants	DSL Giants

CODE	TEAM	LG	AFF	NAME
GIB				Black
DSL GIO	DSL Giants Orange	DSL	Giants	DSL Giants Orange
DSL GIT	DSL Giants2	DSL	Giants	DSL Giants2
DSL IND	DSL Guardians	DSL	Guardians	DSL Guardians
DSL IND1	DSL Guardians1	DSL	Guardians	DSL Guardians1
DSL IND2	DSL Guardians2	DSL	Guardians	DSL Guardians2
DSL INDB	DSL Guardians Blue	DSL	Guardians	DSL Guardians Blue
DSL INDR	DSL Guardians Red	DSL	Guardians	DSL Guardians Red
DSL MET1	DSL Mets1	DSL	Mets	DSL Mets1
DSL MET2	DSL Mets2	DSL	Mets	DSL Mets2
DSL MIA	DSL Marlins	DSL	Marlins	DSL Marlins
DSL NAT	DSL Nationals	DSL	Nationals	DSL Nationals
DSL NYY	DSL Yankees	DSL	Yankees	DSL Yankees
DSL NYY1	DSL Yankees1	DSL	Yankees	DSL Yankees1
DSL NYY2	DSL Yankees2	DSL	Yankees	DSL Yankees2
DSL OR1	DSL Orioles1	DSL	Orioles	DSL Orioles1
DSL OR2	DSL Orioles2	DSL	Orioles	DSL Orioles2
DSL PAD	DSL Padres	DSL	Padres	DSL Padres
DSL PHR	DSL Phillies Red	DSL	Phillies	DSL Phillies Red
DSL PHW	DSL Phillies White	DSL	Phillies	DSL Phillies White
DSL PIR1	DSL Pirates1	DSL	Pirates	DSL Pirates1
DSL PIR2	DSL Pirates2	DSL	Pirates	DSL Pirates2
DSL PIRB	DSL Pirates Black	DSL	Pirates	DSL Pirates Black
DSL PIRG	DSL Pirates Gold	DSL	Pirates	DSL Pirates Gold
DSL RAN2	DSL Rangers2	DSL	Rangers	DSL Rangers2
DSL REDS	DSL Reds	DSL	Reds	DSL Reds
DSL RGR1	DSL Rangers1	DSL	Rangers	DSL Rangers1
DSL RNG1	DSL Rangers1	DSL	Rangers	DSL Rangers1
DSL RNG2	DSL Rangers2	DSL	Rangers	DSL Rangers2
DSL ROC	DSL Rockies	DSL	Rockies	DSL Rockies
DSL ROY1	DSL Royals1	DSL	Royals	DSL Royals1

CODE	TEAM	LG	AFF	NAME
DSL ROY2	DSL Royals2	DSL	Royals	DSL Royals2
DSL ROYB	DSL Royals Blue	DSL	Royals	DSL Royals Blue
DSL ROYW	DSL Royals White	DSL	Royals	DSL Royals White
DSL RS1	DSL Red Sox1	DSL	Red Sox	DSL Red Sox1
DSL RS2	DSL Red Sox2	DSL	Red Sox	DSL Red Sox2
DSL RSB	DSL Red Sox Blue	DSL	Red Sox	DSL Red Sox Blue
DSL RSR	DSL Red Sox Red	DSL	Red Sox	DSL Red Sox Red
DSL SEA	DSL Mariners	DSL	Mariners	DSL Mariners
DSL SHO	DSL Dodgers Shoemaker	DSL	Dodgers	Dodgers Shoemaker
DSL TB1	DSL Rays1	DSL	Rays	DSL Rays1
DSL TB2	DSL Rays2	DSL	Rays	DSL Rays2
DSL TIG	DSL Tigers	DSL	Tigers	DSL Tigers
DSL TIG1	DSL Tigers1	DSL	Tigers	DSL Tigers1
DSL TIG2	DSL Tigers2	DSL	Tigers	DSL Tigers2
DSL TWI	DSL Twins	DSL	Twins	DSL Twins
DSL WSX	DSL White Sox	DSL	White Sox	DSL White Sox
DUN	Dunedin	A SE	Blue Jays	Blue Jays
DUR	Durham	AAA E	Rays	Bulls
DUR	Durango	MEX	-	Generales
ELP	El Paso	AAA W	Padres	Chihuahuas
ELZ	Elizabethton	APP	Twins	Twins
ERI	Erie	AA NE	Tigers	SeaWolves
ESC	Escogido	LIDOM	-	Leones
EST	Estrellas	LIDOM	-	Estrellas
EUG	Eugene	A+ W	Giants	Emeralds
EVE	Everett	A+ W	Mariners	AquaSox
FAY	Fayetteville	A E	Astros	Woodpeckers
FBG	Fredericksburg	A E	Nationals	Nationals
FLO	Florida	FSL	Braves	Fire Frogs
FRE	Frederick	CAR	Orioles	Keys
FRE	Fresno	A W	Rockies	Grizzlies
FRI	Frisco	AA C	Rangers	RoughRiders
FTM	Fort Myers	A SE	Twins	Mighty Mussels
FTM	Fort Myers	FSL	Twins	Miracle
FW	Fort Wayne	A+ C	Padres	TinCaps
GBO	Greensboro	A+ E	Pirates	Grasshoppers
GDD	Glendale	AFL	-	Desert Dogs
GEE	Geelong-Korea	ABL	-	Geelong-Korea
GIB	AZL Giants Black	AZL	Giants	AZL Giants Black
GIG	Gigantes	LIDOM	-	Gigantes
GIO	AZL Giants Orange	AZL	Giants	AZL Giants Orange

CODE	TEAM	LG	AFF	NAME
GJ	Grand Junction	PIO	Rockies	Rockies
GL	Great Lakes	A+ C	Dodgers	Loons
GNTB	ACL Giants Black	ACL	Giants	ACL Giants Black
GNTO	ACL Giants Orange	ACL	Giants	ACL Giants Orange
GRN	Greeneville	APP	Reds	Reds
GSV	Guasave	LMP	-	Guasave
GTF	Great Falls	PIO	White Sox	Voyagers
GVL	Greenville	A+ E	Red Sox	Drive
GWN	Gwinnett	AAA E	Braves	Stripers
HAG	Hagerstown	SAL	Nationals	Suns
HBG	Harrisburg	AA NE	Nationals	Senators
HER	Hermosillo	LMP	-	Hermosillo
HFD	Hartford	AA NE	Rockies	Yard Goats
HIC	Hickory	A+ E	Rangers	Crawdads
HIL	Hillsboro	A+ W	D-backs	Hops
HOU	Houston	AL	-	Astros
HV	Hudson Valley	A+ E	Yankees	Renegades
IDF	Idaho Falls	PIO	Royals	Chukars
IE	Inland Empire	A W	Angels	66ers
IND	ACL Guardians	ACL	Guardians	ACL Guardians
IND	Indianapolis	AAA E	Pirates	Indianapolis
INDB	AZL Guardians Blue	AZL	Guardians	AZL Guardians Blue
INDR	AZL Guardians Red	AZL	Guardians	AZL Guardians Red
IOW	Iowa	AAA E	Cubs	Cubs
JAL	Jalisco	LMP	-	Jalisco
JAX	Jacksonville	AAA E	Marlins	Jumbo Shrimp
JC	Johnson City	APP	Cardinals	Cardinals
JS	Jersey Shore	A+ E	Phillies	BlueClaws
JUP	Jupiter	A SE	Marlins	Hammerheads
JXN	Jackson	SOU	D-backs	Generals
KAN	Kannapolis	A E	White Sox	Cannon Ballers
KAN	Kannapolis	SAL	White Sox	Intimidators
KC	Kane County	MID	D-backs	Cougars
KC	Kansas City	AL	-	Royals
KNG	Kingsport	APP	Mets	Mets
LAA	LA Angels	AL	-	Angels
LAD	LA Dodgers	NL	-	Dodgers
LAG	Laguna	MEX	-	Algodoneros
LAG	La Guaira	LVBP	Tiburones	Tiburones
LAK	Lakeland	A SE	Tigers	Flying Tigers
LAN	Lancaster	CAL	Rockies	JetHawks
LAN	Lansing	A+ C	Athletics	Lugnuts
LAR	Lara	LVBP	Cardenales	Cardenales
LAR	Dos Laredos	MEX	-	Tecolotes
LC	Lake County	A+ C	Guardians	Captains
LE	Lake Elsinore	A W	Padres	Storm
LEO	Leon	MEX	-	Bravos
LEX	Lexington	SAL	Royals	Legends
LHV	Lehigh Valley	AAA E	Phillies	IronPigs
LIC	Licey	LIDOM	-	Tigres
LOU	Louisville	AAA E	Reds	Bats
LOW	Lowell	NYP	Red Sox	Spinners
LV	Las Vegas	AAA W	Athletics	Aviators

CODE	TEAM	LG	AFF	NAME
LWD	Lakewood	SAL	Phillies	BlueClaws
LYN	Lynchburg	A E	Guardians	Hillcats
MAG	Magallanes	LVBP	Navegantes	Navegantes
MAN	Manati	PWL	Manati	Manati
MAR	AZL Mariners	AZL	Mariners	AZL Mariners
MAR	Margarita	LVBP	Bravos	Bravos
MAY	Mayaguez	PWL	Mayaguez	Mayaguez
MAZ	Mazatlan	LMP	-	Mazatlan
MB	Myrtle Beach	A E	Cubs	Pelicans
MEL	Melbourne	ABL	Aces	Aces
MEM	Memphis	AAA E	Cardinals	Redbirds
MET	FCL Mets	FCL	Mets	FCL Mets
MEX	Mexico	MEX	-	Diablos Rojos
MEX	Mexico	CS	-	Mexico
MIA	Miami	NL	-	Marlins
MID	Midland	AA C	Athletics	RockHounds
MIL	Milwaukee	NL	-	Brewers
MIN	Minnesota	AL	-	Twins
MIS	Mississippi	AA S	Braves	Braves
MIS	Missoula	PIO	D-backs	Osprey
MOB	Mobile	SOU	Angels	BayBears
MOC	Los Mochis	LMP	-	Los Mochis
MOD	Modesto	A W	Mariners	Nuts
MRL	FCL Marlins	FCL	Marlins	FCL Marlins
MRL	GCL Marlins	GCL	Marlins	GCL Marlins
MRN	ACL Mariners	ACL	Mariners	ACL Mariners
MSS	Mesa	AFL	-	Solar Sox
MTG	Montgomery	AA S	Rays	Biscuits
MTS	GCL Mets	GCL	Mets	GCL Mets
MTY	Monterrey	LMP	-	Sultanes
MV	Mahoning Valley	NYP	Guardians	Scrappers
MVA	Monclova	MEX	-	Acereros
MXC	Mexicali	LMP	-	Mexicali
NAS	Nashville	AAA E	Brewers	Sounds
NAT	FCL Nationals	FCL	Nationals	FCL Nationals
NAT	GCL Nationals	GCL	Nationals	GCL Nationals
NAV	Navojoa	LMP	-	Navojoa
NH	New Hampshire	AA NE	Blue Jays	Fisher Cats
NO	New Orleans	PCL	Marlins	Baby Cakes
NOR	Norfolk	AAA E	Orioles	Tides
NWA	NW Arkansas	AA C	Royals	Naturals
NYM	NY Mets	NL	-	Mets
NYY	NY Yankees	AL	-	Yankees
OAK	Oakland	AL	-	Athletics
OAX	Oaxaca	MEX	-	Guerreros
OBR	Obregon	LMP	-	Obregon
OGD	Ogden	PIO	Dodgers	Raptors
OKC	Okla. City	AAA W	Dodgers	Dodgers
OMA	Omaha	AAA E	Royals	Storm Chasers
ORI	Caribes	LVBP	Caribes	Caribes
ORI	GCL Orioles	GCL	Orioles	GCL Orioles
ORIB	FCL Orioles Black	FCL	Orioles	FCL Orioles Black
ORIO	FCL Orioles Orange	FCL	Orioles	FCL Orioles Orange
ORM	Orem	PIO	Angels	Owlz

CODE	TEAM	LG	AFF	NAME
PAD	ACL Padres	ACL	Padres	ACL Padres
PAN	Panama	CS	-	Panama
PAW	Pawtucket	INT	Red Sox	Red Sox
PEJ	Peoria	AFL	-	Javelinas
PEO	Peoria	A+ C	Cardinals	Chiefs
PER	Perth	ABL	Heat	Heat
PHE	GCL Phillies East	GCL	Phillies	GCL Phillies East
PHI	FCL Phillies	FCL	Phillies	FCL Phillies
PHI	Philadelphia	NL	-	Phillies
PHW	GCL Phillies West	GCL	Phillies	GCL Phillies West
PIR	GCL Pirates	GCL	Pirates	GCL Pirates
PIRB	FCL Pirates Black	FCL	Pirates	FCL Pirates Black
PIRG	FCL Pirates Gold	FCL	Pirates	FCL Pirates Gold
PIT	Pittsburgh	NL	-	Pirates
PMB	Palm Beach	A SE	Cardinals	Cardinals
PNS	Pensacola	AA S	Marlins	Blue Wahoos
POR	Portland	AA NE	Red Sox	Sea Dogs
POT	Potomac	CAR	Nationals	Nationals
PRN	Princeton	APP	Rays	Rays
PUE	Puebla	MEX	-	Pericos
PUL	Pulaski	APP	Yankees	Yankees
PUR	Puerto Rico	CS	-	Puerto Rico
QC	Quad Cities	A+ C	Royals	River Bandits
RA12	RA12	PWL	-	RA12
RAN	ACL Rangers	ACL	Rangers	ACL Rangers
RAN	AZL Rangers	AZL	Rangers	AZL Rangers
RAY	FCL Rays	FCL	Rays	FCL Rays
RAY	GCL Rays	GCL	Rays	GCL Rays
RC	Rancho Cuca.	A W	Dodgers	Quakes
RCK	ACL Rockies	ACL	Rockies	ACL Rockies
RCT	Rocket City	AA S	Angels	Trash Pandas
REA	Reading	AA NE	Phillies	Fightin Phils
RED	ACL Reds	ACL	Reds	ACL Reds
RED	AZL Reds	AZL	Reds	AZL Reds
RIC	Richmond	AA NE	Giants	Flying Squirrels
RMV	Rocky Mountain	PIO	Brewers	Vibes
RNO	Reno	AAA W	D-backs	Aces
ROC	Rochester	AAA E	Nationals	Red Wings
ROM	Rome	A+ E	Braves	Braves
ROY	AZL Royals	AZL	Royals	AZL Royals
ROYB	ACL Royals Blue	ACL	Royals	ACL Royals Blue
ROYG	ACL Royals Gold	ACL	Royals	ACL Royals Gold
RR	Round Rock	AAA W	Rangers	Express
RSX	FCL Red Sox	FCL	Red Sox	FCL Red Sox
RSX	GCL Red Sox	GCL	Red Sox	GCL Red Sox
SA	San Antonio	AA C	Padres	Missions
SAC	Sacramento	AAA W	Giants	River Cats
SAL	Salem	A E	Red Sox	Red Sox
SAL	Saltillo	MEX	-	Saraperos
SAN	Santurce	PWL	Santurce	Santurce
SB	South Bend	A+ C	Cubs	Cubs
SC	State College	NYP	Cardinals	Spikes
SCO	Scottsdale	AFL	-	Scorpions

CODE	TEAM	LG	AFF	NAME
SD	San Diego	NL	-	Padres
SD1	AZL Padres 1	AZL	Padres	AZL Padres 1
SD2	AZL Padres 2	AZL	Padres	AZL Padres 2
SEA	Seattle	AL	-	Mariners
SF	San Francisco	NL	-	Giants
SI	Staten Island	NYP	Yankees	Yankees
SJ	San Jose	A W	Giants	Giants
SK	Salem-Keizer	NWL	Giants	Volcanoes
SL	Salt Lake	AAA W	Angels	Bees
SLU	St. Lucie	A SE	Mets	Mets
SOM	Somerset	AA NE	Yankees	Patriots
SPO	Spokane	A+ W	Rockies	Spokane
SPR	Springfield	AA C	Cardinals	Cardinals
SRR	Salt River	AFL	-	Rafters
STK	Stockton	A W	Athletics	Ports
STL	St. Louis	NL	-	Cardinals
STL	St. Lucie	FSL	Mets	Mets
STP	St. Paul	AAA E	Twins	Saints
SUG	Sugar Land	AAA W	Astros	Skeeters
SUR	Surprise	AFL	-	Saguaros
SWB	Scranton/WB	AAA E	Yankees	RailRiders
SYD	Sydney	ABL	Blue Sox	Blue Sox
SYR	Syracuse	AAA E	Mets	Mets
TAB	Tabasco	MEX	-	Olmecas
TAC	Tacoma	AAA W	Mariners	Rainiers
TAM	Tampa	A SE	Yankees	Tarpons
TB	Tampa Bay	AL	-	Rays
TDN	Tren del Norte		-	Tren del Norte
TEX	Texas	AL	-	Rangers
TIG	GCL Tigers East	GCL	Tigers	GCL Tigers East
TIG	Quintana Roo	MEX	-	Tigres
TIGE	FCL Tigers East	FCL	Tigers	FCL Tigers East
TIGW	FCL Tigers West	FCL	Tigers	FCL Tigers West
TIJ	Tijuana	MEX	-	Toros
TIW	GCL Tigers West	GCL	Tigers	GCL Tigers West
TNS	Tennessee	AA S	Cubs	Smokies
TOL	Toledo	AAA E	Tigers	Mud Hens
TOR	Toronto	AL	-	Blue Jays
TOR	Toros	LIDOM	-	Toros
TRI	Tri-City	A+ W	Angels	Dust Devils
TRI	Tri-City	NYP	Astros	ValleyCats
TRN	Trenton	EAS	Yankees	Thunder
TUL	Tulsa	AA C	Dodgers	Drillers
TWI	FCL Twins	FCL	Twins	FCL Twins
TWI	GCL Twins	GCL	Twins	GCL Twins
VAN	Vancouver	A+ W	Blue Jays	Canadians
VEN	Venezuela	CS	-	Venezuela
VER	Vermont	NYP	Athletics	Lake Monsters
VIS	Visalia	A W	D-backs	Rawhide
WCH	Wichita	AA C	Twins	Wind Surge
WIL	Williamsport	NYP	Phillies	Crosscutters
WIL	Wilmington	A+ E	Nationals	Blue Rocks
WIS	Wisconsin	A+ C	Brewers	Timber Rattlers
WM	West Michigan	A+ C	Tigers	Whitecaps
WOR	Worcester	AAA E	Red Sox	Red Sox
WS	Winston-Salem	A+ E	White Sox	Dash

CODE	TEAM	LG	AFF	NAME
WAS	Washington	NL	-	Nationals
WSX	ACL White Sox	ACL	White Sox	ACL White Sox
WSX	AZL White Sox	AZL	White Sox	AZL White Sox
WV	West Virginia	NYP	Pirates	Black Bears
WV	West Virginia	SAL	Mariners	Power
YAE	GCL Yankees East	GCL	Yankees	GCL Yankees East
YAW	GCL Yankees West	GCL	Yankees	GCL Yankees West
YNK	FCL Yankees	FCL	Yankees	FCL Yankees
YUC	Yucatan	MEX	-	Leones
ZUL	Zulia	LVBP	Aguilas	Aguilas

Index of Names